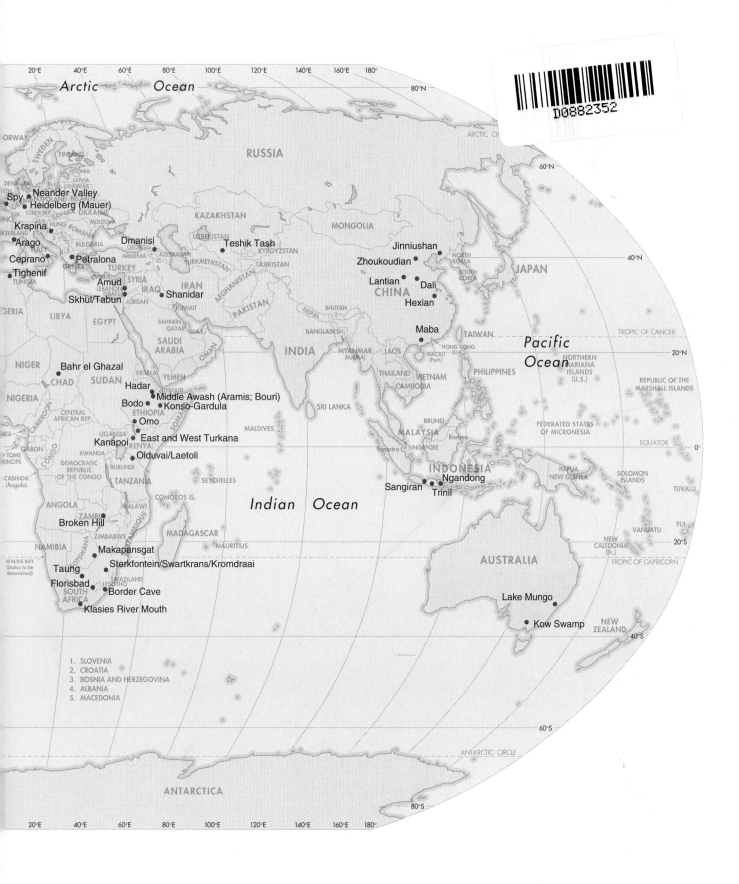

www.wadsworth.com

wadsworth.com is the World Wide Web site for Wadsworth and is your direct source to dozens of online resources.

At *wadsworth.com* you can find out about supplements, demonstration software, and student resources. You can also send email to many of our authors and preview new publications and exciting new technologies.

wadsworth.com
Changing the way the world learns®

Understanding Physical Anthropology and Archaeology

EIGHTH EDITION

William A. Turnbaugh
University of Rhode Island

Robert Jurmain
San Jose State University

Lynn Kilgore
Colorado State University

Harry Nelson

WADSWORTH
™
THOMSON LEARNING

Australia • Canada • Mexico • Singapore • Spain
United Kingdom • United States

WADSWORTH

THOMSON LEARNING

Anthropology Editor: Lin Marshall
Sr. Development Editor: Robert Jucha
Editorial Assistant: Reilly O'Neal
Assistant Editor: Analie Barnett
Marketing Manager: Matthew Wright
Marketing Assistant: Kasia Zagorski
Technology Project Manager: Dee Dee Zobian
Project Manager, Editorial Production: Lisa Weber
Print/Media Buyer: Karen Hunt
Permissions Editor: Stephanie Keough-Hedges
Production Service: Hespenheide Design
Text Designer: Stephanie Davila, Hespenheide Design

Art Editor: Hespenheide Design
Photo Researcher: Hespenheide Design
Copy Editor: Janet Greenblatt
Illustrators: Alexander Productions, DLF Group, Hespenheide
    Design: Leslie Weller, Randy Miyake, Paragon 3, Sue Seelars,
    Cyndie Wooley, Ellen Yamauchi
Cover Designer: Stephen Rapley
Cover Image: Drimolen archaeological site in Africa
    © Kenneth Garrett/National Geographic Image Collection
Cover Printer: Transcontinental Printing, Inc.
Compositor: Hespenheide Design
Printer: Transcontinental Printing, Inc.

Printed in Canada
1 2 3 4 5 6 7 05 04 03 02 01

For permission to use material from this text, contact us by
Web: http://www.thomsonrights.com **Fax:** 1-800-730-2215
Phone: 1-800-730-2214

Library of Congress Cataloging-in-Publication Data
Understanding physical anthropology and archaeology / William Turnbaugh . . . [et al.].—8th ed.
    p. cm.
Includes bibliographical references and index.
ISBN 0-534-58194-3 (alk. paper)
1. Physical anthropology. 2. Archaeology.
I. Title: Physical anthropology and archaeology.
II. Turnbaugh, Willam A.

GN60 .J84 2001
599.9—dc21   2001026230

Wadsworth/Thomson Learning
10 Davis Drive
Belmont, CA 94002-3098
USA

For more information about our products, contact us:
Thomson Learning Academic Resource Center
1-800-423-0563
http://www.wadsworth.com

International Headquarters
Thomson Learning
International Division
290 Harbor Drive, 2nd Floor
Stamford, CT 06902-7477
USA

UK/Europe/Middle East/South Africa
Thomson Learning
Berkshire House
168-173 High Holborn
London WC1V 7AA
United Kingdom

Asia
Thomson Learning
60 Albert Street, #15-01
Albert Complex
Singapore 189969

Canada
Nelson Thomson Learning
1120 Birchmount Road
Toronto, Ontario M1K 5G4
Canada

Brief Contents

Contents

Courtesy, Fred Jacobs

CHAPTER 11
Homo erectus and Contemporaries 257

PHOTO ESSAY
Paleoanthropology 282

CHAPTER 12
Neandertals and Other Archaic *Homo sapiens* 287

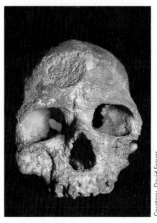

Courtesy, David Frayer

Harry Nelson

Preface

Since its debut in 1981, *Understanding Physical Anthropology and Archaeology* continues to evolve. Each new edition incorporates significant changes in content and organization in response to the rapid pace of discovery in the field *and* in recognition of the changing needs of the many students and professors who have used the book over the years. This new eighth edition represents the culmination of more than two decades of refinement.

As always, the book's major objective continues to be to provide introductory students with a current and comprehensive understanding of human biological and cultural development from an evolutionary perspective, as well as a thorough introduction to the scientific methods by which such information is derived. We have attempted to explain, in a step-by-step progression, how scientific inquiry is conducted, which methodologies are especially relevant to physical anthropology and archaeology, and what specific data researchers have found to support their current conclusions. This approach, we believe, aids students in more fully grasping and appreciating the information presented in these pages.

Additionally, and most basic to our entire approach, the writing style is carefully designed to be clear and understandable, while not insulting the intelligence of college-level readers. To assist students who may have had only minimal prior exposure to scientific topics, we provide a number of learning aids to promote comprehension. For example, a running glossary provides definitions in the margins when key terms are first presented and a full glossary appears at the back of the text. Numerous full-color images, diagrams, and maps have been carefully selected to enhance the narrative. Other helpful features are listed in the section below.

Major Features

Photo Essays There are four photo essays placed throughout the book. Each essay introduces topics to stimulate student interest in contemporary applied research done by physical anthropologists and archaeologists. The first photo essay, following Chapter 1, is entirely new for the eighth edition and presents a portrait of the varied careers pursued by individuals with degrees in physical anthropology and archaeology.

Issues are major boxed features, which are found at the end of selected odd number chapters. Issues focus on current controversial topics being discussed and debated within the field of physical anthropology and archaeology. Examples include:

- Following Chapter 3, Genetic Screening: A Double-Edged Sword?
- Following Chapter 7, Primates in Biomedical Research: Ethics and Concerns
- Following Chapter 17, Who Invented Writing?

Digging Deeper are high-interest boxed features found throughout the book. They expand upon the topic under discussion in the chapter by providing a more in-depth look.

In-Chapter Learning Aids

- **Chapter outlines**, at the beginning of each chapter, list all major topics covered.
- A **running glossary** in the margins provides definitions of terms immediately adjacent to the text when the term is first introduced. A **full glossary** is provided at the back of the book.
- **Figures**, including numerous photographs, line drawings, and maps, most in full color, are carefully selected and placed to directly support discussion in the text.
- **Questions for Review** at the end of each chapter reinforce key points and encourage students to think critically about what they have read.
- **Suggested Further Readings**, also found at the end of each chapter, are carefully selected to direct interested students toward accessible and authoritative resources for further reading.
- **Full bibliography** supports the citations provided throughout the text and gives students a demonstration of standard referencing style in scientific/scholarly presentation as well as guiding them to published source materials.
- **Resources on the Internet** is a new feature for the eighth edition. This learning aid is found at the end of each chapter. Resources include **Internet Exercises** incorporating specific sites on the Internet. These exercises are designed to help students become more competent in using the Internet. New to this edition also are the **InfoTrac® College Edition Exercises**, which utilize the free online library.
- Last, a major new addition to this edition is the systematic integration with the **Virtual Laboratories for Physical Anthropology CD-ROM**, Second Edition,

prepared by John Kappelman of the University of Texas at Austin. In the margins throughout the text there are icons linking the concepts discussed in the book with specific virtual labs on the CD-ROM.

The species concept is presented in Virtual Lab 1, section II.

Organization of the Eighth Edition

A primary strength of this text is that it introduces students both to the processes and to the consequences of human biological and cultural evolution. Following an introduction (Chapter 1) that briefly sets forth the field of anthropology and explains the authors' biocultural approach, the early part of the book (Chapters 2 and 3) provides the historical context for the development of evolutionary theory, both before and after Darwin, and examines the key role that genes play in biological inheritance and variation. Human population genetics and adaptive responses to environmental factors are explored in Chapters 4 and 5 to help understand differences found among modern humans.

The next section begins with a comprehensive overview of modern primate morphological and behavioral characteristics (Chapters 6 and 7), which helps the reader to understand how primates are distinguished from other mammals. Then follows a summary of primate evolution from the early Cenozoic era to the Pliocene epoch (Chapter 8), leading to a completely updated account of the relentless paleoanthropological search for the earliest hominid traces, primarily in southern and eastern Africa (Chapters 9 and 10). The record of *Homo erectus* and related forms in Africa, Asia, and Europe is considered in Chapter 11, while Chapter 12 deals with the evolutionary trends of the earliest *Homo sapiens* and of Neandertals. The eighth edition now covers the origin, dispersal, and cultural achievements of the earliest anatomically modern humans in a separate chapter, Chapter 13.

The final section of the text examines the subsequent biocultural course of our species. Because archaeology plays such a prominent role in revealing post-Pleistocene prehistory, a newly added Chapter 14 discusses the principal methods that archaeologists use to discover, excavate, date, and interpret cultural sites and artifacts. Chapter 15 presents current archaeological perspectives on the intriguing topic of Native American origins and early lifeways and also provides an overview of early Holocene hunters and gatherers in several other parts of the globe. Chapter 16 focuses on the key human invention of food production and the appearance of agricultural lifeways, which, in a few regions of the Old World and the Americas, promoted the rise of early preindustrial civilizations, the topic of Chapters 17 and 18. We end with a short epilogue that considers humankind's contemporary situation from an evolutionary perspective.

What's New in the Eighth Edition?

Through its many editions, this text's authors have endeavored to achieve a balance between physical anthropology and archaeology that reflects our *biocultural* point of view. In part, this symmetry has been achieved through an emphasis on *paleoanthropology*, a multidisciplinary approach combining the methodologies of physical anthropology and archaeology in the discovery and study of early hominids. The eighth edition builds on this focus.

The addition of a new Chapter 14, "Understanding Prehistory: Archaeological Approaches," further enhances the representation of archaeology by introducing readers to the research objectives, standard field methods, and specialized analytical and dating techniques commonly employed by archaeologists (those working in Plio-Pleistocene contexts as well as in more recent situations, including the practice of *cultural resource management*). Some topics previously covered in the paleoanthropology chapter have been combined in this new chapter (e.g., dating methods, reconstructions of stone tool manufacturing techniques). In this way, we have sought to present a more coordinated introduction to archaeological techniques and methods. The paleoanthropology chapter itself—Chapter 9—has also been substantially reorganized to incorporate more material on behavioral and ecological interpretations of early hominids (as reflected in the new chapter title). Moreover, as in each successive edition previous to this one, additional pages have been allocated to the discussion of archaeological data bearing on our species' geographic dispersal and cultural elaboration, including the invention of food production and the emergence of complex societies in both the Old World and the New World. Several new box features on archaeological topics are found in Chapters 14 and 15.

Coverage of topics in physical anthropology has also been augmented in this edition. Chapter 5 expands the focus on infectious disease with an emphasis on HIV/AIDS. The discussion also deals with the role of cultural factors such as population growth, human-induced climate change, and overuse of antibiotics in the reemergence of some infectious diseases.

We have, of course, continued to incorporate the latest information on fossil hominids, including recent discoveries of Plio-Pleistocene species (*Ardipithecus; Australopithecus garhi; Kenyanthropus*) in Chapter 10; new discoveries of *Homo erectus* (or contemporaries) from Spain and Italy (Chapter 11); and recent finds of Neandertals or early modern *H. sapiens* from Portugal, France, and Croatia (Chapters 12 and 13). In addition, since many contemporary scholars recognize considerable complexity in the evolution of *Homo*, a new section in Chapter 11 presents varied interpretations and species designations (i.e., *H. rudolfensis, H. ergaster, H. heidelbergensis, H. neanderthalensis*). This eighth edition now devotes individual chapters to the archaic *Homo sapiens* such as Neandertals (Chapter 12) and the earliest anatomically modern humans and their Upper Paleolithic culture (Chapter 13). The exciting new attempts to extract and sequence Neandertal DNA are also covered in Chapter 12.

Chapter 15 has been extensively rewritten to incorporate exciting developments in the search for the earliest Americans, particularly in light of recently recalibrated radiocarbon chronologies. The latter part of the same chapter now examines Middle Stone Age foraging and food collecting from a more explicitly ecological perspective that anticipates our expanded consideration of food production and its consequences in Chapter 16. The distinguishing characteristics of civilizations receive more detailed treatment in Chapter 17, as does the rise of urbanism and the influential role of early cities in Old World societies. The treatment of New World civilizations in Chapter 18 has been thoroughly updated. An epilogue, new to this edition, considers our modern human situation from a biocultural and evolutionary perspective. The book's epilogue reinforces the contemporary relevance of the long human past that is the subject of this text, connecting it to the present and future of our species, with an evolutionary perspective on issues such as population growth, poverty, and environmental decline.

Acknowledgments

Each edition of this text has benefited directly from the assistance and suggestions of many friends and colleagues. We are particularly indebted to the following reviewers of this edition:

James M. Calcagno
Loyola University of Chicago

Ellis E. McDowell-Loundan
SUNY at Cortland

William Engelbrecht
SUNY Buffalo State College

T. Cregg Madrigal
Rutgers University

George Fulford
University of Winnipeg

Renee B. Walker
Skidmore College

Mary F. Gallagher
Montgomery College

Nancy Marie White
University of South Florida

Lisa J. Lucero
New Mexico State University

The authors also wish to thank the reviewers of the previous edition: Charles A. Bollong, Pima Community College; Douglas E. Crews, Ohio State University; Kenneth Kelly, Northern Arizona University; Dean H. Knight, Wilfried Laurier University; Jack H. Prost, University of Illinois at Chicago; Tal Simmons, Western Michigan University; and Maria O. Smith, Northern Illinois University.

We also wish to thank at Wadsworth Publishing Lin Marshall, Anthropology Editor; Robert Jucha, Development Editor; Matthew Wright, Marketing Manager, Analie Barnett, Assistant Editor, Dee Dee Zobian, Technology Project Manager, and Lisa Weber, Project Editor. We are also grateful to Eve Howard, Publisher; and Susan Badger,

President and CEO. Moreover, for their unflagging expertise and patience we are grateful to Gary Hespenheide and his staff at Hespenheide Design: Patti Zeman, production coordinator; Bridget Neumayr, proofreader/editor; and Stephanie Davila, design. We, as always, are most appreciative of our copy editor, Janet Greenblatt.

In addition, for their help with the photo essays, we thank Art Aufderheide, Don Johanson, Anne Rademacher, Donna Raymond, Ann Silver, and the staff of the Photography Department, San Jose State University Instructional Resources Center.

We also express our continued great appreciation to the many friends and colleagues who have generously provided photographs: Jennifer Hope Antes, C. K. Brain, Günter Bräuer, Desmond Clark, Stephanie Collins, Raymond Dart, Henri DeLumley, Jean DeRousseau, Tom Dillehay, Aaron Elkins, Denis Etler, Diane France, David Frayer, George Frison, Helle Goldman, Mark Gutchen, David Haring, Darden Hood, Ellen Ingmanson, Fred Jacobs, Susan Johnston, Peter Jones, Arlene Kruse, Alan Leveillee, Scott Madry, Rod Mather, Jill McLaughlin, Richard Meadow, John Oates, Bonnie Pedersen, Lorna Pierce, David Pilbeam, Katherine Pomonis, Whitney Powell-Cummer, William Pratt, William Rathje, Judith Regensteiner, Paul Richmond, David Robinson, Sastrohamijoyo Sartono, Rose Sevcik, Elwyn Simons, Lena Sisco, Paul Sledzik, Meredith Small, Fred Smith, H. Dieter Steklis, Peter Storck, Judy Suchey, Li Tianyuan, Phillip Tobias, Sarah Peabody Turnbaugh, Alan Walker, Milford Wolpoff, Xinzhi Wu, and John Yellen.

William A. Turnbaugh
Robert Jurmain
Lynn Kilgore

This edition of *Understanding Physical Anthropology and Archaeology* is dedicated to our coauthor and friend, Harry Nelson.

1915–2000

Supplements

A full array of supplements for both instructors and students accompanies *Understanding Physical Anthropology and Archaeology*, Eighth Edition.

Supplements for Instructors

For the following supplements please contact your Wadsworth/Thomson Learning representative.

Instructor's Manual with Test Bank Written by the main text authors, each chapter includes a chapter outline and overview, learning objectives, lecture suggestions and enrichment topics. The Test Bank provides 40 to 70 questions per chapter.

A detailed media resource guide and a concise InfoTrac College Edition user guide are included as appendixes.

Wadsworth Physical Anthropology Transparency Acetates A selection of full-color acetates is available to help prepare lecture presentations. Free to qualified adopters.

Physical Anthropology Slides A selection of art found in the text is available as color slides.

ExamView® Computerized and Online Testing from Wadsworth/ Thomson Learning Create, deliver, and customize tests and study guides (both print and online) in minutes with this easy-to-use assessment and tutorial system. ExamView offers both a Quick Test Wizard and an Online Test Wizard that guide you step-by-step through the process of creating tests, while its unique "WYSIWYG" capability allows you to see the test you are creating on the screen exactly as it will print or display online. You can build tests of up to 250 questions using up to 12 question types. Using ExamView's complete word processing capabilities, you can enter an unlimited number of new questions or edit existing questions.

AnthroLink 2002 CD-ROM: A Microsoft® PowerPoint® Presentation Tool. AnthroLink 2002 is an easy-to-use CD-ROM with which instructors can create customized lecture Power Point presentations for class. AnthroLink 2002 includes nearly 500 pieces of graphic art from all Wadsworth cultural and physical and archaeological titles. In addition, the user may choose from 400 photographs grouped by standard chapter categories. A unique feature of AnthroLink 2002 is the ability to choose and integrate video segments into lec-tures. AnthroLink 2002 gives instructors the ability to utilize images from the text to create their own lecture presentations *or* to use and manipulate the pre-made lecture presentation already on the CD-ROM.

Wadsworth Anthropology Video Library Qualified adopters may select full-length videos from an extensive library of offerings drawn from such excellent educational video sources such as *NOVA*, *Films for the Humanities and Sciences*, *The Disappearing World Video Series*, and *In Search of Human Origins*.

CNN® Today: Physical Anthropology Video Series Vol. 1, 2, and 3. The *CNN Today Physical Anthropology Videos Series* is an exclusive series jointly created by Wadsworth and CNN for the physical anthropology course. Instructors may choose between three 45-minute videotapes composed of short clips from recent CNN broadcasts. The videos illuminate the principles of physical anthropology and archaeology and their impact on today's world.

Web-Based Resources

Anthropology Online: Wadsworth Anthropology Resource Center http://anthropology.wadsworth.com Perhaps the most exciting new development in the complete supplementary package to accompany *Understanding Physical Anthropology and Archaeology*, Eighth Edition, is the newly developed and expanded website. The Wadsworth Anthropology Resource Center contains a wealth of information and useful tools for both instructors and students. After logging on, click on Turnbaugh, Eighth Edition, and proceed to the Student Resources section. There you will find extra Internet and InfoTrac College Edition exercises, flashcards, and online practice quizzes for each chapter. Anthropology Online contains this special feature:

A Virtual Tour of Applying Anthropology This special section of the website serves as an online resource center for the anthropology student. There is an essay, illustrated with video clips, on careers in anthropology written by Wadsworth author Gary Ferraro. The Applying Anthropology site includes information on careers in anthropology outside the academic setting, including advice on organizations which provide student internships, and hot links to graduate programs in applied anthropology.

Supplements for Students

Virtual Laboratories for Physical Anthropology CD-ROM, Second Edition, by John Kappelman The new version of this Interactive CD-ROM provides students with a hands-on computer component for doing lab assignments at school or at home. It encourages students to actively participate in their physical anthropology lab or course through the taking of measurements and the plotting of data, as well as giving them a format for testing their knowledge of important concepts. Contains full-color images, video clips, 3-D animations, sound, and more. In addition, students can link between this CD and the web page to access additional tutorial quizzes.

Researching Anthropology on the Internet Guide by David L. Carlson, Texas A&M University This useful guide is designed to assist anthropology students with doing research on the Internet. Part One contains general information necessary to get started and answers questions about security, the type of anthropology material available on the Internet, the information that is reliable and the sites that are not, the best ways to find research, and the best links to take students where they want to go. Part Two looks at each main discipline in the area of anthropology, and refers students to sites where the most enlightening research can be obtained.

InfoTrac College Edition InfoTrac College Edition (available as a free option with newly purchased texts) gives you and your students four months of free access to an easy-to-use online database of reliable, full-length articles (not abstracts) from hundreds of top academic journals and popular sources. Among the journals which are available 24 hours a day, seven days a week, are *American Anthropologist, Current Anthropology, Discover,* and *Science.* Contact your Wadsworth/Thomas learning representative for more information.

Lab Manual and Workbook for Physical Anthropology, Fourth Edition, by Diane L. France, Colorado State University This lab manual emphasizes human osteology, forensic anthropology, anthropometry, primates, human evolution, and genetics. It provides students with hands-on lab assignments to help make the concepts of physical anthropology clear. It contains short-answer questions, identification problems, and observation exercises.

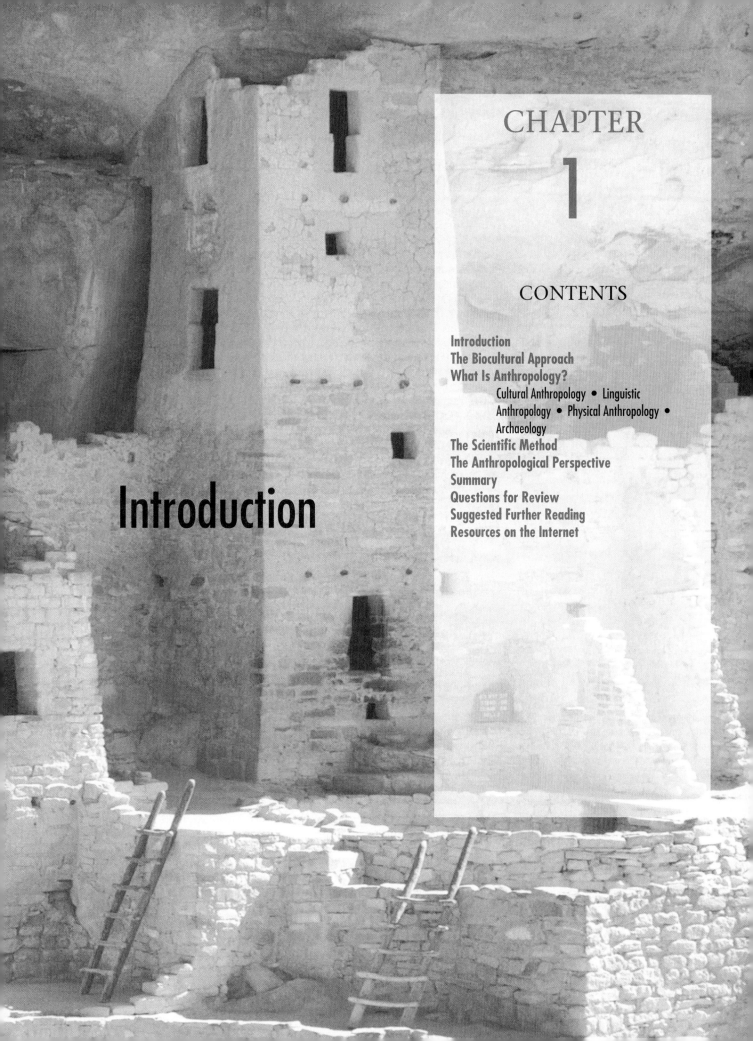

CHAPTER 1

Introduction

CONTENTS

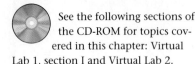

See the following sections of the CD-ROM for topics covered in this chapter: Virtual Lab 1, section I and Virtual Lab 2.

Anthropology
The field of inquiry that studies human culture and evolutionary aspects of human biology; includes cultural anthropology, archaeology, linguistics, and physical anthropology.

Culture
All aspects of human adaptation, including technology, traditions, language, and social roles. Culture is learned and transmitted from one generation to the next by nonbiological (i.e., not genetic) means.

Biocultural evolution
The mutual, interactive evolution of human biology and culture; the concept that biology makes culture possible and that culture further influences the direction of biological evolution; a basic concept in understanding the unique components of human evolution.

Introduction

With notebook in hand, a young man peers intently through the tangled bushes to catch a glimpse of a chimpanzee mother playing with her infant. Seated before a computer in her university laboratory, a white-coated scientist closely compares the DNA sequences of a pair of fraternal twins. In a far-off tropical village, a researcher interviews a tribal elder, carefully recording the old woman's comments as she continues to plait a basket of plant fiber. On a dusty mesa top in New Mexico, an excavator brushes away the sand to expose fragments of a boldly decorated pottery vessel. Manila folders and cardboard boxes clutter a long library table, at which an earnest-looking student peruses a letter describing an early encounter with an indigenous group of people living along the Sepik River in New Guinea. At a Smithsonian museum, a small group of curators and graduate students uses a caliper-like instrument to measure a bone, entering the results into a laptop computer.

Each of these people is an anthropologist, and all are engaged in anthropological research. **Anthropology** is the study of human beings, and as a scientific discipline anthropology is concerned with all aspects of what it is to be human. Such a broad focus encompasses all topics related to behavior including: social relationships (e.g., kinship and marriage patterns), religion, ritual, technology, subsistence techniques, and economic and political systems. Anthropology is also concerned with the numerous biological dimensions of our species such as: genetics, anatomy, skeletal structure, blood types and other biochemical factors, adaptation to disease and other environmental factors, body build, pigmentation, nutrition, and ultimately, all the evolutionary processes that have resulted in the development of modern humans. Anthropology, therefore, is a holistic science, with the entire scope of humankind, past and present, as its focus.

In contrast, an economist, for example, might study market systems—the production, distribution, and consumption of goods—and only rarely, if ever, consider the effects of religion or kinship on economic systems. But anthropology's holistic approach recognizes that many factors contribute to whatever we humans do, even including economic transactions. Anthropologists incorporate findings from many academic fields as they seek to understand and explain what being human is all about. In a practical sense, however, no single anthropologist can hope to encompass the entire discipline.

The Biocultural Approach

While no one specialist can adequately cover the entire breadth of anthropology, there is a unifying theme that helps give all anthropologists a shared perspective: As humans have evolved over the last several million years, the interdependent influences of biology and **culture** have shaped our evolutionary history. Indeed, over time, biology and culture have interacted in such a way that humans are said to be the product of **biocultural evolution**. It is by tracing the interaction between biology and culture and attempting to understand *how* the process has occurred that we are able to come to grips scientifically with what we are and how we came to be.

As this book will emphasize, human organisms are but one recent and fairly short chapter in the book of life composed by evolution. However, a component that has come to dominate human biological evolution to an extent unknown among other organisms is culture. Culture is an extremely important concept, not only as it pertains to modern human beings, but also in terms of its critical role in human evolution. It has been said that there are as many definitions of culture as there are people who attempt to define it. Quite simply, culture can be considered the strategy by which humans adapt to the natural environment. In this sense, culture includes technologies that range from stone tools to computers; subsistence patterns ranging from hunting and gathering to agribusiness on a global scale; housing types, from thatched huts to skyscrapers; and clothing, from animal skins to high-tech synthetic fibers (Fig. 1–1). Because religion, values, social organization,

(a)   (b)

(c)   (d)

language, kinship, marriage rules, gender roles, and so on, are all aspects of culture, each culture shapes people's perceptions of the external environment, or world-view, in particular ways that distinguish that culture from all others.

One fundamental point to remember is that culture is *learned* and not biologically determined. Culture is transmitted from generation to generation independent of biological factors (i.e., genes). For example, if a young girl of Vietnamese ancestry is raised in the United States by English-speaking parents, she will acquire English as her native language. She will eat Western foods with Western utensils and will wear Western clothes. In short, she will be a product of Western culture, because that is the culture she will have learned. We are all products of the culture in which we are socialized, and since most human behavior is learned, it clearly is also culturally patterned.

But as biological organisms, humans are subject to the same evolutionary forces as all other species. On hearing the term **evolution**, many people think of the appearance of new species. Certainly, new species formation is one consequence of

FIGURE 1–1

(a) An early stone tool from East Africa. This artifact represents the oldest type of stone tools found anywhere. (b) Assortment of implements available today in a modern hardware store. (c) A Samburu woman in Kenya building a traditional dwelling of sticks, plant fibers, and mud. (d) A modern high-rise apartment complex, typical of industrialized cities.

Evolution

A change in the genetic structure of a population from one generation to the next. The term is also frequently used to refer to the appearance of a new species.

3

evolution; however, biologists see evolution as an ongoing biological process with a precise genetic meaning. Quite simply, *evolution* is a change in the genetic makeup of a population from one generation to the next. It is the accumulation of such changes, over considerable periods of time, that can result in the appearance of a new species. Thus, evolution can be defined and studied at two different levels. At one level there are genetic alterations *within* populations. Although this type of change may not lead to the development of new species, it frequently results in variation between populations with regard to the frequency of certain traits. Evolution at this level is referred to as *microevolution*. At the other level is long-term genetic change that does result in the appearance of a new species, a process sometimes termed *macroevolution* or *speciation*. Evolution at both these levels will be addressed in this textbook.

In the course of human evolution, biocultural interactions have resulted in such anatomical, biological, and behavioral changes as increased brain size, reorganization of neurological structures, decreased tooth size, and development of language, to list a few. And they have been critical in changing disease patterns as well. As a contemporary example, rapid culture change (e.g., in Africa) and changing social and sexual mores may have influenced evolutionary rates of HIV, the virus that causes AIDS. Certainly, these cultural factors influenced the spread of HIV throughout populations in both developed and developing countries.

The study of many of the biological aspects of humankind, including **adaptation** and evolution, could certainly be the purview of biologists, and indeed, it frequently is. However, when such research also considers the role of cultural factors, in the United States it is placed within the discipline of anthropology. This approach recognizes the fact that the human predisposition to assimilate a culture and to function within it is influenced by biological factors. But in the course of human evolution, as you will see, the role of culture increasingly assumed an added importance. In this respect, humans are unique among biological organisms.

What Is Anthropology?

Stated ambitiously but simply, anthropology is the study of humankind. (The term *anthropology* is derived from the Greek words *anthropos*, meaning "human," and *logos*, meaning "word" or "study of.") Anthropologists are not the only scientists who study humans, and the goals of anthropology are shared by other disciplines within the social, behavioral, and biological sciences. As noted, the main difference between anthropology and other related fields is that anthropology integrates the findings of many disciplines, including sociology, economics, history, psychology, and biology.

In the United States, anthropology comprises three main subfields: cultural or social anthropology; archaeology; and physical or biological anthropology. Additionally, many universities include linguistic anthropology as a fourth area. Each of these subdisciplines, in turn, is divided into more specialized areas of interest. Following is a brief discussion of the main subdisciplines of anthropology.

Cultural Anthropology

Cultural anthropology is the study of all aspects of human behavior. It could reasonably be argued that cultural anthropology began in the fourth century B.C. with the Greek philosopher Aristotle, or even earlier. But for practical purposes, the beginnings of cultural anthropology are found in the nineteenth century, when Europeans became increasingly aware of what they termed "primitive societies" in Africa and Asia. Likewise, in the New World, there was much interest in the rapidly vanishing cultures of Native Americans.

The interest in traditional societies led numerous early anthropologists to study and record lifeways that unfortunately are now mostly extinct. These studies pro-

Adaptation
A physiological and/or behavioral adjustment made by organisms in response to environmental circumstances. Adaptations may be short-term or long-term, and strictly defined, they are the results of evolutionary factors, particularly natural selection.

duced many descriptive **ethnographies** that became the basis for later comparisons between groups. Early ethnographies emphasized various phenomena, such as religion, ritual, myth, use of symbols, subsistence strategies, technology, gender roles, child-rearing practices, dietary preferences, taboos, medical practices, and how kinship was reckoned, to list a few.

The focus of cultural anthropology changed considerably over the course of the twentieth century. But traditional ethnographic techniques, wherein anthropologists spend months or years living in and studying various societies, are still employed, although the nature of the study groups may have changed. For example, in recent decades, ethnographic techniques have been applied to the study of diverse subcultures and their interactions with one another in contemporary metropolitan areas. The subfield of cultural anthropology that deals with issues of inner cities is appropriately called *urban anthropology*. Among the many issues addressed by urban anthropologists are relationships between various ethnic groups, those aspects of traditional cultures that are maintained by immigrant populations, poverty, labor relations, homelessness, access to health care, and problems facing the elderly.

Medical anthropology is the subfield of cultural anthropology that explores the relationship between various cultural attributes and health and disease. One area of interest is how different groups view disease processes and how these views affect treatment or the willingness to accept treatment. When a medical anthropologist focuses on the social dimensions of disease, physicians and physical anthropologists may also collaborate. Indeed, many medical anthropologists have received much of their training in physical anthropology.

Economic anthropologists are concerned with factors that influence the distribution of goods and resources within and between cultures. Areas of interest include such topics as division of labor (by gender and age), factors that influence who controls resources and wealth, and trade practices and regulations.

Many cultural anthropologists are involved in *gender studies*. Such studies may focus on gender norms, how such norms are learned, and the specific cultural factors that lead to individual development of gender identity. It is also valuable to explore the social consequences if gender norms are violated.

There is also increasing interest in the social aspects of development and aging. This field is particularly relevant in industrialized nations, where the proportion of elderly individuals is higher than ever before. As populations age, the needs of the elderly, particularly in the area of health care, become social issues that require more and more attention.

Many of the subfields of cultural anthropology (e.g., medical anthropology) have practical applications and are pursued by anthropologists working both within and outside the university setting. This approach is aptly termed *applied anthropology*. While most applied anthropologists regard themselves as cultural anthropologists, the designation is also sometimes used to describe the activities of archaeologists and physical anthropologists. Indeed, the various fields of anthropology, as they are practiced in the United States, overlap to a considerable degree, which, after all, was the rationale for combining them under the umbrella of anthropology in the first place.

Linguistic Anthropology

Linguistic anthropology is the study of human speech and language, including the origins of language in general as well as specific languages. By examining similarities between contemporary languages, linguists have been able to trace historical ties between languages and groups of languages, thus facilitating the identification of language families and perhaps past relationships between human populations.

There is also much interest in the relationship between language and culture: how language reflects the way members of a society perceive phenomena and how the use of language shapes perceptions in different cultures. For instance, vocabulary

Ethnographies
Detailed descriptive studies of human societies. In cultural anthropology, *ethnography* is traditionally the study of a non-Western society.

provides important clues as to the importance of certain items and concepts in particular cultures. The most famous example of this fact is the use of some 50 terms for snow among the Inuit (Eskimos), reflecting their need to convey specific information about the properties of this form of frozen precipitation. (For that matter, skiers also employ many more increasingly precise terms for snow than do nonskiers.)

Because the spontaneous acquisition and use of language is a uniquely human characteristic, it is a topic that holds considerable interest for linguistic anthropologists, who, along with specialists in other fields, study the process of language acquisition in infants. Since insights into the process may well have implications for the development of language skills in human evolution, as well as in growing children, it is also an important subject to physical anthropologists.

Physical Anthropology

The place of physical anthropology within the discipline of anthropology is discussed in Virtual Lab 1, section I.

Physical anthropology, as has already been stated, is the study of human biology within the framework of evolution, with an emphasis on the interaction between biology and culture. Physical anthropology is composed of several subdisciplines, or areas of specialization, the most significant of which are briefly described in the following paragraphs.

The origins of physical anthropology arose from two principal areas of interest among nineteenth-century scholars. First, there was increasing interest among many scientists (at the time called *natural historians*) in the mechanisms by which modern species had come to be. In other words, increasing numbers of intellectuals were beginning to doubt the literal, biblical explanation of creation. This does not mean that all natural historians had abandoned all religious explanations of natural occurrences. But scientific explanations emphasizing natural, rather than supernatural, phenomena were becoming increasingly popular in scientific circles. Although few scientists were actually prepared to believe that humans had evolved from earlier forms, discoveries of several Neandertal fossils in the 1800s led to questions regarding the origins and antiquity of the human species.

The sparks of interest in biological change over time were fueled into flames by the publication of Charles Darwin's *Origin of Species* in 1859. Today, **paleoanthropology**, or the study of human evolution, particularly as evidenced in the fossil record, is one of the major subfields of physical anthropology (Fig. 1–2). There are now thousands of fossilized specimens of human ancestors housed in museum and research collections. Taken together, these fossils cover a span of more than 4 million years of human prehistory, and although incomplete, they provide us with significantly more knowledge than was available even 15 years ago. It is the ultimate goal of paleoanthropological research to identify the various early **hominid** species and establish a chronological sequence of relationships among them. Only then will there emerge a clear picture of how and when humankind came into being.

Paleoanthropology
The interdisciplinary approach to the study of earlier hominids—their chronology, physical structure, archaeological remains, habitats, etc.

A second nineteenth-century interest that had direct relevance to anthropology was observable physical variation, particularly as seen in skin color, body build, shape of the face, and so on. Enormous effort was aimed at describing and explaining the differences among human populations. Although some endeavors were misguided and indeed racist, they gave birth to literally thousands of body measurements that could be used to compare people. Physical anthropologists use many of the techniques of **anthropometry** today, not only to study living groups (Fig. 1–3), but also to study skeletal remains from archaeological sites. Moreover, anthropometric techniques have had considerable application in the design of everything from airplane cockpits to office furniture.

Hominid
Member of the family Hominidae, the classificatory group to which humans belong; also includes other, now extinct, bipedal relatives.

Anthropologists today are concerned with human variation partly because of its *adaptive significance*. In other words, some traits are seen as having evolved as biological adaptations, or adjustments, to local environmental conditions. Examining biological variation between and within populations of any species provides valuable information regarding the mechanisms of genetic change in

Anthropometry
Measurement of human body parts. When osteologists measure skeletal elements, the term *osteometry* is often used.

FIGURE 1–2
Paleoanthropological research at Hadar, in Ethiopia, during a recent field season.

Institute of Human Origins

groups over time, and genetic change is precisely what the evolutionary process is all about.

Modern population studies also examine other important aspects of human variation, including how various groups respond physiologically to different kinds of environmentally induced stress (Fig. 1–4). Such stresses may include high altitude, cold, or heat.

Courtesy, Eugenie Scott

FIGURE 1–3
Dr. Eugenie Scott measures stature in a Garifuna (Black Carib) girl in Belize.

Courtesy, Judy Regensteiner

FIGURE 1–4
Researcher using a treadmill test to assess a subject's heart rate, blood pressure, and oxygen utilization.

Introduction

Genetics
The study of gene structure and action and of the patterns of inheritance of traits from parent to offspring. Genetic mechanisms are the underlying foundation for evolutionary change.

Primate
A member of the order of mammals Primates (pronounced "pry-may-tees"), which includes prosimians, monkeys, apes, and humans.

Other physical anthropologists conduct nutritional studies, investigating the relationships between various dietary components, cultural practices, physiology, and certain aspects of health and disease. Closely related to the topic of nutrition are investigations of human fertility, growth, and development. These fields of inquiry are fundamental to studies of adaptation in modern human populations, and they can provide insights into hominid evolution as well.

It would be impossible to study evolutionary processes, and therefore adaptation, without a knowledge of genetic principles. For this reason and others, **genetics** is a crucial field for physical anthropologists. Modern physical anthropology could not exist as an evolutionary science were it not for advances in the understanding of genetic principles.

Not only does genetics allow us to explain how evolutionary processes work, but anthropologists use recently developed genetic technologies to investigate evolutionary distances between living **primate** species (including humans). Moreover, genetic techniques have been used (with much debate) to explain, among other things, the origins of modern *Homo sapiens*.

Primatology, the study of nonhuman primates, has become increasingly important since the late 1950s for several reasons. Behavioral studies, especially those conducted on free-ranging groups, have implications for numerous scientific disciplines. Because nonhuman primates are our closest living relatives, the identification of underlying factors related to social behavior, communication, infant care, reproductive behavior, and so on, aids in developing a better understanding of the natural forces that have shaped so many aspects of modern human behavior. But it is even more important that nonhuman primates be studied in their own right, because the majority of primate species are threatened or seriously endangered. Only through study will scientists be able to recommend policies that can better ensure the survival of many nonhuman primates and thousands of other species as well.

Primate paleontology, the study of the primate fossil record, has implications not only for nonhuman primates but also for hominid research. Virtually every year, fossil-bearing beds in Africa, Asia, Europe, and North America yield important new discoveries. Through the study of fossil primates, we are able to learn much about factors such as diet or locomotion in earlier forms. And through comparisons with anatomically similar living species, primate paleontologists can make reasoned inferences regarding behavior in earlier groups as well. Moreover, we hope to be able to clarify what we know about evolutionary relationships between extinct and modern species, including ourselves.

Osteology
The study of all aspects of the skeleton, including bone composition, growth, and response to disease and trauma. Human osteology focuses on the interpretation of the skeletal remains of past groups. The same techniques are used in paleoanthropology to study early hominids.

Osteology, the study of the skeleton, is central to physical anthropology. Indeed, it is so important that when many people think of physical anthropology, the first thing that comes to mind is bones. The emphasis on osteology exists in part because of the concern with the analysis of fossil material. Certainly, a thorough knowledge of the structure and function of the skeleton is critical to the interpretation of fossil remains.

Bone biology and physiology are of major importance to several other aspects of physical anthropology, in addition to paleontology. Many osteologists specialize in metric studies that emphasize various measurements of skeletal elements. This type of research is essential, for example, to the identification of stature and growth patterns in archaeological populations.

Paleopathology
The branch of osteology that studies the traces of disease and injury in human skeletal (or, occasionally, mummified) remains.

One subdiscipline of osteology is the study of disease and trauma in skeletons from archaeological sites. **Paleopathology** is the subfield that investigates the incidence of trauma, certain infectious diseases (such as syphilis and tuberculosis), nutritional deficiencies, and numerous other conditions that leave evidence in bone. In this area of research, a detailed knowledge of bone physiology and response to insult is required.

Forensic anthropology
An applied anthropological approach dealing with legal matters. Forensic anthropologists work with coroners and law enforcement agencies in the recovery, analysis, and identification of human remains.

A field directly related to osteology and paleopathology is **forensic anthropology**. Technically, this approach is the application of anthropological (usually osteological and sometimes archaeological) techniques to the law. Forensic anthropologists are commonly called on to help identify skeletal remains in cases of disaster or other situations where a human body has been found.

Forensic anthropologists have been instrumental in a number of cases having important legal and historical consequences. They assisted medical examiners in 1993 in the identification of human remains at the Branch Davidian compound in Waco, Texas. They have also been prominent in the identification of remains of missing American soldiers in Southeast Asia and the skeletons of the Russian imperial family, executed in 1918.

One other important area of interest for physical anthropologists is anatomy. In the living organism, bone and dental structures are intimately linked to the soft tissues that surround and act on them. Thus, a thorough knowledge of soft tissue anatomy is essential to the understanding of biomechanical relationships involved in movement. Such relationships are important to the development of conditions, such as arthritis, that are frequently encountered in paleopathology. Moreover, accurate assessment of the structure and function of limbs and other components in fossilized remains requires expertise in anatomical relationships. For these reasons, many physical anthropologists specialize in anatomical studies. In fact, several physical anthropologists hold professorships in anatomy departments at universities and medical schools.

Archaeology

Archaeology is the study of earlier cultures and lifeways by anthropologists who specialize in the scientific recovery, analysis, and interpretation of the material remains of past societies. Although archaeology often deals with cultures that existed before the invention of writing (the era commonly known as **prehistory**), many archaeologists also examine the artifactual and structural evidence of later highly developed civilizations that produced written records.

Archaeologists are concerned with culture, but they differ from other cultural anthropologists in that their data sources are not living people but rather the **artifacts** and other **material culture** left behind by earlier societies. Of course, no one has ever excavated a spoken language, a set of religious beliefs, or a political system. But archaeologists consider that the surviving artifacts and structures reflect some of these less tangible aspects of the culture that created them. Therefore, the residue of a given ancient society may inform us about the nature of that society.

Like the other subfields of anthropology, modern archaeology traces its roots to nineteenth-century Europe. A fascination with antiquity, especially the classical Mediterranean civilizations and ancient Egypt and Mesopotamia, fed an initial frenzy of excavation (sometimes controlled, most often not) that yielded literally tons of objects for museums and the private collections of wealthy Europeans. Where such rich finds were less common, as in western Europe and many parts of America, diggers simply plundered more modest graves and structures for their contents. To his credit, as long ago as 1782, Thomas Jefferson conducted one of the first controlled excavations when he opened a burial mound on his property in Virginia (Fig. 1–5). Jefferson's goal was not simply to recover artifacts, but specifically to learn how and perhaps why the mound was constructed.

Few of Jefferson's immediate successors adopted such an enlightened and systematic approach, however, and archaeology for most of the next century continued to resemble a treasure hunt. Fortunately, by the twentieth century, more rigorous and scientific practices replaced such indiscriminate digging.

Especially since the mid-twentieth century, archaeology has become much more methodologically and theoretically sophisticated. Modern archaeologists recognize the need for precise excavation and recording techniques, knowing that as they dig a **site**, they are also destroying it. Because sites are finite resources, as are the funds required to excavate them, archaeologists obtain and preserve as much information as possible every time they dig. The bold excavation work of even such a renowned nineteenth-century archaeologist as Heinrich Schliemann, who used hordes of workers wielding pickaxes and shovels to attack the site of ancient Troy, would be wholly unsuitable by modern standards. Today's meticulous excavators

 Archaeology is discussed in Virtual Lab 11 and includes many 3-D animations of stone tools.

Prehistory
The several million years between the emergence of bipedal hominids and the availability of written records.

Artifacts
Objects or materials made or modified for use by hominids. The earliest artifacts tend to be tools made of stone or, occasionally, bone.

Material culture
The physical manifestations of human activities, such as tools, art, and structures. As the most durable aspects of culture, material remains make up the majority of archaeological evidence of past societies.

William Turnbaugh; painting by Gilbert Stuart

FIGURE 1–5
Thomas Jefferson conducted early archaeological excavations before becoming president of the United States.

Site
A location of past human activity, often associated with artifacts and structures; also, a location of modern archaeological research.

use small hand tools to carefully dissect plotted excavation units. Photographs, drawings, and precise measurements record each find in relation to all others in the context of the site as a whole (Fig. 1–6). Often, an intelligent sampling of the site is sufficient, so that the remainder can be preserved for future researchers.

Another important trend has been the establishment of modern archaeology as a scientific endeavor. In addition to the social science perspective of anthropology, archaeology also maintains strong ties with the natural and physical sciences. Contemporary archaeological research often involves the specialized expertise of many disciplines. Remote-sensing technology, including even NASA satellite imagery, may be used to locate or define sites. Computers are standard equipment, assisting archaeologists with both the management and analysis of vast amounts of data normally collected from even relatively small sites. Geologists, soil scientists, **palynologists**, and others assist in determining a site's ancient environment. Physicists and chemists are called on to use their complex laboratory procedures to determine the age of selected materials. Physical anthropologists examine any human skeletal remains for the overall health status, diet, and physical traits of ancient individuals, a specialization sometimes labeled *bioarchaeology*. Some archaeology students combine their studies with scientific training that prepares them to work with ancient plant or animal remains (*archaeobotany* or *archaeozoology*), ceramics, textiles, and other materials (Fig. 1–7).

A commitment to the scientific method is also evident in the field of *experimental archaeology*, where researchers attempt to replicate ancient techniques and processes under controlled conditions. Using these approaches, archaeologists have reproduced the entire range of ancient stone tools and employed them in many of the tasks presumably performed by prehistoric peoples.

Compared to their predecessors, contemporary archaeologists have more explicitly formulated research goals to justify their activities. These goals are (1) to establish chronology, (2) to reconstruct and describe ancient lifeways, and (3) to explain culture change. Determining a site's age remains an essential first step. Recent refinements in a number of dating techniques, based on the steady decay rate of certain naturally occurring substances, produce dates of great reliability and accuracy. The second goal, to reconstruct and describe the lifeways of the people who lived in the past, requires researchers to determine the original functions of their artifacts and sites. Intensive scrutiny of wear patterns on stone tools, experimental work in re-creating activities and structures, and comparative studies of surviving traditional cultures can all provide useful clues.

Palynologists
Scientists who identify ancient plants from pollen samples unearthed at archaeological sites.

FIGURE 1–6
Excavating a Roman settlement in Canterbury, England.

Courtesy, James D. Loy

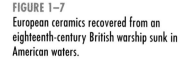

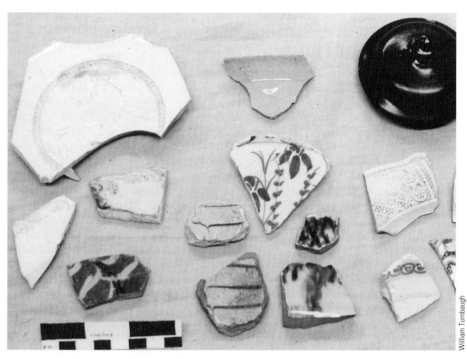

William Turnbaugh

FIGURE 1–7
European ceramics recovered from an eighteenth-century British warship sunk in American waters.

Ultimately, archaeologists seek to explain the past by fashioning models of culture change to account for what has been recovered archaeologically. Archaeologists are far from agreement on the most appropriate philosophical viewpoint for their discipline—or on the basic "meaning" of the past—and the dialogue has been animated at times. In viewing the "big picture," archaeologists propose various evolutionary, political, economic, and environmental models to explain the course of the ancient and more recent human past, but so far no single approach commands a clear consensus.

As we noted earlier, considerable archaeological effort applies toward a fuller understanding of prehistory, the more than 99 percent of the human story for which no written documentation exists. The fossilized bones of remarkable creatures, the likes of which no longer roam the earth, came to light from time to time in western Europe in the nineteenth century. Even more startling, human bones and crudely flaked stone implements sometimes turned up among the fossils of extinct rhinos and mammoths. By the 1860s, such discoveries, along with publications by geologist Charles Lyell and by Darwin, had convinced many to accept the notion of prehistory. *Prehistoric archaeologists* (also known as *prehistorians*) deal with the major issues of early human cultural development: When and where were the first tools made? Were our early ancestors hunters or scavengers? Under what circumstances did farming begin? What were the effects of major cultural inventions such as pottery or metallurgy? How did people accommodate population increases? What was the nature of trade between two or more cultures? What were the advantages or drawbacks of early urban life? Why did warfare develop? In short, what was life like for people in the past? (Note that archaeologists do not study the fossils of nonprimate species such as dinosaurs or mammoths, a field properly claimed by **paleontologists**.)

During the past several thousand years, a growing number of cultures have developed writing systems and maintained at least some primary records of their economy, history, or philosophy by cutting symbols into stone, marking clay tablets, or writing on animal skins, bark, or other prepared surfaces. Descriptive accounts compiled by adventurers and travelers (and later by anthropologists) provide glimpses of still other peoples who had not yet developed writing on their own, including various western European tribes encountered by Julius Caesar over

Paleontologists
Scientists whose study of ancient life forms is based on fossilized remains of extinct animals and plants.

2,000 years ago and the many Native American groups met by the explorers Lewis and Clark about 200 years ago. These historical descriptions usually offer a rather fleeting and narrow view, but they nevertheless augment sites and artifactual remains as sources of information about earlier societies.

Archaeologists who supplement their research and interpretations with the use of written records are called *historical archaeologists*. Those who excavate sites pertaining to the expansion of European civilization in the Americas, Africa, and elsewhere after the fifteenth century likewise fall into this category. Excavations of the remains of colonial farms in New England, slave cabins in Georgia, and sugar plantations in Jamaica are typical historical archaeology projects (Fig. 1–8).

Archaeologists who work with the literate civilizations of the Old World, such as ancient Greece, Rome, and Egypt, are *classical archaeologists*. Their specialized training for work with these cultures emphasizes ancient languages, the study of historical texts, and an intimate familiarity with art styles and architecture (Fig. 1–9). Many classical archaeologists are trained in departments of fine arts, classics, or Near Eastern studies rather than in anthropology. Classical archaeologists who specialize in the study of Near Eastern sites associated with events mentioned in the Old and New Testaments may be considered *biblical archaeologists*.

Archaeological specialties do not stop there. *Underwater archaeology* is a growing field, with an emphasis on the study of shipwrecks and other submerged sites. Using diving equipment, archaeologists in this domain carry out surveys and excavations using techniques specially developed for the unusual surroundings (Fig.1–10). They are able to recover numerous details of the structure of sunken ships and their cargoes, and they even may excavate terrestrial sites that have been submerged by coastal subsidence, dams, or other processes.

In the United States, archaeological activity in recent years has expanded with the growth of *public archaeology*. This field includes efforts to reach out and involve wider audiences in archaeology through education and the media. Most public archaeologists are engaged in cultural resource management (CRM). As mandated by government environmental legislation since the 1970s, archaeologists in this field are contracted to evaluate sites that may be threatened with damage from development and construction. CRM work utilizes a wide range of archaeological expertise, including prehistorians, historical archaeologists, field technicians, archaeological illustrators and writers, and laboratory specialists. Many contract archaeologists in the CRM field are affiliated with environmental study firms in the private sector,

FIGURE 1–8
Historical archaeologist excavates a colonial house foundation in Rhode Island.

William Turnbaugh

FIGURE 1–9
Classical archaeologists study architectural details at the Roman marketplace built by the emperor Trajan in the first century A.D.

Whitney Powell-Cummer

while others are employed by state or federal agencies or by educational institutions. About 40 percent of the respondents in a 1994 membership survey conducted by the Society for American Archaeology fill such positions (Zeder, 1997).

Public and private museums and research organizations support a smaller number of archaeologists, who serve primarily as curators, exhibits specialists, conservators, or researchers. Today, about two in five American archaeologists hold college and university teaching and research positions. Those in academic settings generally instruct interested students, conduct fieldwork, and write scholarly publications, often balancing all three activities.

Most archaeologists define their research topics according to a given geographical region (Turkey, Southeast Asia, central California), a specific issue (early food production, Paleolithic art, toolmaking technology), or some combination of these (e.g., town life of Iron Age Germany).

Many American archaeologists have maintained a long involvement with the impressive pre-Columbian civilizations of Mexico and Central and South America (the Aztecs, Maya, and Inka*). Although scholars still admire the artwork and architecture that initially attracted excavators to these sites, modern archaeologists seek to understand more fully the social, economic, and political dynamics that contributed to the development and downfall of these and other ancient cultures (Fig. 1–11). For example, recent

Gordon P. Watts, Jr.

FIGURE 1–10
Underwater archaeologists map the wooden framing and ballast of a British vessel that sank off Bermuda about 200 years ago.

---

*Because it is consistent with current usage among the native Quechua speakers of Peru, the spelling of "Inka" we have adopted here is becoming generally preferred over the once-standard "Inca."

FIGURE 1–11
The Caracol, a late Maya observatory at Chichén Itzá, in the Yucatán region of Mexico, attracts both archaeologists and tourists.

Harry Nelson

A discussion of the scientific method can be found in Virtual Lab 3, section III.

Science
A body of knowledge gained through observation and experimentation; from the Latin *scientia*, meaning "knowledge."

Empirical
Relying on experiment or observation; from the Latin *empiricus*, meaning "experienced."

Scientific method
A research method whereby a problem is identified, a hypothesis (or hypothetical explanation) is stated, and that hypothesis is tested through the collection and analysis of data. If the hypothesis is verified, it becomes a theory.

Data (*sing.*, datum)
Facts from which conclusions can be drawn; scientific information.

Quantitatively (quantitative)
Pertaining to measurements of quantity and including such properties as size, number, and capacity. When data are quantified, they are expressed numerically and are capable of being tested statistically.

advances in translating Maya inscriptions reveal that the society was held together by exchange networks and royal alliances that occasionally lapsed into warfare.

Elsewhere in the New World where such large-scale prehistoric societies never emerged, archaeologists examine a great diversity of Native American cultures, from the widely dispersed sites of hunters and gatherers to the ancient farming villages along major river courses, the temple and burial mound complexes in the southeastern United States, and the well-preserved prehistoric townsites of the Southwest. Some North American archaeologists are trying to answer questions about the origin and timing of the first arrivals in the New World. Some examine issues relating to cultural contact and culture change, including the rise and spread of farming or civilizations. Many trace the prehistory of individual native societies that were present at the time of European exploration. And still others focus on the dynamic episodes of contact between the peoples of Europe and the Americas or the subsequent historical period.

The Scientific Method

Science is a process of understanding phenomena through observation, generalization, and verification. By this we mean that there is an **empirical** approach to gaining information through the use of systematic and explicit techniques. Because physical anthropologists and archaeologists are engaged in scientific pursuits, they adhere to the principles of the **scientific method**, whereby a research problem is identified and information subsequently gathered to solve it.

The gathering of information is referred to as **data** collection, and when researchers use a rigorously controlled approach, they are able to describe precisely their techniques and results in a manner that facilitates comparisons with the work of others. For example, when scientists collect data on tooth size in hominid fossils, they must specify precisely which teeth are being measured, how they are being measured, and what the results of the measurements are (expressed numerically, or **quantitatively**). Subsequently, it is up to the investigators to draw conclusions as to the meaning and significance of their measurements. This body of information then becomes the basis of future studies, perhaps by other researchers, who can compare their own results with those already obtained. The eventual outcome of this type of inquiry may be the acceptance or rejection of certain proposed facts and explanations.

Once facts have been established, scientists attempt to explain them. First, a **hypothesis**, or provisional explanation of phenomena, is developed. But before a hypothesis can be accepted, it must be tested by means of data collection and analysis. Indeed, the testing of hypotheses with the possibility of proving them false is the very basis of the scientific method.

Scientific testing of hypotheses may take several years (or longer) and may involve researchers who were not connected with the original work. In subsequent studies, other investigators may attempt to obtain the original results, but such repetition may not occur. For example, repeated failures to duplicate the results of highly publicized cold fusion experiments led most scientists to question and ultimately reject the claims made in the original research. While it is easier to duplicate original studies conducted in laboratory settings, it is equally important to verify data collected outside tightly controlled situations. In the latter circumstance, results are tested relative to other, often larger samples. The predicted patterns will either be confirmed through such further research or be viewed as limited or even incorrect.

If a hypothesis cannot be falsified, it is accepted as a **theory**. There is a popular misconception that theories are nothing more than hunches or unfounded explanations. But in scientific terms, a theory is a statement of relationships that has a firm basis as demonstrated through testing and the accumulation of evidence. As such, it not only helps organize current knowledge, but should also predict how new facts may fit into the established pattern.

Use of the scientific method not only allows for the development and testing of hypotheses, but also permits various types of *bias* to be addressed and controlled. It is important to realize that bias occurs in all studies. Sources of bias include how the investigator was trained and by whom; what particular questions interest the researcher; what specific skills and talents he or she possesses; what earlier results (if any) have been established in this realm of study and by whom (e.g., the researcher, close colleagues, or those with rival approaches or even rival personalities); and what sources of data are available (e.g., accessible countries or museums) and thus what samples can be collected (at all or at least conveniently).

Trained scientists must be vigilant of various (and often personal) biases, and you, the reader, should be, too. In this book, certain views are presented that we, the authors, might not personally favor. However, we include those views because scientists should not simply dismiss views or ideas of which they are skeptical. Similarly, you should be reluctant to accept or reject an idea based solely on your personal feelings or biases. Science is an approach—indeed, a *tool*—used to eliminate (or at least minimize) bias.

Application of the scientific method thus requires constant vigilance by all who practice it. The goal is not to establish "truth" in any absolute sense, but rather to generate ever more accurate and consistent depictions and explanations of phenomena in our universe. At its very heart, scientific methodology is an exercise in rational thought and critical thinking.

The Anthropological Perspective

Perhaps the most important benefit you will derive from this textbook (and this course) is a wider appreciation of the human experience. To better understand human beings and how our species came to be, it is necessary to broaden our viewpoint across space (comparing individuals, populations, and even species) and through time (considering the past, with special emphasis on evolutionary factors). In their own ways, all branches of anthropology seek to do this in an approach we call the *anthropological perspective*.

Hypothesis (*pl.*, **hypotheses**)
A provisional explanation of a phenomenon. Hypotheses require verification.

Scientific testing
The precise repetition of an experiment or expansion of observed data to provide verification; the procedure by which hypotheses and theories are verified, modified, or discarded.

Theory
A broad statement of scientific relationships or underlying principles that has been at least partially verified.

Exercises in which you formulate and test hypotheses with data that you collect are found in nearly all of the Virtual Lab exercises.

Continuum
A set of relationships in which all components fall along a single integrated spectrum. All life reflects a single *biological* continuum.

From the brief overview presented in this chapter, we can see that physical anthropologists focus on varied aspects of the biological nature of *Homo sapiens* and that archaeologists discover and interpret the cultural evidence of hominid (including modern human) behavior from sites ranging in age from over 2 million years old up to the present day. Modern humans are products of the same forces that produced all life on earth. As such, we represent one contemporary component of a vast biological **continuum** at one point in time. In this regard, we are not particularly unique. Stating that humans are part of a continuum does not imply that we are at the peak of development on that continuum. Depending on which criteria one uses, humans can be seen to exist at one end of the continuum or the other, or somewhere in between, but humans do not occupy a position that is inherently superior to other species.

There is, however, one dimension in which humans are truly unique, and that is intellect. Humans are the only species to develop complex culture as a means of buffering the challenges posed by nature, and we are the only species that spontaneously acquires and uses spoken language as a very complex form of communication. Consequently, physical anthropologists are keenly interested in how humans differ from and are similar to other animals, especially nonhuman primates. For example, in Chapters 5 and 16, we will discuss some aspects of human nutrition and how it has been influenced by various evolutionary factors. Today, the majority of foods people eat are derived from domesticated plants and animals, but these dietary items were unavailable prior to the development of agriculture some 10,000 years ago. However, human physiological mechanisms for chewing and digesting, as well as the types of foods humans are predisposed to eat, are variations of patterns that had been well established in nonhuman primate ancestors long before 10,000 years ago. Indeed, these adaptive complexes probably go back millions of years.

In addition to differences in diet prior to the development of agriculture, earlier hominids might well have differed from modern humans in average body size, metabolism, and activity patterns. How, then, does the basic evolutionary "equipment" (i.e., physiology) inherited from our hominid and prehominid forebears accommodate our modern diets? Clearly, the way to understand such processes is not simply to look at contemporary human responses, but also to place them within the context of evolution and adaptation through time. Indeed, throughout this book, we will focus on the biocultural interactions that came about after the development of agriculture, an event that was one of the most fundamental revolutions in all of human prehistory. By studying human behavior and anatomy from the broader perspective provided by an evolutionary context, we are better able to understand the factors that led to the development of the human species.

Archaeologists trace the evolution of culture and its ever-expanding role in human affairs over the past 2 million years. Information from archaeological research is frequently combined with biological data to elucidate how cultural and biological factors have interacted in the past to produce variations in human adaptive response, disease patterns, and even the genetic diversity that we see today. From such a perspective, we can begin to appreciate the diversity of the human experience and, in so doing, more fully understand human constraints and potentials. Furthermore, by extending the breadth of our knowledge, it is easier to avoid the **ethnocentric** pitfalls inherent in a more limited view of humanity, a view that isolates modern humans from other human groups and places them outside the context of evolution.

Ethnocentric
Viewing other cultures from the inherently biased perspective of one's own culture. Ethnocentrism often results in other cultures being seen as inferior to one's own.

SUMMARY

In this chapter, we have introduced the fields of physical anthropology and archaeology and have placed them within the overall context of anthropological studies. Anthropology as a major academic area within the social sciences also includes cultural anthropology and linguistics within its major subfields.

CHAPTER 1

Physical anthropology itself includes aspects of human biology (emphasizing evolutionary perspectives), the study of nonhuman primates, and the hominid fossil record. Physical anthropologists are interested in how hominids came to possess culture and how this process has influenced the direction of human evolution. Especially in regard to the study of early hominids (as incorporated within the interdisciplinary field of paleoanthropology), physical anthropologists work in close collaboration with many other scientists from the fields of archaeology, geology, chemistry, and so forth.

Archaeology provides time depth for our understanding of humans as biocultural organisms. Archaeologists systematically recover and study the artifacts and sites of past societies to shed light on extinct lifeways, provide cultural chronologies, and suggest explanations for observable change. As with paleoanthropology (of which prehistoric archaeology is a key component), archaeological research also involves other input from many related disciplines. This collaborative work accounts for nearly all we now know about prehistoric human behavior and activities.

QUESTIONS FOR REVIEW

1. What is anthropology? What are the major subfields of anthropology?
2. How does physical anthropology differ from other disciplines interested in human biology?
3. What is meant by biocultural evolution, and why is it important in understanding human evolution?
4. What are some of the primary areas of research within physical anthropology? Give two or three examples of the types of research pursued by physical anthropologists.
5. What is meant by the term *hominid*? Be specific.
6. What fields, in addition to physical anthropology, contribute to paleo-anthropology?
7. Discuss some of the varied specializations and research areas within archaeology. Give examples of the types of research pursued by archaeologists within several of these specializations.
8. Discuss what is meant by the term *anthropological perspective*. How does this approach differ from that of a sociologist or historian?

SUGGESTED FURTHER READING

Bahn, Paul G. 1996. *The Cambridge Illustrated History of Archaeology*. Cambridge: Cambridge University Press.

Fagan, Brian M. (ed.). 1996. *Eyewitness to Discovery*. New York: Oxford University Press.

Ferraro, Gary, Wenda Trevathan, and Janet Levy. 1994. *Anthropology, an Applied Perspective*. St. Paul:West.

Schnapp, Alain. 1997. *The Discovery of the Past*. New York: Abrams.

Spencer, Frank (ed.). 1982. *A History of Physical Anthropology*. New York: Academic Press.

Willey, Gordon R., and Jeremy A. Sabloff. 1993. *A History of American Archaeology*. San Francisco: Freeman.

RESOURCES ON THE INTERNET

 Wadsworth Anthropology Resource Center
http://anthropology.wadsworth.com

The companion website for this text includes a range of enrichment material focused on the chapter's topic. While online you can enhance your understanding of the chapter by exploring one of the several additional Internet Exercises, by researching topics, and by accessing full articles on InfoTrac College Edition. You can also reinforce the concepts by taking online practice exams.

Internet Exercises

Visit the major association of anthropologists in the United States, the American Anthropological Association. (If your search did not provide the link, try **http://www.aaanet.org**.) The American Anthropological Association represents anthropologists in all subdisciplines, and this site serves as a good indicator of the breadth of anthropology. Take time to explore the site thoroughly. Visit "About AAA" to learn more about the field and the association. Read "Careers in Anthropology." What could you do with a major in anthropology without going to graduate school?

 InfoTrac College Edition
http://www.infotrac-college.com/wadsworth

Anthropology is a very broad discipline. Search InfoTrac College Edition for the subject *anthropology*. How many different topics are there? How many are related to biological or physical anthropology? How many are there for archaeology? Choose one subject not introduced in the text and read some of the articles about it. What makes this topic anthropological?

Careers in Physical Anthropology and Archaeology

A background in anthropology can help prepare students for a wide variety of careers, and many of these extend well beyond traditional academic settings. Featured below are a number of individuals who have used their anthropological education to pursue varied and interesting careers. These archaeologists and physical anthropologists display in diverse ways how anthropology has influenced their career choices and ongoing commitment to contribute to their communities.

Cindy Fleming

Sarah Peabody Turnbaugh, Museum of Primitive Art and Culture

Cindy Fleming earned both her bachelor's and master's degrees from Oberlin College, where she studied anthropology, sociology, and art history. After first working as an aide at her children's schools and at a public library in Alabama, Cindy moved to southern Rhode Island. For several years she has been an educator at the Museum of Primitive Art and Culture, a community-based anthropology museum in Peace Dale, Rhode Island. Through outreach programs to area schools and in the museum gallery, Cindy enjoys interacting with enthusiastic youngsters as she introduces them to Native American and Inuit lifeways, African cultures, and early civilizations through stories, artifacts, and hands-on activities.

Donna Raymond (left)

Museum of Primitive Art and Culture

Since earning her bachelor's degree in anthropology with a focus on archaeology, Donna Raymond has been in charge of the day-to-day laboratory operations of the Public Archaeology Laboratory, Inc., a major cultural resource management firm specializing in archaeological assessment and mitigation projects. At the PAL facilities in Pawtucket, Rhode Island, Donna and her colleagues use an array of technical processes to analyze samples and specimens recovered by dozens of archaeological field projects each year. But Donna never tires of her work, sometimes even volunteering her time to demonstrate basic excavation techniques to some budding archaeologists.

Careers in Physical Anthropology and Archaeology (continued)

Judy Regensteiner

Many people who begin with an interest in physical anthropology find themselves doing biomedical research. Dr. Judy Regensteiner was in high school when a general anthropology class captured her imagination and sent her on a course she would pursue throughout her career. Her Ph.D. dissertation on elderly residents of high-altitude areas (over 8,000 feet) concerned the effects of altitude on out-migration due to heart and lung disease. After earning a Ph.D. at the University of Colorado, with an emphasis in physical anthropology, she completed a two-year post-doctoral fellowship in cardiovascular physiology at the University of Colorado Health Sciences Center in Denver. She has remained at the UCHSC, where she is now an associate professor of medicine and director of the clinical treadmill lab. She has conducted considerable research in peripheral arterial disease—a focus of her current research, along with car-diovascular disease and diabetes in women. In particular, she has exam-ined the effects of peripheral arterial disease and diabetes on the ability to perform exercise as well as carry out normal daily physical activities.

When asked how anthropology has influenced her career choices, Dr. Regensteiner replied, "Anthropology has always influenced the direction my career has taken because of its focus on human adaptation. In fact, all of my research, beginning with my dissertation, has been influenced by this emphasis. In all subsequent work, I have emphasized the physiological ability of human beings to adapt functionally in the presence of a disease state."

Russell Mittermeier

Although he undertook a fairly typical academic education, first at Dartmouth College (B.A. in anthropology) and later at Harvard University (M.A., Ph.D., both in biological anthropology), Russell Mittermeier has pursued anything but a typical academic career. Indeed, he has spent his entire adult life either trouping through rain forests all around the world or working for conservation groups dedicated to protecting these habitats.

Currently, Dr. Mittermeier is president of Conservation International, a nonprofit organization headquartered in Washington, D.C., which pro-motes the preservation of biodiversity in those habitats ("hot spots") presently under the most threat. Founded in 1987, Conservation International appointed Dr. Mittermeier its president in 1989. Over the last three decades, Russell Mittermeier has come to be recognized as one of the most dynamic conservation biologists in the world. His dedication, energy, and passion have helped to mobilize industrial and financial lead-ers, government policy makers, and the general public.

In the face of seemingly overwhelming odds, Russell Mittermeier's commitment to preserving the earth's biodiversity has never wavered. Recently, he said, "As we enter the new millennium, we risk losing our closest living relatives in the Animal Kingdom. But while they are under tremendous threats, there is still hope if we can take action now."*

---

*Quoted from the Conservation International website. Find out more about Conservation International at www.conservation.org.

Whitney Powell-Cummer

Whitney Powell-Cummer combines artistic talent and archaeological knowledge in her career as an archaeological illustrator, much of it having been spent at Harvard University's Peabody Museum of Archaeology and Ethnology. Her meticulous pen-and-ink artifact renderings have appeared in numerous scientific publications. Whitney occasionally offers instruction in archaeological illustration, a skill that remains essential even today, since cameras and computer graphics cannot capture and convey significant details as clearly as a high-quality drawing. In this photo, Whitney traces ancient inscriptions found on a wall fragment at Tiryns, Greece.

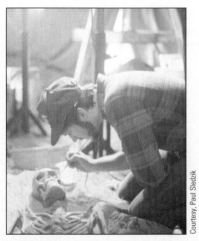

Paul Sledzik

Forensic anthropologist Paul Sledzik writes: "When I took my first anthropology course in 1982—an introductory course in physical anthropology—I had just shifted away from a focus in pre-medicine. I had always had an interest in anthropology, and my undergraduate professors supported my desire to attend graduate school. In 1985, I started my master's degree training, choosing a biological anthropology program in an ecology and evolutionary biology department. In 1986, I was offered a temporary job in Washington, D.C., at the National Museum of Health and Medicine. The museum is part of the Armed Forces Institute of Pathology, a distinguished research facility in pathology and forensic medicine. After the year was up, I was asked to stay on. I've been there ever since, eventually becoming curator of the anatomical collections in 1991.

It is a unique job, overseeing a collection of 5,000 skeletal specimens and 7,000 gross pathology specimens. I've learned about Civil War medicine, medical history, anatomical preparation, and other intriguing areas of study. The collection includes the remains of presidents, and some 2,000 Civil War soldiers, as well as examples of rare diseases.

Although I had worked on forensic cases while a student, the museum and AFIP has offered a rare opportunity to learn about forensics and become involved in research and teaching in the field. In the early 1990s, I became involved in issues related to the identification of the dead in mass disasters. The more I learned, the more it became clear that this area of victim identification could benefit from an approach that looked at the physical aspects of humans, the religious and cultural aspects of death, and the methods of archaeology in the search and recovery of remains. I've been promoting this approach since 1993. The satisfaction of applying my training in anthropology to directly assist people during a critical time is extremely rewarding.

My job allows me to teach, conduct research, and make a meaningful impact on people's lives. No two days have ever been the same. I travel, meet new people, and promote science on a regular basis. I've had the chance to affect national policy in the area of disaster response and victim identification."

Careers in Physical Anthropology and Archaeology (continued)

Aaron Elkins

Mystery novelist Aaron Elkins writes: "I began writing after a some-what unfocused work life of government employment and teaching (University of Maryland, California State University, Golden Gate University, and other schools), mostly in nontenured positions. My first book, published in 1982, featured Gideon Oliver, the skeleton detective, who was a better physical anthropologist than I was ever going to be. I promptly made the resolution to drop my own anthropological career and hitch my wagon to his, and I've never been sorry.

I didn't realize it at the time, but it was physical anthropology—oste-ology and skeletal analysis in particular—that served as my introduction to the joys of the kind of detective work that I've been writing happily about for the last 20 years. The mystery and fascination of sitting down with a few skeletal fragments, whether two years old or two hundred thou-sand years old—actually holding in one's hand these last remnants of a once-living human being—and trying through them to "connect" with the individual they belonged to has never left me. Was this a man or a woman? How old was he? How did she die? How tall, how strong, how healthy? Are there clues to what she ate or how he looked or what kind of hardships she endured?"

David S. Robinson

David S. Robinson often finds himself in deep water, but that's just fine with him. Upon graduation, David combined his undergraduate stud-ies in anthropology with his diving skills and a penchant for maritime his-tory by participating in archaeological work in the waters of Rhode Island Sound, the Great Lakes, Chesapeake Bay, and the Gulf of Mexico. Now he holds a master's degree from Texas A & M University's graduate program in nautical archaeology and has his own Vermont-based consulting firm, David S. Robinson & Associates, specializing in terrestrial and marine remote sensing survey, underwater archaeology, and archaeological con-servation. Though many of his projects have been historical American shipwrecks from the Revolution to the Civil War period, David recently worked as a guest of the Danish National Museum's Center for Maritime Archaeology and raised a twelfth-century wreck from the bottom of Kolding Fjord, in Denmark.

For more information on careers for physical anthropologists and archaeologists, visit the website of the American Anthropological Association, http://www.ameranthassn.org, and click Careers.

You can also find helpful information by visiting www.wadsworth.anthropology.com and clicking the Applying Anthropology button.

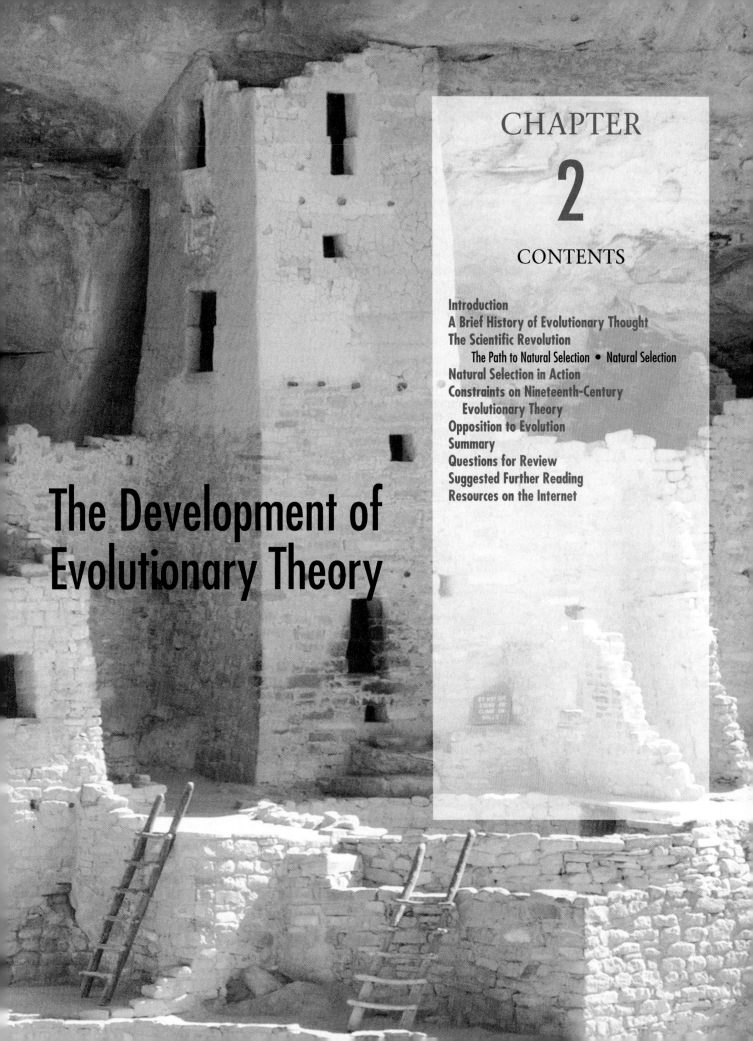

CHAPTER 2

CONTENTS

The Development of Evolutionary Theory

Evolution
A change in the genetic structure of a population. The term is also frequently used to refer to the appearance of a new species.

 See the following sections of the CD-ROM for topics covered in this chapter: Virtual Lab 1, section II and Virtual Lab 2, section I, part B.

Natural selection
The mechanism of evolutionary change first articulated by Charles Darwin; refers to genetic change, or to changes in the frequencies of certain traits in populations due to differential reproductive success between individuals.

Worldview
General cultural orientation or perspective shared by members of a society.

Fixity of species
The notion that species, once created, can never change; an idea diametrically opposed to theories of biological evolution.

Introduction

The term **evolution** is sometimes charged with emotion. The concept is often controversial, particularly in the United States, because some religious views hold that evolutionary statements run counter to biblical teachings. In fact, as you are probably aware, there continues to be much opposition to the teaching of evolution in public schools.

Those who wish to denigrate evolution frequently insist that it is "only a theory" in an attempt to reduce its status to supposition. Actually, to refer to a concept as "theory" is to lend it support. As we noted in Chapter 1, theories are general hypotheses that have been tested and subjected to verification through accumulated evidence. Evolution *is* a theory, one that has increasingly been supported by a mounting body of genetic evidence. It is a theory that has stood the test of time, and today it stands as the most fundamental unifying force in biological science.

Because physical anthropology is concerned with all aspects of how humans came to be and how we adapt physiologically to the external environment, the details of the evolutionary process are crucial to the field. Moreover, given the central importance of evolution to physical anthropology, it is valuable to know how the mechanics of the process came to be discovered. Additionally, to appreciate the nature of the controversy that continues to surround the issue today, it is important to examine the basic evolutionary principles within the social and political context in which the theory emerged.

A Brief History of Evolutionary Thought

The individual most responsible for the elucidation of the evolutionary process is Charles Darwin. But while Darwin was formulating his theory of **natural selection**, his ideas were being duplicated by another English naturalist, Alfred Russel Wallace.

That natural selection, the single most important mechanism of evolutionary change, should be proposed at more or less the same time by *two* British men in the mid-nineteenth century may seem highly improbable. But actually, it is not all that surprising. Indeed, if Darwin and Wallace had not made their simultaneous discoveries, someone else would have done so in short order. That is to say, the groundwork had already been laid, and many within the scientific community were prepared to accept explanations of biological change that would have been unacceptable even 25 years before.

Like other human endeavors, scientific knowledge is usually gained through a series of small steps rather than giant leaps. Just as technological innovation is based on past achievements, scientific knowledge builds on previously developed theories. (One does not build a space shuttle without first having invented the airplane.) Given this stepwise aspect of scientific discovery, it is informative to examine the development of ideas that led Darwin and Wallace independently to develop the theory of evolution by natural selection.

Throughout the Middle Ages, one predominant component of the European **worldview** was *stasis*. That is, all aspects of nature, including all forms of life and their relationships to one another, were fixed and unchanging. This view of natural phenomena was shaped in part by a feudal society that was very much a hierarchical arrangement supporting a rigid class system that had changed little for several centuries.

The worldview of Europeans during the Middle Ages was also shaped by a powerful religious system. The teachings of Christianity were taken quite literally, and it was generally accepted that all life on earth had been created by God exactly as it existed in the present. This belief that life forms could not change eventually came to be known in European intellectual circles as **fixity of species**.

Accompanying the notion of fixity of species was the belief that all God's creations were arranged in a hierarchy that progressed from the simplest organisms to the most complex. At the top of this linear sequence were humans. This concept of

a ranked order of living things is termed the *Great Chain of Being* and was first proposed in the fourth century B.C. by the Greek philosopher Aristotle. Although position within the chain was based on physical similarities between species, no evolutionary or biological relationships were implied. Moreover, "lower" forms could not move up the scale to become "superior" ones.

In addition, there was the common notion that the earth was "full" and that nothing new (such as species) could be added. Thus, it was believed that since the creation, no new species had appeared and none had disappeared, or become extinct. And since all of nature and the Great Chain of Being were created by God in a fixed state, change was inconceivable. Questioning the assumptions of fixity was ultimately seen as a challenge to God's perfection and could be considered heresy.

The plan of the entire universe was seen as the Grand Design—that is, God's design. In what is called the "argument from design," anatomical structures were viewed as planned to meet the purpose for which they were required. Wings, arms, eyes—all these structures were interpreted as neatly fitting the functions they performed, and nature was considered to be a deliberate plan of the Grand Designer.

The date the Grand Designer had completed his works was relatively recent—4004 B.C., according to Archbishop James Ussher (1581–1656), an Irish scholar who worked out the date of creation by analyzing the "begat" chapter of Genesis. The idea of a recent origin of the earth did not begin with Archbishop Ussher, but he was responsible for providing a precise and late date for it.

The prevailing notion of the earth's brief existence, together with fixity of species, provided a formidable obstacle to the development of evolutionary theory because evolution requires time. Thus, in addition to overcoming the concept of fixity of species, scientists needed a theory of immense geological time in order to formulate evolutionary principles. In fact, until these prior concepts of fixity and time were fundamentally altered, it would have been unlikely that the idea of natural selection could even have been conceived.

The Scientific Revolution

What, then, upset the medieval belief in a rigid universe of planets, stars, plants, and animals? How did the scientific method as we know it today develop and, with the help of Newton and Galileo in the seventeenth century, demonstrate a moving, not static, universe?

The discovery of the New World and circumnavigation of the globe in the fifteenth century overturned some very fundamental ideas about the planet. For one thing, the earth could no longer be perceived as flat. Also, as Europeans began to explore the New World, their awareness of biological diversity was greatly expanded through exposure to plants and animals previously unknown to them.

There were other attacks on the complacency of traditional beliefs. In 1514, a Polish mathematician named Copernicus challenged Aristotle's long-believed assertion that the earth, circled by the sun, moon, and stars, was the center of the universe. Copernicus removed the earth as the center of all things by proposing a *heliocentric* (sun-centered) solar system.

Copernicus' theory did not attract widespread attention at the time, but in the early 1600s, it was restated and further substantiated by an Italian mathematics professor, Galileo Galilei. Galileo came into direct confrontation with the Catholic Church over his publications, to the extent that he spent the last nine years of his life under house arrest. Even so, in intellectual circles, the universe had changed from one of fixity to one of motion, although most scholars still believed that change was impossible for living forms.

Scholars of the sixteenth and seventeenth centuries developed methods and theories that revolutionized scientific thought. The seventeenth century, in particular, was a beehive of scientific activity. The works of such individuals as Kepler, Descartes, and Newton established the laws of physics, motion, and gravity. Other achievements included the discovery of the circulation of blood and the

development of numerous scientific instruments, including the telescope, barometer, and microscope. These technological advances permitted investigations of natural phenomena and opened up entire worlds for discoveries such as had never before been imagined.

Scientific achievement increasingly came to direct as well as reflect the changing views of Europeans. Investigations of stars, planets, animals, and plants came to be conducted without significant reference to the supernatural. In other words, nature was seen as a mechanism functioning according to certain universal physical laws, and it was these laws that scientists were seeking. Yet, most scientists still insisted that a First Cause initiated the entire system. The argument from design was still defended, and support for it continued well into the nineteenth century and persists even today.

The Path to Natural Selection

Before early naturalists could begin to understand the forms of organic life, it was necessary to list and describe those forms. As attempts in this direction were made, scholars became increasingly impressed with the amount of biological diversity that confronted them.

John Ray   By the sixteenth century, a keen interest in nature's variation had developed, and by the mid-1500s, there were a few descriptive works on plants, birds, fish, and mammals. But it was not until the seventeenth century that the concept of species was clearly defined by Englishman John Ray (1627–1705), an ordained minister trained at Cambridge University.

Ray was the first to recognize that groups of plants and animals could be distinguished from other groups by their ability to reproduce with one another and produce offspring. Such groups of reproductively isolated organisms were placed into a single category he called *species* (*pl.*, species). Thus, by the late 1600s, the biological criterion of reproduction was used to define species much as it is today (Young, 1992), and upon its publication, the concept was enthusiastically received by the scientific community.

Ray also recognized that species frequently shared similarities with other species, and these he grouped together in a second level of classification he called the *genus* (*pl.*, genera). Ray was the first to use the labels *genus* and *species* in this manner, and they are the terms still in use today. But Ray was very much an adherent of fixity of species. His 1691 publication, *The Wisdom of God Manifested in the Works of Creation*, was intended to demonstrate God's plan in nature, and in this work Ray stressed that nature was a deliberate outcome of a Grand Design.

Carolus Linnaeus   One of the leading naturalists of the eighteenth century was Carolus Linnaeus (1707–1778) of Sweden (Fig. 2–1). He is best known for developing a classification of plants and animals, the *Systema Naturae* (Systems of Nature), first published in 1735.

Linnaeus standardized Ray's more sporadic use of two names (genus and species) for organisms, thus firmly establishing the use of **binomial nomenclature**. Moreover, he added two more categories: class and order. Linnaeus' four-level system of classification became the basis for **taxonomy**, the system of classification still used today.

Another of Linnaeus' innovations was to include humans in his classification of animals, placing them in the genus *Homo* ("human") and species *sapiens* ("wise"). The inclusion of humans in this scheme was controversial because it defied contemporary thought that humans, made in God's image, should be considered separately and outside the animal kingdom.

Linnaeus was also a believer in fixity of species, although in later years, faced with mounting evidence to the contrary, he came to question this long-held

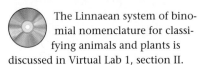

The species concept is presented in Virtual Lab 1, section II.

The Linnaean system of binomial nomenclature for classifying animals and plants is discussed in Virtual Lab 1, section II.

Binomial nomenclature
(*Binomial* means "two names.") In taxonomy, the convention established by Carolus Linnaeus whereby genus and species names are used to refer to species. For example, *Homo sapiens* refers to human beings.

Taxonomy
The branch of science concerned with the rules of classifying organisms on the basis of evolutionary relationships.

Courtesy, Dept. of Library Services, American Museum of Natural History #318607

FIGURE 2–1
Linnaeus developed a classification system for plants and animals.

assumption. Indeed, fixity of species was being challenged on many fronts, especially in France, where voices were being raised in favor of a universe based on change and, more to the point, in favor of biological relationships between similar forms based on descent from a common ancestor.

Comte de Buffon Georges-Louis Leclerc (1707–1788), who was elevated to the rank of count under the name Buffon, was Keeper of the King's Gardens in Paris (Fig. 2–2). He believed neither in the perfection of nature nor in the idea that nature had a purpose, as declared by the argument from design, but he did recognize the dynamic relationship between the external environment and living forms. In his *Natural History*, first published in 1749, he repeatedly stressed the importance of change in the universe, and he underlined the changing nature of species.

Buffon believed that when groups of organisms migrated to new areas of the world, each group would subsequently be influenced by local climatic conditions and would gradually change as a result of adaptation to the environment. Buffon's recognition of the external environment as an agent of change in species was an important innovation. However, he rejected the idea that one species could give rise to another.

Erasmus Darwin Erasmus Darwin (1731–1802) is today best known as Charles Darwin's grandfather (Fig. 2–3). But during his life, this freethinking, high-living physician was well known in literary circles for his poetry and other writings. Chief among the latter was his *Zoonomia*, in which evolutionary concepts were expressed in verse.

More than 50 years before his grandson was to startle the world with his views on natural selection, Erasmus Darwin had expressed similar ideas and had even commented on *human* evolution. From letters and other sources, it is known that Charles Darwin had read and was fond of his grandfather's writings, but the degree to which the grandson's theories were influenced by the grandfather is not known.

Jean-Baptiste Lamarck Neither Buffon nor Erasmus Darwin codified his beliefs into a comprehensive system that attempted to *explain* the evolutionary process. The first scientist to do so was the French scholar Jean-Baptiste Pierre Antoine de Monet Chevalier de Lamarck (1744–1829). (Thankfully, most references to Lamarck use only his surname.)

Expanding beyond the views of Buffon, Lamarck (Fig. 2–4) attempted to *explain* evolution. He postulated a dynamic interaction between organic forms and the environment, such that organic forms could become altered in the face of changing environmental circumstances. Thus, as the environment changed, an animal's activity patterns would also change, resulting in increased or decreased use of certain body parts. As a result of this use or disuse, body parts became altered.

Physical alteration occurred as a function of perceived bodily "needs." If a particular part of the body felt a certain need, "fluids and forces" would be directed toward that point and the structure would be modified to satisfy the need. Because the modification would render the animal better suited to its habitat, the new trait would be passed on to offspring. This theory is known as the *inheritance of acquired characteristics*, or the *use-disuse* theory.

One of the most frequently given examples of Lamarck's theory is that of the giraffe, who, having stripped all the leaves from the lower branches of a tree (environmental change), strives to reach the leaves on the upper branches. As vital forces progress to tissues of the neck, the neck increases slightly in length, thus enabling the giraffe to obtain more food. The longer neck is subsequently transmitted to offspring, with the eventual result that all giraffes have longer necks than did their predecessors (Fig. 2–5a). Thus, according to the theory of inheritance of acquired characteristics, *a trait acquired by an animal during its lifetime can be passed on to offspring.* Today we know this explanation to be inaccurate, for only those traits coded for by genetic information contained within sex cells (eggs and sperm) can be inherited (see Chapter 3).

FIGURE 2–2
Buffon recognized the influence of the environment on life forms.

FIGURE 2–3
Erasmus Darwin, grandfather of Charles Darwin, believed in species change.

FIGURE 2–4
Lamarck believed that species change was influenced by environmental change. He is known for his theory of the inheritance of acquired characteristics.

Because Lamarck's explanation of species change was not genetically correct, his theories are frequently derided. Actually, Lamarck deserves much credit. He was the first to recognize and stress the importance of interactions between organisms and the environment in the evolutionary process. Moreover, Lamarck was one of the first to acknowledge the need for a distinct branch of science that dealt solely with living things (i.e., separate from geology). For this new science, Lamarck coined the term *biology*, and a central feature of this new science was the notion of evolutionary change.

Georges Cuvier   The most vehement opponent of Lamarck was a young colleague, Georges Cuvier (1769–1832). Cuvier (Fig. 2–6) specialized in vertebrate paleontology, and it was he who introduced the concept of extinction to explain the disappearance of animals represented by fossils. Although a brilliant anatomist, Cuvier never grasped the dynamic concept of nature, and he adamantly insisted on the fixity of species. Just as the abundance of fossils in geological strata was becoming increasingly apparent, it also became more important to explain what they were. But rather than assume that similarities between certain fossil forms and living species indicated evolutionary relationships, Cuvier proposed a variation of a theory known as **catastrophism**.

Proponents of catastrophism held that the earth's geological features were the result of sudden, worldwide cataclysmic events, such as the Noah flood. Cuvier's version of catastrophism also postulated a series of regional disasters that destroyed

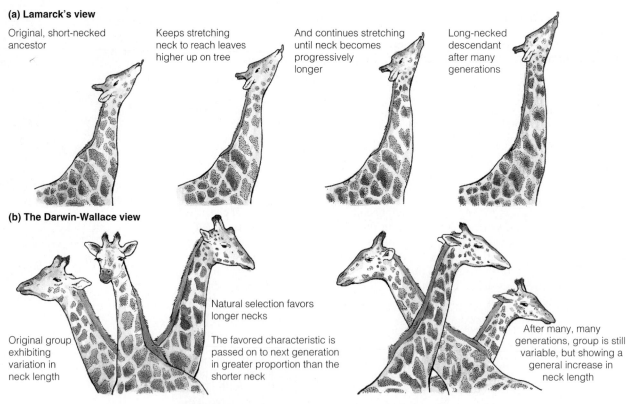

FIGURE 2–5
Contrasting ideas about the mechanism of evolution. (a) According to Lamarck's theory, acquired characteristics can be passed to subsequent generations. Thus, short-necked giraffes stretched their necks to reach higher into trees for food, and, according to Lamarck, this acquired trait was passed on to offspring, who were born with longer necks. (b) According to the Darwin-Wallace theory of natural selection, among giraffes there is variation in neck length. If having a longer neck provides an advantage for feeding, this trait will be passed on to a greater number of offspring, leading to an increase in the length of giraffe necks over many generations.

most or all of the plant and animal life within a region but not worldwide. These areas of destruction were subsequently restocked with new forms that migrated in from neighboring, unaffected regions.

To be consistent with the fossil evidence, Cuvier also proposed that destroyed regions were repopulated by new organisms of a more modern appearance and that these forms were the result of more recent creation events. (The last of these creations was said to be the one depicted in Genesis.) Thus, Cuvier's explanation of increased complexity over time avoided any notion of evolution, while still being able to account for the evidence of change as preserved in the fossil record.

Charles Lyell   Charles Lyell (1797–1875), the son of Scottish landowners, is considered the founder of modern geology (Fig. 2–7). He was a barrister by training, a geologist by avocation, and for many years Charles Darwin's friend and mentor. Before he met Darwin in 1836, Lyell had earned wide popular acclaim as well as acceptance in Europe's most prestigious scientific circles, thanks to his highly praised *Principles of Geology*, first published in three volumes in 1830–1833.

In this immensely important work, Lyell argued that the geological processes observed in the present are the same as those that occurred in the past. This theory, which has come to be known as **uniformitarianism**, did not originate entirely with Lyell, but had been proposed by James Hutton in the late 1700s. Nevertheless, it was Lyell who demonstrated that such forces as wind, water erosion, local flooding, frost, the decomposition of vegetable matter, volcanoes, earthquakes, and glacial movements all had contributed in the past to produce the geological landscape that exists in the present. Moreover, the fact that these processes could still be observed in operation indicated that geological change continued to occur and that the forces that drove such change were consistent, or *uniform*, over time. In other words, although various aspects of the earth's surface (e.g., climate, flora, fauna, and land surfaces) are variable through time, the underlying *processes* that influence them are constant.

The theory of uniformitarianism flew in the face of Cuvier's catastrophism and did not go unopposed. Additionally, and every bit as controversially, Lyell emphasized the obvious: namely, that for such slow-acting forces to produce momentous change, the earth must indeed be far older than anyone had previously suspected.

By providing an immense time scale and thereby altering perceptions of the earth's history from a few thousand to many millions of years, Lyell changed the framework within which scientists viewed the geological past. Thus, the concept of "deep time" (Gould, 1987) remains as one of Lyell's most significant contributions to the discovery of evolutionary principles. The immensity of geological time permitted the necessary time depth for the inherently slow process of evolutionary change.

Thomas Malthus   In 1798, Thomas Robert Malthus (1766–1834), an English clergyman and economist, wrote *An Essay on the Principle of Population*, which inspired both Charles Darwin and Alfred Wallace in their separate discoveries of the principle of natural selection (Fig. 2–8). In his essay, Malthus pointed out that if not kept in check by limited food supplies, human populations could double in size every 25 years. That is, population size increases exponentially while food supplies remain relatively stable.

Malthus focused on humans because the ability to increase food supplies artificially reduces constraints on population growth, and he was arguing for population control. However, the same logic could be applied to nonhuman organisms. In nature, the tendency for populations to increase is continuously checked by resource availability. Thus, there is constant competition for food and other resources. In time, the extension of Malthus' principles to all organisms would be made by both Darwin and Wallace.

Charles Darwin   Charles Darwin (1809–1882) was one of six children of Dr. Robert and Susanna Darwin (Fig. 2–9). Being the grandson of wealthy Josiah Wedgwood

Catastrophism
The view that the earth's geological landscape is the result of violent cataclysmic events. This view was promoted by Cuvier, especially in opposition to Lamarck.

FIGURE 2–6
Cuvier explained the fossil record as the result of a succession of catastrophes followed by new creation events.

FIGURE 2–7
Lyell, the father of geology, stated the theory of uniformitarianism in his *Principles of Geology*.

Uniformitarianism
The theory that the earth's features are the result of long-term processes that continue to operate in the present as they did in the past. Elaborated on by Lyell, this theory opposed catastrophism and provided for immense geological time.

FIGURE 2–8
Thomas Malthus' *Essay on the Principle of Population* led both Darwin and Wallace to the principle of natural selection.

Transmutation
The change of one species to another. The term *evolution* did not assume its current meaning until the late nineteenth century.

FIGURE 2–9
Charles Darwin as a young man.

(of Wedgwood pottery fame) as well as of Erasmus Darwin, he grew up enjoying the lifestyle of the landed gentry in rural England.

As a boy, Darwin displayed a keen interest in nature and spent his days fishing and collecting shells, birds' eggs, and rocks. However, this developing interest in natural history did not dispel the generally held view of family and friends that he was not in any way remarkable. In fact, his performance at school was no more than ordinary.

After the death of his mother when he was eight, Darwin's upbringing was guided by his rather stern father and his older sisters. Because he showed little interest in, or aptitude for, anything except hunting, shooting, and perhaps science, his father, fearing Charles would sink into dissipation, sent him to Edinburgh University to study medicine. It was at Edinburgh that Darwin first became acquainted with the evolutionary theories of Lamarck and others.

During this time (the 1820s), notions of evolution were becoming much feared in England and elsewhere. Certainly, anything identifiable with postrevolutionary France was viewed with grave suspicion by the established order in England. Lamarck, especially, was vilified by most English academicians, the majority of whom were also members of the Anglican clergy.

This was also a time of growing political unrest in Britain. The Reform Movement, which sought to undo many of the wrongs of the class system, was under way, and as with most social movements, this one contained a radical faction. Because many of the radicals were atheists and socialists who also supported Lamarck's evolutionary theory, evolution came to be associated, in the minds of many, with atheism and political subversion. Such was the growing fear of evolutionary ideas that many believed that if it were generally accepted that nature evolved unaided by God, "the Church would crash, the moral fabric of society would be torn apart, and civilized man would return to savagery" (Desmond and Moore, 1991, p. 34). It is unfortunate that some of the most outspoken early proponents of **transmutation** were so vehemently anti-Christian, because their rhetoric helped establish the entrenched suspicion and misunderstanding of evolutionary theory that persists today, especially in the United States.

While at Edinburgh, young Darwin spent endless hours studying with professors who were outspoken supporters of Lamarck. Darwin's second year in Edinburgh saw him examining museum collections and attending natural history lectures. Therefore, although he hated medicine and left Edinburgh after two years, his experience there was a formative period in his intellectual development.

Subsequently, Darwin took up residence at Christ's College, Cambridge, to study theology. (Although he was rather indifferent to religion, theology was often seen as a last resort by parents who viewed their sons as having no discernible academic leanings.) It was during his Cambridge years that Darwin seriously cultivated his interests in natural science, and he often joined the field excursions of botany classes. He also was immersed in geology and was a frequent and serious participant in geological expeditions.

It was no wonder that following his graduation in 1831 at age 22, he was recommended to accompany a scientific expedition that would circle the globe. Thus it was, after overcoming his father's objections, that Darwin set sail aboard the HMS *Beagle* on December 17, 1831 (Fig. 2–10). The famous voyage of the *Beagle* was to last almost five years and would forever change not only the course of Darwin's life but also the history of biological science.

Darwin went aboard the *Beagle* still believing in fixity of species. But during the voyage, he privately began to have doubts. As early as 1832, for example, he noted in his diary that a snake with rudimentary hind limbs marked "the passage by which Nature joins the lizards to the snakes." He came across fossils of ancient giant animals that looked, except for size, very much like living forms in the same vicinity, and he wondered whether the fossils were the ancestors of those living forms.

During the famous stopover at the Galápagos Islands (see Fig. 2–10), Darwin noted that the flora and fauna showed striking similarities to those of South

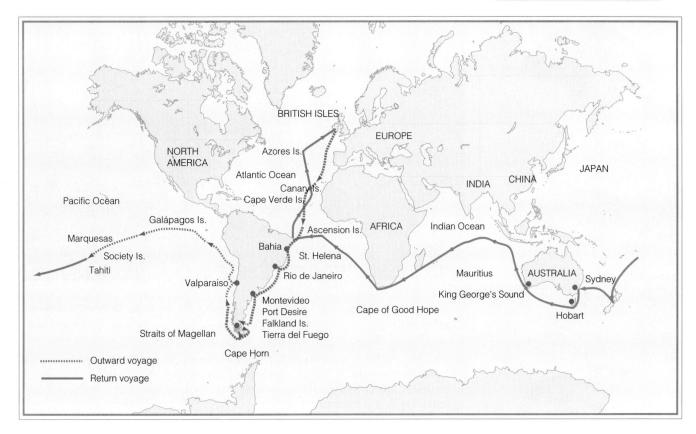

FIGURE 2–10
The route of the HMS *Beagle*.

America, as well as some intriguing differences. Even more surprising, the inhabitants of the various islands differed slightly from one another.

For example, Darwin collected 13 different varieties of Galápagos finches. These varieties shared many structural similarities, and clearly they represented a closely affiliated group. But at the same time, they differed with regard to certain physical traits, particularly in the shape and size of their beaks (Fig. 2–11). Darwin also collected finches from the South American mainland, and these appeared to represent only one group, or species.

The insight that Darwin gained from the finches is legendary. He recognized that the various Galápagos finches had all descended from a common mainland ancestor and had become modified in response to the varying island habitats and to altered dietary preferences. But actually, it was not until *after* he had returned to England that Darwin recognized the significance of the variation in beak structure. In fact, during the voyage, Darwin had paid little attention to his finches. It was only in retrospect that he considered the factors that could lead to the modification of 1 species into 13 (Gould, 1985; Desmond and Moore, 1991).

Darwin returned to England in October 1836 and almost immediately was accepted into the most eminent of scientific circles. He married his cousin Emma Wedgwood and moved to the village of Down, near London, where he spent the rest of his life writing on topics ranging from fossils to orchids (Fig. 2–12). But his overriding concern was the question of species change.

At Down, Darwin began developing his views on what he termed *natural selection*. This concept was borrowed from animal breeders, who "select" as breeding stock those animals that exhibit specific traits they hope to emphasize in offspring. Animals with undesirable traits are "selected against," or prevented from breeding.

Darwin was keenly interested in domestic animals—pigeons, in particular—and he wanted to know how breeders could develop distinctive varieties in just a few

 An example of artificial selection is presented in Virtual Lab 2, section I, part B.

(a) Ground finch
   Main food: seeds
   Beak: heavy

(b) Tree finch
   Main food: leaves, buds,
   blossoms, fruits
   Beak: thick, short

(c) Tree finch (called
   woodpecker finch)
   Main food: insects
   Beak: stout, straight

(d) Ground finch (known as
   warbler finch)
   Main food: insects
   Beak: slender

FIGURE 2–11
Beak variation in Darwin's Galápagos finches.

The case of Darwin's finches is
presented in Virtual Lab 2,
section I, part B.

Lynn Kilgore

FIGURE 2–12
The Darwin home, Down House, in the village of Down, as seen from the rear garden. *On the Origin of Species* was written here.

generations. (The variations seen in domestic dog breeds may be the best example of the effects of selective breeding.) He applied his knowledge of domesticated species to naturally occurring ones, recognizing that in undomesticated organisms, the selective agent was nature, not humans.

By the late 1830s, Darwin recognized that biological variation within a species was critically important. Furthermore, he acknowledged the importance of sexual reproduction in increasing variation. Then, in 1838, Darwin read Malthus' essay, and in it he found the answer to his question of how new species came to be. He accepted from Malthus that populations increase at a faster rate than do resources, and he inferred that in nonhuman animals, increase in population size is continuously checked by limited food supplies. He also accepted Lyell's observation that in nature there is a constant "struggle for existence." The idea that in each generation more offspring were born than survived to adulthood, coupled with the notions of competition for resources and biological diversity, was all Darwin needed to develop his theory of natural selection. He wrote: "It at once struck me that under these circumstances favourable variations would tend to be preserved, and unfavourable ones to be destroyed. The result of this would be the formation of a new species" (F. Darwin, 1950, pp. 53–54). Basically, this quotation summarizes the whole of natural selection theory.

Darwin wrote a short summary of his views on natural selection in 1842 and revised it in 1844. The 1844 sketch is similar to the argument he presented 15 years later in *On the Origin of Species*, but in 1844 he did not feel he had sufficient data to support his views, so he continued his research without publishing.

Darwin had another reason for not publishing what he knew would be, to say the least, a highly controversial work. As a member of the established order, Darwin knew that many of his friends and associates were concerned with threats to the status quo, and evolutionary theory was viewed as a serious threat indeed. In addition, Darwin was a man to whom reputation was of paramount importance, and he was tormented by fears of bringing dishonor and public criticism to those he loved. So, he hesitated.

Alfred Russel Wallace   Unlike Darwin, Alfred Russel Wallace (1823–1913) was born into a family of modest means (Fig. 2–13). He went to work at the age of 14, and without any special talent and little formal education, he moved from one job to the next. He became interested in collecting plants and animals, and in 1848 he joined an expedition to the Amazon, where he acquired firsthand knowledge of natural phenomena. Then, in 1854, he sailed for Southeast Asia and the Malay Peninsula to continue his study and to collect bird and insect specimens.

In 1855, Wallace published an article suggesting that species were descended from other species and that the appearance of new species was influenced by environmental factors (Trinkaus and Shipman, 1992). The Wallace paper spurred Lyell and others to urge Darwin to publish, but still Darwin hesitated. Wallace and Darwin even corresponded briefly.

Then, in 1858, Wallace sent Darwin another paper titled "On the Tendency of Varieties to Depart Indefinitely from the Original Type." In this paper, Wallace described evolution as a process driven by competition and natural selection. Upon receipt of Wallace's paper, Darwin despaired. He feared that Wallace might be credited for a theory (natural selection) that he himself had formulated. He quickly wrote a paper presenting his ideas, and both the paper by Darwin and the one by Wallace were read before the Linnean Society of London in 1858. Neither author was present. Wallace was not in the country, and Darwin was mourning the very recent death of his young son.

The papers received little notice at the time, but at the urging of Lyell and others, Darwin completed and published his greatest work, *On the Origin of Species*,* in December 1859. Upon publication, the storm broke, and it has not abated even to this day. While there was much praise for the book, the gist of opinion was negative. Scientific opinion gradually came to Darwin's support, assisted by Darwin's able friend, Thomas Huxley, who for years wrote and spoke in favor of natural selection. The riddle of species was now explained: Species were mutable, not fixed; and they evolved from other species through the mechanism of natural selection.

FIGURE 2–13
Alfred Russel Wallace independently uncovered the key to the evolutionary process.

Natural Selection

Early in his research, Darwin had realized that selection was the key to evolution. With the help of Malthus' ideas, he saw *how* selection in nature could be explained. In the struggle for existence, those *individuals* with favorable variations would survive and reproduce; those with unfavorable variations would not.

For Darwin, the explanation of evolution was simple. The basic processes, as he understood them, are as follows:

1. All species are capable of producing offspring at a faster rate than food supplies increase.
2. There is biological variation within all species; except for identical twins, no two individuals are exactly alike.
3. Because in each generation more individuals are produced than can survive, owing to limited resources, there is competition between individuals. (*Note:* This statement does not imply that there is constant fighting.)
4. Those individuals that possess favorable variations or traits (e.g., speed, disease resistance, protective coloration) have an advantage over individuals that do not possess them. By virtue of the favorable characteristic, these individuals are more likely to survive to produce more offspring than are others.
5. The environmental context determines whether or not a trait is beneficial. That is, what is favorable in one setting may be a liability in another. In this way, which traits become most advantageous is the result of a natural process.
6. Traits are inherited and are passed on to the next generation. Because individuals possessing favorable characteristics contribute more offspring to the next generation than do others, over time, such traits become more common in the population; less favorable traits are not passed on as frequently and become less common. Those individuals that produce more offspring, compared to others, are said to have greater **reproductive success.**

Reproductive success
The number of offspring an individual produces and rears to reproductive age; an individual's genetic contribution to the next generation as compared to the contributions of other individuals.

---

*The full title is *On the Origin of Species by Means of Natural Selection, or the Preservation of Favoured Races in the Struggle for Life.*

7. Over long periods of geological time, successful variations accumulate in a population, so that later generations may be distinct from ancestral ones. Thus, in time, a new species may appear.

8. Geographical isolation may also lead to the formation of new species. As populations of a species become geographically isolated from one another, for whatever reasons, they begin to adapt to different environments. Over time, as populations continue to respond to different **selective pressures** (i.e., different ecological circumstances), they may become distinct species, descended from a common ancestor. The 13 species of Galápagos finches, presumably all descended from a common ancestor on the South American mainland, are an example of the role of geographical isolation.

Before Darwin, scientists thought of species as entities that could not change. Because individuals within the species did not appear to be significant, they were not the object of study; therefore, it was difficult for many scientists to imagine how change could occur. Darwin, as we have pointed out, saw that variation among individuals could explain how selection occurred. Favorable variations were selected for survival by nature; unfavorable ones were eliminated.

This emphasis on the uniqueness of the individual led Darwin to natural selection as the mechanism that made evolution work. *Natural selection operates on individuals*, favorably or unfavorably, but it is the population that evolves. The unit of natural selection is the individual; the unit of evolution is the population.

Natural Selection in Action

The best-documented case of natural selection acting in modern populations concerns changes in pigmentation among peppered moths near Manchester, England (Fig. 2–14). Before the nineteenth century, the common variety of moth was a mottled gray color. This light, mottled coloration provided extremely effective camouflage against lichen-covered tree trunks. Also present, though less common, was a dark variety of the same species. While resting on light, lichen-covered trees, the dark, uncamouflaged moths were more visible to birds and were therefore eaten more often. (In this example, birds are the *selective agent*.) Thus, in the end, the dark moths produced fewer offspring than the light, camouflaged moths. Yet, by the end of the nineteenth century, the common gray form had been almost completely replaced by the black variety.

What had brought about this rapid change? The answer lies in the swiftly changing environment of industrialized nineteenth-century England. Coal dust in the area settled on trees, killing the lichen and turning the bark a dark color. Moths continued to rest on trees, but the gray (light) variety was increasingly conspicuous as the trees became darker. Consequently, they began to be preyed on more fre-

Selective pressures
Forces in the environment that influence reproductive success in individuals. In the example of the peppered moth, birds applied the selective pressure.

FIGURE 2–14
Variation in the peppered moth. (a) The dark form is more visible on the light, lichen-covered tree. (b) On trees darkened by pollution, the lighter form is more visible.

(a)   (b)

quently by birds and thus contributed fewer genes to the next generation. In the late twentieth century, increasing control of pollutants allowed trees to return to their lighter, lichen-covered, preindustrial condition. As would be expected, darker moths are being supplanted by gray ones.

The substance that produces pigmentation is called *melanin*, and the evolutionary shift in the peppered moth, as well as in many other moth species, is termed *industrial melanism*. Such evolutionary shifts in response to environmental change are called *adaptations*.

This example of the peppered moths provides numerous insights into the mechanism of evolutionary change by natural selection:

1. *A trait must be inherited in order to have importance in natural selection.* A characteristic that is not hereditary (such as a temporary change in hair pigmentation brought about by dye) will not be passed on to succeeding generations. In moths, pigmentation is a demonstrated hereditary trait.
2. *Natural selection cannot occur without variation in inherited characteristics.* If all the moths had initially been gray (you will recall that some dark moths were always present) and the trees had become darker, the survival and reproduction of all moths could have been so low that the population might have become extinct. Species extinction is not unusual and without variation would nearly always occur. *Selection can work only when variation already exists.*
3. *Fitness is a relative measure that will change as the environment changes.* Fitness is simply differential reproductive success. In the initial stage, the gray moth was the more fit variety because gray moths produced more offspring. But as the environment changed, the black moths became more fit. Then a further environmental change reversed the adaptive pattern yet again. It should be obvious that statements regarding the "most fit" life form mean nothing without reference to specific environments.

Fitness
Pertaining to natural selection, a measure of *relative* reproductive success of individuals. Fitness can be measured by an individual's genetic contribution to the next generation compared to that of others.

The example of the peppered moths shows how different death rates influence natural selection, since moths that die early tend to leave fewer offspring. But mortality is not the entire picture. Another important aspect of natural selection is fertility, for an animal that gives birth to more young would pass its genes on at a faster rate than one that bears fewer offspring. However, fertility is not the entire picture either, for the crucial element is the number of young raised successfully to the point at which they themselves reproduce. We may state this simply as *differential net reproductive success*. The way this mechanism works can be demonstrated through another example.

In a variety of birds called swifts, data show that producing more offspring does not necessarily guarantee that more young will be successfully raised. The number of eggs hatched in a breeding season is a measure of fertility. The number of birds that mature and are eventually able to leave the nest is a measure of net reproductive success, or offspring successfully raised. The following tabulation shows the correlation between the number of eggs hatched (fertility) and the number of young that leave the nest (reproductive success) averaged over four breeding seasons (Lack, 1966):

Number of eggs hatched (fertility)	2 eggs	3 eggs	4 eggs
Average number of young raised (reproductive success)	1.92	2.54	1.76
Sample size (number of nests)	72	20	16

As the tabulation shows, the most efficient number is three eggs, since that number yields the highest reproductive success. Raising two is less beneficial to the parents, since the end result is not as successful as with three eggs. Trying to raise more than three young is actually detrimental, since the parents may not be able to provide adequate nourishment for all the offspring. An offspring that dies before reaching reproductive age is, in evolutionary terms, equivalent to never having

been born in the first place. Actually, such a result may be an evolutionary minus to the parents, for this offspring will drain their resources and may inhibit their ability to raise other offspring, thereby lowering their reproductive success even further. Selection will favor those genetic traits that yield the maximum net reproductive success. If the number of eggs laid* is a trait that is influenced by genetic factors in birds (and it seems to be), natural selection in swifts should act to favor the laying of three eggs as opposed to two or four.

Constraints on Nineteenth-Century Evolutionary Theory

Darwin argued eloquently for the notion of evolution in general and the role of natural selection in particular, but he did not entirely comprehend the exact mechanisms of evolutionary change.

As we have seen, natural selection acts on *variation* within species. But neither Darwin nor anyone else in the nineteenth century understood the source of this variation. Consequently, Darwin speculated about variation arising from "use"—an idea similar to Lamarck's. Darwin, however, was not as dogmatic in his views as Lamarck and most emphatically argued against inner "needs" or "effort." Darwin had to confess that when it came to explaining variation, he simply did not know: "Our ignorance of the laws of variation is profound. Not in one case out of a hundred can we pretend to assign any reason why this or that part differs, more or less, from the same part in the parents" (Darwin, 1859, pp. 167–168).

In addition to his inability to explain the origins of variation, Darwin also did not completely understand the mechanism by which parents transmitted traits to offspring. Almost without exception, nineteenth-century scholars were confused about the laws of heredity, and the popular consensus was that inheritance was *blending* by nature. In other words, offspring were expected to express intermediate traits as a result of a blending of their parents' contributions. Without any viable alternatives, Darwin accepted this popular misconception. As it turned out, a contemporary of Darwin's had systematically worked out the rules of heredity. However, the work of Gregor Mendel (whom you will meet in Chapter 3) was not recognized until the beginning of the twentieth century.

Opposition to Evolution

The publication of *On the Origin of Species* fanned the flames of controversy over evolution into an inferno, but the question had already been debated in intellectual circles for some years, with most people vehemently opposed to evolutionary theory. The very idea that species could give rise to other species was particularly offensive to many Christians because it appeared to be in direct conflict with the special creation event depicted in Genesis. People were (and many still are) horrified at the notion that humans might be biologically related to other animals and especially that they might share a common ancestor with the great apes. Even to make such a claim was degrading, for it denied humanity its unique and exalted place in the universe; in the minds of many, it denied the very existence of God.

The debate has not ended even now, some 140 years later. For the majority of scientists today, evolution is fact. Indeed, the genetic evidence for it is indisputable, and anyone who appreciates and understands genetic mechanisms cannot avoid the conclusion that populations and species evolve. Moreover, the majority of Christians do not believe that biblical depictions are to be taken literally. But at the same time, surveys show that almost half of all Americans believe that evolution does not occur. There are a number of reasons for this.

---

*The number of eggs hatched is directly related to the number of eggs laid.

The mechanisms of evolution are complex and do not lend themselves to simple explanations. To understand these mechanisms requires some familiarity with genetics and biology, a familiarity that most people unfortunately do not possess. Moreover, people who have not been exposed to scientific training want definitive answers to complicated questions. But as you learned in Chapter 1, science does not prove truths, and it frequently does not provide definitive answers.

Another fact to consider is that while all religions offer explanations for natural phenomena, and some even feature the transformation of individuals from one form to another, none really proposes biological change over time. Most people, regardless of their culture, are raised in belief systems that do not emphasize biological continuity between species or offer scientific explanations for natural phenomena.

The relationship between science and religion has never been easy. While both serve, in their own ways, to explain phenomena, scientific explanations are based on data analysis and interpretation and hypothesis testing. Religion, meanwhile, is a system of beliefs not amenable to scientific testing and falsification; it is based on faith. Religion and science concern different aspects of the human experience, and although they use different approaches in areas where they overlap, they are not inherently mutually exclusive. In fact, many people see them as two sides of the same coin. Moreover, evolutionary theories are not considered anathema by all religions (or even by all forms of Christianity). Some years ago, the Vatican hosted an international conference on human evolution, and in 1996, Pope John Paul II issued a statement to the Pontifical Academy of Sciences acknowledging that "fresh knowledge leads to recognition of the theory of evolution as more than just a hypothesis." Today, the official position of the Catholic Church is that evolutionary processes do occur but that the human soul is of divine creation and not subject to evolutionary processes. Likewise, mainstream Protestants do not generally see a conflict. Unfortunately, those who believe in a literal interpretation of the Bible (frequently termed fundamentalists) do not accept any form of compromise.

Reacting to rapid cultural changes after World War I, conservative Christians in the United States sought a revival of what they considered traditional values. In their view, one way to do this was to prevent any mention of Darwinism in public schools. The Butler Act, passed in Tennessee in 1925, was one result of this effort, and it banned the teaching of evolution in public schools in that state. To test the validity of the law, the American Civil Liberties Union persuaded John Scopes, a high school teacher, to be arrested and ultimately tried for teaching evolution.

The subsequent trial was the famous Scopes Monkey Trial, in which the well-known orator William Jennings Bryan was the prosecuting attorney. The lawyer for the defense was Clarence Darrow, a nationally known labor and criminal lawyer. The trial ended with the conviction of Scopes, who was fined $100. The case was appealed to the Tennessee Supreme Court, which upheld the law, and the teaching of evolution remained illegal in Tennessee. Eventually, several other states, mostly in the South, passed similar laws, and it was not until 1967 that the last two states (Tennessee and Arkansas) ceased to prohibit the teaching of evolution.

But the story does not end there. In the more than 75 years since the Scopes trial, religious fundamentalists have persisted in their attempts to remove evolution from public school curricula. Known as creationists because they explain the existence of the universe as a result of a sudden creation, they are determined either to eliminate the teaching of evolution or to introduce antievolutionary material into public school classes. In the past 20 years, creationists have insisted that "creation science" is just as valid a scientific endeavor as is the study of evolution. They argue that in the interest of fairness, a balanced view should be offered: If evolution is taught as science, then creationism should also be taught as science. But "creation science" is, by definition, not science at all. Creationists assert that their view is absolute and infallible. Consequently, creationism is not a hypothesis that can be tested, nor is it amenable to falsification. Because such testing is the basis of all science, creationism, by its very nature, cannot be considered science. It is religion.

Still, creationists have been active in state legislatures, promoting the passage of laws mandating the inclusion of creationism in school curricula. To this effect, the Arkansas state legislature passed such a law in 1981, but this law was overturned in 1982. Judge William Ray Overton, in his ruling against the state, found that "a theory that is by its own terms dogmatic, absolutist and never subject to revision is not a scientific theory." And he added: "Since creation is not science, the conclusion is inescapable that the only real effect of such a law is the advancement of religion." In 1987, the United States Supreme Court struck down a similar law in Louisiana.

So far, these and related laws have been overturned because they violate the provision for separation of church and state in the First Amendment to the Constitution. But this has not stopped the creationists, who have encouraged teachers to claim "academic freedom" to teach creationism. Also, they have dropped the term *creationism* in favor of less religious sounding terms, such as *intelligent design theory*. And as recently as August 1999, the Kansas state legislature adopted a policy that, had it not been overturned, could have eliminated the teaching of evolution from standardized public school curricula. Moreover, anti-evolution feeling remains strong among politicians. In 1999, one very prominent U.S. congressman went so far as to say that the teaching of evolution is one of the factors behind violence in America today!

Although the courts have consistently ruled against the creationists, religious fundamentalists have nevertheless had an impact on the teaching of evolution. Many public school teachers, seeking to avoid controversy, simply do not cover evolution, or they refer to it as "just a theory" (see p. 15). Thus, students may not be exposed to theories of evolution until they go to college—and only then if they take related courses. This consequence is ultimately to the detriment of the biological sciences (and education in general) in the United States.

SUMMARY

Our current understanding of evolutionary processes is directly traceable to developments in intellectual thought in western Europe over the last 300 years. In particular, the contributions of Linnaeus, Lamarck, Buffon, Lyell, and Malthus all had a significant impact on Darwin. The year 1859 marks a watershed in evolutionary theory, for in that year, the publication of Darwin's *On the Origin of Species* crystallized the understanding of the evolutionary process (particularly the crucial role of natural selection) and for the first time thrust evolutionary theory into the consciousness of the common person. Debates both inside and outside the sciences continued for several decades and, as you have seen, persist today, but the theory of evolution irrevocably changed the tide of intellectual thought. Gradually, Darwin's formulation of evolutionary principles became accepted almost universally by scientists as the very foundation of all the biological sciences, physical anthropology included. As we begin the twenty-first century, contributions from genetics allow us to demonstrate the mechanics of evolution in a way unknown to Darwin and his contemporaries.

Natural selection is the central determining factor influencing the long-term direction of evolutionary change. How natural selection works can best be explained as differential reproductive success—in other words, how successful individuals are in leaving offspring to succeeding generations.

QUESTIONS FOR REVIEW

1. Trace the history of intellectual thought immediately leading to Darwin's theory.
2. What is fixity of species? Why did it pose an obstacle to the development of evolutionary thinking?

3. What was John Ray's major contribution to biology and the development of evolutionary theories?
4. In what ways did Linnaeus and Buffon differ in their approach to the concept of evolution?
5. What are the bases of Lamarck's theory of acquired characteristics? Why is this theory incorrect?
6. What was Lamarck's contribution to nineteenth-century evolutionary ideas?
7. Explain Cuvier's catastrophism.
8. What did Malthus and Lyell contribute to Darwin's thinking on evolution?
9. Darwin approached the subject of species change by emphasizing individuals within populations. Why was this significant to the development of the concept of natural selection?
10. What evidence did Darwin use to strengthen his argument concerning evolution?
11. How did Darwin's explanation of evolution differ from Lamarck's?
12. What is meant by adaptation? Illustrate through the example of industrial melanism.
13. Define natural selection. What is a selective agent?
14. Explain why the changes in coloration in populations of peppered moths serve as a good example of natural selection.

SUGGESTED FURTHER READING

Burke, James. 1985. *The Day the Universe Changed*. Boston: Little, Brown.

Desmond, Adrian, and James Moore. 1991. *Darwin*. New York: Warner Books.

Gould, Stephen Jay. 1987. *Time's Arrow, Time's Cycle*. Cambridge, MA: Harvard University Press.

Mayr, Ernst. 2000. "Darwin's Influence on Modern Thought." *Scientific American* 283 (1): 78–83.

Ridley, Mark. 1993. *Evolution*. Boston: Blackwell Scientific Publications.

Scott, Eugenie C. 1997. "Antievolutionism and Creationism in the United States." *Annual Review of Anthropology* 2: 263–289.

Trinkaus, Eric, and Pat Shipman. 1993. *The Neandertals*. New York: Knopf.

Young, David. 1992. *The Discovery of Evolution*. London: Natural History Museum Publications, Cambridge University Press.

RESOURCES ON THE INTERNET

 Wadsworth Anthropology Resource Center
http://anthropology.wadsworth.com

The companion website for this text includes a range of enrichment material focused on the chapter's topic. While online you can enhance your understanding of the chapter by exploring one of the several additional Internet Exercises, by researching topics, and by accessing full articles on InfoTrac College Edition. You can also reinforce the concepts by taking online practice exams.

Internet Exercises

As you learned in this chapter, Charles Darwin's theory of natural selection was influenced by the writings of numerous other naturalists. You can either use your search engine or go to **www.ucmp.berkeley.edu/history/evolution.html** to read more about these influential people and the development of evolutionary thought.

Scroll down to "Preludes to Evolution" and click on the name of someone discussed in this chapter (perhaps Lamarck). What additional facts did you learn? Then choose someone not discussed in the textbook and write one or two paragraphs describing that person's contributions.

 InfoTrac College Edition
http://www.infotrac-college.com/wadsworth

A subject search in InfoTrac College Edition for *natural selection* will yield at least 100 current periodical references. Explore these references, and select and read at least one article (not just the abstract) pertaining to a topic you find especially interesting. How does this article illustrate and elaborate on the basic principles of natural selection as presented in Chapter 2?

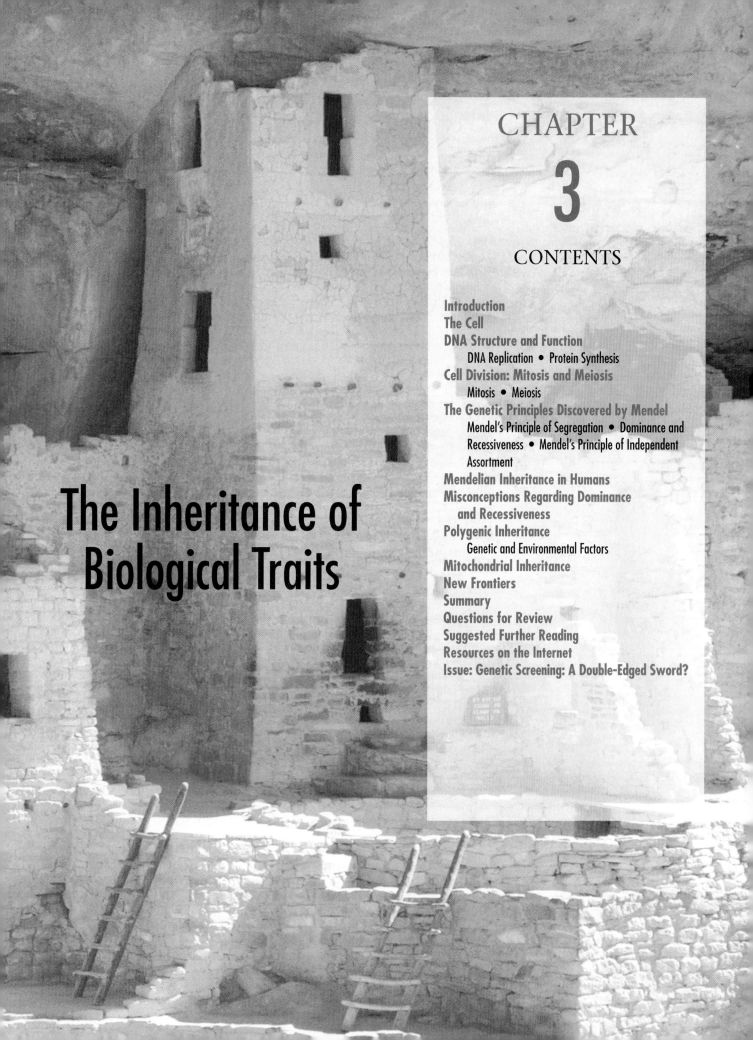

CHAPTER

3

CONTENTS

The Inheritance of Biological Traits

Introduction

In Chapter 2, you learned that in his efforts to explain how natural selection worked, Charles Darwin was confounded by his inability to account for the physical variation that exists in populations and species. We, the beneficiaries of a century of research, know that this inability resulted from an unawareness of the principles of **genetics**.

As we mentioned at the conclusion of Chapter 2, it was not until Gregor Mendel addressed the question of inheritance in the mid-nineteenth century that the basic principles of heredity were discovered. However, because Mendel's research was largely unknown until 1900, the field of genetics has been almost exclusively a twentieth-century development. In fact, most of our current knowledge has been acquired just within the last 50 years, most especially since the 1980s.

Today, insights into the numerous aspects of inheritance are increasing at an exponential rate, with new discoveries being made every day, and as genetic technologies develop and come into use, they assume an ever greater and more pervasive role in society. Therefore, it is more important than ever that we acquire a basic understanding of these factors that can so dramatically influence our lives. Moreover, from an anthropological perspective, it is only through the further elucidation of genetic principles that we can hope to understand fully the evolutionary mechanisms that have permitted humans to become the species we are today.

However interesting the topic may be, it is not within the scope of this text to provide an in-depth discussion of even the most fundamental aspects of genetics. Instead, what we have attempted to do is discuss the basic concepts in a manner that will permit you to apply them to the topics of evolution, adaptation, and variation covered in subsequent chapters. Thus, we begin this chapter with a brief overview of the molecular aspects of genetics. Although some of these phenomena were not revealed until the 1950s and later, we are presenting them prior to our discussion of Mendel to establish a contemporary framework within which to describe the principles he discovered. The chapter concludes with a section on patterns of inheritance other than those described by Mendel.

The Cell

To discuss genetic and evolutionary principles, we must first have some understanding of cell function. Cells are the basic units of life in all living things. In some forms, such as bacteria, a single cell constitutes the entire organism. However, more complex *multicellular forms*, such as plants, insects, birds, and mammals, are composed of billions of cells. Indeed, an adult human is made up of perhaps as many as 1,000 billion (1,000,000,000,000) cells, all functioning in complex ways to promote the survival of the individual.

Life on earth can be traced back at least 3.7 billion years, in the form of *prokaryotic* cells. Prokaryotes are single-celled organisms, represented today by bacteria and blue-green algae. Structurally more complex cells appeared approximately 1.2 billion years ago, and these are referred to as *eukaryotic* cells. Because eukaryotic cells are found in all multicellular organisms, they are the focus of the remainder of this discussion. In spite of the numerous differences between various life forms and the cells that constitute them, it is important to understand that the cells of all living organisms share many similarities as a result of their common evolutionary past.

In general, a eukaryotic cell is a three-dimensional entity composed of *carbohydrates*, *lipids*, *nucleic acids*, and *proteins*. It contains a variety of structures called organelles contained within a *cell membrane* (Fig. 3–1). One of these organelles is the **nucleus** (*pl.*, nuclei), a discrete unit surrounded by a thin nuclear membrane. Within the nucleus are two acids that contain the genetic information that controls the cell's functions. These two critically important **molecules** are **deoxyribonucleic acid (DNA)** and **ribonucleic acid (RNA)**. Surrounding the nucleus is the **cytoplasm**, which contains numerous other types of organelles involved in various

---

Genetics
The branch of science that deals with the inheritance of biological characteristics; the study of how traits are transmitted from one generation to the next.

See the following sections of the CD-ROM for topics covered in this chapter: Virtual Lab 2, section II, parts A, B, C, and E.

Nucleus
A structure (organelle) found in all eukaryotic cells. The nucleus contains chromosomes (nuclear DNA).

Molecules
Structures made up of two or more atoms. Molecules can combine with other molecules to form more complex structures.

Deoxyribonucleic acid (DNA)
The double-stranded molecule that contains the genetic code. DNA is a main component of chromosomes.

Ribonucleic acid (RNA)
A single-stranded molecule, similar in structure to DNA. The three forms of RNA are essential to protein synthesis.

Cytoplasm
The portion of the cell contained within the cell membrane, excluding the nucleus. The cytoplasm consists of a semifluid material and contains numerous structures involved with cell function.

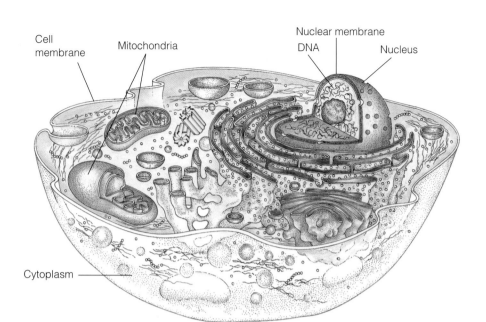

Cell membrane

Mitochondria

Nuclear membrane

DNA

Nucleus

Cytoplasm

FIGURE 3–1
Structure of a generalized eukaryotic cell, illustrating the cell's three-dimensional nature. Although various organelles are shown, for the sake of simplicity only those we discuss in this text are labeled.

activities, such as breaking down nutrients and converting them to other substances (*metabolism*), storing and releasing energy, eliminating waste, and manufacturing **proteins (protein synthesis)**.

There are basically two types of cells: **somatic cells** and **gametes**. Somatic cells are the cellular components of body tissues, such as muscle, bone, skin, nerve, heart, and brain. Gametes, or sex cells, are specifically involved in reproduction and are not important as structural components of the body. There are two types of gametes: *ova*, or egg cells, produced in the ovaries in females; and *sperm*, which develop in male testes. The sole function of a sex cell is to unite with a gamete from another individual to form a **zygote**, which has the potential of developing into a new individual. By so doing, gametes transmit genetic information from parent to offspring.

DNA Structure and Function

As already mentioned, cellular functions are directed by DNA. If we are to understand these functions and how characteristics are inherited, we must first know something about the structure and function of DNA. It was not until 1944 that DNA was shown to be the material responsible for the transmission of inherited traits (Avery, MacLeod, and McCarty, 1944). Subsequently, in 1953, Francis Crick and James Watson revolutionized the fields of biology and medicine by publishing their structural and functional model of DNA (Watson and Crick, 1953a, 1953b).

The DNA molecule is composed of two chains of even smaller molecules called **nucleotides**. A nucleotide, in turn, is made up of three components: a sugar molecule (deoxyribose), a phosphate, and one of four bases (Fig. 3–2). In DNA, nucleotides are stacked on one another to form a chain that is bonded along its bases to another **complementary** nucleotide chain. Together the two twist to form a spiral, or helical, shape. The resulting DNA molecule, then, is two-stranded and is described as forming a *double helix* that resembles a twisted ladder. If we follow the twisted ladder analogy, the sugars and phosphates represent the two sides, while the bases and the bonds that join them form the rungs.

The secret of how DNA functions lies within the four bases. These bases are *adenine*, *guanine*, *thymine*, and *cytosine*, frequently referred to by their initial letters, A, G, T, and C. In the formation of the double helix, it is possible for one type of base to pair or bond with only one other type. Thus, base pairs can form only between

Proteins
Three-dimensional molecules that serve a wide variety of functions through their ability to bind to other molecules.

Protein synthesis
The assembly of chains of amino acids into functional protein molecules. The process is directed by DNA.

Somatic cells
Basically, all the cells in the body except those involved with reproduction.

Gametes
Reproductive cells (eggs and sperm in animals) developed from precursor cells in ovaries and testes.

Zygote
A cell formed by the union of an egg and a sperm cell. It contains the full complement of chromosomes (in humans, 46) and has the potential of developing into an entire organism.

Nucleotides
Basic units of the DNA molecule, composed of a sugar, a phosphate, and one of four DNA bases.

Complementary
Referring to the fact that DNA bases form base pairs in a precise manner. For example, adenine can bond only to thymine. These two bases are said to be *complementary* because one requires the other to form a complete DNA base pair.

FIGURE 3–2
Part of a DNA molecule. The illustration shows the two DNA strands with the sugar and phosphate backbone and the bases extending toward the center.

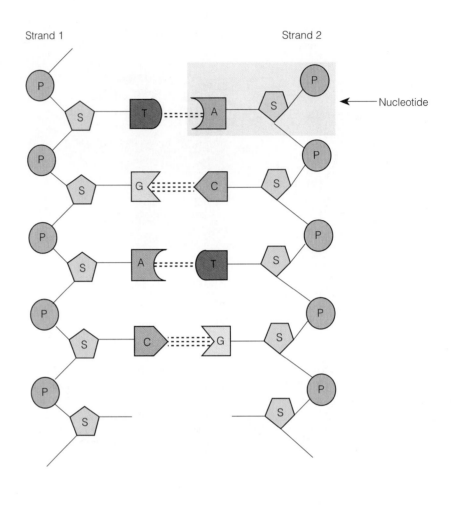

Strand 1   Strand 2

Nucleotide

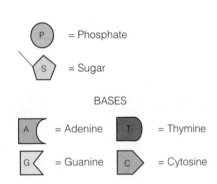

P = Phosphate

S = Sugar

BASES

A = Adenine   T = Thymine

G = Guanine   C = Cytosine

Replicate
To duplicate. The DNA molecule is able to make copies of itself.

Enzymes
Specialized proteins that initiate and direct chemical reactions in the body.

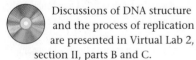
Discussions of DNA structure and the process of replication are presented in Virtual Lab 2, section II, parts B and C.

adenine and thymine and between guanine and cytosine (see Fig. 3–2). This specificity is essential to the DNA molecule's ability to **replicate**, or make an exact copy of itself, and DNA is the only molecule known to have this capacity.

DNA Replication

Growth and development of organisms and tissue repair following injury or disease are among the crucial processes made possible by cell division. Cells multiply by dividing in such a way that each new cell receives a full complement of genetic material. This is a crucial point, since a cell cannot function properly without the appropriate amount of DNA, and for new cells to receive the essential amount of DNA, it is first necessary for the DNA to replicate.

Prior to cell division, specific **enzymes** break the bonds between bases in the DNA molecule, leaving the two previously joined strands of nucleotides with their bases exposed (Fig. 3–3). The exposed bases attract unattached nucleotides, which are free-floating in the cell nucleus.

Because one base can be joined to only one other, the attraction between bases occurs in a complementary fashion. Thus, the two previously joined parental nucleotide chains serve as models, or *templates*, for the formation of a new strand of nucleotides. As each new strand is formed, its bases are joined to the bases of an original strand. When the process is completed, there are two double-stranded DNA molecules exactly like the original one, and each newly formed molecule consists of one original nucleotide chain joined to a newly formed chain (see Fig. 3–3).

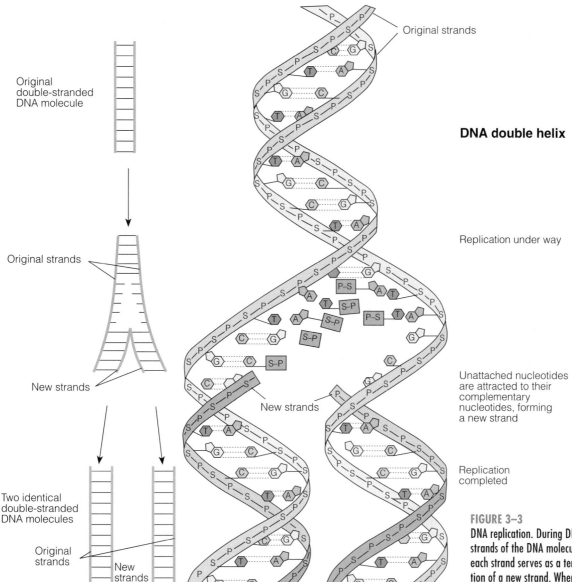

Original double-stranded DNA molecule

Original strands

New strands

Two identical double-stranded DNA molecules

Original strands

New strands

Original strands

DNA double helix

Replication under way

Unattached nucleotides are attracted to their complementary nucleotides, forming a new strand

Replication completed

FIGURE 3–3
DNA replication. During DNA replication, the two strands of the DNA molecule are separated, and each strand serves as a template for the formation of a new strand. When replication is complete, there are two DNA molecules. Each molecule consists of one new and one original DNA strand.

Protein Synthesis

One of the most important functions of DNA is the manufacture of proteins (protein synthesis) within the cell. Proteins are complex, three-dimensional molecules that function through their ability to bind to other molecules. For example, the protein **hemoglobin**, found in red blood cells, is able to bind to oxygen and serves to transport oxygen to cells throughout the body.

Proteins function in myriad ways. Some are structural components of tissues. Collagen, for example, is the most common protein in the body and is a major component of all connective tissues. Aside from mineral components, it is the most abundant structural material in bone. Enzymes are also proteins, and their function is to initiate and enhance chemical reactions. An example of a digestive enzyme is *lactase*, which breaks down *lactose*, or milk sugar, into two simpler sugars. Another class of proteins includes many types of **hormones**. Specialized cells produce and release hormones into the bloodstream to circulate to other areas of the body,

Hemoglobin
A protein molecule that occurs in red blood cells and binds to oxygen molecules.

Hormones
Substances (usually proteins) that are produced by specialized cells and that travel to other parts of the body, where they influence chemical reactions and regulate various cellular functions.

where they produce specific effects in tissues and organs. A good example of this type of protein is *insulin*, produced by cells in the pancreas. Insulin causes cells in the liver and certain types of muscle tissue to absorb glucose (sugar) from the blood. (Enzymes and hormones will be discussed in more detail in Chapter 5.)

As you can see, proteins make us what we are. Not only are they the major constituents of all body tissues, but they also direct and perform physiological and cellular functions. It is therefore critical that protein synthesis occur accurately, because, if it does not, physiological development and activities can be disrupted or even prevented.

Proteins are composed of linear chains of smaller molecules called **amino acids**. In all, there are 20 amino acids, which are combined in different amounts and sequences to produce potentially millions of proteins. What makes proteins different from one another is the number of amino acids involved and the *sequence* in which they are arranged. For a protein to function properly, its amino acids must be arranged in the proper sequence.

DNA serves as a recipe for making a protein, because it is the sequence of DNA bases that ultimately determines the order of amino acids in a protein molecule. In the DNA instructions, a *triplet*, or group of three bases, specifies a particular amino acid. For example, if a triplet includes the bases cytosine, guanine, and adenine (CGA), it specifies the amino acid *alanine*. If the next triplet in the chain contains guanine, thymine, and cytosine (GTC), it refers to another amino acid—*glutamine*. Therefore, a DNA recipe might look like this: AGA CGA ACA ACC TAC TTT TTC CTT AAG GTC, and so on, as it directs the cell in assembling proteins.

Protein synthesis is a little more complicated than the preceding few sentences would imply, and it involves an additional molecule similar to DNA called RNA (ribonucleic acid). While DNA provides the instructions for protein synthesis, it is RNA that reads the instructions and actually assembles amino acids to form proteins.

The entire sequence of DNA bases responsible for the synthesis of a protein or, in some cases, a portion of a protein, is referred to as a **gene**. Or, put another way, a gene is a segment of DNA that specifies the sequence of amino acids in a particular protein. A gene may comprise only a few hundred bases, or it may be composed of thousands. If the sequence of DNA bases is altered through **mutation** (a change in the DNA), the manufacture of some proteins may not occur, and the cell (or indeed the organism) may not function properly, if at all.

This definition of a gene is a functional one and is technically correct. But it is important to emphasize that gene action is a complex phenomenon that is only partly understood. For example, although we usually think of genes as coding for the production of structural proteins, some genes function primarily to influence the expression of other genes. Basically, these *regulatory genes* produce enzymes and other proteins that either switch on or off other segments of DNA. Consequently, this mechanism is critical for individual organisms and also has important evolutionary implications.

All somatic cells contain the same genetic information, but in any given cell, only a fraction of the DNA is actually involved in protein synthesis. For example, bone cells carry the same DNA that directs the production of digestive enzymes produced by cells of the stomach lining. But bone cells do not produce digestive enzymes. Instead, they manufacture collagen, the major organic component of bone. The reason bone cells do not produce digestive enzymes is because, during early embryonic development, cell lines differentiate (i.e., bone cells become distinct from skin cells or nerve cells). During this process, cells undergo changes in form, their functions become specialized, and most of their DNA is permanently deactivated through the action of regulatory genes.

On a larger scale, alterations in the behavior of regulatory genes that influence the activities of the structural genes involved in growth and development may be responsible for some of the physical differences between species. For example, some of the anatomical differences between humans and chimpanzees, who share some 98 percent of their DNA, may be the results of evolutionary changes in regulatory genes in one or both lineages.

Amino acids
Small molecules that are the components of proteins.

Gene
A sequence of DNA bases that specifies the order of amino acids in an entire protein or, in some cases, a portion of a protein. A gene may be made up of hundreds or thousands of DNA bases.

Mutation
A change in DNA. Technically, mutation refers to changes in DNA bases as well as changes in chromosome number and/or structure.

A final point is that the genetic code is said to be universal in that, at least on earth, DNA is the genetic material in all forms of life. Moreover, the DNA of all organisms, from bacteria to oak trees to human beings, is composed of the same molecules using the same kinds of instructions. Consequently, the DNA triplet CGA, for example, specifies the amino acid alanine, regardless of species. These similarities imply biological relationships among, and an ultimate common ancestry for, all forms of life. What makes oak trees distinct from humans is not differences in the DNA material, but differences in how that material is arranged.

Cell Division: Mitosis and Meiosis

Throughout much of a cell's life, its DNA exists as an uncoiled, threadlike substance. (Incredibly, there are an estimated 6 feet of DNA in the nucleus of every one of your somatic cells!) However, at various times in the life of most types of cells, normal functions are interrupted and the cell divides. Cell division results in the production of new cells, and it is during this process that the DNA becomes tightly coiled and is visible under a light microscope as a set of discrete structures called **chromosomes** (Fig. 3–4).

A chromosome is composed of a DNA molecule and associated proteins (Fig. 3–5). During normal cell function, if chromosomes were visible, they would appear as single-stranded structures. However, during the early stages of cell division, they are made up of two strands, or two DNA molecules, joined together at a constricted area called the **centromere**. There are two strands because the DNA molecules have *replicated*. Therefore, one strand of a chromosome is an exact copy of the other.

Every species is characterized by a specific number of chromosomes in somatic cells. In humans there are 46, organized into 23 pairs. Chimpanzees and gorillas possess 48. This difference in chromosome number does not necessarily mean that humans have less DNA; it only shows that DNA is packaged differently in the three species.

One member of each chromosomal pair is inherited from the father (paternal), and the other member is inherited from the mother (maternal). Members of chromosomal pairs are alike in size and position of the centromere, and they carry genetic information influencing the same traits (e.g., ABO blood type). This does

Chromosomes
Discrete structures composed of DNA and protein found only in the nuclei of cells. Chromosomes are visible only under magnification during certain stages of cell division.

Centromere
The constricted portion of a chromosome. After replication, the two strands of a double-stranded chromosome are joined at the centromere.

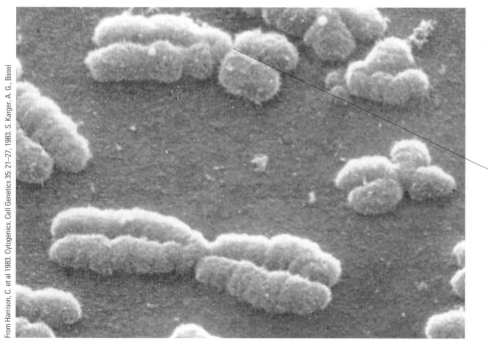

FIGURE 3–4
Scanning electron micrograph of human chromosomes during cell division. Note that these chromosomes are composed of two strands, or two DNA molecules.

Centromere

From Harrison, C. et al 1983. Cytogenics. Cell Genetics 35: 21–27, 1983. S. Karger, A. G., Basel

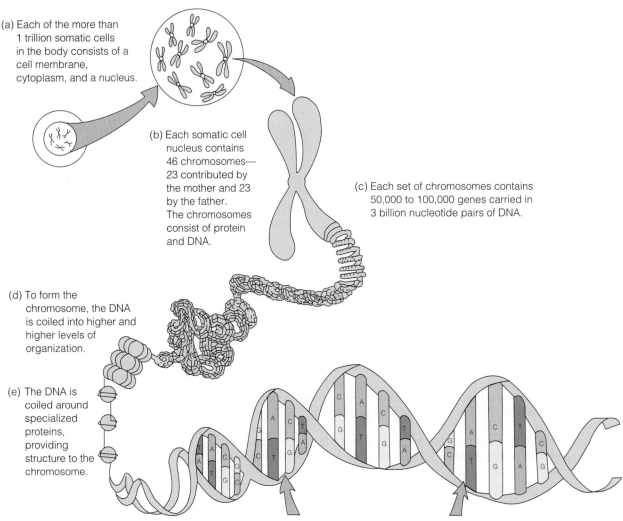

(a) Each of the more than 1 trillion somatic cells in the body consists of a cell membrane, cytoplasm, and a nucleus.

(b) Each somatic cell nucleus contains 46 chromosomes— 23 contributed by the mother and 23 by the father. The chromosomes consist of protein and DNA.

(c) Each set of chromosomes contains 50,000 to 100,000 genes carried in 3 billion nucleotide pairs of DNA.

(d) To form the chromosome, the DNA is coiled into higher and higher levels of organization.

(e) The DNA is coiled around specialized proteins, providing structure to the chromosome.

(f) A specific sequence of nucleotide base pairs constitutes a gene.

FIGURE 3–5

A model of a human chromosome, illustrating the relationship of chromosomes to DNA.

Autosomes
All chromosomes except the sex chromosomes.

Sex chromosomes
The X and Y chromosomes.

not imply that partner chromosomes are genetically identical; it simply means that the traits they govern are the same.

There are two basic types of chromosomes: **autosomes** and **sex chromosomes**. Autosomes carry genetic information that governs all physical characteristics except primary sex determination. The two sex chromosomes are the X and Y chromosomes. The Y chromosome carries genes that are directly involved with determining maleness. The X chromosome, although termed a "sex chromosome," is larger and functions more like an autosome in that it is not actually involved in primary sex determination but does influence a number of other traits. Among mammals, all genetically normal females have two X chromosomes (XX), and they are female simply because the Y chromosome is absent. All genetically normal males have one X and one Y chromosome (XY).

It is extremely important to note that *all* autosomes occur in pairs. Normal human somatic cells have 22 pairs of autosomes and one pair of sex chromosomes. It should also be noted that abnormal numbers of autosomes, with few exceptions, are fatal to the individual, usually soon after conception. Although abnormal numbers of sex chromosomes are not usually fatal, they may result in sterility and frequently have other consequences as well. Therefore, to function normally, it is essential for a human cell to possess both members of each chromosomal pair, or a total of 46 chromosomes.

Mitosis

Cell division in somatic cells is called **mitosis**. Mitosis occurs during growth of the individual. It also acts to promote healing of injured tissues and to replace older cells with newer ones. In short, it is the way somatic cells reproduce.

In the early stages of mitosis, the cell possesses 46 double-stranded chromosomes, which line up in random order along the center of the cell (Fig. 3–6). As the cell wall begins to constrict at the center, the chromosomes split apart at the centromere, so that the two strands are separated. Once the two strands are apart, they pull away from each other and move to opposite ends of the dividing cell. At this point, each strand is now a distinct chromosome, *composed of one DNA molecule.*

Mitosis

Simple cell division; the process by which somatic cells divide to produce two identical daughter cells.

FIGURE 3–6
Mitosis.

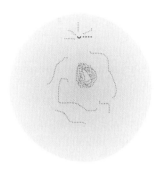

(a) The cell is involved in metabolic activities. DNA replication occurs, but chromosomes are not visible.

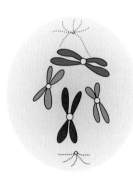

(b) The nuclear membrane disappears, and double-stranded chromosomes are visible.

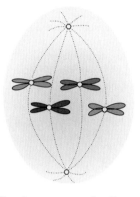

(c) The chromosomes align themselves at the center of the cell.

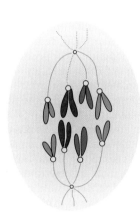

(d) The chromosomes split at the centromere, and the strands separate and move to opposite ends of the dividing cell.

(e) The cell membrane pinches in as the cell continues to divide. The chromosomes begin to uncoil (not shown here).

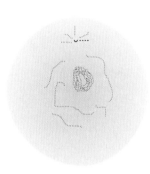
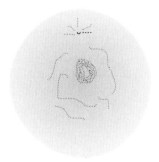

(f) After mitosis is complete, there are two identical daughter cells. The nuclear membrane is present, and chromosomes are no longer visible.

Following the separation of chromosome strands, the cell wall pinches in and becomes sealed, so that two new cells are formed, each with a full complement of DNA, or 46 chromosomes (see Fig. 3–6).

Mitosis is referred to as "simple cell division" because a somatic cell divides one time to produce two daughter cells that are genetically identical to each other and to the original cell. In mitosis, the original cell possesses 46 chromosomes, and each new daughter cell inherits an exact copy of all 46. This precise arrangement is made possible by the ability of the DNA molecule to replicate. Thus, it is DNA replication that ensures that the quantity and quality of the genetic material remain constant from one generation of cells to the next.

Meiosis

Meiosis
Cell division in specialized cells in ovaries and testes. Meiosis involves two divisions and results in four daughter cells, each containing only half the original number of chromosomes. These cells can develop into gametes.

While mitosis produces new cells, **meiosis** may lead to the development of new individuals, since it produces reproductive cells, or gametes. Although meiosis is another form of cell division and is in some ways similar to mitosis, it is a more complicated process (Fig. 3–7).

During meiosis, specialized cells in male testes and female ovaries divide and develop, eventually to produce sperm or egg cells. Meiosis is characterized by *two divisions* that result in *four daughter cells*, each of which contains only 23 chromosomes, or half the original number.

Reduction of chromosome number is a critical feature of meiosis, because the resulting gamete, with its 23 chromosomes, may ultimately unite with another gamete that also carries 23 chromosomes. The product of this union is a *zygote*, or fertilized egg, which in humans receives a total of 46 chromosomes. In other words, the zygote inherits the full complement of DNA it needs (half from each parent) to develop and function normally. If it were not for reduction division (the first division) in meiosis, it would not be possible to maintain the correct number of chromosomes from one generation to the next.

In the first division of meiosis, partner chromosomes come together, forming pairs of double-stranded chromosomes. In this way, then, *pairs* of chromosomes line up along the cell's equator (see Fig. 3–7). Pairing of partner chromosomes is highly significant, for while they are together, members of pairs exchange genetic information in a critical process called **recombination** or *crossing over*. Pairing is also important because it facilitates the accurate reduction of chromosome number by ensuring that each new daughter cell will receive only one member of each pair.

Recombination
The exchange of DNA between paired chromosomes during meiosis; also called "crossing over."

As the cell begins to divide, the chromosomes themselves remain intact (i.e., double-stranded), *but members of pairs* separate and migrate to opposite ends of the cell. After the first division, there are two new daughter cells, but they are not identical to each other or to the parental cell because each contains only one member of each chromosome pair and therefore only 23 chromosomes, each of which still has two strands (see Fig. 3–7).

The second meiotic division proceeds in much the same way as cell division in mitosis. In the two newly formed cells, the 23 double-stranded chromosomes align themselves at the cell's center, and as in mitosis, the strands of each chromosome separate at the centromere and move apart. Once this second division is completed, there are four daughter cells, each with 23 single-stranded chromosomes. (For a diagrammatic representation of the differences between mitosis and meiosis, see Fig. 3–8.)

 The importance of meiosis to random assortment and inheritance is discussed in Virtual Lab 2, section II, part E.

The Evolutionary Significance of Meiosis

The Evolutionary Significance of Meiosis   Meiosis occurs in all sexually reproducing organisms, and it is a highly important evolutionary innovation, since it increases genetic variation in populations at a faster rate than mutation alone can do. Individual members of sexually reproducing species are not genetically identical clones of other individuals. Rather, they result from the contribution of genetic information from two parents. Therefore, each individual represents a unique combination of genes that, in all likelihood, has never occurred before and will never

FIGURE 3–7
Meiosis.

Chromosomes are not visible as DNA replication occurs in a cell preparing to divide.

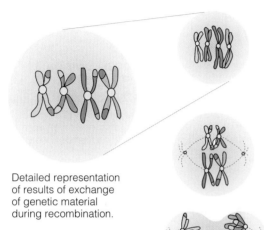

Double-stranded chromosomes become visible, and partner chromosomes exchange genetic material in a process called "recombination" or "crossing over."

Chromosome pairs migrate to the center of the cell.

Detailed representation of results of exchange of genetic material during recombination.

FIRST DIVISION (REDUCTION DIVISION)

Partner chromosomes separate, and members of each pair move to opposite ends of the dividing cell. This results in only half the original number of chromosomes in each new daughter cell.

After the first meiotic division, there are two daughter cells, each containing only one member of each original chromosomal pair, or 23 nonpartner chromosomes.

SECOND DIVISION

In this division, the chromosomes split at the centromere, and the strands move to opposite sides of the cell.

After the second division, meiosis results in four daughter cells. These may mature to become functional gametes, containing only half the DNA in the original cell.

occur again. The genetic uniqueness of individuals is further enhanced by recombination between partner chromosomes during meiosis, since recombination ensures that chromosomes are not transmitted intact from one generation to the next. Instead, in every generation, parental contributions are reshuffled in an almost infinite number of combinations, thus altering the genetic composition of chromosomes even before they are passed on.

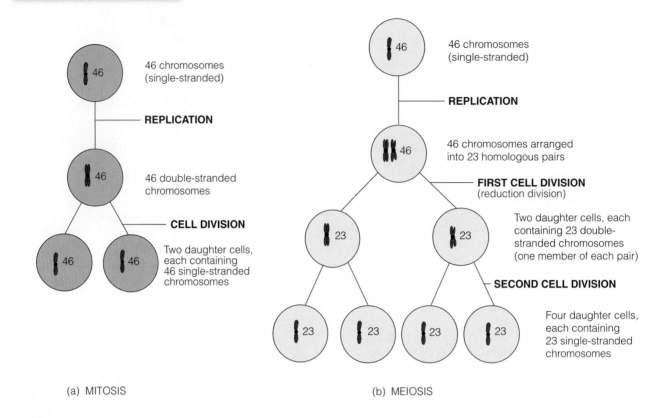

(a) MITOSIS

(b) MEIOSIS

FIGURE 3–8
Mitosis and meiosis compared. In mitosis, one division produces two daughter cells, both of which contain 46 chromosomes. Meiosis is characterized by two divisions. After the first, there are two cells, each containing only 23 chromosomes (one member of each original chromosome pair). Each daughter cell divides again, so that the final result is four cells, each with only half the original number of chromosomes.

Hybrids
Offspring of mixed ancestry; heterozygotes.

Genetic diversity is therefore considerably enhanced by meiosis. As was mentioned in Chapter 2, natural selection acts on genetic variation in populations. If all individuals in a population are genetically identical over time, then natural selection (and evolution) cannot occur. Although there are other sources of variation (mutation being the only source of *new* variation), sexual reproduction and meiosis are of major evolutionary importance because they contribute to the role of natural selection in populations.

The Genetic Principles Discovered by Mendel

It was not until Gregor Mendel (1822–1884) addressed the issue that the question of heredity began to be resolved (Fig. 3–9). Mendel was a monk living in the Augustinian abbey at Brno in what is now the Czech Republic. At the time he began his research, he had already acquired scientific expertise in botany, physics, and mathematics at the University of Vienna, and he had also conducted various experiments in the monastery gardens. These experiments led him to explore the various ways in which physical traits, such as color or height, could be expressed in plant **hybrids**. He hoped that by making crosses between two strains of *purebred* plants (plants that were alike with regard to certain traits) and examining their offspring, he could determine and predict how many different forms of hybrids there were, arrange the forms according to generation, and evaluate the proportion of each type in each generation.

Mendel's Principle of Segregation

Mendel chose to work with common garden peas, and unlike previous researchers, he chose to consider only one trait at a time. In all, he focused on seven traits, each of which could be expressed in two different ways (Table 3–1). Because the genetic

TABLE 3–1   The Seven Garden Pea Characteristics Studied by Mendel

Characteristic	Dominant Trait	Recessive Trait
1. Form of ripe seed	Smooth	Wrinkled
2. Color of seed albumen	Yellow	Green
3. Color of seed coat	Gray	White
4. Form of ripe pods	Inflated	Constricted
5. Color of unripe pods	Green	Yellow
6. Position of flowers	Axial	Terminal
7. Length of stem	Tall	Dwarf

FIGURE 3–9
Gregor Mendel.

principles Mendel discovered apply to humans (and all other biological organisms) as well as to peas, we discuss his work to illustrate the basic rules of inheritance.

Mendel began by crossing plants that produced only tall plants with others that produced only short ones. The result was that the first generation of offspring, called F_1 plants, were all tall. But when he conducted crosses between the F_1 plants, the second generation of offspring (F_2 plants) showed variation. In this generation, approximately $3/4$ of the plants were tall and $1/4$ were short. Thus, it appeared that one expression (shortness) of the trait (height) had completely disappeared in the F_1 plants and reappeared in the second generation (the F_2 plants). Moreover, the expression that was universal in the F_1 generation was more common in the F_2 generation, occurring in a ratio of approximately 3:1, or three tall plants for every short one.

These results led Mendel to conclude that the characteristics of offspring were not the result of a blending of parental traits, as was commonly believed. In fact, Mendel was the first to demonstrate that inheritance was *particulate* in nature—that the different expressions of traits, such as seed color in peas, were controlled by discrete *units* (what we now call genes) that occurred in pairs. He also determined that offspring inherited one unit from each parent and that the members of a pair of units somehow separated into different sex cells and were united with another member during fertilization of the egg. This discovery was the basis of Mendel's *first principle of inheritance*, known as the **principle of segregation**.

Today we know that meiosis explains Mendel's principle of segregation. You will remember that during meiosis, paired chromosomes, and the genes they carry, separate from one another and are distributed to different gametes. However, in the zygote, the full complement of chromosomes is restored, and both members of each chromosome pair are present in the offspring.

Dominance and Recessiveness

Mendel also recognized that the expression that was absent in the first generation had not actually disappeared at all. It had remained present, but somehow it was masked and could not be expressed. To describe the trait that seemed to be lost, Mendel used the term **recessive**; the trait that was expressed was said to be **dominant**. Thus, the important principles of *dominance* and *recessiveness* were formulated, and they remain today as important concepts in the field of genetics.

As you already know, a *gene* is a segment of DNA that directs the production of a specific protein or part of a protein. Furthermore, the location of a gene on a chromosome is its **locus** (*pl.*, loci). At numerous genetic loci, however, there is more than one possible form of the gene, and these variations of genes at specific loci are called **alleles**. Therefore, alleles are alternate forms of a gene that can direct the cell to produce slightly different forms of the same protein and, ultimately, different expressions of traits.

Principle of segregation
Genes (alleles) occur in pairs (because chromosomes occur in pairs). During gamete production, the members of each gene pair separate, so that each gamete contains one member of each pair. During fertilization, the full number of chromosomes is restored, and members of gene or allele pairs are reunited.

Recessive
Describing a trait that is not expressed in heterozygotes; also refers to the allele that governs the trait. For a recessive allele to be expressed, there must be two copies of the allele (i.e., the individual must be homozygous).

Dominant
Describing a trait governed by an allele that can be expressed in the presence of another, different allele (i.e., in heterozygotes). Dominant alleles prevent the expression of recessive alleles in heterozygotes. (This is the definition of *complete* dominance.)

Locus (*pl.*, loci)
(lo´-kus, lo-sigh´) The position on a chromosome where a given gene occurs. The term is sometimes used interchangeably with *gene*.

Alleles
Alternate forms of a gene. Alleles occur at the same locus on paired chromosomes and thus govern the same trait. However, because they are different, their action may result in different expressions of that trait. The term *allele* is often used synonymously with *gene*.

As it turns out, plant height in garden peas is controlled by two different alleles at one genetic locus. The allele that determines that a plant will be tall is dominant to the allele for short. (It is worth mentioning that height is not governed in this manner in all plants.)

In Mendel's experiments, all the parent (P) plants had two copies of the same allele, either dominant or recessive, depending on whether they were tall or short. When two copies of the same allele are present, the individual is said to be **homozygous**. Thus, all the tall P plants were homozygous for the dominant allele, and all the short P plants were homozygous for the recessive allele. (This homozygosity explains why tall plants crossed with tall plants produced only tall offspring, and short plants crossed with short plants produced all short offspring; they were "pure lines" and lacked genetic variation at this locus.) However, all the F_1 plants (hybrids) had inherited one allele from each parent plant; therefore, they all possessed two different alleles at specific loci. Individuals that possess two different alleles at a locus are **heterozygous**.

Figure 3–10 illustrates the crosses that Mendel initially performed. Geneticists use standard symbols to refer to alleles. Uppercase letters refer to dominant alleles

Homozygous
Having the same allele at the same locus on both members of a chromosome pair.

Heterozygous
Having different alleles at the same locus on members of a chromosome pair.

FIGURE 3–10
Results of crosses when only one trait at a time is considered.

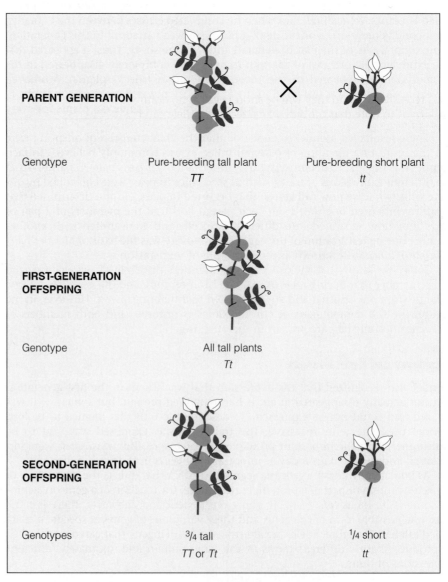

F03.10

(or dominant traits), and lowercase letters refer to recessive alleles (or recessive traits). Therefore,

T = the allele for tallness
t = the allele for shortness (dwarfism)

The same symbols are combined to describe an individual's actual genetic makeup, or **genotype**. The term *genotype* can be used to refer to an organism's entire genetic makeup or to the alleles at a specific genetic locus. Thus, the genotypes of the plants in Mendel's experiments were

TT = homozygous tall plants
Tt = heterozygous tall plants
tt = homozygous short plants

Figure 3–11 is a *Punnett square*. It represents the different ways the alleles can be combined when the F_1 plants are self-fertilized to produce an F_2 generation. In this way, the figure shows the *genotypes* that are possible in the F_2 generation, and it also demonstrates that approximately $1/4$ of the F_2 plants are homozygous dominant (TT); $1/2$ are heterozygous (Tt); and the remaining $1/4$ are homozygous recessive (tt).

The Punnett square can also be used to show (and predict) the proportions of F_2 **phenotypes**, or the observed physical manifestations of genes. Moreover, the Punnett square illustrates why Mendel observed three tall plants for every short plant in the F_2 generation. By examining the Punnett square, you can see that $1/4$ of the F_2 plants will be tall because they have the TT genotype. Furthermore, an additional $1/2$, which are heterozygous (Tt), will also be tall because T is dominant to t and will therefore be expressed in the phenotype. The remaining $1/4$ are homozygous recessive (tt), and they will be short because no dominant allele is present. It is important to note that the *only* way a recessive allele can be expressed is if it occurs with another recessive allele—that is, if the individual is homozygous recessive at the particular locus in question.

In conclusion, $3/4$ of the F_2 generation will express the dominant phenotype, and $1/4$ will show the recessive phenotype. This relationship is expressed as a **phenotypic ratio** of 3:1 and typifies all **Mendelian traits** (characteristics governed by only one genetic locus) when only two alleles are involved, one of which is completely dominant to the other.

Mendel's Principle of Independent Assortment

Mendel also made crosses in which two characteristics were considered simultaneously to determine whether there was a relationship between them. Two such characteristics were plant height and seed (pea) color. Mendel's peas came in two colors: yellow (dominant) and green (recessive).

In the P generation, crosses were made between pure-breeding tall plants with yellow seeds and short plants with green seeds. As expected, the recessive expression of each trait was not seen in the F_1 generation; all these plants were tall and produced

Genotype
The genetic makeup of an individual. Genotype can refer to an organism's entire genetic makeup or to the alleles at a particular locus.

Phenotypes
The observable or detectable physical characteristics of an organism; the detectable expressions of genotypes.

Phenotypic ratio
The proportion of one phenotype to other phenotypes in a group of organisms. For example, Mendel observed that there were approximately three tall plants for every short plant in the F_2 generation. This is expressed as a phenotypic ratio of 3:1.

Mendelian traits
Characteristics that are influenced by alleles at only one genetic locus. Examples include many blood types, such as ABO. Many genetic disorders, including sickle-cell anemia and Tay-Sachs disease, are also Mendelian traits.

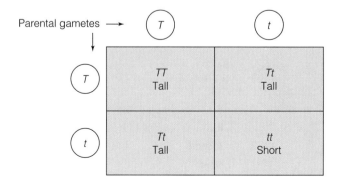

FIGURE 3–11
Punnett square representing possible genotypes and phenotypes and their proportions in the F_2 generation. The circles across the top and at the left of the Punnett square represent the gametes of the F_1 parents. The four squares illustrate that $1/4$ of the F_2 plants will be homozygous tall (TT); another $1/2$ also will be tall but will be heterozygous (Tt); and the remaining $1/4$ will be short (tt). Thus, $3/4$ can be expected to be tall and $1/4$ will be short.

yellow seeds. However, in the next (F₂) generation, both recessive traits reappeared in a small proportion of plants. Moreover, the allele for tallness had the same chance (50-50) of ending up with the allele for yellow seeds or with the allele for green seeds. These results demonstrated that there was no relationship between the two traits; that is, there is nothing to dictate that a tall plant must have yellow (or green) seeds. The expression of one trait is not influenced by the expression of the other trait.

Mendel stated this relationship as the **principle of independent assortment**, which says that the units (genes) that code for different traits assort independently of each other during gamete formation. Today, we know this to be true because we know that the genetic loci controlling these two characteristics are located on different chromosomes, and during meiosis, chromosomes travel to newly forming cells independently of one another. But if Mendel had used just *any* two traits, his results would have been quite different. For example, if the two traits in question were influenced by genes located on the same chromosome, then they would be more likely to be inherited together and, if so, would not conform to Mendel's ratios. The ratios came out as he predicted because the loci governing most of the traits he chose were carried on different chromosomes.

In 1866, Mendel's results were published, but their methodology and statistical nature were beyond the thinking of the time, and the significance of his work was unappreciated. However, by the end of the nineteenth century, several investigators had made important contributions to the understanding of chromosomes and cell division. These discoveries paved the way for the acceptance of Mendel's work by 1900, when three different groups of scientists came across his paper. Unfortunately, Mendel had died 16 years earlier and never saw his work vindicated.

Mendelian Inheritance in Humans

Mendelian traits (also referred to as *discrete traits* or *traits of simple inheritance*) are controlled by alleles at *one* genetic locus. Currently, more than 4,500 human traits are known to be inherited according to simple Mendelian principles. Examples include several blood group systems, such as ABO.

The ABO system is governed by three alleles, *A*, *B*, and *O*, found at the ABO locus on the ninth chromosome. Although three alleles are present in populations, each individual can possess only two. These alleles determine which ABO blood type an individual has by coding for the production of special substances, called **antigens**, on the surface of red blood cells. If only antigen A is present, the blood type (phenotype) is A; if only B is present, the blood type is B; if both are present, the blood type is AB; and when neither is present, the blood type is O (Table 3–2).

Dominance and recessiveness are clearly illustrated by the ABO system. The *O* allele is recessive to both *A* and *B*; therefore, if a person has type O blood, he or she must be homozygous for (have two copies of) the *O* allele. Since both *A* and *B* are dominant to *O*, an individual with blood type A can have one of two genotypes: *AA* or *AO*. The same is true of type B, which results from the genotypes *BB* and *BO*. However, type AB presents a slightly different situation and is an example of **codominance**.

Principle of independent assortment
The distribution of one pair of alleles into gametes does not influence the distribution of another pair. The genes controlling different traits are inherited independently of one another.

Virtual Lab 2, section II, part E, provides a Punnett square exercise for you to complete.

An example of human blood groups is given in Virtual Lab 2, section II, part E.

Antigens
Large molecules found on the surface of cells. Several different loci governing antigens on red and white blood cells are known. (Foreign antigens provoke an immune response in individuals.)

Codominance
The expression of two alleles in heterozygotes. In this situation, neither is dominant or recessive, so that both influence the phenotype.

TABLE 3–2 ABO Genotypes and Associated Phenotypes

Genotype	Antigens on Red Blood Cells	ABO Blood Type (Phenotype)
AA, AO	A	A
BB, BO	B	B
AB	A and B	AB
OO	None	O

Codominance is seen when two different alleles occur in heterozygotes, but instead of one having the ability to mask the expression of the other, the products of *both* are expressed in the phenotype. Therefore, when both *A* and *B* alleles are present, both A and B antigens can be detected on the surface of red blood cells.

A number of genetic disorders are inherited as dominant traits (Table 3–3). This means that if a person inherits only one copy of a harmful dominant allele, the condition it causes will be present, regardless of the existence of a different, recessive allele on the corresponding chromosome.

Recessive conditions (see Table 3–3) are commonly associated with the lack of a substance, usually an enzyme. For a person actually to have a recessive disorder, he or she must have *two* copies of the recessive allele that causes it. Heterozygotes who have only one copy of a harmful recessive allele are unaffected. Such individuals are frequently called *carriers*.

Although carriers do not actually have the recessive condition they carry, they can pass the allele that causes it to their children. (Remember, half their gametes

TABLE 3–3 Some Mendelian Disorders in Humans

Dominant Traits		Recessive Traits	
Condition	**Manifestations**	**Condition**	**Manifestations**
Achondroplasia	Dwarfism due to growth defects involving the long bones of the arms and legs; trunk and head size usually normal.	Cystic fibrosis	Among the most common genetic (Mendelian) disorders among whites in the United States; abnormal secretions of the exocrine glands, with pronounced involvement of the pancreas; most patients develop obstructive lung disease. Until the recent development of new treatments, only about half of all patients survived to early adulthood.
Brachydactyly	Shortened fingers and toes.		
Familial hyper-cholesterolemia	Elevated cholesterol levels and cholesterol plaque deposition; a leading cause of heart disease, with death frequently occurring by middle age.		
		Tay-Sachs disease	Most common among Ashkenazi Jews; degeneration of the nervous system beginning at about 6 months of age; lethal by age 2 or 3 years.
Neurofibromatosis	Symptoms range from the appearance of abnormal skin pigmentation to large tumors resulting in gross deformities; can, in extreme cases, lead to paralysis, blindness, and death.	Phenylketonuria (PKU)	Inability to metabolize the amino acid phenylalanine; results in mental retardation if left untreated during childhood; treatment involves strict dietary management and some supplementation.
Marfan syndrome	The eyes and cardiovascular and skeletal systems are affected; symptoms include greater than average height, long arms and legs, eye problems, and enlargement of the aorta; death due to rupture of the aorta is common. (Abraham Lincoln may have had Marfan syndrome.)	Albinism	Inability to produce normal amounts of the pigment melanin; results in very fair, untannable skin, light blond hair, and light eyes; may also be associated with vision problems. (There is more than one form of albinism.)
Huntington disease	Progressive degeneration of the nervous system accompanied by dementia and seizures; age of onset variable but commonly between 30 and 40 years.	Sickle-cell anemia	Abnormal form of hemoglobin (Hb^S) that results in collapsed red blood cells, blockage of capillaries, reduced blood flow to organs, and, without treatment, death.
Camptodactyly	Malformation of the hands whereby the fingers, usually the little finger, is permanently contracted.	Thalassemia	A group of disorders characterized by reduced or absent alpha or beta chains in the hemoglobin molecule; results in severe anemia and, in some forms, death.

will carry the recessive allele.) If their mate is also a carrier, then it is possible for them to have a child who will possess two copies of the allele, and that child will be affected. In fact, in a mating between two carriers, the risk of having an affected child is 25 percent (refer back to Fig. 3–11).

Misconceptions Regarding Dominance and Recessiveness

Traditional methods of teaching genetics have led to some misunderstanding of dominance and recessiveness. Thus, virtually all introductory students (and most people in general) have the impression that these phenomena are all-or-nothing situations. This misconception especially pertains to recessive alleles, and the general view is that when these alleles occur in heterozygotes (i.e., carriers), they have absolutely no effect on the phenotype—that is, they are completely inactivated by the presence of another (dominant) allele. Certainly, this is how it appeared to Gregor Mendel and, until the last two or three decades, to most geneticists.

However, various biochemical techniques, unavailable in the past but in wide use today, have demonstrated that recessive alleles do indeed exert some influence on phenotype, although these effects are not always apparent through simple observation. In fact, in heterozygotes, many recessive alleles act to reduce, but not eliminate, the gene products they influence. Thus, it is now clear that our *perception* of recessive alleles greatly depends on whether we examine them at the directly observable phenotypic level or the biochemical level.

Scientists now know of several recessive alleles that produce phenotypic effects in heterozygotes. Consider Tay-Sachs disease, a lethal condition that results from the inability to produce the enzyme hexosaminidase A (see Table 3–3). This inability, seen in people who are homozygous for a recessive allele (*ts*) on chromosome 15, invariably results in death by early childhood. Carriers do not have the disease, and practically speaking, they are unaffected. However, in 1979, it was shown that Tay-Sachs carriers, although functionally normal, have only about 40 to 60 percent of the amount of the enzyme seen in normal people. In fact, there are now voluntary tests to screen carriers in populations at risk for Tay-Sachs disease.

Similar misconceptions also relate to dominant alleles. The majority of people see dominant alleles as somehow "stronger" or "better," and there is always the mistaken notion that dominant alleles are more common in populations. These misconceptions undoubtedly stem partly from the label "dominant" and the connotations that the term carries. But in genetic usage, those connotations are somewhat misleading. If dominant alleles were always more common, then a majority of people would be affected by such conditions as achondroplasia and Marfan syndrome (see Table 3–3).

Clearly, the relationships between recessive and dominant alleles and their functions are more complicated than they would appear at first glance. Previously held views of dominance and recessiveness were guided by available technologies; as genetic technologies continue to change, new theories may emerge, and, if so, our perceptions will be further altered. Therefore, it is just possible that one day the concepts of dominance and recessiveness, as they have traditionally been taught, will be obsolete.

Polygenic Inheritance

Mendelian traits are said to be *discrete*, or *discontinuous*, because their phenotypic expressions do not overlap, but rather fall into clearly defined categories (Fig 3–12a). For example, Mendel's pea plants were either short or tall, but none was intermediate in height. In the ABO system, the four phenotypes are completely distinct from one another; that is, there is no intermediate form between type A and type B to represent a gradation between the two. In other words, Mendelian traits do not show *continuous* variation.

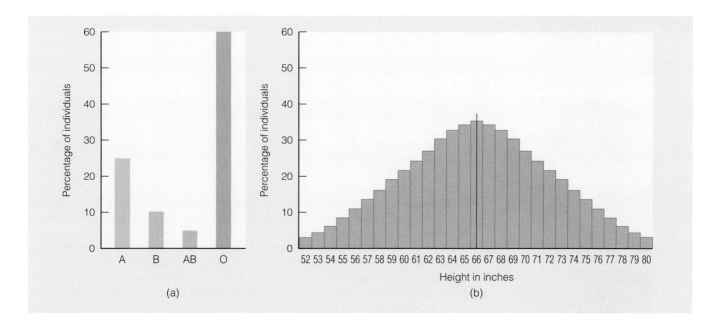

(a)

(b)

However, many traits do have a wide range of phenotypic expressions that form a graded series. These are called **polygenic**, or *continuous*, traits (Fig. 3–12b). While Mendelian traits are governed by only one genetic locus, polygenic characteristics are influenced by alleles at two or more loci, with each locus making a contribution to the phenotype. For example, one of the most frequently cited instances of polygenic inheritance in humans is skin color, and the single most important factor influencing skin color is the amount of the pigment melanin present.

Melanin production is believed to be influenced by between three and six genetic loci, with each locus having at least two alleles, neither of which is dominant. Individuals having only alleles for maximum melanin production (i.e., they are homozygous at all loci) have the darkest skin. Those having only alleles that code for reduced melanin production have very fair skin.

As there are perhaps six loci and at least 12 alleles, there are numerous ways in which these alleles can combine in individuals. If an individual inherits 11 alleles coding for maximum pigmentation and only 1 for reduced melanin production, skin color will be very dark. A person who inherits a higher proportion of reduced pigmentation alleles will have lighter skin color. This is because in this system, as in some other polygenic systems, there is an *additive effect*. This means that each allele that codes for melanin production makes a contribution to increased melanization (although for some characteristics the contributions of the alleles are not all equal). Likewise, each allele coding for less melanin production contributes to reduced pigmentation. Therefore, the effect of multiple alleles at several loci is to produce continuous variation from very dark to very fair skin within the species. (Skin color is also discussed in Chapter 5.)

Polygenic traits actually account for most of the readily observable phenotypic variation seen in humans and they have traditionally served as a basis for racial classification (see Chapter 5). In addition to skin color, polygenic inheritance in humans is seen in hair color, weight, stature, eye color (Fig. 3–13), shape of face, shape of nose, and fingerprint pattern. Because they exhibit continuous variation, most polygenic traits can be measured on a scale composed of equal increments (see Fig. 3–12b). For example, height (stature) is measured in feet and inches (or meters and centimeters). If one were to measure height in a large number of individuals, the distribution of measurements would continue uninterrupted from the shortest extreme to the tallest. That is what is meant by the term *continuous traits*.

FIGURE 3–12

(a) This histogram shows the discontinuous distribution of a Mendelian trait (ABO blood type) in a hypothetical population. The expression of the trait is described in terms of frequencies. (b) This histogram represents the continuous expression of a polygenic trait (height) in a large group of people. Note that the percentage of extremely short or tall individuals is low, where the majority of people are closer to the mean, or average, height, represented by the vertical line at the center of the distribution.

Polygenic
Referring to traits that are influenced by genes at two or more loci. Examples of such traits are stature, skin color, and eye color. Many polygenic traits are also influenced by environmental factors.

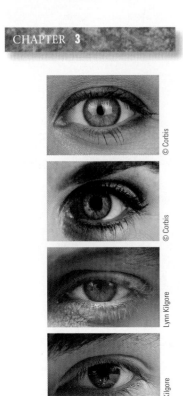

© Corbis

© Corbis

Lynn Kilgore

Lynn Kilgore

FIGURE 3–13
Examples of the continuous variation seen in human eye color.

Because polygenic traits usually lend themselves to metric analysis, biologists, geneticists, and physical anthropologists treat them statistically. Although statistical analysis can be complicated, the use of simple summary statistics, such as the *mean* (average) or *standard deviation* (a measure of within-group variation), permits basic descriptions of, and comparisons between, populations. For example, one might be interested in average height in two different populations and whether or not differences between the two are significant, and if so, why. Or a researcher might determine that in the same geographical area, one group shows significantly more variation in skin color than another, and it would be useful to explain this variability. (You should also note that *all* physical traits measured and statistically treated in fossils are polygenic in nature.)

However, these particular statistical manipulations are not possible with Mendelian traits because those traits cannot be measured in the same manner. They are either present or they are not; they are expressed one way or another. But just because Mendelian traits are not amenable to the same statistical tests used to study polygenic characters does not mean that Mendelian traits are less worthy of study or less informative of genetic processes. It simply means that scientists must approach the study of these two types of inheritance from different perspectives.

Mendelian characteristics can be described in terms of frequency within populations, thus yielding between-group comparisons regarding incidence. Moreover, these characteristics can also be analyzed for mode of inheritance (dominant or recessive). Finally, for many Mendelian traits, the approximate or exact positions of genetic loci have been identified, thus making it possible to examine the mechanisms and patterns of inheritance at these loci. Because polygenic characters are influenced by several loci, they cannot, as yet, be traced to specific loci; therefore, such analysis is currently not possible.

Genetic and Environmental Factors

From the preceding discussion, it might appear that phenotype is solely the expression of the genotype, but this is not true. (Here we use the terms *genotype* and *phenotype* in a broader sense to refer to an individual's entire genetic makeup and *all* observable or detectable characteristics.) The genotype sets limits and potentials for development, but it also interacts with the environment, and many aspects of phenotype are influenced by this genetic-environmental interaction. For many traits, scientists have developed statistical methods for calculating what proportion of phenotypic variation is due to genetic or environmental components. However, it is usually not possible to identify the *specific* environmental factors affecting the phenotype.

Many polygenic traits are quite obviously influenced by environmental conditions. Adult stature is strongly affected by the individual's nutritional status during growth and development. Other important environmental factors include exposure to sunlight, altitude, temperature, and, unfortunately, increasing levels of exposure to toxic waste and airborne pollutants. All these and many more contribute in complex ways to the continuous phenotypic variation seen in characteristics governed by multiple loci.

Mendelian traits are less likely to be influenced by environmental factors. For example, ABO blood type is determined at fertilization and remains fixed throughout the individual's lifetime, regardless of diet, exposure to ultraviolet radiation, temperature, and so forth.

Mendelian and polygenic inheritance produce different kinds of phenotypic variation. In the former, variation occurs in discrete categories, while in the latter, it is continuous. However, it is important to understand that even for polygenic characteristics, Mendelian principles still apply at individual loci. In other words, if a trait is influenced by seven loci, each one of those loci may have two or more alleles, with one perhaps being dominant to the other or with the alleles being codominant. It is the combined action of the alleles at all seven loci, interacting with the environment, that results in observable phenotypic expression.

Mitochondrial Inheritance

There is another component of inheritance that has gained much attention in recent years, and it involves organelles called **mitochondria** (see Fig. 3–1). All cells contain several hundred of these oval-shaped structures that convert energy (derived from the breakdown of nutrients) into a form that can be used by the cell.

Each mitochondrion contains several copies of a ring-shaped DNA molecule, or chromosome. While **mitochondrial DNA (mtDNA)** is distinct from the DNA found within cell nuclei, its molecular structure and functions are the same. The entire molecule has been sequenced and is known to contain around 40 genes that direct the conversion of energy within the cell.

Mitochondrial DNA is subject to mutations just like nuclear DNA, and such mutations can lead to certain genetic disorders, some of which have been traced to specific loci. In general, these disorders result from impaired energy conversion and can produce a wide range of symptoms. Importantly, mitochondrial DNA is transmitted to offspring only from the mother; it is thus the mother who transmits all mitochondrial traits to her offspring of both sexes. This is so because mitochondria occur in cellular cytoplasm, and while egg cells retain their cytoplasm, sperm cells lose theirs prior to fertilization.

Mitochondrial mutation rates have been used as a basis for constructing evolutionary relationships between species. They have also been used, with much controversy, to establish ancestral relationships within the human lineage (see Chapter 12). While these techniques are still being refined and remain the topic of debate, it is clear that we have much to learn from mitochondrial DNA.

Mitochondria (*sing.,* **mitochondrion)** (my´-tow-kond´-dree-uh) Structures contained within the cytoplasm of eukaryotic cells that convert energy, derived from nutrients, into a form that is used by the cell.

Mitochondrial DNA (mtDNA) DNA found in the mitochondria that is inherited through the maternal line.

New Frontiers

Since the discovery of DNA structure and function in the 1950s, the field of genetics has revolutionized biological science and reshaped our understanding of inheritance, genetic disease, and evolutionary processes. For example, a technique developed in 1986 called **polymerase chain reaction (PCR)** now enables scientists to produce multiple copies of DNA, making it possible to analyze segments of DNA as small as one molecule. This ability is critically important because samples of DNA, such as those obtained at crime scenes or from fossils, are frequently too small to permit reliable analysis of nucleotide sequences.

In PCR, the two strands of a DNA sample are separated, and an enzyme synthesizes complementary strands on the exposed bases, as in DNA replication. Because this process can be repeated many times, it is possible to produce over a million copies of the original DNA material! Thus, scientists have been able to identify nucleotide sequences in, for example, fossils (including Neandertals), Egyptian mummies, and members of the Russian royal family murdered in 1918. As you can imagine, PCR has limitless potential for many disciplines, including forensic science, medicine, and evolutionary biology.

Over the last two decades, using the techniques of recombinant DNA, scientists have been able to transfer genes from the cells of one species into those of another. The most common method has been to insert genes that direct the production of various proteins into bacterial cells, thus causing the altered bacteria to produce human gene products. There are numerous commercial applications for this technology, many of which are aimed at treating genetic disease in humans. For example, until the early 1980s, diabetic patients relied on insulin derived from nonhuman animals. However, this insulin was not plentiful; moreover, some patients developed allergies to it. But since 1982, abundant supplies of human insulin, produced by bacteria, have been available; and bacteria-derived insulin does not cause allergic reactions in patients.

Human genes may also be inserted into the fertilized eggs of some nonhuman animals. The eggs are then implanted into the uteri of females who subsequently give birth to genetically altered offspring. These offspring serve as a source of various

Polymerase chain reaction (PCR) A method of producing copies of a DNA segment using the enzyme DNA polymerase.

substances needed in medical practice. For example, genetically altered female sheep can carry a human gene that causes them to produce an enzyme that is present in most people and which prevents a serious form of emphysema. This enzyme is produced in the sheep's milk, and once extracted and purified, it can be administered to people who do not normally produce it.

Genetic transfer techniques have also been used to improve crops in a variety of ways. For instance, genetically altered strawberries are able to withstand temperatures of 10–12°F below freezing without being damaged. Likewise, some tomatoes can be ripened on the vine before being shipped because they carry a gene that inhibits the potentially damaging softness that normally develops during ripening.

In recent years, genetic manipulation has become increasingly controversial owing to questions related to product safety, environmental concerns, and animal welfare, among others. For example, the insertion of bacterial DNA into certain crops has made them toxic to leaf-eating insects, thus reducing the need for pesticide use. And cattle and pigs are commonly treated with genetically engineered growth hormone to increase growth rates. Although there is no current evidence that humans are susceptible to the insect-repelling bacterium or adversely affected by the consumption of meat and dairy products from animals treated with growth hormone, there are concerns over the unknown effects of such long-term exposure.

But regardless of how intriguing these new techniques may be, nothing has generated as much controversy as the birth of Dolly, a **clone** of a female sheep, in 1997 (Wilmut et al., 1997). Actually, cloning is not as new as you might think. Anyone who has ever taken a cutting from a plant and rooted it to grow a new plant has produced a clone. In the 1950s, plant biologists developed methods of cloning carrots by culturing cells taken from mature plants. In the 1960s, an African toad became the first animal to be cloned, but for a number of reasons, cloning a mammal remained an elusive goal. Then, in 1981, a Swiss team of geneticists successfully produced cloned mice, and these experiments were followed by cloned cattle and sheep. So, you might ask, why was Dolly such a big deal? The furor was partly due to the fact that earlier cloning results had not been well publicized. But in the scientific community, the enthusiasm was due to the techniques that were used.

The Dolly research was unique because the donor nucleus was derived not from an undifferentiated embryonic cell (standard practice) but from a cell of a *mature* animal. This demonstrated that DNA derived from a specialized somatic cell is capable of returning to an embryonic state, where it can direct cell division and ultimately orchestrate the development of an entire organism. Until now, this ability had been questioned.

Since the original reports of the Dolly experiment were published, it has emerged that the donor cell for Dolly may inadvertently have been a fetal cell and not one taken from an adult sheep after all. But teams of Japanese scientists have now reported cloning cattle and mice using donor cells from adult animals (Wakayama et al., 1998). Thus, while it is possible that Dolly was not derived from an adult somatic cell, other animals have been. These experiments have demonstrated that DNA derived from a specialized somatic cell is capable of being "turned back on" so that it can orchestrate the development of an entire organism.

As exciting as these innovations are, probably the single most important advance in genetics has been the progress made by the **Human Genome Project**. The goal of this international effort, begun in 1990, is the sequencing of the entire human **genome**, which consists of some 3 billion bases comprising approximately 30,000 genes. At a White House press conference in July 2000, two years earlier than projected deadlines, scientists announced that they had produced a "working draft" of the entire human DNA sequence. Actually, about 87 percent of the genome had been sequenced at that time, and scientists are still several years away from sorting out which DNA segments operate as functional genes and which do not. It will also be years before the identity and function of many of the proteins produced by these newly identified genes are ascertained. Put another way, it is one thing to know the

Clone
An organism that is genetically identical to another organism. The term may also be used to refer to genetically identical DNA segments and molecules.

Human Genome Project
An international effort aimed at sequencing and mapping the entire human genome.

Genome
The entire genetic makeup of an individual or species. In humans, it is estimated that each individual possesses approximately 3 billion DNA nucleotides.

chemical makeup of a gene but quite another to know what that gene does. Nevertheless, the magnitude and importance of the achievement cannot be overstated, because it will ultimately transform biomedical and pharmaceutical research and will change forever how many human diseases are diagnosed and treated.

Moreover, at the same time scientists were sequencing human genes, the genomes of other organisms were also being studied. As of September 2000, the genomes of over 600 species (mostly viruses) had been either partially or completely identified. This research has enormous implications not only for biomedical research but also for studies of evolutionary relationships among species. We already know that humans share many genes with other organisms, but just how many and which ones will partly be clarified by upcoming projects aimed at sequencing nonhuman primate (especially chimpanzee) genomes. Eventually, comparative genome analysis should provide a thorough assessment of genetic similarities and differences, and thus the evolutionary relationships, between humans and other primates. Indeed, it would not be an exaggeration to say that this is the most exciting time in the history of evolutionary biology since Darwin published *On the Origin of Species*.

SUMMARY

The topics covered in this chapter relate almost entirely to discoveries made after Darwin and Wallace described the fundamentals of natural selection. But all the issues presented here are basic to an understanding of biological evolution, adaptation, and human variation.

It has been shown that cells are the fundamental units of life and that they are essentially classified into two types. Somatic cells make up body tissues, while gametes (eggs and sperm) are reproductive cells that transmit genetic information from parent to offspring.

Genetic information is contained in the DNA molecule, found in the nuclei of cells. The DNA molecule is capable of replication, or making copies of itself, and it is the only molecule known to have this ability. DNA also controls protein synthesis by directing the cell to arrange amino acids in the proper sequence for each particular type of protein. Also involved in the process of protein synthesis is another, similar molecule called RNA.

Cells multiply by dividing, and during cell division, DNA is visible under a microscope in the form of chromosomes. In humans, there are 46 chromosomes, or 23 pairs.

Somatic cells divide during growth or tissue repair or to replace old or damaged cells. Somatic cell division is called mitosis. During mitosis, a cell divides one time to produce two daughter cells, each possessing a full and identical set of chromosomes.

Sex cells are produced when specialized cells in the ovaries and testes divide in meiosis. Unlike mitosis, meiosis is characterized by two divisions that produce four nonidentical daughter cells, each containing only half the amount of DNA (23 chromosomes) contained within the original cell.

Traits that are influenced by only one genetic locus are called Mendelian traits. At many genetic loci, two or more alleles may interact in dominant/recessive or codominant fashion with one another. Examples of Mendelian traits in humans include ABO blood type and cystic fibrosis. In contrast, many characteristics such as stature and skin color are said to be polygenic, or continuous, because they are influenced by more than one genetic locus and show a continuous range of expression.

In addition to nuclear DNA, we have discussed mitochondrial DNA, which is found within cellular structures called mitochondria and which is transmitted to offspring only through the maternal line. Mitochondrial DNA directs the production of energy used by the cells, and mitochondrial mutations result in a variety of disorders, several of which have now been identified. Mitochondrial mutation rates

have been used to construct evolutionary relationships between species and to trace ties between early human ancestors.

The expression of all biological traits is, to varying degrees, under genetic control. Genes, then, can be said to set limits and potentials for human growth, development, and achievement. However, these limits and potentials are not written in stone, so to speak, because many characteristics are also very much influenced by such environmental factors as temperature, diet, and sunlight. Thus, ultimately it is the interaction between genetic and environmental factors that produces phenotypic variation in all species, including *Homo sapiens*.

Lastly, we discussed the advances in genetics of the latter part of the twentieth century. The techniques used in PCR, cloning, and sequencing the genomes of humans and other species will have profound effects on the lives of everyone in the twenty-first century.

QUESTIONS FOR REVIEW

1. Name the four DNA bases. Which pairs with which?
2. What are proteins? Give two examples.
3. What are the building blocks of protein? How many different kinds are there?
4. What is the function of DNA in protein synthesis?
5. How many cell divisions occur in mitosis? In humans, how many chromosomes does each new cell have?
6. How many cell divisions occur in meiosis? How many daughter cells are produced when meiosis is complete? In humans, how many chromosomes does each new cell contain?
7. Why is meiosis important to the process of natural selection?
8. What is Mendel's principle of segregation?
9. How does meiosis explain the principle of segregation?
10. Explain dominance and recessiveness. What are some misconceptions about these phenomena?
11. Define allele.
12. What is phenotype, and what is its relationship to genotype?
13. Why were all of Mendel's F_1 pea plants phenotypically the same?
14. Why are polygenic traits said to be continuous?
15. What factors, other than genetic, contribute to phenotypic variation in populations?
16. Explain the difference between Mendelian and polygenic traits.
17. What is mitochondrial DNA? What is its primary function?
18. From which parent is mitochondrial DNA inherited?
19. What is the Human Genome Project, and why is it important?

SUGGESTED FURTHER READING

"The Business of the Human Genome." 2000. *Scientific American* 283(1): 48–69. Special Report.

Collins, Francis S., and Karin G. Jegalian. 1999. "Deciphering the Code of Life." *Scientific American* 281(6): 86–91.

Cummings, Michael R. 2000. *Human Heredity*. 4th ed. Belmont, CA: Brooks/Cole.

Wallace, Douglas C. 1997. "Mitochondrial DNA in Aging and Disease." *Scientific American*, 277(2): 40–47.

See entire issue of *Scientific American*, vol. 253(4), (October 1985), for numerous articles pertaining to molecular genetics and evolution.

RESOURCES ON THE INTERNET

 Wadsworth Anthropology Resource Center

http://anthropology.wadsworth.com

The companion website for this text includes a range of enrichment material focused on the chapter's topic. While online you can enhance your understanding of the chapter by exploring one of the several additional Internet Exercises, by researching topics, and by accessing full articles on InfoTrac College Edition. You can also reinforce the concepts by taking online practice exams.

Internet Exercises

The subject of genetics is well represented on the Internet. Use your search engine to do a word search for *genetics*. See if you can find the original 1953 article by Watson and Crick that describes the structure of the DNA molecule. Read this very short Nobel Prize–winning article and make a list of facts that are not presented in Chapter 3. What is your overall impression of the Watson and Crick paper?

 InfoTrac College Edition

http://www.infotrac-college.com/wadsworth

Conduct a subject search for *DNA*. Choose at least one article, read it, and write a short summary. In your summary, discuss some aspect of the article that pertains to one of the topics discussed in Chapter 3.

Genetic Screening: A Doubled-Edged Sword?

Genetic screening involves the use of several techniques to identify individuals who possess deleterious alleles that may eventually lead to debilitating illness and, perhaps, death. Screening can also identify carriers for certain recessive disorders who, though not affected themselves, can nevertheless pass a defective allele on to their offspring. The applications of genetic screening are numerous, but primarily all are aimed at decreasing the incidence of genetic disorders.

For a number of reasons, chief among which are reducing human suffering and cutting health costs, genetic screening has become a powerful diagnostic tool since the 1970s. Moreover, as new technologies are developed and as more genetic markers for disease are identified, use of such technologies in assessing individual risk will certainly continue to increase.

The benefits of genetic screening both to the individual and to society are enormous but they carry a price tag. The ability to identify individuals at risk for potentially fatal conditions raises numerous difficult questions never before asked. Currently, advances in genetic technology are proceeding at a rate that has far outpaced our legal and ethical systems. Thus, the purpose of this Issue is to explore some of the beneficial applications of genetic screening as well as some of the difficult choices such screening may pose.

Detection of an individual's carrier status is possible through blood testing combined with genetic counseling. Clearly, this ability is of enormous benefit for those who have a family history of some recessive disorder, and who

are making family planning decisions of their own.

The same techniques are also increasingly used today to identify persons with a genetic *predisposition* to problems associated with exposure to certain environmental agents. These results permit avoidance of potentially harmful substances especially in the workplace. Employers are especially interested in identifying those employees who might potentially suffer from contact with particular materials. (This raises obvious issues related to the rights of employees to privacy and job security.)

Newborn infants can be tested for several metabolic disorders to aid in early diagnosis and treatment. The most widespread use of newborn testing is for *phenylketonuria (PKU)* (see Table 3–3, p. 57), a recessive disorder that prevents production of the enzyme phenylalanine hydroxylase. Without this enzyme, the body cannot properly metabolize the amino acid phenylalanine, common in meat and dairy products, and the resulting accumulation of phenylalanine eventually leads to brain damage and severe mental retardation.

PKU testing is mandatory in most states and involves a simple blood test to detect abnormal levels of phenylalanine. For those infants who test positive, the severe consequences of PKU are avoidable by strict adherence to a low-phenylalanine diet throughout childhood and adolescence. The important point here is that treatment depends on early detection made possible through genetic screening.

But diagnosis of such conditions as PKU does not have to occur after birth. *Prenatal testing* permits detection of over 200

genetically determined metabolic disorders and all chromosomal abnormalities in a developing fetus. Currently, the two most commonly used methods of detecting such conditions in fetuses are *amniocentesis* and *chorionic villus sampling (CVS)*.

Prenatal testing is controversial for the obvious reason that test results may lead to termination of a pregnancy. Although therapeutic abortion may be the outcome, the notion that amniocentesis and CVS are aimed at the elimination of all abnormal fetuses is inaccurate. Not all negative findings result in abortion, and in fact, prenatal diagnosis can be highly beneficial in preparing physicians and parents for *in utero* surgery, or for the birth of an infant who requires immediate treatment.

Individuals must make personal decisions as to where to draw the line if they are told their fetus has a genetic disorder. Tay-Sachs (see Table 3–3, p. 57) carriers can be identified through screening prior to beginning a pregnancy. But if both prospective parents are carriers and they choose to conceive, they face a 25 percent risk of having an affected fetus. Because Tay-Sachs is such a devastating condition with no chance of survival beyond childhood, 80 to 90 percent of diagnosed pregnancies are terminated.

Likewise, the majority of pregnancies *with* a *diagnosis* of trisomy 21 also end in abortion. This fact does not mean, however, that the majority of all trisomy 21 pregnancies are terminated. Most pregnant women over the age of 35 (who are at increased risk) are not screened. Moreover, at least 65 percent of trisomy 21 infants are born to women younger than 35 who are not usually tested. Since trisomy 21 is variably expressed, with many affected persons leading fairly normal lives, the certainty of outcome is not as clear as with Tay-Sachs. Because of this uncertainty, some parents who would terminate a Tay-Sachs pregnancy would not do so in the case of trisomy 21.

Other situations are even more ambiguous. Does one choose abortion if a fetus has PKU, cystic fibrosis, or sickle-cell anemia? All three are treatable to some extent, though at considerable costs, both financial and otherwise.

Another serious question is faced by individuals who learn that they themselves possess an allele that will eventually cause illness and death. What does one do with such knowledge? For example, it is possible to identify people at risk for *Huntington disease*, a fatal, degenerative disorder of the central nervous system (see Table 3–3, p. 57). Huntington disease is inherited as an autosomal dominant trait and usually produces no symptoms until middle age. Symptoms include progressive degeneration of the central nervous system, mental deterioration, and eventually, after 5 to 15 years, death.

Because Huntington disease is a dominant trait, all affected people (barring new mutations) will have an affected parent. Additionally, anyone who has a parent with Huntington disease has a 50 percent chance of inheriting the allele and thus of developing symptoms by middle age. However, until the development of reliable methods of detecting genetic markers, children of affected parents could not know for certain if they had the defective allele or not. Such a test exists today, and it is possible to learn if, in later life, one will succumb to this tragic disease.

People who have a parent with Huntington disease face a most terrible dilemma. They can go untested and continue hoping, but not knowing, that they do not have the allele. Or they can be tested and either be tremendously relieved, or plan the rest of their lives in anticipation of catastrophic debilitating disease and early death. Unless one has faced such a horrific decision, one cannot comprehend the uncertainty and fear that accompanies it. Unfortunately, technology has given us the tools with which to answer many painful questions, but it has not prepared us for how to cope with what we may learn.

The fact that many genetic disorders are treatable but, as yet, not curable, raises another issue: cost. With medical costs soaring out of reach for anyone without health care coverage, financial considerations must be addressed, and this obviously raises many painful questions.

How does an individual or the state place a monetary value on a human life? Can we morally establish limits on public expenditures for the treatment of genetic disease when those diseases can be prevented by prenatal testing and selective abortion? Is society obligated to bear the costs of preventable hereditary conditions? Do people have a fundamental right to have children regardless of circumstances? Or, do they have an obligation to society to be personally responsible for the financial costs of medical treatment?

Does a fetus have a right to be born free of disease? If so, can an afflicted child later sue the parents for having given birth? (Such a case actually has come before the courts.) Is it indeed desirable for

society to be free of "imperfect" people? If so, who defines "perfect," and what does such a policy say about our tolerance of diversity? (One should note that a goal of the Nazi regime in Germany was to rid society of imperfection, as it was defined by the Nazis.)

These are only a few of the many discomforting ethical questions that have accompanied advances in genetic screening and prenatal testing. There are numerous other questions as well as considerable potential for abuse. For example, after screening programs for the sickle-cell trait were instituted in the United States in 1972, persons testing positive as heterozygotes were, in some cases, reportedly denied health insurance or employment opportunities. Do employers or insurance companies have the right to refuse opportunities to people because, due to potential health problems, they ostensibly constitute an economic risk? This issue raises the question of whether or not individual rights, including rights to privacy, are violated by government or corporate policies that institute genetic screening programs.

These examples illustrate the conflicts between technology, ethical standards, and the legal system. The questions raised are disturbing because they challenge traditionally held views about fundamental aspects of life. In the past, people with hereditary disorders frequently died. They still do. But now, there are treatments, however costly, for some conditions. In addition, we now have the means to detect genetic defects or determine their risk of occurrence. How we come to terms with the ethical and legal issues surrounding our new technologies will increasingly

Genetic Screening: A Doubled-Edged Sword? (continued)

become social, religious, and, ultimately, political concerns. Solutions will not come easily and, most assuredly, they will not please everyone.

Critical Thinking Questions

1. Do you approve of technologies that permit a person to learn if he or she has inherited a lethal allele, such as the one that causes Huntington disease? Why or why not? If one of your parents developed Huntington disease, would you be tested to see if you had inherited the allele that causes it?

2. What do you see as the most disturbing aspect of genetic screening? Which do you think is the most positive? Explain.

3. If you were an employer providing health benefits to employees, would you hire someone who carried the allele for Huntington disease? Since appropriate genetic tests are available, do you think you should have the right to obtain test results for employees? Explain your answer.

4. Do you think it is desirable for society to attempt to eliminate all or some genetic diseases? If your answer is "all," explain why. If your answer is "some," where do you draw the line and why? If your answer is "no" to any elimination, explain why.

Microevolution in Modern Human Populations

See the following sections of the CD-ROM for topics covered in this chapter: Virtual Lab 2, sections I, II, and III.

Introduction

How is evolution defined and measured in contemporary species? In the last chapter, we discussed the mechanisms of inheritance. How does the transmission of such heritable characteristics influence evolutionary change? In this chapter, we will demonstrate how genetic principles lie at the very foundation of the evolutionary process. Moreover, we will show how these factors interact to produce evolutionary change in contemporary human populations. In the twentieth century, a *synthetic* theory of evolution, incorporating genetic principles, has become the major cornerstone of modern biology. As with all other organisms, the variation exhibited by *Homo sapiens* can be understood within this contemporary evolutionary framework. Evolutionary change not only characterizes the human past; it also continues as a major factor shaping human beings today.

The Modern Theory of Evolution

By the beginning of the twentieth century, the two essential foundations of modern evolutionary theory were in place. Darwin and Wallace had articulated the crucial role of natural selection 40 years earlier, and in 1900, Mendel's pioneering work was rediscovered, clearly establishing the mechanisms for inheritance.

We might expect that the two basic contributions would have been joined rather quickly into one consistent theory of evolution. However, such was not the case. For the next 30 years, rival "camps" advocated what seemed to be opposing viewpoints. One, supported by experimental biologists working with such organisms as fruit flies, emphasized the central role of mutation. The other school of thought continued with the more traditional Darwinian view, pointing to the key role of natural selection.

A combination of these two views, in what is called the *Modern Synthesis*, was not achieved until the mid-1930s, and we owe much of our current understanding of evolutionary change to this important intellectual breakthrough. Biologists working primarily on mathematical models came to realize that mutation and selection processes were not opposing themes, but that a comprehensive explanation of organic evolution required *both*. Small changes in the genetic material (i.e., mutations) are transmitted from parent to child according to the rules first discovered by Mendel. Mutations do not usually, by themselves, produce evolutionary change, but are selected for (or against) in particular environments. Indeed, mutation is the origin of variation, and it is the only original source of "fuel" for natural selection.

Using such a perspective, evolution is described by the Modern Synthesis as a two-stage process:

1. Production and redistribution of **variation** (inherited differences between individuals)
2. **Natural selection** (whereby genetic differences in some individuals lead to their higher reproductive success)

The Definition of Evolution

Darwin saw evolution as the gradual emergence of new life forms derived from earlier ones. Such a depiction is in accordance with the common understanding of evolutionary change and indeed is one result of the evolutionary process. However, such long-term effects—called **macroevolution**—can only come about by the accumulation of many small evolutionary changes—called **microevolution**—which unfold every generation. To understand how the process of evolution works, we must study the short-term events. Using such a modern *population genetics* perspective, we define evolution as a change in **allele frequency** from one generation to the next. This concept is really very simple. As we have seen, *alleles* are alternative

Variation
Inherited (i.e., genetically influenced) differences between individuals.

Natural Selection
The differential reproductive success of certain phenotypes (and their underlying genotypes) relative to others in a population.

Macroevolution
Large-scale evolutionary changes (especially speciation) that may require many hundreds of generations and are usually only detectable paleontologically (in the fossil record).

Microevolution
Small-scale evolutionary changes that occur over the span of a few generations and can therefore be detected in living populations.

Allele frequency
The proportion of one allele to all alleles at a given locus in a population.

forms of genes that occur at the same locus. For example, the ABO blood type in humans is governed by a single locus on chromosome 9. As such, it is a good example of a *Mendelian* trait in humans. As we have seen in Chapter 3, this locus has three alternative forms (alleles): *A*, *B*, or *O*.

Allele frequencies are simply the proportions of alleles in a population. If 70 percent of all alleles at the ABO locus are *O*, the frequency of the *O* allele is .70. If *A* and *B* constitute, respectively, 10 percent and 20 percent of alleles at this locus, their frequencies are .10 and .20. In any genetic system, the total of allele frequencies for a locus must equal 1.0 (100 percent).

Evolution, then, is a *change* in these proportions. For example, if the allele frequencies noted above were to shift, over a few generations, to *O* = .50, *A* = .30, and *B* = .20, then we would say that evolution had occurred (*O* had decreased in frequency, *A* had increased, and *B* had stayed the same).

What causes allele frequencies to change in human populations? In the following section, you will find the answer to this question.

Population Genetics

What do we mean by "population"? A **population** is a group of interbreeding individuals. More precisely, a population is the group within which one is most likely to find a mate. As such, a population is marked by a degree of genetic relatedness, and its members share a common **gene pool**.

In theory, this is a straightforward concept. In every generation, the genes (alleles) are mixed by recombination and rejoined through mating. What emerges in the next generation is a direct product of the genes going into the pool, which in turn is a product of who is mating with whom.

In practice, however, isolating and describing human populations is difficult. The largest population of *Homo sapiens* that could be described is the entire **species**. All members of a species are *potentially* capable of interbreeding, but are incapable of mating and producing fertile offspring with members of other species. Our species is thus a *genetically closed system*. The problem arises not in describing who potentially can interbreed, but in isolating exactly the pattern of those individuals who are doing so.

Factors that determine mate choice are geographical, ecological, and social. If individuals are isolated on a remote island in the middle of the Pacific, there is not much chance of their finding a mate outside the immediate vicinity. Such **breeding isolates** are fairly easily defined and are a favorite target of microevolutionary studies. Geography plays a dominant role in producing these isolates by rather strictly determining the range of available mates. But even within these limits, cultural rules strongly influence the choice of partners among those who are potentially available.

Human population segments within the species are defined as groups with relative degrees of **endogamy** (marrying/mating within the group). These are, however, not totally closed systems. Migration often occurs between groups, and individuals may choose mates from distant localities. With the modern advent of rapid transportation, greatly accelerated rates of **exogamy** (marrying/mating outside the group) have emerged.

Most humans today are not so clearly identified as members of particular populations as they would be if they belonged to a breeding isolate. Inhabitants of large cities may appear to be members of a single population, but within the city borders, social, ethnic, and religious boundaries crosscut in a complex fashion to form smaller population segments. In addition to being members of these highly open local population groupings, we are simultaneously members of overlapping gradations of larger populations—the immediate geographical region (a metropolitan area or perhaps an entire state), a section of the country, the whole nation, and ultimately, again, the whole species.

 See Virtual Lab 2, sections I and II for discussions of populations and an example of the Hardy-Weinberg equilibrium.

Population
Within a species, the community of individuals where mates are usually found.

Gene pool
The total complement of genes shared by reproductive members of a population.

Species
A group of organisms that can interbreed to produce fertile offspring. Members of one species are reproductively isolated from all other species.

Breeding isolates
Populations that are clearly isolated geographically and/or socially from other breeding groups.

Endogamy
Mating with others from the same group.

Exogamy
Mating with individuals from other groups.

Hardy-Weinberg equilibrium
The mathematical relationship expressing—under ideal conditions—the predicted distribution of genes in populations; the central theorem of population genetics.

Once specific human populations have been identified, the next step is to ascertain what evolutionary forces, if any, are operating on this group. To determine whether evolution is taking place at a given locus, we measure allele frequencies for specific traits and compare these observed frequencies with a set predicted by a mathematical model: the **Hardy-Weinberg equilibrium** equation. The approach used by physical anthropologists to measure evolution using this model is called *population genetics*. Just how the equation is used is illustrated in Appendix B.

The Hardy-Weinberg formula provides the tool to establish whether allele frequencies in a human population are indeed changing. What factors initiate changes in allele frequencies? There are a number of such factors, including those that

1. Produce new variation (i.e., *mutation*)
2. Redistribute variation through *gene flow*
3. Redistribute variation through *genetic drift*
4. Select "advantageous" allele combinations that promote reproductive success (i.e., *natural selection*)

Note that factors 1, 2, and 3 constitute the first stage of the evolutionary process, as emphasized by the Modern Synthesis, while factor 4 is the second stage.

Mutation

In Chapter 3, we defined mutation as a change in DNA that can occur either as a change in the sequence of bases or at a larger, chromosomal level. From an evolutionary perspective, mutation is the only way totally *new* variation can be produced. Effects on any one gene should be minor, however, since mutation rates for any given locus are quite low (estimated at about 1 per 10,000 gametes per generation). In fact, because mutation occurs so infrequently at any particular locus, it would rarely have any significant effect on allele frequencies. Certainly, mutation occurs every generation, but unless we sample a huge number of subjects, we are unlikely to detect any noticeable effect.

However, because we each have many loci (estimated at about 30–40 thousand), we all possess numerous mutations that have accumulated over recent generations. Most of these are not expressed in the phenotype, but are "hidden" as recessive alleles. (See Chapter 3 for a discussion of recessive inheritance.) An example of such a recessive mutation is the allele for PKU (phenylketonuria). About 1 in 12,000 babies born in the United States carry this allele in homozygous form and thus are affected phenotypically. Without early detection and treatment, this condition leads to severe mental retardation (see p. 57).

Several dominant alleles that produce phenotypic effects are also well known. An example of such a condition is a type of dwarfism called achondroplasia. Individuals with one copy of the responsible mutant allele have abnormally shortened limbs but normal-sized head and trunk. The incidence of achondroplasia among newborns in the United States is about 1 in 10,000. (See Chapter 3 for further examples of dominant alleles.)

Gene Flow

Gene flow
The exchange of genes between populations; also called migration.

Gene flow is the movement of alleles between populations. The term *migration* is frequently used synonymously with gene flow; however, migration, strictly defined, means movement of people, whereas gene flow refers to the exchange of *genes*—which can occur only if the migrants interbreed. In the last 500 years especially, population movements have reached enormous proportions, and few breeding isolates remain. It should not, however, be assumed that significant population movements did not occur prior to modern times. Our hunting and gathering ancestors probably lived in small groups that were mobile as well as flexible in membership. Early farmers may well have been fairly mobile, moving from area to area as

the land wore out. Intensive, highly sedentary agricultural communities came later, but even then, significant migration was still possible. From the Near East, one of the early farming centers, populations spread gradually in a "creeping occupation of Europe, India, and northern and eastern Africa" (Bodmer and Cavalli-Sforza, 1976, p. 563).

An interesting application of how gene flow influences microevolutionary change in modern human populations is seen in the population history of African Americans over the last three centuries. In the United States, African Americans are largely of West African descent, but there has also been considerable influx of alleles from non-African populations. By measuring allele frequencies for specific genetic loci (such as those influencing the Rh blood group), we can estimate the amount of gene flow of non-African alleles being incorporated into an African American gene pool. By using different methods, the percentage of gene flow from one population to another has been estimated. From these analyses, a variety of data from northern and western U.S. cities (including New York, Detroit, and Oakland) have shown the migration rate (i.e., the proportion of *non*-African genes in the African American gene pool) at 20 to 25 percent (Cummings, 1997). However, more restricted data from the southern United States (Charleston and rural Georgia) have suggested a lower degree of gene flow (4 to 11 percent). The most consistent of these studies employ new genetic techniques, especially those involving direct DNA comparisons (discussed later in this chapter).

It would be a misconception to conclude that human gene flow can occur only through large-scale movements of groups. In fact, significant alterations in allele frequencies can come about through long-term patterns of mate selection. If exchanges of mates were consistently in one direction over a long period of time, allele frequencies would ultimately be altered. Because of demographic, social, or economic pressures, an individual may choose a mate from outside the immediate vicinity.

Transportation plays an obvious role in determining the manageable geographical distance for finding available mates. When people were limited to walking or using the horse, transportation ranges were typically limited to about a 10-mile radius. With the spread of affordable railway transportation through rural England in the nineteenth century, a dramatic increase in the mean marital distance* of 20 to 30 miles was seen. Today, with even more efficient means of transportation, the potential range has become worldwide. Actual patterns are, however, somewhat more restricted. For example, data from Ann Arbor, Michigan, indicate a mean marital distance of close to 160 miles—not worldwide by any means, but still including a tremendous number of potential marriage partners.

Genetic Drift

Genetic drift is the purely chance factor in evolution and is tied directly to population size. The term *drift* is used because, as a completely random process, the allele frequencies can change in any direction. A particular kind of drift seen in modern populations is called **founder effect**. Founder effect operates when an unusually small number of individuals contributes genes to the next generation. This phenomenon can occur when a small migrant band of "founders" colonizes a new and separate area away from the parent group. Small founding populations may also be left as remnants when famine, war, or other diasters ravage a normally larger group. In these situations, the reduced group size is called a population bottleneck, and the process is sometimes designated as a type of drift called the *bottleneck effect*. In reality, as we can see, each generation is the founder of all succeeding generations in any population. Consequently, many researchers (e.g., Ridley, 1993) do not draw a distinction between founder effect and bottleneck effect.

Genetic drift
Evolutionary changes—that is, changes in allele frequencies—produced by random factors. Genetic drift is a result of small population size.

Founder effect
Also called the *Sewall-Wright effect*, a type of genetic drift in which allele frequencies are altered in small populations that are taken from, or are remnants of, larger populations.

---

*The average distance between husband's and wife's birthplace.

The cases of founder effect producing evolutionary change in human populations are necessarily seen in small groups. For example, an island in the South Atlantic, Tristan da Cunha, has unusually high frequencies of a hereditary eye disorder. First settled in 1817 by one Scottish family, this isolated island's indigenous inhabitants include only descendants of this one family and a few other individuals. All in all, only about two dozen founders established this population. A fortuitous opportunity to study the descendants occurred in 1961 when, owing to an imminent volcanic eruption, all 294 residents were evacuated to England. There, extensive medical tests were performed that revealed four individuals with the rare recessive eye disease retinitis pigmentosa. The allele frequency for the mutant allele was unusually high in this population, and no doubt, a high proportion of individuals were carriers.

How did this circumstance come about? Apparently, just by chance, one of the initial founders carried the allele and later passed it on to descendants who, with some inbreeding, occasionally produced affected offspring. The fact that so few individuals founded this population allowed the one person who carried the retinitis pigmentosa allele to make a disproportionate contribution to the incidence of this condition in future generations. An important point to keep in mind is that the larger the population, the smaller the effect of drift. Drift can exert immediate influence *only* when the population is relatively small.

Genetic drift has probably played an important role in human evolution, influencing genetic changes in small groups. From studies of recent hunter-gatherers in Australia, we know that the range of available mates was restricted to within the linguistic tribe, usually consisting of about 500 individuals. In groups of this size, drift can have significant effects, particularly if drought, disease, and so on, should temporarily reduce the population still further.

While drift has been a factor over the long term, the effects have been irregular and nondirectional (for drift is *random* in nature). Certainly, the pace of evolutionary change could have been accelerated if many small populations were isolated and thus subject to drift. By modifying such populations, drift can provide significantly greater opportunities for the truly directional force in evolution—natural selection.

It is important to emphasize that natural selection need not be the inevitable and *only* prime mover of evolutionary change. As we have seen, both gene flow and genetic drift can produce some evolutionary changes by themselves. However, these changes are usually *microevolutionary* ones; that is, they produce changes within species over the short term. To yield the kind of evolutionary changes that ultimately result in entire new groups (e.g., the diversification of the first primates, the appearance of the hominids), natural selection most likely would play the major role. Remember, however, that natural selection does not and cannot operate independently of the other evolutionary factors—mutation, gene flow, and genetic drift. All four factors (sometimes called the "four forces of evolution") work interactively.

Additional insight concerning the relative influences of the different evolutionary factors has emerged in recent studies of the early dispersal of modern *Homo sapiens* (discussed in Chapter 13). New evidence suggests that in the last 100,000 to 200,000 years, our species experienced a genetic bottleneck, which considerably influenced the pattern of genetic variation seen in all human populations today. In this sense, modern humans can be seen as the fairly recent product of a form of genetic drift acting on a somewhat grand scale. Such evolutionary changes could be potentially significant over tens of thousands of years and could cause substantial genetic shifts within species.

Natural Selection

 See Virtual Lab 2, section I for a discussion of natural selection and variation.

In the long run, the most important factor influencing the *direction* of evolutionary change is natural selection. As you will recall, we have defined natural selection as differential net reproductive success (see p. 33). Controlled observations of laboratory animals or natural populations of quickly reproducing organisms, such as moths (see Chapter 2), have demonstrated how differential reproductive success eventually leads to adaptive shifts within populations.

Human beings are neither quickly reproducing nor amenable to controlled laboratory manipulations. Therefore, unambiguous examples of natural selection in action among contemporary humans are extremely difficult to find.

The best-documented case concerns the *sickle-cell allele*, which is the result of a single amino acid substitution in the hemoglobin molecule. If inherited in homozygous form, this gene causes severe anemia and frequently early death. Even with aggressive medical treatment, life expectancy in the United States today is less than 45 years for victims of the severe recessive disease, sickle-cell anemia (also called sickle-cell disease). Worldwide, sickle-cell disease is estimated to cause 100,000 deaths each year.

With such obviously harmful effects, it is surprising to find the sickle-cell allele so frequent in some populations (Fig. 4–1). The highest allele frequencies are found in western and central African populations, reaching levels close to 20 percent; values are also moderately high in some Greek and Asiatic Indian populations. How do we explain such a phenomenon? Obviously, the allele originated from a simple mutation, but why did it increase in frequency?

The answer lies in yet another kind of disease, one that exerts enormous selective pressure. In those areas of the world where the sickle-cell allele is found in highest frequency, *malaria* is also found (Fig. 4–2). Caused by a single-celled parasite, this debilitating infectious disease is transmitted to humans by mosquitoes. In areas that are **endemically** infected, many individuals suffer sharply lower reproductive success, owing to high infant mortality rates or to lowered vitality as adults.

Such a geographical correlation between malarial incidence and distribution of the sickle-cell allele is indirect evidence of a biological correlation. Further confirmation was provided by British biologist A. C. Allison in the 1950s. Volunteers from

Endemically (endemic)
Continuously present in a population. With regard to disease, refers to populations in which there will always be some infected individuals.

FIGURE 4–1
Map of the sickle-cell allele distribution in the Old World.

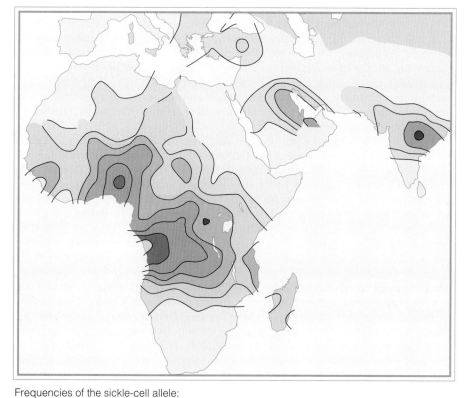

Frequencies of the sickle-cell allele:

Greater than .14	.08–.10	.02–.04
.12–.14	.06–.08	.00–.02
.10–.12	.04–.06	

FIGURE 4–2
Malaria distribution in the Old World.

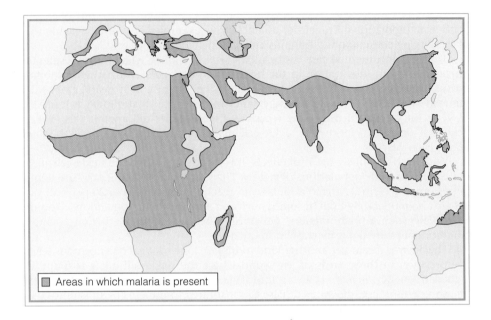

☐ Areas in which malaria is present

the Luo tribe of eastern Africa with known genotypes were injected with the malarial parasite. The ethics concerning human subjects would preclude such experimentation today; even when the original study was conducted, its justification was questionable. A short time following infection, results showed that heterozygous carriers of the sickle-cell allele were much more resistant to malarial infection than the homozygous "normals." Apparently, carriers resist infection because their red blood cells provide a less conducive environment for the malarial parasite to reproduce itself. As a result, the parasite often dies before widely infecting the body of a carrier. But for the homozygous "normals," the infection usually persists.

A genetic trait (such as sickle-cell trait) that provides a reproductive advantage in certain environments is a clear example of natural selection in action among human populations. The precise evolutionary mechanism in the sickle-cell example is termed a **balanced polymorphism**.

Balanced polymorphism
The maintenance of two or more alleles in a population due to the selective advantage of the heterozygote.

Polymorphism
A genetic trait (the locus governing the trait) with more than one allele in appreciable frequency (i.e., greater than 1 percent).

A genetic trait is called a **polymorphism** "when two or more alleles at a given genetic locus occur with appreciable frequencies in a population" (Bodmer and Cavalli-Sforza, 1976, p. 308). How much is "appreciable" is a fairly arbitrary judgment, but it is usually placed at 1 percent. In other words, if a population is sampled for a particular trait, and frequencies for more than one allele are higher than 1 percent, the trait (more precisely, the locus that governs the trait) is polymorphic.

The limit of 1 percent is an attempt by population geneticists to control for mutation effects, which normally add new alleles at rates far below our 1 percent level. So when an allele like that for the sickle-cell trait is found in a population in frequencies approaching 10 percent, the locus is clearly polymorphic. The frequency is higher than can be accounted for by mutation *alone* and thus demands a fuller evolutionary explanation. In this case, the additional mechanism is natural selection.

This brings us back to the other part of the term *balanced polymorphism*. By "balanced," we are referring to the interaction of selective pressures operating in a malarial environment. Some individuals (mainly homozygous normals) will be removed by the infectious disease malaria, and some (homozygous recessives) will die of the inherited disease sickle-cell anemia. Those with the highest reproductive success are the heterozygous carriers. But what alleles do they carry? Clearly, they are passing *both* the "normal" allele and the sickle-cell allele to offspring, thus maintaining both alleles at fairly high frequencies (above the minimum level for polymorphism). Since one allele in this population will not significantly increase in frequency over the other allele, this situation will reach a balance and persist, at least as long as malaria continues to be a selective factor.

Human Biocultural Evolution

We have defined culture as the human strategy of adaptation. Human beings live in cultural environments that are continually modified by human activity; thus, evolutionary processes are understandable only within this *cultural* context. You will recall that natural selection pressures operate within specific environmental settings. For humans and many of our hominid ancestors, this means an environment dominated by culture. For example, the sickle-cell allele has not always been an important genetic factor in human populations. In fact, human cultural modification of the environment apparently provided the initial stimulus. Before the development of agriculture, humans rarely, if ever, lived close to mosquito-breeding areas. With the development and spread to Africa of **slash-and-burn agriculture**, perhaps in just the last 2,000 years, penetration and clearing of tropical rain forests occurred. As a result of deforestation, open, stagnant pools provided prime mosquito-breeding areas in close proximity to human settlements. (Here we see another example of the major impact of agriculture on human populations.)

As a result of these agricultural changes, malaria now struck human populations with its full impact, and as a selective force it was powerful indeed. No doubt, humans attempted to adjust culturally to these circumstances, and numerous biological adaptations also probably came into play. The sickle-cell trait is one of these biological (genetic) adaptations. However, there is a definite cost involved with such an adaptation. Carriers have increased resistance to malaria and presumably higher reproductive success, but some of their offspring may be lost through the genetic disease sickle-cell anemia. So there is a counterbalancing of selective forces with an advantage for carriers *only* in malarial environments. The genetic patterns of recessive traits such as sickle-cell anemia are discussed in Chapter 3.

Following World War II, extensive DDT spraying by the World Health Organization began systematically to wipe out mosquito-breeding areas in the tropics. As would be expected, malaria decreased sharply, and also as would be expected, the frequency of the sickle-cell allele also seemed on the decline. The intertwined story of human cultural practices, mosquitoes, malarial parasites, and the sickle-cell allele is still not finished. Forty years of DDT spraying killed many mosquitoes, but natural selection is also acting on these insect populations. Facilitated by the tremendous amount of genetic diversity among insects, as well as their short generation span, several DDT-resistant strains have arisen and spread in the last few years (Fig. 4–3). Accordingly, malaria is again on the rise, with several hundred thousand new cases reported in India, Africa, and Central America.

Two other traits that may also be influenced by the selective agent of malaria are G-6-PD deficiency* and the thalassemias (results of several different mutations that block hemoglobin production). However, in both these cases, evidence of natural selection is not as strong as with the sickle-cell allele. The primary evidence suggesting a link with malaria is the geographical concordance of increased frequency of these traits with areas (especially around the Mediterranean) that historically have had a high incidence of malarial infection.

Another example of human biocultural evolution concerns the ability to digest milk. In all human populations, infants and young children can digest milk, an obvious necessity for any young mammal. A major ingredient of milk is the sugar *lactose*, which is broken down by humans and other mammals by the enzyme *lactase*. In most mammals, including humans, the gene coding for lactase production "switches off" by adolescence. If too much milk is then ingested, it ferments in the large intestine, leading to diarrhea and severe gastrointestinal upset. Among many African and Asian populations—a majority of humankind today—most adults are intolerant of milk (Table 4–1).

Slash-and-burn agriculture
A traditional land-clearing practice whereby trees and vegetation are cut and burned. In many areas, fields were abandoned after a few years and clearing occurred elsewhere.

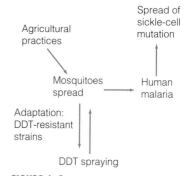

FIGURE 4–3
Evolutionary interactions affecting the frequency of the sickle-cell trait.

TABLE 4–1 Frequencies of Lactose Intolerance

Population Group	Percent
U.S. whites	2–19
Finnish	18
Swiss	12
Swedish	4
U.S. blacks	70–77
Ibos	99
Bantu	90
Fulani	22
Thais	99
Asian Americans	95–100
Native Australians	85

Source: Lerner and Libby, 1976, p. 327.

---

*G-6-PD is an abbreviation for the enzyme glucose-6-phosphate dehydrogenase. Individuals affected with G-6-PD deficiency are homozygous for the recessive allele and do not produce the enzyme.

Lactose intolerance
The inability to digest fresh milk products; caused by the discontinued production of lactase, the enzyme that breaks down lactose (milk sugar).

Recent evidence has suggested a simple dominant mode of inheritance for **lactose intolerance**. The environment also plays a role in expression of the trait—that is, whether a person will be lactose-intolerant—since intestinal bacteria can somewhat buffer the adverse effects. Because these bacteria will increase with previous exposure, some tolerance can be acquired, even in individuals who genetically have become lactase-deficient.

Why do we see variation in lactose tolerance among human populations? Throughout most of hominid evolution, no milk was available after weaning. Perhaps, in such circumstances, continued action of an unnecessary enzyme might inhibit digestion of other foods. Therefore, there *may* be a selective advantage for the gene coding for lactase production to switch off. The question can then be asked, Why can some adults (the majority in some populations) tolerate milk? The distribution of lactose-tolerant populations is very interesting, revealing the probable influence of cultural factors on this trait.

European groups, who are generally lactose-tolerant, are partially descended from groups of the Middle East. Often economically dependent on pastoralism, these groups raised cows and/or goats and no doubt drank considerable quantities of milk. In such a cultural environment, strong selection pressures would act to shift allele frequencies in the direction of more lactose tolerance. Modern European descendants of these populations apparently retain this ancient ability.

Even more informative is the distribution of lactose tolerance in Africa. For example, groups such as the Fulani and Tutsi, who have been pastoralists probably for thousands of years, have much higher rates of lactose tolerance than nonpastoralists.

As we have seen, the geographical distribution of lactose tolerance is related to a history of cultural dependence on milk products. There are, however, some populations that rely on dairying but are not characterized by high rates of lactose tolerance. It has been suggested that such populations traditionally have consumed their milk produce as cheese and other derivatives in which the lactose has been broken down by bacterial action (Durham, 1981).

The interaction of human cultural environments and changes in lactose tolerance among human populations is another example of biocultural evolution. In the last few thousand years, cultural factors have initiated specific evolutionary changes in human groups. Such cultural factors have probably influenced the course of human evolution for at least 3 million years, and today they are of paramount importance.

Human Polymorphisms

Variance of hemoglobin and the production of the enzyme lactase are both *Mendelian* traits. That is, the phenotype of each of these traits can unambiguously be linked to the action of a single locus. These simple genetic mechanisms are much more straightforward than the polygenic traits usually associated with traditional studies of human variation (discussed in Chapter 5). In fact, the difficulty in tracing the genetic influence on such characteristics as skin color or face shape has led some human biologists to avoid investigations of such polygenic traits. Although anthropologists, by tradition, have been keenly interested in explaining such variation, we have seen a trend among physical anthropologists and other biological scientists toward greater concentration on those traits with a clearly demonstrated genetic mechanism (i.e., Mendelian characteristics).

Simple Polymorphisms

Of greatest use in contemporary studies of human variation are those traits that can be used to document genetic differences among various populations. Such genetic traits are what we have defined as polymorphisms, which, as noted, must have more than one allele in appreciable frequency. To explain this pattern of variation beyond mutation, some *additional* evolutionary factor (gene flow, drift, natural selection) must also have been at work.

Clearly, then, the understanding of human genetic polymorphisms demands evolutionary explanations. As students of human evolution, physical anthropologists use these polymorphisms as their principal tool to understand the dynamics of evolution in modern populations. Moreover, by utilizing these simple polymorphisms and comparing allele frequencies in different populations, we can begin to reconstruct the evolutionary events that link human populations with one another.

ABO In addition to some components of hemoglobin, there are many other polymorphisms known in human blood. Because samples can easily be obtained and transported, blood has long been a favorite tissue for studying human polymorphisms. Consequently, we know a great deal regarding genetic traits found in red blood cells, white blood cells, and blood serum. The first of these to be described, and certainly the best known, is the ABO blood group system. As we have seen, ABO is expressed phenotypically in individuals as molecules called antigens on the surface of red blood cells. A person's blood group (i.e., which antigens are on the red blood cells) is directly determined by his or her genotype at the ABO locus. The complications that result from mismatched blood transfusions are the result of antigen-antibody reactions. The body has a finely tuned capacity to recognize foreign antigens and to produce antibodies to deactivate them. Such an immune response is normally beneficial (indeed, indispensable), as it allows the body to fight infections—especially those caused by viruses or bacteria. Usually, antibodies are produced only after foreign antigens have been introduced and recognized. However, in the case of ABO, antibodies are already present in the blood serum at birth, having been stimulated in fetal life. (Some of the relationships within the ABO system are shown in Table 3–2, p. 56.)

The ABO system is interesting from an anthropological perspective because the frequencies of the three alleles (*A*, *B*, *O*) vary tremendously among human populations. In most groups, *A* and *B* are only rarely found in frequencies greater than 50 percent; usually, frequencies for these two alleles are considerably below this figure (Fig. 4–4). Most human groups, however, are polymorphic for all three alleles. Occasionally, as in native South American Indians, frequencies of *O* reach 100 percent, and this allele is said to be "fixed" in this population. Indeed, in most native New World populations, the frequency of *O* is at least 80 percent and is usually considerably higher. Unusually high frequencies of *O* are also found in northern Australia, and some islands off the Australian coast show frequencies exceeding 90 percent. Since these figures are higher than presumably closely related mainland populations, genetic drift (founder effect) is probably the evolutionary factor responsible. That is, in both the New World and Australia, groups with such unusually high frequencies of the *O* allele are probably descendants of fairly small groups of founders who by chance contained individuals mostly of blood type O.

HLA Another important polymorphic system is found on the surface of certain white blood cells. Called HLA, this genetic system influences histocompatibility (i.e., tissue type) and is the reason that organ transplants are usually rejected if not properly matched. Genetically, the HLA system is exceedingly complex, and researchers are still discovering more details about it. There are four major and several associated loci on chromosome 6 that make up the HLA system. Taken together, there are already well over 100 antigens known within the system, with a potential of at least 30 million different genotypes (Williams, 1985; Bodmer, 1995). By far, this is the most polymorphic of any known human genetic system.

Because the system has only fairly recently been discovered, the geographical distribution of many of the alleles is still not well known. Some interesting patterns, however, are apparent. For example, Lapps, Sardinians, and Basques display frequencies for some HLA alleles that differ from the frequencies seen in other European populations, paralleling evidence from ABO. In addition, many areas of

See Virtual Lab 2, section III for a discussion of ABO.

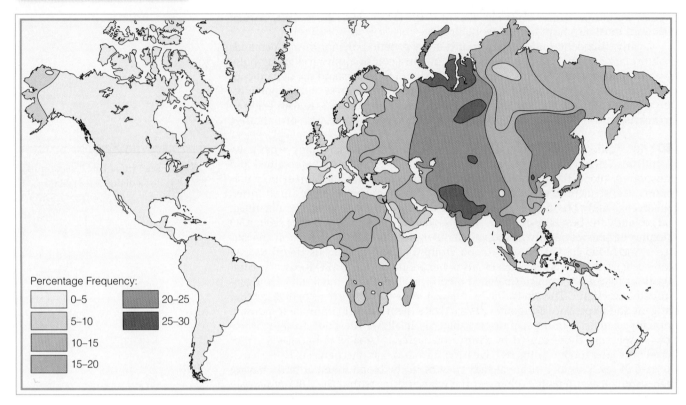

FIGURE 4–4
Distribution of the *B* allele in the indigenous populations of the world. (After Mourant et al., 1976.)

New Guinea and Australia are quite divergent, possibly resulting from past effects of genetic drift. It is imperative, however, that care be taken in postulating genetic relatedness on the basis of very restricted polymorphic data; otherwise, such ridiculous links as some proposed for HLA (e.g., Tibetans with native Australians; Inuit with some New Guineans) would confound our attempts to understand human microevolution (Livingstone, 1980). Because HLA is involved in the superfine detection of foreign antigens, selection relative to infectious disease, especially viruses, may also play a significant role in the distribution (and past evolution) of HLA alleles. The further understanding of these processes promises to be among the most exciting frontiers of medical and evolutionary biology.

Miscellaneous Polymorphisms An interesting genetically controlled variation in human populations was discovered by accident in 1931. When the artificially synthesized chemical phenylthiocarbamide (PTC) was dropped in a laboratory, some researchers were able to smell it, while others could not. It was later established that there is a dichotomy among humans regarding those who can versus those who cannot taste PTC. Although tasters vary considerably in sensitivity, most report a very bitter, unpleasant sensation. The pattern of inheritance follows a Mendelian model, with the inability to taste behaving as a simple recessive. In most populations, a majority of individuals are tasters, but the frequency of nontasters varies dramatically—from as low as 5 percent in Africa to as high as 40 percent in India.

The evolutionary function of this polymorphism is not known, although the fact that it is also seen in some other primates argues that it has a long history. Obviously, evolution has not acted to produce discrimination for an artificial substance recently concocted by humans. The observed variation *may* reflect selection for taste discrimination of other, more significant substances. Indeed, taste discrimination, which may allow the avoidance of many toxic plants (which frequently are bitter), may well be an important evolutionary consideration.

Another puzzling human polymorphism is the variability seen in earwax, or cerumen. Earwax is found in human groups in two basic varieties: (1) yellow and sticky with a good deal of lipids (fats and fatlike substances), and (2) gray and dry with fewer lipids. Cerumen variation appears also to be inherited as a simple Mendelian trait with two alleles (sticky is dominant; dry is recessive). Interestingly, frequencies of the two varieties of earwax vary considerably among human populations. In European populations, about 90 percent of individuals typically have the sticky variety, while in northern China, only about 4 percent are of this type.

How do we explain these differences? Even between very large groups there are consistent differences in cerumen type, arguing that drift is an unlikely causal mechanism. However, it is difficult to imagine what kind of selective pressure would act directly on earwax. Perhaps, as previously suggested for PTC discrimination, earwax variation is an incidental expression of a gene controlling something more adaptively significant. Suggestions along these lines have pointed to the relation of cerumen to other body secretions, especially those affecting odor. Certainly, other mammals, including nonhuman primates, pay considerable attention to smell stimuli. Although the sense of smell is not as well developed in humans as in other mammals, humans still process and utilize olfactory (smell) stimuli. Thus, it is not impossible that during the course of human evolution, genes affecting bodily secretions (including earwax) came under selective influence.

Polymorphisms at the DNA Level

Geneticists and physical anthropologists over the last 50 years have used somewhat indirect techniques to study human polymorphisms, observing some *phenotypic* product. For example, the ABO antigens are phenotypic products (quite immediate ones) of the DNA locus coding for them. In the last decade, with the revolution in DNA technology, much more *direct* means have become available by which to study human genetic variation.

mtDNA   In addition to the DNA found in the nucleus (nuclear DNA), human (and other eukaryotic) cells contain another kind of DNA. This DNA, found in the cytoplasm, is contained within the organelles called mitochondria and is thus called mitochondrial DNA (mtDNA). While the nuclear DNA is extraordinarily long, containing an estimated 3 billion nucleotides, the mtDNA is much shorter, containing only 16,569 nucleotides. Using special enzymes (restriction enzymes, derived from bacteria) that cut the DNA in specific locations, researchers have been able to sequence the entire mtDNA genome. Thus, it has become possible to compare variation among individuals and among populations. Ongoing work is establishing that some mtDNA regions are more variable than others but that for the *total* mtDNA genome, variation within *Homo sapiens* is apparently much less pronounced than in other species (e.g., chimpanzees). The possible evolutionary reasons for this surprising finding might relate to a quite recent origin of all modern *Homo sapiens* from a restricted ancestral population base (thus producing, as noted earlier, genetic drift/founder effect). We will return to this topic in our discussion of the evolutionary origin of modern humans in Chapter 13.

Nuclear DNA   As with mtDNA analysis, the use of restriction enzymes has permitted much greater precision in direct study of the DNA contained within human chromosomes—that is, nuclear DNA. This work has been greatly facilitated as part of the continuing intense research of the **Human Genome Project**. Untangling the entire human genetic complement is obviously an enormous undertaking, but to date, considerable insight has been gained regarding human variation *directly at the DNA level*. By cutting the DNA of different individuals and comparing the results, researchers have observed great variation in the length of the DNA fragments at numerous DNA sites. Accordingly, these genetic differences (caused by variable

Human Genome Project
A multinational effort designed to map (and ultimately sequence) the complete genetic complement of *Homo sapiens*.

Restriction fragment length polymorphisms (RFLPs)
Variation among individuals in the length of DNA fragments produced by enzymes that break the DNA at specific sites.

Cline
A gradient of genotypes (usually measured as allele frequencies) over geographical space; more exactly, the depiction of allele distribution produced by connecting points of equal frequency (as on a temperature map).

DNA sequences) are referred to as **restriction fragment length polymorphisms (RFLPs)**. In addition to providing direct evidence of human genetic variation, the RFLPs are also of vital importance in mapping other loci (e.g., that for cystic fibrosis) to specific regions of specific chromosomes.

Patterns of Human Population Diversity

A fairly simple approach to help understand human genetic diversity is to look at the pattern of allele frequencies over space for *one* polymorphic trait at a time. Here, allele frequencies are shown geographically on a map in what is called a **cline**. Although we did not label it as such in our previous discussion, the distribution of the *B* allele in Eurasia (see Fig. 4–4) is a good example of a cline.

Utilizing single traits can be informative regarding potential influences of natural selection or gene flow, but this approach has limitations when we try to sort out population relationships. As noted in our discussion of the HLA polymorphisms, single traits *by themselves* often can yield confusing interpretations regarding likely population relationships. What is needed, then, is a method to analyze a larger, more consistent body of data—that is, to look at several traits simultaneously. Such a *multivariate* approach makes ready use of digital computers. (In the next chapter, we will discuss the more traditional approach using polygenic characteristics and some of the controversies surrounding "racial" classification.)

An excellent example of the contemporary multivariate approach to human diversity was undertaken by Harvard population geneticist R. D. Lewontin (1972), and his results are most informative. Lewontin calculated population differences in allele frequency for 17 polymorphic traits. In his analysis, Lewontin immediately faced a dilemma: Which groups (populations) should he contrast and how should they be weighted? That is, should larger population segments, such as Arabs, carry the same weight in the analysis as small populations, such as the one from the island Tristan da Cunha? After considerable deliberation, Lewontin decided to break down his sample into seven geographical areas, and he included several equally weighted population samples within each (Table 4–2). He then calculated how much of the total genetic variability within our species could be accounted for by these population subdivisions.

The results are surprising. Only 6.3 percent of the total genetic variation is explained by differences among major "races" (Lewontin's seven geographical units). In other words, close to 94 percent of human genetic diversity occurs *within* these very large groups. The larger population subdivisions within the geographical clusters (e.g., within Caucasians: Arabs, Basques, Welsh) account for another 8.3 percent. Thus, geographical and local "races" together account for just 15 percent of all human genetic variation, leaving the remaining 85 percent unaccounted for.

TABLE 4–2 Population Groupings Used by Lewontin in Population Genetics Study (1972)

Geographical Group	Examples of Populations Included
Caucasians	Arabs, Armenians, Tristan da Cunhans
Black Africans	Bantu, San, U.S. blacks
Asians	Ainu, Chinese, Turks
South Asians	Andamanese, Tamils
Amerinds	Aleuts, Navaho, Yanomama
Oceanians	Easter Islanders, "Micronesians"
Australians	All treated as a single group

The vast majority of genetic differences among human beings is explicable in terms of differences from one village to another, one family to another, and, to a very significant degree, one person to another—even within the same family. Of course, when you recall the high degree of genetic polymorphism (discussed in this chapter) combined with the vast number of combinations resulting from recombination during meiosis (discussed in Chapter 3), all this individual variation should not be that surprising.

Our visual perceptions superficially suggest to us that race does exist. But the visible phenotypic traits most frequently used to make racial distinctions (skin color, hair form, nose shape, etc.) may very well produce a highly biased sample, not giving an accurate picture of the actual pattern of *genetic variation*. The simple polymorphic traits discussed in this chapter (many of the same used by Lewontin) are a more objective basis for accurate biological comparisons of human groups, and they indicate that the traditional concept of race is very limited. Indeed, Lewontin concludes his analysis with a ringing condemnation of traditional studies: "Human racial classification is of no social value and is positively destructive of social and human relations. Since such racial classification is now seen to be of virtually no genetic or taxonomic significance either, no justification can be offered for its continuance" (Lewontin, 1972, p. 397).

If one feels compelled to continue to classify humankind into large geographical segments, population genetics offers some aid in isolating consistent patterns of genetic variation. Following and expanding on the approach used by Lewontin, population geneticist L. L. Cavalli-Sforza, of Stanford University, and colleagues evaluated 44 different polymorphic traits ascertained in 42 different human sample populations. From the results, these researchers constructed a "tree" (technically called a dendrogram) depicting the relationships of these samples as part of larger populations (Cavalli-Sforza et al., 1988) (Fig. 4–5). Analysis of mitochondrial DNA has produced similar results, especially showing greater genetic diversity among African populations than among other groups (Stoneking, 1993). Because mtDNA is passed solely through the maternal line (and thus does not undergo recombination), it has certain advantages in reconstructing population relationships. Nevertheless, as a single genetic component, it acts like one large locus; thus, mtDNA results must be supplemented by other genetic data.

Comparative data from nuclear DNA studies (RFLPs) in conjunction with the studies discussed here are thus potentially illuminating. Initial analysis comparing 80 RFLPs in eight different groups (Mountain et al., 1993) again produced patterns quite similar to those established for the traditional polymorphisms and for mtDNA. However, another recent large-scale study (Jia and Chakraborty, 1993) of DNA markers among 59 different groups (and including about 12,000 individuals) found the vast majority of variation (up to 98.5 percent) occurring *within* populations at the *individual* level. These latest data dramatize even further the results obtained by Lewontin, leading one geneticist to conclude, "These results indicate that individual variation in DNA profiles overwhelm any interpopulational differences, no matter how the populations are ethnically or racially classified" (Cummings, 1994, p. 500). And while not quite as overwhelming, *all* the genetically based studies cited here support Lewontin's initial results, strongly indicating that the great majority of human variation does occur within human populations—not between them. How, then, do these genetic data compare and articulate with the traditional concept of race? We turn to this topic in the next chapter.

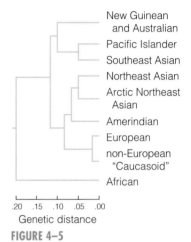

New Guinean
and Australian
Pacific Islander
Southeast Asian
Northeast Asian
Arctic Northeast
Asian
Amerindian
European
non-European
"Caucasoid"
African

.20　.15　.10　.05　.00
Genetic distance

FIGURE 4–5

Genetic tree (dendrogram) showing population relationships. This dendrogram was constructed by population geneticists (Cavalli-Sforza et al., 1988) using 44 polymorphic traits.

SUMMARY

In this chapter, we have discussed human variation from an evolutionary perspective. Modern evolutionary theory views evolutionary change as a two-stage process in what has come to be known as the Modern Synthesis. In this theory, the factors of mutation, gene flow, and genetic drift, acting in concert with natural selection, come together to produce evolutionary change.

We have focused on the contemporary trend to describe simple genetic polymorphisms that can be measured for allele frequencies as well as emphasizing genetic data obtained directly from analysis of mitochondrial and nuclear DNA. Data on such polymorphic traits can then be used to understand aspects of human microevolution. For humans, of course, culture also plays a crucial evolutionary role, and the sickle-cell trait and lactose intolerance are thus discussed from an explicitly biocultural perspective.

QUESTIONS FOR REVIEW

1. How is a population defined? Discuss why, in human groups, defining particular populations can be very difficult.
2. What are the two stages of the evolutionary process as postulated by the Modern Synthesis?
3. What role does variation play in natural selection?
4. Give a concise *genetic* definition of evolution. Discuss an example in human populations.
5. What is meant by gene flow? Discuss an example derived from human population studies.
6. How has the sickle-cell allele come to be common in some parts of the world? Why is it thought to be a good example of natural selection?
7. What biocultural interactions have occurred that help explain the distribution of lactose intolerance?
8. Discuss how genetic drift may have influenced the geographical distribution of the *A*, *B*, and *O* alleles.

SUGGESTED FURTHER READING

Cavalli-Sforza, L. L., P. Menozzi, and A. Piazza. 1994. *The History and Geography of Human Genes*. Princeton: Princeton University Press.

Cummings, Michael. 2000. *Human Heredity: Principles and Issues*. 5th ed. Belmont, CA: Brooks/Cole.

Durham, W. 1991. *Coevolution: Genes, Culture and Human Diversity*. Stanford: Stanford University Press.

Lewontin, R. 1974. *The Genetic Basis of Evolutionary Change*. New York: Columbia University Press.

RESOURCES ON THE INTERNET

 Wadsworth Anthropology Resource Center
http://anthropology.wadsworth.com

The companion website for this text includes a range of enrichment material focused on the chapter's topic. While online you can enhance your understanding of the chapter by exploring one of the several additional Internet Exercises, by researching topics, and by accessing full articles on InfoTrac College Edition. You can also reinforce the concepts by taking online practice exams.

Internet Exercises

Visit Online Mendelian Inheritance in Man (OMIM—**http://www3.ncbi.nlm.nih .gov/Omim/**) and search for one of the Mendelian traits discussed in Chapter 4, such as sickle-cell anemia, thalassemia, G-6-PD, or lactase deficiency (lactose intolerance). Read part of the discussion and note how complicated the genetic effects of the relevant alleles are. Make a list of facts you learned from this site.

InfoTrac College Edition
http://www.infotrac-college.com/wadsworth

On InfoTrac College Edition, search for *human population genetics*. What does this search find? Choose one article and report on the gene(s) studied and the distribution of that gene in the population investigated. Is an explanation offered for the distribution seen?

CONTENTS

Human Variation and Adaptation

Introduction

In Chapter 3, we saw how physical characteristics are influenced by the DNA in our cells. Furthermore, we discussed how individuals inherit genes from parents and how variations in genes (alleles) can produce different expressions of phenotypic traits. In Chapter 4, we emphasized the study of Mendelian traits in our discussion of evolutionary factors in human populations.

In this chapter, our focus shifts to polygenic traits—traits that express continuous variation. In particular, we examine how these traits have been used as a basis for traditional racial classification, and we look at some of the issues that currently surround the topic of race in physical anthropology.

Following the discussion of historical attempts at racial classification, we look at more recent explanations of certain polygenic traits; but instead of emphasizing their utility as "racial markers," we focus on their adaptive value in specific environmental contexts and various genetic factors that influence their expression. We also examine how populations and individuals differ in their adaptive responses to such environmental factors as heat, cold, and high altitude. Finally, we consider the role of infectious disease in human evolution and adaptation.

See the following sections of the CD-ROM for topics covered in this chapter: Virtual Lab 2, section III, and Virtual Lab 2, section IV.

Historical Views of Human Variation

The first step toward understanding natural phenomena is the ordering of variation into categories that can then be named, discussed, and perhaps studied. Historically, when different groups of people came into contact with one another, they offered explanations for the phenotypic variations they saw. Because skin color was so noticeable, it was one of the more frequently discussed traits, and most systems of racial classification were based on it.

As early as 1350 B.C., the ancient Egyptians had classified humans on the basis of skin color: red for Egyptian, yellow for people to the east, white for those to the north, and black for Africans from the south (Gossett, 1963, p. 4). In the sixteenth century, after the discovery of the New World, Europe embarked on a period of intense exploration and colonization in both the New and Old Worlds. Resulting from this contact was an increased awareness of human diversity.

As you learned in Chapter 2, the discovery of the New World was of major importance in altering the views of Europeans who had perceived the world as static and nonchanging. One of the most influential discoveries of the early European explorers was that the Americas were inhabited by people, some of whom were dark-skinned (compared to most Europeans). Furthermore, these people were not Christian and, because of this and numerous other cultural differences, were not considered "civilized" by Europeans. At first, Native Americans were thought to be Asian, and since Columbus believed that he had discovered a new route to India, he called them "Indians." This term was later applied to indigenous, dark-skinned populations of Australia as well.

By the late eighteenth century, Europeans and European Americans were asking questions that challenged traditional Christian beliefs. They wanted to know if other populations belonged to the same species as themselves; that is, were Native Americans and other indigenous peoples indeed human? Were they descendants of Adam and Eve, or had there been separate creations of non-Europeans? If the latter were true, then Native Americans had to represent different species, or else the Genesis account of creation could not be taken literally.

Two schools of thought, known as **monogenism** and **polygenism**, devised responses. In the monogenist view, all humans were descended from a single, original pair (Adam and Eve). Insisting on the **plasticity** of human structure, monogenists contended that local environmental conditions, such as climate and terrain, could modify the original form, resulting in observable phenotypic differences between populations. Monogenist views were initially attractive to many because they did not conflict with the Genesis version of creation.

Monogenism
The theory that all human races are descended from one pair (Adam and Eve), but they differ from one another because they have occupied different habitats. This concept was an attempt to explain phenotypic variation between populations, but did not imply evolutionary change.

Polygenism
A theory, opposed to monogenism, that states that human races are not all descended from Adam and Eve. Instead, there had been several original human pairs, each giving rise to a different group. Thus, human races were considered separate species.

Plasticity
The capacity to change; in a physiological context, the ability of systems or organisms to make alterations in order to respond to differing conditions.

The polygenist view, on the other hand, argued that all populations did not descend from a single, original pair, but from a number of pairs. Also, polygenists saw such a wide gap in the physical, mental, and moral attributes between themselves and other peoples that they were sure that outsiders belonged to different species. Furthermore, polygenists did not accept the monogenist notion of plasticity of physical traits, and they rejected the proposition that climate and environment were modifying influences.

Throughout the eighteenth and nineteenth centuries, European and American scientists concentrated primarily on describing and classifying the biological variation in humans as well as in nonhuman species. The first scientific attempt to describe the newly discovered variation between human populations was Linnaeus' taxonomic classification, which placed humans into four separate categories (Linnaeus, 1758) (Table 5–1). Linnaeus assigned behavioral and intellectual qualities to each group, with the least complimentary descriptions going to African blacks. This ranking was typical of the period and reflected the almost universal European view that Europeans were superior to all other peoples.

Johann Friedrich Blumenbach (1752–1840), a German anatomist, classified humans into five races (see Table 5–1). Although Blumenbach's categories came to be described simply as white, yellow, red, black, and brown, he also used criteria other than skin color. Moreover, Blumenbach emphasized that racial categories based on skin color were arbitrary and that many traits, including skin color, were not discrete phenomena. Blumenbach pointed out that to attempt to classify all humans using such a system would be to omit completely all those who did not neatly fall into a specific category. Furthermore, it was recognized by Blumenbach

TABLE 5–1 Racial Classification Schemes

Linnaeus, 1758	Stanley M. Garn, 1965
Homo europaeus (SAPIENS) *Homo afer* (Africans) *Homo asiaticus* *Homo americanus* (Native Americans)	**GEOGRAPHICAL RACES:** "a collection of race populations, separated from other such collections by major geographical barriers." Amerindian Melanesian-Papuan Indian Polynesian Australian European Micronesian Asiatic African
Blumenbach, 1781 Caucasoid Ethiopian Mongoloid American Malay	**LOCAL RACE:** "a breeding population adapted to local selection pressures and maintained by either natural or social barriers to gene interchange." These are some examples of local races; there are many others: Northwest European East African North Chinese Northeast European Bantu Extreme Mongoloid Alpine Tibetan Hindu Mediterranean

E. A. Hooton, 1926
 	
PRIMARY RACE
 	
White
  Mediterranean
  Ainu
  Keltic
  Nordic
  Alpine
  East Baltic
 	
Negroid
  African Negro
  Nilotic Negro
  Negrito
	Mongoloid
	  Classic Mongoloid
	  Arctic Mongoloid
	  Malay-Mongoloid
	  Indonesian

	MICRORACES: Not well defined but apparently refers to neighborhoods within a city or a city itself, since "marriage or mating is a mathematical function of distance. With millions of potential mates, the male ordinarily chooses one near at hand."

and others that traits such as skin color showed overlapping expression between populations. At the time, it was thought that racial taxonomies should be based on characteristics unique to particular groups and uniformly expressed within them. Some scientists, taking the polygenist view, began attempting to identify certain physical traits that were thought to be stable or that did not appear to be influenced by external environmental factors. Therefore, these so-called *nonadaptive* traits should exhibit only minimal within-group variation and could thus be used to typify entire populations. Shape of the skull was incorrectly believed to be one such characteristic, and the fallacy of this assumption was not demonstrated until the early twentieth century (Boas, 1912).

In 1842, Anders Retzius, a Swedish anatomist, developed the *cephalic index* as a method of describing the shape of the head. The cephalic index, derived by dividing maximum head breadth by maximum length and multiplying by 100, gives the ratio of head breadth to length. (It is important to note that the cephalic index does not measure head size.) Compared to the statistical methods in use today, the cephalic index seems rather simplistic; but in the nineteenth century it was seen as an important scientific tool, and because people could be neatly categorized by a single number, it provided an efficient method for describing variation. Individuals with an index of less than 75 had long, narrow heads and were termed **dolichocephalic**. **Brachycephalic** individuals, with broad heads, had an index of over 80; and those whose indices were between 75 and 80 were *mesocephalic*.

Studies showed that northern Europeans tended to be dolichocephalic, while southern Europeans were brachycephalic, and these findings led to heated and nationalistic debate over whether one group was superior to another. But when it was shown that northern Europeans shared their tendency to long, narrow heads with several African populations, the cephalic index ceased to be considered a reliable indicator of race.

By the mid-nineteenth century, monogenists were beginning to reject their somewhat egalitarian concept of race in favor of a more hierarchical view. Populations were ranked essentially on a scale based on skin color (along with size and shape of the head), with Africans placed at the bottom. Moreover, Europeans themselves were ranked so that northern, light-skinned populations were considered superior to their southern, more olive-skinned neighbors.

The fact that non-Europeans were viewed as "uncivilized" implied an inferiority of character and intellect. This view was based in a concept now termed **biological determinism**, which in part holds that there is an association between physical characteristics and such attributes as intelligence, morals, values, abilities, and even social and economic differences between groups. In other words, cultural variations are *inherited* in the same manner as biological variations. It follows, then, that there are inherent behavioral and cognitive differences between groups, and therefore, some groups are *by nature* superior to others. Following this logic, it is a simple matter to justify the persecution and even enslavement of other peoples simply because their appearance and cultural practices differ from what is familiar.

After 1850, biological determinism was a constant theme underlying common thinking as well as scientific research in Europe and the United States. Deterministic (and what we today would call racist) views were held to some extent by most people, including such notable figures as Thomas Jefferson, Georges Cuvier, Benjamin Franklin, Charles Lyell, Abraham Lincoln, Charles Darwin, and Oliver Wendell Holmes. Commenting on this usually deemphasized characteristic of notable historical figures, Stephen J. Gould (1981, p. 32), of Harvard University, emphasizes that "all American culture heroes embraced racial attitudes that would embarrass public-school mythmakers."

Francis Galton (1822–1911), a cousin of Charles Darwin, shared the increasingly common fear among Europeans that "civilized society" was being weakened by the failure of natural selection to completely eliminate unfit and inferior members (Greene, 1981, p. 107). Galton wrote and lectured on the necessity of "race improvement" and suggested governmental regulation of marriage and family size, an approach he called **eugenics**.

Dolichocephalic
Having a long, narrow head in which the width measures less than 75 percent of the length.

Brachycephalic
Having a broad head in which the width measures more than 80 percent of the length.

Biological determinism
The concept that various attributes and behaviors (e.g., intelligence, values, morals) are governed by biological (genetic) factors; the inaccurate association of various behavioral attributes with certain biological traits, such as skin color.

Eugenics
The philosophy of "race improvement" through the forced sterilization of members of some groups and encouraged reproduction among others; an overly simplified, often racist view that is now discredited.

Galton's writings attracted a considerable following in both Europe and the United States, and a number of eugenics societies were formed. The eugenics movement had a great deal of snob appeal, for fitness was deemed to be embodied in the upper classes, while the lower classes were associated with criminality, illness, and mental impairment. Moreover, many eugenics groups sought to rid society of crime and poverty through mandatory sterilization programs of the poorer classes.

Although eugenics had its share of critics, its popularity flourished throughout the 1930s, but nowhere was it more attractive than in Germany, where the viewpoint took a disastrous turn. The false idea of pure races was increasingly extolled as a means of reestablishing a strong and prosperous state. Eugenics was seen as scientific justification for purging Germany of its "unfit," and many of Germany's scientists continued to support the views of racial purity and eugenics during the Nazi period (Proctor, 1988, p. 143), when these policies served as justification for condemning millions of people to death.

But at the same time, many were turning away from racial typologies and classification in favor of a more evolutionary approach. No doubt for some, this shift in direction was motivated by their growing concerns over the goals of the eugenics movement. Probably more important, however, was the synthesis of Mendelian genetics and Darwin's theories of natural selection during the 1930s. This breakthrough influenced all the biological sciences, and some physical anthropologists began to apply evolutionary principles to the study of human variation.

The Concept of Race

Polytypic
Referring to species composed of populations that differ with regard to the expression of one or more traits.

All contemporary humans are members of the same **polytypic** species, *Homo sapiens*. A polytypic species is one composed of local populations that differ from one another with regard to the expression of one or more traits. Moreover, *within* local populations there is a great deal of phenotypic and genotypic variation between individuals. Many species are polytypic.

In discussions of human variation, people have traditionally clumped together various attributes such as skin color, shape of the face, shape of the nose, hair color, hair form (curly, straight), and eye color. People possessing particular *combinations* of these and other traits have been placed together into categories associated with specific geographical localities. Such categories are called *races*.

We all think we know what we mean by the word *race*, but in reality, the term has had a number of meanings since it gained common usage in English in the 1500s. It has been used synonymously with *species*, as in "the human race," or to refer to a more limited grouping of individuals all descended from a single individual (e.g., "the race of Abraham").

Since the 1600s, race has also referred to various culturally defined groups, and this meaning still enjoys popular usage. For example, one hears "the English race" or "the Japanese race," where the reference is actually to nationality. Another often-heard phrase is "the Jewish race," when the speaker is really talking about a particular ethnic and religious identity.

Thus, while *race* is commonly used as a biological term, or at least one with biological connotations, it is also one with enormous social significance. This is partly because there is still a widespread and unfortunate perception that there is an association between certain physical traits (skin color, in particular) and numerous cultural attributes (such as language, occupational preferences, or even morality). Therefore, in many cultural contexts, a person's social identity is strongly influenced by the manner in which he or she expresses those physical traits traditionally used to define "racial groups." Characteristics such as skin color are highly visible, and they facilitate an immediate and superficial designation of individuals into socially defined categories. However, so-called racial traits are not the only phenotypic expressions that contribute to social identity. Sex and age are also critically important. But aside from these two variables, an individual's racial and/or *ethnic*

background is still inevitably a factor that influences how he or she is initially perceived and judged by others, especially in diverse societies.

References to national origin (e.g., African, Asian) as substitutes for racial labels have become more common in recent years, both within and outside anthropology. Within anthropology, the term *ethnicity* was proposed in the early 1950s as a means of avoiding the more emotionally charged term *race*. Strictly speaking, ethnicity refers to cultural factors, and for this reason, some have objected to its use in discussions that also include biological characteristics. However, the fact that the words *ethnicity* and *race* are used interchangeably reflects the social importance of phenotypic expression and demonstrates once again how phenotype is associated with culturally defined variables.

In its most common biological usage, the term "race" refers to geographically patterned phenotypic variation within a species. By the seventeenth century, naturalists began to describe races in plants and nonhuman animals, because they recognized that when populations of a species occupied different regions, they sometimes differed from one another in the expression of one or more traits. But even today, there are no established criteria by which races of plants and animals are to be assessed. To a biologist studying nonhuman forms, the degree of genetic difference necessary for racial distinctions is somewhat arbitrary and can be only partially determined. Moreover, if we are to apply the term to humans, we must precisely elucidate the degree of genetic difference that exists between individuals *within* populations as well as *between* populations, and this has not really been done.

Prior to World War II, most studies of human variation focused on observable phenotypic variation between large, geographically defined populations, and these studies were largely descriptive. Since that time, the emphasis has shifted to the examination of differences in allele frequencies within and between populations as well as the adaptive significance of phenotypic and genotypic variation. This shift in focus occurred partly as the outcome of historical trends in biological science in general and physical anthropology in particular. Especially crucial to this shift was the emergence of the Modern Synthesis in biology (see p. 70), which was based on the recognition of the fundamental importance of the *interaction* of natural selection and other factors, such as gene flow, mutation, and drift, to the process of evolution.

Application of evolutionary principles to the study of modern human variation replaced the superficial nineteenth-century view of race *based solely on observed phenotype*. Additionally, the genetic emphasis dispelled previously held misconceptions that races were fixed biological units that did not change over time and that were composed of individuals who all conformed to a particular *type*.

Clearly, there are phenotypic differences between humans, and some of these differences roughly correspond to particular geographical locations. It is unlikely that anyone would mistake a person of Asian descent for one of northern European ancestry. But certain questions must be asked. Is there any adaptive significance attached to observed phenotypic variation? What is the degree of underlying genetic variation that influences it? What is the role of such factors as genetic drift? These questions place considerations of human variation within a contemporary evolutionary framework.

Although, in part, physical anthropology has its roots in attempts to explain human diversity, anthropologists have never been in complete agreement on the topic of race. Even attempts to reach a consensus in defining the term have frequently failed. Among physical anthropologists there is still sometimes heated debate over whether it is justifiable to apply racial concepts to humans at all.

Today, some anthropologists recognize population patterning corresponding to at least three major racial groups, each composed of several subgroupings. However, no contemporary scholar subscribes to pre-Darwinian and pre–Modern Synthesis concepts of races (human and nonhuman) as fixed biological entities, the members of which all conform to specific types. And many who continue to use broad racial categories do not view them as particularly important, especially from a genetic perspective, because the amount of genetic variation accounted for by differences

BOX 5–1   DIGGING DEEPER

Racial Purity: A False and Dangerous Ideology

During the late nineteenth and early twentieth centuries, a growing sense of nationalism was sweeping Europe and the United States. At the same time, an increased emphasis on "racial purity" had been coupled with the more dangerous aspects of biological determinism. The concept of pure races is based, in part, on the notion that in the past, races were composed of individuals who conformed to idealized types and who were similar in appearance and intellect. Over time, some variation had been introduced into these pure races through interbreeding with other groups, and increasingly, this type of "contamination" was seen as a threat to be avoided.

In today's terminology, pure races would be said to be genetically homogenous, or to possess little genetic variation. Everyone would have the same alleles at most of their loci. Actually, we do see this situation in "pure breeds" of domesticated animals and plants, developed *deliberately* by humans through selective breeding. We also see many of the detrimental consequences of such genetic uniformity in various congenital abnormalities, such as hip dysplasia in some breeds of dogs.

With our current understanding of genetic principles, we are able to appreciate the potentially negative outcomes of matings between genetically similar individuals. For example, we know that inbreeding increases the likelihood of offspring who are homozygous for certain deleterious recessive alleles. We also know that decreased genetic variation in a species diminishes the potential for natural selection to act,

thus compromising that species' ability to adapt to certain environmental fluctuations. Furthermore, in highly genetically uniform populations, individual fertility can be seriously reduced, potentially with disastrous consequences for the entire species. Thus, even if pure human races did exist at one time (and they did not), theirs would not have been a desirable condition genetically, and they most certainly would have been at an evolutionary disadvantage.

During the latter half of the nineteenth century, many Americans and Europeans had come to believe that nations could be ranked according to technological achievement. In their view, the United States and Europe attained a "higher level of civilization" owing to the "biological superiority" of their northern European forebears. This concept arose in part from the writings of Herbert Spencer, a British philosopher who misapplied the principles of natural selection to societies in a doctrine termed "social Darwinism." Spencer believed that societies evolved, and through competition, "less endowed" cultures and the "unfit" people in them would be weeded out. Indeed, it was Spencer who coined the much misused (and almost always abused) phrase, "survival of the fittest," and his philosophy became widely accepted on both sides of the Atlantic, where its principles accorded well with notions of racial purity.

In northern Europe, particularly Germany, and in the United States, "racial superiority" was increasingly embodied in the so-called "aryan race." *Aryan* is a term that is still widely used, albeit erroneously, with biological connotations. Actually, "aryan" does not refer to a

between groups is vastly exceeded by the variation that exists *within* groups (see p. 82). In fact, as a species, humans are remarkably genetically uniform, and some studies now suggest that we exhibit less genetic variation than do chimpanzees. But given these considerations, there are those who see variation in outwardly expressed phenotype, because of its potential adaptive value or because it may represent genetic drift in some groups, as worthy of investigation and explanation within the framework of evolutionary principles (Brues, 1991).

Forensic anthropologists in particular find the phenotypic criteria associated with race to have practical applications because they are frequently called on by law enforcement agencies to assist in the identification of human skeletal remains. Inasmuch as unidentified human remains are often those of crime victims, and forensic analysis may lead to courtroom testimony, identification must be as accurate as possible. The most important variables in such identification are the indi-

biological unit or Mendelian population, as the majority of people who use the term intend it. Rather, it is a linguistic term that refers to an ancient language group that was ancestral to the Indo-European family of languages.

By the early twentieth century, the "aryans" had been transformed into a mythical super race of people whose noble traits were embodied in an extremely idealized "nordic type." The true "aryan" was held to be tall, blond, blue-eyed, strong, industrious, and "pure in spirit." "Nordics" were extolled as the developers of all ancient "high" civilizations and as the founders of modern industrialized nations. In Europe, there was growing emphasis on the superiority of northwestern Europeans as the modern representatives of "true nordic stock," while southern and eastern Europeans were viewed as inferior.

In the United States, there prevailed the strongly held opinion that America was originally settled by Christian "nordics." Prior to about 1890, the majority of newcomers to the United States had come from Germany, Scandinavia, and Britain (including Ireland). But by the 1890s, the pattern of immigration had changed. The arrival of increasing numbers of Italians, Turks, Greeks, and Jews among the thousands of newcomers raised fears that society was being contaminated by immigration from southern and eastern Europe.

Moreover, in the United States, there were additional concerns about the large population of former black slaves and their descendants. As African Americans left the South in increasing numbers to work in the factories of the North, many unskilled white workers felt economically threatened by new competition. It was no coincidence that the Ku Klux Klan, which had been inactive for a number of years, was revived in 1915 and by the 1920s was preaching vehement opposition to African Americans, Jews, and Catholics in support of the supremacy of the white Protestant "nordic race."

To avoid the further "decline of the superior race," many states practiced policies of racial segregation until the mid-1950s. Particularly in the South, segregation laws resulted in an almost total separation of whites and African Americans, except where African Americans were employed as servants or laborers. Moreover, *antimiscegenation* laws prohibited marriage between whites and blacks in over half the states, and unions between whites and Asians were frequently illegal as well. Astonishingly, some of these laws were not repealed until the late 1950s or early 1960s. Likewise, in Germany by 1935, the newly instituted Nuremberg Laws forbade marriage or sexual intercourse between so-called "aryan" Germans and Jews.

The fact that belief in racial purity and superiority led ultimately to the Nazi death camps in World War II is undisputed (except for continuing efforts by certain white supremacist and neo-Nazi organizations). It is one of the great tragedies of the twentieth century that some of history's most glaring examples of discrimination and viciousness were perpetrated by people who believed that their actions were based in scientific principles. In reality, such beliefs constitute nothing more than myth. Indeed, the notion of racial purity flies in the face of everything we know about natural selection, recombination, and gene flow. The degree of genetic uniformity throughout our species (compared to some other species), as evidenced by mounting data from mitochondrial and nuclear DNA analysis, argues strongly that there has always been gene flow between human populations and that genetically homogenous races are nothing more than fabrication.

vidual's sex, age, stature, and ancestry. Using metric and nonmetric criteria, forensic anthropologists employ a number of techniques for establishing broad population affinity, and they are generally able to do so with about 80 percent accuracy.

On the other side of the issue, there are numerous physical anthropologists who argue that race is a meaningless concept when applied to humans. Race is an outdated creation of the human mind that attempts to simplify biological complexity by organizing it into categories. Thus, human races are a product of the human tendency to superimpose order on complex natural phenomena. While classification may have been an acceptable approach some 150 years ago, it is viewed as no longer valid given the current state of genetic and evolutionary science.

Objections to racial taxonomies have also been raised because classification schemes are *typological* in nature, meaning that categories are discrete and based on stereotypes or ideals that comprise a specific set of traits. Thus, in general, typologies are inherently misleading, because there are always many individuals in any grouping who do not conform to all aspects of a particular type.

In any "racial" group, there will be individuals who fall into the normal range of variation for another group with regard to one or several characteristics. For example, two people of different ancestry might vary with regard to skin color, but they could share any number of other traits, such as height, shape of head, hair color, eye color, or ABO blood type. In fact, they could easily share more similarities with each other than they do with many members of their own populations. (Remember, at most, only about 6 percent of genetic difference among humans has been shown to be due to differences between large geographical groups.)

Moreover, as we have stressed, because the characteristics that have traditionally been used to define races are polygenic, they exhibit a continuous range of expression. It thus becomes difficult, if not impossible, to draw discrete boundaries between races with regard to many traits. This limitation becomes clear if you ask yourself, "At what point is hair color no longer dark brown but medium brown, or no longer light brown but blond?"

The scientific controversy over race is not likely to disappear. It has received considerable attention outside academia in popular publications such as *Newsweek* and *Discover*. But in spite of all the scientific discussion that has ensued, among the general public, variations on the theme of race will undoubtedly continue to be the most common view toward human biological and cultural variation. Given this fact, it falls to anthropologists and biologists to continue to explore the issue so that, to the best of our abilities, accurate information regarding human variation is available for anyone who seeks informed explanations of complex phenomena.

Intelligence

As we have shown, belief in the relationship between race and specific behavioral attributes is popular even today, but evidence is lacking that personality or any other behavioral trait differs genetically *between* human groups. Most scientists would agree with this last statement, but one question that has produced controversy both inside scientific circles and among laypeople is whether population affinity and **intelligence** are associated.

Both genetic and environmental factors contribute to intelligence, although it is not yet possible to measure accurately the percentage each contributes. What can be said is that IQ scores and intelligence are not the same thing. IQ scores can change during a person's lifetime, and average IQ scores of different populations overlap. Such differences in IQ scores as do exist between groups are difficult to interpret, given the problems inherent in the design of the IQ tests. Moreover, complex cognitive abilities, however measured, are influenced by multiple loci and they are strongly influenced by environmental factors.

Innate factors set limits and define potentials for behavior and cognitive ability in any species. In humans, the limits are broad and the potentials are not fully known. Individual abilities result from complex interactions between genetic and environmental factors. One product of this interaction is learning, and the ability to learn is influenced by genetic and other biological components. Undeniably, there are differences between individuals regarding these biological components. However, elucidating what proportion of the variation in test scores is due to biological factors probably is not possible. Moreover, innate differences in abilities reflect individual variation *within* populations, not inherent differences *between* groups. Comparing populations on the basis of IQ test results is a misuse of testing procedures, and there is no convincing evidence *whatsoever* that populations vary with regard to cognitive abilities, regardless of the assertions in some popular books. Unfortunately, it appears that no matter what is said about the lack of evidence of the mental inferiority of some populations (and the mental superiority of others) and the questionable validity of intelligence tests, racist attitudes toward the topic continue to flourish.

Intelligence
Mental capacity; ability to learn, reason, or comprehend and interpret information, facts, relationships, meanings, etc.; the capacity to solve problems, whether through the application of previously acquired knowledge or through insight.

The Adaptive Significance of Human Variation

Today, physical anthropologists view human variation as the result of such evolutionary factors as genetic drift, founder effect, gene flow, and adaptations to environmental conditions, both past and present. Cultural adaptations have also played an important role in the evolution of *Homo sapiens*, and although in this discussion we are primarily concerned with biological issues, we must still consider the influence of cultural practices on human adaptive response.

All organisms must maintain the normal functions of internal organs, tissues, and cells in order to survive, and this task must be accomplished within the context of an ever-changing environment. Even during the course of a single, seemingly uneventful day, there are numerous fluctuations in temperature, wind, solar radiation, humidity, and so on. Physical activity also places **stress** on physiological mechanisms. The body must accommodate all these changes by compensating in some manner to maintain internal constancy, or **homeostasis**, and all life forms have evolved physiological mechanisms that, within limits, achieve this goal.

Physiological response to environmental change is, to some degree, influenced by genetic factors. We have already defined adaptation as a functional response to environmental conditions in populations and individuals. In a narrower sense, adaptation refers to *long-term* evolutionary (i.e., genetic) changes that characterize all individuals within a population or species.

Examples of long-term adaptations in *Homo sapiens* include some physiological responses to heat (sweating) and deeply pigmented skin in tropical regions. Such characteristics are the results of evolutionary change in species or populations, and they do not vary as the result of short-term environmental change. For example, the ability to sweat is not lost in people who spend their entire lives in predominantly cool areas. Likewise, individuals born with deeply pigmented skin will not become pale, even if never exposed to intense sunlight.

Short-term physiological response to environmental change, which occurs in all people, is called **acclimatization**. Tanning is a form of acclimatization. Another example is the very rapid increase in hemoglobin production that occurs when lowland natives travel to higher elevations. This increase provides the body with more oxygen in an environment where oxygen is less available. In both these examples, the physiological change is temporary. Tans fade once exposure to sunlight is reduced; and hemoglobin production drops to original levels following a return to lower altitudes.

In the following discussion, we present some examples of how humans respond to environmental challenges. Some of these examples illustrate adaptations that characterize the entire species. Others illustrate adaptations seen in only some populations. And still others illustrate the process of acclimatization.

Solar Radiation, Vitamin D, and Skin Color

Skin color is often cited as an example of adaptation and natural selection in human populations. In general, skin color in populations, prior to European contact, follows a particular geographical distribution, especially in the Old World. Figure 5–1 illustrates that populations with the greatest amount of pigmentation are found in the tropics, while lighter skin color is associated with more northern latitudes, particularly the inhabitants of northwestern Europe.

Skin color is influenced by three substances: hemoglobin, carotene, and most important, the pigment *melanin*. Melanin is a granular substance produced by specialized cells (*melanocytes*) found in the epidermis. All humans appear to have approximately the same number of melanocytes. It is the amount of melanin and the size of the melanin granules that vary.

Melanin has the capacity to absorb potentially dangerous ultraviolet (UV) rays present, although not visible, in sunlight. Therefore, melanin provides protection from overexposure to ultraviolet radiation, which can cause genetic mutations in

Stress
In a physiological context, any factor that acts to disrupt homeostasis; more precisely, the body's response to any factor that threatens its ability to maintain homeostasis.

Homeostasis
A condition of balance or stability within a biological system, maintained by the interaction of physiological mechanisms that compensate for changes (both external and internal).

Acclimatization
Physiological response to changes in the environment that occurs during an individual's lifetime. Such responses may be short-term. The capacity for acclimatization may typify an entire population or species. This capacity is under genetic influence and thus is subject to evolutionary factors such as natural selection.

The adaptive significance of skin color is presented as a virtual exercise in Virtual Lab 2, section IV.

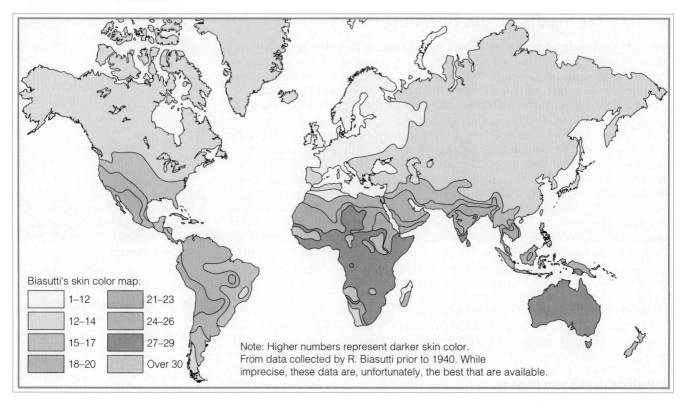

Biasutti's skin color map:

1–12	21–23
12–14	24–26
15–17	27–29
18–20	Over 30

Note: Higher numbers represent darker skin color.
From data collected by R. Biasutti prior to 1940. While imprecise, these data are, unfortunately, the best that are available.

FIGURE 5–1
Geographical distribution of skin color among the indigenous populations of the world. (After Biasutti, 1959.)

Norman Lightfoot/PhotoResearchers #7V3198

FIGURE 5–2
An African albino.

skin cells. These mutations may ultimately lead to skin cancer, which, if left untreated, can eventually spread to other organs and result in death.

As already mentioned, exposure to sunlight triggers a protective mechanism in the form of tanning, which results from temporarily increased melanin production (acclimatization). This protective response occurs in all humans except albinos, who carry a genetic mutation that prevents their melanocytes from producing melanin (Fig. 5–2). Moreover, tanning is limited in many fair-complexioned people of northern European descent who do produce small amounts of melanin but have a reduced capacity for temporary increases in melanin production.

Natural selection appears to have favored dark skin in areas nearest the equator, where the sun's rays are most direct and thus where exposure to UV light is most intense. However, as hominids migrated out of Africa into Europe and Asia, selective pressures changed. Not only were these populations moving away from the tropics, where ultraviolet rays were most direct, but they were also moving into areas where it was cold and cloudy during winter. Bear in mind, too, that physiological adaptations were not sufficient to meet the demands of living in colder climates. Therefore, we must assume that these populations had adopted certain cultural practices, such as wearing animal skins or other types of clothing. Although clothing would have added necessary warmth, it also would have effectively blocked exposure to sunlight. Consequently, the advantages provided by deeply pigmented skin in the tropics were no longer important, and selection for melanin production may have been relaxed (Brace and Montagu, 1977).

However, relaxed selection favoring dark skin may not be adequate to explain the very depigmented skin seen especially in some northern Europeans. Perhaps another factor, the need for adequate amounts of vitamin D, was also critical. The theory concerning the possible role of vitamin D, known as the *vitamin D hypothesis*, offers the following explanation.

Vitamin D is produced in the body partly as a result of the interaction between ultraviolet radiation and a substance similar to cholesterol. It is also available in some foods, including liver, fish oils, egg yolk, butter, and cream. Vitamin D is necessary for normal bone growth and mineralization, and some exposure to ultraviolet radiation is therefore essential. Insufficient amounts of vitamin D during childhood result in *rickets*, which often leads to bowing of the long bones of the legs and deformation of the pelvis. Pelvic deformities are of particular concern for women, for they can lead to a narrowing of the birth canal, which, in the absence of surgical intervention, frequently results in the death of both mother and fetus during childbirth.

This example illustrates the potential for rickets as a significant selective factor favoring less pigmented skin in regions where climate and other factors operate to reduce exposure to UV radiation. It is obvious how reduced exposure to sunlight due to climate and increased use of clothing could have been detrimental to dark-skinned individuals in more northern latitudes. In these individuals, melanin would have blocked absorption of the already reduced amounts of available ultraviolet radiation required for vitamin D synthesis. Therefore, selection pressures would have shifted over time to favor individuals with lighter skin. There is substantial evidence, both historically and in contemporary populations, to support this theory.

During the latter decades of the nineteenth century in the United States, black inhabitants of northern cities suffered a higher incidence of rickets than whites. Northern blacks were also more commonly affected than blacks living in the South, where exposure to sunlight is greater. (The supplementation of milk with vitamin D was initiated to alleviate this problem.) Another example is seen in Britain, where darker-skinned East Indians and Pakistanis show a higher incidence of rickets than people with lighter skin (Molnar, 1983).

Perhaps more social importance has been attached to variation in skin color than to any other single human biological trait. But aside from its probable adaptive significance relative to UV radiation, skin color is no more important physiologically than many other biological characteristics. Still, from an evolutionary perspective, skin color provides a good example of how the forces of natural selection have produced geographically patterned variation as the consequence of two conflicting selective forces: the need for protection from overexposure to UV radiation, on the one hand, and the need for adequate UV exposure for vitamin D synthesis on the other.

The Thermal Environment

Mammals and birds have evolved complex mechanisms to maintain a constant internal body temperature. While reptiles must rely on exposure to external heat sources to raise body temperature and energy levels, mammals and birds possess physiological mechanisms that, within certain limits, increase or reduce the loss of body heat. The optimum internal body temperature for normal cellular functions is species-specific, and for humans it is approximately 98.6°F.

Homo sapiens is found in a wide variety of habitats, with thermal environments ranging from exceedingly hot (in excess of 120°F) to bitter cold (less than −60°F). In such extremes, particularly cold, human life would not be possible without cultural innovations. But even accounting for the artificial environments in which we live, such external conditions place the human body under enormous stress.

Response to Heat All available evidence suggests that the earliest hominids evolved in the warm-to-hot savannas of East Africa. The fact that humans cope better with heat than they do with cold is testimony to the long-term adaptations to heat that evolved in our ancestors.

In humans, as well as certain other species, such as horses, sweat glands are distributed throughout the skin. This wide distribution of sweat glands makes possible the loss of heat at the body surface through evaporative cooling, a mechanism that has evolved to the greatest degree in humans.

Vasodilation
Expansion of blood vessels, permitting increased blood flow to the skin. Vasodilation permits warming of the skin and also facilitates radiation of warmth as a means of cooling. Vasodilation is an involuntary response to warm temperatures, various drugs, and even emotional states (blushing).

The capacity to dissipate heat by sweating is seen in all humans to an almost equal degree, with the average number of sweat glands per individual (approximately 1.6 million) being fairly constant. However, there is variation in that persons not generally exposed to hot conditions do experience a period of acclimatization that initially involves significantly increased perspiration rates (Frisancho, 1993). An additional factor that enhances the cooling effects of sweating is increased exposure of the skin through reduced amounts of body hair. We do not know when in our evolutionary history loss of body hair began, but it represents a species-wide adaptation.

Heat reduction through evaporation can be expensive, and indeed dangerous, in terms of water and sodium loss. Up to 3 liters of water can be lost by a human engaged in heavy work in high heat. The importance of this fact can be appreciated if you consider that the loss of 1 liter of water is approximately equivalent to losing 1.5 percent of total body weight, and loss of 10 percent of body weight can be life threatening.

Another mechanism for radiating body heat is **vasodilation**, whereby capillaries near the skin's surface widen to permit increased blood flow to the skin. The visible effect of vasodilation is flushing, or increased redness of the skin, particularly of the face, accompanied by warmth. But the physiological effect is to permit heat, carried by the blood from the interior of the body, to be emitted from the skin's surface to the surrounding air. (Some drugs, including alcohol, also produce vasodilation, which accounts for the increased redness and warmth of the face in some people.)

Body size and proportions are also important in regulating body temperature. Indeed, there seems to be a general relationship between climate and body size and shape in birds and mammals. In general, within a species, body size (weight) increases as distance from the equator increases. In humans, this relationship holds up fairly well, but there are numerous exceptions.

Two rules that pertain to the relationship between body size, body proportions, and climate are *Bergmann's rule* and *Allen's rule*.

1. *Bergmann's rule (concerning the relationship of body mass or volume to surface area):* In mammalian species, body size tends to be greater in populations that live in colder climates. This is because as mass increases, the relative amount of surface area decreases proportionately. Because heat is lost at the surface, it follows that increased mass allows for greater heat retention and reduced heat loss.
2. *Allen's rule (concerning shape of the body, especially appendages):* In colder climates, shorter appendages, with increased mass-to-surface ratios, are adaptive because they are more effective at preventing heat loss. Conversely, longer appendages, with increased surface area relative to mass, are more adaptive in warmer climates because they promote heat loss.

According to these rules, the most suitable body shape in hot climates is linear with long arms and legs. In a cold climate, a more suitable body type is stocky with shorter limbs. Considerable data gathered from several human populations generally conform to these principles. In colder climates, body mass tends, on average, to be greater and characterized by a larger trunk relative to arms and legs (Roberts, 1973). People living in the Arctic tend to be short and stocky, while many sub-Saharan Africans, especially East African pastoralists, tend to be taller and more linear (Fig. 5–3). But there is much human variability regarding body proportions, and not all populations conform so readily to Bergmann's and Allen's rules.

Response to Cold   Human physiological responses to cold combine factors that increase heat retention with those that enhance heat production. Of the two, heat retention is more efficient because it requires less energy. This is an important point because energy is derived from dietary sources. Unless food resources are abundant, and in winter they frequently are not, any factor that conserves energy can have adaptive value.

(a)   (b)

FIGURE 5–3
(a) This African woman has the linear proportions characteristic of many inhabitants of sub-Saharan Africa. (b) By comparison, the Inuit woman is short and stocky. These two individuals serve as good examples of Bergmann's and Allen's rules.

Short-term responses to cold include increased metabolic rate and shivering, both of which generate body heat, at least for a short time. **Vasoconstriction**, another short-term response, restricts heat loss and conserves energy. In addition, humans possess a subcutaneous (beneath the skin) fat layer that provides an insulative layer throughout the body. Behavioral modifications include increased activity, wearing warmer clothing, increased food consumption, and assuming a curled-up position.

Increases in metabolic rate (the rate at which cells break up nutrients into their components) release energy in the form of heat. Shivering also generates muscle heat, as does voluntary exercise. But these methods of heat production are expensive, because they require an increased intake of nutrients to provide energy. (Perhaps this explains why we tend to have a heartier appetite during the winter and why we also tend to increase our intake of fats and carbohydrates, the very sources of energy our bodies require.)

In general, people exposed to chronic cold (meaning much or most of the year) maintain higher metabolic rates than those living in warmer climates. The Inuit (Eskimo) people living in the Arctic maintain metabolic rates between 13 and 45 percent higher than observed in non-Inuit control subjects (Frisancho, 1993). Moreover, the highest metabolic rates are seen in inland Inuit, who are exposed to even greater cold stress than coastal populations. Traditionally, the Inuit had the highest animal protein and fat diet of any human population in the world. Such a diet, necessitated by the available resource base, served to maintain the high metabolic rates required by exposure to chronic cold.

Vasoconstriction restricts capillary blood flow to the surface of the skin, thus reducing heat loss at the body surface. Because retaining body heat is more economical than creating it, vasoconstriction is very efficient, provided temperatures do not drop below freezing. However, if temperatures do fall below freezing, continued vasoconstriction can allow the skin temperature to decline to the point of frostbite or worse.

Long-term responses to cold vary among human groups. For example, in the past, desert-dwelling native Australian populations were subjected to wide temperature fluctuations from day to night. As they wore no clothing and did not build shelters, their only protection from temperatures that hovered only a few degrees

Vasoconstriction
Narrowing of blood vessels to reduce blood flow to the skin. Vasoconstriction is an involuntary response to cold and reduces heat loss at the skin's surface.

above freezing was provided by sleeping fires. They experienced continuous vaso-constriction throughout the night, and this permitted a degree of skin cooling most people would find extremely uncomfortable. But there was no threat of frostbite, and continued vasoconstriction helped to prevent excessive internal heat loss.

By contrast, the Inuit experience intermittent periods of vasoconstriction and vasodilation. This compromise provides periodic warmth to the skin that helps prevent frostbite in below-freezing temperatures. At the same time, because vasodilation is intermittent, energy loss is restricted, with more heat retained at the body's core.

The preceding examples illustrate but two of the many ways in which human populations vary with regard to adaptation to cold. Although all humans respond to cold stress in much the same manner, there is variation in how adaptation and acclimatization are manifested.

High Altitude

Today, perhaps as many as 25 million people live at altitudes above 10,000 feet. In Tibet, permanent settlements exist above 15,000 feet, and in the Andes, they can be found as high as 17,000 feet (Fig. 5–4).

At such altitudes, multiple factors produce stress on the human body. These include **hypoxia** (reduced available oxygen), more intense solar radiation, cold, low humidity, wind (which amplifies cold stress), a reduced nutritional base, and rough terrain. Of these, hypoxia exerts the greatest amount of stress on human physiological systems, especially the heart, lungs, and brain.

Hypoxia results from reduced barometric pressure. It is not that there is less oxygen in the atmosphere at high altitudes; rather, it is less concentrated. Therefore, to obtain the same amount of oxygen at 9,000 feet as at sea level, people must make certain physiological alterations aimed at increasing the body's ability to transport and utilize efficiently the oxygen that is available.

People who reside at higher elevations, especially recent immigrants, display a number of manifestations of their hypoxic environment. Reproduction, in particular, is affected through increased rates of infant mortality, miscarriage, and prematurity. Low birth weight is also more common and is attributed to decreased

Hypoxia
Lack of oxygen. Hypoxia can refer to reduced amounts of available oxygen in the atmosphere (due to lowered barometric pressure) or to insufficient amounts of oxygen in the body.

FIGURE 5–4
(a) La Paz, Bolivia, at just over 12,000 feet above sea level, is home to more than 1 million people. (b) A household in northern Tibet, situated at an elevation of over 15,000 feet above sea level.

Courtesy, William Pratt

(a)

Courtesy, L.G. Moore

(b)

fetal growth due to impaired maternal-fetal transport of oxygen (Moore and Regensteiner, 1983). But there is also some evidence to suggest that low birth weight may actually have some adaptive value in high-altitude natives.

Compared to populations at lower elevations, lifelong residents of high altitude display slowed growth and maturation. Other differences include larger chest size, associated, in turn, with greater lung volume and larger hearts.

Compared to high-altitude natives, nonnatives exhibit some differences in acclimatization and adaptation to hypoxia. Frisancho (1993) terms these different responses "adult acclimatization" and "developmental acclimatization." *Adult acclimatization* occurs upon exposure to high altitude in people born at low elevation. The responses may be short-term modifications, depending on duration of stay, but they begin within hours of the altitude change. These changes include an increase in respiration rate, heart rate, and production of red blood cells. (Red blood cells contain hemoglobin, the protein responsible for transporting oxygen to organs and tissues.)

Developmental acclimatization occurs in high-altitude natives whose adaptations are acquired during growth and development. (Note that this type of acclimatization is present only in people who grow up in high-altitude areas, not in those who moved there as adults.) In addition to greater lung capacity, people born at high altitudes are more efficient than migrants at diffusing oxygen from the blood to bodily tissues. Hence, they do not rely as heavily on increased red cell formation as do newcomers. Developmental acclimatization serves as a good example of physiological plasticity by illustrating how, within the limits set by genetic factors, development can be influenced by environment.

There is some evidence that entire populations have adapted to high altitudes. Indigenous peoples of Tibet who have inhabited regions higher than 12,000 feet for around 25,000 years may have made genetic (i.e., evolutionary) accommodations to hypoxia. Altitude does not appear to affect reproduction in these people to the degree it does in other populations. Infants have birth weights as high as those of lowland Tibetan groups and higher than those of recent (20 to 30 years) Chinese immigrants. This fact may be the result of alterations in maternal blood flow to the uterus during pregnancy (Moore et al., 1994).

Another line of evidence concerns the utilization of glucose (blood sugar). Glucose is critical in that it is the only source of energy used by the brain, and it is also utilized, although not exclusively, by the heart. Both highland Tibetans and the Quechua (inhabitants of high-altitude regions of the Peruvian Andes) burn glucose in a way that permits more efficient use of oxygen. This implies the presence of genetic mutations in the mitochondrial DNA that directs how cells use glucose. It also implies that natural selection has acted to increase the frequency of these advantageous mutations in these groups.

There is no certain evidence that Tibetans and Quechua have made evolutionary changes to accommodate high-altitude hypoxia. Moreover, the genetic mechanisms that underlie these populations' unique abilities have not been identified. The data are intriguing, however, and they strongly suggest that selection has operated to produce evolutionary change in these two groups. If further study supports these findings, we will have an excellent example of evolution in action producing long-term adaptation at the population level.

Infectious Disease

Infection, as opposed to other disease categories, such as degenerative or genetic disease, is a category that includes those pathological conditions caused by microorganisms (viruses, bacteria, or fungi). Throughout the course of human evolution, infectious disease has exerted enormous selective pressures on populations and thus has influenced the frequency of certain alleles that affect the immune response. But as important as infectious disease has been as an agent of natural selection in human populations, its role in this regard is not very well documented.

Human Variation and Adaptation

Virtual Lab 2, section III, part B, provides a discussion of the human adaptive response to malaria.

Pathogens
Substances or microorganisms, such as bacteria, fungi, or viruses, that cause disease.

Malaria provides perhaps the best-documented example of the evolutionary role of disease. In Chapter 4, you saw how malaria has operated in some African and Mediterranean populations to alter allele frequencies at the locus governing hemoglobin formation. In spite of extensive long-term eradication programs, malaria still poses a serious threat to human health. Indeed, the World Health Organization estimates the number of people currently infected with malaria to be between 300 and 500 million worldwide. This number is increasing, too, as drug-resistant strains of the disease-causing microorganism become more common (Olliaro et al., 1995).

Another example of the selective role of infectious disease is indirectly provided by AIDS (acquired immune deficiency syndrome). In the United States, the first cases of AIDS were reported in 1981. Since that time, perhaps as many as 1.5 million have been infected by HIV (human immunodeficiency virus), the agent that causes AIDS. As of June, 2000, about 439,000 had died in the United States, but worldwide, 21 million had died and more than 36 million were infected.

HIV is transmitted from person to person through the exchange of bodily fluids, usually blood or semen. It is not spread through casual contact. Within six months of infection, most persons test positive for anti-HIV antibodies, meaning that their immune system has recognized the presence of foreign antigens and has responded by producing antibodies. However, serious HIV-related symptoms may not appear in infected people for years, and in the United States, the average "latency period" is over 11 years.

Like all viruses, HIV must invade certain types of cells and alter the functions of those cells to produce more virus particles in a process that eventually leads to cell destruction. (The manner in which HIV accomplishes this task is different from that of many other viruses.) HIV can attack various types of cells, but it especially targets so-called T4 helper cells, which are major components of the immune system. As HIV infection spreads and T4 cells are destroyed, the patient's immune system begins to fail. Consequently, he or she begins to exhibit symptoms caused by various **pathogens** that are commonly present but usually kept in check by a normal immune response. When an HIV-infected person's T cell count drops to a level that indicates immune suppression, and when symptoms of "opportunistic" infections appear, the patient is said to have AIDS.

By the early 1990s, scientists were aware of a number of patients who had been HIV positive for 10 to 15 years but continued to show few if any symptoms. Awareness of these patients led researchers to suspect that some individuals possess a natural immunity or resistance to HIV infection. This was shown to be true in late 1996 with the publication of two different studies (Dean et al., 1996; Samson et al., 1996) that demonstrated a mechanism for resistance to HIV.

These two reports describe a genetic mutation that concerns a major protein "receptor site" on the surface of certain immune cells, including T4 cells. (Receptor sites are protein molecules that enable HIV and other viruses to invade cells.) In this particular situation, the mutant allele results in a malfunctioning receptor site, and current evidence now strongly suggests that individuals who are homozygous for this allele may be completely resistant to many types of HIV infection. In heterozygotes, infection may still occur, but the course of HIV disease is markedly slowed.

Interestingly, and for unknown reasons, the mutant allele occurs mainly in people of European descent, among whom its frequency is about 10 percent. Samson and colleagues (1996) reported that in the Japanese and West African samples they studied, the mutation was absent, but Dean and colleagues (1996) reported an allele frequency of about 2 percent among African Americans. These researchers speculate that the presence of the allele in African Americans may be entirely due to genetic admixture (gene flow) with American whites. Moreover, they suggest that this polymorphism exists in Europeans as a result of selective pressures favoring an allele that originally occurred as a rare mutation. But it is critical to note that the original selective agent was *not* HIV. Instead, it was some other, as yet unidentified, pathogen that requires the same receptor site as HIV. Researchers may be close to identifying which pathogen, or group of pathogens, it was. In

December 1999, a group of scientists reported that the myxoma poxvirus, which is related to the virus that causes smallpox, can use the same receptor site as does HIV. These authors (Lalani, et al., 1999) suggest that the agent that selected for the altered form of the receptor site may have been smallpox. While this conclusion has not yet been proven, or even really investigated, it offers a most exciting avenue of research with the possibility of revealing how a mutation that has been favored by selection because it provides protection against one disease can be shown to increase resistance to another malady (AIDS) as well.

Examples such as AIDS and the relationship between malaria and sickle-cell anemia are continuously revealing new insights into the complex interactions between disease organisms and their host populations. These insights in turn provide a growing basis for understanding the many variations between individuals and populations that have arisen as adaptive responses to infectious disease.

Smallpox, once a deadly viral disease, may provide a good example of how exposure to infectious agents can produce polymorphisms in host populations. During the eighteenth century, smallpox is estimated to have accounted for 10 to 15 percent of all deaths in parts of Europe. But today, this once devastating killer is the only condition to have been successfully eliminated by modern medical technology. By 1977, through massive vaccination programs, the World Health Organization was able to declare the smallpox virus to be extinct.

Smallpox had a higher incidence in persons with either blood type A or AB than in type O individuals, a fact that has been explained by the presence of an antigen on the smallpox virus that is similar to the A antigen. It follows that when some type A individuals were exposed to smallpox, their immune systems failed to recognize the virus as foreign and thus did not mount an adequate immune response. Consequently, in regions where smallpox was common in the past, it could have altered allele frequencies at the ABO locus by selecting against the *A* allele.

The effects of infectious disease on humans are mediated culturally as well as biologically. Innumerable cultural factors, such as architectural styles, subsistence techniques, exposure to domesticated animals, and even religious practices, all affect how infectious disease develops and persists within and between populations (see pp. 442–444).

As will be discussed further in Chapter 16, until about 10,000 to 12,000 years ago, all humans lived in small nomadic hunting and gathering groups. As these groups rarely remained in one location more than a few days at a time, they had minimal contact with refuse heaps that housed disease **vectors**. But with the domestication of plants and animals, people became more sedentary and began living in small villages. Gradually, villages became towns, and towns, in turn, developed into densely crowded, unsanitary cities.

As long as humans lived in small isolated bands, there was little opportunity for infectious disease to have much impact on large numbers of people. Even if an entire local group or band were wiped out, the effect on the overall population in a given area would have been negligible. Moreover, for a disease to become **endemic** in a population, sufficient numbers of people must be present. Therefore, small bands of hunter-gatherers were not faced with continuous exposure to endemic disease. However, with the advent of settled living and association with domesticated animals, opportunities for disease increased.

It is important to realize that humans and pathogens exert selective pressures on each other, creating a dynamic relationship between disease organisms and their human (and nonhuman) hosts. Just as disease exerts selective pressures on host populations to adapt, microorganisms also evolve and adapt to various pressures exerted on them by their hosts.

Evolutionarily speaking, it is to the advantage of any pathogen not to be so virulent as to kill its host too quickly. If the host dies shortly after becoming infected, the viral or bacterial agent may not have time to reproduce and infect other hosts.

Selection sometimes acts to produce resistance in host populations and/or to reduce the virulence of disease organisms, to the benefit of both. However, prior to

Vectors
Agents that serve to transmit disease from one carrier to another. Mosquitoes are vectors for malaria, just as fleas are vectors for bubonic plague.

Endemic
Continuously present in a population.

this occurrence, hosts exposed for the first time to a new disease frequently die in huge numbers. This is the case with the current worldwide spread of HIV. Initial exposure to a pathogen was also a major factor in the decimation of indigenous New World populations after contact with Europeans exposed Native American groups to smallpox.

Through the adoption of various cultural practices, humans have radically altered patterns of infectious disease. Here, then, is another example of biocultural evolution in our species. The interaction of cultural and biological factors has influenced microevolutionary change in humans (as in the example of sickle-cell anemia) to accommodate altered relationships with disease organisms.

Fundamentals of Growth and Development

Another good place to explore the relationship between human variation and the interaction of culture and biology is human growth and development. The terms *growth* and *development* are often used interchangeably, but they actually refer to different processes. **Growth** refers to an increase in mass or number of cells, whereas **development** refers to the differentiation of cells into different types of tissues and their subsequent maturation.

There is much variation in the extent to which cultural factors interact with genetically based biological characteristics; these variable interactions greatly influence how characteristics are expressed in individuals. Some genetically based characteristics will be exhibited no matter what the cultural context of growth and development happen to be. If a person inherits two alleles for albinism, for example, he or she will be deficient in melanin production. This deficiency will emerge regardless of the cultural environment in which the person lives.

But as we have said, other characteristics, such as intelligence, body shape, and growth, will reflect the interaction of environment and genes. We know, for example, that each of us is born with a genetic makeup that influences the maximum stature we can achieve in adulthood. But to reach that maximum stature, we must be properly nourished while growing. What factors determine whether we are well fed and receive good medical care? In the United States, socioeconomic status is probably the primary determinant of nutrition and health. Thus, socioeconomic status is an example of a cultural factor that affects growth.

Stature

Increased stature is a common indicator of health status in children because it is easy to assess under most circumstances. Growth spurts occur in early infancy and at puberty. Typically, well-nourished humans grow fairly rapidly during the first two trimesters (six months) of fetal development, but growth slows during the third trimester. After birth, the rate of development increases and remains fairly rapid for about four years, at which time it decreases again to a relatively slow, steady level that is maintained until puberty. At puberty, there is, once again, a very pronounced increase in growth. During this so-called **adolescent growth spurt**, Western teenagers typically grow 9 to 10 cm per year. Subsequent to the adolescent growth spurt, the rate of development declines again and remains slower until adult stature is achieved by the late teens (Fig. 5–5).

Growth curves for boys and girls are significantly different, with the adolescent growth spurt occurring approximately two years earlier in girls than in boys At birth, there is slight **sexual dimorphism** in many body measures (e.g., height, weight, head circumference, and body fat), but the major divergence in these characteristics does not occur until puberty. Table 5–2 shows the differences between these measures for boys and girls at birth and at age 18. Boys are slightly larger than girls at birth and are even more so at age 18, except in the last two measures, triceps skinfold and subscapular skinfold. These two measurements give information on body fat content and are determined by a special skinfold-measuring caliper. The

Growth
Increase in mass or number of cells.

Development
Differentiation of cells into different types of tissues and their maturation.

Adolescent growth spurt
The period during adolescence in which well-nourished teens typically increase in stature at greater rates than at other points in the life cycle.

Sexual dimorphism
Differences in physical characteristics between males and females of the same species. For example, humans are slightly sexually dimorphic for body size, with males being taller, on average, than females of the same population.

(a)

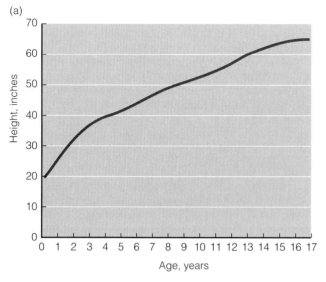

(b)

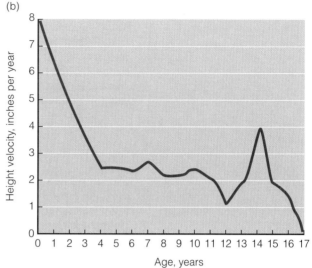

FIGURE 5–5
Distance and velocity curves of growth in height for a healthy American girl.

TABLE 5–2 Some Measurements of Size at Birth and at Age 18 for Children Born in the United States

	Boys		Girls	
	Birth	**18**	**Birth**	**18**
Body length (cm)*	49.9	181.1	49.3	166.7
Weight (kg)*	3.4	69.9	3.3	55.6
Head circumference (cm)[†]	34.8	55.9	34.1	54.9
Triceps skinfold (mm)	3.8[††]	8.5[§]	4.1[††]	17.5[§]
Subscapular skinfold (mm)	3.5[††]	10.0[§]	3.8[††]	12.0[§]

* Hamill et al., 1977
[†] Nellhaus, 1968.
[††] Johnston and Beller, 1976.
[§] Johnson et al., 1981.

Source: From Bogin, 1988, p.22.

triceps skinfold measure is taken by gently pinching the skin and fat underneath the upper arm, and the subscapular measurement is taken by gently pinching the skin and fat below the shoulder blade. These measures reflect differences not only in the more obvious characteristics of height and weight, but also in body composition, with girls generally having more body fat than boys at all ages.

Brain Growth

The head is a relatively large part of the body at birth. The continued growth of the brain after birth occurs at a rate far greater than that of any other part of the body, with the exception of the eyeball. At birth, the human brain is about 25 percent of its adult size. By 6 months of age, the brain has doubled in size, reaching 50 percent of adult size. It reaches 75 percent of adult size at age $2^{1}/_{2}$ years, 90 percent at age 5 years, and 95 percent by age 10 years. There is only a very small spurt at adolescence, making the brain an exception to the growth curves characteristic of most

other parts of the body. As we will see, this pattern of brain growth, including the relatively small amount of growth before birth, is unusual among primates and other mammals. By contrast, the typical pattern for most mammalian species is that at least 50 percent of adult brain size has been attained prior to birth. For humans, however, the narrow pelvis, necessary for bipedality, imposes limits on the size of the fetal head that can pass through it. This limitation, in addition to the value of having most brain growth occur in the more stimulating environment outside the womb, has resulted in human infants being born with far less of their total adult brain size than most other mammals.

Nutritional Effects on Growth and Development

Nutrition has an impact on human growth at every stage of the life cycle. During pregnancy, for example, a woman's diet can have a profound effect on the development of her fetus and the eventual health of the child. Moreover, the effects are transgenerational, because a woman's own supply of eggs is developed while she herself is *in utero*. Thus, if a woman is malnourished during pregnancy, the eggs that develop in her female fetus may be damaged in a way that will impact the health of her future grandchildren.

Basic Nutrients for Growth and Development

Nutrients needed for growth, development, and body maintenance are organized into five major categories: proteins, carbohydrates, lipids (fats), vitamins, and minerals. As you learned in Chapter 3, *proteins*, composed of amino acids (see p. 45), are the major structural components of such structures as muscles, skin, hair, and most of the organs of the body. Antibodies and enzymes are proteins, as are most hormones. When you eat a meal, stomach and pancreatic enzymes break the protein down into the 20 amino acids mentioned in Chapter 3. The amino acids are then absorbed into the bloodstream through the walls of the small intestine and are transported to other cells in the body, where they will be used in the synthesis of new proteins (the process by which this occurs is described in Chapter 3).

Carbohydrates are important sources of energy needed to run the body. Good sources of carbohydrates are potatoes, beans, and grains. Carbohydrate digestion begins in the mouth and continues in the small intestine, where simple sugars are absorbed into the bloodstream through the walls of the small intestine in a manner similar to that for amino acids. From there they are transported to the liver, where all are converted into glucose, the primary source of energy for the body. Indeed, glucose is the only source of energy utilized by the brain, and the hormone insulin is responsible for regulating glucose levels in the blood and tissues.

Lipids comprise the third major nutrient category and include fats and oils. Fats are broken down into fatty acids and are absorbed into the bloodstream through the walls of the small intestine. These fatty acids are then further broken down and stored until needed for energy.

Vitamins are another category of nutrients needed for growth and for a healthy, functioning body. Vitamins serve as components of enzymes that speed up chemical reactions. There are two categories of vitamins: those that are water-soluble (the B vitamins and vitamin C) and those that are not soluble in water but are soluble in fat (vitamins A, D, E, and K). The fat-soluble vitamins can be stored, so a deficiency of any of them is slow to develop. Because water-soluble vitamins are excreted in urine, very little is stored; these vitamins must be consumed almost daily to maintain health.

Unlike other nutrients, *minerals* are not organic, but they, too, contribute to normal functioning and health. The minerals needed in the greatest quantity include calcium (this mineral alone makes up 2 percent of our body weight, mostly in the skeleton and teeth), phosphorus, potassium, sulfur, sodium, chlorine, and magnesium. Our requirements for iron are comparatively low, but this mineral plays a critical role in oxygen transport. Iron-deficiency anemia is one of the most common nutritional deficiency diseases worldwide, especially in women of reproductive age, whose iron needs are greater than those of men. Other essential minerals include iodine, zinc, manganese, copper, cobalt, fluoride, molybdenum, selenium, and chromium.

Evolution of Nutritional Needs

Our nutritional needs have coevolved with the types of food that were available to human ancestors throughout our evolutionary history. Because the earliest mammals and the first primates were probably insect eaters, humans have inherited the ability to digest and process animal protein. Early primates also evolved the ability to process most vegetable material, and some incorporated fruits into their diets. Consequently, vegetables and fruits are important dietary items for modern humans, just as they were for our early primate ancestors. Furthermore, human needs for specific vitamins and minerals reflect these ancestral nutritional adaptations. A good example is our requirement for vitamin C, also known as ascorbic acid. Vitamin C plays an important role in the metabolism of all foods and in the production of energy. It is a crucial organic compound for all animals—so crucial, in fact, that most animals are able to manufacture, or *synthesize*, it internally and need not depend on dietary sources. It is likely that most of the early primates were able to make their own vitamin C. As the monkeys evolved, however, they began to eat more leaves and fruits and less animal protein; thus, they were getting adequate amounts of vitamin C dietarily. It is hypothesized that at some point in early primate evolution some individuals "lost" the ability to synthesize vitamin C, probably through genetic mutation. This loss would not have been disadvantageous as long as dietary sources of vitamin C were regularly available. In fact, it may have been selectively advantageous to conserve the energy required for the manufacture of vitamin C, so that natural selection favored those individuals in a species who were unable to synthesize it. Eventually, all descendants of these early primates were unable to synthesize vitamin C and became dependent entirely on external (food) sources.

Through much of the course of human evolution, the inability to manufacture vitamin C was not a problem because of the abundance of the vitamin in the diet. It has been estimated that the average daily intake of vitamin C for preagricultural people was about 440 mg, compared to an approximate 90 mg in the current American diet (Eaton and Konner, 1985). When people get insufficient amounts of vitamin C, they often develop **scurvy**, a disease that was probably extremely rare or absent in preagricultural populations (agriculture arose approximately 10,000 to 12,000 years ago). Symptoms of scurvy include abnormal bleeding of gums, slowed healing of wounds, loss of energy, anemia, and abnormal formation of bones and teeth. Scurvy was probably not very common in the past except in extreme northern regions. Today, the condition occasionally appears in infants who are fed exclusively on powdered or canned milk that does not have added vitamin C.

Humans also lack the ability to synthesize some of the amino acids that are necessary for growth and maintenance of the body. As noted in Chapter 3, there are 20 amino acids that make up the proteins of all living things. Plants synthesize all the amino acids, but animals must get some or all (in the case of some bacteria) from the foods they consume. Because adult humans cannot synthesize eight of the amino acids in sufficient quantities, we must obtain them from the foods we eat; they are thus referred to as the eight **essential amino acids** (for infants, there are nine). Interestingly, the amounts of each of the amino acids we need parallel the amounts present in animal protein, suggesting that food from animal sources may have been an important component of ancestral hominid and prehominid diets when our specific nutrient requirements were evolving. Biologically, most humans can best meet their needs for protein from animal sources, but meat consumption is expensive, in both ecological and economic terms. By combining vegetables such

Scurvy
A disease resulting from a dietary deficiency of vitamin C. It may result in anemia, poor bone growth, abnormal bleeding and bruising, and muscle pain.

Essential amino acids
The eight (nine for infants) amino acids that must be ingested by humans for normal growth and body maintenance. These include tryptophan, leucine, lysine, methionine, phenylalanine, isoleucine, valine, and threonine (plus histidine for infants).

FIGURE 5–6
Complementarity of beans and wheat. (Adapted from *Scientific American*, 1976.)

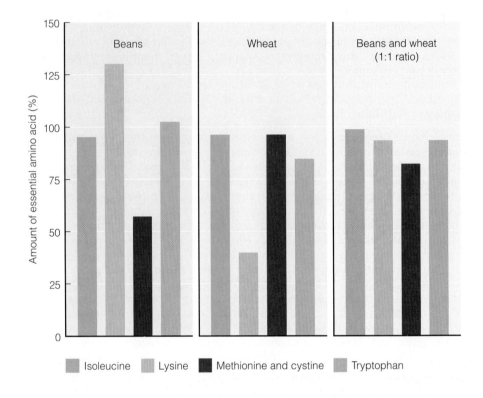

Pellagra
Disease resulting from a dietary deficiency of niacin (vitamin B3). Symptoms include dermatitis, diarrhea, dementia, and death (the "four Ds").

as legumes and grains, humans can obtain the eight essential amino acids in the correct proportions (Fig. 5–6). Thus, most contemporary populations meet their need for protein by eating enough variety of vegetable foods so that adequate proportions of amino acids are achieved. Examples of familiar cuisines that reflect these combinations include beans and corn in Mexico, beans and rice in Caribbean cultures, rice and lentils in India, and black-eyed peas and cornbread in the southern United States.

An example of biological and cultural interaction in meeting nutritional requirements is seen in the traditional methods for processing corn into tortillas or hominy. Wherever corn is a major part of the diet, it is usually associated with a high incidence of the disease **pellagra**, which results from a deficiency of the vitamin niacin (vitamin B_3). The exception to this pattern is the Americas, where corn was originally domesticated and where pellagra is not common. The reason for the lower prevalence of pellagra appears to be the practice of adding lime or ashes to the cornmeal when making tortillas or hominy. These additives increase the availability of niacin in the corn so that it can be absorbed by the body (Katz et al., 1974). Unfortunately, when corn was exported to the rest of the world, this particular technology was not exported with it.

Because humans can use cultural responses to adapt to environmental challenges, does that mean that culture has enabled us as a species to transcend the limitations placed on us by our biology? At this stage of human history, it seems that we are still constrained by nutritional needs that are the products of several million years of evolution. These needs reflect an adaptation to a food base that included a great deal of variety. Not only did humans evolve against a background of variety, we are now "stuck with" requirements for variety. As agriculture has evolved and population size expanded, however, the human food base has become narrower, leading to the appearance of nutritional deficiency disease, which, like scurvy and pellagra, probably did not commonly exist prior to the development of agriculture.

Genetics

No matter how much you eat in your lifetime or how excellent your health is, you will not be able to exceed your genetic potential for stature and a number of other physiological parameters. As we stated in Chapter 3, genetic factors set the underlying limitations and potentialities for growth and development, but the life experience and environment of the organism influence how the body grows within those parameters. How do we assess the relative contributions of genes and the environment in their effects on growth? Much of our information comes from studies of monozygotic and dizygotic twins. Monozygotic (identical) twins come from the union of a single sperm and ovum and share 100 percent of their genes. Dizygotic (fraternal) twins come from separate ova and sperm and share the same proportion of their genes (half) as any two siblings from the same parents. If monozygotic twins with identical genes but different growth environments were exactly the same in stature at various ages (i.e., showed perfect correlation or *concordance* for stature), then we could conclude that genes are the primary, if not the only, determinants of stature. Most studies of twins reveal that under normal circumstances, stature is "highly correlated" for monozygotic twins, leading to the conclusion that stature is under fairly strong genetic control (Table 5–3). Weight, on the other hand, seems to be more strongly influenced by diet, environment, and individual experiences than by genes.

Hormones

Hormones are substances (usually proteins) that are produced by cells within endocrine glands and then transmitted through the bloodstream to other tissues, where they exert powerful influences on specific cellular functions (see p. 45). Although several hormones influence stature in various ways, *growth hormone* (*GH*) is primarily responsible for the growth of bone and muscle. Growth hormone is one of many hormones produced in the pituitary gland, a pea-sized structure situated at the base of the brain, and the amount of GH produced during growth phases strongly influences how tall an individual will be. (Abnormal levels of GH during growth phases can produce various conditions, such as dwarfism or gigantism, among others.)

Testosterone is another hormone that influences growth and development. By about the sixth week of embryonic development, testosterone begins to initiate processes that result in sexual dimorphism in a variety of physical characteristics. In

TABLE 5–3 Correlation Coefficients for Height Between Monozygotic (MZ) and Dizygotic (DZ) Twin Pairs from Birth to Age 8

Age	Total *N*	MZ	DZ Same Sex	DZ Different Sex
Birth	629	0.62	0.79	0.67
3 months	764	0.78	0.72	0.65
6 months	819	0.80	0.67	0.62
12 months	827	0.86	0.66	0.58
24 months	687	0.89	0.54	0.61
3 years	699	0.93	0.56	0.60
5 years	606	0.94	0.51	0.68
8 years	444	0.94	0.49	0.65

Source: From Wilson, 1979, after Bogin, 1988, p. 163.

fact, it is the production of testosterone by newly formed testicular tissues that directs the subsequent development of a fetus as male rather than female. In addition to these most basic functions, testosterone also stimulates bone and muscle growth, and this effect becomes more pronounced in males at puberty, when the testes begin producing increased amounts of the hormone. Consequently, testosterone contributes to the adolescent growth spurt in teenage boys and to a considerable degree is responsible for the overall greater muscle mass of males, in humans as well as in other species. (It should be noted that females also produce testosterone, but in reduced amounts compared to males.)

Environmental Factors

As you have seen, environmental factors, such as altitude and climate, also have effects on growth and development. Perhaps the primary influence of such external factors comes from their effects on nutrition, but there is evidence of independent effects as well. For example, as previously noted, infant birth weight is lower at high altitude, and this is so even when such factors as nutrition, smoking, and socioeconomic status are taken into consideration. In the United States, the percentage of low-birth-rate (LBW) infants (those weighing less than 2,500 g, or 5.7 pounds) is about 6.5 percent at sea level, rising to 10.4 percent at 5,000 feet and almost 24 percent above 10,000 feet. In a Bolivian study, the mean birth weight was 3,415 g (7.8 pounds) at low elevations and 3,133 g (7.1 pounds) at high elevations (Hass et al., 1980). Most studies of children have found that those at high elevations are shorter and lighter than those at low elevations.

In general, populations in cold climates tend to be heavier and have longer trunks and shorter extremities than populations in tropical areas. This reflects Bergmann's and Allen's rules. Exposure to sunlight also appears to have an effect on growth, most likely through its effects on vitamin D production. Children tend to grow more rapidly in times of high sunlight concentration (i.e., in the summer in temperate regions and in the dry season in monsoonal tropical regions). Vitamin D, necessary for skeletal growth, requires sunlight for its synthesis.

The influences of environmental, genetic, and biocultural factors (which, when taken together, produce evolution and adaptation) on such traits as body proportions and skin color illustrate the fundamental concepts of this chapter. For example, body size and proportions are affected not just by genetic factors (as they govern hormone production, etc.), but also by diet, disease, and exposure to sunlight. These three elements are in turn affected by cultural practices and the natural environment. Moreover, it is important to consider that all these factors interact with one another through a number of physiological and behavioral mechanisms to produce human variation and adaptation.

SUMMARY

In this chapter, we have explored a seemingly wide array of topics, all of which are related to evolutionary aspects of variation, adaptation, growth, and development in modern humans. We investigated some of the ways in which humans differ from one another, both within and between populations. We explored how this variation has been approached in terms of racial typologies and as a function of adaptation to a number of environmental factors, including solar radiation, heat, cold, and high altitude. We have also briefly looked at the role of infectious disease in human adaptation.

This chapter has also reviewed the fundamental concepts of growth and development and how these processes occur within the contexts of both biology and culture. Diet has an important effect on growth, and human nutritional needs themselves result from biological and biocultural evolution.

The topics of human variation and growth and development are complex, and the biological and cultural factors that have contributed to that variation, and con-

tinue to influence it, are manifold. But it is from an explicitly evolutionary perspective—that is, through the investigation of changes in allele frequencies in response to environmental conditions—that we will continue to elucidate the diverse adaptive potential that characterizes our species. Likewise, we can fully understand the nutritional needs of our own species only through an appreciation of the dietary habits and adaptations of our prehominid ancestors. Equally important in this regard are the many biocultural factors that have been critical both before and after the adoption of agriculture.

QUESTIONS FOR REVIEW

1. What is a polytypic species?
2. What is biological determinism?
3. What was the eugenics movement, and what were its goals?
4. How did eighteenth- and nineteenth-century European scientists deal with human phenotypic variation?
5. What is homeostasis?
6. Under what conditions might light skin color be adaptive? Under what conditions might dark skin color be adaptive?
7. What physiological adjustments do humans show in coping with cold stress?
8. What physiological adjustments do humans show in coping with heat stress?
9. What do body size and shape have to do with adaptation to climate?
10. What are Bergmann's and Allen's rules?
11. How has infectious disease influenced human evolution?
12. How has susceptibility to HIV been shown to vary between populations? What genetic and biological factors have led to this variation?
13. What is sexual dimorphism? List some examples in humans.
14. Briefly describe human brain growth.
15. What are essential amino acids? Develop a scenario for how our need for these amino acids might have evolved.
16. Describe human diets before the development of agriculture. How do they differ from human diets today?
17. What factors, in addition to nutrition, affect growth?

SUGGESTED FURTHER READING

Bodmer, W. F., and L. L. Cavalli-Sforza. 1976. *Genetics, Evolution and Man*. San Francisco: Freeman.

Bogin, Barry. 1988. *Patterns of Human Growth*. Cambridge: Cambridge University Press.

Cohen, Mark Nathan. 1989. *Health and the Rise of Civilization*. New Haven: Yale University Press.

Diamond, Jared. 1992. *The Third Chimpanzee: The Evolution and Future of the Human Animal*. New York: Harper Collins.

Discover. 1994. Special Issue: The Science of Race, 15 (November).

Eaton, S. Boyd, Marjorie Shostak, and Melvin Konner. 1988. *The Paleolithic Prescription*. New York: Harper & Row.

Gould, Stephen Jay. 1981. *The Mismeasure of Man*. New York: Norton.

Jacoby, R., and N. Glauberman (eds.). 1995. *The Bell Curve Debate*. New York: Times Books.

Journal of the American Medical Association. 1996. Entire issue, 275 (January 17). (Numerous articles pertaining to climate change and reemergence of infectious diseases.)

Leffell, David J., and Douglas E. Brash. 1996. "Sunlight and Skin Cancer." *Scientific American* 275(1): 52–59.

Nesse, Randolph M., and George C. Williams. 1998. "Evolution and the Origins of Disease." *Scientific American* 279(5): 86–93.

Plomin, Robert, and John C. DeFries. 1998. "The Genetics of Cognitive Abilities and Disabilities." *Scientific American* 278(5): 62–69.

Ramenofsky, Ann F. 1992. "Death by Disease." *Archaeology* 45(2): 47–49.

Sinclair, D. 1989. *Human Growth After Birth*. New York: Oxford University Press.

Tanner, James M. 1990. *Foetus into Man: Physical Growth from Conception to Maturity*. 2nd ed. Cambridge, MA: Harvard University Press.

Trevathan, Wenda R. 1987. *Human Birth: An Evolutionary Perspective*. Hawthorne, NY: Aldine de Gruyter.

RESOURCES ON THE INTERNET

Wadsworth Anthropology Resource Center
http://anthropology.wadsworth.com

The companion website for this text includes a range of enrichment material focused on the chapter's topic. While online you can enhance your understanding of the chapter by exploring one of the several additional Internet Exercises, by researching topics, and by accessing full articles on InfoTrac College Edition. You can also reinforce the concepts by taking online practice exams.

Internet Exercises

Both the American Anthropological Association (AAA) and the American Association of Physical Anthropologists (AAPA) have issued policy statements on the subject of *race*. Go to the AAA home page (**http://www.aaanet.org/**) and, on the side bar, click on the search option, and conduct a search for *race*. Read the AAA statement, then go to the AAPA Web site at **http://www.physanth.org/** and read the statement entitled, *Biological Aspects of Race*. Write a short summary of the two statements showing how they are similar and also how they differ.

InfoTrac College Edition
http://www.infotrac-college.com/wadsworth

InfoTrac College Edition provides many articles about eugenics and its effects on public policy. Search for *eugenics*, and read at least one article. A number of issues are raised by these articles. Write a one-page discussion of these issues. You should also address how eugenics has affected politics and public policy.

Paleopathology: Diseases and Injuries of Bone

In Chapter 4, we discussed microevolutionary processes acting on contemporary humans. An important component of such studies relates to an understanding of the role of *disease* as it has influenced adaptations in *Homo sapiens*. This topic will also be a major focus of our discussion in the next chapter. Indeed, in the last few thousand years especially, infectious disease has likely been the single most important selective influence on recent human populations.

Some of the most significant biocultural adaptive shifts occurred with the development of agriculture. We have already noted in Chapter 4 some of the biocultural dynamics that influenced the spread of the sickle-cell allele over the last 2,000 years.

In the study of human disease, how do we obtain some time depth, thus extending our perspective back from strictly contemporary contexts? The primary source of information relating to the relative recent history of disease (i.e., over the last few thousand years) comes from skeletons. Archaeological skeletal material provides evidence on a variety of pathological conditions, making it possible to expand our knowledge both *through time* and *across space*

to include a wide array of different human populations. In this way, physical anthropologists and archaeologists working together maximize the clear advantages of an anthropological perspective.

The branch of physical anthropology that studies injury and disease in earlier populations is called *paleopathology*. Within this subdiscipline, anthropologists, often working with medical specialists, contribute to our knowledge of the history and geographical distribution of human diseases such as rheumatoid arthritis, tuberculosis, and syphilis. In addition, patterns of disease and trauma in specific groups can further illuminate how these peoples were affected by various environmental and cultural factors.

In most cases, paleopathologists work exclusively with skeletonized specimens. Occasionally, however, under unusual circumstances, soft tissues—such as skin, hair, cartilage, or even internal organs—may also be preserved. For example, artificial mummification was practiced in ancient Egypt and Chile, and natural mummification may also occur in extremely dry and/or cold climates (such as in the American Southwest, parts of North Africa, and Peru).

FIGURE 1
Naturally mummified tissue on a cranium from Nubia (part of the modern country of the Sudan; c. A.D. 700–1400).

Lynn Kilgore

Paleopathology: Diseases and Injuries of Bone (continued)

In addition, in permanently wet environments such as bogs, where bacterial action is forestalled, soft tissues can endure. For example, there are the famous bog bodies discovered in Denmark and England. In such circumstances, preservation may be quite extraordinary.

One major category of pathological process that leaves its mark on bone is trauma. Injuries in ancient human populations may be manifested in the skeleton as fractures (which frequently are well healed), dislocations, or wounds (e.g., from projectile points).

FIGURE 3
Embedded piece of obsidian projectile point in a lumbar vertebra from a central California male, 25 to 40 years old. The portion being held was found with the burial and may have been retained during life in soft tissue (muscle?). The injury shows some healing.

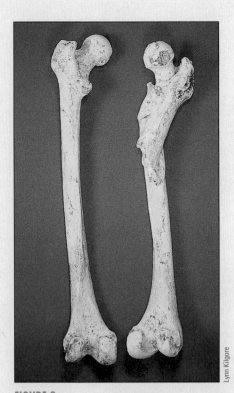

FIGURE 2
Fracture of a right femur (thigh bone) seen from the rear. (The normal left femur is shown for comparison.) Such an injury is extremely severe, even life threatening, but in this individual the bone healed remarkably well although it was poorly aligned.

FIGURE 4
Unfused portion along the midline of a sacrum from a central California male, 16 to 18 years old. This condition, called spina bifida occulta, is a fairly common, genetically influenced, asymptomatic condition.

Other categories of skeletal abnormality include those that are *congenital* (present at birth) and *hereditary* (genetically determined). Rarely in skeletal collections are severe hereditary maladies (such as dwarfism) clearly diagnostic. More commonly, modifications are subtle and probably asymptomatic (i.e., not producing symptoms).

Tumors are another category of bone pathology, and, very rarely, malignant, life-threatening conditions can reliably be diagnosed from skeletal remains. (Usually, conditions such as lung or colon cancer kill the person *before* the skeleton becomes involved.)

A very common condition seen in all skeletal populations is degenerative arthritis. Bone changes

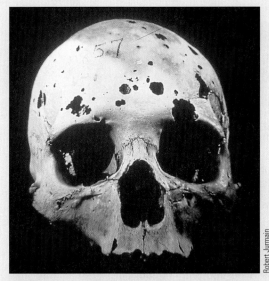

Robert Jurmain

FIGURE 5
Numerous lesions of the cranium (such erosive lesions were also found in other bones), probably the result of a disseminated (metastasized) cancer, possibly originating from the breast, shown here in an Inuit female.

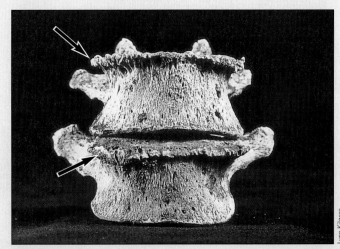

Lynn Kilgore

FIGURE 6
Bony lipping around the margins of two lumbar vertebrae (see arrows).

Paleopathology: Diseases and Injuries of Bone (continued)

are most visible around the margins of vertebral body surfaces or are either peripheral to the margins or on the articular surfaces of appendicular joints (such as the knee).

In common conditions such as arthritis (seen in all human groups), the most informative approach is to compare *frequencies* of involvement in different populations. Such an approach is called *paleoepi-*

demiology and is best controlled when the study samples are partitioned by sex and age (the latter is especially important in age-related diseases, such as arthritis).

Because infectious disease has been such an important selective factor in human evolution and adaptation, it is an important disease category for paleopathological inquiry. Unfortunately, many infec-

Lynn Kilgore

FIGURE 7
Extreme degenerative arthritis of a knee joint in an adult female from Nubia.

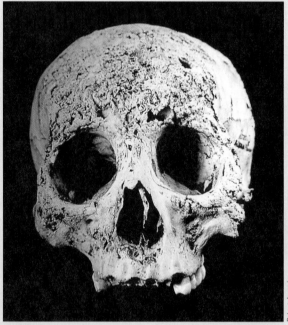

Robert Jurmain

FIGURE 9
Extreme reaction in a cranium from an Alaskan Inuit (Eskimo), diagnostic of syphilis (although other possibilities must be considered).

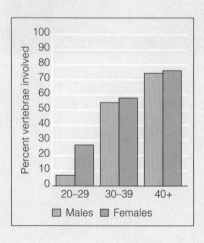

FIGURE 8
Bar graph showing incidence of vertebral body arthritis (osteophytosis), controlling for age and sex. The frequencies shown here are for a medieval Nubian population, and such information can be compared with data from other groups.

116

tious processes do not leave evidence in bone, because affected individuals either recover or die before bone tissue becomes involved. But some conditions, such as syphilis or tuberculosis, occasionally produce bone reaction. Interpretation of such processes in skeletons from varied geographical and chronological contexts provides some of the best biological data regarding the history of significant human diseases.

In recent years, the techniques of DNA fingerprinting have been added to the arsenal of tools to be used in the identification of infectious disease in archaeological populations. Perhaps the most

FIGURE 10
Probable case of tuberculosis, as seen in the thoracic vertebrae of an individual from Pueblo Bonito, New Mexico. As the disease progresses, one or more vertebrae can collapse (see arrow), producing a severe forward angulation of the spine.

FIGURE 11
Dr. Wilmar Salo (left) and Dr. Arthur Aufderheide (right) examine DNA fingerprints obtained by PCR. From this analysis these researchers were the first to obtain such clear molecular evidence of tuberculosis in the pre-Columbian New World.

117

Paleopathology: Diseases and Injuries of Bone (continued)

successful of these investigations to date has been the recovery of a segment of DNA that is unique to *Mycobacterium tuberculosis*, the bacterium that causes tuberculosis, from a 1,000-year-old mummy from Peru. This discovery, which would have been impossible without the use of PCR amplification techniques, has provided the most definitive evidence to date for the existence of tuberculosis in the New World prior to European contact.

Probably the most common conditions seen in ancient human groups are those that affect the teeth. In some groups, abrasive diets (and perhaps use of the teeth as tools) resulted in severe wear throughout the dentition.

Other types of dental lesions include caries (popularly called "cavities"), abscesses, loss of teeth (with resorbed sockets and loss of bone in the jaws), and improperly erupted teeth.

Courtesy, Arthur Aufderheide

FIGURE 12
Lung tissue from which *Mycobacterium tuberculosis* DNA samples were taken.

Robert Jurmain

FIGURE 13
Severe dental wear in the upper jaw (maxilla) of a central California male, 30+ years old. There is almost no enamel left on most of the teeth.

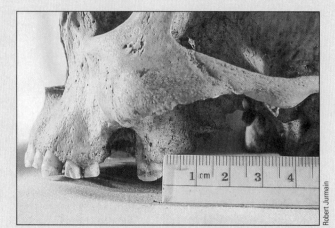

Robert Jurmain

FIGURE 14
Severe abscess in the maxilla of a California Indian male, 31 to 40 years old. Despite the degree of bone reaction, such lesions can be asymptomatic.

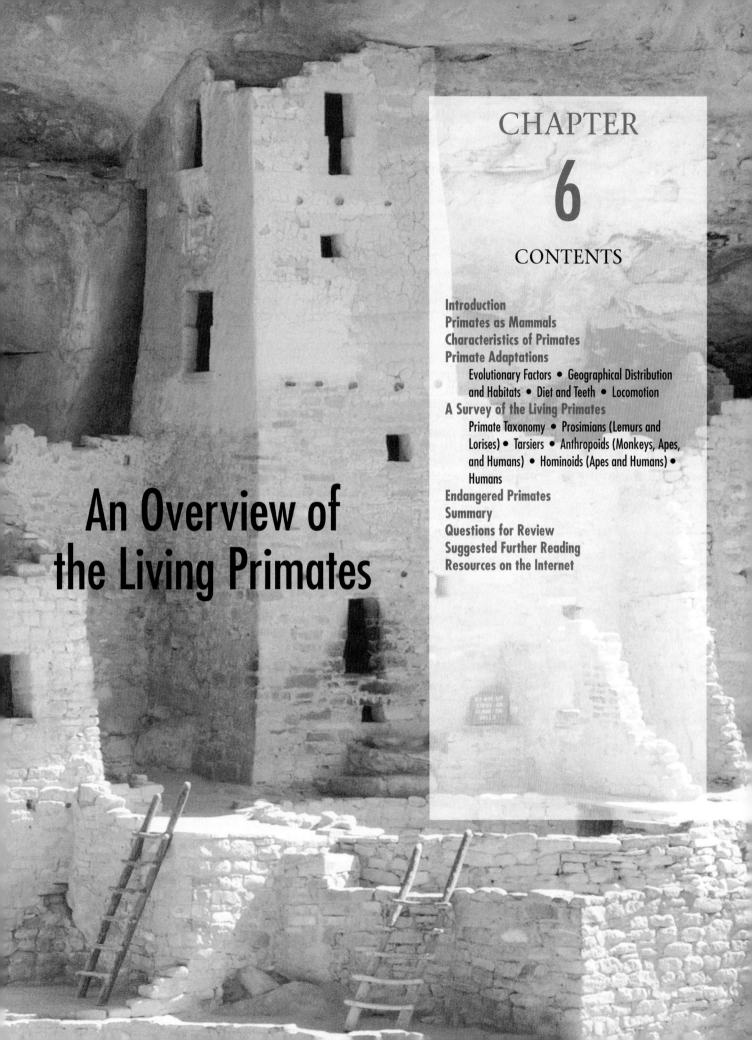

CHAPTER

6

CONTENTS

An Overview of
the Living Primates

See the following sections of the CD-ROM for topics covered in this chapter: Virtual Lab 1, sections II and III; Virtual Labs 3 and 4.

Prosimians
Members of a suborder of Primates, the *Prosimii* (pronounced "pro-sim´-ee-eye"). Traditionally, the suborder includes lemurs, lorises, and tarsiers.

Anthropoids
Members of a suborder of Primates, the *Anthropoidea* (pronounced "ann-throw-poid´-ee-uh"). Traditionally, the suborder includes monkeys, apes, and humans.

Mammalia
The technical term for the formal grouping (class) of mammals.

Introduction

Thus far, we have presented the basic biological background for understanding human evolution. The remainder of this textbook is devoted to explaining what it is to be human—that is, the kind of animal we are and how we got to be this way.

Evolution has produced a continuum of life forms, as demonstrated genetically, anatomically, and behaviorally. To gain an understanding of any organism, it is necessary, whenever possible, to compare its anatomy and behavior with those of other, closely related forms. This comparative approach helps elucidate the significance of physiological and behavioral systems as adaptive responses to various selective pressures throughout the course of evolution. This statement applies to *Homo sapiens* just as surely as to any other species, and if we are to identify the components that have shaped hominid evolution, the starting point must be a systematic comparison between humans and our closest living relatives, the approximately 190 species of nonhuman primates (**prosimians**, monkeys, and apes). This chapter describes the physical characteristics that define the order Primates, gives a brief overview of the major groups of living primates, and introduces some methods of comparing living primates through genetic data. (For a detailed comparison of human and nonhuman skeletons, see Appendix A.) This chapter and the one that follows concentrate on various anatomical and behavioral features that characterize primates.

Before proceeding further, we must call attention to a few common misunderstandings about evolutionary processes. Evolution is not a goal-directed process; thus, the fact that prosimians evolved before **anthropoids** does not mean that prosimians "progressed," or "advanced," to become anthropoids. Living primate species are in no way "superior" to their evolutionary predecessors or to one another. Consequently, in discussions of major groupings of contemporary nonhuman primates, there is no implied superiority or inferiority of any of these groups. Each grouping (lineage, or species) has come to possess unique qualities that make it better suited than others to a particular habitat and lifestyle. Given that all contemporary organisms are "successful" results of the evolutionary process, it is best to avoid altogether the use of such loaded terms as "superior" and "inferior."

Finally, you should not make the mistake of thinking that contemporary primates (including humans) necessarily represent the final stage or apex of a lineage. Remember, the only species that represent final evolutionary stages of particular lineages are those that become extinct.

Primates as Mammals

The order *Primates* is a subgroup of a larger group of organisms, the mammals (technically, the class **Mammalia**). Today there are over 4,000 species of mammals, which can be further subdivided into three major subgroups: (1) the egg-laying mammals, (2) the pouched mammals (i.e., marsupials), and (3) the placental mammals. We will discuss mammalian evolution in more detail in Chapter 8. For the moment, you should recognize that primates are members of the placental subgroup, by far the most common of living mammals (and including other common orders such as rodents and carnivores). Placental mammals today are distributed over most of the world in a wide variety of forms. In fact, biologists recognize more than 20 orders of mammals, including flying, swimming, and burrowing varieties and a host of other adaptations as well. Sizes range from the tiny dwarf shrews (just a few grams) to the whales, the largest animals ever to inhabit the earth.

Characteristics of Primates

All primates possess numerous characteristics they share in common with other placental mammals. Such traits include body hair; a relatively long gestation period followed by live birth; mammary glands (thus the term *mammal*); different types of teeth; the ability to maintain a constant internal body temperature through physiological means (*homeothermy*); increased brain size; and a considerable capacity for learning and behavioral flexibility. Therefore, to differentiate primates, as a group, from other mammals, we must describe those characteristics that, taken together, set primates apart from other mammalian groups.

This is not a simple task, for among mammals, primates have remained quite *generalized*. That is, primates have retained many **primitive** mammalian traits that some other mammalian species have lost over time. In response to particular selective pressures, many mammalian groups have become increasingly **specialized**. For example, through the course of evolution, horses and cattle have undergone a reduction of the number of digits (fingers and toes) from the primitive pattern of five to one and two, respectively. Moreover, these species have developed hard, protective coverings over their feet in the form of hooves. While this type of limb structure is adaptive in prey species, whose survival depends on speed and stability, it restricts the animal to only one type of locomotion. Moreover, limb function is limited entirely to support and movement, while the ability to manipulate objects is completely lost.

Primates, precisely because they are *not* so specialized, cannot be simply defined by one or even two traits they share in common. As a result, biologists have pointed to a group of characteristics that, taken together, more or less characterize the entire order. Keep in mind that these are a set of *general* tendencies and are not all equally expressed in all primates. Indeed, this is what we would expect in a diverse group of generalized animals. Moreover, while some of these traits are unique to primates, many others are retained primitive mammalian characteristics. These latter are useful in contrasting the generalized primates with the more specialized varieties of other placental mammals.

Thus, the following list is intended to give an overall structural and behavioral picture of that kind of animal we call "primate," focusing on those characteristics that tend to set primates apart from other mammals. Concentrating on certain retained (ancestral) mammalian traits, along with more specific ones, has been the traditional approach of **primatologists**. Some contemporary primatologists (Fleagle, 1999) feel that it is useful to enumerate all these features to better illustrate primate adaptations. Thus, a common evolutionary history with adaptations to similar environmental challenges is seen to be reflected in the limbs and locomotion, teeth and diet, senses, brain, and behaviors of those animals that make up the primate order.

A. *Limbs and Locomotion*
  1. *A tendency toward erect posture (especially in the upper body).* Shown to some degree in all primates, this tendency is variously associated with sitting, leaping, standing, and, occasionally, bipedal walking.
  2. *A flexible, generalized limb structure, permitting most primates to engage in a number of locomotor behaviors.* Primates have retained some bones (e.g., the clavicle, or collarbone) and certain abilities, (e.g., rotation of the forearm) that have been lost in some more specialized mammals. Various aspects of hip and shoulder **morphology** also provide primates with a wide range of limb movement and function. Thus, by maintaining a generalized locomotor anatomy, primates are not restricted to one form of movement, as are many other mammals. Primate limbs are also used for activities other than locomotion.
  3. *Hands and feet with a high degree of **prehensility** (grasping ability).* All primates use the hands, and frequently the feet, to grasp and manipulate objects (Fig. 6–1). This capability is variably expressed and is enhanced by a number of characteristics, including:
     a. *Retention of five digits on hands and feet.* This varies somewhat throughout the order, with some species showing marked reduction of the thumb or of the second digit.

Primitive
Referring to a trait or combination of traits present in an ancestral form.

Specialized
Evolved for a particular function; usually refers to a specific trait (e.g., incisor teeth), but may also refer to the entire way of life of an organism.

Primatologists
Scientists who study the evolution, anatomy, and behavior of nonhuman primates. Those who study behavior in noncaptive animals are usually trained as physical anthropologists.

Morphology
The form (shape, size) of anatomical structures; can also refer to the entire organism.

Prehensility
Grasping, as by the hands and feet of primates.

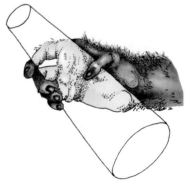

FIGURE 6–1
Primate (macaque) hand.

 Virtual Lab 1, section II, presents a discussion of the characteristics typically used to define primates.

Omnivorous
Having a diet consisting of many food types (i.e., plant materials, meat, and insects).

Diurnal
Active during the day.

Nocturnal
Active during the night.

Stereoscopic vision
The condition whereby visual images are, to varying degrees, superimposed on one another. This provides for depth perception, or the perception of the external environment in three dimensions. Stereoscopic vision is partly a function of structures in the brain.

Binocular vision
Vision characterized by overlapping visual fields provided by forward-facing eyes; essential to depth perception.

   b. *An opposable thumb and, in most species, a divergent and partially opposable big toe.* Most primates are capable of moving the thumb so that it comes in contact (in some fashion) with the second digit or the palm of the hand.

   c. *Nails instead of claws.* This characteristic is seen in all primates except some New World monkeys. Some prosimians also possess a claw on one digit.

   d. *Tactile pads enriched with sensory nerve fibers at the ends of digits.* This trend serves to enhance the sense of touch.

B. *Diet and Teeth*

  1. *Lack of dietary specialization.* This is typical of most primates, who tend to eat a wide assortment of food items.

  2. *A generalized dentition.* The teeth are not specialized for processing only one type of food, a pattern correlated with the lack of dietary specialization. In general, primates are **omnivorous**.

C. *The senses and the brain.* Primates (**diurnal** ones in particular) rely heavily on the visual sense and less on the sense of smell, especially compared to many other mammals. This emphasis is reflected in evolutionary changes in the skull, eyes, and brain.

  1. *Color vision.* This is characteristic of all diurnal primates. **Nocturnal** primates lack color vision.

  2. *Depth perception.* **Stereoscopic vision**, or the ability to perceive objects in three dimensions, is made possible through a variety of mechanisms, including:

   a. *Eyes positioned toward the front of the face (not to the sides).* This configuration provides for overlapping visual fields, or **binocular vision** (Fig. 6–2).

   b. *Visual information from each eye transmitted to visual centers in both hemispheres of the brain.* In nonprimate mammals, most optic nerve fibers cross to the opposite hemisphere through a structure at the base of the brain. In primates, about 40 percent of the fibers remain on the same side (see Fig. 6–2).

   c. *Visual information organized into three-dimensional images by specialized structures in the brain itself.* The capacity for stereoscopic vision is dependent on each hemisphere of the brain having received visual information from both eyes and from overlapping visual fields.

  3. *Decreased reliance on the sense of smell (olfaction).* This trend is seen in an overall reduction in the size of olfactory structures in the brain. Corresponding reduction of the entire olfactory apparatus has also resulted in decreased size of the snout (Fig. 6–3). (In some species, such as baboons, the large muzzle is not related to olfaction, but to the presence of large teeth, especially the canines.)

  4. *Expansion and increased complexity of the brain.* This is a general trend among placental mammals, but it is especially true of primates. In primates, this expansion is most evident in the visual and association areas of the neocortex (portions of the brain where information from different sensory modalities is integrated). Expansion in regions involved with the hand (both sensory and motor) is seen in many species, particularly humans.

D. *Maturation, learning, and behavior*

  1. *A more efficient means of fetal nourishment, longer periods of gestation, reduced numbers of offspring (with single births the norm), delayed maturation, and extension of the entire life span.*

  2. *A greater dependence on flexible, learned behavior.* This trend is correlated with delayed maturation and consequently longer periods of infant and child dependency on the parent. As a result of both these trends, parental invest-

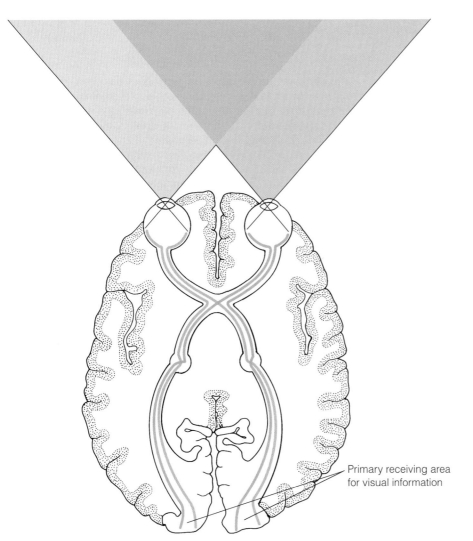

FIGURE 6–2
Simplified diagram showing overlapping visual fields (binocular vision) in primates (and some predators) with eyes positioned at the front of the face. (The green shaded area represents the area of overlap.) Stereoscopic vision (three-dimensional vision) is provided in part by binocular vision and in part by the transmission of visual stimuli from each eye to *both* hemispheres of the brain. (In nonprimate mammals, most, if not all, visual information crosses over to the hemisphere opposite the eye in which it was initially received.)

Primary receiving area
for visual information

FIGURE 6–3 (below)
The skull of a gibbon, a small-bodied ape (left), compared to that of a red wolf (right). Note the forward-facing eye orbits of the gibbon and the eye orbits placed more to the side in the wolf. Also, in the gibbon, the proportional size of the snout is smaller than in the wolf.

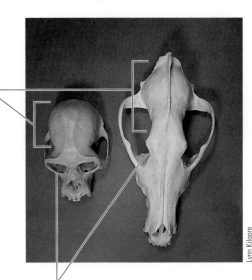

Braincase

Eye socket

ment in each offspring is increased, so that although fewer offspring are born, they receive more intense and efficient rearing.

3. *The tendency to live in social groups and the permanent association of adult males with the group.* Except for some nocturnal forms, primates tend to associate with other individuals. The permanent association of adult males with the group is uncommon in mammals but widespread in primates.

4. *The tendency to diurnal activity patterns.* This is seen in most primates; only one monkey species and some prosimians are nocturnal.

Primate Adaptations

Evolutionary Factors

Traditionally, the suite of characteristics shared by primates has been explained as the result of adaptation to **arboreal** living. While other placental mammals were adapting to various ground-dwelling lifestyles and even marine environments, the primates found their **adaptive niche** in the trees. Indeed, some other mammals were also adapting to arboreal living, but while many of these species nested in trees, they continued to come to the ground to forage for food. But throughout the course of evolution, primates came increasingly to exploit foods (leaves, seeds, fruits, nuts, insects, and small mammals) found in the branches themselves. The exploitation of these varied foods enhanced the general trend toward *omnivory* in primates and toward the primate generalized dentition.

We can also see this adaptive process reflected in the primate reliance on vision. In a complex, three-dimensional environment with uncertain footholds, acute color vision with depth perception is extremely beneficial. The presence of grasping hands and feet is also an indicator of the adaptation to living in the trees. Climbing can be accomplished by either digging in with claws (as in many species, such as squirrels or raccoons) or grasping around branches with prehensile hands and feet. Primates adopted this latter strategy, which allowed a means of moving about, sometimes very rapidly, on small, unstable surfaces, and grasping abilities were further enhanced by the appearance of flattened nails instead of claws.

An alternative to this traditional **arboreal hypothesis**, called the *visual predation hypothesis* (Cartmill, 1972, 1992), acknowledges that forward-facing eyes are characteristic not only of primates, but also of predators, such as cats and owls, that prey on small animals. Cartmill points out that the most significant primate trends (forward-facing eyes, grasping hands and feet, and the presence of nails instead of claws) may *not* have arisen as adaptive advantages in a purely arboreal environment. According to the visual predation hypothesis, primates may first have adapted to shrubby forest undergrowth and the lowest tiers of the forest canopy, where they exploited insects and other small prey that they captured primarily through stealth.

A third scenario (Sussman, 1991) proposes that the basic primate traits developed in conjunction with another major evolutionary occurrence, the rise of the *angiosperms* (flowering plants). Flowering plants provided numerous resources, including nectar, seeds, and fruits, and their appearance and diversification were accompanied by the appearance of ancestral forms of major groups of modern birds and mammals. Sussman argues that visual predation is not common among modern primates and that forward-facing eyes, grasping extremities, and omnivory may have arisen in response to the demand for fine visual and tactile discrimination, necessary when feeding on small food items such as fruits, berries, and seeds among branches and stems.

These hypotheses are not mutually exclusive. The complex of primate characteristics might well have begun in nonarboreal settings and certainly may have been stimulated by the new econiches provided by evolving angiosperms. But one thing is certain. At some point, the primates did take to the trees, and that is where the vast majority of nonhuman primates still live today. Whereas the basic primate structural complexes may have been adapted for visual predation and/or omnivory in shrubby undergrowth and terminal branches, they became ideally suited for the arboreal adaptations that followed. We would say, then, that the early primates were "preadapted" for arboreal living and that those early adaptations have served them long and well in the trees.

Geographical Distribution and Habitats

With just a couple of exceptions, primates are found in tropical or semitropical areas of the New and Old Worlds. In the New World, these areas include southern

Arboreal
Tree-living; adapted to life in the trees.

Adaptive niche
The entire way of life of an organism: where it lives, what it eats, how it gets food, how it avoids predators, etc.

Arboreal hypothesis
The traditional view that primate characteristics can be explained as a consequence of primate diversification into arboreal habitats.

Mexico, Central America, and parts of South America. Old World primates are found in Africa, India, Southeast Asia (including numerous islands), and Japan (Fig. 6–4 on pp. 126–127).

The majority of primates are, as we have discussed, mostly arboreal and live in forest or woodland habitats. However, some Old World monkeys (e.g., baboons) have, to varying degrees, adapted to life on the ground in areas where trees are sparsely distributed. Moreover, among the apes, gorillas and chimpanzees spend a considerable amount of time on the ground in forested and wooded habitats. Nevertheless, no nonhuman primate is adapted to a fully terrestrial lifestyle, and all spend some time in the trees.

Diet and Teeth

As noted, primates are generally *omnivorous*. Indeed, the tendency toward omnivory is one example of the overall lack of specialization in primates. Although the majority of primate species tend to emphasize some food items over others, most eat a combination of fruit, leaves and other plant materials, and insects. Many obtain animal protein from birds and amphibians as well. Some (baboons and especially chimpanzees) occasionally kill and eat small mammals, including other primates. Others, such as African colobus monkeys and the leaf-eating monkeys (langurs) of India and Southeast Asia, have become more specialized and subsist primarily on leaves. Such an array of choices is highly adaptive even in fairly predictable environments.

Like the majority of other mammals, most primates have four kinds of teeth: incisors and canines for biting and cutting and premolars and molars for chewing. Biologists use a device called a *dental formula* to describe the number of each type of tooth that typifies a species. A dental formula indicates the number of each tooth type in each quadrant of the mouth (Fig. 6–5). For example, all Old World *anthropoids* have two incisors, one canine, two premolars, and three molars on each side of the **midline** in both the upper and lower jaws, or a total of 32 teeth. This is represented as a dental formula of

$$\frac{2.1.2.3.}{2.1.2.3.} \text{ (upper)} \atop \text{(lower)}$$

The dental formula for a generalized placental mammal is 3.1.4.3. (three incisors, one canine, four premolars, and three molars). Primates have fewer teeth than this ancestral pattern because there has been a general evolutionary trend toward reduction of the number of teeth in many mammal groups. Consequently, the number of each type of tooth varies between lineages. For example, in the majority of New World monkeys, the dental formula is 2.1.3.3. (two incisors, one canine, three premolars, and three molars).

Correlated with an overall lack of dietary specialization in primates is a lack of specialization with regard to the size and shape of the teeth because tooth form is directly related to diet. For example, carnivores typically have premolars and molars with high pointed **cusps** adapted for tearing meat, while the premolars of herbivores, such as cattle and horses, have broad, flat surfaces suited to chewing tough grasses and other plant materials. Most primates possess premolars and molars that have low, rounded cusps, a molar morphology that enables them to process most types of foods. Thus, throughout their evolutionary history, the primates have developed a dentition adapted to a varied diet, and the capacity to exploit many foods has contributed to their overall success during the last 50 million years.

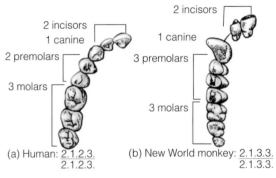

2 incisors
1 canine
2 premolars
3 molars

(a) Human: 2.1.2.3.
2.1.2.3.

2 incisors
1 canine
3 premolars
3 molars

(b) New World monkey: 2.1.3.3.
2.1.3.3.

FIGURE 6–5
Dental formulae. The number of each kind of tooth is given for one-quarter of the mouth.

Midline
An anatomical term referring to a hypothetical line that divides the body into right and left halves.

Cusps
The elevated portions (bumps) on the chewing surfaces of premolar and molar teeth.

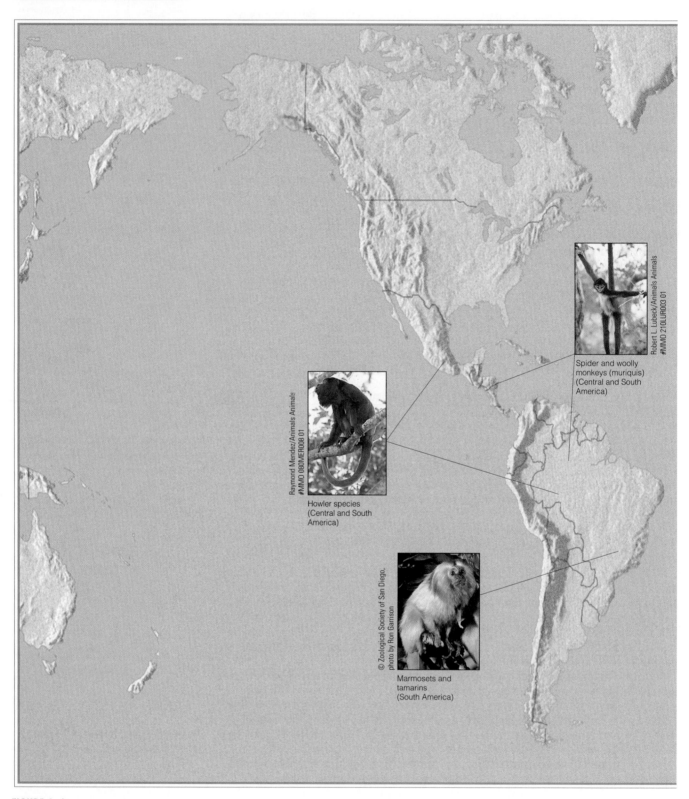

FIGURE 6–4
Geographical distribution of living nonhuman primates. Much original habitat is now very fragmented.

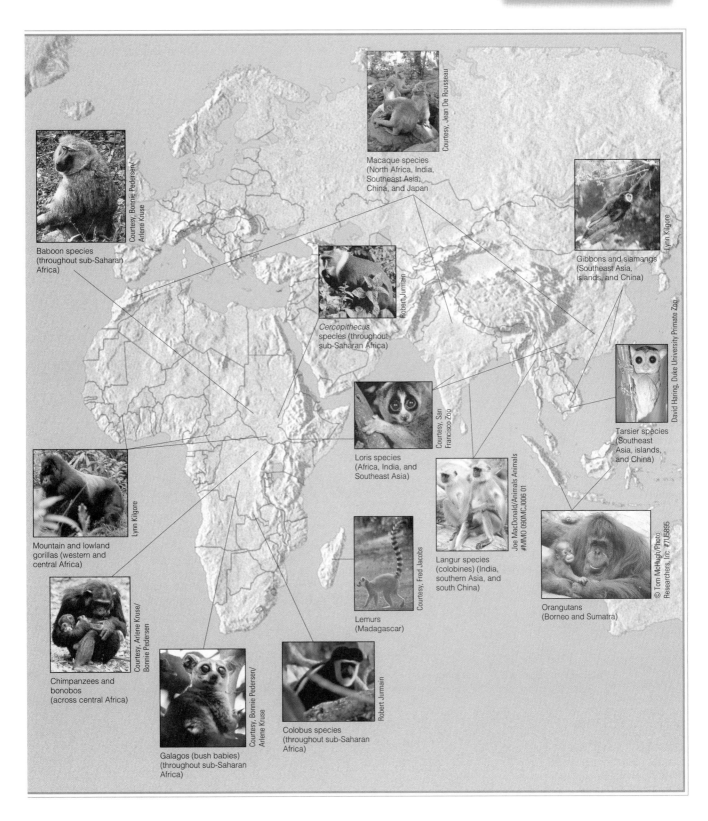

Macaque species
(North Africa, India,
Southeast Asia,
China, and Japan)

Courtesy, Jean De Rousseau

Baboon species
(throughout sub-Saharan
Africa)

Courtesy, Bonnie Pedersen/
Arlene Kruse

Gibbons and siamangs
(Southeast Asia,
islands, and China)

Lynn Kilgore

Cercopithecus
species (throughout
sub-Saharan Africa)

Robert Jurmain

Loris species
(Africa, India, and
Southeast Asia)

Courtesy, San
Francisco Zoo

Tarsier species
(Southeast
Asia, islands,
and China)

David Haring, Duke University Primate Zoo

Mountain and lowland
gorillas (western and
central Africa)

Lynn Kilgore

Langur species
(colobines) (India,
southern Asia, and
south China)

Joe MacDonald/Animals Animals
#MMO 090MCJ006 01

Orangutans
(Borneo and Sumatra)

© Tom McHugh/Photo
Researchers, Inc; #7U5895

Chimpanzees and
bonobos
(across central Africa)

Courtesy, Arlene Kruse/
Bonnie Pedersen

Lemurs
(Madagascar)

Courtesy, Fred Jacobs

Galagos (bush babies)
(throughout sub-Saharan
Africa)

Courtesy, Bonnie Pedersen/
Arlene Kruse

Colobus species
(throughout sub-Saharan
Africa)

Robert Jurmain

Locomotion

Quadrupedal
Using all four limbs to support the body during locomotion; the basic mammalian (and primate) form of locomotion.

Macaques
(muh-kaks´) Group of Old World monkeys comprising several species, including rhesus monkeys.

FIGURE 6–6a–d
Differences in skeletal anatomy and limb proportions reflect differences in locomotor patterns. (Redrawn from original art by Stephen Nash. In John G. Fleagle, *Primate Adaptation and Evolution*, 1988, 1999. New York: Academic Press.)

 Discussions of primate locomotion are provided in Virtual Labs 3 and 4.

Almost all primates are, at least to some degree, **quadrupedal**, meaning they use all four limbs to support the body during locomotion. However, to describe most primate species in terms of only one or even two forms of locomotion would be to overlook the wide variety of methods they may use to move about. Many primates employ more than one form of locomotion, and they owe this important ability to their generalized structure.

Although the majority of quadrupedal primates are arboreal, terrestrial quadrupedalism is fairly common and is displayed by some lemurs, baboons, and **macaques**. Typically, the limbs of terrestrial quadrupeds are approximately of equal length, with forelimbs being 90 percent (or more) as long as hind limbs (Fig. 6–6a).

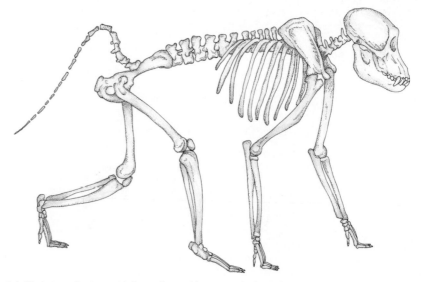

(a) Skeleton of a terrestrial quadruped (savanna baboon).

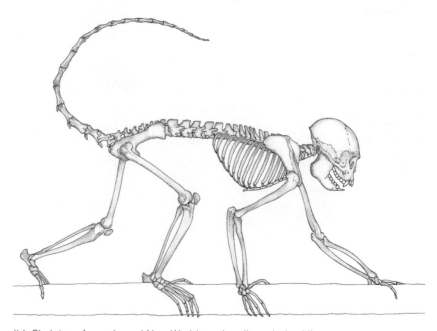

(b) Skeleton of an arboreal New World monkey (bearded saki).

In arboreal quadrupeds, forelimbs are shorter and may be only 70 to 80 percent as long as hind limbs (Fig. 6–6b).

Quadrupeds are also characterized by a relatively long and flexible *lumbar spine* (lower back). This lumbar flexibility permits the animal to bend the body during running, thus positioning the hind limbs and feet well forward under the body and enhancing their ability to propel the animal forward. (Watch for this the next time you see slow-motion footage of cheetahs or lions on television.)

Another form of locomotion is *vertical clinging and leaping*, seen in many prosimians. As the term implies, vertical clingers and leapers support themselves vertically by grasping onto trunks of trees while their knees and ankles are tightly flexed (Fig. 6–6c). Forceful extension of their long hind limbs allows them to spring powerfully away in either a forward or backward direction. Once in midair, the body rotates so that the animal lands feet first on the next vertical support.

Yet another type of primate locomotion is **brachiation**, or arm swinging, where the body is alternatively supported under either forelimb. Because of anatomical modifications at the shoulder joint, apes and humans are capable of true brachiation. However, only the small gibbons and siamangs of Southeast Asia use this form of locomotion almost exclusively (Fig. 6–6d).

Brachiation is seen in species characterized by arms longer than legs, a short stable lumbar spine, long curved fingers, and reduced thumbs. Because these are traits seen in all the apes, it is believed that although none of the great apes (orang-utans, gorillas, and chimpanzees) habitually brachiates today, they most likely inherited these characteristics from brachiating or perhaps climbing ancestors.

Brachiation
A form of locomotion in which the body is suspended beneath the hands and support is alternated from one forelimb to the other; arm swinging.

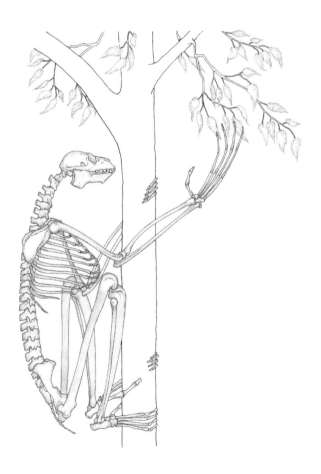

(c) Skeleton of a vertical clinger and leaper (indri).

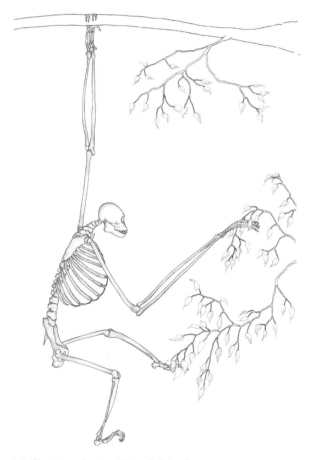

(d) Skeleton of a brachiator (gibbon).

Some monkeys, particularly New World monkeys, are termed *semibrachiators*, as they practice a combination of leaping with some arm swinging. In a few New World species, arm swinging and other suspensory behaviors are enhanced by use of a *prehensile tail*, which in effect serves as a marvelously effective grasping fifth "hand." It should be noted that prehensile tails are strictly a New World phenomenon and are not seen in any Old World primate species.

A Survey of the Living Primates

Primate Taxonomy

An interactive discussion of primate taxonomy is presented in Virtual Lab 1, section II.

The living primates are commonly categorized into their respective subgroups as shown in Figure 6–7. This taxonomy is based on the system originally established by Linnaeus. (Remember that the primate order, which includes a diverse array of approximately 190 species, belongs to a larger group, the class *Mammalia*.)

In any taxonomic system, organisms are organized into increasingly specific categories. For example, the order *Primates* includes *all* primates. However, at the next level down—the *suborder*—the primates have conventionally been divided into two large categories, Prosimii (all the prosimians: lemurs, lorises, and, customarily, the tarsiers) and Anthropoidea (all the monkeys, apes, and humans). Therefore, the suborder distinction is more specific and more precise than the order.

At the level of the suborder, the prosimians are distinct as a group from all the other primates, and this classification makes the biological and evolutionary statement that all the prosimian species are more closely related to one another than they are to any of the anthropoids. Likewise, all anthropoid species are more closely related to one another than to the prosimians.

At each succeeding level (infraorder, superfamily, family, subfamily, genus, and species), finer distinctions are made between categories until, at the species level, only those animals that can interbreed and produce viable offspring are included. In this manner, taxonomies not only organize diversity into categories, but also illustrate evolutionary and genetic relationships between species and groups of species.

The taxonomy presented in Figure 6–7 is the traditional one and is based on physical similarities between species and lineages. However, this technique can be problematic. For example, two primate species that superficially resemble each other (e.g., some New and Old World monkeys) may in fact not be closely related at all. Using external morphology alone overlooks the unknown effects of separate evolutionary history. But evidence such as biochemical data avoids these pitfalls and indeed shows Old and New World monkeys to be genetically and evolutionarily quite distinct.

This relatively new perspective has enormous potential for clarifying taxonomic problems by making between-species comparisons of chromosomes and amino acid sequences in proteins. Direct comparisons of proteins (products of DNA) are excellent indicators of shared evolutionary history. If two primate species are similar with regard to protein structure, we know that their DNA sequences are also similar. It also follows that if two species share similar DNA, it is highly probable that both inherited their blueprint from a common ancestor.

Detailed comparisons of protein structure can be achieved by isolating the amino acid sequences. Comparisons between humans and the African great apes for the approximately half dozen proteins analyzed in this manner show striking similarities: They are either identical or show a difference of only one or two amino acids in the entire sequence.

Another technique called DNA hybridization matches DNA strands from two species to determine what percentage of bases match. The higher the percentage, the closer the genetic relationship between the two. The results of this technique show that 98.4 percent of the human and chimpanzee DNA base sequences examined are identical.

FIGURE 6–7
Primate taxonomic classification. This abbreviated taxonomy illustrates how primates are grouped into increasingly specific categories. Only the more general categories are shown, except for the great apes and humans.

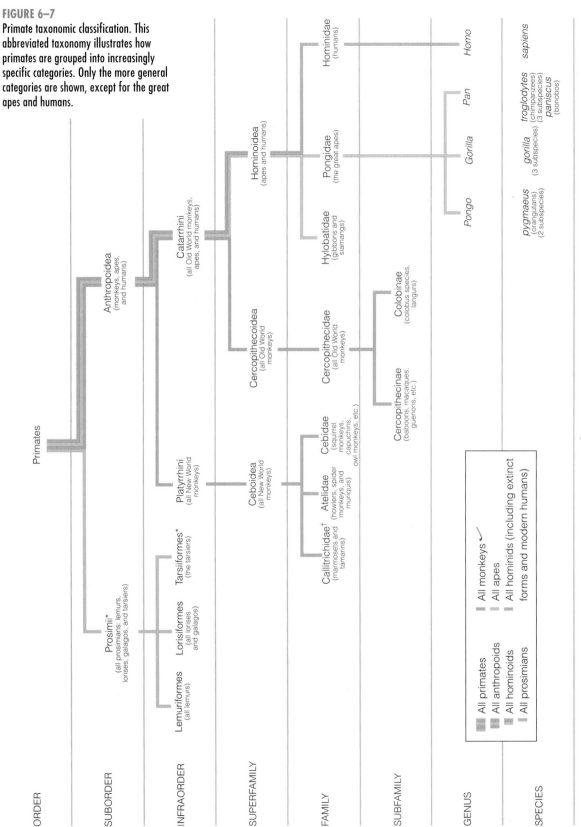

*There is some disagreement among primatologists concerning where to place tarsiers. Many researchers suggest that they more properly belong closer to the anthropoids and thus revise the primate classification to reflect this view. Here, for simplicity, we continue to use the traditional classifications.

†Fleagle (1999) and others have recently eliminated the family Callitrichidae and included marmosets and tamarins in the family Cebidae.

As useful as they are, these techniques are *indirect* methods of examining the DNA code. But today there are procedures that make it possible to sequence the nucleotides *directly* from the DNA molecule. However, the technologies of *DNA sequencing* used in the Human Genome Project (see p. 62) have not been extensively used to compare the DNA of nonhuman species. But there is strong support for such research, and once this approach is more widely applied, it will be possible to ascertain even more clearly the precise genetic and evolutionary relationships among the primates (McConkey and Vavki, 2000).

At present, amino acid sequencing and DNA hybridization, as well as other techniques, have reaffirmed the basic tenets of traditional primate classification. Moreover, they have shown how genetically close humans and the African great apes are. A systematic application of DNA hybridization (Sibley and Ahlquist, 1984) demonstrated that humans and chimpanzees are closer genetically than either is to the gorilla. For that matter, chimpanzees and humans share more genetic similarities than do zebras and horses or goats and sheep. On the basis of these results, it would be entirely consistent to classify humans and chimpanzees (perhaps gorillas as well) within the same genus. Humans would continue to be called *Homo sapiens*, whereas chimpanzees would be classed as *Homo troglodytes*.

We have presented the traditional system of primate classification here, even though we acknowledge the need for modification. At present, not all anthropologists and biologists have completely accepted the revised terminology. Until consensus is reached and new designations are formally adopted, we think it appropriate to use the standard taxonomy along with discussion of some proposed changes. It is also important to point out that while specific details and names have not yet been worked out, the vast majority of experts do accept the evolutionary implications of the revised groupings.

Another area where modifications have been suggested concerns tarsiers. Tarsiers are highly specialized animals that display several unique physical characteristics. Because they possess a number of prosimian traits, tarsiers traditionally have been classified as prosimians (with lemurs and lorises); but they also share certain anthropoid features. Moreover, biochemically, tarsiers are more closely related to anthropoids than to prosimians (Dene et al., 1976); but with regard to chromosomes and several anatomical traits, they are distinct from both groups.

Today, most primatologists recognize tarsiers as more closely related to anthropoids than to prosimians. But instead of simply moving them into the suborder Anthropoidea, one proposed scheme places lemurs and lorises in a new suborder, Strepsirhini (instead of Prosimii), and includes tarsiers with monkeys, apes, and humans in another new suborder, Haplorhini (Szalay and Delson, 1979) (Fig. 6–8). Thus, in this classification, the conventionally named suborders Prosimii and Anthropoidea are replaced by Strepsirhini and Haplorhini, respectively. As yet, this designation has not been universally accepted, but the terminology has become common, especially in technical publications.

Prosimians (Lemurs and Lorises)

The most primitive of the primates are the lemurs and lorises. (We do not include tarsiers here, because their status is not as clear.) By "primitive" we mean that prosimians, taken as a group, are more similar anatomically to their earlier mam-

FIGURE 6–8
Revised partial classification of the primates. In this system, the terms *Prosimii* and *Anthropoidea* have been replaced by *Strepsirhini* and *Haplorhini*, respectively. The tarsier is included in the same suborder with monkeys, apes, and humans to reflect a closer relationship with these forms than with lemurs and lorises. (Compare with Fig. 6–7.)

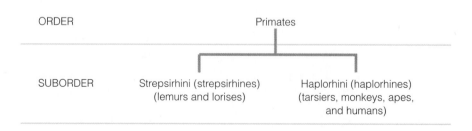

malian ancestors than are the other primates (monkeys, apes, and humans). Therefore, they tend to exhibit certain more ancestral characteristics, such as a more pronounced reliance on *olfaction* (sense of smell). Their greater olfactory capabilities (compared to other primates) are reflected in the presence of a moist, fleshy pad (**rhinarium**) at the end of the nose and in a relatively long snout. Moreover, prosimians mark territories with scent in a manner not seen in many other primates.

There are numerous other characteristics that distinguish lemurs and lorises from the anthropoids, including somewhat more laterally placed eyes, differences in reproductive physiology, and shorter gestation and maturation periods. Lemurs and lorises also possess a dental specialization known as the "dental comb." The dental comb is formed by forward-projecting lower incisors and canines, and together these modified teeth are used in both grooming and feeding (Fig. 6–9). One other characteristic that sets lemurs and lorises apart from anthropoids is the retention of a claw (called a "grooming claw") on the second toe.

Lemurs   Lemurs are found only on the island of Madagascar and adjacent islands off the east coast of Africa (Fig. 6–10). As the only nonhuman primates on Madagascar, which comprises some 227,000 square miles, lemurs diversified into numerous and varied ecological niches without competition from monkeys and apes. Thus, while lemurs became extinct elsewhere, the 22 surviving species of Madagascar represent an evolutionary pattern that has vanished elsewhere.

Lemurs range in size from the small mouse lemur, with a body length (head and trunk) of only 5 inches, to the indri, with a body length of a little over 2 feet (Napier and Napier, 1985). While the larger lemurs are diurnal and exploit a wide variety of dietary items, such as leaves, fruit, buds, bark, and shoots, the smaller forms (mouse and dwarf lemurs) are nocturnal and insectivorous.

Lemurs display considerable variation regarding numerous other aspects of behavior. While many are primarily arboreal, others, such as the ring-tailed lemur (Fig. 6–11), are more terrestrial. Some arboreal species are quadrupeds, and others (sifakas and indris) are vertical clingers and leapers (Fig. 6–12). Socially, several species (e.g., ring-tailed lemurs and sifakas) are gregarious and live in groups of 10 to 25 animals composed of males and females of all ages. Others (the indris) live in monogamous family units, and several nocturnal forms are mostly solitary.

Lorises   Lorises (Fig. 6–13), which are similar in appearance to lemurs, were able to survive in mainland areas by adopting a nocturnal activity pattern at a time when most other prosimians became extinct. In this way, they were (and are) able to avoid competition with more recently evolved primates (the diurnal monkeys).

Rhinarium
(rine-air´-ee-um) The moist, hairless pad at the end of the nose seen in most mammalian species. The rhinarium enhances an animal's ability to smell.

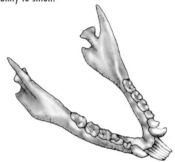

FIGURE 6–9
Prosimian dental comb, formed by forward-projecting incisors and canines.

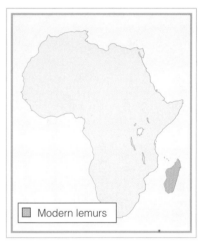

Modern lemurs

FIGURE 6–10
Geographical distribution of modern lemurs.

Courtesy, Fred Jacobs

FIGURE 6–11
Ring-tailed lemur.

Courtesy, Fred Jacobs

FIGURE 6–12
Sifakas in their native habitat in Madagascar.

FIGURE 6–13
Slow loris.

FIGURE 6–14
Galago, or "bush baby."

FIGURE 6–15
Tarsier.

FIGURE 6–16
Geographical distribution of tarsiers.

There are at least eight loris species, all of which are found in tropical forest and woodland habitats of India, Sri Lanka, Southeast Asia, and Africa. Also included in the same general category are six to nine (Bearder, 1987) galago species (Fig. 6–14), which are widely distributed throughout most of the forested and woodland savanna areas of sub-Saharan Africa.

Locomotion in lorises is a slow, cautious climbing form of quadrupedalism, and flexible hip joints permit suspension by hind limbs while the hands are used in feeding. All galagos, however, are highly agile and active vertical clingers and leapers. Some lorises and galagos are almost entirely insectivorous; others supplement their diet with various combinations of fruit, leaves, gums, and slugs. Lorises and galagos frequently forage for food alone (females leave infants behind in nests until they are older). However, ranges overlap, and two or more females occasionally forage together or share the same sleeping nest.

Lemurs and lorises represent the same general adaptive level. Both groups exhibit good grasping and climbing abilities and a fairly well developed visual apparatus, although vision is not completely stereoscopic, and color vision may not be as well developed as in anthropoids. Most lemurs and lorises also have prolonged life spans as compared to most other small-bodied mammals, averaging about 14 years for lorises and 19 years for lemurs.

Tarsiers

There are three recognized species of tarsier (Fig. 6–15), all restricted to island areas in Southeast Asia (Fig. 6–16), where they inhabit a wide range of forest types, from tropical forest to backyard gardens. Tarsiers are nocturnal insectivores, leaping onto prey (which may also include small vertebrates) from lower branches and shrubs. They appear to form stable pair bonds, and the basic tarsier social unit is a mated pair and their young offspring (MacKinnon and MacKinnon, 1980).

As we have already mentioned, tarsiers present a complex blend of characteristics not seen in other primates. Moreover, they are unique in that their enormous eyes, which dominate much of the face, are immobile within their sockets. To compensate for this inability to move the eyes, tarsiers are able to rotate their heads 180° in a decidedly owl-like manner.

Anthropoids (Monkeys, Apes, and Humans)

Although there is much variation among anthropoids, there are certain features that, when taken together, distinguish them as a group from prosimians (and other placental mammals). Here is a partial list of these traits:

1. Generally larger body size
2. Larger brain (in absolute terms and relative to body weight)

3. Reduced reliance on the sense of smell, indicated by absence of rhinarium and other structures
4. Increased reliance on vision, with forward-facing eyes placed at front of face
5. Greater degree of color vision
6. Back of eye socket formed by a bony plate
7. Blood supply to brain different from that of prosimians
8. Fusion of the two sides of the mandible at the midline to form one bone (in prosimians and tarsiers they are joined by fibrous tissue)
9. Less specialized dentition, as seen in absence of dental comb and some other features
10. Differences with regard to female internal reproductive anatomy
11. Longer gestation and maturation periods
12. Increased parental care
13. More mutual grooming

Approximately 70 percent of all primates (about 130 species) are monkeys. It is frequently impossible to give precise numbers of species because the taxonomic status of some primates remains in doubt, and primatologists are still making new discoveries. Monkeys are divided into two groups separated by geographical area (New World and Old World), as well as by several million years of separate evolutionary history.

New World Monkeys The New World monkeys exhibit a wide range of size, diet, and ecological adaptation. In size, they vary from the tiny marmosets and tamarins (about 12 ounces) to the 20-pound howler monkey (Figs. 6–17 and 6–18). New World monkeys are almost exclusively arboreal, and some never come to the ground. Like Old World monkeys, all except one species (the douroucouli, or owl monkey) are diurnal. Although confined to the trees, New World monkeys can be found in a wide range of arboreal environments throughout most forested areas in southern Mexico and Central and South America (Fig. 6–19).

One of the characteristics distinguishing New World monkeys from those found in the Old World is shape of the nose. New World forms have broad noses with outward-facing nostrils. Conversely, Old World monkeys have narrower noses with downward-facing nostrils. This difference in nose form has given rise to the terms *platyrrhine* (flat-nosed) and *catarrhine* (downward-facing nose) to refer to New and Old World anthropoids, respectively.

© Zoological Society of San Diego, photo by Ron Garrison

FIGURE 6–17
A pair of golden lion tamarins.

Raymond Mendez/Animals Animals #MMO 080MER008 01

FIGURE 6–18
Howler monkeys.

EQUATOR

☐ New World monkeys

FIGURE 6–19
Geographical distribution of modern New World monkeys.

Callitrichidae
(kal-eh-trick´-eh-dee)

Cebidae
(see´-bid-ee)

Robert L. Lubeck/Animals Animals #MMO 210LUR003 01

FIGURE 6–20
Spider monkey. Note the prehensile tail.

New World monkeys have traditionally been divided into two families: **Callitrichidae** (marmosets and tamarins) and **Cebidae** (all others). Some authors have suggested that molecular data along with recently reported fossil evidence indicate that a major regrouping of New World monkeys is in order (Fleagle, 1999).*

Marmosets and tamarins are the most primitive of monkeys, retaining claws instead of nails and usually giving birth to twins instead of one infant. They are mostly insectivorous, although marmoset diet includes gums from trees, and tamarins also rely heavily on fruit. Locomotion is quadrupedal, and their claws aid in climbing vertical tree trunks, much in the manner of squirrels. Moreover, some tamarins employ vertical clinging and leaping as a form of travel. Socially, these small monkeys live in family groups composed usually of a mated pair, or a female and two adult males, and their offspring. Indeed, marmosets and tamarins are among the few primate species in which males are heavily involved in infant care.

There are at least 30 cebid species ranging in size from the squirrel monkey (body length 12 inches) to the howler (body length 24 inches). Diet varies, with most relying on a combination of fruit and leaves supplemented, to varying degrees, by insects. Most cebids are quadrupedal, but some—for example, the spider monkey (Fig. 6–20)—are semibrachiators. Some cebids, including the spider and howler, also possess powerful prehensile tails that are used not only in locomotion but also for suspension under branches while feeding on leaves and fruit. Socially, most cebids are found either in groups of both sexes and all age categories or in monogamous pairs with subadult offspring.

Old World Monkeys   The monkeys of the Old World display more morphological and behavioral diversity than is seen in New World monkeys. Except for humans, Old World monkeys are the most widely distributed of all living primates. They are found throughout sub-Saharan Africa and southern Asia, ranging from tropical jungle habitats to semiarid desert and even to seasonally snow-covered areas in northern Japan (Fig. 6–21).

FIGURE 6–21
Geographical distribution of modern Old World monkeys.

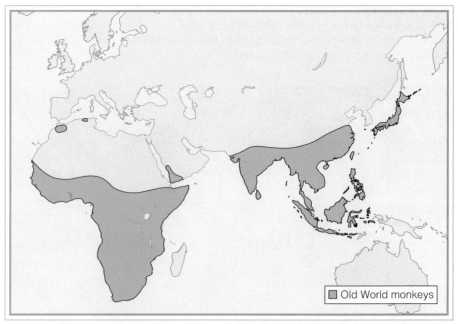

Old World monkeys

---

*One possibility is to include spider monkeys, howler monkeys, and muriquis (woolly spider monkeys) in a third family, Atelidae (see taxonomic chart, p. 131). Another is to eliminate the family Callitrichidae altogether and include marmosets and tamarins as a subfamily within the family Cebidae.

Most Old World monkeys are quadrupedal and primarily arboreal, but some (e.g., baboons) are also adapted to life on the ground. Whether in trees or on the ground, these monkeys spend a good deal of time sleeping, feeding, and grooming while sitting with their upper bodies held erect. Usually associated with this universal sitting posture are areas of hardened skin on the buttocks (**ischial callosities**) that serve as sitting pads.

Within the entire group of Old World monkeys there is only one recognized taxonomic family: **Cercopithecidae**. This family, in turn, is divided into two subfamilies: the **cercopithecines** and **colobines**.

The cercopithecines are the more generalized of the two groups, showing a more omnivorous dietary adaptation and distinctive cheek pouches for storing food. As a group, the cercopithecines eat almost anything, including fruit, seeds, leaves, grasses, tubers, roots, nuts, insects, birds' eggs, amphibians, small reptiles, and small mammals (the last seen in baboons).

The majority of cercopithecine species, such as the mostly arboreal guenons (Fig. 6–22) and the more terrestrial savanna (Fig. 6–23) and hamadryas baboons are found in Africa. However, the several species of macaque, which include the well-known rhesus monkey, are widely distributed in southern Asia and India.

Colobine species are more limited dietarily, specializing on mature leaves, a behavior that has led to their designation as "leaf-eating monkeys." The colobines are found mainly in Asia, but both the red colobus and the black-and-white colobus are exclusively African (Fig. 6–24). Other colobines include several species of Asian langur and the proboscis monkey of Borneo.

Ischial callosities
Patches of tough, hard skin on the buttocks of Old World monkeys and chimpanzees.

Cercopithecidae
(serk-oh-pith´-eh-sid-ee)

Cercopithecines
(serk-oh-pith´-eh-seens) The subfamily of Old World monkeys that includes baboons, macaques, and guenons.

Colobines
(kole´-uh-beans) The subfamily of Old World monkeys that includes the African colobus monkeys and Asian langurs.

FIGURE 6–22
Adult male sykes monkey, one of several guenon species.

Robert Jurmain

(a)

(b)

Courtesy, Bonnie Pedersen/Arlene Kruse

Courtesy, Bonnie Pedersen/Arlene Kruse

FIGURE 6–23
Savanna baboons. (a) Male. (b) Female.

FIGURE 6–24
Black-and-white colobus monkey.

Robert Jurmain

Sexual dimorphism
Differences in physical characteristics between males and females of the same species. For example, humans are slightly sexually dimorphic for body size, with males being taller, on average, than females of the same population.

Estrus
(ess´-truss) Period of sexual receptivity in female mammals (except humans), correlated with ovulation. When used as an adjective, the word is spelled "estrous."

Hominoidea
The formal designation for the superfamily of anthropoids that includes apes and humans.

Hylobatidae
(high-lo-baht´-id-ee)

Pongidae
(ponj´-id-ee)

Locomotor behavior among Old World monkeys includes arboreal quadrupedalism in guenons, macaques, and langurs; terrestrial quadrupedalism in baboons, patas, and macaques; and semibrachiation and acrobatic leaping in colobus monkeys.

Marked differences in body size or shape between the sexes, referred to as **sexual dimorphism**, are typical of some terrestrial species and are particularly pronounced in baboons and patas. In these species, male body weight (up to 80 pounds in baboons) may be twice that of females.

Females of several species (especially baboons and some macaques) exhibit pronounced cyclical changes of the external genitalia. These changes, including swelling and redness, are associated with **estrus**, a hormonally initiated period of sexual receptivity in female nonhuman mammals correlated with ovulation.

Several types of social organization characterize Old World monkeys, and there are uncertainties among primatologists regarding some species. In general, colobines tend to live in small groups, with only one or two adult males. Savanna baboons and most macaque species are found in large social units comprising several adults of both sexes and offspring of all ages. Monogamous pairing is not common in Old World monkeys, but is seen in a few langurs and possibly one or two guenon species.

Hominoids (Apes and Humans)

The other large grouping of anthropoids, the hominoids, includes apes and humans. The superfamily **Hominoidea** includes the "lesser" apes in the family **Hylobatidae** (gibbons and siamangs); the great apes in the family **Pongidae** (orangutans, gorillas, bonobos, and chimpanzees); and humans in the family Hominidae.

Apes and humans differ from monkeys in numerous ways:

1. Generally larger body size, except for gibbons and siamangs
2. Absence of a tail
3. Shortened trunk (lumbar area shorter and more stable)
4. Differences in position and musculature of the shoulder joint (adapted for suspensory locomotion)
5. More complex behavior
6. More complex brain and enhanced cognitive abilities
7. Increased period of infant development and dependency

Gibbons and Siamangs   The eight gibbon species and the closely related siamang are today found in the southeastern tropical areas of Asia (Fig. 6–25). These animals are the smallest of the apes, with a long, slender body weighing 13 pounds in the gibbon (Fig. 6–26) and 25 pounds in the larger siamang.

The most distinctive structural feature of gibbons and siamangs is related to an adaptation for brachiation. They have extremely long arms, long, permanently curved fingers, short thumbs, and powerful shoulder muscles. These highly specialized locomotor adaptations may be related to feeding behavior while hanging beneath branches. The diet of both species is largely composed of fruit. Both (especially the siamang) also eat a variety of leaves, flowers, and insects.

The basic social unit of gibbons and siamangs is the monogamous pair with dependent offspring. As in marmosets and tamarins, male gibbons and siamangs are very much involved in rearing their young. Both males and females are highly territorial and protect their territories with elaborate whoops and sirenlike "songs."

Orangutans   Orangutans (*Pongo pygmaeus*) (Fig. 6–27) are represented by two subspecies found today only in heavily forested areas on the Indonesian islands of Borneo and Sumatra (see Fig. 6–25). Due to poaching by humans and continuing habitat loss on both islands, orangutans are threatened by extinction in the wild.

Orangutans are slow, cautious climbers whose locomotor behavior can best be described as "four-handed," referring to the tendency to use all four limbs for grasping and support. Although they are almost completely arboreal, orangutans do sometimes travel quadrupedally on the ground. Orangutans are also very large animals with pronounced sexual dimorphism (males may weigh 200 pounds or more and females less than 100 pounds).

In the wild, orangutans lead largely solitary lives, although adult females are usually accompanied by one or two dependent offspring. They are primarily **frugivorous**, but bark, leaves, insects, and meat (on rare occasions) may also be eaten.

Gorillas   The largest of all living primates, gorillas (*Gorilla gorilla*) are today confined to forested areas of western and eastern equatorial Africa (Fig. 6–28). There are three generally recognized subspecies, although molecular data suggest that one of these, the western lowland gorilla (Fig. 6–29), is perhaps sufficiently genetically distinct to warrant designation as a separate species (Ruvolo et al., 1994; Garner and

FIGURE 6–25
Geographical distribution of modern Asian apes.

Lynn Kilgore

FIGURE 6–26
White-handed gibbon.

Frugivorous
(fru-give´-or-us) Having a diet composed primarily of fruit.

Robert Jurmain, photo by Jill Matsumoto/Jim Anderson

FIGURE 6–27
Female orangutan.

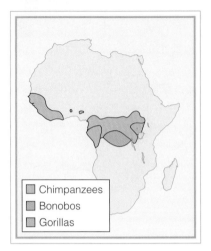

FIGURE 6–28
Geographical distribution of modern African apes.

Chimpanzees
Bonobos
Gorillas

FIGURE 6–29
Western lowland gorillas. (a) Male. (b) Female.

Ryder, 1996). The western lowland gorilla is found in several countries of western central Africa and is the most numerous of the three subspecies, with a population size of perhaps 110,000 (Doran and McNeilage, 1998). The eastern lowland gorilla is found near the eastern border of the Democratic Republic of the Congo (formerly Zaire) and numbers about 12,000. Mountain gorillas (Fig. 6–30), the most extensively studied of the three subspecies, are found in the mountainous areas of central Africa in Rwanda, the Democratic Republic of the Congo, and Uganda. Mountain gorillas have probably never been very numerous, and today they are among the more endangered primates, numbering only about 600.

Gorillas exhibit marked sexual dimorphism, with males weighing up to 400 pounds and females around 150 to 200 pounds. Because of their weight, adult gorillas, especially males, are primarily terrestrial and adopt a semiquadrupedal (knuckle-walking) posture on the ground.

Mountain gorillas live in groups consisting of one (or sometimes two) large *silverback* males, a variable number of adult females, and their subadult offspring. The

FIGURE 6–30
Mountain gorillas. (a) Male. (b) Female.

term *silverback* refers to the saddle of white hair across the back of full adult (at least 12 or 13 years of age) male gorillas. Additionally, the silverback male may tolerate the presence of one or more young adult *blackback* males, probably his sons. Typically, but not always, both females and males leave their natal group as young adults. Females join other groups, and males, who appear to be less likely to emigrate, may live alone for a while, or they may join an all-male group before eventually forming their own group.

Systematic studies of free-ranging western lowland gorillas were not initiated until the mid-1980s; thus, our knowledge of their social structure and behavior is still in its infancy. In general, it appears that their social structure is similar to that of mountain gorillas, but groups are smaller and somewhat less cohesive.

All gorillas are almost exclusively vegetarian. Mountain gorillas concentrate primarily on leaves, pith, and stalks. These foods are also important for western lowland gorillas, but western lowland gorillas also eat considerably more fruit, depending on seasonal availability. Recent studies also report that western lowland gorillas, unlike mountain gorillas (which avoid water), frequently wade through swamps while foraging on aquatic plants.

Perhaps because of their large body size and enormous strength, gorillas have long been considered ferocious monsters; but in reality, they are shy and gentle. This is not to imply that gorillas are never aggressive. Indeed, male-male competition for females can be extremely violent. Moreover, when threatened, males will attack, and they will certainly defend their group from any perceived danger, whether it be another male gorilla or a human hunter. Still, the reputation of gorillas as murderous beasts is the result of uninformed myth making and little else.

Chimpanzees   Chimpanzees are probably the best known of all nonhuman primates (Fig. 6–31). Often misunderstood because of zoo exhibits, circus acts, television shows, and movies, the true nature of chimpanzees did not become known until years of fieldwork with wild groups provided a reliable picture. Today, chimpanzees are found in equatorial Africa, stretching in a broad belt from the Atlantic Ocean in the west to Lake Tanganyika in the east. Their range, however, is patchy within this large geographical area, and with further habitat destruction, it is becoming even more so (see Fig. 6–28).

Chimpanzees are in many ways structurally similar to gorillas, with corresponding limb proportions and upper-body shape. This similarity is due to commonalities in locomotion when on the ground (quadrupedal knuckle walking). However, the ecological adaptations of chimpanzees and gorillas differ, with chimpanzees spending more time in the trees. Moreover, whereas gorillas are typically placid and quiet, chimpanzees are highly excitable, active, and noisy.

Chimpanzees are smaller than orangutans and gorillas, and although they are sexually dimorphic, sex differences are not as pronounced as in these other species. While male chimpanzees may weigh over 100 pounds, females may weigh at least 80.

In addition to quadrupedal knuckle walking, chimpanzees (particularly youngsters) may brachiate while in the trees. When on the ground, they frequently walk bipedally for short distances when carrying food or other objects. One adult male at Jane Goodall's study area in Tanzania frequently walked bipedally because one arm was paralyzed by polio (Goodall, 1986).

Chimpanzees eat an amazing variety of items, including fruit, leaves, insects, nuts, birds' eggs, berries, caterpillars, and small mammals. Moreover, both males and females occasionally take part in group hunting efforts to kill such small mammals as red colobus, young baboons, bushpigs, and antelope. When hunts are successful, the prey is shared by the group members.

Chimpanzees live in large, fluid communities of as many as 50 individuals or more. At the core of a chimpanzee community is a group of bonded males. Although relationships between them are not always peaceful or stable, these males nevertheless act as a group to defend their territory and are highly intolerant of unfamiliar chimpanzees, especially nongroup males.

(a)

(b)

FIGURE 6–31
Chimpanzees. (a) Male. (b) Female.

Even though chimpanzees are said to live in communities, there are few times, if any, when all members are together. Indeed, it is the nature of chimpanzees to come and go, so that the individuals they encounter vary from day to day. Moreover, adult females tend to forage either alone or in the company of their offspring. The latter foraging group could comprise several chimpanzees, as females with infants sometimes accompany their own mothers and their younger siblings. A female may also leave her community, either permanently to join another community or temporarily while she is in estrus. This behavioral pattern may reduce the risk of mating with close male relatives, because males apparently never leave the group in which they were born.

Chimpanzee social behavior is complex, and individuals form lifelong attachments with friends and relatives. Indeed, the bond between mothers and infants often remains strong until one or the other dies. This may be a considerable period, because some chimpanzees live into their mid-30s and a few into their 40s.

Bonobos Bonobos (*Pan paniscus*) are found only in an area south of the Zaire River in the Democratic Republic of the Congo (formerly Zaire) (see Fig. 6–28). Not officially recognized by European scientists until the 1920s, they remain among the least studied of the great apes. Although ongoing field studies have produced much information (Susman, 1984; Kano, 1992), research has been periodically hampered by political unrest. There are no accurate counts of bonobos, but their numbers are believed to be between 10,000 and 20,000 (IUCN, 1996), and these are threatened by human hunting, warfare, and habitat loss.

Because bonobos bear a strong resemblance to chimpanzees but are somewhat smaller, they have been called "pygmy chimpanzees." However, differences in body size alone are not sufficient to warrant this designation, and in fact, bonobos exhibit several anatomical and behavioral differences from chimpanzees. Physically, they have a more linear body build, longer legs relative to arms, a relatively smaller head, a dark face from birth, and tufts of hair at the side of the face (Fig. 6–32).

Bonobos are more arboreal than chimpanzees, and they appear to be less excitable and aggressive. While aggression is not unknown, it appears that physical violence both within and between groups is uncommon. Like chimpanzees, bonobos live in geographically based, fluid communities, and they exploit many of the same foods, including occasional meat derived from killing small mammals (Badrian and Malinky, 1984). But bonobo communities are not centered around a

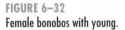
FIGURE 6–32
Female bonobos with young.

Courtesy, Ellen Ingmanson

group of closely bonded males. Rather, male-female bonding is more important than in chimpanzees (and most other nonhuman primates), and females are not as peripheral to the group (Badrian and Badrian, 1984). This may be related to bonobo sexuality, which differs in expression from that of other nonhuman primates in that copulation is frequent and occurs throughout a female's estrous cycle.

Bonobos are relatively late to arrive on the scene of primate research. But it is crucial that studies of this intriguing species be allowed to progress. Not only do bonobos have the potential of providing information about human behavior and evolution, but they are of considerable interest in their own right and they are highly endangered. In fact, without research and protection, they, like so many other nonhuman primates, are in danger of extinction.

Humans

Humans are the only living representatives of the family Hominidae (genus *Homo*, species *sapiens*). Our primate heritage is evident in our overall anatomy and genetic makeup and in many aspects of human behavior. With the exception of reduced canine size, human teeth are typical primate teeth; indeed, in overall morphology, they very much resemble ape teeth. The human dependence on vision and decreased reliance on olfaction, as well as flexible limbs and grasping hands, are rooted in our primate, arboreal past. Humans can even brachiate, and playgrounds often accommodate this ability in children.

Humans in general are omnivorous, although all societies observe certain culturally based dietary restrictions. Nevertheless, as a species with a rather generalized digestive system, we are physiologically adapted to digest an extremely wide assortment of foods. Perhaps to our detriment, given how humans tend to go to extremes, we also share with our relatives a fondness for sweets that originates from the importance of high-energy fruits in the diets of many nonhuman primates.

But quite obviously, humans are unique among primates and indeed among all animals. For example, no member of any other species has the ability to write or think about issues such as how they differ from other life forms. This ability is rooted in the fact that human evolution, during the last 800,000 years or so, has been characterized by dramatic increases in brain size and other neurological changes.

Humans are also completely dependent on culture. Without cultural innovation, it would have been impossible for us to have ever left the tropics. As it is, humans inhabit every corner of the planet with the exception of Antarctica, and we have even established outposts there. And lest we forget, a fortunate few have even walked on the moon. None of the technologies (indeed, none of the other aspects of culture) that humans have developed over the last several thousand years would have been possible without the highly developed cognitive abilities we alone possess. Nevertheless, the neurological basis for intelligence is something we share with other primates. Indeed, research has demonstrated that several nonhuman primate species—most notably chimpanzees, bonobos, and gorillas—display a level of problem solving and insight that most people would have considered impossible 25 years ago (see Chapter 7).

Humans are uniquely predisposed to use spoken language, and for the last 5,000 years or so, we have used written language as well. This ability exists because human evolution has modified certain neurological and anatomical structures in ways not observed in any other animal. But while nonhuman primates are not anatomically capable of producing speech, research has demonstrated that to varying degrees, the great apes are able to communicate through the use of symbols. And basically, that is a foundation for language that humans and the great apes (to a limited degree) have in common.

Aside from cognitive abilities, the one other trait that sets humans apart from other primates is our unique (among mammals) form of *habitual* bipedal locomotion. This particular trait appeared early in the evolution of our lineage, and over time, we have become more efficient at it because of related changes in the musculoskeletal anatomy of the pelvis, leg, and foot (see Chapter 10). But for whatever

Virtual Lab 1, section III, provides a contrast between the restricted geographical ranges of nonhuman primates versus that of humans.

143

reasons, early hominids increasingly adopted bipedalism because they were already preadapted for it. That is, as primates, and especially as apelike primates, they were already behaviorally predisposed to, and anatomically capable of, at least short-term bipedal walking before they adopted it wholeheartedly.

Thus, while it is certainly true that human beings are unique intellectually and in some ways anatomically, we are still primates. In fact, it is quite reasonable to say that fundamentally, humans are exaggerated primates.

Endangered Primates

In September 2000, scientists announced that a subspecies of red colobus, named Miss Waldron's red colobus, had officially been declared extinct. This announcement came after a six-year search for the 20-pound monkey that had not been seen for 20 years (Oates, 2000). Thus, this species, indigenous to the West African countries of Ghana and the Ivory Coast, has the distinction of being the first nonhuman primate to be declared extinct in the twenty-first century. But it will certainly not be the last. In fact, as of this writing, over half of all nonhuman primate species are now in jeopardy, and some face almost immediate extinction in the wild.

There are three basic reasons for the worldwide depletion of nonhuman primates: habitat destruction, hunting for food, and live capture for export or local trade. Underlying these three causes is one major factor: unprecedented human population growth, which is occurring at a faster rate in developing countries than in the developed world. The developing nations of Africa, Asia, and Central and South America are home to over 90 percent of all nonhuman primate species, and these countries, aided in no small part by the industrialized countries of Europe and the United States, are cutting their forests at a rate of about 30 million acres per year. In Brazil, the Atlantic rain forest originally covered some 385,000 square miles. Today, an estimated 7 percent is all that remains of what was once home to countless New World monkeys and thousands of other species.

Much of the motivation behind the devastation of the rain forests is, of course, economic: the short-term gains from clearing forests to create immediately available (but poor) farmland or ranchland; the use of trees for lumber and paper products; and large-scale mining operations (with their necessary roads, digging, etc., all of which cause habitat destruction). And, of course, the demand for tropical hardwoods (e.g., mahogany, teak, and rosewood) in the United States, Europe, and Japan creates an enormously profitable market for rain forest products.

Primates have also been captured live for zoos, biomedical research, and the exotic pet trade. Live capture has declined dramatically since the implementation of the Convention on Trade in Endangered Species of Wild Flora and Fauna (CITES) in 1973. Currently, 87 countries have signed this treaty, agreeing not to allow trade in species listed by CITES as being endangered. However, even some CITES members are still occasionally involved in the illegal primate trade (Japan and Belgium, among others).

In most areas, habitat loss has been, and continues to be, the single greatest cause of declining numbers of nonhuman primates. But in parts of western and central Africa, human hunting for food now poses an even greater threat. This tragic turn of events occurred rather quickly, but during the 1990s, primatologists became increasingly aware of the immense scope of the slaughter.

Wherever they occur, nonhuman primates have traditionally been an important source of food for people. In the past, subsistence hunting by indigenous peoples, armed with snares, bows and arrows, and other traditional weapons, did not usually constitute a serious threat to nonhuman primate populations, and certainly not to entire species. But increased demand for food by ever-growing numbers of people has combined with other factors to produce disastrous consequences. The construction of logging roads, mainly by French, German, and Belgian companies, has opened up vast tracts of forest that, until recently, offered sanctuary to thousands of animals. What has emerged is an unprecedented trade in "bush meat," a trade in which logging company employees participate along with local hunters. In contrast to hunters of the past, today's hunters are armed with automatic weapons, and they can wipe out an entire group of monkeys, gorillas, or chimpanzees in minutes. Consequently, the hunting of nonhuman primates, particularly in Africa, has shifted from being a subsistence activity to a commercial practice. Indeed, it is now common to see bush meat for sale in markets, where a monkey carcass can be bought for $5 and a dead gorilla for $40 (McRae, 1997). Most disturbingly, primate meat (including that of chimpanzees and gorillas) is served in restaurants not only in West Africa but reportedly in some Belgian and French restaurants as well (Fig. 6–33).

There are no accurate numbers, but it is estimated that each year, thousands of nonhuman primates are killed and sold for meat, as well as for commercial products such as skins and body parts. And, if animals other than primates are taken into account, an estimated 1 million metric tons of meat are taken annually from the forests of Africa.

Clearly, with the low reproductive rate characteristic of most nonhuman primates, and in the face of such massive slaughter, it is impossible for populations to sustain themselves. Some observers have likened the killing in parts of Africa to the slaying of the American bison in the nineteenth century (Strier, 1999), and unless the hunting stops, many primate species, certainly gorillas, chimpanzees and bonobos, could well be exterminated from central Africa by the year 2010.

But the problem extends well beyond Africa. As we previously mentioned, destruction of forests continues throughout the tropics at an unprecedented rate. And in South America, hunting nonhuman primates for food is also common. For example, one report documents that in less than two years, one family of Brazilian rubber tappers killed almost 500 members of various large-bodied species, including spider monkeys, woolly monkeys, and howler monkeys (Peres, 1990). Moreover, live capture and (illegal) trade in endangered primate species continues unabated in China and Southeast Asia, where nonhuman primates are eaten and also funneled into the exotic pet trade. Primate body parts also figure prominently in traditional medicines, and with increasing human population size, the demand for these products (and products from other, nonprimate species, such as tigers) has placed many species in jeopardy.

Fortunately, steps are being taken to ensure the survival of some species. Many developing countries, such as Costa Rica and the Malagasy Republic (Madagascar), are designating national parks and other reserves for the protection of natural resources, including primates. There are also now several private international efforts aimed at curbing the bush meat trade. It is only through such practices and through educational programs that many primate species have a chance of escaping extinction, at least in the immediate future.

If you are in your 20s or 30s, you will live to hear of the extinction of some of our marvelously unique and clever cousins. Many more will undoubtedly slip away unnoticed. Tragically, this will occur, in most cases, before we have even had the opportunity to get to know them.

Each species on earth is the current result of a unique set of evolutionary events that, over millions of years, has produced a finely adapted component of a diverse ecosystem. When it becomes extinct, that adaptation and that part of biodiversity is lost forever. What a tragedy it will be if, through our own mismanagement and greed, we awaken to a world without chimpanzees, mountain gorillas, or the tiny, exquisite lion tamarin. When this day comes, we truly will have lost a part of ourselves, and we will be the poorer for it.

Courtesy, J. Oates

FIGURE 6–33
Red-eared guenons (with red tails) and Preuss's guenons for sale in bushmeat market, Malabo, Equatorial Guinea.

SUMMARY

In this chapter, we have briefly introduced you to the primates, the mammalian order that includes humans. As a group, the primates are generalized in terms of diet and locomotor patterns, and these behavioral generalizations are reflected in the morphology of the teeth and limbs.

We have also discussed some of the anatomical similarities and differences between the major groupings of primates: prosimians, monkeys (New and Old World), and hominoids. In the next chapter, we will turn our attention to primate social behavior and cognitive abilities. These are extremely important topics, for it is through better understanding nonhuman primate behavior that we can make more general statements about human behavior. Moreover, increasing our knowledge is essential if we are to prevent many of these uniquely adapted and marvelous relatives of ours from being lost forever.

QUESTIONS FOR REVIEW

1. Discuss why primates are said to be "generalized mammals."
2. Summarize the major evolutionary trends that characterize the primate order.
3. How does adaptation to an arboreal environment help explain primate evolution?
4. What is the geographical distribution of the nonhuman primates?
5. What are the two major subdivisions of the order Primates?
6. Which major groups of primates are included within the anthropoids?
7. What is a dental formula? What is the dental formula of all the Old World anthropoids?
8. What are quadrupedalism, vertical clinging and leaping, and brachiation? Name at least one primate species that is characterized by each of these.
9. What are the major differences between prosimians and anthropoids?
10. What are at least three anatomical differences between monkeys and apes?
11. Name the two major categories (subfamilies) of Old World monkeys. In general, what is the geographical distribution of each?
12. Explain how a taxonomic classification scheme reflects biological relationships.
13. Where are lemurs and lorises found today?
14. In general, which primates have prehensile tails?
15. What are the two family divisions of New World monkeys? Name at least one species for each.
16. In which taxonomic family are the great apes placed?
17. Define estrus.
18. Describe the type of social organization seen in chimpanzees (*Pan troglodytes*) and gorillas.
19. How do bonobos (*Pan paniscus*) differ from "common" chimpanzees (*Pan troglodytes*)?

SUGGESTED FURTHER READING

Fleagle, John. 1999. *Primate Adaptation and Evolution*. New York: Academic Press.

Mittermeier, Russell A., Ian Tattersall, William R. Konstant, David M. Meyers, and Roderick B. Mast. 1994. *Lemurs of Madagascar*. Washington, DC: Conservation International.

Napier, J. R., and P. H. Napier. 1985. *The Natural History of the Primates*. Cambridge, MA: MIT Press.

Sussman, Robert W. 1991. "Primate Origins and the Evolution of the Angiosperms." *American Journal of Primatology* 23: 209–223.

RESOURCES ON THE INTERNET

 ## Wadsworth Anthropology Resource Center
http://anthropology.wadsworth.com

The companion website for this text includes a range of enrichment material focused on the chapter's topic. While online you can enhance your understanding of the chapter by exploring one of the several additional Internet Exercises, by researching topics, and by accessing full articles on InfoTrac College Edition. You can also reinforce the concepts by taking online practice exams.

Internet Exercises

Because many primate species are endangered, conservation is a major topic. To learn more about conservation, visit Primate Info Net (**www.primate.wisc.edu/ pin**). Click on "Resources in Primatology," then go to "Conservation," and choose one of the conservation links. Read the link and write a short summary. What species and its habitat is discussed at the link? What can we do, or what can you do, to improve the chances of survival for this species?

 ## InfoTrac College Edition
http://www.infotrac-college.com/wadsworth

Search InfoTrac College Edition for a nonhuman primate species. You will probably find more references if you search for *chimpanzee, gorilla, orangutan,* or *baboon*, but you need not limit your search to these. Does the article you found contain much of the information presented in Chapter 6? If so, list the topics the two share. Also list those topics not included in the chapter.

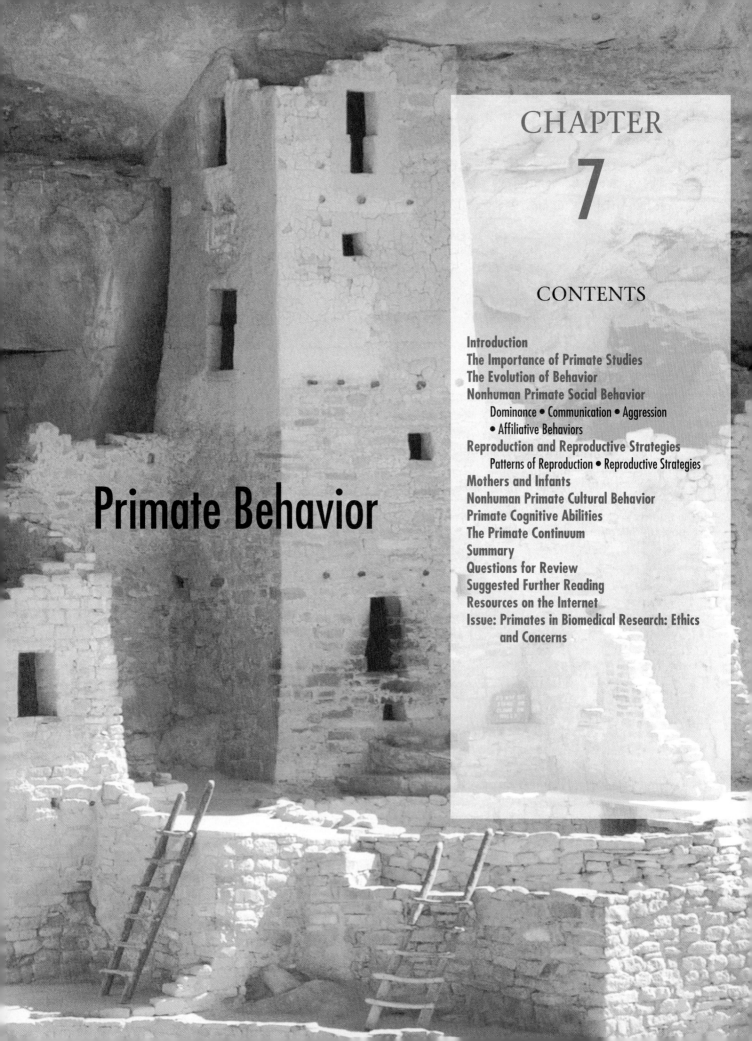

CHAPTER

7

CONTENTS

Primate Behavior

Introduction

In this chapter, discussion shifts to various aspects of nonhuman primate behavior and cognitive abilities. These are extremely important topics for anthropologists. One method of gaining a fuller understanding of human and early hominid behavior is to become more familiar with the behavior and intellectual capacities of living nonhuman primates. For that reason, as you read this chapter, you should be thinking of ways to apply some of the behavioral principles presented here to the early ancestors of *Homo sapiens*.

Because primates live in highly complex natural and social environments, they have evolved increasingly complex neurological structures. That is to say, there is a *feedback mechanism* between the biosocial environment and neurological complexity, so that over time, complex lifestyles have selected for increased neurological complexity, or intelligence. Intelligence, in turn, permits increasingly complex lifestyles. We know that all primates, including many prosimians, are extremely clever when compared to most other mammals. In this chapter, we will examine evidence that illustrates just how complex and intelligent are the other members of the order to which we ourselves belong.

The Importance of Primate Studies

Modern African apes and humans last shared a common ancestor between 5 and 8 million years ago. Although ape behavior has undoubtedly changed since that time, the behavior of hominids, who developed culture as an adaptive strategy, has changed much more dramatically. Accordingly, if we want to know what hominid behavior was like before culture became a factor, and if we wish to speculate as to which behaviors may have led to culture, we must look for clues in nonhuman primate behavior.

One approach is to correlate specific aspects of **social structure** with elements of primate habitats, since all living organisms must adapt to their environment. Because there are limits to the ways in which adaptation can occur, it follows that all organisms are to some degree governed by the same principles. By elucidating the various environmental pressures involved and understanding how they have influenced nonhuman primate behavior, we can better comprehend those factors that led to human emergence.

In addition to studying nonhuman primates to learn more about ourselves, it is just as important to learn more about them in their own right. Only within the past four decades have they been systematically studied, and we still have much to learn about them. Indeed, many species, especially several arboreal monkeys, have scarcely been studied at all. The beginning of the twenty-first century is an especially critical time for much of life on our planet. If we hope to save even some of the many threatened and endangered species from extinction, we must understand their needs (space, diet, group organization, etc.) in the wild. Without this knowledge, we can neither preserve sufficient natural habitat for their survival in the wild nor re-create it in captivity.

The Evolution of Behavior

Scientists who study behavior in free-ranging primates do so within an **ecological** framework, focusing on the relationship between behavior, the natural environment, and numerous factors related to the biology of the species in question. This approach is called **behavioral ecology**, and it is based on the underlying assumption that the various components of ecological systems have evolved together.

Briefly, the cornerstone of this perspective is that *behavior has evolved through the operation of natural selection*. That is, natural selection acts on behavior in the same way that it acts on physical characteristics. Therefore, individuals whose genotypes influence behaviors that lead to greater reproductive success will be more fit and should pass on their genes at a faster rate than others.

See the following sections of the CD-ROM for topics covered in this chapter: Virtual Lab 2, section I; Virtual Lab 5, section I; and Virtual Lab 6.

Social structure
The composition, size, and sex ratio of a group of animals. Social structures, in part, are the result of natural selection in specific habitats, and they function to guide individual interactions and social relationships.

A discussion of reproductive success is presented in Virtual Lab 2, section I.

Ecological
Pertaining to the relationship between organisms and all aspects of their environment (temperature, predators, other animals, vegetation, availability of food and water, types of food, etc.)

Behavioral ecology
The study of the evolution of behavior, emphasizing the role of ecological factors as agents of natural selection. Behaviors and behavioral patterns have been selected for because they increase reproductive fitness in individuals (i.e., they are adaptive) in specific ecological contexts.

 Ecological factors are discussed in Virtual Lab 5, section I.

Plasticity
The capacity to change; in a physiological context, the ability of systems or organisms to make alterations in order to respond to differing conditions.

Sociobiological
Pertaining to *sociobiology*, the study of the relationship between natural selection and behavior. Unlike the approach of behavioral ecology, sociobiological theory does not strongly emphasize ecological factors.

FIGURE 7–1
Hanuman langurs.

Joe MacDonald/Animals Animals #MM0 090MCJ006 01

Superficially, such an explanation implies the existence of genes that code for specific behaviors (e.g., a gene for aggression, another for cooperation). Such conclusions result, in part, from misinterpretation, but they have caused much controversy when applied to humans. The concern partly arises out of fear that if specific human behaviors could be explained in terms of genes, and if populations varied with regard to the frequency of these genes, then such evolutionarily based theories could be used by some people to support racist and other discriminatory views.

Much of the behavior of insects and other invertebrates, as well as that of lower vertebrates, is largely under genetic control. In other words, most behavioral patterns in these species are *innate*, not learned. However, in many vertebrates, particularly birds and mammals, the proportion of behavior that is due to *learning* is substantially increased. Accordingly, the proportion that is under genetic influence is reduced. This phenomenon is especially true of primates; and in humans, who are so much a product of culture, most behavior results from learning. Nevertheless, it is also clear that in higher organisms, some behaviors are partly influenced by certain gene products, (e.g., hormones). For example, numerous studies have shown that increased levels of testosterone increase aggressive behavior in many nonhuman species.

Behavior is a highly complex trait and must be seen not only as being influenced by specific gene products, but also as the product of *interactions between genetic and environmental factors* that are not yet fully elucidated. Indeed, the ability to learn is ultimately based in the genome inherited by individuals of any species. Between species, there is considerable variation in the limits and potentials for learning and behavioral **plasticity**. But for any given species, those limits and potentials are ultimately influenced by genetic factors that have been shaped by the evolutionary history of that species. The evolutionary history of any species is shaped by the ecological setting, not only of that species, *but of ancestral species as well*. Thus, behaviors are viewed as adaptations to environmental circumstances, and it is important to note that behavioral flexibility is also a form of adaptation.

A problem arises when trying to establish the actual mechanics of behavioral evolution in complex social animals such as primates. There is a need to determine which primate behaviors have a genetic basis and how these behaviors influence reproductive success. To accomplish these goals, we must learn considerably more about genotype-phenotype interactions in complex traits. We also need accurate data on reproductive success in primate groups, and so far, such long-term data are almost completely lacking. Thus, rather than offering precise explanations, an evolutionary approach provides a set of hypotheses for explaining primate behavior, and it remains for these hypotheses to be tested.

Obtaining conclusive data for primates and other mammals is not easy. A good starting point, however, is to frame hypotheses concerning behavioral evolution on the basis of the evidence that does exist. A good example of such a perspective is Sarah Blaffer Hrdy's (1977) **sociobiological** explanation of infanticide among Hanuman langurs of India (Fig. 7–1). Hanuman langurs typically live in social groups composed of one adult male, several females, and their offspring. Other males without mates associate in "bachelor" groups. These peripheral males occasionally attack and defeat a reproductive male and drive him from his group. Sometimes, following such takeovers, the group's infants (fathered by the previous male) are attacked and killed by the new male.

It would certainly seem that such behavior is counterproductive, especially from the species' perspective. However, individuals act to maximize their *own* reproductive success, no matter what the effect may be on the population or ultimately the species. Ostensibly, that is exactly what the male langur is doing, albeit unknowingly. While a female is lactating, she does not come into estrus, and therefore she is not sexually available. But when an infant dies, its mother ceases to lactate, and within two or three months, she resumes cycling and becomes sexually receptive. Therefore, by killing the infants, the male avoids a two- to three-year wait until they are weaned. This could be especially advantageous to him, as chances are good that his tenure in the group will not even last two or three years. Moreover, he does not expend energy and put himself at risk defending infants who do not carry his genes.

Hanuman langurs are not the only primates that engage in infanticide. Indeed, infanticide has been observed (or surmised) in many primate species, such as redtail monkeys, red colobus, blue monkeys, savanna baboons, howlers, orangutans, gorillas, chimpanzees (Struhsaker and Leyland, 1987), and humans. It also occurs in numerous nonprimate species, including rodents and cats. In the majority of nonhuman primate examples, infanticide occurs in conjunction with the transfer of a new male into a group or, as in chimpanzees, an encounter with an unfamiliar female and infant.

Numerous objections to this explanation of infanticide have been raised. Alternative explanations have included competition for resources (Rudran, 1973), aberrant behaviors related to human-induced overcrowding (Curtin and Dohlinow, 1978), and inadvertent killing during aggressive episodes, where it was not clear that the infant was actually the target animal (Bartlett et al., 1993). Sussman and colleagues (1995), as well as others, have questioned the actual prevalence of the practice, arguing that although it does occur, it is not particularly common. These authors have also postulated that if indeed male fitness is increased through the practice, such increases are negligible. Yet others (Struhsaker and Leyland, 1987; Hrdy, 1995) maintain that the incidence and patterning of infanticide by males are not only significant, but consistent with the assumptions established by theories of behavioral evolution.

Hrdy's well-known explanation of infanticide is an excellent example of the emphasis sociobiology placed on genes and individual reproductive success. But while primatologists still emphasize the importance of individual reproductive success, the focus of *behavioral ecology* has broadened to include ecological interactions that were largely ignored by sociobiology. For example, to understand the function of one particular behavioral element, such as the social organization of a given species, it is necessary to determine how that species is influenced by numerous factors, including:

1. Quantity and quality of different kinds of foods (i.e., net value to the individual in terms of calories and nutrients relative to energy requirements)
2. Spatial distribution of food resources (e.g., dense, scattered, clumps, or seasonal availability)
3. Distribution and reliability of water sources
4. Body size
5. Distribution and types of predators
6. Distribution of sleeping sites
7. Activity patterns (nocturnal, diurnal, **crepuscular**)
8. Relationships with other nonpredator species, both primate and nonprimate
9. Impact of human activities

Crepuscular
Active during the evening or dawn.

Although all the relationships between ecological variables, social organization, and behavior have not yet been thoroughly elucidated, there is certainly a relationship between, for example, group size, group dynamics, and the problems of obtaining food and avoiding predators. Indeed, average group size and composition are adaptive responses to these problems (Pulliam and Caraco, 1984). For example, groups composed of several adult males and females (multimale, multifemale groups) have traditionally been viewed as advantageous in areas where predation pressure is high. This is because where members of prey species occur in larger groups, there is increased likelihood of early predator detection and thus predator avoidance.

These assumptions are supported by reports that groups of red colobus monkeys and Diana monkeys (a guenon species) form interspecific aggregations in response to predation by chimpanzees in the Tai National Forest in the Ivory Coast. Normally, these two species do not form close associations with each other. However, when chimpanzee predation increases, new groupings develop and preexisting

FIGURE 7–2
Group of savanna baboons, which includes adult males and females as well as youngsters of various ages. Note adult male carrying infant in foreground.

ones remain intact for longer than normal periods of time. This same response was also seen when human observers played recordings of chimpanzee vocalizations (Noe and Bshary, 1997).

Savanna baboons (Fig. 7–2) have long been used as another example of these principles. They are found in semiarid grassland and broken woodland habitats throughout sub-Saharan Africa. To avoid nocturnal predators, savanna baboons sleep in trees; however, they spend much of the day on the ground foraging for food. In the presence of nonhuman predators, baboons flee to the safety of trees. However, if they are at some distance from safety, or if a predator is nearby, adult males may join forces to chase an intruder away. The effectiveness of male baboons in this regard should not be underestimated, for baboons have been known to kill domestic dogs and even to attack leopards and lions (Altmann and Altmann, 1970).

As you have already learned, not all primates are found in large groups. Solitary foraging is typical of many species, and it is probably related to diet and distribution of resources. In the case of the slow-moving, insectivorous loris, for example, solitary feeding reduces competition, which allows for less distance traveled (and thus less expenditure of energy) in the search for prey. Moreover, because insects usually do not occur in dense patches, they are more efficiently exploited by widely dispersed individuals rather than by groups. Solitary foraging is also related to predator avoidance, and it is particularly effective in species that rely chiefly on concealment rather than escape. Again, the loris serves as a good example.

Foraging alone or with offspring is also seen in females of some diurnal anthropoid species (e.g., orangutans, chimpanzees). These females, being relatively large-bodied, have little to fear from predators, and by feeding alone or with only one or two youngsters, they maximize their access to food, free from competition with others.

The various solutions that primate species have developed to deal with the problems of survival differ in complicated ways. Closely related species living in proximity to one another and exploiting many of the same resources can have very different types of social structure. It is only through continued research that primatologists will be able to sort out the intricate relationships between society and the natural environment.

 Primate behavior is discussed in Virtual Lab 6.

Nonhuman Primate Social Behavior

Because primates solve their major adaptive problems in a social context, we might expect them to participate in a number of activities to reinforce the integrity of the group. The better known of these activities are described in the sections that follow.

Dominance

Many primate societies are organized into **dominance hierarchies**. Dominance hierarchies impose a certain degree of order within groups by establishing parameters of individual behavior. Although aggression is frequently a means of increasing one's status, dominance usually serves to reduce the amount of actual physical violence. Not only are lower-ranking animals unlikely to attack or even threaten a higher-ranking one, but dominant animals are also frequently able to exert control simply by making a threatening gesture.

Individual rank or status may be measured by access to resources, including food items and mating partners. Dominant individuals are given priority by others, and they usually do not give way in confrontations.

Many primatologists postulate that the primary benefit of dominance is the increased reproductive success of the individual. This observation would be true if it could be demonstrated that dominant males compete more successfully for mates than do subordinate males. However, there is also good evidence that lower-ranking males of some species successfully mate; they just do so surreptitiously. Likewise, increased reproductive success can be postulated for high-ranking females, who have greater access to food than subordinate females. High-ranking females are provided with more energy for offspring production and care (Fedigan, 1983), and presumably their reproductive success is greater.

An individual's rank is not permanent and changes throughout life. It is influenced by many factors, including sex, age, level of aggression, amount of time spent in the group, intelligence, perhaps motivation, and the mother's social position (particularly true of macaques and baboons).

In species organized into groups containing a number of females associated with one or several adult males, the males are generally dominant to females. Within such groups, males and females have separate hierarchies, although very high ranking females can dominate the lowest-ranking males (particularly young males). There are exceptions to this pattern of male dominance. Among many lemur species, females are the dominant sex. Moreover, among species that form monogamous pairs (e.g., indris, gibbons), males and females are codominant.

All primates *learn* their position in the hierarchy. From birth, an infant is carried by its mother, and it observes how she responds to every member of the group. Just as importantly, it sees how others react to her. Dominance and subordination are indicated by gestures and behaviors, some of which are universal throughout the primate order (including humans), and this gestural repertoire is part of every youngster's learning experience.

Young primates also acquire social rank through play with age peers. As they spend more time with play groups, their social interactions widen. Competition and rough-and-tumble play allow them to learn the strengths and weaknesses of peers, and they carry this knowledge with them throughout their lives. Thus, through early contact with the mother and subsequent exposure to peers, young primates learn to negotiate their way through the complex web of social interactions that make up their daily lives.

Communication

Communication is universal among animals and includes scents and unintentional, **autonomic** responses and behaviors that convey meaning. Such attributes as body posture convey information about an animal's emotional state. For example, a crouched position indicates a certain degree of insecurity or fear, while a purposeful striding gait implies confidence. Moreover, autonomic responses to threatening or novel stimuli, such as raised body hair (most species) or enhanced body odor (gorillas), indicate excitement.

Many intentional behaviors also serve as communication. In primates, these include a wide variety of gestures, facial expressions, and vocalizations, some of which we humans share. Among many primates, a mild threat is indicated by an

Dominance hierarchies
Systems of social organization wherein individuals within a group are ranked relative to one another. Higher-ranking individuals have greater access to preferred food items and mating partners than lower-ranking individuals. Dominance hierarchies have sometimes been referred to as "pecking orders."

Communication
Any act that conveys information, in the form of a message, to another individual. Frequently, the result of communication is a change in the behavior of the recipient. Communication may not be deliberate but may be the result of involuntary processes or a secondary consequence of an intentional action.

Autonomic
Pertaining to physiological responses not under voluntary control. An example in chimpanzees would be the erection of body hair during excitement. An example in humans is blushing. Both convey information regarding emotional states, but neither is a deliberate behavior, and communication is not intended.

FIGURE 7–3
Adolescent male savanna baboon threatens photographer with a characteristic "yawn" that shows the canine teeth. Note also that the eyes are closed briefly to expose light, cream-colored eyelids. This has been termed the "eyelid flash."

Displays
Sequences of repetitious behaviors that serve to communicate emotional states. Nonhuman primate displays are most frequently associated with reproductive or agonistic behavior.

intense stare, and indeed, we humans find prolonged eye contact with strangers very uncomfortable. For this reason, people should avoid eye contact with captive primates. Other threat gestures are a quick yawn to expose canine teeth (baboons, macaques) (Fig. 7–3); bobbing back and forth in a crouched position (patas monkeys); and branch shaking (many monkey species). High-ranking baboons *mount* the hindquarters of subordinates to express dominance (Fig. 7–4). Mounting may also serve to defuse potentially tense situations by indicating something like, "It's okay, I accept your apology, I know you didn't intend to offend me."

There are also a number of behaviors to indicate submission, reassurance, or amicable intentions. Submission is indicated by a crouched position (most primates) or presenting the hindquarters (baboons). Reassurance takes the form of touching, patting, and, in chimpanzees, hugging and holding hands. Grooming also serves in a number of situations to indicate submission or reassurance.

A wide variety of facial expressions indicating emotional states is seen in chimpanzees and bonobos (Fig. 7–5). These include the well-known play face (also seen in several other species), associated with play behavior, and the fear grin (seen in *all* primates) to indicate fear and submission.

Primates also use a wide array of vocalizations for communication. Some, such as the bark of a baboon that has just spotted a leopard, are unintentional startled reactions. Others, such as the chimpanzee food grunt, are heard only in specific contexts. Nevertheless, both serve the same function: They inform others, although not necessarily deliberately, of the possible presence of predators or food.

Primates (and other animals) also communicate through **displays**, which are more complicated, frequently elaborate combinations of behaviors. For example, the exaggerated courtship dances of many male birds, often enhanced by colorful plumage, are displays. Common gorilla displays are chest slapping and the tearing of vegetation to indicate threat. Likewise, an angry chimpanzee, with hair bristling, may charge an opponent while screaming, waving its arms, and tearing vegetation.

All nonhuman animals employ various vocalizations, body postures, and, to some degree, facial expressions that transmit information. However, the array of communicative devices is much richer among nonhuman primates, even though they do not use language in the manner of humans. Communication is important,

FIGURE 7–4
One young male savanna baboon mounts another as an expression of dominance.

Relaxed   Relaxed with dropped lip Horizontal pout face   Fear grin   Full play face
                (distress)   (fear/excitement)

for it truly is what makes social living possible. Through submissive gestures, aggression is reduced and physical violence is less likely. Likewise, friendly intentions and relationships are reinforced through physical contact and grooming. Indeed, it is in the familiar methods of nonverbal communication that we humans can see ourselves in other primate species most clearly.

Aggression

Within primate societies, there is an interplay between **affiliative** behaviors that promote group cohesion and aggressive behaviors that can lead to group disruption. Conflict within a group frequently develops out of competition for resources, including mating partners and food items. Instead of actual attacks or fighting, most intragroup aggression occurs in the form of various signals and displays, frequently within the context of a dominance hierarchy. The majority of such situations are resolved through various submissive and appeasement behaviors.

But conflict is not always resolved peacefully, and it can have serious consequences. For example, high-ranking female macaques frequently intimidate, harass, and even attack lower-ranking females, particularly to restrict their access to food. High-ranking females consistently chase subordinates away from food and have even been observed to take food from their mouths; these behaviors can result in weight loss and poorer nutrition in low-ranking females.

Competition between males for mates frequently results in injury and occasionally in death. In species that have a distinct breeding season (e.g., squirrel monkeys), conflict between males is most common during that time. Male squirrel monkeys form coalitions to compete with other males, and when outright fighting occurs, injuries can be severe. In species not restricted to a mating season, competition between males can be an ongoing process.

Aggressive encounters occur *between* groups as well as within groups. Between groups, aggression occurs in the defense of **territories**. Primate groups are associated with a **home range**, where they remain permanently. Within this home range is a portion called the **core area**, which contains the highest concentration of predictable resources and where the group is most frequently found. Although portions of the home range may overlap with the home range of one or more other groups, core areas of adjacent groups do not overlap. The core area can also be said to be a group's territory, and it is the portion of the home range that is usually defended against intrusion by others. However, in some species, such as chimpanzees, other areas of the home range may also be defended. Whatever area is defended, this portion is termed the *territory*.

Beginning in 1974, Jane Goodall and her colleagues witnessed at least five unprovoked and extremely brutal attacks by groups of chimpanzees (usually, but not always, males) on lone individuals. To explain these attacks, it is necessary to point out that by 1973, the original Gombe community had divided into two distinct groups. The larger group was located in the north of the original home range.

FIGURE 7–5

Chimpanzee facial expressions. (Adapted with permission of the publishers from *The Chimpanzees of Gombe* by Jane Goodall, Cambridge, Mass.: Harvard University Press, © 1986 by the President and Fellows of Harvard College.)

Affiliative
Pertaining to amicable associations between individuals. Affiliative behaviors, such as grooming, reinforce social bonds and promote group cohesion.

Territories
Areas that will be aggressively protected against intrusion, particularly by other members of the same species.

Home range
The entire area exploited by an animal or group of animals.

Core area
The portion of a home range containing the highest concentration of resources.

The smaller offshoot group established itself in the southern portion, effectively denying the others access to part of their former territory.

By 1977, all seven males and one female of the splinter group were either known or suspected to have been killed. All observed incidents involved several animals who attacked lone individuals. Although it is not possible to know exactly what motivated the attackers, it was clear that they intended to incapacitate their victims (Goodall, 1986).

A situation similar to that at Gombe has been reported for a group of chimpanzees in the Mahale Mountains south of Gombe. Over a 17-year period, all the males of a small community disappeared. Although no attacks were actually observed, there was circumstantial evidence that most of these males met the same fate as the Gombe attack victims (Nishida et al., 1985; Nishida et al., 1990).

In addition to territoriality, Manson and Wrangham (1991) have proposed a number of other factors that may contribute to male chimpanzee aggression, including acquisition of females from other groups. While the precise motivation of chimpanzee intergroup violence may never be fully elucidated, it is clear that a number of interrelated factors are involved. Moreover, although chimpanzees do not meet all the criteria developed for true territorial behavior (Goodall, 1986), it appears that various aspects of resource acquisition and protection are involved.

Affiliative Behaviors

Even though conflict can be destructive, a certain amount of aggression is useful in maintaining order within groups and protecting either individual or group resources. Fortunately, to minimize actual violence and to defuse potentially dangerous situations, there is an array of affiliative, or friendly, behaviors that serve to reinforce bonds between individuals and enhance group stability.

Common affiliative behaviors include reconciliation, consolation, and simple amicable interactions between friends and relatives. Most such behaviors involve various forms of physical contact, such as touching, hand holding, hugging, and, among chimpanzees, kissing (Fig. 7–6). In fact, physical contact is one of the most important factors in primate development and is crucial in promoting peaceful relationships in many primate social groups.

Grooming is one of the most important affiliative behaviors in many primate species. Although grooming occurs in other animal species, social grooming is mostly a primate activity, and it plays an important role in day-to-day life (Fig. 7–7). Because grooming involves using the fingers to pick through the fur of another individual (or one's own) to remove insects, dirt, and other materials, it serves hygienic functions. But it is also an immensely pleasurable activity that individuals of some species (especially chimpanzees) engage in for considerable periods of time.

Grooming occurs in a variety of contexts. Mothers groom infants. Males groom sexually receptive females. Subordinate animals groom dominant ones, sometimes to gain favor. Friends groom friends. In general, grooming is comforting. It restores peaceful relationships between animals who have quarreled and provides reassurance during tense situations. In short, grooming reinforces social bonds and consequently helps to maintain and strengthen the structure of the group. For this reason, it has been called "the social cement of primates from lemur to chimpanzee" (Jolly, 1985, p. 207).

Conflict resolution through reconciliation is another important aspect of primate social behavior. Following a conflict, chimpanzee opponents frequently move, within minutes, to reconcile (de Waal, 1982). Reconciliation takes many forms, including hugging, kissing, and grooming. Even uninvolved individuals may take part, either grooming one or both participants or forming their own grooming parties. In addition, bonobos are unique in their use of sex to promote group cohesion, restore peace after conflicts, and relieve tension within the group (de Waal, 1987, 1989).

FIGURE 7–6
Adolescent savanna baboons holding hands.

Grooming
Picking through fur to remove dirt, parasites, and other materials that may be present. Social grooming is common among primates and reinforces social relationships.

Lynn Kilgore

Courtesy, Meredith Small

Robert Jurmain

Lynn Kilgore

Courtesy, Arlene Kruse/Bonnie Pedersen

(a)

(b)

(c)

(d)

FIGURE 7–7

Grooming primates. (a) Patas monkeys; female grooming male. (b) Longtail macaques. (c) Savanna baboons. (d) Chimpanzees.

Relationships are crucial to nonhuman primates, and the bonds between individuals can last a lifetime. These relationships serve a variety of functions. Individuals of many species form alliances in which one supports another against a third. Alliances, or coalitions, as they are also called, can be used to enhance the status of members. For example, at Gombe, the male chimpanzee Figan achieved alpha status because of support from his brother (Goodall, 1986, p. 424). In fact, chimpanzees so heavily rely on coalitions and are so skillful politically that an entire book, appropriately titled *Chimpanzee Politics* (de Waal, 1982), is devoted to the topic.

There are other behaviors that also illustrate the importance of social relationships, some of which can perhaps be described as examples of caregiving or compassion. When discussing nonhuman animal (or indeed, human) behavior, it is impossible to know with certainty what an individual's motivation is. Thus, the use of the term *compassion* is risky, because in humans, compassion is motivated by empathy for another. Whether nonhuman primates can empathize with the suffering or misfortune of another is not really known, but certainly there are numerous examples, mostly from chimpanzee studies, of caregiving actions that resemble

Altruism
Any behavior or act that benefits another individual but poses some potential risk or cost to oneself.

compassionate behavior in humans. Examples include protection of others during attacks, helping younger siblings, and staying near ill or dying relatives or friends.

Altruism, behavior that benefits another while involving some risk or sacrifice to the performer, is common in many primate species, and altruistic acts sometimes contain elements of compassion and cooperation. The most fundamental of altruistic behaviors, the protection of dependent offspring, is ubiquitous among mammals and birds, and in the majority of species, altruistic acts are confined to this context. However, among primates, recipients of altruistic acts may include individuals who are not offspring and who may not even be closely related to the performer. Chimpanzees routinely come to the aid of relatives and friends; female langurs join forces to protect infants from males; and male baboons cooperate to chase predators. In fact, the primate literature abounds with examples of altruistic acts, whereby individuals place themselves at some risk to protect others from attacks by conspecifics or predators.

Adoption of orphans is a form of altruism that has been reported for macaques and baboons and is common in chimpanzees. When chimpanzee youngsters are orphaned, they are routinely adopted, usually by older siblings who are solicitous and highly protective. Adoption is crucial to the survival of orphans, who would certainly not survive on their own. In fact, it is extremely rare for a chimpanzee orphan less than three years of age to survive even if it is adopted.

Reproduction and Reproductive Strategies

Patterns of Reproduction

In most primate species, sexual behavior is tied to the female's reproductive cycle, with females sexually receptive to males only when they are in estrus. Estrus is characterized by behavioral changes that indicate a female is receptive. In Old World monkeys and apes that live in multimale groups, estrus is also accompanied by swelling and changes in color of the skin around the genital area. These changes serve as visual cues of a female's readiness to mate (Fig. 7–8).

FIGURE 7–8
Estrous swelling of genital tissues in a female chimpanzee.

Lynn Kilgore

Permanent bonding between males and females is not common among nonhuman primates. However, male and female savanna baboons sometimes form mating *consortships*. These temporary relationships last while the female is in estrus, and the two spend most of the time together, mating frequently. Moreover, lower-ranking baboon males often form "friendships" (Smuts, 1985) with females and occasionally may mate with them, although they may be driven away by high-ranking males when the female is most receptive.

Mating consortships are sometimes seen in chimpanzees and are particularly common among bonobos. In fact, a male and female bonobo may spend several weeks primarily in each other's company. During this time, they mate often, even when the female is not in estrus. These relationships of longer duration are not typical of chimpanzee (*Pan troglodytes*) males and females.

Such a male-female bond may result in increased reproductive success for both sexes. For the male, there is the increased likelihood that he will be the father of any infant the female conceives. At the same time, the female potentially gains protection from predators or others of her group and perhaps assistance in caring for offspring she may already have.

Reproductive Strategies

Reproductive strategies, and especially how they differ between the sexes, have been a primary focus of primate research. The goal of such strategies is to produce and successfully rear to adulthood as many offspring as possible.

Primates are among the most **K-selected** of mammal species. By this we mean that individuals produce only a few young, in whom they invest a tremendous amount of parental care. Contrast this pattern with **r-selected** species, where individuals produce large numbers of offspring but invest little or no energy in parental care. Good examples of r-selected species include insects, most fish, and, among mammals, mice and rabbits.

When we consider the degree of care required by young, growing primate offspring, it is clear that enormous investment by at least one parent is necessary, and it is usually the mother who carries most of the burden both before and after birth. Primates are totally helpless at birth. They develop slowly and are thus exposed to expanded learning opportunities within a *social* environment. This trend has been elaborated most dramatically in great apes and humans, and especially in the latter. Thus, what we see in ourselves and our close primate kin (and presumably in our more recent ancestors as well) is a strategy wherein a few "high-quality," slowly maturing offspring are produced through extraordinary investment by at least one parent, usually the mother.

Finding food and mates, avoiding predators, and caring for and protecting dependent young represent difficult challenges for nonhuman primates. Moreover, in most species, males and females employ different strategies to meet these challenges.

Female nonhuman primates spend almost all their adult lives either pregnant, lactating, and/or caring for offspring, and the resulting metabolic demands are enormous. A pregnant or lactating female, although perhaps only half the size of her male counterpart, may require about the same number of calories per day. Even if these demands are met, her physical resources may be drained. For example, analysis of chimpanzee skeletons from Gombe National Park, in Tanzania, shows significant loss of bone and bone mineral in older females (Sumner et al., 1989).

Given these physiological costs, a female's best strategy is to maximize the amount of resources available to her and her offspring. Indeed, females of many primate species (gibbons, marmosets, and macaques, to name a few) are viciously competitive with other females and aggressively protect resources and territories. In other species, as we have seen, females distance themselves from others to avoid competition.

Reproductive strategies
The complex of behavioral patterns that contributes to individual reproductive success. The behaviors need not be deliberate, and they often vary considerably between males and females.

K-selected
Pertaining to an adaptive strategy whereby individuals produce relatively few offspring, in whom they invest increased parental care. Although only a few infants are born, chances of survival are increased for each individual because of parental investments in time and energy. Examples of nonprimate K-selected species are birds and canids (e.g., wolves, coyotes, and dogs).

r-selected
Pertaining to an adaptive strategy that emphasizes relatively large numbers of offspring and reduced parental care (compared to K-selected species). (*K-selection* and *r-selection* are relative terms; e.g., mice are r-selected compared to primates but K-selected compared to many fish species.)

Primate Behavior

Males, however, face a separate set of challenges. Having little investment in the rearing of offspring (except in the case of monogamous pairs), it is to the male's advantage to secure as many mates and produce as many offspring as possible. By so doing, he is effectively increasing his genetic contribution to the next generation relative to other males.

One outcome of different mating strategies is **sexual selection**, a phenomenon first described by Charles Darwin. Sexual selection is a type of natural selection that operates on only one sex, usually males, whereby the selective agent is male competition for mates and, in some species, mate choice in females. The long-term effect of sexual selection is to increase the frequency of those traits that lead to greater success in acquiring mates.

In the animal kingdom there are numerous male attributes that result from sexual selection. In some bird species, for example, males are much more brightly colored than females. For various reasons, female birds find those males with more vividly colored plumage more attractive as mates; thus, selection has increased the frequency of alleles that influence brighter coloration in males.

Sexual selection in primates is most important in species characterized by multimale social groups, but it is a factor in any species where mating is polygynous and male competition for females is prominent. In these species, sexual selection produces dimorphism with regard to a number of traits, most noticeably body size. The males of many primate species are considerably larger than females (indeed, male gorillas and orangutans can be twice as large), and males also have larger canine teeth. Conversely, in species where mating is monogamous (e.g., gibbons) or where male competition is reduced, dimorphism in canine and body size is either reduced or nonexistent. For these reasons, the presence or absence of sexually dimorphic traits in a species is a reasonably good indicator of mating structure.

Mothers and Infants

The basic social unit among all primates is the female and her infants (Fig. 7–9). Except in those species in which monogamy or **polyandry** occurs, males do not participate greatly in the rearing of offspring. Observations both in the field and in captivity suggest that the mother-offspring core provides the social group with its stability.

The mother-infant bond, one of the most basic themes running throughout primate social relations, begins at birth. Although the exact nature of the bonding process is not fully known, there appear to be predisposing innate factors that strongly attract the female to her infant, so long as she herself has had sufficiently normal experiences with her own mother. This does not mean that primate mothers possess innate knowledge of how to care for an infant. Indeed, they do not. Monkeys and apes raised in captivity without contact with their own mothers not only do not know how to care for a newborn infant, but may also be afraid of it and attack and kill it. Even if they do not directly attack the infant, they may kill it indirectly through mishandling or improper nursing.

The crucial role of bonding between primate mothers and infants was clearly demonstrated by the Harlows (1959), who raised infant monkeys with surrogate mothers fashioned from wire or a combination of wire and cloth. Other monkeys were raised with no mothers at all. In one experiment, infants retained an attachment to their cloth-covered surrogate mother (Fig. 7–10). But those raised with no mother were incapable of forming lasting affectional ties. These deprived monkeys sat passively in their cages and stared vacantly into space. None of the motherless males ever successfully copulated, and those females who were (somewhat artificially) impregnated either paid little attention to offspring or reacted aggressively toward them (Harlow and Harlow, 1961). The point is that monkeys reared in isolation were denied opportunities to *learn* the rules of social behavior. Moreover, and just as essential, they were denied the all-important physical contact so necessary for normal primate psychological and emotional development.

Sexual selection
A type of natural selection that operates on only one sex within a species. It is the result of competition for mates, and it can lead to sexual dimorphism with regard to one or more traits.

Polyandry
A mating system wherein a female continuously associates with more than one male (usually two or three) with whom she mates. Among nonhuman primates, this pattern is seen only in marmosets and tamarins.

(a)

(b)

(c)

(d)

(e)

The importance of a normal relationship with the mother is demonstrated by field studies as well. From birth, infant primates are able to cling to their mother's fur, and they are in more or less constant physical contact with her for several months. During this critical period, the infant develops a closeness with the mother that does not always end with weaning. This closeness is often maintained throughout life (especially among some Old World monkeys). It is reflected in grooming behavior that continues between mother and offspring even after the young reach adulthood and have infants of their own.

FIGURE 7–9 (above)
Primate mothers with young. (a) Mongoose lemur. (b) Chimpanzee. (c) Patas monkey. (d) Orangutan. (e) Sykes monkey.

FIGURE 7–10
Infant macaque clinging to cloth mother.

Nonhuman Primate Cultural Behavior

One important trait that makes nonhuman primates, and especially chimpanzees and bonobos, attractive as models for behavior in early hominids may be called *cultural behavior*. Although many cultural anthropologists and others prefer to use the term *culture* to refer specifically to human activities, most biological anthropologists consider it appropriate to use the term in discussions of nonhuman primates as well (McGraw, 1992, 1998; de Waal, 1999; Whiten et al., 1999).

Undeniably, there are many aspects of culture that are uniquely human, and one must be cautious when interpreting nonhuman animal behavior. But again, since humans are products of the same evolutionary forces that have produced other species, they can be expected to exhibit some of the same *behavioral patterns* seen in other species, particularly primates. However, because of increased brain size and learning capacities, humans express many characteristics to a greater degree. We would argue that the *aptitude for culture* as a means of adapting to the natural environment is one such characteristic.

Among other things, cultural behavior is *learned*, and it is passed from generation to generation not biologically, but through learning. Whereas humans deliberately teach their young, free-ranging nonhuman primates (with the exception of a few reports) do not generally appear to do so. But human children also acquire tremendous knowledge not from instruction, but through observation in the same manner as young nonhuman primates. Nonhuman primate infants, through observing their mothers and others, learn about food items, appropriate behaviors, and how to use and modify objects to achieve certain ends. In turn, their own offspring will observe their activities. What emerges is a *cultural tradition* that may eventually come to typify an entire group or even a species.

A famous example of cultural behavior was seen in a study group of Japanese macaques on Koshima Island. In 1952, Japanese researchers began provisioning the 22-member troop with sweet potatoes. The following year, a young female named Imo began washing her potatoes in a freshwater stream prior to eating them. Within three years, several monkeys had adopted the practice, but they had switched from using the stream to taking their potatoes to the ocean nearby. Perhaps they liked the salt seasoning!

The researchers proposed that dietary habits and food preferences are learned and that potato washing was an example of nonhuman culture. Because this practice arose as an innovative solution to a problem and was imitated by others until it became a tradition, it was seen as resembling human culture.

Among chimpanzees we see more elaborate examples of cultural behavior in the form of *tool use*. This point is very important, for traditionally, tool use (along with language) was said to set humans apart from other animals.

Chimpanzees insert twigs and grass blades into termite mounds in a practice called "termite fishing." When termites seize the twig, the chimpanzee withdraws it and eats the attached insects. Chimpanzees modify some of their stems and twigs by stripping the leaves—in effect, manufacturing a tool from the natural material. To some extent, chimpanzees even alter objects to a "regular and set pattern" and have been observed preparing objects for later use at another location (Goodall, 1986, p. 535). For example, a chimpanzee will very carefully select a piece of vine, bark, twig, or palm frond and modify it by removing leaves or other extraneous material, then break off portions until it is the proper length. Chimpanzees have also been seen making these tools even before the termite mound is in sight.

All this preparation has several implications. First, the chimpanzees are engaged in an activity that prepares them for a future (not immediate) task at a somewhat distant location, and this action implies planning and forethought. Second, attention to the shape and size of the raw material indicates that chimpanzee toolmakers have a preconceived idea of what the finished product needs to be in order to be useful. To produce a tool, even a simple tool, based on a concept is an extremely complex behavior. Scientists previously believed that such behavior was the exclusive domain of humans, but now we must question this very basic assumption.

Chimpanzees also crumple and chew handfuls of leaves, which they dip into the hollow of a tree where water has accumulated. Then they suck the water from their newly made "leaf sponges," water that otherwise would have been inaccessible to them. Leaves are also used to wipe substances from fur; twigs are sometimes used as toothpicks; stones may be used as weapons; and various objects, such as branches and stones, may be dragged or rolled to enhance displays. Lastly, sticks or leaves are used as aids in processing mammalian prey, but with one exception these practices appear to be incidental. The one exception, observed in chimpanzees in the Tai forest (Ivory Coast), is the frequent use of sticks to extract marrow from long bones (Boesch and Boesch, 1989).

Chimpanzees in numerous West African study groups use hammerstones with platform stones to crack nuts and hard-shelled fruits (Boesch et al, 1994). However, it is important to note that neither the hammerstone nor the platform stone was deliberately manufactured.* Wild capuchin monkeys use leaves to extract water from cavities in trees (Phillips, 1998) and also smash objects against stones (Izawa and Mizuno, 1977), and their use of stones in captivity (both as hammers and anvils) has been reported (Visalberghi, 1990). (Stones serve as anvils when fruit or other objects are bashed against the rock surface.) In nature, chimpanzees are the only nonhuman animal to use stones both as hammers and anvils to obtain food. They are also the only nonhuman primate that consistently and habitually makes and uses tools (McGrew, 1992).

Importantly, chimpanzees exhibit regional variation regarding both the types and methods of tool use. Use of stone hammers and platforms is confined to West African groups. And at central and eastern African sites, termites are obtained by means of stems and sticks, while at some West African locations, it appears that no tools are used in this context (McGrew, 1992).

Regional dietary preferences are also noted for chimpanzees (Nishida et al., 1983; McGrew, 1992, 1998). For example, oil palms are exploited for their fruit and nuts at many locations, including Gombe, but even though they are present in the Mahale Mountains, they are not utilized by the chimpanzees there. Such regional patterns in tool use and food preferences that are not due to environmental variation are reminiscent of the cultural variations characteristic of humans.

Using sticks, twigs, and stones enhances chimpanzees' ability to exploit resources. Learning these behaviors occurs during infancy and childhood, partly as a function of prolonged contact with the mother. Also important in this regard is the continued exposure to others provided by living in social groupings. These statements also apply to early hominids. While sticks and unmodified stones do not remain to tell tales, our early ancestors surely used these same objects as tools in much the same manner as do chimpanzees.

While chimpanzees in the wild have not been observed modifying the stones they use, a male bonobo named Kanzi (see p. 167) has learned to strike two stones together to produce sharp-edged flakes. In a study conducted by Sue Savage-Rumbaugh and archaeologist Nicholas Toth, Kanzi was allowed to watch as Toth produced stone flakes, which were then used to open a transparent plastic food container (Savage-Rumbaugh and Lewin, 1994). Although bonobos apparently do not commonly use objects as tools in the wild, Kanzi readily appreciated the utility of the flakes in obtaining food. Moreover, he was able to master the basic technique of producing flakes without having been taught the various components of the process, even though initially his progress was slow. Eventually, Kanzi realized that he could overcome his difficulties by throwing a stone onto a hard floor, causing it

---

*Observers of nonhuman primates rarely distinguish natural objects used as tools from modified objects deliberately manufactured for specific purposes. The term *tool* is usually employed in both cases.

Primate Behavior

to shatter, thus providing an abundance of cutting implements. Although his solution was not necessarily the one that Savage-Rumbaugh and Toth expected, it nevertheless provided an excellent example of bonobo insight and problem-solving capability. Moreover, Kanzi did eventually learn to produce flakes by striking two stones together, and these flakes were then used to obtain food. Not only is this behavior an example of tool manufacture and tool use, albeit in a captive situation; it is also a very sophisticated goal-directed activity.

Human culture has become the environment in which modern *Homo sapiens* lives. Quite clearly, the use of sticks in termite fishing and hammerstones to crack nuts is hardly comparable to modern human technology. However, modern human technology had its beginnings in these very types of behaviors we observe in other primates. This does not mean that nonhuman primates are "on their way" to becoming human. Remember, evolution is not goal directed, and if it were, there is nothing to dictate that modern humans necessarily constitute an evolutionary goal. Such a conclusion is a purely **anthropocentric** view, and it has no validity in discussions of evolutionary processes.

Moreover, nonhuman primates have probably been capable of certain cultural behaviors for millions of years. As we have stated, the common ancestor that humans share with chimpanzees may have used sticks and stones to exploit resources and perhaps even as weapons. These behaviors are not newly developed in our close relatives simply because we have only recently discovered and documented them. Thus, we must continue to study these capabilities in nonhuman primates in their social and ecological context so that we may eventually understand more clearly how cultural traditions emerged in our own lineage.

Primate Cognitive Abilities

As we have already seen, primates are extremely intelligent, as demonstrated by their complicated social interactions and problem-solving abilities. Indeed, their use of tools represents solutions to such problems as how to get termites out of their mounds or how to gain access to water in difficult places.

Although numerous studies have demonstrated the abilities of nonhuman primates, probably no research has had the impact, certainly on the general public, that the language acquisition studies have had. As previously discussed, all animals communicate through a variety of modalities, including scent, vocalizations, touch, and visual indicators (gestures, facial expressions, and body posture). However, the amount and kinds of information that nonhuman animals are able to convey are limited.

The view traditionally held by most linguists and behavioral psychologists has been that nonhuman communication consists of mostly involuntary vocalizations and actions that convey information about the emotional state of the animal (anger, fear, etc.). Nonhuman animals have not been considered capable of communicating about external events, objects, or other animals, either in close proximity or removed in space or time. For example, when a startled baboon barks, its fellow baboons know only that it is startled. What they do not know is what elicited the bark, and this they can only ascertain by looking around. In general, then, it has been assumed that nonhuman animals, including primates, use a *closed system* of communication, one in which use of vocalizations and other modalities does not include references to specific external phenomena.

In recent years, these views have been challenged (Steklis, 1985; King, 1994). Vervets (Fig. 7–11) have been shown to use specific vocalizations for particular categories of predators such as snakes, eagles, and leopards (Struhsaker, 1967; Seyfarth, Cheney, and Marler, 1980a, 1980b). When researchers made tape recordings of various vervet alarm calls and played them back within hearing distance of free-ranging vervets, they observed differing responses to various calls. In response to leopard alarm calls, the monkeys climbed trees; eagle alarm calls caused them to

Anthropocentric
Viewing nonhuman phenomena in terms of human experience and capabilities; emphasizing the importance of humans over everything else.

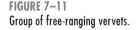

Lynn Kilgore

FIGURE 7–11
Group of free-ranging vervets.

look upward and run into bushes; and snake alarm calls elicited looking around in the nearby grass.

These results demonstrate that vervets use distinct vocalizations to refer to specific components of the external environment. These calls are not involuntary, and they do not refer solely to the emotional state of the individual animal, although this information is also conveyed. While these significant findings dispel certain long-held misconceptions about nonhuman communication (at least for some species), they also indicate certain limitations. Vervet communication is restricted to the present; as far as we know, no vervet can communicate about a predator it saw yesterday or one it might see in the future.

Other studies have now shown that numerous other nonhuman primates, including cottontop tamarins (Cleveland and Snowdon, 1982), red colobus (Struhsaker, 1975), and gibbons (Tenaza and Tilson, 1977), also produce distinct calls that have specific references. There is also growing evidence that many birds and some nonprimate mammals use distinct predator alarm calls as well (Seyfarth, 1987).

In contrast, humans use *language*, a set of written and spoken symbols that refer to concepts, other humans, objects, and so on. This set of symbols is said to be *arbitrary* in that the symbol itself has no relationship to whatever it represents. For example, the English word *flower* when written or spoken neither looks, smells, nor feels like the thing it represents. Moreover, humans can recombine their linguistic symbols in an infinite number of ways to create new meanings, and we can use language to refer to events, places, objects, and people far removed in both space and time. For these reasons, language is described as an *open system* of communication, based on the human ability to think symbolically.

Language, as distinct from other forms of communication, has been considered a uniquely human achievement, one that sets humans apart from the rest of the animal kingdom. But work with captive apes has raised some doubts about that supposition. While many people were skeptical about the capacity of nonhuman primates to use language, reports from psychologists who work with apes, especially chimpanzees, leave little doubt that these primates can learn to interpret signs and use them to communicate with their trainers and companions in their own group.

No mammal, other than humans, has the ability to speak. However, the fact that apes cannot speak has less to do with lack of intelligence than to differences in the anatomy of the vocal tract and *language-related structures in the brain*. Quite clearly, communication became increasingly important in hominid evolution, and natural selection increasingly favored anatomical and neurological changes that enhanced our ancestors' ability to use spoken language.

Because of failed attempts at teaching young chimpanzees to speak, psychologists Beatrice and Allen Gardner designed a study to test language capabilities in chimpanzees by teaching an infant female named Washoe to use ASL (American sign language for the deaf). Beginning in 1966, the Gardners began teaching Washoe signs in the same way parents would teach a deaf human infant. In just over three years, Washoe had acquired at least 132 signs. "She asked for goods and services, and she also asked questions about the world of objects and events around her" (Gardner et al., 1989, p. 6).

Years later, an infant chimpanzee named Loulis was placed in Washoe's care. Researchers wanted to know if Loulis would acquire signing skills from Washoe and other chimpanzees in the study group. Within just eight days, Loulis began to imitate the signs of others. Moreover, Washoe also deliberately *taught* Loulis some signs. For example, teaching him to sit, "Washoe placed a small plastic chair in front of Loulis, and then signed CHAIR/SIT to him several times in succession, watching him closely throughout" (Fouts et al., 1989, p. 290).

There have been other ape language experiments. The chimpanzee Sara, for instance, was taught by Professor David Premack to recognize plastic chips as symbols for various objects. The chips did not resemble the objects they represented. For example, the chip that represented an apple was neither round nor red. Sara's ability to associate chips with concepts and objects to which they bore no visual similarity implies some degree of symbolic thought.

At the Yerkes Regional Primate Research Center in Atlanta, Georgia, another chimpanzee, Lana, worked with a specially designed computer keyboard with chips attached to keys. After six months, Lana recognized symbols for 30 words and was able to ask for food and answer questions through the machine (Rumbaugh, 1977). Also at Yerkes, two male chimpanzees, Sherman and Austin, learned to communicate using a series of lexigrams, or geometric symbols, imprinted on a computer keyboard (Savage-Rumbaugh, 1986b).

Dr. Francine Patterson, who taught ASL to Koko, a female lowland gorilla, reports that Koko uses more than 500 signs. Furthermore, Michael, an adult male who was also involved in the gorilla study until his death in 2000, had a considerable sign vocabulary, and the two gorillas communicated with each other via signs.

In the late 1970s, a male orangutan, Chantek (also at Yerkes), began to use signs after one month of training when he was two years old. Chantek eventually acquired a total of approximately 140 signs, which in some situations were used to refer to objects and persons not present. Chantek also invented signs and recombined them in novel ways, and he appeared to understand that his signs were *representations* of items, actions, and people (Miles, 1990).

Questions have been raised about this type of experimental work. Do the apes really understand the signs they learn? Are they merely imitating their trainers? Do they learn that a symbol is a name for an object or simply that executing a symbol will produce a desired object? Other unanswered questions concern the apes' use of grammar, especially when they combine more than just a few "words" to communicate.

Partly in an effort to address some of these questions and criticisms, Dr. Sue Savage-Rumbaugh taught the chimpanzees Sherman and Austin to use symbols to categorize *classes* of objects, such as "food" or "tool." This was done in recognition of the fact that in previous studies, apes had been taught symbols for *specific* items. Savage-Rumbaugh reasoned that simply using a symbol as a label is not the same thing as understanding the *representational value* of the symbol.

Sherman and Austin were taught to recognize familiar food items, for which they routinely used symbols, as belonging to a broader category referred to by yet another symbol, "food." They were then introduced to unfamiliar food items, for which they had no symbols, to see if they would place them in the food category. The fact that they both had perfect or nearly perfect scores further substantiated that they could categorize unfamiliar objects. More importantly, it was clear that they were capable of assigning to unknown objects symbols that denoted member-

ship in a broad grouping. This ability was a strong indication that the chimpanzees understood that the symbols were being used referentially.

However, subsequent work with Lana, who had different language experiences, did not prove as successful. Although Lana was able to sort actual objects into categories, she was unable to assign generic symbols to novel items (Savage-Rumbaugh and Lewin, 1994). Thus, it became apparent that the manner in which chimpanzees are introduced to language influences their ability to understand the representational value of symbols.

Chimpanzees learn language differently than do human children in that they must be taught. Human children learn language spontaneously, through exposure, without needing to be deliberately taught. Therefore, it is significant that Savage-Rumbaugh and her colleagues reported that the infant male bonobo Kanzi (Fig. 7–12), much prior to his toolmaking days, was spontaneously acquiring and using symbols at the age of 2$\frac{1}{2}$ years (Savage-Rumbaugh et al., 1986a). Kanzi's younger half-sister began to use symbols spontaneously at 11 months of age. Both animals had been exposed to the use of lexigrams when they accompanied their mother to training sessions. But neither youngster had received instruction and in fact were not involved in the sessions.

The scientists involved in ape language research are convinced that apes are capable, to varying degrees, of employing symbols to communicate. It has been strongly suggested that bonobos are superior in this ability to chimpanzees and gorillas (Savage-Rumbaugh, 1986, 1994).

These statements do not mean that apes acquire and use language in the same way humans do. In general, apes must be taught to use symbols to communicate. Moreover, it appears that not all signing apes understand the referential relationship between symbol and object, person, or action. Nonetheless, there is abundant evidence that humans are not the only species capable of some degree of symbolic thought and complex communication.

From an evolutionary perspective, the ape language experiments may suggest clues to the origins of human language. Quite possibly, the last common ancestor that hominids shared with the great apes possessed communication capabilities similar to those we see now in modern **pongids**. If so, we need to elucidate the factors that enhanced the adaptive significance of these characteristics in our own lineage. It is equally important to explore why these pressures did not operate to the same degree in gorillas, chimpanzees, and bonobos.

Pongids
Members of the family Pongidae, including orangutans, gorillas, chimpanzees, and bonobos.

FIGURE 7–12
The bonobo Kanzi, as a youngster, using lexigrams to communicate with human observers. (Photograph by Elizabeth Pugh.)

Courtesy, Rose A. Sevcik, Language Research Center, Georgia State University; photo by Elizabeth Pugh

It would be difficult to overstate the significance of human cognitive abilities, as evidenced in our reliance on complex patterns of communication and our technological manipulations of the natural environment. But these capacities should not be used to set humankind apart from the rest of nature, as they almost universally are. In fact, the genetic and behavioral similarities we share with the great apes, as well as ape proficiency at symbolic communication, indicate that the very qualities we have traditionally considered unique to our species are in reality expressed in other species, too, but to a lesser degree.

The Primate Continuum

For decades, behavioral psychology taught that animal behavior represents nothing more than a series of conditioned responses to specific stimuli (Fig. 7–13). (This perspective is very convenient for those who wish to exploit nonhuman animals, for whatever purposes, and remain free of guilt.) Fortunately, this attitude has begun to change in recent years to reflect a growing awareness that humans, although in many ways unquestionably unique, are nevertheless part of a **biological continuum**.

Where do humans fit, then, in this biological continuum? Are we at the top? The answer depends on the criteria used, and we must also bear in mind that evolution is not a goal-directed process. Certainly, we are the most intelligent species, if we define intelligence in terms of problem-solving abilities and abstract thought. However, if we look more closely, we recognize that the differences between ourselves and our primate relatives, especially chimpanzees and bonobos, are primarily quantitative and not qualitative.

Although human brains are absolutely and relatively larger, neurological processes are functionally the same. The necessity of close bonding with at least one parent and the need for physical contact are essentially the same. Developmental stages and dependence on learning are strikingly similar. Indeed, even in the chimpanzee's capacity for cruelty and aggression combined with compassion, tenderness, and altruism, we see a close parallel to the dichotomy between "evil" and "good" so long recognized in ourselves. The main difference between how chimpanzees and humans express these qualities (and therefore the dichotomy) is one of degree. Humans are much more adept at both cruelty and compassion, and humans reflect on their behavior in ways that chimpanzees do not. While chimpanzees may not understand the suffering they inflict on others, humans do.

Biological continuum
The fact that organisms are related through common ancestry and that behaviors and traits seen in one species are also seen in others to varying degrees. (When expressions of a phenomenon continuously grade into one another so that there are no discrete categories, they are said to exist on a continuum. For example, color is such a phenomenon.)

FIGURE 7–13
This unfortunate advertising display is a good example of how humans misunderstand and thus misrepresent our closest relatives.

Lynn Kilgore

Likewise, while an adult chimpanzee may sit next to and protect a dying relative or friend, it does not appear to feel intense grief and a sense of loss to the extent a human normally does.

To arrive at any understanding of what it is to be human, it is vastly important to recognize that many of our behaviors are but elaborate extensions of those of our hominid ancestors and close primate relatives. We share 98 percent of our DNA with chimpanzees. The fact that so many of us prefer to bask in the warmth of the "sun belt" with literally millions of others reflects our heritage as social animals adapted to life in the tropics. Likewise, it is no mistake that industry has invested millions of dollars in the development of low-calorie, artificial sweeteners. The "sweet tooth" that afflicts so many humans is a direct result of our earlier primate ancestors' predilection for high-energy sugar contained in desirably sweet, ripe fruit.

The fact that humans are part of an evolutionary continuum is the entire basis for animal research aimed at benefiting our species. Yet, even with our growing awareness of the similarities we share, we continue to cage nonhuman primates with little regard for the very needs they share with us. We would argue that nonhuman primates should be maintained in social groups and that habitat enrichment programs should be introduced. It would seem the very least we can do for our close relatives, from whom we continue to derive so many benefits.

SUMMARY

We have discussed many aspects of nonhuman primate behavior, such as social organization and dominance hierarchies, communication, reproduction, intra- and intergroup relationships (including mothers and infants), aggression, friendship, and culture (in the form of tool use). These behaviors have been treated, to considerable extent, from an evolutionary perspective; specifically, we have attempted to show what features of the environment are most likely to be important in shaping primate social behavior.

Group size and composition are influenced by such environmental components as diet, resource availability, and predators. Moreover, many behaviors are seen as the result of natural selection; that is, they promote increased likelihood of survival and reproduction. Therefore, individuals, ideally, should behave in ways that will maximize their own reproductive success relative to others. Although this does not imply that in mammals, and especially primates, there are genes for specific behaviors, it does suggest that genes may have mediating effects on behavior—perhaps through such products as hormones.

We have emphasized that humans are part of a biological continuum that includes all the primates. It is this evolutionary relationship, then, that accounts for many of the behaviors we have in common with prosimians, monkeys, and apes.

QUESTIONS FOR REVIEW

1. What factors should be considered if one approaches the study of nonhuman primate behavior from an evolutionary perspective?
2. What are some of the environmental factors believed to influence group size and social organization? Give two examples.
3. How could multimale, multifemale groupings be advantageous to species living in areas where predation pressure is high?
4. How may solitary foraging be advantageous to primates? Discuss two examples.
5. How may genetic factors influence behavior?
6. Discuss a primate behavior that has traditionally been used as an example of behavioral evolution.
7. What are reproductive strategies, and what is their basic goal?

8. Primates are said to be K-selected. What is meant by this? What is r-selection? Give an example of r-selection.
9. Explain male and female differences with regard to parental investment.
10. What are dominance hierarchies? What is their function in primate groups?
11. What is believed to be the primary benefit of being a high-ranking individual? What are three factors that influence an individual's rank in a group?
12. What is grooming? Why is it so important in many primate species; that is, what functions does it serve?
13. Discuss three ways nonhuman primates can communicate information to other group members. Name at least two "threat gestures."
14. Name two ways in which nonhuman primates communicate reassurance.
15. What is meant by an open system of communication? How does it differ from a closed system?
16. What is seen as the basic social unit among all primates? Why is it so important?
17. Discuss an example of between-group aggression. What is thought to have motivated the violence between two groups of chimpanzees at Gombe?
18. Discuss two examples of nonhuman primate cultural behavior. Why is our discovery of these behaviors important to studies of early human evolution?
19. Discuss the language acquisition studies using chimpanzees, bonobos, and gorillas. What are the implications of this research?
20. What do we mean when we state that humans are a part of a biological continuum? How does the view expressed in this statement differ from traditional views expressed by most people?

SUGGESTED FURTHER READING

Cartmill, Matt. 1990. "Human Uniqueness and Theoretical Content in Paleoanthropology." *International Journal of Primatology* 11(3): 173–192.

Cheney, Dorothy L., and Robert M. Seyfarth. 1990. *How Monkeys See the World.* Chicago: University of Chicago Press.

Goodall, Jane. 1986. *The Chimpanzees of Gombe.* Cambridge, MA: The Belknap Press of Harvard University Press.

King, Barbara J. 1994. *The Information Continuum: Social Information Transfer in Monkeys, Apes, and Hominids.* Santa Fe: SAR Press.

McGrew, W. C. 1992. *Chimpanzee Material Culture.* Cambridge, MA: Cambridge University Press.

_____. 1998. "Culture in Nonhuman Primates?" *Annual Review of Anthropology* 27: 301–328.

Napier, J. R., and P. H. Napier. 1985. *The Natural History of the Primates.* Cambridge, MA: The MIT Press.

Packer, C., and A. E. Pusey. 1997. "Divided We Fall: Cooperation Among Lions." *Scientific American* 276(5): 52–59.

Savage-Rumbaugh, S., and Roger Lewin. 1994. *Kanzi: The Ape at the Brink of the Human Mind.* New York: Wiley.

Smuts, Barbara B., Dorothy L. Cheney, Robert M. Seyfarth, Richard W. Wrangham, and Thomas T. Struhsaker (eds.). 1987. *Primate Societies.* Chicago: University of Chicago Press.

Strier, Karen B. 2000. *Primate Behavioral Ecology.* Boston: Allyn Bacon.

RESOURCES ON THE INTERNET

Wadsworth Anthropology Resource Center
http://anthropology.wadsworth.com

The companion website for this text includes a range of enrichment material focused on the chapter's topic. While online you can enhance your understanding of the chapter by exploring one of the several additional Internet Exercises, by researching topics, and by accessing full articles on InfoTrac College Edition. You can also reinforce the concepts by taking online practice exams.

Internet Exercises

Living Links is a website at the Yerkes Regional Primate Research Center dedicated to research on the great apes. Visit this site at **www.emory.edu/LIVING_LINKS/** and explore the various topics presented there. Topics include behavior, communication, and conservation, to name a few. There are also audios of some nonhuman primate vocalizations. Choose any topic, and after reading the available information, make a list of facts you have learned.

InfoTrac College Edition
http://www.infotrac-college.com/wadsworth

Do a search for *primatology* and go to *primates*, then the subdivision *behavior*. Select an article from this list of references that relates to some aspect of primate behavior. Do the behaviors described in this article have any relevance for studies of human or early hominid behavior?

Primates in Biomedical Research: Ethics and Concerns

The use of nonhuman animals for experimentation is an established practice, long recognized for its benefits to human beings as well as to nonhuman animals. Currently, an estimated 17 to 22 million animals are used annually in the United States for the testing of new vaccines and other methods of treating or preventing disease, as well as for the development of innovative surgical procedures. Nonhuman animals are also used in psychological experimentation and in the testing of consumer products.

Because of biological and behavioral similarities shared with humans, nonhuman primates are among those species most desired for biomedical research. According to figures from the United States Department of Agriculture (USDA), 42,620 primates were used in laboratory studies in 1991. On average, about 50,000 are used annually, with approximately 3,000 being involved in more than one study. The most commonly used primates are baboons, vervets, various macaque species, squirrel monkeys, marmosets, and tamarins. Because they are more costly than other species (such as mice, rats, rabbits, cats, and dogs), primates are usually reserved for medical and behavioral studies and not for the testing of consumer goods such as cosmetics or household cleaners. (It should be noted that many cosmetic companies assert that they no longer perform tests on animals.)

Although work with primates has certainly benefited humankind, these benefits are expensive, not only monetarily but in terms of suffering and animal lives lost. The development of the polio vaccine in the 1950s serves as one example of the costs involved. Prior to the 1950s, polio had killed and crippled millions of people worldwide. Now the disease is almost unheard of, at least in developed nations. But included in the price tag for the polio vaccine were the lives of 1.5 *million* rhesus macaques, mostly imported from India.

Unquestionably, the elimination of polio and other diseases is a boon to humanity, and such achievements are part of the obligation of medical research to promote the health and well-being of humans. But at the same time, serious questions have been raised about medical advances made at the expense of millions of nonhuman animals, many of whom are primates. Indeed, one well-known primatologist, speaking at a conference some years ago, questioned whether we can morally justify depleting populations of threatened species solely for the benefit of a single, highly overpopulated one.

This question will seem extreme, if not absurd, to many readers, especially in view of the fact that the majority of people would argue that *whatever* is necessary to promote human health and longevity is justified.

Leaving the broader ethical issues aside for a moment, one area of controversy regarding laboratory primates is housing. Traditionally, lab animals have been kept in small metal cages, usually one or two per cage. Cages are usually bare, except for food and water, and they are frequently stacked one on top of another, so that their inhabitants find themselves in the unnatural situation of having animals above and below them, as well as on each side.

The primary reason for small cage size is simple. Small cages are less expensive than large ones and they require less space (space is also costly). Moreover, sterile, unenriched cages (i.e., lacking objects for manipulation or play) are easier and therefore cheaper to clean. But for such curious, intelligent animals as primates, these easy-to-maintain facilities result in a deprivation that leads to depression, neurosis, and psychosis. (The application of these terms to a nonhuman context is criticized as being anthropomorphic by many who believe that nonhuman animals, including primates, cannot be said to have psychological needs.)

Chimpanzees, reserved primarily for AIDS and hepatitis B research, probably suffer more than any other species from inadequate facilities. In 1990, Jane Goodall published a description of conditions she encountered in one lab she visited in Maryland. In this facility, she saw two- and three-year-old chimpanzees housed, two together, in cages measuring 22 inches square and 24 inches high. Obviously, movement for these youngsters was virtually impossible, and they had been housed in this manner for over three months. At this same lab and others, adult chimps, infected with HIV or hepatitis, were confined alone for several years in small isolation chambers, where they rocked back and forth, seeing little and hearing nothing of their surroundings.

Fortunately, conditions are improving. There has been increased public awareness of existing conditions; and there is, among some members of the biomedical community, a growing sensitivity toward the special requirements of primates.

In 1991, amendments to the Animal Welfare Act were enacted to require all labs to provide minimum standards for the humane care of all "warm-blooded" animals. (Birds and rodents were not included in this category, but this situation has been amended and is now under appeal.) These minimum standards provide specific requirements for cage size based on weight of the animal. For example, primates weighing less than 2.2 pounds must have 1.6 square feet of floor space per animal, and the cage must be at least 20 inches high. Those weighing more than 55 pounds are allotted at least 25.1 square feet of floor space per animal and at least 84 inches (7 feet) of vertical space.

Clearly, the enclosures described above are not sufficiently large for normal locomotor activities, and this could certainly contribute to psychological stress. One method of reducing such stress is to provide cages with objects and climbing structures. (Even part of a dead branch is a considerable improvement and costs nothing.) Several facilities are now implementing such procedures. Also, many laboratory staffs are now trained to provide enrichment for the animals in their care. Moreover, the Maryland lab that Dr. Goodall observed no longer maintains chimpanzees in isolation chambers. Rather, they are now housed with other animals in areas measuring 80 cubic feet and are provided with enrichment devices.

Aside from the treatment of captive primates, there continues to be concern over the depletion of wild populations in order to provide research animals. Actually, the number of wild-caught animals used in research today is small compared to the numbers lost to habitat destruction and hunting for food. However, in the past, particu-

larly in the 1950s and 1960s, the numbers of animals captured for research were staggering. In 1968, for example, 113,714 primates were received in the United States alone!

Fortunately, the number of animals imported into the United States has declined dramatically since the Convention on Trade in Endangered Species (CITES) was ratified in 1973. In 1984, for example, the United States imported 13,148 primates (Mittermeier and Cheney, 1987). More recently the United States annually imports an estimated 20,000 animals (some from breeding colonies in the country of origin). Although it would be best if no free-ranging primates were involved, at least these figures represent a substantial improvement since the 1960s.

It is important to note that biomedical research accounts for only a small part of the demand for primates captured in the wild. The exotic pet trade provides a much greater share of the market, both locally and internationally. But even more important is the hunting or live capture of primates for human consumption. This is especially true in parts of West Africa and Asia. Moreover, in several Asian countries, there is a growing demand for animal (including primate) products (body parts such as bones or brain tissue) for medicinal purposes.

In response to concerns for diminishing wild populations and regulations to protect them, a number of breeding colonies have been established in the United States and other countries to help meet demands for laboratory animals. Additionally, in 1986, the National Institutes of Health established the National Chimpanzee Breeding Program to provide chim-

panzees primarily for AIDS and hepatitis B research.

Furthermore, in 1989, the United States Fish and Wildlife Service upgraded the status of wild chimpanzees from "threatened" to "endangered." The endangered status was not applied to animals born in captivity; the upgrade was intended to provide additional protection for free-ranging populations. Unfortunately, even with all the policies now in place, there is no guarantee that some wild-born chimpanzees will not find their way into research labs.

The animal rights movement has been described by many in the scientific community as "antiscience" or "anti-intellectual." Certainly, there are extremists in the animal rights movement for whom these labels are appropriate. But to categorize in this manner all who have concern for animals and, in this case, primates is unjustified. There are many concerned members of the biomedical and scientific communities, including the authors of this text, to whom these labels do not apply.

It is neither antiscience nor anti-intellectual to recognize that humans who derive benefits from the use of nonhuman species have an obligation to reduce suffering and provide adequate facilities for highly intelligent, complex animals. This obligation does not necessitate laboratory break-ins. But improvement does mean that individual members of the biomedical community must become even more aware of the requirements of captive primates. Moreover, those involved in primate testing, as well as the granting agencies that fund them, should be kept well informed as to the status of wild primate populations. Lastly, and

Primates in Biomedical Research: Ethics and Concerns (continued)

perhaps most importantly, existing laws that regulate the capture, treatment, and trade of wild-caught animals *must* be more strictly enforced.

Undoubtedly, humankind has much to gain by using nonhuman primates for experimentation. But we also have a moral obligation to ensure their survival in the wild, as well as to provide them with humane treatment and enriched captive environments. But most of all, we owe them respect as complex, intelligent, and sensitive animals who are not that different from ourselves. If we grant them this, the rest should follow.

Critical Thinking Questions

1. What do you see as the benefits derived from using nonhuman primates in biomedical research? Have you personally benefited from this type of research? If so, how?

2. Do you personally have concerns regarding the use of nonhuman primates in biomedical research? Explain your views.

3. Delineate the issues surrounding habitat enrichment for laboratory primates. Do you think enrichment is an important concern? Why or why not? If so, how would you address this issue, bearing in mind that there are constraints on funding?

4. What do you see as solutions to the problem of depletion of wild populations of nonhuman primates? Your answer should be practical and should take into consideration the needs of humans and limited financial resources.

Sources

Goodall, Jane. 1990. *Through a Window*. Boston: Houghton-Mifflin.

Holden, Constance. 1988. "Academy Explores Use of Laboratory Animals." *Science* 242 (October): 185.

Mittermeier, R. A., and D. Cheney. 1987. "Conservation of Primates in their Habitats," in B. Smuts et al., eds., *Primate Societies*, pp. 477–496. Chicago: University of Chicago Press.

United States Department of Agriculture. Subchapter A—Animal Welfare. Washington, D.C.: U.S. Government Printing Office, Publication Number 311–364/60638, 1992.

Note: We would like to express special appreciation to Dr. Shirley MacGreal, President, International Primate Protection League, and to Dr. Thomas L. Wolfle, Director, Institute of Laboratory Animal Resources, for providing information for this issue.

CHAPTER

8

CONTENTS

Mammalian/Primate Evolutionary History

See the following sections of the CD-ROM for topics covered in this chapter: Virtual Lab 7, sections I, II, and III.

Introduction

In the two preceding chapters, we surveyed the structure, ecology, and social behavior of *living* primates. In this chapter, we shift our focus to primate evolution. To place primates, and more specifically, hominids, in their proper evolutionary context, we first give a brief summary of vertebrate and mammalian evolution.

In addition to the broad trends of evolutionary history, we also discuss some contemporary issues relating to evolutionary theory. In particular, we emphasize concepts that relate to large-scale evolutionary processes, that is, *macroevolution* (in contrast to the microevolutionary focus of Chapter 4). The fundamental perspectives reviewed here concerning geological history, principles of classification, and modes of evolutionary change will serve as a basis for topics covered throughout the remainder of the text.

The Human Place in the Organic World

There are millions of species living today; if we were to include microorganisms, the total would surely exceed tens of millions. And if we then added in the vast multitudes of species that are now extinct, the total would be staggering—perhaps hundreds of millions!

How do biologists cope with all this diversity? As is typical for *Homo sapiens*, scientists approach complexity through simplification. Thus, biologists group life forms together; that is, they construct a **classification**. For example, today there are probably more than 15 million species of animals, most of them insects. No one knows exactly how many species there are, because more than 90 percent have yet to be scientifically described or named. Nevertheless, even with the tens of thousands of species that biologists do know something about, there is still too much diversity to handle conveniently—indeed, too many names for the human brain to remember. Thus, the solution is to organize the diversity into groups to (1) reduce the complexity and (2) indicate evolutionary relationships.

Organisms that move about and ingest food (but do not photosynthesize, as do plants) are called animals. More precisely, the multicelled animals are placed within the group called the **Metazoa** (Fig. 8–1). Within the Metazoa there are more than 20 major groups termed *phyla* (*sing.*, phylum). One of these phyla is the **Chordata**, animals with a nerve cord, gill slits (at some stage of development), and a stiff supporting cord along the back called a *notochord*. Most chordates today are **vertebrates**, in which the notochord has become a vertebral column (which gives its name to the group); in addition, vertebrates have a developed brain and paired sensory structures for sight, smell, and balance.

The vertebrates themselves are subdivided into six classes: bony fishes, cartilaginous fishes, amphibians, reptiles, birds, and mammals. We will discuss mammal classification later in this chapter.

Principles of Classification

Before we go any further, it would be useful to discuss the bases of animal classification. The field that specializes in delineating the rules of classification is called *taxonomy*. As mentioned in Chapter 6, organisms are classified first, and most traditionally, on the basis of physical similarities. Such was the basis of the first systematic classification devised by Linnaeus in the eighteenth century (see Chapter 2).

Today, basic physical similarities are still considered a good starting point in postulating schemes of organic relationships. For similarities to be useful, however, they *must* reflect evolutionary descent. For example, the bones of the forelimb of all terrestrial air-breathing vertebrates (tetrapods) are so similar in number and form (Fig. 8–2) that the obvious explanation for the striking resemblance is that all four kinds of air-breathing vertebrates ultimately derived their forelimb structure from a common ancestor.

Classification
In biology, the ordering of organisms into categories, such as phyla, orders, and families, to show evolutionary relationships.

Metazoa
Multicellular animals; a major division of the animal kingdom.

Chordata
The phylum of the animal kingdom that includes vertebrates.

Vertebrates
Animals with bony backbones; includes fishes, amphibians, reptiles, birds, and mammals.

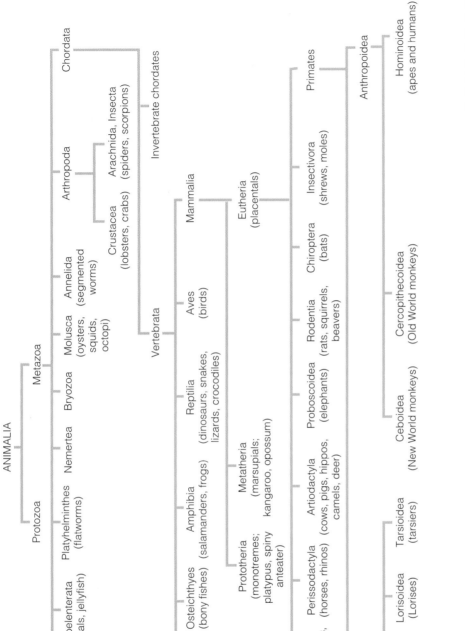

FIGURE 8–1
Classification chart, modified from Linnaeus. All animals are placed in certain categories based on structural similarities. Not all members of categories are shown. For example, there are up to 20 orders of placental mammals (8 are depicted). A more comprehensive classification of the primate order was presented in Chapter 6.

FIGURE 8–2
Homologies. The similarities in the bones of these animals can be most easily explained by descent from a common ancestor.

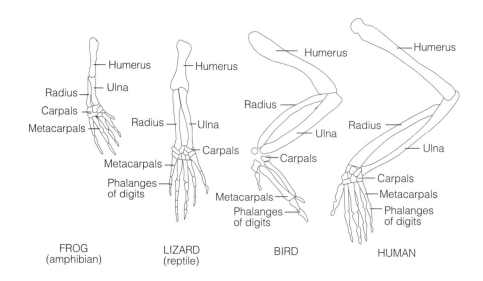

FROG (amphibian)   LIZARD (reptile)   BIRD   HUMAN

Homologies
Similarities between organisms based on descent from a common ancestor.

Analogies
Similarities between organisms based strictly on common function with no assumed common evolutionary descent.

Homoplasy
(*homo*, meaning "same," and *plasy*, meaning "growth") The separate evolutionary development of similar characteristics in different groups of organisms.

Evolutionary systematics
A traditional approach to classification (and evolutionary interpretation) in which presumed ancestors and descendants are traced in time by analysis of homologous characters.

Cladistics
An approach to classification that seeks to make rigorous evolutionary interpretations based solely on analysis of certain types of homologous (i.e., derived) characters.

Structures that are shared by species on the basis of descent from a common ancestor are called **homologies**. Homologies alone are reliable indicators of evolutionary relationship. But we must be careful not to draw hasty conclusions from superficial similarities.

For example, both birds and butterflies have wings, but they should not be grouped together on the basis of this single characteristic; butterflies (as insects) differ dramatically from birds in a number of other, even more fundamental ways. (For example, birds have an internal skeleton, central nervous system, and four limbs; insects do not.).

What has happened in evolutionary history is that from quite distant ancestors, both butterflies and birds have developed wings *independently*. Thus, their (superficial) similarities are a product of separate evolutionary response to roughly similar functional demands; such similarities, based on independent functional adaptation and *not* on shared evolutionary descent, are called **analogies**. The process that leads to the development of analogies (also called analogous structures) such as wings in birds and butterflies is termed **homoplasy**. In the case of butterflies and birds, the homoplasy has occurred in evolutionary lines that share only very remote ancestry. Here, homoplasy has produced analogous structures separately from any homology. In some cases, however, homoplasy can occur in lineages that are more closely related (and which thus share considerable homology as well). Examples of homoplasy in closely related lineages are evident among the primates (e.g., among New and Old World monkeys and also among the great apes; see Chapter 6).

Constructing Classifications and Interpreting Evolutionary Relationships

There are two major approaches, or "schools," by which evolutionary biologists interpret evolutionary relationships and thus produce classifications. The first of these, called **evolutionary systematics**, is a more traditional approach, whereas the second approach, called **cladistics**, has emerged primarily in the last two decades. While aspects of both approaches are still utilized by most evolutionary biologists, in recent years cladistic methodologies have predominated among anthropologists. Indeed, one noted primate evolutionist recently commented that "virtually all current studies of primate phylogeny involve the methods and terminology" of cladistics (Fleagle, 1998, p. 1).

Before drawing distinctions between these two approaches, it is first helpful to note features shared by both evolutionary systematics and cladistics. First, both schools are interested in tracing evolutionary relationships and constructing classifications that reflect these relationships. Second, both schools recognize that organisms must be compared for specific features (called *characters*) and that some of these characters are more informative than others. And third (and deriving directly from the previous two points), both approaches focus exclusively on homologies.

However, there are also significant differences between these approaches in terms of how characters are chosen, which groups are compared, and how the results are interpreted and eventually incorporated into evolutionary schemes and classifications. The primary difference is that cladistics more explicitly and more rigorously defines the kinds of homologies that yield the most useful information. For example, at a very basic level, all life (except for some viruses) shares DNA as the molecule underlying all organic processes. However, beyond inferring that all life most likely derives from a single origin (a most intriguing point), the presence of DNA tells us nothing further regarding more specific relationships among different kinds of life forms. To draw further conclusions, we need to look at particular characters that are shared by certain groups as the result of more recent ancestry.

This perspective emphasizes an important point: Some homologous characters are much more informative than others. We saw earlier that all terrestrial vertebrates share homologies in the number and basic arrangement of bones in the forelimb. Thus, while these similarities are broadly useful in showing that these large evolutionary groups (amphibians, reptiles, birds, and mammals) are all related through a distant ancestor, they do not provide any usable information by which to distinguish one from another (a reptile from a mammal, for example). Such characters (also called traits) that are shared through such remote ancestry (i.e., more remote than the common ancestor of each of the groups being compared) are said to be **primitive**, or **ancestral**. We prefer the term *ancestral*, because it does not carry a negative connotation regarding the evolutionary value of the character in question. In physical anthropology, the term *primitive* or *ancestral* simply means that a character seen in two organisms is derived in both of them from a distant ancestor.

In most circumstances, analysis of ancestral characters does not provide enough information to make accurate evolutionary interpretations regarding relationships between different groups. In fact, misinterpretation of ancestral characters can easily lead to quite inaccurate evolutionary conclusions! The traits that cladistics focuses on, and which are far more informative, are those that distinguish particular evolutionary lineages. Such characters are said to be **derived**, or **modified**. Thus, while the general ancestral bony pattern of the forelimb in land animals with backbones does not allow us to distinguish among them, the further modification in certain groups (as hooves, flippers, or wings, for instance) does.

A simplified example might help clarify the basic principles used in cladistic analysis. Figure 8–3a shows a hypothetical "lineage" of passenger vehicles. All of the "descendant" vehicles share a common ancestor, the prototype passenger vehicle. The first major division (I) is that differentiating passenger cars from trucks. The second split (i.e., diversification) is between luxury cars and sports cars (you could, of course, imagine many other subcategories). Modified (derived) traits that distinguish trucks from cars might include type of frame, suspension, wheel size, and, in some forms, an open cargo bed. Derived characters that might distinguish sports cars from luxury cars could include engine size and type, wheel base size, and a decorative racing stripe.

Now let us assume that you are presented with an "unknown" vehicle (i.e., one as yet unclassified). How do you decide what kind of vehicle it is? You might note such features as four wheels, a steering wheel, and a seat for the driver, but these are *ancestral* characters of all passenger vehicles (and ones found in the common ancestor). If, however, you note that the vehicle lacks a cargo bed and raised suspension (i.e., is not a truck) but has a racing stripe, you might conclude that it is a car, and more than that, a sports car (since it has a derived feature presumably of *only* that group).

 See Virtual Lab 7, section II for a discussion of taxonomy and classification.

Ancestral (primitive)
Referring to characters inherited by a group of organisms from a remote ancestor and thus not diagnostic of groups (lineages) branching subsequent to the time the character first appeared.

Derived (modified)
Referring to characters that are modified from the ancestral condition and thus *are* diagnostic of particular evolutionary lineages.

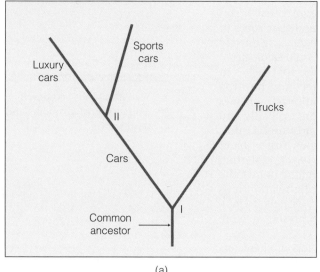

(a)

(b)

From a common ancestor of all passenger vehicles, the first major divergence is that between cars and trucks (I). A later divergence also occurs between luxury cars and sports cars (II). Derived features of each grouping ("lineage") appear only after its divergence from other groups (e.g., cargo beds are found only in trucks, cushioned suspension only in cars; likewise, only sports cars have a decorative racing stripe).

In this "tree," SUVs diverge from trucks, but like sports cars, they have a decorative racing stripe. This feature is a homoplasy and does *not* make SUVs sports cars. The message is that classifications based on just one characteristic that can appear independently in different groups can lead to an *incorrect* conclusion.

FIGURE 8–3
Evolutionary "trees" showing development of passenger vehicles.

All this seems fairly obvious, and you probably have noticed that this simple type of decision making characterizes much of human mental organization. Still, there are frequently complications that are not so obvious. What if you are presented with a sports utility vehicle (SUV) with a racing stripe (Fig. 8–3b)? SUVs are basically trucks, but the presence of the racing stripe could be seen as a homoplasy with sports cars. The lesson here is that we need to be careful, to look at several traits, to decide which are ancestral and which are derived, and finally to try to recognize the complexity (and confusion) introduced by homoplasy.

The preceding example is useful up to a point. Because it concerns human inventions, the groupings possess characters that humans can add and delete in almost any combination. Naturally occurring organic systems are more limited in this respect. Any species can only possess characters that have been inherited from its ancestor or that have been subsequently modified (derived) from those shared with the ancestor. Thus, any modification in *any* species is constrained by that species' evolutionary legacy—that is, what the species starts out with.

Another example, one drawn from paleontological (fossil) evidence of actual organisms, can help clarify these points. Most people know something about dinosaur evolution, and some of you may know about the recent controversies surrounding this topic. There are a number of intriguing issues concerning the evolutionary history of dinosaurs, and recent fossil discoveries have shed considerable light on them. We will mention some of these issues later in the chapter, but here we will consider one of the more fascinating: the relationship of dinosaurs to birds.

Traditionally, it had been thought that birds were a quite distinct group from reptiles and not especially closely related to any of them (including extinct forms, such as the dinosaurs) (Fig. 8–4a). However, the early origins of birds were clouded in mystery and have been much debated for more than a century. In fact, the first fossil evidence of a very primitive bird (now known to be about 150 million years old) was discovered in 1861, just two years following Darwin's publication of *Origin of Species*. Despite some initial and quite remarkably accurate interpretations by Thomas Huxley linking these early birds to dinosaurs, most experts concluded that there was no close relationship. This view persisted through most of the twentieth

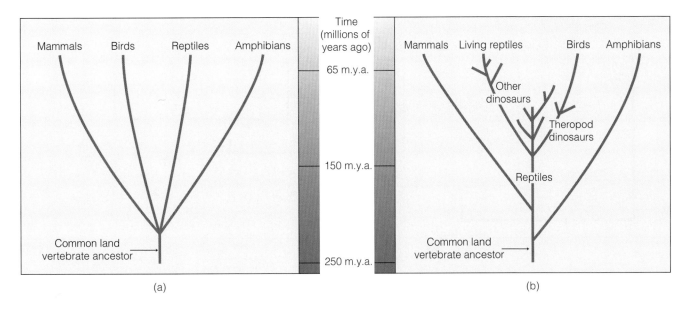

(a)

(b)

Time
(millions of
years ago)

65 m.y.a.

150 m.y.a.

250 m.y.a.

FIGURE 8–4
Evolutionary relationships of birds and
dinosaurs. (a) Traditional view, showing no close
relationship. (b) Revised view, showing common
ancestry of birds and dinosaurs.

century, but events of the last two decades have swung the consensus back to the hypothesis that birds *are* closely related to some dinosaurs. Two developments in particular have influenced this change of opinion: the remarkable discoveries in the 1990s from China, Madagascar, and elsewhere and the application of cladistic methods to the interpretation of these and other fossils.

Recent finds from Madagascar of chicken-size very primitive birds dated to 70–65 million years ago (m.y.a.) show an elongated second toe (similar, in fact, to that in the dinosaur *Velociraptor*, made infamous in the film *Jurassic Park*). Indeed, these primitive birds from Madagascar show many other similarities to *Velociraptor* and its close cousins, which together comprise a group of small- to medium-sized ground-living, carnivorous dinosaurs called **theropods**. Even more extraordinary finds have been found recently in China, where embossed in fossilized sediments are traces of what were once *feathers*! For many researchers, these new finds have finally solved the mystery of bird origins, leading some experts to conclude that this evidence "shows that birds are not only *descended* from dinosaurs, they *are* dinosaurs (and reptiles)—just as humans are mammals, even though people are as different from other mammals as birds are from other reptiles" (Padian and Chiappe, 1998, p. 43) (Fig. 8–4b).

There are some doubters who remain concerned that the presence of feathers in dinosaurs (145–125 m.y.a.) might simply be a homoplasy (i.e., these creatures developed the trait independently from its appearance in birds). Certainly, the possibility of homoplasy must always be considered, as it can add considerably to the complexity of what seems like a straightforward evolutionary interpretation. Indeed, strict cladistic analysis assumes that homoplasy is not a common occurrence; if it were, perhaps no evolutionary interpretation could be very straightforward! In the case of the proposed relationship between some (theropod) dinosaurs and birds, the presence of feathers looks like an excellent example of a shared derived characteristic, which therefore *does* link the forms. Moreover, cladistic analysis emphasizes that several characteristics should be examined, since homoplasy might muddle an interpretation based on just one or two shared traits. In the bird-dinosaur case, several other characteristics further suggest their evolutionary relationship.

As we already noted, dinosaur paleontology continues to be a hotbed, fueled by dramatic new discoveries, reinterpretations, and ongoing disputes. Another spectacular new analysis (using ultraviolet light) of a 100 m.y.a. Italian theropod has revealed the presence of internal organs, including the intestines, liver, trachea, and some muscles (Ruben et al., 1999). Initial analysis has suggested that this theropod

Theropods
Small- to medium-sized ground-living dinosaurs, dated to approximately 150 million years ago and thought to be related to birds.

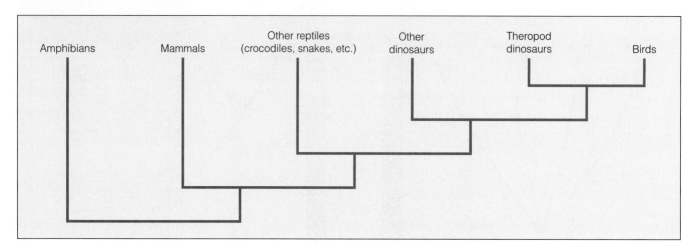

FIGURE 8–5
Cladogram showing relationships of birds, dinosaurs, and other terrestrial vertebrates. Note that no time scale is utilized, and both living and fossil forms are shown along the same dimension (i.e., there is *no* indication of ancestor-descendant relationships).

Phylogenetic tree
A chart showing evolutionary relationships as determined by phylogenetic systematics. It contains a time component and implies ancestor-descendant relationships.

Cladogram
A chart showing evolutionary relationships as determined by cladistic analysis. It is based solely on interpretation of shared derived characters. No time component is indicated, and ancestor-descendant relationships are *not* inferred.

Geological time scale
The organization of earth history into eras, periods, and epochs; commonly used by geologists and paleoanthropologists.

dinosaur had a breathing mechanism quite different from birds but in some ways similar to that of living crocodiles. Some researchers have thus argued that this new evidence casts some doubt on the theropod-bird link. For the moment, however, the overall cladistic analysis of several other traits (following Padian and Chiappe, 1998) argues for a fairly close theropod-bird evolutionary relationship. (*Note:* To falsify this hypothesis, a great deal of homoplasy in theropods and birds would have had to take place.)

One last point needs to be mentioned. Traditional phylogenetic systematics illustrates the hypothesized evolutionary relationships using a *phylogeny*, more properly called a **phylogenetic tree**. Strict cladistic analysis, however, shows relationships in a **cladogram** (Fig. 8–5). If you examine these charts, you will see some obvious differences. A phylogenetic tree incorporates the dimension of time, shown approximately in Figure 8–4. (Numerous other examples can be found in this and subsequent chapters.) A cladogram does not indicate time; all forms (fossil and modern) are indicated along one dimension. Phylogenetic trees usually attempt to make some hypotheses regarding ancestor-descendant relationships (e.g., theropods are ancestral to modern birds). Cladistic analysis (through cladograms) makes no attempt whatsoever to discern ancestor-descendant relationships. In fact, strict cladists are quite skeptical that the evidence really permits such specific evolutionary hypotheses to be scientifically confirmed (since there are many more extinct species than living ones).

In practice, most physical anthropologists (and other evolutionary biologists) utilize cladistic analysis to identify and assess the utility of traits and to make testable hypotheses regarding the relationships of groups of organisms. Moreover, they frequently extend this basic cladistic methodology to further hypothesize likely ancestor-descendant relationships shown relative to a time scale (i.e., in a phylogenetic tree). In this way, aspects of both traditional evolutionary systematics and cladistic analyses are combined to produce a more complete picture of evolutionary history.

Vertebrate Evolutionary History: A Brief Summary

In addition to the staggering array of living and extinct life forms, biologists must also contend with the vast amount of time that life has been evolving on earth. Again, scientists have devised simplified schemes—but in this case to organize *time*, not organic diversity.

Geologists have formulated the **geological time scale** (Fig. 8–6), in which very large time spans are organized into eras and periods. Periods, in turn, can be broken down into epochs (as we will do later in our discussion of primate evolution). For

ERA	PERIOD	(Began m.y.a.)	EPOCH	(Began m.y.a.)
CENOZOIC	Quaternary	1.8	Holocene Pleistocene	0.01 1.8
CENOZOIC	Tertiary	65	Pliocene Miocene Oligocene Eocene Paleocene	5 23 34 55 65
MESOZOIC	Cretaceous	136		
MESOZOIC	Jurassic	190		
MESOZOIC	Triassic	225		
PALEOZOIC	Permian	280		
PALEOZOIC	Carboniferous	345		
PALEOZOIC	Devonian	395		
PALEOZOIC	Silurian	430		
PALEOZOIC	Ordovician	500		
PALEOZOIC	Cambrian	570		
PRE-CAMBRIAN				

FIGURE 8–6
Geological time scale.

 See Virtual Lab 7, section I, for a discussion of geological time.

the time span encompassing vertebrate evolution, there are three eras: the Paleozoic, the Mesozoic, and the Cenozoic. The first vertebrates are present in the fossil record dating to early in the Paleozoic 500 m.y.a. and probably go back considerably further. It is the vertebrate capacity to form bone that accounts for their more complete fossil record *after* 500 m.y.a.

During the Paleozoic, several varieties of fishes (including the ancestors of modern sharks and bony fishes), amphibians, and reptiles appeared. In addition, at the end of the Paleozoic, close to 250 m.y.a., several varieties of mammal-like reptiles were also diversifying. It is widely thought that some of these forms gave rise to the mammals.

The evolutionary history of vertebrates and other organisms during the Paleozoic and Mesozoic was profoundly influenced by geographical events. We know that the positions of the earth's continents have dramatically shifted during the last several hundred million years. This process, called **continental drift**, is explained by the geological theory of *plate tectonics*, which views the earth's crust as a series of gigantic moving and colliding plates. Such massive geological movements can induce volcanic activity (as, for example, all around the Pacific rim), mountain

Continental drift
The movement of continents on sliding plates of the earth's surface. As a result, the positions of large landmasses have shifted dramatically during earth's history.

building (e.g., the Himalayas), and earthquakes. Living on the edge of the Pacific and North American plates, residents of the Pacific coast of the United States are acutely aware of some of these consequences, as illustrated by the explosive volcanic eruption of Mt. St. Helens or the frequent earthquakes in Alaska and California.

Geologists, in reconstructing the earth's physical history, have established the prior (significantly altered) positions of major continental landmasses. During the late Paleozoic, the continents came together to form a single colossal landmass called *Pangea*. In actuality, the continents had been drifting on plates, coming together and separating, long before the end of the Paleozoic (c. 225 m.y.a.), and to be more precise, the large landmass at this time should be called Pangea II. During the early Mesozoic, the southern continents (South America, Africa, Antarctica, Australia, and India) began to split off from Pangea, forming a large southern continent called *Gondwanaland* (Fig. 8–7a). Similarly, the northern continents (North America, Greenland, Europe, and Asia) were consolidated into a northern landmass called *Laurasia*. During the Mesozoic, Gondwanaland and Laurasia continued to drift apart and to break up into smaller segments. By the end of the Mesozoic (c. 65 m.y.a.), the continents were beginning to assume their current positions (Fig. 8–7b).

The evolutionary ramifications of this long-term continental drift were profound. Groups of land animals became effectively isolated from each other by large water boundaries, and the distribution of reptiles and mammals was significantly influenced by continental movements. Although not producing such dramatic continental realignments, the process continued into the Cenozoic. The more specific effects of continental drift on early primate evolution are discussed later in this chapter.

During most of the Mesozoic, reptiles were the dominant land vertebrates, and they exhibited a broad expansion into a variety of **ecological niches**, which included aerial and marine habitats. No doubt, the most famous of these highly successful Mesozoic reptiles were the dinosaurs, which themselves evolved into a wide array of sizes and lifestyles. Dinosaur paleontology, never a boring field, has advanced several startling notions in recent years: that many dinosaurs were warm-blooded; that some varieties were quite social and probably also engaged in considerable parental care; that many forms became extinct as the result of major climatic changes to the earth's atmosphere from collisions with comets or asteroids; and finally, as previously discussed, that not all dinosaurs became entirely extinct, with many descendants still living today (i.e., all modern birds). (See Figure 8–8 for a summary of major events in early vertebrate evolutionary history.)

Ecological niches
The positions of species within their physical and biological environments, together making up the *ecosystem*. A species' ecological niche is defined by such components as diet, terrain, vegetation, type of predators, relationships with other species, and activity patterns, and each niche is unique to a given species.

FIGURE 8–7
Continental drift. Changes in positions of the continental plates from late Paleozoic to the early Cenozoic. (a) The positions of the continents during the Mesozoic (c. 125 m.y.a.). Pangea is breaking up into a northern landmass (Laurasia) and a southern landmass (Gondwanaland). (b) The positions of the continents at the beginning of the Cenozoic (c. 65 m.y.a.).

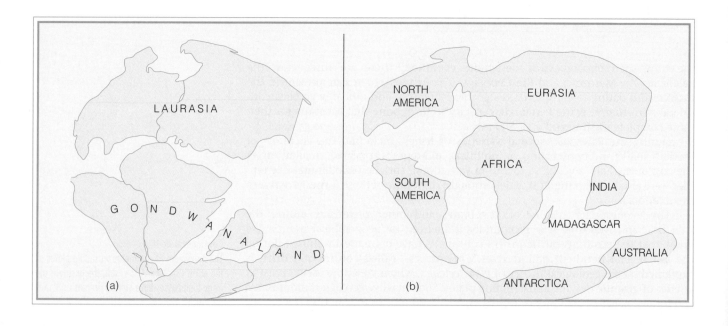

PALEOZOIC							MESOZOIC		
Cambrian	Ordovician	Silurian	Devonian	Carbon-iferous	Permian		Triassic	Jurassic	Cretaceous
Trilobites abundant; also brachiopods, jellyfish, worms, and other invertebrates	First fishes; trilobites still abundant; graptolites and corals become plentiful; possible land plants	Jawed fishes appear; first air-breathing animals; definite land plants	Age of Fish; first amphibians; first forests	First reptiles; radiation of amphibians; modern insects diversify	Reptile radiation; mammal-like reptiles	*Major extinction event*	Reptiles further radiate; first dinosaurs; egg-laying mammals	Great Age of Dinosaurs; flying and swimming dinosaurs; first toothed birds	Placental and marsupial mammals appear; first modern birds	*Major extinction event*

570 m.y.a   500 m.y.a   430 m.y.a   395 m.y.a   345 m.y.a   280 m.y.a   225 m.y.a   190 m.y.a   136 m.y.a   65 m.y.a

The earliest mammals are known from fossil traces fairly early in the Mesozoic, but the first *placental* mammals cannot be positively identified until quite late in the Mesozoic, approximately 70 m.y.a. This highly successful mammalian adaptive radiation is thus almost entirely within the most recent era of geological history, the Cenozoic.

The Cenozoic is divided into two periods, the Tertiary (about 63 million years duration) and the Quaternary, from about 1.8 m.y.a. up to and including the present. Because this division is rather imprecise, paleontologists more frequently refer to the next level of subdivision within the Cenozoic, the **epochs**. There are seven epochs within the Cenozoic: the Paleocene, Eocene, Oligocene, Miocene, Pliocene, Pleistocene, and Holocene, the last often referred to as the Recent (see Fig 8–6).

Mammalian Evolution

Following the extinction of dinosaurs and many other Mesozoic forms (at the end of the Mesozoic), there was a wide array of ecological niches open for the rapid expansion and diversification of mammals. The Cenozoic was an opportunistic time for mammals, and it is known as the Age of Mammals. Mesozoic mammals were small animals, about the size of mice, which they resembled superficially. The wide diversification of mammals in the Cenozoic saw the rise of the major lineages of all modern mammals. Indeed, mammals, along with birds, replaced reptiles as the dominant terrestrial vertebrates.

How do we account for the rapid success of the mammals? Several characteristics relating to learning and general flexibility of behavior are of prime importance. To process more information, mammals were selected for larger brains than those typically found in reptiles. In particular, the cerebrum became generally enlarged, especially the outer covering, the neocortex, which controls higher brain functions (Fig. 8–9). In some mammals, the cerebrum expanded so much that it came to comprise the majority of brain volume; moreover, the number of surface convolutions increased, creating more surface area and thus providing space for even more nerve cells (neurons). As we have already seen (in Chapter 7), this is a trend even further emphasized among the primates.

For such a large and complex organ as the mammalian brain to develop, a longer, more intense period of growth is required. Slower development can occur internally (*in utero*) as well as after birth. While internal fertilization and internal development are not unique to mammals, the latter is a major innovation among

FIGURE 8–8
Time line of major events in early vertebrate evolution.

Epochs
Categories of the geological time scale; subdivisions of periods. In the Cenozoic, epochs include Paleocene, Eocene, Oligocene, Miocene, Pliocene (from the Tertiary), and the Pleistocene and Holocene (from the Quaternary).

FIGURE 8–9
Lateral view of the brain. The illustration shows the increase in the cerebral cortex of the brain. The cerebral cortex integrates sensory information and selects responses.

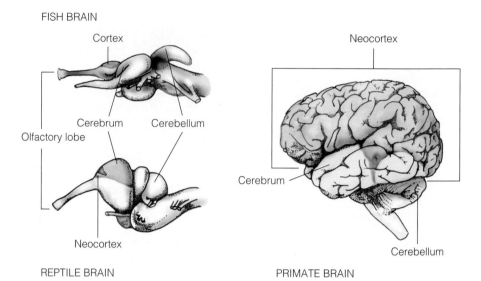

FISH BRAIN

Cortex

Olfactory lobe

Cerebrum   Cerebellum

Neocortex

REPTILE BRAIN

Neocortex

Cerebrum

Cerebellum

PRIMATE BRAIN

Viviparous
Giving birth to live young.

REPTILIAN (alligator): homodont

MAMMALIAN: heterodont

Incisors

Canine

Premolars   Molars

Cheek teeth

FIGURE 8–10
Reptilian and mammalian teeth.

Heterodont
Having different kinds of teeth; characteristic of mammals, whose teeth consist of incisors, canines, premolars, and molars.

Endothermic
(*endo*, meaning "within" or "internal")
Able to maintain internal body temperature through the production of energy by means of metabolic processes within cells; characteristic feature of mammals, birds, and perhaps some dinosaurs.

terrestrial vertebrates. Other forms (birds, most fishes, and reptiles) incubate their young externally by laying eggs (i.e., they are oviparous), while mammals, with very few exceptions, give birth to live young and are thus said to be **viviparous**. Even among mammals, however, there is considerable variation among the major groups in how mature the young are at birth. As you will see, it is in mammals like ourselves, the *placental* forms, where development *in utero* goes the furthest.

Another distinctive feature of mammals is seen in the dentition. While living reptiles consistently have similarly shaped teeth (called a *homodont* dentition), mammals have differently shaped teeth (Fig. 8–10). This varied pattern, termed a **heterodont** dentition, is reflected in the primitive (ancestral) mammalian array of dental elements, which includes 3 incisors, 1 canine, 4 premolars, and 3 molars for each quarter of the mouth. Since the upper and lower jaws are usually the same and are symmetrical for both sides, the "dental formula" is conventionally illustrated by dental quarter (see p. 125 for a more complete discussion of dental patterns as they apply to primates). Thus, with 11 teeth per quarter segment, the primitive mammalian dental complement includes a total of 44 teeth. Such a heterodont arrangement allows mammals to process a wide variety of foods. Incisors can be used for cutting, canines for grasping and piercing, and premolars and molars for crushing and grinding.

A final point regarding teeth relates to their disproportionate representation in the fossil record. As the hardest, most durable portion of a vertebrate skeleton, teeth have the greatest likelihood of becoming fossilized (i.e., mineralized). As a result, the vast majority of the available fossil data for most vertebrates, including primates, consists of teeth.

Another major adaptive complex that distinguishes contemporary mammals from reptiles is the maintenance of a constant internal body temperature. Also colloquially (and incorrectly) called warm-bloodedness, this central physiological adaptation is also seen in contemporary birds (and was also perhaps characteristic of many dinosaurs as well). In fact, many contemporary reptiles are able to approximate a constant internal body temperature through behavioral means (especially by regulating activity and exposing the body to the sun). In this sense, reptiles (along with birds and mammals) could be said to be *homeothermic*. Thus, the most important distinction in contrasting mammals (and birds) with reptiles is how the energy to maintain body temperature is produced and channeled. In reptiles, this energy is obtained directly from exposure (externally) to the sun; reptiles are thus said to be *ectothermic*. In mammals and birds, however, the energy is generated *internally* through metabolic activity (by processing food or by muscle action); mammals and birds are hence referred to as **endothermic**.

Major Mammalian Groups

As briefly mentioned in Chapter 6, there are three major subgroups of living mammals: the egg-laying mammals, or monotremes (Fig. 8–11), the pouched mammals, or marsupials (Fig. 8–12), and the placental mammals. The monotremes are extremely primitive and are considered more distinct from marsupials or placentals than these latter are from each other.

The most notable distinction differentiating the marsupials from the placentals is the type of fetal development. In marsupials, the young are born extremely immature and must complete development in an external pouch. It has been suggested (Carroll, 1988) that such a reproductive strategy is more energetically costly than retaining the young for a longer period *in utero*. In fact, the latter is exactly what placental mammals have done through a more advanced placental connection (from which the group gets its popular name). But perhaps even more basic than fetal nourishment are the means to allow the mother to *tolerate* her young internally over an extended period. Marsupial young are born so quickly after conception that there is little chance for the mother's system to recognize and have an immune rejection of the fetal "foreign" tissue. But in placental mammals, such an immune response would occur were it not for the development of a specialized tissue that isolates the fetus from the mother's immune detection, thus preventing tissue rejection. Quite possibly, this innovation is the central factor in the origin and initial rapid success of placental mammals (Carroll, 1988).

In any case, with a longer gestation period, the central nervous system could develop more completely in the fetus. Moreover, after birth, the "bond of milk" between mother and young also would allow more time for complex neural structures to form. It should also be emphasized that from a *biosocial* perspective, this dependency period not only allows for adequate physiological development, but also provides for a wider range of learning stimuli. That is, the young mammalian brain receives a vast amount of information channeled to it through observation of the mother's behavior and through play with age-mates. It is not sufficient to have evolved a brain capable of learning. Collateral evolution of mammalian social systems has ensured that young mammal brains are provided with ample learning opportunities and are thus put to good use.

FIGURE 8–11
The spiny anteater (a monotreme).

FIGURE 8–12
A wallaby with an infant in the pouch (marsupials).

Early Primate Evolution

The roots of the primate order go back to the beginnings of the placental mammal radiation circa 65 m.y.a. Thus, the earliest primates were diverging from quite early primitive placental mammals. We have seen (in Chapter 6) that strictly defining living primates using clear-cut derived features is not an easy task. The further back we go in the fossil record, the more primitive and, in many cases, the more generalized the fossil primates become. Such a situation makes classifying them all the more difficult.

As a case in point, the earliest identifiable primates were long thought to be a Paleocene group known as the plesiadapiforms. You must remember, however, that much of our understanding, especially of early primates, is based on quite fragmentary evidence, mostly jaws and teeth. In just the last few years, much more complete remains of plesiadapiforms from Wyoming have been discovered, including a nearly complete skull and elements of the hand and wrist.

As a result of this more complete information, the plesiadapiforms have been removed from the primate order altogether. From distinctive features (shared derived characteristics) of the skull and hands, these Paleocene mammals are now thought to be closely related to the colugo (Fig. 8–13). The colugo is sometimes called a "flying lemur," a misnomer, really, as it is not a lemur, nor does it fly (it glides). This group of unusual mammals is probably closely linked to the roots of primates, but apparently was already diverged by Paleocene times.

Given these new and major reinterpretations, we are left with extremely scarce traces of the beginnings of primates. Scholars have suggested that some other recently discovered bits and pieces from North Africa *may* be those of a very small primitive primate. Until more evidence is found, and remembering the lesson of the plesiadapiforms, we will just have to wait and see.

A large array of fossil primates from the Eocene (55–34 m.y.a.) have been discovered and now total more than 200 recognized species. Unlike the available Paleocene forms, those from the Eocene display distinctive primate features. Indeed, primatologist Elwyn Simons (1972, p. 124) has called them "the first primates of modern aspect." These animals have been found primarily in sites in North America and Europe (which were then still connected). It is important to recall that the landmasses that connect continents, as well as the water boundaries that separate them, have obvious impact on the geographical distribution of such terrestrially bound animals as primates.

Some interesting late Eocene forms have also been found in Asia, which was joined to Europe by the end of the Eocene epoch. Looking at the whole array of Eocene primates, it is certain that they were (1) primates, (2) widely distributed, and (3) mostly extinct by the end of the Eocene. What is less certain is how any of them might be related to the living primates. Some of these forms are probably ancestors of the *prosimians*—the lemurs and lorises. Others are probably related to the tarsier. New evidence of *anthropoid* origins has also recently been discovered in several sites from North Africa, the Persian Gulf, and China. These newly discovered fossils of late Eocene anthropoids have now shown that anthropoid origins were well established by 35 m.y.a.

Some new discoveries of very small primates from China are particularly interesting. These 45-million-year-old fossils have been suggested as representing early anthropoids (Gebo et al., 2000), but this hypothesis is still very tentative (there are, as yet, no cranial remains discovered, and the traits that are present are primitive rather than derived in the anthropoid direction). The most intriguing aspect of this recent discovery is the extremely small body size estimated for these primates, considerably smaller, in fact, than any living primate (see Box 8–1).

The Oligocene (34–23 m.y.a.) has yielded numerous additional fossil remains of several different species of early anthropoids. Most of these forms are *Old World anthropoids*, all discovered at a single locality in Egypt, the Fayum (Fig. 8–14). In addition, from North and South America, there are a few known bits that relate

FIGURE 8–13
Colugo.

Doug Wechsler/Animals Animals #MAM 130WED001 01

FIGURE 8–14
Location of the Fayum, an Oligocene primate site in Egypt.

BOX 8–1 DIGGING DEEPER

Telling It Like It Isn't

The discovery of new fossil primates often provokes dramatic media coverage. As we will see in subsequent chapters, when the fossils are hominids, public interest is even keener. When in spring 2000, the discovery of two tiny species of primates from China was first published (Gebo et al., 2000), it quickly received national coverage in the news media. The scientific publication (in a professional journal) provided photographs of the fossils (two small ankle bones) and quantitative estimates of the likely size of the animals. Appropriately, given the very incomplete nature of the remains (Fig. 1), no visual reconstructions of the new species were attempted. However, newspapers, magazines, and Internet sources are not as constrained by scientific considerations. Indeed, a widely published and speculative full-body reconstruction was reproduced in many of these popular news sources (Fig. 3). Interestingly, images of the actual fossil finds were usually omitted, so the average reader would easily con-

clude that the reconstruction derived from reasonable scientific inference. Apparently, the popular media generally assume that the average reader is too unsophisticated to be concerned with actual fossils and is content merely to see what the animal looked like ("in the flesh"). We think this attitude underestimates the intelligence of many readers. We ask you to compare Figures 1 and 2 with Figure 3 and draw your own conclusions.

The most conservative scientific conclusion here would be that no such complete reconstruction is attainable. What is perhaps even more startling than the baseless attempt to depict such a reconstruction is that in almost every significant detail (body proportions, size of head, position of eyes, length of snout, length of tail), it is almost certainly wildly inaccurate, as evidenced from what is actually known from other fossils already discovered. It seems that some illustrator decided simply to draw a little monkey (one, in fact, very reminiscent of a modern squirrel monkey).

FIGURE 1
Actual size
(left) 4.5 mm ($^3/_{16}$")
(right) 4.1 mm ($^5/_{32}$")

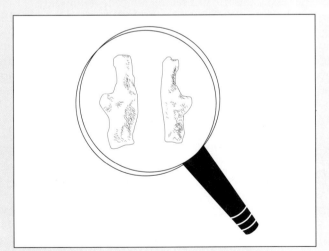

FIGURE 2
Enlargement of fossil ankle bones shown in Figure 1 (magnification approximately 500% of actual size).

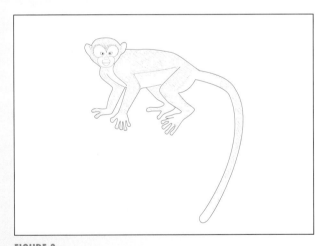

FIGURE 3
Reconstruction of fossil primate (from fossil bones shown in Figure 1). This reconstruction was widely used by popular media (shown to approximate size).

only to the ancestry of New World monkeys. By the early Oligocene, continental drift had separated the New World (i.e., the Americas) from the Old World (Africa and Eurasia). Some of the earliest Fayum forms, nevertheless, *may* potentially be close to the ancestry of both Old and New World anthropoids. It has been suggested that late in the Eocene or very early in the Oligocene, the first anthropoids (primitive "monkeys") arose in Africa and later reached South America by "rafting" over the water separation on drifting chunks of vegetation. What we call "monkey," then, may have a common Old World origin, but the ancestry of New and Old World varieties remains separate after about 35 m.y.a. Our closest evolutionary affinities after this time are with other Old World anthropoids, that is, with Old World monkeys and apes.

The possible roots of anthropoid evolution are illustrated by different forms from the Fayum; one is the **genus** *Apidium*. By *genus* (*pl.*, genera) we mean a group of species that are closely related. In Chapter 2, we discussed Linnaeus' binomial system for designating different organisms (e.g., *Equus callabus* for the horse, *Pan troglodytes* for the chimp, and *Homo sapiens* for humans). The first term (always capitalized—*Equus, Pan, Homo*) is the genus. In paleontological contexts, when remains are fragmentary and usually separated by long time spans, often the best that can be achieved is to make genus-level distinctions (see p. 198 for further discussion).

Apidium, well known at the Fayum, is represented by several dozen jaws or partial dentitions and more than 100 specimens from the limb and trunk skeleton. Because of its primitive dental arrangement, some paleontologists have suggested that *Apidium* may lie near or even before the evolutionary divergence of Old and New World anthropoids. As so much fossil material of teeth and limb bones of *Apidium* has been found, some informed speculation regarding diet and locomotor behavior is possible. It is thought that this small, squirrel-sized primate ate mostly fruits and some seeds and was most likely an arboreal quadruped, adept at leaping and springing (Table 8–1).

The other genus of importance from the Fayum is *Aegyptopithecus*. This genus, also well known, is represented by several well-preserved crania and abundant jaws and teeth. The largest of the Fayum anthropoids, *Aegyptopithecus* is roughly the size of a modern howler monkey (13 to 20 pounds) (Fleagle, 1983) and is thought to have been a short-limbed, slow-moving arboreal quadruped (see Table 8–1). *Aegyptopithecus* is important because, better than any other known form, it bridges the gap between the Eocene fossils and the succeeding Miocene hominoids.

Nevertheless, *Aegyptopithecus* is a very primitive Old World anthropoid, with a small brain and long snout and not showing any derived features of either Old World monkeys or hominoids. Thus, it may be close to the ancestry of *both* major groups of living Old World anthropoids. Found in geological beds dating to 35–33 m.y.a., *Aegyptopithecus* further suggests that the crucial evolutionary divergence of hominoids from other Old World anthropoids occurred *after* this time (Fig. 8–15).

Genus
A group of closely related species.

TABLE 8–1 Inferred General Paleobiological Aspects of Oligocene Primates

	Weight Range	Substratum	Locomotion	Diet
Apidium	750–1,600 g (2–3 lb)	Arboreal	Quadruped	Fruit, seeds
Aegyptopithecus	6,700 g (15 lb)	Arboreal	Quadruped	Fruit, some leaves?

Source: After Fleagle, 1999.

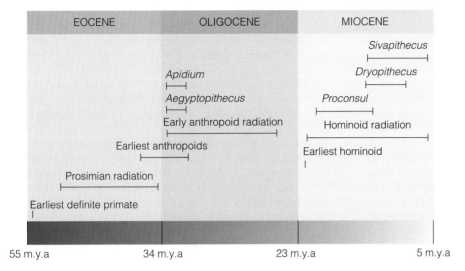

FIGURE 8–15
Major events in early primate evolution.

Miocene Fossil Hominoids

During the approximately 18 million years of the Miocene (23–5 m.y.a.), a great deal of evolutionary activity took place. In Africa, Asia, and Europe, a diverse and highly successful group of hominoids emerged (Fig. 8–16). Indeed, there were many more forms of hominoids from the Miocene than are found today (now represented by the highly restricted groups of apes and one species of humans). In fact, the Miocene could be called "the golden age of hominoids." Many thousands of fossils have been found from dozens of sites scattered in East Africa, southwest Africa, southwest Asia, into western and southern Europe, and extending into southern Asia and China.

During the Miocene, significant transformations relating to climate and repositioning of landmasses took place. By 23 m.y.a., *major* continental locations approximated those of today (except that North and South America were separate). Nevertheless, the movements of South America and Australia further away from

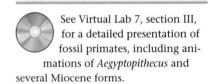

See Virtual Lab 7, section III, for a detailed presentation of fossil primates, including animations of *Aegyptopithecus* and several Miocene forms.

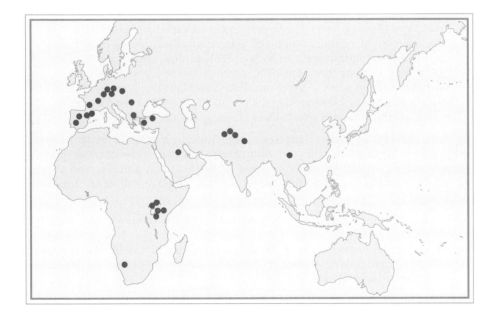

FIGURE 8–16
Miocene hominoid distribution, from fossils thus far discovered.

Antarctica significantly altered ocean currents. Likewise, the continued impact of the South Asian plate into Asia produced the Himalayan Plateau. Both of these paleogeographical modifications had considerable impact on the climate, and the early Miocene was considerably warmer than the preceding Oligocene. Moreover, by 16 m.y.a., the Arabian Plate (which had been separate) "docked" with northeastern Africa. As a result, migrations of animals from Africa directly into southwest Asia (and in the other direction as well) became possible. Among the earliest transcontinental migrants (soon after 16 m.y.a.) were African hominoids who colonized Asia and later Europe.

A problem arises in any attempt to simplify the complex evolutionary situation regarding Miocene hominoids. For example, for many years paleontologists tended to think of these fossil forms as either "apelike" or "humanlike" and used modern examples as models. But as we have just noted, there are very few hominoids remaining. We should not rashly generalize from the living forms to the much more diverse fossil forms; otherwise, we obscure the evolutionary uniqueness of these animals. In addition, we should not expect all fossil forms to be directly or even particularly closely related to living varieties. Indeed, we should expect the opposite; that is, most lines vanish without descendants.

Over the last three decades, the Miocene hominoid assemblage has been interpreted and reinterpreted. As more fossils are found, the evolutionary picture grows more complicated. The vast array of fossil forms has not yet been completely studied, so conclusions remain tenuous. Given this uncertainty, it is probably best, for the present, to group Miocene hominoids geographically:

1. *African forms (23–14 m.y.a.)* Known especially from western Kenya, these include quite generalized, in many ways primitive, hominoids. The best-known genus is *Proconsul* (Fig. 8–17). In addition to the well-known East African early Miocene hominoids, a more recent discovery (in 1992) from Namibia has further extended by over 1,800 miles the known range of African Miocene hominoids (Conroy et al., 1992).

2. *European forms (13–11 m.y.a.)* Known from widely scattered localities in France, Spain, Italy, Greece, Austria, and Hungary, most of these forms are quite derived. However, this is a varied and not well understood lot. The best known of the forms are placed in the genus *Dryopithecus*; the Hungarian and Greek fossils are usually assigned to other genera. The latter of these, from Greece, is called *Ouranopithecus* and remains date to sites 9 to 10 million years of age. Evolutionary relationships are uncertain, but several researchers have suggested a link with the African ape/hominid group.

3. *Asian forms (16–7 m.y.a.)* The largest and most varied group from the Miocene fossil hominoid assemblage, geographically dispersed from Turkey through India/Pakistan and east to the highly prolific site Lufeng, in southern China, most of these forms are *highly* derived. The best-known genus is *Sivapithecus* (known from Turkey and Pakistan). The Lufeng material (now totaling more than 1,000 specimens) is usually placed in a separate genus from *Sivapithecus* (and is referred to as *Lufengpithecus*).

Four general points are certain concerning Miocene hominoid fossils: They are widespread geographically; they are numerous; they span a considerable portion of the Miocene, with *known* remains dated between 23 and 6 m.y.a.; and at present, they are poorly understood. However, we can reasonably draw the following conclusions:

1. These are hominoids—more closely related to the ape-human lineage than to Old World monkeys.

2. Moreover, they are mostly **large-bodied hominoids**, that is, more akin to the lineages of orangutans, gorillas, chimpanzees, and humans than to smaller-bodied apes (i.e., gibbons).

3. Most of the Miocene forms thus far discovered are so derived as to be improbable ancestors of *any* living form.

Robert Jurmain

FIGURE 8–17

Proconsul africanus skull (from early Miocene deposits on Rusinga Island, Kenya).

Large-bodied hominoids

Those hominoids including the great apes (orangutans, chimpanzees, gorillas) and hominids, as well as all ancestral forms back to the time of divergence from small-bodied hominoids (i.e., the gibbon lineage).

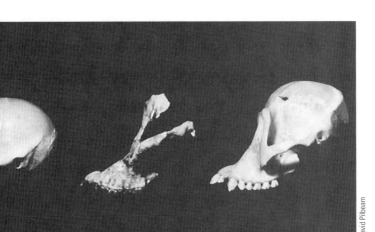

Courtesy, David Pilbeam

FIGURE 8–18
Comparison of *Sivapithecus* cranium (center)
with that of modern chimpanzee (left)
and orangutan (right). The *Sivapithecus* fossil is
specimen GSP 15000 from the Potwar Plateau,
Pakistan, c. 8 m.y.a.

4. One lineage that appears well established relates to Sivapithecus from Turkey and Pakistan. This form shows some highly derived facial features similar to the modern orangutan, suggesting a fairly close evolutionary link (Fig. 8–18).

5. There are no definite **hominids** yet discerned from any Miocene-dated locale. All the confirmed members of our family come from Pliocene beds and later. (The detailed story of hominid evolution will encompass much of the remainder of this text.)

Hominids
Colloquial term for members of the family
Hominidae, which includes all bipedal hominoids
back to the divergence from African great apes.

Processes of Macroevolution

As noted earlier, evolution operates at both microevolutionary and macroevolutionary levels. We discussed evolution primarily from a microevolutionary perspective in Chapter 4; in this chapter our focus is on macroevolution. In this section, we discuss some macroevolutionary mechanisms that operate more on the whole species than on individuals or populations and that also take much longer than microevolutionary processes to have a noticeable impact.

Adaptive Radiation

The potential capacity of a group of organisms to multiply is practically unlimited; its ability to increase its numbers, however, is regulated largely by the available resources of food, shelter, and space. As the size of a population increases, its food supply, shelter, and space decrease, and the environment will ultimately prove inadequate. Depleted resources engender pressures that will very likely induce some members of the population to seek an environment in which competition is considerably reduced and the opportunity for survival and reproductive success increased. This evolutionary tendency to exploit unoccupied habitats may eventually produce an abundance of diverse species.

A good example of the evolutionary process known as **adaptive radiation** is seen in the divergence of the stem reptiles into the profusion of different forms of the late Paleozoic and especially those of the Mesozoic. It is a process that has taken place many times in evolutionary history when a life form has rapidly taken advantage, so to speak, of the many newly available ecological niches.

The principle of evolution illustrated by adaptive radiation is fairly simple, but important. It may be stated thus: *A species, or group of species, will diverge into as many variations as two factors allow: (1) its adaptive potential and (2) the adaptive opportunities of the available zones.*

Adaptive radiation
The relatively rapid expansion and diversification of life forms into new ecological niches.

In the case of reptiles, there was little divergence in the very early stages of evolution, when the ancestral form was little more than one among a variety of amphibian water dwellers. In reptiles, a more efficient egg than that of amphibians (i.e., one that could incubate out of water) had developed, but although it had great adaptive potential, there were few zones to invade. However, once reptiles became fully terrestrial, there was a sudden opening of available zones—ecological niches— accessible to them.

This new kind of egg provided the primary adaptive trait that freed reptiles from their attachment to water. The adaptive zones for reptiles were not limitless; nevertheless, continents were now open to them with no serious competition from any other animal. The reptiles moved into the many different ecological niches on land (and to some extent in the air and sea), and as they adapted to these areas, they diversified into a large number of species. This spectacular radiation burst forth with such evolutionary rapidity that it may well be termed an adaptive explosion.

The rapid expansion of placental mammals at the beginning of the Cenozoic and the diversification of lemurs in Madagascar are other good examples of adaptive radiation. This latter (primate) example is particularly instructive. As we noted in Chapter 6, the contemporary array of 32 lemur species shows considerable diversity, both in size and in lifestyle (diet, degree of arboreality, etc.). Indeed, if we also include several other species that have become extinct in the last 1,000 years (following intensive human occupation of the island), the degree of lemur biodiversity was even greater—even including a ground-living form the size of a gorilla! The diversification of so many different kinds of lemur in Madagascar is explained by their adaptive radiation from a common ancestor, beginning up to 50 m.y.a. Without competition from other types of mammals, the lemurs fairly rapidly diversified and expanded into a number of varied niches in their isolated island home.

Generalized and Specialized Characteristics

Another aspect of evolution closely related to adaptive radiation involves the transition from generalized characteristics to specialized characteristics. These two terms refer to the adaptive potential of a particular trait: a trait that is adapted for many functions is said to be generalized, whereas a trait that is limited to a narrow set of ecological functions is said to be specialized.

For example, a generalized mammalian limb has five fairly flexible digits adapted for many possible functions (grasping, weight support, digging). In this respect, our hands are still quite generalized. On the other hand (or foot), there have been many structural modifications in our feet suited for the ecologically specialized function of stable weight support in an upright posture.

The terms *generalized* and *specialized* are also sometimes used when speaking of the adaptive potential of whole organisms. For example, the aye-aye of Madagascar is a highly specialized animal structurally adapted in its dentition for an ecologically narrow rodent/woodpecker-like niche—digging holes with prominent incisors and removing insect larvae with an elongated finger.

The notion of adaptive potential is a relative judgment and can estimate only crudely the likelihood of one form evolving into one or more other forms. Adaptive radiation is a related concept, for only a generalized ancestor can provide the flexible evolutionary basis for such rapid diversification. Only a generalized species with potential for adaptation into varied ecological niches can lead to all the later diversification and specialization of forms into particular ecological niches.

An issue that we have already raised also bears on this discussion: the relationship of ancestral and derived characters. While not always the case, ancestral characters *usually* tend to be more generalized than specialized. And specialized characteristics are almost always also derived ones.

Modes of Evolutionary Change

The single most important evolutionary factor underlying macroevolutionary change is **speciation**, the process whereby new species first arise. As you will recall, we have defined a species as a group of *reproductively isolated* organisms, a characterization that follows the biological species concept (Mayr, 1970). According to this same view, the way new species are first produced involves some form of isolation. Picture a single species (baboons, for example) composed of several populations distributed over a wide geographical area. Gene exchange between populations (gene flow) will be limited if a geographical barrier such as an ocean or mountain range effectively separates these populations. This extremely important form of isolating mechanism is termed *geographical isolation*.

If one baboon population (A) is separated from another baboon population (B) by a mountain range, individual baboons of population A will not be able to mate with individuals from B (Fig. 8–19). As time passes (several generations), genetic differences will accumulate in both populations. If population size is small, we can predict that genetic drift will cause allele frequencies to change in both populations. Moreover, since drift is *random* in nature, we would not expect the effects to be the same. Consequently, the two populations will begin to diverge.

As long as gene exchange is limited, the populations can only become more genetically different with time. Moreover, further difference would be expected if the baboon groups are occupying slightly different habitats. These additional genetic differences would be incorporated through the process of natural selection. Certain individuals in population A may be most reproductively fit in their own environment, but would show less reproductive success in the environment occupied by population B. Thus, allele frequencies will shift further, and the results, again, will be divergent in the two groups.

With the cumulative effects of genetic drift and natural selection acting over many generations, the result will be two populations that—even if they were to come back into geographical contact—could no longer interbreed. More than just geographical isolation might now apply. There may, for instance, be behavioral differences interfering with courtship—what we call *behavioral isolation*. Using our *biological* definition of species, we now would recognize two distinct species, where initially only one existed.

Until recently, the general consensus among evolutionary biologists was that microevolutionary mechanisms could be translated directly into the larger-scale macroevolutionary changes, especially speciation (also called *transspecific evolution*). A smooth gradation of change was assumed to run directly from microevolution into macroevolution. A representative view was expressed by a leading synthesist, Ernst Mayr: "The proponents of the synthetic theory maintain that all evolution is due to accumulation of small genetic changes, guided by natural selection, and that

Speciation
The process by which new species are produced from earlier ones; the most important mechanism of macroevolutionary change.

FIGURE 8–19
A speciation model.

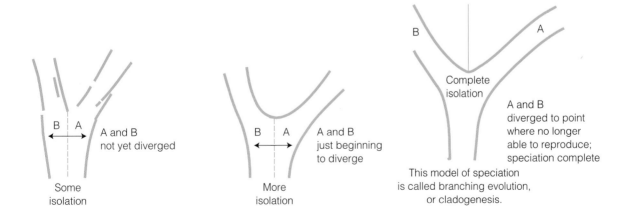

B   A — A and B not yet diverged

Some isolation

B   A — A and B just beginning to diverge

More isolation

B   A   Complete isolation

A and B diverged to point where no longer able to reproduce; speciation complete

This model of speciation is called branching evolution, or cladogenesis.

transspecific evolution is nothing but an extrapolation and magnification of events that take place within populations and species" (Mayr, 1970, p. 351).

In the last two decades, this view has been seriously challenged. Many theorists now believe that macroevolution cannot be explained solely in terms of accumulated microevolutionary changes. Consequently, these researchers are convinced that macroevolution is only partly understandable through microevolutionary models.

Gradualism vs. Punctuated Equilibrium   The traditional view of evolution has emphasized that change accumulates gradually in evolving lineages—the idea of phyletic gradualism. Accordingly, the complete fossil record of an evolving group (if it could be recovered) would display a series of forms with finely graded transitional differences between each ancestor and its descendant. The fact that such transitional forms are only rarely found is attributed to the incompleteness of the fossil record, or, as Darwin called it, "a history of the world, imperfectly kept, and written in changing dialect."

For more than a century, this perspective dominated evolutionary biology, but in the last 25 years, some biologists have called this notion into serious question. The evolutionary mechanisms operating on species over the long run are often not continuously gradual. In some cases, species persist for thousands of generations basically unchanged. Then, rather suddenly, at least in evolutionary terms, a "spurt" of speciation occurs. This uneven, nongradual process of long stasis and quick spurts has been termed **punctuated equilibrium** (Gould and Eldredge, 1977).

What the advocates of punctuated equilibrium are disputing are the tempo (rate) and mode (manner) of evolutionary change as commonly understood since Darwin's time. Rather than a slow, steady tempo, this alternate view postulates long periods of no change punctuated only occasionally by sudden bursts. From this observation, it was concluded that the mode of evolution, too, must be different from that suggested by classical Darwinists. Rather than gradual accumulation of small changes in a single lineage, advocates of punctuated equilibrium believe that an additional evolutionary mechanism is required to push the process along. They thus postulate *speciation* as the major influence in bringing about rapid evolutionary change.

How well does the paleontological record agree with the predictions of punctuated equilibrium? Indeed, considerable fossil data show long periods of stasis punctuated by occasional quite rapid changes (on the order of 10,000 to 50,000 years). The best supporting evidence for punctuated equilibrium has come from the fossilized remains of marine invertebrates. Intermediate forms are rare, not so much because the fossil record is poor, but because the speciation events and longevity of these transitional species were so short that we should not expect to find them very often.

How well, then, does the primate fossil record fit the punctuated equilibrium model? In studies of Eocene primates, rates of evolutionary change were shown to be quite gradual (Gingerich, 1985; Brown and Rose, 1987; Rose, 1991). In another study, here of Paleocene plesiadapiforms, evolutionary changes were also quite gradual. Although no longer considered primates, these forms show a gradual tempo of change in another, closely related group of mammals. The predictions consistent with punctuated equilibrium have thus far not been substantiated in those evolving lineages of primates for which we have adequate data to test the theory.

It would, however, be a fallacy to assume that evolutionary change in primates or in any other group must therefore be of a completely gradual tempo. Such is clearly not the case. In all lineages, the pace assuredly speeds up and slows down as a result of factors that influence the size and relative isolation of populations. In addition, environmental changes that influence the pace and direction of natural selection must also be considered. Nevertheless, in general accordance with the Modern Synthesis, microevolution and macroevolution need not be "decoupled," as some evolutionary biologists have recently suggested.

Punctuated equilibrium
The concept that evolutionary change proceeds through long periods of stasis punctuated by rapid periods of change.

The Meaning of Genus and Species

Our discussion of fossil primates has introduced a variety of taxonomic names. We should pause at this point and ask why we use so many names like *Aegyptopithecus*, *Proconsul*, and *Sivapithecus*. What do such names mean in evolutionary terms?

Our goal when applying genus, species, or other taxonomic labels to groups of organisms is to make meaningful biological statements about the variation that is present. When looking at populations of living or long-extinct animals, we are assuredly going to see variation. The situation is true of *any* sexually reproducing organism because of the factors of recombination (see Chapter 3). As a result of recombination, each individual organism is a unique combination of genetic material, and the uniqueness is usually reflected to some extent in the phenotype.

In addition to such *individual variation*, we see other kinds of systematic variation in all biological populations. *Age changes* certainly alter overall body size as well as shape in many mammals. One pertinent example for fossil hominoid studies is the great change in number, size, and shape of teeth from deciduous (milk) teeth (only 20 present) to the permanent dentition (32 present). It would be an obvious error to differentiate fossil forms solely on the basis of such age-dependent criteria. If one individual were represented just by milk teeth and another (seemingly very different) individual were represented just by adult teeth, they easily could be different-aged individuals from the *same* population. Variation due to sex also plays an important role in influencing differences among individuals observed in biological populations. Differences in structural traits between males and females of the same population are called *sexual dimorphism* and can result in marked variance in body size and proportions in adults of the same species.

Keeping in mind all the types of variation present within interbreeding groups of organisms, the minimum biological category we would like to define in fossil primate samples is the *species*. As already defined, a species is a group of interbreeding or potentially interbreeding organisms that is reproductively isolated from other such groups. In modern organisms, this concept is theoretically testable by observations of reproductive behavior. In animals long dead, such observations are obviously impossible. Therefore, to get a handle on the interpretation of variation seen in fossil groups, we must refer to living animals.

We know without doubt that variation is present. The question is, What is its biological significance? Two immediate choices occur: Either the variation is accounted for by individual, age, and sex differences seen within every biological species (it is **intraspecific**) or the variation represents differences between reproductively isolated groups (it is **interspecific**). How do we decide which alternative is at work? We clearly must refer to already defined groups where we can observe reproductive behavior—in other words, contemporary species.

If the amount of morphological variation observed in fossil samples is comparable to that seen today *within species of closely related forms*, then we should not "split" our sample into more than one species. We must, however, be careful in choosing modern analogues, for rates of morphological evolution vary widely among different groups of mammals. In interpreting past primates, we do best when comparing them with well-known species of modern primates.

Nevertheless, studies of such living groups have shown that delimiting exactly where species boundaries begin and end is often difficult. In dealing with extinct species, the uncertainties are even greater. In addition to the overlapping patterns of variation *over space*, variation also occurs *through time*. In other words, even more variation will be seen in such **paleospecies**, since individuals may be separated by thousands or even millions of years. Applying strict Linnaean taxonomy to such a situation presents an unavoidable dilemma. Standard Linnaean classification, designed to take account of variation present at any given time, describes a static situation. However, when we deal with paleospecies, the time frame is expanded, and the situation can be dynamic (i.e., later forms might be different from earlier ones). In such a dynamic situation, taxonomic decisions (where to draw species boundaries) are ultimately going to be somewhat arbitrary.

Intraspecific
Within species; refers to variation seen within the same species.

Interspecific
Between species; refers to variation beyond that seen within the same species to include additional aspects seen between two different species.

Paleospecies
Species defined from fossil evidence, often covering a long time span.

The next level of formal taxonomic classification, the *genus*, presents another problem. To have more than one genus, we obviously must have at least two species (reproductively isolated groups), and the species of one genus must differ in a basic way from the species of another genus. A genus is therefore defined as a group of species composed of members more closely related to each other than they are to species from any other genus.

Grouping species together into genera is largely a subjective procedure wherein the degree of relatedness becomes a relative judgment. One possible test for contemporary animals is to check for results of hybridization between individuals of different species—rare in nature but quite common in captivity. If two normally separate species interbreed and produce live, though not necessarily fertile, offspring, they probably are not too different genetically and should therefore be grouped together in the same genus. A well-known example of such a cross is horses with donkeys (*Equus callabus* × *Equus asinus*), which normally produces live, sterile offspring (mules).

As previously mentioned, we cannot perform breeding experiments with extinct animals, but another definition of genus becomes highly relevant. Species that are members of the same genus share the same broad adaptive zone. What this represents is a general ecological lifestyle more basic than the narrower ecological niches characteristic of individual species. This ecological definition of genus can be an immense aid in interpreting fossil primates. Teeth are the most frequently preserved parts, and they often can provide excellent general ecological inferences. Moreover, cladistic analysis (see pp. 178–182) also provides assistance in making judgments about evolutionary relationships. That is, members of the *same* genus should all share derived characters not seen in members of other genera.

As a final comment, we should point out that classification by genus is not always a straightforward decision. Indeed, the argument among primatologists over whether the chimpanzee and gorilla represent one genus (*Pan troglodytes, Pan gorilla*) or two different genera (*Pan troglodytes, Gorilla gorilla*) demonstrates that even with living, breathing animals, the choices are not always clear. For that matter, many current researchers, pointing to the very close genetic similarities between humans and chimpanzees, would place both in the same genus (*Homo sapiens, Homo troglodytes*). When it gets this close to home, it is even more difficult to remain objective!

SUMMARY

This chapter has surveyed the basics of mammalian/primate evolution, emphasizing a macroevolutionary perspective. Given the huge amount of organic diversity displayed, as well as the vast time involved, two major organizing perspectives prove indispensable: schemes of formal classification to organize organic diversity and the geological time scale to organize geological time. The principles of classification were reviewed in some detail, contrasting two differing approaches: evolutionary systematics and cladistics. Because primates are vertebrates and, more specifically, mammals, these broader organic groups were briefly reviewed, emphasizing major evolutionary trends. The fossil history of primates was taken up in more detail with surveys of earliest traces from the Paleocene and Eocene epochs. The beginnings of anthropoid radiation can be traced to the end of the Eocene and to the Oligocene (the Fayum in Egypt), and the broad, complex radiation of hominoids during the Miocene is even more central to understanding human evolution.

Theoretical perspectives relating to contemporary understanding of macroevolutionary processes (especially the concept of speciation) are crucial to interpreting any long-term aspect of evolutionary history, be it mammalian, primate, hominoid, or hominid. In this context, evolutionary biologists have postulated two different modes of evolutionary change: gradualism and punctuated equilibrium. At present, the available primate evolutionary record does not conform to the predictions of punctuated equilibrium, but one should not conclude that evolutionary tempo was necessarily strictly gradual (which it certainly was not). Finally, as genus and species designation is the common form of reference for both living and extinct organisms (and will be used frequently throughout the next five chapters), its biological significance was discussed in depth.

QUESTIONS FOR REVIEW

1. What are the two primary goals of organic classification?
2. What are the six major groups of vertebrates?
3. What are the two main approaches to the classification of organisms? Compare them.
4. What are the major eras of geological time over which vertebrates have evolved?
5. What primary features distinguish mammals—especially placental mammals—from other vertebrates?
6. What is meant by a homology? Contrast with analogy, using examples.
7. Why do evolutionary biologists concentrate on derived features rather than primitive ones? Give an example of each.
8. What are the seven epochs of the Cenozoic?
9. Why is it difficult to identify clearly very early primates from other primitive placental mammals?
10. How diversified and geographically widespread were hominoids in the Miocene?
11. Humans are Old World anthropoids. What other groups are also Old World anthropoids?
12. Contrast the gradualist view of evolutionary change with that of punctuated equilibrium. Give an example from primate evolution that supports one view or the other.
13. How are species defined? Discuss how the definition applies to both living and fossil groups.

SUGGESTED FURTHER READING

Carroll, Robert L. 1988. *Vertebrate Paleontology and Evolution*. New York: Freeman.
Conroy, G. C. 1990. *Primate Evolution*. New York: Norton.
Fleagle, John. 1999. *Primate Adaptation and Evolution*. 2nd ed. New York: Academic Press.
Jones, Steve, Robert Martin, and David Pilbeam (eds.). 1992. *The Cambridge Encyclopedia of Human Evolution*. New York: Cambridge University Press.

RESOURCES ON THE INTERNET

 Wadsworth Anthropology Resource Center
http://anthropology.wadsworth.com

The companion website for this text includes a range of enrichment material focused on the chapter's topic. While online you can enhance your understanding of the chapter by exploring one of the several additional Internet Exercises, by researching topics, and by accessing full articles on InfoTrac College Edition. You can also reinforce the concepts by taking online practice exams.

Internet Exercises

Visit the University of California Museum of Paleontology (**http://www.ucmp .berkeley.edu/**). This site provides extensive online exhibits on geology, phylogeny, and mammalian evolution. Explore the site and see what you can find to supplement the information in the text on mammalian evolution. When did mammals first appear? When did they begin to differentiate into the modern orders? When and where did primates first appear?

InfoTrac College Edition

http://www.infotrac-college.com/wadsworth

On InfoTrac College Edition, search for the keywords *evolution* and *mammals*. Choose one of the articles found by this search and read through it. What does this research reveal about evolution?

CONTENTS

Paleoanthropology: Reconstructing Early Hominid Behavior and Ecology

See the following sections of the CD-ROM for topics covered in this chapter: Virtual Lab 7, sections I, II; Virtual Lab 8, section I; and Virtual Lab 11.

See Virtual Lab 7, section II, for a discussion of definitions of hominids and hominoids.

Mosaic evolution
A pattern of evolution in which the rates of evolution in one functional system vary from those in other systems. For example, in hominid evolution, the dental system, locomotor system, and neurological system (especially the brain) all evolved at markedly different rates.

Introduction

In the last three chapters, we have seen how humans are classed as primates, both structurally and behaviorally, and how our evolutionary history coincides with that of other mammals and, specifically, with other primates. However, we are a unique kind of primate, and our ancestors have been adapted to a particular lifestyle for several million years. Some primitive hominoid may have begun this process more than 8 m.y.a., but there is much more definite hominid fossil evidence from Africa after 5 m.y.a. The hominid nature of these remains is revealed by more than the morphological structure of teeth and bones; we know that these animals are hominids also because of the way they behaved—emphasizing once again the *biocultural* nature of human evolution. In this chapter, we discuss the methods scientists use to explore the secrets of early hominid behavior and ecology, and we demonstrate these methods through the example of the best-known early hominid site in the world: Olduvai Gorge in East Africa.

Definition of Hominid

If any of the Miocene hominoid fossils represent the earliest stages of hominid diversification, our definition of them as hominid must primarily be a *dental* one, for teeth and jaws are most of what we have of these Miocene forms. In fact, as we have seen in the previous chapter, *none* of the Miocene hominoid fossils discovered thus far is clearly hominid. Dentition is not the only way to describe the special attributes of our particular evolutionary radiation, and it certainly is not the most distinctive characteristic of the later stages of human evolution. Modern humans and our hominid ancestors are distinguished from our closest living relatives (the great apes) by more obvious features than tooth and jaw dimensions. For example, various scientists have pointed to such hominid characteristics as large brain size, bipedal locomotion, and toolmaking behavior as being significant (at some stage) in defining what makes a hominid a hominid (as opposed to a pongid or anything else).

It must be emphasized that not all these characteristics developed simultaneously. Quite the opposite, in fact, has been apparent in hominid evolution over the last 5 million years. This pattern, in which different physiological systems (and behavioral correlates) evolve at different rates, is called **mosaic evolution**. As we first pointed out in Chapter 1 and will discuss in more detail in Chapter 10, the most defining characteristic for all of hominid evolution is *bipedal locomotion*. Certainly for the earliest stages of the hominid lineage, skeletal evidence of bipedal locomotion is the only truly reliable indicator of hominid status. However, in later stages of hominid evolution, other features, especially those relating to neurology and behavior, do become highly significant (Fig. 9–1).

These behavioral aspects of hominid emergence—particularly toolmaking capacity—is what we wish to emphasize in this chapter. The important structural attributes of the hominid brain, teeth, and especially locomotor apparatus will be discussed in the next chapter, where we investigate early hominid anatomical adaptations in greater detail.

Biocultural Evolution: The Human Capacity for Culture

When compared with other animals, the most distinctive behavioral feature of humans is our extraordinary elaboration of and dependence on culture. Certainly, other primates, and many other animals for that matter, modify their environments. As we saw in Chapter 7, chimpanzees especially are known for such behaviors as using termite sticks and sponges and even transporting rocks to crush nuts. Given such observations, it becomes tenuous to draw sharp lines between hominid toolmaking behavior and that exhibited by other animals.

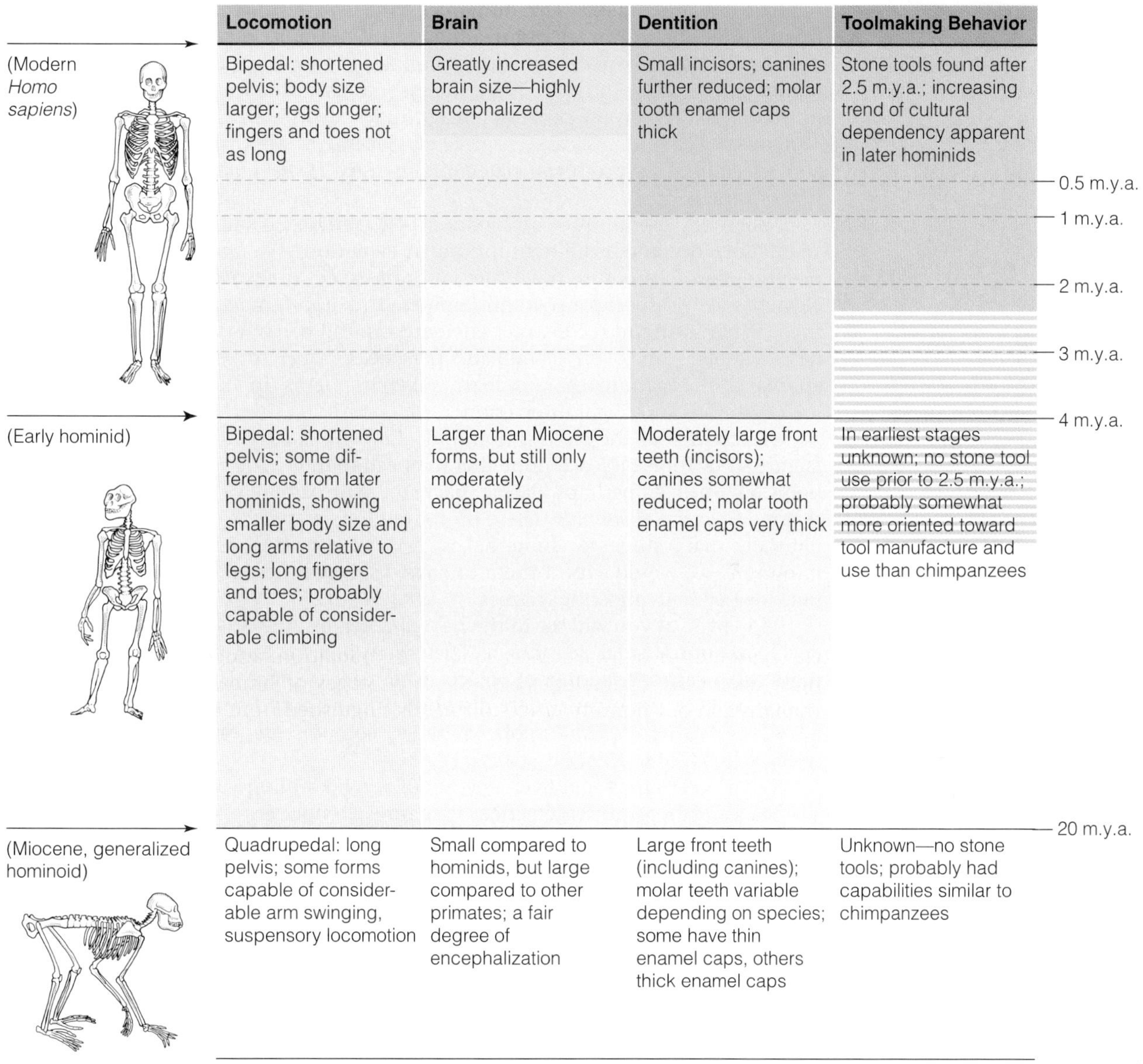

	Locomotion	Brain	Dentition	Toolmaking Behavior	
(Modern *Homo sapiens*)	Bipedal: shortened pelvis; body size larger; legs longer; fingers and toes not as long	Greatly increased brain size—highly encephalized	Small incisors; canines further reduced; molar tooth enamel caps thick	Stone tools found after 2.5 m.y.a.; increasing trend of cultural dependency apparent in later hominids	— 0.5 m.y.a. — 1 m.y.a. — 2 m.y.a. — 3 m.y.a. — 4 m.y.a.
(Early hominid)	Bipedal: shortened pelvis; some differences from later hominids, showing smaller body size and long arms relative to legs; long fingers and toes; probably capable of considerable climbing	Larger than Miocene forms, but still only moderately encephalized	Moderately large front teeth (incisors); canines somewhat reduced; molar tooth enamel caps very thick	In earliest stages unknown; no stone tool use prior to 2.5 m.y.a.; probably somewhat more oriented toward tool manufacture and use than chimpanzees	— 20 m.y.a.
(Miocene, generalized hominoid)	Quadrupedal: long pelvis; some forms capable of considerable arm swinging, suspensory locomotion	Small compared to hominids, but large compared to other primates; a fair degree of encephalization	Large front teeth (including canines); molar teeth variable depending on species; some have thin enamel caps, others thick enamel caps	Unknown—no stone tools; probably had capabilities similar to chimpanzees	

Another point to remember is that human culture, at least as it is defined in contemporary contexts, involves much more than toolmaking capacity. For humans, culture integrates an entire adaptive strategy involving cognitive, political, social, and economic components. The *material culture*, the tools and other items humans use, is but a small portion of this cultural complex.

Nevertheless, when examining the archaeological record of earlier hominids, what is available for study is almost exclusively certain remains of material culture, especially residues of stone tool manufacture. Thus, it is extremely difficult to learn anything about the earliest stages of hominid cultural development prior to the regular manufacture of stone tools. As you will see, this most crucial cultural development has been traced to approximately 2.5 m.y.a. Yet, hominids undoubtedly were using other kinds of tools (such as sticks) and displaying a whole array of other cultural behaviors long before this time. However, without any "hard" evidence preserved in the archaeological record, the development of these nonmaterial cultural components remains elusive.

FIGURE 9–1
Mosaic evolution of hominid characteristics: a postulated time line.

The fundamental basis for human cultural elaboration relates directly to cognitive abilities. Again, we are not dealing with an absolute distinction, but a relative one. As you have learned, some other primates possess some of the symboling capabilities exhibited by humans. Nevertheless, modern humans display these abilities in a complexity several orders of magnitude beyond that of any other animal. Moreover, only humans are so completely dependent on symbolic communication and its cultural by-products that contemporary *Homo sapiens* could not survive without them.

When did the unique combination of cognitive, social, and material cultural adaptations become prominent in human evolution? We must be careful to recognize the manifold nature of culture and not expect it always to contain the same elements across species (as when compared to nonhuman primates) or through time (when trying to reconstruct ancient hominid behavior). Richard Potts (1993) has critiqued this overly simplistic perspective and suggests a more dynamic approach, one that incorporates many subcomponents (including aspects of behavior, cognition, and social interaction).

We know that the earliest hominids almost certainly did *not* regularly manufacture stone tools (at least, none that has been found!). The earliest members of the hominid lineage, perhaps dating back to approximately 7–5 m.y.a., could be referred to as *protohominids*. These protohominids may have carried objects such as naturally sharp stones or stone flakes, parts of carcasses, and pieces of wood. At minimum, we would expect them to have displayed these behaviors to at least the same degree as living chimpanzees.

Moreover, as you will see in the next chapter, by at least 4 m.y.a., hominids had developed one crucial advantage: They were bipedal and could therefore much more easily carry all manner of objects from place to place. Ultimately, the efficient exploitation of resources widely distributed in time and space would most likely have led to using "central" spots where key components, especially stone objects, were cached (Potts, 1991).

What is certain is that over a period of several million years, during the formative stages of hominid emergence, numerous components interacted, but not all developed simultaneously. As cognitive abilities developed, more efficient means of communication and learning resulted. Largely as a result of such neural reorganization, more elaborate tools and social relationships also emerged. These, in turn, selected for greater intelligence, which in turn selected for further neural elaboration. Quite clearly, then, these mutual dynamics are at the very heart of what we call hominid *biocultural* evolution.

The Strategy of Paleoanthropology

To understand human evolution adequately, we obviously need a broad base of information. The task of recovering and interpreting all the clues left by early hominids is the work of paleoanthropologists. Paleoanthropology is defined as the study of ancient humans. As such, it is a diverse *multidisciplinary* pursuit seeking to reconstruct every possible bit of information concerning the dating, structure, behavior, and ecology of our hominid ancestors. In the last few decades, the study of early humans has marshaled the specialized skills of many different kinds of scientists. Included in this growing and exciting adventure are geologists, archaeologists, physical anthropologists, and **paleoecologists** (Table 9–1).

Geologists, usually working with anthropologists, do the initial surveys to locate potential early hominid sites. Many sophisticated techniques can aid in this search, including aerial and satellite photography. Paleontologists are usually involved in this early survey work, for they can help find fossil beds containing faunal remains. Where conditions are favorable for the preservation of bone from such species as pigs and elephants, conditions may also be favorable for the preservation of hominid remains. In addition, paleontologists can (through comparison with known faunal sequences) give fairly quick estimates of the approximate age of fos-

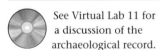

See Virtual Lab 11 for a discussion of the archaeological record.

Paleoecologists
(*paleo*, meaning "old," and *ecology*, meaning "environmental setting") Scientists who study ancient environments.

TABLE 9–1   Contributing Scientific Fields to Paleoanthropology

Physical Sciences	Biological Sciences	Social Sciences
Geology	Physical anthropology	Archaeology
Stratigraphy	Ecology	Ethnoarchaeology
Petrology	Paleontology (fossil	Cultural anthropology
(rocks, minerals)	animals)	Ethnography
Pedology (soils)	Palynology (fossil pollen)	Psychology
Geomorphology	Primatology	
Geophysics		
Chemistry		
Taphonomy		

sil sites without having to wait for the more expensive and time-consuming analyses. In this way, fossil beds of appropriate geological ages (i.e., where hominid finds are most likely) can be isolated.

Once potential early hominid localities have been identified, much more extensive surveying begins. At this point, at least for some sites postdating 2.5 m.y.a., archaeologists take over in the search for hominid "traces." We do not necessarily have to find remains of early hominids themselves to know that they consistently occupied a particular area. Preserved material clues, or **artifacts**, also inform us directly and unambiguously about early hominid activities. Modifying rocks according to a consistent plan or simply carrying them around from one place to another (over fairly long distances) is characteristic of no other animal but a hominid. Therefore, when we see such behavioral evidence at a site, we know absolutely that hominids were present.

Because organic materials such as sticks and bones do not usually preserve in the archaeological record, we have no solid evidence of the earliest stages of hominid cultural modifications. On the other hand, our ancestors at some point showed a veritable fascination with stones, for these provided not only easily accessible and transportable materials (to use as convenient projectiles to throw or to hold down objects, such as skins and windbreaks) but also the most durable and sharpest cutting edges available at that time. Luckily for us, stone is almost indestructible, and some early hominid sites are strewn with thousands of stone artifacts. The earliest artifact sites now documented are from the Gona and Bouri areas in northeastern Ethiopia, dating to 2.5 m.y.a. (Semaw et al., 1997; de Heinzelin et al., 1999). Other contenders for the "earliest" stone assemblage come from the adjacent Hadar and Middle Awash areas, immediately to the south in Ethiopia, dated 2.5–2 m.y.a.

If an area is clearly demonstrated to be a hominid site, much more concentrated research will then begin. We should point out that a more mundane but very significant aspect of paleoanthropology not reflected in Table 9–1 is the financial one. Just the initial survey work in usually remote areas costs many thousands of dollars, and mounting a concentrated research project costs several hundred thousand dollars. Therefore, for such work to go on, massive financial support is required from government agencies and private donations. A significant amount of a paleoanthropologist's efforts and time is necessarily devoted to writing grant proposals or speaking on the lecture circuit to raise the required funds for this work.

Once the financial hurdle has been cleared, a coordinated research project can commence. Usually headed by an archaeologist or physical anthropologist, the field crew will continue to survey and map the target area in great detail. In addition, field crew members will begin to search carefully for bones and artifacts eroding out of the soil, take pollen and soil samples for ecological analysis, and carefully recover rock samples for use in various dating techniques. If, in this early stage of exploration, members of the field crew find a fossil hominid, they will feel very lucky indeed. The international press usually considers human fossils the most

Artifacts
Objects or materials made or modified for use by hominids. The earliest artifacts are usually made of stone or, occasionally, bone.

exciting kind of discovery, a situation that produces wide publicity, often ensuring future financial support. More likely, the crew will accumulate much information on geological setting, ecological data (particularly faunal remains), and, with some luck, archaeological traces (hominid artifacts).

After long and arduous research in the field, even more time-consuming and detailed analysis is required back in the laboratory. Archaeologists must clean, sort, label, and identify all artifacts, and paleontologists must do the same for all faunal remains. Knowing the kinds of animals represented, whether forest browsers, woodland species, or open-country forms, will greatly help in reconstructing the local *paleoecological* settings in which early hominids lived. In addition, analysis of pollen remains by a palynologist will further aid in a detailed environmental reconstruction. All these paleoecological analyses can assist in reconstructing the diet of early humans. Also, the **taphonomy** of the site must be worked out in order to understand its depositional history—that is, whether the site is of a *primary* or *secondary* **context**.

In the concluding stages of interpretation, the paleoanthropologist will draw together the following essentials:

1. *Dating*
    geological
    paleontological
    geophysical
2. *Paleoecology*
    paleontology
    palynology
    geomorphology
    taphonomy
3. *Archaeological traces of behavior*
4. *Anatomical evidence from hominid remains*

From all this information, scientists will try to "flesh out" the kind of animal that may have been our direct ancestor, or at least a very close relative. In this final analysis, still further comparative scientific information may be needed. Primatologists may assist here by showing the detailed relationships between the anatomical structure and behavior of humans and that of contemporary non-human primates (see Chapters 6 and 7). Cultural anthropologists may contribute ethnographic information concerning the varied nature of human behavior, particularly ecological adaptations of those contemporary hunter-gatherer groups exploiting roughly similar environmental settings as those reconstructed for a hominid site.

The end result of years of research by dozens of scientists will (we hope) produce a more complete and accurate understanding of human evolution—how we came to be the way we are. Both biological and cultural aspects of our ancestors pertain to this investigation, each process developing in relation to the other.

Paleoanthropology in Action—Olduvai Gorge

Several paleoanthropological projects of the scope just discussed have recently been pursued in diverse places in the Old World (Fig. 9–2). The most important of these include David Pilbeam's work in the Miocene beds of the Potwar Plateau of western Pakistan (circa 13–7 m.y.a.); Don Johanson's projects at Hadar and other areas of Ethiopia (circa 3.7–1.6 m.y.a.), sponsored by the Institute of Human Origins; a recently intensified effort just south of Hadar in Ethiopia in an area called the Middle Awash (circa 5–4 m.y.a.), led by Berkeley paleoanthropologists Tim White and Desmond Clark; a now completed research project along the Omo River of southern Ethiopia (circa 4–1.5 m.y.a.), directed by F. Clark Howell; Richard and Meave Leakey's fantastically successful research near Lake Turkana (formerly Lake

---

Taphonomy

(*taphos*, meaning "dead") The study of how bones and other materials came to be buried in the earth and preserved as fossils. A taphonomist studies the processes of sedimentation, the action of streams, preservation properties of bone, and carnivore disturbance factors.

Context

The environmental setting where an archaeological trace is found. *Primary* context is the setting in which the archaeological trace was originally deposited. A *secondary* context is one to which it has been moved (e.g., by the action of a stream).

See Virtual Lab 7, section I, for a discussion of taphonomy and factors influencing formation of sites.

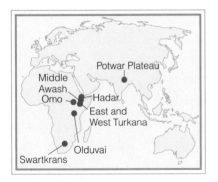

FIGURE 9–2
Major paleoanthropological projects.

Rudolf) in northern Kenya (circa 4.2–1.5 m.y.a.); Mary Leakey's famous investigations at Olduvai Gorge in northern Tanzania (circa 1.85 m.y.a. to present); and finally the recent exploration by Phillip Tobias of hominid localities in southern Africa (the most important being Swartkrans, discussed in Chapter 10).

Of all these localities, the one that has yielded the finest quality and greatest abundance of paleoanthropological information concerning the behavior of early hominids has been Olduvai Gorge. First "discovered" in the early twentieth century by a German butterfly collector, Olduvai was soon scientifically surveyed and its wealth of paleontological evidence recognized. In 1931, Louis Leakey made his first trip to Olduvai Gorge and almost immediately realized its significance for studying early humans. From 1935, when she first worked there, until she retired in 1984, Mary Leakey directed the archaeological excavations at Olduvai.

Located in the Serengeti Plain of northern Tanzania, Olduvai is a steep-sided valley resembling a miniature version of the Grand Canyon. A deep ravine cut into an almost mile-high grassland plateau of East Africa, Olduvai extends more than 25 miles in total length. Climatically, the semiarid pattern of present-day Olduvai is believed to be similar to what it has been for the last 2 million years. The surrounding countryside is a grassland savanna broken occasionally by scrub bushes and acacia trees. It is noteworthy that this environment presently (as well as in the past) supports a vast number of mammals (such as zebra, wildebeest, and gazelle), representing an enormous supply of "meat on the hoof."

Geographically, Olduvai is located on the eastern branch of the Great Rift Valley of Africa. The geological processes associated with the formation of the Rift Valley make Olduvai (and other East African sites) extremely important to paleoanthropological investigation. Three results of geological rifting are most significant:

1. Faulting, or earth movement, exposes geological beds near the surface that are normally hidden by hundreds of feet of accumulated overburden.
2. Active volcanic processes cause rapid sedimentation, which often yields excellent preservation of bone and artifacts that normally would be scattered by carnivore activity and erosion forces.
3. Volcanic activity provides a wealth of materials datable by chronometric techniques.

As a result, Olduvai is the site of superb preservation of ancient hominids, portions of their environment, and their behavioral patterns in datable contexts, all of which are readily accessible.

The greatest contribution Olduvai has made to paleoanthropological research is the establishment of an extremely well documented and correlated *sequence* of geological, paleontological, archaeological, and hominid remains over the last 2 million years. At the very foundation of all paleoanthropological research is a well-established geological context. At Olduvai, the geological and paleogeographical situation is known in minute detail. Olduvai is today a geologist's delight, containing sediments in some places 350 feet thick, accumulated from lava flows (basalts), tuffs (windblown or waterborne fine deposits from nearby volcanoes), sandstones, claystones, and limestone conglomerates, all neatly stratified (Fig. 9–3). A hominid site can therefore be accurately dated relative to other sites in the Olduvai Gorge by cross-correlating known marker beds. At the most general geological level, the stratigraphic sequence at Olduvai is broken down into four major beds (Beds I–IV).

Paleontological evidence of fossilized animal bones also has come from Olduvai in great abundance. More than 150 species of extinct animals have been recognized, including fishes, turtles, crocodiles, pigs, giraffes, horses, and many birds, rodents, and antelopes. Careful analysis of such remains has yielded voluminous information concerning the ecological conditions of early human habitats. In addition, the precise analysis of bones directly associated with artifacts can sometimes tell us about the diets and bone-processing techniques of early hominids. (There are some reservations, however; see Issue, pp. 220–221.)

FIGURE 9–3
View of the main gorge at Olduvai. Note the clear sequence of geological beds. The discontinuity to the right is a major fault line.

Robert Jurmain

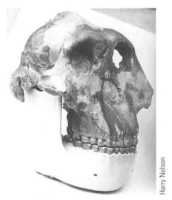

Harry Nelson

FIGURE 9–4
Zinjanthropus skull, discovered by Mary Leakey at Olduvai Gorge in 1959. The skull and reconstructed jaw depicted here are casts at the National Museums of Kenya, Nairobi. As we will see in Chapter 10, this fossil is now included as part of the genus *Australopithecus.*

See Virtual Lab 7, section I, for a discussion of dating techniques.

The archaeological sequence is also well documented for the last 2 million years. Beginning at the earliest hominid site (circa 1.85 m.y.a.), there is already a well-developed stone tool kit, including chopping tools and some small flake tools (Leakey, 1971). Such a tool industry is called *Oldowan* (after Olduvai), and it continues into later beds with some small modifications, where it is called *Developed Oldowan.*

Finally, partial remains of several fossilized hominids have been found at Olduvai, ranging in time from the earliest occupation levels to fairly recent *Homo sapiens.* Of the more than 40 individuals represented, many are quite fragmentary, but a few are excellently preserved. While the center of hominid discoveries has now shifted to other areas of East Africa, it was the initial discovery by Mary Leakey of the *Zinjanthropus* skull at Olduvai in July 1959 that focused the world's attention on this remarkably rich area (see Fig. 9–4 and Box 9–1). "Zinj" provides an excellent example of how financial ramifications directly result from hominid fossil discoveries. Prior to 1959, the Leakeys had worked sporadically at Olduvai on a financial shoestring, making marvelous paleontological and archaeological discoveries. Yet, there was little support available for much needed large-scale excavations. However, following the discovery of "Zinj," the National Geographic Society funded the Leakeys' research, and within a year, more than twice as much dirt had been excavated than during the previous 30 years! (See Box 9–2.)

Dating Methods

Other than the location of sites and recovery of fossils, artifacts, and other materials, the most fundamental goal of paleoanthropological research is to establish the *age* of the finds. By placing discoveries in a firm chronological context, paleoanthropologists are able to more accurately interpret the relationships of sites to each other and ultimately construct a more complete picture of human evolution.

A variety of dating techniques have been developed to allow chronological estimates of paleoanthropological/archaeological discoveries, in some cases with considerable precision. In Chapter 14, we will discuss in more detail the physical basis and interpretive frameworks of these dating techniques. Here, it is useful to mention some aspects of dating relevant to the most ancient of hominid sites.

DIGGING DEEPER

Mary Leakey (1913–1996)

Mary Leakey, one of the leading prehistorians of this century, spent most of her professional life living in the shadow of her famous husband. But to a considerable degree, Louis' fame is directly attributable to Mary. Justly known for his extensive fieldwork in Miocene sites along the shores of Lake Victoria in Kenya, Louis Leakey is quite often associated with important hominoid discoveries.

Courtesy of the L.S.B. Leakey Foundation

However, it was Mary who, in 1948, found the best-preserved *Proconsul* skull ever discovered.

The names Louis Leakey and Olduvai Gorge are almost synonymous, but here, too, it was Mary who made the most significant single discovery—the "Zinj" skull in 1959. Mary had always been the supervisor of archaeological work at Olduvai while Louis was busily engaged in traveling, lecturing, or tending to the National Museums in Nairobi.

Mary Leakey did not come upon her archaeological career by chance. A direct descendant of John Frere (who, because of his discoveries in 1797, is called the father of Paleolithic archaeology), Mary always had a compelling interest in prehistory. Her talent in illustrating stone tools provided her entry into African prehistory and was the reason for her introduction to Louis in 1933. Throughout her career, she did all the tool illustrations for her publications and has set an extremely high standard of excellence for all would-be illustrators of Paleolithic implements.

A committed, hard-driving woman of almost inexhaustible energy, Mary spent most of each year at Olduvai. Busily engaged seven days a week, she supervised ongoing excavations, as well as working on the monumental publications detailing the fieldwork already done.

Following her retirement from active fieldwork, Mary continued her research and writing at her home in Nairobi. As one of the great pioneers of modern archaeological research, her death in 1996 left a void for friends, colleagues, and admirers worldwide.

Generally, there are two types of dating techniques: *relative dating*, which places finds in a sequence but provides no actual estimate in number of years, and *chronometric dating*, which does provide estimates in actual numbers of years.

Chronometric dating in paleoanthropology has allowed much more precise dating of ancient localities, especially in East Africa. In other areas (e.g., South Africa), the nature of the sediments does not permit application of the more accurate dating techniques. Consequently, the chronology of early South African sites is not as definitely known as the chronology of sites from the eastern part of the continent.

Relative techniques also have their uses, and both relative and chronometric methods are employed at most sites, both ancient and more recent (see Chapter 14 for further discussion). Table 9–2 summarizes the more important dating techniques used at early hominid sites. Wherever possible, more than one type of dating technique is used to determine scientifically reliable dates. Because a variety of errors can distort the results from any one of the methods, the best way to corroborate

BOX 9-2 · DIGGING DEEPER

Discovery of *Zinjanthropus*, July 17, 1959

That morning I woke with a headache and a slight fever. Reluctantly I agreed to spend the day in camp.

With one of us out of commission, it was even more vital for the other to continue the work, for our precious seven-week season was running out. So Mary departed for the diggings with Sally and Toots [two of their dalmatians] in the Land-Rover, and I settled back to a restless day off.

Some time later—perhaps I dozed off—I heard the Land-Rover coming up fast to camp. I had a momentary vision of Mary stung by one of our hundreds of resident scorpions or bitten by a snake that had slipped past the dogs.

The Land-Rover rattled to a stop, and I heard Mary's voice calling over and over: "I've got him! I've got him! I've got him!"

Still groggy from the headache, I couldn't make her out.

"Got what? Are you hurt?" I asked.

"Him, the man! Our man," Mary said. "The one we've been looking for (for 23 years). Come quick, I've found his teeth!"

Magically, the headache departed. I somehow fumbled into my work clothes while Mary waited.

As we bounced down the trail in the car, she described the dramatic moment of discovery. She had been searching the slope where I had found the first Oldowan tools in 1931, when suddenly her eye caught a piece of bone lodged in a rock slide. Instantly, she recognized it as part of a skull—almost certainly not that of an animal.

Her glance wandered higher, and there in the rock were two immense teeth, side by side. This time there was no question: They were undeniably human. Carefully, she marked the spot with a cairn of stones, rushed to the Land-Rover, and sped back to camp with the news.

The gorge trail ended half a mile from the site, and we left the car at a dead run. Mary led the way to the cairn, and we knelt to examine the treasure.

I saw at once that she was right. The teeth were premolars, and they had belonged to a human. I was sure they were larger than anything similar ever found, nearly twice the width of modern man's.

I turned to look at Mary, and we almost cried with sheer joy, each seized by that terrific emotion that comes rarely in life. After all our hoping and hardship and sacrifice, at last we had reached our goal—we had discovered the world's earliest known human.

Source:

"Finding the World's Earliest Man," by L. S. B. Leakey, *National Geographic*, 118 (September 1960):431. Reprinted with permission of the publisher.

---

data is to have cross-correlations of several different techniques. In other words, we can be much more confident of results when dating estimates closely agree between at least two separate methods.

Excavations at Olduvai

Because the vertical cut of the Olduvai Gorge provides a ready cross section of 2 million years of earth history, sites can be excavated by digging "straight in" rather than first having to remove tons of overlying dirt (Fig. 9–5). In fact, sites are usually discovered by merely walking the exposures and observing what bones, stones, and so forth, are eroding out.

Several dozen hominid sites (at a minimum, they are bone and tool scatters) have been surveyed at Olduvai, and Mary Leakey extensively excavated close to 20 of these. An incredible amount of paleoanthropological information has come from these excavated areas, data that can be generally grouped into three broad categories of site types, depending on implied function:

TABLE 9–2   Dating Techniques Most Commonly Used at Paleoanthropological Sites

Technique	Type	Basis	Limitations	Comments
Potassium-argon (K/Ar) method	Chronometric	Regular radioactive decay of potassium isotope	Contamination can occur; usually requires corroboration from other independent methods	Can be used only on sediments that have been super-heated (usually volcanic deposits)
Argon-argon (Ar/Ar) method	Chronometric	Radioactive decay of argon isotope, which has artificially been substituted for potassium atoms	Same as above	Same as above
Fission-track method	Chronometric	Regular fission of uranium atoms, leaving microscopic tracks	Usually derived from volcanic deposits; estimates generally less accurate than for K/Ar	Very important corroboratory technique in East Africa
Biostratigraphy	Relative	Estimates of consistent modifications in evolving lineages of animals; presence/absence of species	Requires very well documented sequences and somewhere *must* be correlated with chronometric results—e.g., with K/Ar	Best estimates in East Africa using pigs, monkeys, antelope, and rodents; has been important technique in South Africa
Paleomagnetism	Relative	Regular shifts in earth's geomagnetic pole; evidence preserved in magnetically charged sediments	Requires precise excavation techniques (see p. 285); both major and minor reversals occur and can easily confuse interpretation	Important corroboratory technique in both East and South Africa
Stratigraphy	Relative	Accumulation of sediments in "layer-cake" fashion; lower sediments are older than upper layers	Earth movements easily disrupt sequences; rarely are very complete sequences found undisturbed; not usable to correlate different sites, but applicable for establishing sequences *within* individual sites	The most basic of all dating techniques; the first method used by geologists, etc. (e.g., Lyell, Darwin)

Robert Jurmain

FIGURE 9–5
Excavations in progress at Olduvai. This site, more than 1 million years old, was located when a hominid ulna (arm bone) was found eroding out of the side of the gorge.

1. *"Butchering" localities*, areas containing one or only a few individuals of a single species of large mammal associated with a scatter of archaeological traces. Two "butchering" sites, one containing an elephant and another containing a *Deinotherium* (a large extinct relative of the elephant), have been found at levels approximately 1.7 m.y.a. Both sites contain only a single animal, and it is impossible to ascertain whether the hominids actually killed these animals or exploited them (either for meat or, perhaps, to extract marrow) after they were already dead. A third butchering locality dated at approximately 1.2 m.y.a. shows perhaps more consistent and efficient exploitation of large mammals by this time. Remains of 24 *Pelorovis* individuals (a giant extinct relative of the buffalo, with horn spans more than 10 feet across!) have been found here, and Louis Leakey suggested they were driven into a swamp by a band of hominids and then systematically slaughtered (Leakey, 1971). (*Note:* This is an interpretation that is no longer widely accepted.)

2. *Quarry localities*, areas where early hominids extracted their stone resources and initially fashioned their tools. At such sites, thousands of small stone fragments of only one type of rock are found, usually associated with no or very little bone refuse. At Olduvai, a 1.6- to 1.7-million-year-old area was apparently a chert (a rock resembling flint) factory site, where hominids came repeatedly to quarry this material.

3. *Multipurpose localities* (also called "campsites"), general-purpose areas where hominids possibly ate, slept, and put the finishing touches on their tools. The accumulation of living debris, including broken bones of many animals of several different species and many broken stones (some complete tools, some waste flakes), is a basic human pattern. As Glynn Isaac noted:

> The fact that discarded artifacts tend to be concentrated in restricted areas is itself highly suggestive. It seems likely that such patches of material reflect the organization of movement around a camp or home base, with recurrent dispersal and reuniting of the group at the chosen locality. Among living primates this pattern in its full expression is distinctive of man. The coincidence of bone and food refuse with the artifacts strongly implies that meat was carried back—presumably for sharing. (Isaac, 1976, pp. 27–28)

(See Issue, pp. 220–221 for a different interpretation.)

Several multipurpose areas have been excavated at Olduvai, including one that is over 1.8 million years old. This site has a circle of large stones forming what at one time was thought to be a base for a windbreak; however, this interpretation is now considered unlikely. Whatever its function, without the meticulous excavation and recording of modern archaeological techniques, the presence of such an archaeological feature would never have been recognized. This point requires further emphasis. Many people assume that archaeologists derive their information simply from analysis of objects (stone tools, gold statues, or whatever). However, it is the *context* and **association** of objects (i.e., precisely where the objects are found and what is found associated with them) that give archaeologists the data they require to understand the behavioral patterns of ancient human populations. Once pot hunters or looters pilfer a site, proper archaeological interpretation is never again possible.

The types of activities carried out at these multipurpose sites remain open to speculation (Fig. 9–6). Archaeologists had thought, as the quote by Glynn Isaac indicates (and as also argued by Mary Leakey), that the sites functioned as "campsites." Lewis Binford has forcefully critiqued this view and has alternatively suggested that much of the refuse accumulated is the result of nonhominid (i.e., predator) activities. Another possibility, suggested by Richard Potts (1984), postulates that these areas served as collecting points (caches) for some tools. This last interpretation has received considerable support from other archaeologists in recent years.

Association
What an archaeological trace is found with.

FIGURE 9–6
A dense scatter of stone and some fossilized animal bone from a site at Olduvai, dated at approximately 1.6 m.y.a. Some of these remains are the result of hominid activities.

A final interpretation, incorporating aspects of the hypotheses proposed by Binford and Potts has been proposed by Robert Blumenschine. He suggests that early hominids were gatherers and scavengers, and the bone and stone scatters reflect these activities (Blumenschine, 1986; Blumenschine and Cavallo, 1992; see Issue, pp. 220–221).

Environmental Explanations for Hominid Origins

As we saw in Chapter 8, there are no *definite* hominid remains yet discovered from any Miocene-dated context. From what we presently know, the earliest hominids did not appear until early in the Pliocene (4–5 m.y.a.). What were the environmental conditions at this time and immediately prior to it? Can these general ecological patterns help explain the origins of the first hominids (as they diversified from other kinds of hominoids)?

Before continuing, we should emphasize a caution. A common misconception that many students have is that a single large environmental change is related clearly to a major adaptive change in a type of organism (in other words, environmental change X produced adaptation Y in a particular life form). This oversimplification is a form of **environmental determinism**, and it grossly underestimates the true complexity of the evolutionary process. It is clear that the environment does influence evolutionary change, as seen in the process of natural selection. But organisms are highly complex systems, composed of thousands of genes, and any adaptive shift to changing environmental circumstances is likely to be a compromise, balancing several selective factors simultaneously (such as temperature requirements, amount and distribution of food and water, predators, and safe sleeping sites). Our discussion of the socioecological dynamics of nonhuman primate adaptations in Chapter 7 made this same point.

There is some evidence that at about the same time the earliest hominids were diverging, there *may* have been some major ecological changes occurring in Africa. Could these ecological and evolutionary changes be related to each other? As we will see, there is much debate regarding such a sweeping generalization. For most of the Miocene, Africa was generally tropical, with heavy rainfall persisting for most of the year; consequently, most of the continent was heavily forested. However, beginning later in the Miocene and intensifying up to the end of the epoch (about 5 m.y.a.), the climate became cooler, drier, and more seasonal.

Environmental determinism
An interpretation that links simple environmental changes directly to a major evolutionary shift in an organism. Such explanations tend to be extreme oversimplifications of the evolutionary process.

Stable carbon isotopes
Isotopes of carbon that are produced in plants in differing proportions, depending on environmental conditions. Through analyzing the proportions of the isotopes contained in fossil remains of animals (who ate the plants), it is possible to reconstruct aspects of ancient environments (particularly temperature and aridity).

We should mention as well that there were other regions of the world where paleoecological evidence reveals a distinct cooling trend at the end of the Miocene. However, our focus is on Africa, particularly East Africa, for it is from this region that we have the earliest evidence of hominid diversification. As already noted, one method used by paleoanthropologists to reconstruct environments is to analyze animal (faunal) remains and fossilized pollen. In addition, an innovative technique also studies the chemical pathways utilized by different plants. In particular, **stable carbon isotopes** are produced by plants in differing proportions, depending partly on temperature and aridity (plants adapted to warmer, wetter climates, such as most trees, shrubs, and tubers, versus plants requiring hotter, drier conditions, as typified by many types of grasses). Animals eat the plants, and the differing concentrations of the stable isotopes of carbon are incorporated into their bones and teeth, thus providing a "signature" of the general type of environment in which they lived.

It is from a combination of these analytical techniques that paleoecologists have gained a reasonably good handle on worldwide and continentwide environmental patterns of the past. For example, one model postulates that as climates grew cooler in East Africa 12–5 m.y.a., forests became less continuous. As a result, forest "fringe" habitats and transitional zones between forests and grasslands became more widespread. It is hypothesized that in such transitional environments, some of the late Miocene hominoids may have exploited more intensively the drier grassland portions of the fringe (these would be the earliest hominids); conversely, other hominoids concentrated more on the wetter portions of the fringe (these presumably were the ancestors of African great apes). In the incipient protohominids, further adaptive strategies would have followed, including bipedalism, increased tool use, dietary specialization (perhaps on hard items such as seeds and nuts), and changes in social organization.

Such assertions concerning interactions of habitat, locomotion, dietary changes, and social organization are not really testable (since we do not know which changes came first). Still, some of the more restricted contentions of this "climatic forcing" theory are amenable to testing; as yet, however, the more basic predictions of the model have not been verified. Most notably, further analyses using stable carbon isotopes from several East African localities suggest that during the late Miocene, environments across the area were consistently quite densely forested (i.e., grasslands never predominated, except perhaps at a local level).

You should be aware that there can be wide fluctuations at the local level pertaining to such factors as temperature, rainfall, vegetation, and the animals exploiting the vegetation. For example, local uplift can produce a rain shadow, dramatically altering rainfall and temperature in a region. River and related lake drainages also have major impacts in some areas, and these topographical features are often influenced by highly localized geological factors. To generalize about climates in Africa, good data from several regions are required.

It would thus appear, given current evidence and available analytical techniques, that our knowledge of the factors influencing the appearance of the *earliest* hominids is very limited. Considering the constraints, most hypotheses relating to potential factors are best kept restricted in scope and directly related to actual data. In this way, their utility can be more easily evaluated and they can be modified and built upon.

Changing Environments and Later Hominid Diversifications

From the Pliocene and early Pleistocene, we have much more data relating to hominids and the environments in which they lived. One innovative explanation has sought to link periods of hominid and other mammalian diversification (when new species appear) with regular shifts in the African environment. From her research in both South and East Africa, Elizabeth Vrba, of Yale University, noticed that the appearance of new species of antelope as well as hominids was correlated with three periods of increased aridity (at 2.5, 1.8, and 1.0 m.y.a.) (Vrba, 1988, 1995). Could the environment have played a significant role in stimulating mammalian (including hominid) evolution at several crucial stages? This view has come to be called the **evolutionary pulse theory** and has been supported from data in Africa and other regions.

However, more recent and highly detailed analyses of more than 400 paleontological sites located around Lake Turkana (in northern Kenya and southern Ethiopia) have cast doubt on some aspects of the evolutionary pulse theory. Anna Behrensmeyer and colleagues from the Smithsonian Institution collected data from more than 10,000 specimens from contexts ranging in age from 4.4 m.y.a. to the present to see if any "spikes" in rates of extinction or appearance of new species were evident (Behrensmeyer et al., 1997). The key period pointed to by many proponents of the evolutionary pulse theory is around 2.5 m.y.a., since this is a time of considerable activity in the hominid lineage (including the first documented evidence of the genus *Homo*). Was there a general evolutionary pulse at 2.5 m.y.a. associated with climate change that impacted a wide variety of African mammals? The evidence for this time period from the Lake Turkana region does not support any such rapid evolutionary event. In fact, species turnover between 3 and 2 million years ago in this area was quite gradual, with no indication of a pulse. Some species associated with drier habitats persisted throughout this million-year time period.

Vrba's hypothesis suggested a series of rapid, continentwide environmental changes, which then stimulated accelerated evolutionary changes in various animals (including hominids) around 2.5 m.y.a. This view is intriguing and was initially bolstered by some paleontological data, especially those from South Africa. However, for the Turkana area, "the absence of a pulse from the best calibrated, fossil-rich deposits from this time period weakens the case for rapid climatic forcing of continent scale ecological change and faunal turnover" (Behrensmeyer et al., 1997, p. 1593). Nevertheless, this region is only one segment of Africa and may not indicate broad climatic trends occurring elsewhere on the continent. The evolutionary pulse theory is thus not yet clearly established, but the proposal has stimulated innovative further research. In this way, we can see scientific methodology working at its best. Better data analyzed with better controls *should* yield better explanations. Indeed, Vrba has suggested two other periods of evolutionary pulses, one of these occurring at 1.8 m.y.a. These periods of increased speciation and extinction are again thought to be associated with significant evolutionary changes among the hominids. Interestingly, the data from the Turkana region lends support to fairly rapid turnover in mammalian species at 1.8 m.y.a. Thus, there may have been a significant role played by broad climatic influences, at least during some stages of hominid evolution.

We should not, however, assume that for any period, environmental explanations can be simply applied. What we should conclude is that such broad environmental changes probably were just one factor among many influencing the evolution of early African hominids at different times and in different regions of the continent.

Why Did Hominids Become Bipedal?

As we have noted several times, the adaptation of hominids to bipedal locomotion was *the* most fundamental adaptive shift among the early members of our family. But what were the factors that initiated this crucial change? Ecological theories, similar to some of those just discussed, have long been thought to be central to the development of bipedalism. Clearly, however, environmental influences would have to occur *before* documented evidence of well-adapted bipedal behavior. In other words, the major shift would have been at the end of the Miocene or beginning of the Pliocene. Although the evidence indicates that no *sudden* wide ecological change took place at this time, locally forests probably did become patchier as rainfall became more seasonal. Given the changing environmental conditions, did hominids come to the ground to seize the opportunities offered in these more open habitats? Did bipedalism then quickly ensue, stimulated by this new way of life? At a very general level, the answer to these questions is yes. Obviously, hominids did at some point become bipedal, and this adaptation took place on the ground. Likewise, hominids are more adapted to mixed and open-country habitats than are our closest

Evolutionary pulse theory
A view that postulates a correlation of periods of hominid diversification during the Pliocene and early Pleistocene with major shifts in several African mammalian species. These changes in mammalian evolution, in turn, are thought to be related to periodic episodes of aridity.

ape cousins. Successful terrestrial bipedalism probably made possible the further adaptation to more arid, open-country terrain. Still, this rendition simply tells us *where* hominids found their niche, not *why*.

As always, one must be cautious when speculating about causation in evolution. It is all too easy to draw superficial conclusions. For example, it is often surmised that the mere fact that ground niches were available (and perhaps lacked direct competitors) inevitably led the earliest hominids to terrestrial bipedalism. But consider this: There are plenty of mammalian species, including some nonhuman primates, that also live mostly on the ground in open country—and they are not bipedal. Clearly, beyond such simplistic environmental determinism, some more complex explanation for hominid bipedalism is required. There must have been something *more* than just an environmental opportunity to explain this adaptation to such a unique lifestyle.

Another issue sometimes overlooked in the discussion of early hominid bipedal adaptation is that these creatures did not suddenly become *completely* terrestrial. We know, for example, that all terrestrial species of nonhuman primates (e.g., savanna baboons, hamadryas baboons, patas monkeys; see Chapter 7) regularly seek out "safe sleeping sites" off the ground. These safe havens help protect against predation and are usually found in trees or on cliff faces. Likewise, early hominids almost certainly sought safety at night *in the trees*, even after they became well adapted to terrestrial bipedalism during daytime foraging. Moreover, the continued opportunities for feeding in the trees would most likely have remained significant to early hominids, well after they were also utilizing ground-based resources.

A variety of hypotheses to explain why hominids initially became bipedal have been suggested and are summarized in Table 9–3. The primary influences claimed to have stimulated the shift to bipedalism include the ability to carry objects (and offspring); hunting on the ground; gathering of seeds and nuts; feeding from bushes; better view of open country (to spot predators); long-distance walking; and provisioning by males of females with dependent offspring.

These are all creative scenarios but once again are not very conducive to rigorous testing and verification. Nevertheless, two of the more ambitious scenarios proposed by Clifford Jolly (1970) and Owen Lovejoy (1981) deserve further mention. Both of these views sought to link several aspects of early hominid ecology, feeding, and social behavior, and both utilized models derived from studies of contemporary nonhuman primates.

Jolly's seed-eating hypothesis used the feeding behavior and ecology of gelada baboons as an analogy for very early hominids. In this view, early hominids are hypothesized to have adapted to open country and bipedalism as consequences of their *primary* adaptation to eating seeds and nuts (found on the ground). The key assumption is that early hominids were eating seeds acquired in similar ecological conditions to those of contemporary gelada baboons.

Lovejoy, meanwhile, has combined *presumed* aspects of early hominid ecology, feeding, pair bonding, infant care, and food sharing to devise his creative scenario. This view hinges on the following assumptions: (1) that the earliest hominids had offspring at least as K-selected (see p. 159) as other large-bodied hominids; (2) that hominid males ranged widely and provisioned females and their young, who remained more tied to a "home base"; and (3) that males were paired *monogamously* with females.

As we have noted, while not strictly testable, such scenarios do make certain predictions (which can be verified). Accordingly, aspects of each scenario can be evaluated in light of more specific data obtained from the paleoanthropological record. As pertaining to the seed-eating hypothesis, predictions relating to size of the back teeth in most early hominids are met; however, the proportions of the front teeth in many forms are not what would be expected in a committed seed eater. Moreover, the analogy with gelada baboons is not as informative as once thought, since these animals actually do not eat that many seeds. Finally, many of the characteristics suggested by Jolly to be restricted to hominids (and geladas) are also found in several late Miocene hominoids (who were not hominids). Thus,

TABLE 9–3 Possible Factors Influencing the Initial Evolution of Bipedal Locomotion in Hominids

Factor	Speculated Influence	Comments
Carrying (objects, tools, weapons, infants)	Upright posture freed the arms to carry various objects (including offspring)	Charles Darwin emphasized this view, particularly relating to tools and weapons; however, evidence of stone tools is found much later in record than first evidence of bipedalism
Hunting	As correlated with above theory, carrying weapons made hunting more efficient; in addition, long-distance walking may have been more energetically efficient (see below)	Systematic hunting is now thought not to have been practiced until after the origin of bipedal hominids
Seed and nut gathering	Feeding on seeds and nuts occurred while standing upright	Model initially drawn from analogy with gelada baboons (see text)
Feeding from bushes	Upright posture provided access to seeds, berries, etc., in lower branches; analogous to adaptation seen in some specialized antelopes	Climbing adaptation already existed as prior ancestral trait in earliest hominids (i.e., bush and tree feeding already was established prior to bipedal adaptation)
Visual surveillance	Standing up provided better view of surrounding countryside (view of potential predators as well as other group members)	Behavior seen occasionally in terrestrial primates (e.g., baboons); probably a contributing factor, but unlikely as "prime mover"
Long-distance walking	Covering long distances was more efficient for a biped than for a quadruped (during hunting or foraging); mechanical reconstructions show that bipedal walking is less energetically costly than quadrupedalism (this is not the case for bipedal *running*)	Same difficulties as with hunting explanation; long-distance foraging on ground also appears unlikely adaptation in *earliest* hominids
Male provisioning	Males carried back resources to dependent females and young	Monogamous bond suggested; however, most skeletal data appear to falsify this part of the hypothesis (see text)

regarding the seed-eating hypothesis, the proposed dental and dietary adaptations do not appear to be linked specifically to hominid origins or bipedalism.

Similarly, further detailed analyses of data have questioned crucial elements of Lovejoy's scenario of male provisioning. The evidence that appears to most contradict this view is that *all* early hominids were quite sexually dimorphic. According to Lovejoy's model (and analogies with contemporary monogamous nonhuman primates such as gibbons), there should not be such dramatic differences in body size between males and females. Moreover, the notions of food sharing (presumably including considerable meat), home bases, and long-distance provisioning are questioned by more controlled interpretations of the archaeological record (see Issue, pp. 220–221).

Another imaginative view is also relevant to this discussion of early hominid evolution, since it relates the adaptation to bipedalism (which was first) to increased brain expansion (which came later). This interpretation, proposed by Dean Falk, of the State University of New York at Albany, suggests that an upright posture put severe constraints on brain size (since blood circulation and drainage would have been altered and thus cooling would have been more limited than in quadrupeds). Falk thus hypothesizes that new brain-cooling mechanisms must have coevolved with bipedalism, articulated in what she calls the "radiator theory" (Falk, 1990). Falk further surmises that the requirements for better brain cooling would have been particularly marked as hominids adapted to open-country ground living on the hot African savanna. Another interesting pattern observed by Falk concerns two different cooling adaptations found in different early hominid species. She thus suggests that the type of "radiator" adapted in the genus *Homo* was particularly significant in reducing constraints on brain size—which presumably limited some other early hominids. The radiator theory works well, since it not only

 See Virtual Lab 8, section I, for a discussion of sexual dimorphism in fossil hominids.

helps explain the relationship of bipedalism to later brain expansion, but also explains why only some hominids became dramatically encephalized.

The radiator theory, too, has been criticized by some paleoanthropologists. Most notably, the presumed species distinction concerning varying cooling mechanisms is not so obvious as suggested by the hypothesis. Both types of venous drainage systems can be found in contemporary *Homo sapiens* as well as within various early hominid species (i.e., the variation is intraspecific, not just interspecific). Indeed, in some early hominid specimens, both systems can be found in the *same* individual (differently expressed i.e., on each side of the skull). Moreover, as Falk herself has noted, the radiator itself did not lead to larger brains; it simply helped reduce constraints on increased encephalization among hominids. It thus requires some *further* mechanism (prime mover) to explain why, in some hominid species, brain size increased in the manner it did.

As with any such ambitious effort, it is all too easy to find holes. Falk aptly reminds us that "the search for such 'prime movers' is highly speculative and these theories do not lend themselves to hypothesis testing" (Falk, 1990, p. 334). Nevertheless, the attempt to interrelate various lines of evidence, the use of contemporary primate models, and predictions concerning further evidence obtained from paleoanthropological contexts all conform to sound scientific methodology. All the views discussed here have contributed to this venture—one not just aimed at understanding our early ancestors, but one also seeking to refine its methodologies and scientific foundation.

SUMMARY

The biocultural nature of human evolution requires that any meaningful study of human origins examine both biological and cultural information. The multidisciplinary approach of paleoanthropology is designed to bring together varied scientific specializations to reconstruct the anatomy, behavior, and environments of early hominids. Such a task is centered around the skills of the geologist, paleontologist, paleoecologist, archaeologist, and physical anthropologist.

Much of what we know about the origins of human culture between 1 and 2 m.y.a. comes from archaeological excavations by Mary Leakey at Olduvai Gorge in East Africa. Olduvai's well-documented stratigraphic sequence, its superior preservation of remains, and the varied dating techniques possible there have made it an information bonanza for paleoanthropologists. Excavated sites have yielded a wealth of bones of fossil animals, as well as artifact traces of hominid behavior. Ecological reconstructions of habitat and dietary preferences are thereby possible and inform us in great detail concerning crucial evolutionary processes affecting early hominid populations.

Broader interpretations, leading to several speculative scenarios, have also been attempted to help us understand the environmental influences and behavioral adaptations exhibited by early hominids. Most notably, attempts have been made to link the earliest origins of hominids as well as somewhat later diversifications to general ecological changes in Africa. Finally, many researchers have speculated concerning the factors influencing that most fundamental of all early hominid adaptations, the development of bipedal locomotion. In the next chapter, we will survey the fossil hominid evidence in South and East Africa that informs us directly about human origins during the Plio-Pleistocene.

QUESTIONS FOR REVIEW

1. Why are cultural remains so important in the interpretation of human evolution?
2. How are early hominid sites found, and what kind of specialist is involved in the excavation and analysis of paleoanthropological data?

3. What kinds of paleoanthropological information have been found at Olduvai Gorge? Why is this particular locality so rich in material?

4. What techniques have been used to date early hominid sites at Olduvai? Why is more than one technique necessary for accurate dating?

5. Why are context and association so important in the interpretation of archaeological remains?

6. What different activities can be inferred from the different kinds of sites at Olduvai? Discuss alternative views in the interpretation of these "sites."

7. What is a scenario? How does it differ from a scientific hypothesis? Give an example.

8. What environmental factors have been postulated as important in influencing the origins of the first hominids? How satisfactory are these explanations?

9. What are some of the factors thought to be important in influencing the early evolution of bipedal locomotion?

SUGGESTED FURTHER READING

Binford, Lewis. 1981. *Bones: Ancient Men and Myths*. New York: Academic Press.

Leakey, Mary. 1984. *Disclosing the Past. An Autobiography*. Garden City, NJ: Doubleday.

Leakey, Richard. 1981. *The Making of Mankind*. New York: Dutton.

Rasmussen, D. T. (ed.). 1993. *The Origin and Evolution of Humans and Humanness*. Boston: Jones and Bartlett.

RESOURCES ON THE INTERNET

 Wadsworth Anthropology Resource Center

http://anthropology.wadsworth.com

The companion website for this text includes a range of enrichment material focused on the chapter's topic. While online you can enhance your understanding of the chapter by exploring one of the several additional Internet Exercises, by researching topics, and by accessing full articles on InfoTrac College Edition. You can also reinforce the concepts by taking online practice exams.

Internet Exercises

The Institute for Human Origins is one of the major research institutes in paleoanthropology. At their website (**http://www.asu.edu/clas/iho**) you can view pictures of some of their field research as well as some of the fossils they have found. Read through the science section and look at the photography section. In particular, spend some time looking at the pictures of the field work at Hadar and Swartkrans. What different fieldwork methods were used at these two sites?

 InfoTrac College Edition

http://www.infotrac-college.com/wadsworth

Search InfoTrac College Edition for *bipedalism*. What hypotheses are offered in these articles for the origins of bipedalism? Do you find any single hypothesis more convincing than the others? Why or why not?

Who Was Doing What at the Olduvai Sites?

The long-held interpretation of the bone refuse and stone tools discovered at Olduvai has been that most, if not all, of these materials are the result of hominid activities. More recently, however, a comprehensive reanalysis of the bone remains from Olduvai localities has challenged this view (Binford 1981, 1983). Archaeologist Lewis Binford criticizes those drawn too quickly to the conclusion that these bone scatters are the remnants of hominid behavior patterns while simultaneously ignoring the possibility of other explanations. For example, he forcefully states:

All the facts gleaned from the deposits interpreted as living sites have served as the basis for making up "just-so-stories" about our hominid past. No attention has been given to the possibility that many of the facts may well be referable to the behavior of nonhominids. (Binford, 1981, p. 251)

From information concerning the kinds of animals present, which body parts were found, and the differences in preservation among these skeletal elements, Binford has concluded that much of what is preserved could be explained by carnivore activity. This conclusion has been reinforced by certain details observed by Binford himself in Alaska—details on animal kills, scavenging, the transportation of elements, and preservation as the result of wolf and dog behaviors. Binford describes his approach thus:

I took as "known," then, the structure of bone assemblages produced in various settings by animal predators and scavengers; and as "unknown" the bone deposits excavated by the

Leakeys at Olduvai Gorge. Using mathematical and statistical techniques I considered to what degree the finds from Olduvai Gorge could be accounted for in terms of the results of predator behavior and how much was "left over." (Binford, 1983, pp. 56–57)

Binford is not arguing that all of the remains found at Olduvai have resulted from nonhominid activity. In fact, he recognizes that "residual material" was consistently found on surfaces with high tool concentration "which could not be explained by what we know about African animals" (Binford 1983).

Support for the idea that at least some of the bone refuse was utilized by early hominids has come from a totally different perspective. Researchers have analyzed (both macroscopically and microscopically) the cut marks left on fossilized bones. By experimenting with modern materials, they have further been able to delineate clearly the differences between marks left by stone tools and those left by animal teeth (or other factors) (Bunn, 1981; Potts and Shipman, 1981). Analysis of bones from several early localities at Olduvai have shown unambiguously that these specimens were utilized by hominids, who left telltale cut marks from stone tool usage. The sites thus far investigated reveal a somewhat haphazard cutting and chopping, apparently unrelated to deliberate disarticulation. It has thus been concluded (Shipman, 1983) that hominids scavenged carcasses (probably of carnivore kills) and did *not* hunt large animals themselves.

Following and expanding on the experimental approaches pioneered by Binford, Bunn, and others, more detailed analysis of the

Olduvai material has recently been done by Robert Blumenschine of Rutgers University. Like his predecessors, Blumenschine has also concluded that the cut marks on animal bones are the result of hominid processing (Blumenschine, 1995). Moreover, Blumenschine and colleagues have surmised that most meat acquisition (virtually all from large animals) was the result of scavenging (from remains of carnivore kills or from animals who died from natural causes). In fact, these researchers suggest that scavenging was a critically important adaptive strategy for early hominids and considerably influenced their habitat usage, diet, and stone tool utilization (Blumenschine and Cavallo, 1992; Blumenschine and Peters, 1998). Of notable scientific merit, Blumenschine and colleagues have developed a model detailing how scavenging and other early hominid adaptive strategies integrate into patterns of land use (i.e., differential utilization of various niches in and around Olduvai). From this model they have formulated specific hypotheses concerning the predicted distribution of artifacts and animal remains in different areas at Olduvai. Ongoing excavations at Olduvai are now aimed specifically at *testing* these hypotheses.

If early hominids (close to 2 m.y.a.) were not hunting consistently, what did they obtain from scavenging the kills of other animals? One obvious answer is, whatever meat was left behind. However, the position of the cut marks suggests that early hominids were often hacking at non-meat-bearing portions of the skeletons. Perhaps they were after bone marrow and brain, substances not fully exploited by other predators and scavengers (Binford, 1981; Blumenschine and Cavallo, 1992).

Exciting new discoveries from the Bouri Peninsula of the Middle Awash of Ethiopia provide the best evidence yet for meat and marrow exploitation by early hominids. Dated to 2.5 m.y.a. (i.e., as old as the oldest known artifacts), antelope and horse fossils from Bouri show telltale incisions and breaks indicating that bones were smashed to extract marrow and also cut, ostensibly to retrieve meat (de Heinzelin et al., 1999). The researchers who analyzed these materials have suggested that the greater dietary reliance on animal products may have been important in stimulating brain enlargement in the lineage leading to genus *Homo*.

Another new research twist relating to the reconstruction of early hominid diets has come from biochemical analysis of hominid teeth from South Africa (dating to about the same time range as hominids from Olduvai— or perhaps slightly earlier). In an innovative application of stable carbon isotope analysis (see p. 214), Matt Sponheimer of Rutgers University and Julia Lee-Thorp of the University of Cape Town found that these early hominid teeth revealed telltale chemical signatures relating to diet (Sponheimer and Lee-Thorp, 1999). In particular, the proportions of stable carbon isotopes indicated that these early hominids either ate grass products (such as seeds) or ate meat/marrow from animals that in turn had eaten grass products (i.e., the hominids might well have derived a significant portion of their diet from meat or other animal products). This evidence comes from an exciting new perspective, for it provides a more *direct* indicator of early hominid diets. While it is not clear how much meat these early hominids consumed, these new data do suggest they were consistently exploiting more open regions of their environment.

Critical Thinking Questions

1. What types of evidence are available to interpret hominid behavior (specifically, meat acquisition) at Olduvai sites?
2. Which of the evidence in question 1 is prehistoric, and which relates to *modern* contexts?
3. What is *known* and what is *inferred* in regard to these behavioral interpretations?
4. Why is it notable that Blumenschine and colleagues have made hypotheses about Olduvai sites that are testable?
5. Using Binford's model, how would you test the hypothesis that the distribution of broken animal bones at a 1.8-million-year-old site at Olduvai is primarily the result of hominid food-processing behavior?

Sources

Binford, Lewis R. 1981. *Bones: Ancient Men and Modern Myths.* New York: Academic Press.
_____. 1983. *In Pursuit of the Past.* New York: Thames and Hudson.
Blumenschine, Robert J. 1995. "Percussion Marks, Tooth Marks, and Experimental Determinants of the Timing of Hominid and Carnivore Access to Long Bones at FLK *Zinjanthropus*, Olduvai Gorge, Tanzania." *Journal of Human Evolution* 29: 21–51.
Blumenschine, Robert J., and John A. Cavallo. 1992. "Scavenging and Human Evolution." *Scientific American* (Oct.): 90–96.
Blumenschine, Robert J., and Charles R. Peters. 1998. "Archaeological Predictions for Hominid Land Use in the Paleo-Olduvai Basin, Tanzania, During Lowermost Bed II Times." *Journal of Human Evolution* 34: 565–607.
Bunn, Henry T. 1981. "Archaeological Evidence for Meat-Eating by Plio-Pleistocene Hominids from Koobi Fora and Olduvai Gorge." *Nature* 291:574–577.
de Heinzelin, Jean, J. Desmond Clark, Tim White, et al. 1999. "Environment and Behavior of 2.5-Million-Year-Old Bouri Hominids." *Science* 284:625–629.
Potts, Richard, and Pat Shipman. 1981. "Cutmarks Made by Stone Tools from Olduvai Gorge, Tanzania." *Nature* 291:577–580.
Shipman, Pat. 1983. "Early Hominid Lifestyle. Hunting and Gathering or Foraging and Scavenging?" Paper presented at 52nd Annual Meeting, American Association of Physical Anthropologists, Indianapolis.
Sponheimer, Matt, and Julia A. Lee-Thorp. 1999. "Isotopic Evidence for the Diet of an Early Hominid, *Australopithecus africanus*." *Science* 283:368–370.

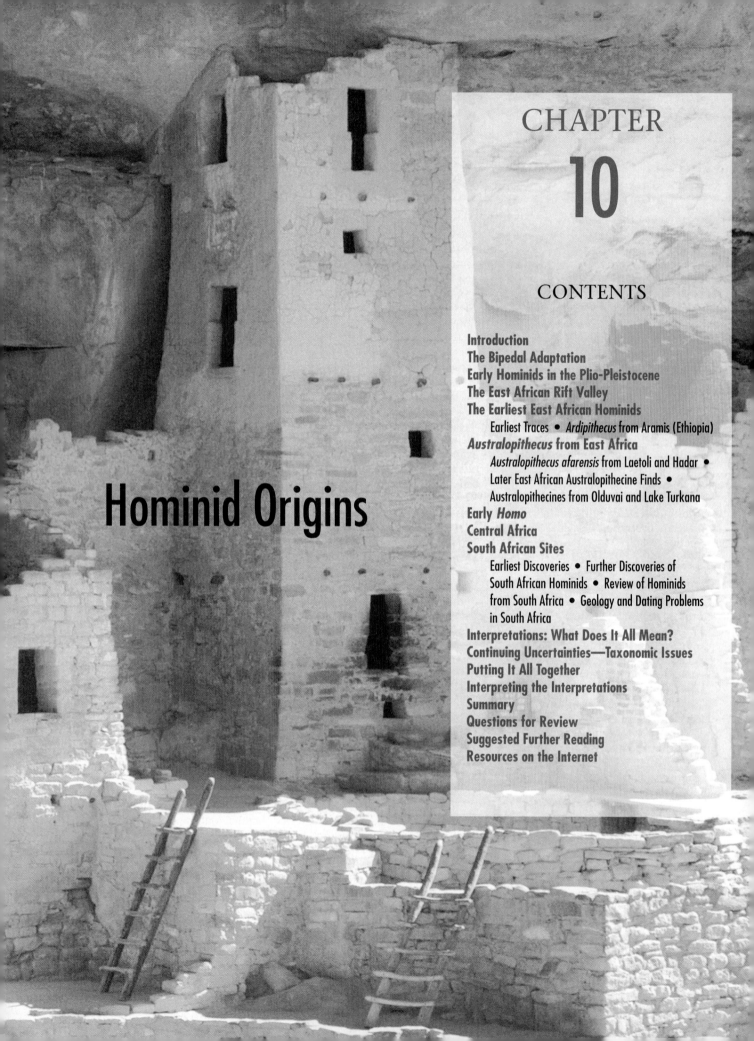

CHAPTER

10

Hominid Origins

CONTENTS

Introduction

In Chapter 9, we discussed the techniques used by paleoanthropologists to collect and interpret basic background data relating to the evolution of early hominids. Such geological, ecological, and archaeological information helps us understand the environments and behaviors of the earliest members of the hominid family.

In this chapter, we turn to the physical evidence of the hominid fossils themselves. From the Pliocene epoch and the first half of the Pleistocene, a very large fossil collection of these early hominids has been found in Africa. Comprising the time span of 5–1 m.y.a., this period is usually referred to as the **Plio-Pleistocene**. These fossil hominids are a rich and varied lot, and their discovery has stimulated a great deal of interest among both the scientific community and the general public. Given these circumstances, it is perhaps no great surprise that the interpretation of these finds has also generated considerable controversy. Thus, in addition to reviewing the anatomical details revealed directly in the fossil material, we will also discuss and attempt to sort out the complex and frequently conflicting interpretations concerning the evolutionary patterns of Plio-Pleistocene hominids.

The Bipedal Adaptation

In our overview of behavioral reconstructions in early hominids, we highlighted several hypotheses that attempt to explain *why* bipedal locomotion first evolved in the hominids. Here we turn to the specific anatomical (i.e., **morphological**) evidence that shows us when, where, and how hominid bipedal locomotion evolved.

In our discussion of primate anatomical trends in Chapter 6, we noted that there is a general tendency in all primates for erect body posture and some bipedalism. However, of all living primates, efficient bipedalism as the primary form of locomotion is seen *only* in hominids. Functionally, the human mode of locomotion is most clearly shown in our striding gait, where weight is alternately placed on a single fully extended hind limb. This specialized form of locomotion has developed to a point where energy levels are used to near peak efficiency. Such is not the case in nonhuman primates, who move bipedally with hips and knees bent and maintain balance in a clumsy and inefficient manner.

Our mode of locomotion is indeed extraordinary, involving as it does an activity in which "the body, step by step, teeters on the edge of catastrophe" (Napier, 1967, p.56). The problem is to maintain balance on the "stance" leg while the "swing" leg is off the ground. In fact, during normal walking, both feet are simultaneously on the ground only about 25 percent of the time, and as speed of locomotion increases, this figure becomes even smaller.

To maintain a stable center of balance in this complex form of locomotion, many drastic structural/anatomical alterations in the basic primate quadrupedal pattern are required. The most dramatic changes are seen in the pelvis. The pelvis is composed of three elements: two *ossa coxae* (*sing.*, os coxae) joined at the back to the sacrum (Fig. 10–1). In a quadruped, the ossa coxae are elongated bones positioned along each side of the lower portion of the spine and oriented more or less parallel to it. In hominids, the pelvis is comparatively much shorter and broader and extends around to the side (Fig. 10–2). This configuration helps to stabilize the line of weight transmission, in a bipedal posture, from the lower back to the hip joint (Fig. 10–3).

A number of consequences resulted from the remodeling of the pelvis during early hominid evolution. Broadening the two sides and extending them around to the side and front of the body produced a basin-shaped structure that helps support the abdominal organs (indeed, *pelvis* means "basin" in Latin). Moreover, these alterations repositioned the attachments of several key muscles that act on the hip and leg, changing their mechanical function. Probably the most important of these altered relationships is that involving the *gluteus maximus*, the largest muscle in the body, which in humans forms the bulk of the buttocks. In quadrupeds, the gluteus maximus is positioned to the side of the hip and functions to pull the thigh to the

See the following sections of the CD-ROM for topics covered in this chapter: Virtual Labs 8, 9, 10, and Virtual Lab 12, section I.

Plio-Pleistocene
Pertaining to the Pliocene and first half of the Pleistocene, a time range of 5–1 m.y.a. During this time period, the earliest fossil hominids have been found in Africa.

Morphological
Pertaining to the form and structure of organisms.

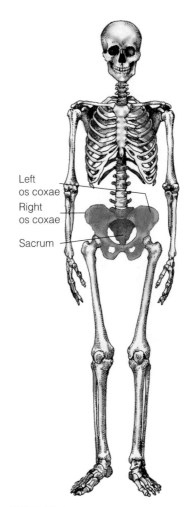

Left
os coxae
Right
os coxae

Sacrum

FIGURE 10–1
The human pelvis. Various elements shown on a modern skeleton.

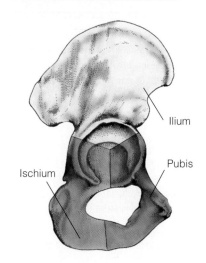

FIGURE 10–2
The human os coxae, composed of three bones (right side shown).

Ilium

Pubis

Ischium

FIGURE 10–3
Ossa coxae. (a) *Homo sapiens.* (b) Early hominid (*Australopithecus*) from South Africa. (c) Chimpanzee. Note especially the length and breadth of the iliac blade and the line of weight transmission (shown in red).

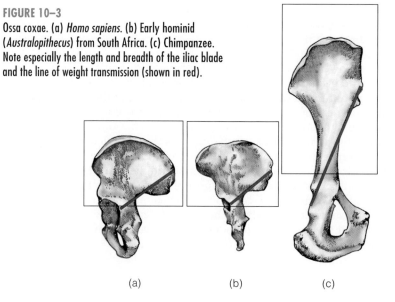

(a)   (b)   (c)

Foramen magnum
The opening at the base of the skull through which the spinal cord passes as it enters the body to descend through the vertebral column. In quadrupeds, it is located more to the rear of the skull, while in bipeds, it is located farther beneath the skull.

side, away from the body. But in humans, this muscle acts, along with the hamstrings, to extend the thigh, pulling it to the rear during walking and running (Fig 10–4). Indeed, the gluteus maximus is a powerful extensor of the thigh and provides additional force, particularly during running and climbing.

Modifications also occurred in other parts of the skeleton as a result of the shift to bipedalism. The most significant of these are summarized in Box 10–1 and include (1) repositioning of the **foramen magnum**, the opening at the base of the skull through which the spinal cord emerges; (2) the addition of spinal curves that facilitate the transmission of the weight of the upper body to the hips in an upright posture; (3) shortening and broadening of the pelvis and the stabilization of weight transmission (discussed earlier); (4) lengthening of the hind limb, thus increasing stride length; (5) angling of the femur (thighbone) inward to bring the knees and

FIGURE 10–4
Comparisons of important muscles that act to extend the hip. Note that the attachment surface (origin, shown in red) of the gluteus maximus in humans (a) is farther in back of the hipbone than in a chimpanzee standing bipedally (b). Conversely, in chimpanzees, the hamstrings are farther in back of the knee.

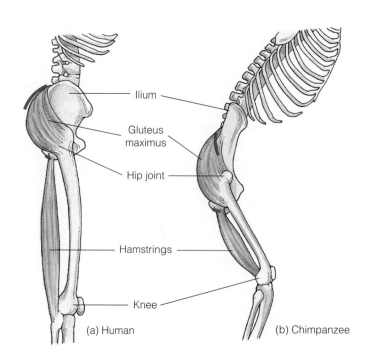

Ilium

Gluteus maximus

Hip joint

Hamstrings

Knee

(a) Human   (b) Chimpanzee

feet closer together under the body; and (6) several structural changes in the foot, including the development of a longitudinal arch and realignment of the big toe in parallel with the other toes (i.e., it was no longer divergent).

As you can appreciate, the evolution of hominid bipedalism required complex anatomical reorganization. For natural selection to produce anatomical change of the magnitude seen in hominids, the benefits of bipedal locomotion must have been significant indeed. We mentioned in Chapter 9 several possible adaptive advantages that bipedal locomotion *may* have conferred upon early hominids. However, these all remain hypotheses (even more accurately, they could be called scenarios), and we lack adequate data with which to test the various proposed alternatives.

Still, given the anatomical alterations that efficient bipedalism necessitated, there must have been some major behavioral stimuli influencing its development. In the interpretation of evolutionary history, biologists are fond of saying that form follows function. In other words, during evolution, organisms do not undergo significant reorganization in structure *unless* these changes (over many generations) assist individuals in some functional capacity (and, in so doing, increase their reproductive success). Such changes did not necessarily occur all at once, but probably evolved over a fairly long period of time. Nevertheless, once behavioral influences initiated certain structural modifications, the process gained momentum and proceeded irreversibly.

We say that hominid bipedalism is *habitual* and *obligate*. By habitual, we mean that hominids, unlike any other primate, move bipedally as their standard and most efficient mode of locomotion. By obligate, we mean that hominids are committed to bipedalism and cannot locomote efficiently in any other manner. For example, the loss of grasping ability in the foot makes climbing much more difficult for humans (although by no means impossible). The central task, then, in trying to understand the earliest members of the hominid family is to identify anatomical features that indicate bipedalism and to interpret to what degree these organisms were committed to this form of locomotion (i.e., was it habitual and was it obligate?).

What structural patterns are observable in early hominids, and what do they imply regarding locomotor function? *All the major structural changes required for bipedalism are seen in early hominids from East and South Africa* (at least insofar as the evidence has thus far been reported). In particular, the pelvis, as clearly documented by several excellently preserved specimens, was dramatically remodeled to support weight in a bipedal stance (see Fig. 10–3b).

In addition, other structural changes shown in even the earliest definitive hominid postcranial remains further confirm the pattern seen in the pelvis. For example, the vertebral column (as known from specimens in East and South Africa) shows the same curves as in modern hominids. The lower limbs were also elongated and were apparently proportionately about as long as in modern humans (although the arms were longer). Further, the carrying angle of weight support from the hip to the knee was also very similar to that seen in *Homo sapiens*.

Fossil evidence of early hominid foot structure has come from two sites in South Africa, and especially important are some recently announced new fossils from Sterkfontein (Clarke and Tobias, 1995). These specimens, consisting of four articulating elements from the ankle and big toe, indicate that the heel and longitudinal arch were both well adapted for a bipedal gait. However, the paleoanthropologists (Ron Clarke and Phillip Tobias) who analyzed these remains also suggest that the large toe was *divergent*, unlike the hominid pattern shown in Box 10–1. If the large toe really did possess this anatomical position, it most likely would have aided the foot in grasping. In turn, this grasping ability (as in other primates) would have enabled early hominids to more effectively exploit arboreal habitats. Finally, since anatomical remodeling is always constrained by a set of complex functional compromises, a foot highly capable of grasping and climbing is *less* capable as a stable platform during bipedal locomotion. Some researchers therefore see early hominids as not necessarily obligate bipeds. Further investigation of the cave site in

 See Virtual Lab 9 for a detailed discussion of the evolution of bipedalism.

BOX 10-1

During hominid evolution, several major structural features throughout the body have been reorganized (from that seen in other primates) to facilitate efficient bipedal locomotion. These are illustrated here, beginning with the head and progressing to the foot: (a) The foramen magnum (shown in red) is repositioned far- ther underneath the head, so that the head is more or less bal- anced on the spine (and thus requires less robust neck muscles to hold the head upright). (b) The spine has two distinctive curves—a backward (thoracic) one and a forward (lumbar) one—that keep the trunk (and weight) centered above the pelvis. (c) The pelvis is

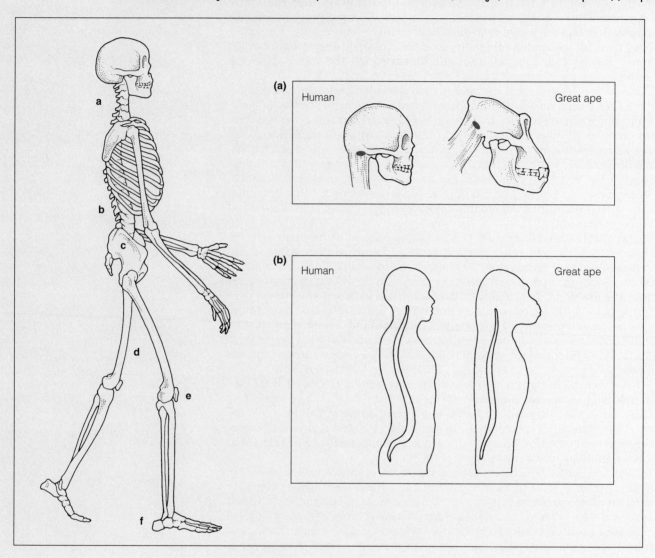

1998 revealed a remarkable find, the remains of a nearly complete skeleton belong- ing to the same individual from which the foot came (see p. 242).

Further evidence for evolutionary changes in the foot skeleton comes from Olduvai Gorge in Tanzania, where a nearly complete hominid foot is preserved, and from Hadar in Ethiopia, where numerous foot elements have been recovered (Fig. 10–5). As in the remains from South Africa, the East African fossils suggest a well- adapted bipedal gait. The arches are developed, but some differences in the ankle also imply that considerable flexibility was possible (again, suggested for continued adaptation to climbing). As we will see, some researchers have recently concluded that many early forms of hominids probably spent considerable time in the trees. Moreover, they may not have been quite as efficient bipeds as has previously been suggested. Nevertheless, to this point, *all* the early hominids that have been identi-

shaped more in the form of a basin to support internal organs; more-over, the ossa coxae (specifically, iliac blades) are shorter and broader, thus stabilizing weight transmission. (d) Lower limbs are elongated, as shown by the proportional lengths of various body segments (e.g., in humans the thigh comprises 20 percent of body height, while in gorillas it comprises only 11 percent). (e) The femur is angled inward, keeping the legs more directly under the body; modified knee anatomy also per-mits full extension of this joint. (f) The big toe is enlarged and brought in line with the other toes; in addition, a distinctive longitudinal arch (shown in red) forms, helping absorb shock and adding propulsive spring.

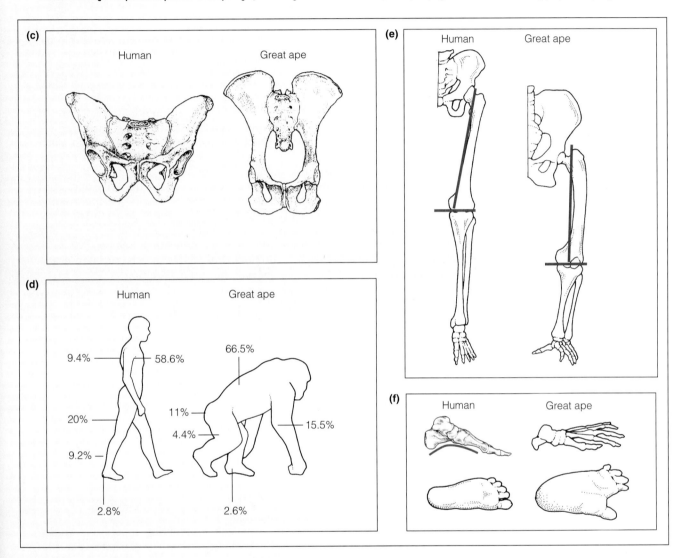

fied from Africa are thought by most researchers to have been both habitual and obligate bipeds (notwithstanding the new evidence from South Africa, which will require further study).

Early Hominids in the Plio-Pleistocene

The beginnings of hominid differentiation almost certainly have their roots in the late Miocene (circa 10–5 m.y.a.). Sometime during the period between 8 and 5 m.y.a., hominids began to adapt more fully to their peculiar ground-living niche, and fossil evidence from this period would be most illuminating, particularly any remains indi-cating a bipedal adaptation. However, scant information is presently available con-cerning the course of hominid evolution during this significant 3-million-year gap.

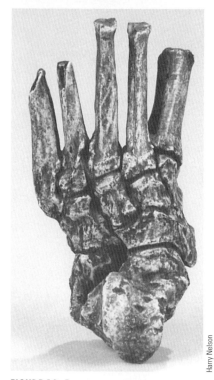

FIGURE 10–5
A nearly complete hominid foot (OH 8) from Olduvai Gorge, Tanzania.

Harry Nelson

See Virtual Lab 8 for an interactive timeline, map, and phylogeny of early hominid evolution.

But beginning around 4.5 m.y.a., the fossil record picks up considerably. We now have a wealth of fossil hominid material from the Pliocene and the earliest stages of the Pleistocene (5–1 m.y.a.), and as noted, this whole span is usually referred to as the Plio-Pleistocene.

The East African Rift Valley

Stretching along a more than 1,200-mile trough extending through Ethiopia, Kenya, and Tanzania from the Red Sea in the north to the Serengeti Plain in the south is the eastern branch of the Great Rift Valley of Africa (Fig. 10–6). This massive geological feature has been associated with active mountain building, faulting, and vulcanism over the last several million years.

Because of these gigantic earth movements, earlier sediments (normally buried under hundreds of feet of earth and rock) were literally thrown to the surface, where they became exposed to the trained eye of the paleoanthropologist. Such earth movements have exposed Miocene beds at sites in Kenya, along the shores of Lake Victoria, where abundant remains of early fossil hominoids have been found. In addition, Plio-Pleistocene sediments are also exposed all along the Rift Valley, and paleoanthropologists in recent years have made the most of this unique opportunity.

More than just exposing normally hidden deposits, rifting has stimulated volcanic activity, which in turn has provided a valuable means of chronometrically dating many sites in East Africa. Unlike the sites in South Africa (see pp. 240–247), those along the Rift Valley are *datable* and have thus yielded much crucial information concerning the precise chronology of early hominid evolution.

The Earliest East African Hominids

The site that focused attention on East Africa as a potential paleoanthropological gold mine was Olduvai Gorge in northern Tanzania. As discussed in great detail in Chapter 9, this site has offered unique opportunities because of the remarkable preservation of geological, paleontological, and archaeological records. Following Mary Leakey's discovery of "Zinj" in 1959 (and the subsequent dating of its site at 1.75 m.y.a.), numerous other areas in East Africa have been surveyed and several intensively explored. We will review the fossil discoveries from these sites as well as briefly discuss their chronological and geological context, beginning with the earliest.

Earliest Traces

The oldest specimen discovered to date, which several authorities identify as a *probable* hominid, comes from a site in northern Kenya (see Fig. 10–6). This fossil is very fragmentary and consists of a portion of a lower jaw (mandible). In addition, in the time range 5–4 m.y.a., there are further scattered finds from two other sites in northern Kenya and from a third locality in northeastern Ethiopia. However, none of this fossil material is very definitive, since, as of yet, only a single (fragmentary) specimen has been recovered from each site (see Table 10–1 for a summary of discoveries).

Still, in the last few years, new and much more abundant discoveries have been made at three other localities, two in northern Kenya and the other in Ethiopia (Aramis) (see Fig. 10–6). Finds from these three sites have added dramatically to our knowledge of the earliest stages of hominid emergence.

Ardipithecus from Aramis (Ethiopia)

One of the most exciting areas for future research in East Africa is the Afar Triangle of northeastern Ethiopia, where the Red Sea, Rift Valley, and Gulf of Aden all intersect. From this area have come many of the most important recent discoveries bearing on human origins. Several areas have yielded fossil remains in recent decades, and many potentially very rich sites are currently being explored. One of these sites

FIGURE 10–6
The East African Rift Valley system and locations of major hominid sites.

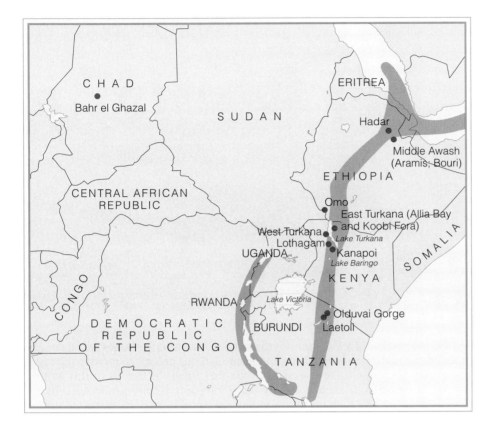

 See Virtual Lab 8, section I, for a comparison of *Ardipithecus* and *Australopithecus*.

just recently discovered, located in the region called the Middle Awash (along the banks of the Awash River), is called **Aramis**. Initial radiometric dating of the sediments places the hominid remains at 4.4 m.y.a., making this the earliest *collection* of hominids yet discovered.

Fossil remains from Aramis were excavated between 1992 and 1995 and include up to 50 different individuals (Wolpoff, 1999). This crucial and quite large collection includes several dental specimens as well as an upper arm bone (humerus) and some fragmentary cranial remains (Fig. 10–7). Most exciting of all,

Aramis
(air´-ah-miss)

TABLE 10–1   Discoveries of Earliest Hominid* Fossil Remains

Site	Dates (m.y.a.)	Taxonomic Designation	Fossil Sample
Belohdelie (Ethiopia)	3.9–3.8	*Australopithecus afarensis*	5 pieces of cranium
Allia Bay (East Turkana) (Kenya)	3.9	*Australopithecus anamensis*	13 specimens
Kanapoi (Kenya)	4.2–3.9	*Australopithecus anamensis*	9 specimens
Aramis (Ethiopia)	4.4	*Ardipithecus ramidus*	More than 50 individuals
Tabarin (Kenya) (Chemeron Beds)	5.0	Uncertain	1 specimen (partial mandible)
Mabaget (Kenya) (Chemeron Beds)	5.1–5.0	Uncertain	1 specimen (partial subadult humerus)
Lothagam (Kenya)	5.8–5.6	Uncertain (possibly, *Ardipithecus*)	1 specimen (partial mandible)

*Note: In some cases, hominid status is not yet well established.

FIGURE 10–7
New hominid discoveries from Aramis. Alemayehu Asfaw is holding his discovery of an upper arm bone (humerus). In the background, team members search for other fragments; parts of all three bones of the upper appendage of one *Ardipithecus ramidus* individual were discovered.
©1994 Tim D. White\Brill Atlanta

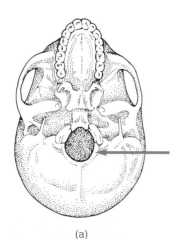

(a)

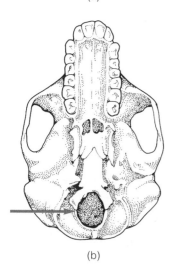

(b)

FIGURE 10–8
Position of the foramen magnum in (a) a human and (b) a chimpanzee. Note the more forward position in the human cranium.

Australopithecus
An early hominid genus, known from the Plio-Pleistocene of Africa, characterized by bipedal locomotion, a relatively small brain, and large back teeth.

in 1995, 40 percent of a skeleton was discovered; however, the bones are all encased in limestone matrix, thus requiring a long and tedious process to remove the fossils intact from the cementlike material surrounding them. In fact, as of this writing, the Aramis remains (including the skeleton) have not yet been fully scientifically described. Nevertheless, details from initial reports are highly suggestive that these remains are, in fact, the *earliest* hominids yet to be found (except, perhaps, for some of the potential early "traces" mentioned earlier).

First of all, in an Aramis partial cranium, the *foramen magnum* is positioned farther forward in the base of the skull than is the case in quadrupeds (Fig. 10–8). Second, features of the humerus also differ from those seen in quadrupeds, indicating that the Aramis humerus did not function in locomotion to support weight (i.e., the upper limbs were free). From these two features, the provisional interpretation by Tim White, of the University of California, Berkeley, and his colleagues was that the Aramis individuals were *bipedal*. Moreover, initial interpretation of the partial skeleton (while not yet fully cleaned and reported) also suggests obligate bipedalism (Wolpoff, 1999).

Nevertheless, these were clearly quite primitive hominids, displaying an array of characteristics quite distinct from other members of our family. These primitive characteristics include flattening of the cranial base and relatively thin enamel caps on the molar teeth. From measurements of the humerus head, Wolpoff (1999) estimates a body weight of 42 kg (93 pounds); if this humerus comes from a male individual, this weight estimate is very similar to that hypothesized for other Plio-Pleistocene hominids (see Table 10–3, p. 243).

Thus, current conclusions (which will be either unambiguously confirmed or falsified as the skeleton is fully cleaned and studied) interpret the Aramis remains as the earliest hominids yet known. These individuals from Aramis, although very primitive hominids, were apparently bipedal, although not necessarily in the same way that later hominids were.

Tim White and colleagues have recently argued (White et al., 1995) that the fossil hominids from Aramis are so primitive and so different from other early hominids that they should be assigned to a new genus (and, necessarily, a new species as well): *Ardipithecus ramidus*. Most especially, the thin enamel caps on the molars are in dramatic contrast to all other early hominids, who show quite thick enamel caps. These other early hominid forms (all somewhat later than *Ardipithecus*) are placed in the genus *Australopithecus*. Moreover, White and his associates have further suggested that as the earliest and most primitive hominid yet discovered, *Ardipithecus* may form the "sister-group" and thus possibly the root species for all later hominids. Another intriguing feature is that unlike the savanna habitat found at Olduvai and other East African hominid sites, the habitat at Aramis 4.4 m.y.a. was woodland. Perhaps we are seeing at Aramis the divergence of hominids very soon after they diverged from the African great apes!

Australopithecus from East Africa

Several sites in Ethiopia, Kenya, and Tanzania have yielded remains of somewhat later hominids than the *Ardipithecus* remains from Aramis. Dating from 4.2 m.y.a. to approximately 1.4 m.y.a., most of these later East African fossils are included in the genus *Australopithecus*.* Note, however, that in the later half of this time span, some other specimens are placed in the genus *Homo*.

The earliest members of *Australopithecus* found to date come from two sites near Lake Turkana in northern Kenya (Allia Bay and Kanapoi). Like Aramis, these localities have only recently been fully explored, with the majority of discoveries coming during 1994 and 1995 (Leakey et al., 1995). Not as many specimens have been found at these two sites as at Aramis (see Table 10–1), but from what has been discovered, Meave Leakey and her colleagues have detected some interesting patterns. First, as with the Aramis specimens, limb bones indicate that these individuals were bipedal. Moreover, the molar teeth have thick enamel, like other members of *Australopithecus*.

However, there are also some primitive characteristics in these still quite early hominid specimens (dated 4.2–3.9 m.y.a.). For example, Leakey and colleagues point to such primitive features as a large canine, a **sectorial** lower first premolar (Fig. 10–9), and a small opening for the ear canal. Since these particular *Australopithecus* individuals have initially been interpreted as more primitive than all the later members of the genus, Meave Leakey and associates have provisionally assigned them to a separate species (*Australopithecus anamensis*). Further study and (with some luck) additional more complete remains will help decide whether such a distinction is warranted.

Slightly later and much more complete remains of *Australopithecus* have come from the sites of Hadar (in Ethiopia) and Laetoli (in Tanzania) (see Fig. 10–6). Much of this material has been known for some time (since the mid-1970s), and the fossils have been very well studied; indeed, in certain instances, they are quite famous. For example, the Lucy skeleton was discovered at Hadar in 1974, and the Laetoli footprints were first found in 1978. Literally thousands of footprints have been found at Laetoli, representing more than 20 different kinds of animals (Pliocene elephants, horses, pigs, giraffes, antelope, hyenas, and an abundance of hares). Several hominid footprints have also been found, including a trail more than 75 feet long, made by at least two—and perhaps three—individuals (Leakey and Hay, 1979) (Fig 10–10).

Such discoveries of well-preserved hominid footprints are extremely important in furthering our understanding of human evolution. For the first time, we can make *definite* statements regarding the locomotor pattern and stature of early hominids. Initial analysis of these Pliocene footprints suggests a stature of about 4 feet 9 inches for the larger individual and 4 feet 1 inch for the smaller individual.

Studies of these impression patterns clearly show that the mode of locomotion of these hominids was bipedal (Day and Wickens, 1980). As we have discussed, the development of bipedal locomotion is the most important defining characteristic of early hominid evolution. Some researchers, however, have concluded that these early hominids were not bipedal in quite the same way that modern humans are. From detailed comparisons with modern humans, estimates of stride length, cadence, and speed of walking have been ascertained, indicating that the Laetoli

Sectorial

Adapted for cutting or shearing; among primates, refers to the compressed (side-to-side) first lower premolar, which functions as a shearing surface with the upper canine.

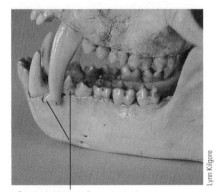

Sectorial lower first premolar

Lynn Kilgore

FIGURE 10–9

Left lateral view of the teeth of a male patas monkey. Note how the large upper canine shears against the elongated surface of the *sectorial* lower first premolar.

---

*Moreover, some paleoanthropologists place portions of the *Australopithecus* sample into another genus designated *Paranthropus* (see p. 252).

FIGURE 10–10
Hominid footprint from Laetoli, Tanzania. Note the deep impression of the heel and the large toe (arrow) in line (adducted) with the other toes.

Courtesy, Peter Jones

hominids moved in a slow-moving ("strolling") fashion with a rather short stride (Chateris et al., 1981).

Two extraordinary discoveries at Hadar are most noteworthy. First, there is the Lucy skeleton (Fig. 10–11), found by Don Johanson eroding out of a hillside. This fossil is scientifically designated as Afar Locality (AL) 288-1, but is usually just called Lucy (after the Beatles' song "Lucy in the Sky with Diamonds"). Representing almost 40 percent of a skeleton, this is one of the three most complete individuals from anywhere in the world for the entire period before about 100,000 years ago.*

The second find, a phenomenal discovery, came to light in 1975 at another Hadar locality. Don Johanson and his amazed crew found dozens of hominid bones scattered along a hillside. These bones represented at least 13 individuals, including 4 infants. Possibly members of one social unit, it has been argued that the members of this group died at about the same time, thus representing a "catastrophic" assemblage (White and Johanson, 1989). However, the precise deposition of the site has not been completely explained, so this assertion must be viewed as quite tentative. (In geological time, an "instant" could represent many decades or centuries.) Considerable cultural material has been found in the Hadar area, mostly washed into stream channels, but some stone tools have been reported in context at a site dated at 2.5 m.y.a., potentially making the findings among the oldest cultural evidence yet discovered.

Because the Laetoli area was covered periodically by ashfalls from nearby volcanic eruptions, accurate dating is possible and has provided dates of 3.7–3.5 m.y.a. Dating from the Hadar region has not proved as straightforward; however, more complete dating calibration, using a variety of techniques (see Chapter 9), has determined a range of 3.9–3.0 m.y.a. for the hominid discoveries from this area (see Table 10–1).

Australopithecus afarensis from Laetoli and Hadar

Several hundred specimens, representing a minimum of 60 individuals (and perhaps as many as 100), have been removed from Laetoli and Hadar. At present, these

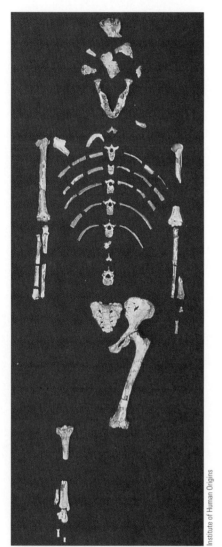

Institute of Human Origins

FIGURE 10–11
"Lucy," a partial hominid skeleton, discovered at Hadar in 1974. This individual is assigned to *Australopithecus afarensis.*

---

*The others are a specimen from Sterkfontein in South Africa (see p. 242) and a *H. erectus* skeleton from west of Lake Turkana, Kenya (see p. 274). Also note that the crushed and embedded skeleton from Aramis may be nearly as complete as Lucy.

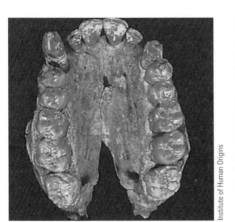

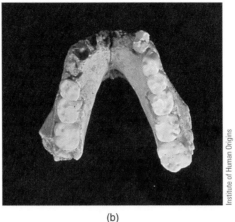

(a) (b)

FIGURE 10–12
Jaws of *Australopithecus afarensis.* (a) Maxilla, AL 200-1a, from Hadar, Ethiopia. (Note the parallel tooth rows and large canines.) (b) Mandible, LH 4, from Laetoli, Tanzania. This fossil is the type specimen for the species *Australopithecus afarensis.*

 See Virtual Lab 8, section I, for a discussion of *Australopithecus afarensis.*

materials represent the largest *well-studied* collection of early hominids known. Moreover, it has been suggested that fragmentary specimens from other locales in East Africa are remains of the same species as that found at Laetoli and Hadar. Most scholars refer to this species as *Australopithecus afarensis.*

Without question, *A. afarensis* is more primitive than any of the other **australopithecine** fossils from South or East Africa (discussed subsequently), although the recently described materials from Aramis (*Ardipithecus*) and Kanapoi and Allia Bay (*Australopithecus anamensis*) are even more primitive yet. By "primitive," we mean that *A. afarensis* is less evolved in any particular direction than are later occurring hominid species. That is, *A. afarensis* shares more primitive features with other early hominoids (such as *Dryopithecus* and *Sivapithecus*) and with living pongids than do later hominids, who display more derived characteristics.

For example, the teeth of *A. afarensis* are quite primitive. The canines are often large, pointed teeth. Moreover, the lower first premolar is semisectorial (i.e., it provides a shearing surface for the upper canine) and the tooth rows are parallel, even converging somewhat toward the back of the mouth (Fig. 10–12).

The cranial portions that are preserved, including a recently discovered specimen (shown in Fig. 10–13), also display several primitive hominoid characteristics, including a compound crest in the back as well as several primitive features of the cranial base. Cranial capacity estimates for *A. afarensis* show a mixed pattern when compared to later hominids. A provisional estimate for the one partially complete cranium—apparently a large individual—gives a figure of 500 cm³, but another, even more fragmentary cranium is apparently quite a bit smaller and has been estimated at about 375 cm³ (Holloway, 1983). Thus, for some individuals (males?), *A. afarensis* is well within the range of other australopithecine species (see Box 10–2), but others (females?) may have a significantly smaller cranial capacity. However, a detailed depiction of cranial size for *A. afarensis* is not possible at this time; this part of the skeleton is unfortunately too poorly represented. One thing is clear: *A. afarensis* had a small brain, probably averaging for the whole species not much over 420 cm³.

On the other hand, a large assortment of postcranial pieces has been found at Hadar. Initial impressions suggest that relative to lower limbs, the upper limbs are longer than in modern humans (also a primitive hominoid condition). (This statement does not mean that the arms of *A. afarensis* were longer than the legs.) In addition, the wrist, hand, and foot bones show several differences from modern humans (Susman et al., 1985). Stature can now be confidently estimated: *A. afarensis* was a short hominid. From her partial skeleton, Lucy is figured to be only 3½ to 4 feet tall. However, Lucy—as demonstrated by her pelvis—was probably a female, and at Hadar and Laetoli, there is evidence of larger individuals as well. The most economical hypothesis explaining this variation is that *A. afarensis* was quite sexually dimorphic: The larger individuals are male and the smaller ones, such as Lucy,

Australopithecine
(os-tra-loh-pith´-e-seen) The colloquial name for members of the genus *Australopithecus.* The term was first used as a subfamily designation, but it is now most commonly used informally.

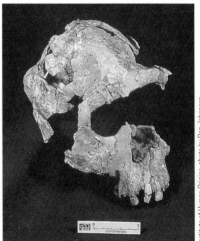

FIGURE 10–13
Australopithecus afarensis cranium discovered at Hadar in 1992. This is the most complete *A. afarensis* cranium yet found.

233

BOX 10–2   DIGGING DEEPER

Cranial Capacity

Cranial capacity, usually reported in cubic centimeters, is a measure of brain size or volume. The brain itself, of course, does not fossilize. However, the space once occupied by brain tissue (the inside of the cranial vault) does sometimes preserve, at least in those cases where fairly complete crania are recovered.

For purposes of comparison, it is easy to obtain cranial capacity estimates for contemporary species (including humans) from analyses of skeletonized specimens in museum collections. From studies of this nature, estimated cranial capacities for modern hominoids have been determined as follows (Tobias, 1971, 1983):

	Range (cm³)	Average (cm³)
Human	1150–1750*	1325
Chimpanzee	285–500	395
Gorilla	340–752	506
Orangutan	276–540	411
Bonobo	—	350

*The range of cranial capacity for modern humans is very large—in fact, even greater than that shown (which approximates cranial capacity for the *majority* of contemporary *H. sapiens*).

These data for living hominoids can then be compared with those obtained from early hominids:

	Averages(s) (cm³)
Ardipithecus	Not presently known
Australopithecus anamensis	Not presently known
Australopithecus afarensis	420
Later australopithecines	410–530
Early members of genus *Homo*	631

As the tabulations indicate, cranial capacity estimates for australopithecines fall within the range of most modern great apes, and gorillas actually average slightly more than *A. afarensis*. It must be remembered, however, that gorillas are very large animals, whereas australopithecines probably weighed on the order of 100 pounds (see Table 10–3). Since brain size is partially correlated with body size, comparing such different-sized animals cannot be justified. Compared to living chimpanzees (most of which are slightly larger than early hominids) and bonobos (which are somewhat smaller), australopithecines had *proportionately* about 10 percent bigger brains, and we would therefore say that these early hominids were more *encephalized*.

 See Virtual Lab 10, section IV, and Virtual Lab 12, section I, for a discussion of the evolution of the brain size.

are female. Estimates of male stature can be approximated from the larger footprints at Laetoli, inferring a height of about 5 feet. If we accept this interpretation, *A. afarensis* was a very sexually dimorphic form. In fact, for overall body size, this species may have been as dimorphic as *any* living primate (i.e., as much as gorillas, orangutans, or baboons).

In a majority of dental and cranial features, *A. afarensis* is clearly more primitive than later hominids. In fact, from the neck up, *A. afarensis* is so primitive that without any evidence from the limbs, one would be hard-pressed to call it a hominid at all (although the back teeth are large and heavily enameled, unlike pongids, and the position of the foramen magnum indicates an upright posture).

What, then, makes *A. afarensis* a hominid? The answer is revealed by its manner of locomotion. From the abundant limb bones recovered from Hadar and those beautiful footprints from Laetoli, we know unequivocally that *A. afarensis* walked bipedally when on the ground. Whether Lucy and her contemporaries still spent considerable time in the trees, and just how efficiently they walked, have become topics of some controversy. Most researchers, however, agree that *A. afarensis* was an efficient habitual biped while on the ground. These hominids were also clearly obligate bipeds, which would have hampered their climbing abilities but would not necessarily have precluded arboreal behavior altogether. As one physical anthropologist has surmised: "One could imagine these diminutive early hominids making maximum use of *both* terrestrial and arboreal resources in spite of their commitment to exclusive bipedalism when on the ground. The contention of a mixed arboreal and terrestrial behavioral repertoire would make adaptive sense of the Hadar australopithecine forelimb, hand, and foot morphology without contradicting the evidence of the pelvis" (Wolpoff, 1983b, p. 451).

Later East African Australopithecine Finds

An assortment of fossil hominids, including many specimens of later members of the genus *Australopithecus*, has been recovered from geological contexts with dates after 3 m.y.a. at several localities in East Africa. Up to 10 different such sites are now known (in the time range of 3–1 m.y.a.), but here we will concentrate on the three most significant ones: East Lake Turkana, West Lake Turkana (both in northern Kenya), and Olduvai Gorge (in northern Tanzania) (Table 10–2).

A significant new hominid discovery from another site in East Africa was announced in 1999 (Asfaw et al., 1999). Behane Asfaw, Tim White, and colleagues have discovered several fossils, dated to 2.5 m.y.a., of what they suggest may be yet another species of *Australopithecus*, termed *A. garhi*, *garhi* meaning "surprise" in the Afar language (Fig. 10–14). These important new finds come from the Bouri site in the Middle Awash region of Ethiopia, just south of Aramis. The hominid fossils, including an incomplete cranium and much of the limb skeleton (from another individual), are in several ways quite different from any other Plio-Pleistocene hominid. For example, the cranium combines a projecting face, fairly large front teeth, and very large back teeth. The limb proportions are also unusual, with long forelimbs (as in *A. afarensis*) but also with quite long hind limbs (as in *Homo*). Finally, the hominids at Bouri were found close to animal bones displaying clear signs of butchering (see p. 221).

Located very near the considerably older Allia Bay site on the east shore of Lake Turkana is Koobi Fora (Fig. 10–15). This latter locality, with sediments dating to

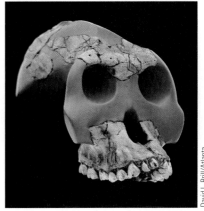

FIGURE 10–14
Reconstructed cranium of *Australopithecus garhi* from Bouri, Ethiopia; estimated date, 2.5 m.y.a.

David L. Brill/Atlanta

TABLE 10–2 Summary of Later East African Hominid Discoveries

Site Name	Location	Age (m.y.a.)	Hominids
Olduvai	N. Tanzania	1.85–1.0	48 specimens; australopithecines; early *Homo*
Turkana	N. Kenya (eastern side of Lake Turkana)	1.9–1.3	More than 150 specimens; many australopithecines; several early *Homo*
	West side of Lake Turkana	2.5–1.6	1 cranium (australopithecine); 1 nearly complete skeleton (*Homo erectus*)
Middle Awash (Bouri)	N.E. Ethiopia	2.5	5 hominids; 1 cranium; parts of limb skeleton; (*A. garhi*)
Hadar	N.E. Ethiopia	3.9–3.0	Minimum of 40 individuals (maximum of 65); early australopithecines (*A. afarensis*)
Laetoli	N. Tanzania	3.7–3.5	24 hominids; early australopithecines (*A. afarensis*)

FIGURE 10-15
Excavations in progress at Koobi Fora, in East Lake Turkana, northern Kenya.

1.8–1.3 m.y.a., has provided specimens representing at least 100 individuals, and this fine sample includes several complete crania, many jaws, and an assortment of postcranial bones. Next to Olduvai, Koobi Fora has yielded the most information concerning the behavior of early hominids. More than 20 archaeological sites have been discovered, and excavation or testing has been done at 10 localities.

Across the lake, on the west side of Lake Turkana, are other deposits that recently have yielded new and very exciting discoveries. In addition, Olduvai Gorge (discussed in detail in Chapter 9) has also yielded a considerable collection of early hominid fossils (see Table 10–2).

Australopithecines from Olduvai and Lake Turkana

Most fossil hominids from Olduvai, West Lake Turkana, and especially Koobi Fora are later in time than the *A. afarensis* remains from Laetoli and Hadar (by at least 500,000 years). It is thus not surprising that they are more derived, in some cases dramatically so. Also, these later hominids are considerably more diverse. Most researchers accept the interpretation that all the hominids from Laetoli and Hadar are members of a single taxon, *A. afarensis*. However, it is clear that the remains from the Turkana area and Olduvai collectively represent multiple taxa—two different genera and perhaps up to five or six different species. Current discussion on how best to sort this complex material is among the most vehement in paleoanthropology. Here we summarize the broad patterns of physical morphology. At the end of this chapter, we will take up the various schemes that attempt to interpret the fossil remains in a broader evolutionary context.

Following 2.5 m.y.a., later (and more derived) representatives of *Australopithecus* are found in East Africa. This is a most distinctive group that has popularly been known for some time as "robust" australopithecines. By "robust" it had generally been meant that these forms—when compared to other australopithecines—were larger in body size. However, more recent, and better controlled studies (Jungers, 1988; McHenry, 1988, 1992) have shown that all the species of *Australopithecus* overlapped considerably in body size. As you will see shortly, "robust" australopithecines have also been found in South Africa.

As a result of these new weight estimates, many researchers have either dropped the use of the term *robust* (along with its opposite, *gracile*) or presented it in quotation marks to emphasize its conditional application. We believe that the term *robust* can be used in this latter sense, as it still emphasizes important differences in the scaling of craniodental traits. In other words, even if they are not larger overall, robust forms are clearly robust in the skull and dentition.

Dating to approximately 2.5 m.y.a., the earliest representative of this robust group comes from northern Kenya on the west side of Lake Turkana. A complete cranium (WT 17000—"the black skull") was unearthed there in 1985 and has proved to be a most important discovery (Fig. 10–16). This skull, with a cranial capacity of only 410 cm^3, has the smallest definitely ascertained brain volume of any hominid yet found and has other primitive traits reminiscent of *A. afarensis*. For example, there is a compound crest in the back of the skull, the upper face projects considerably, the upper dental row converges in back, and the cranial base is extensively pneumatized—that is, it possesses air pockets (Kimbel et al., 1988).

What makes the black skull so fascinating, however, is that mixed with this array of distinctively primitive traits are a host of derived ones linking it to other members of the robust group (including a broad face, a very large palate, and a large area for the back teeth). This mosaic of features seems to place skull WT 17000 between earlier *A. afarensis* on the one hand and the later robust species on the other. Because of its unique position in hominid evolution, WT 17000 (and the population it represents) has been placed in a new species, *Australopithecus aethiopicus*.

Around 2 m.y.a., different varieties of even more derived members of the robust lineage were on the scene in East Africa. As well documented by finds at Olduvai and Koobi Fora, robust australopithecines have relatively small cranial capacities (ranging from 510 to 530 cm^3) and very large, broad faces with massive back teeth and lower jaws. The larger (probably male) individuals also show a raised ridge, called a **sagittal crest**, along the midline of the cranium. The first find of a recognized Pio-Pleistocene hominid in East Africa, in fact, was of a nearly complete robust australopithecine cranium, discovered in 1959 by Mary Leakey at Olduvai Gorge (see p. 208). As a result of Louis Leakey's original naming of the fossil (as *Zinjanthropus*), this find is still popularly referred to as "Zinj." However, it and other members of the same species in East Africa are now usually classified as *Australopithecus boisei*.

FIGURE 10–16
The "black skull," WT 17000, discovered at West Lake Turkana in 1985. This specimen is provisionally assigned to *Australopithecus aethiopicus*. It is called the "black skull" owing to the dark color from the fossilization (mineralization) process.

Sagittal crest
Raised ridge along the midline of the cranium where the temporal muscle (which closes the jaw) is attached.

Early *Homo*

In addition to the robust australopithecine remains in East Africa, there is another contemporaneous Plio-Pleistocene hominid that is quite distinctive. In fact, as best documented by fossil discoveries from Olduvai and Koobi Fora, these materials have been assigned to the genus *Homo*—and thus are different from all species assigned to *Australopithecus*.

The earliest appearance of genus *Homo* in East Africa may be as ancient as that of the robust australopithecines. (As we have discussed, the black skull from West Turkana has been dated to approximately 2.5 m.y.a.) Recent reinterpretations of a temporal fragment from the Lake Baringo region of central Kenya have suggested that early *Homo* may also be close to this same antiquity (estimated age of 2.4 m.y.a) (Hill et al., 1992). More diagnostic remains of a lower jaw of early *Homo* have also recently been reported from Hadar, in Ethiopia, and are dated to 2.3 m.y.a. (Kimbel et al., 1996). Given that the robust australopithecine lineage was probably diverging at this time, it is not surprising to find the earliest representatives of the genus *Homo* also beginning to diversify.

The presence of a Plio-Pleistocene hominid with a significantly larger brain than seen in *Australopithecus* was first suggested by Louis Leakey in the early 1960s on the basis of fragmentary remains found at Olduvai Gorge. Leakey and his colleagues gave a new species designation to these fossil remains, naming them **Homo habilis**.

The *Homo habilis* material at Olduvai ranges in time from 1.85 m.y.a. for the earliest to about 1.6 m.y.a. for the latest. Due to the fragmentary nature of the fossil remains, interpretations have been difficult and much disputed. The most immediately obvious feature distinguishing the *H. habilis* material from the

See Virtual Lab 10 for a detailed discussion of the evolution of *Homo*.

Homo habilis
(hab´-ih-liss) A species of early *Homo*, well known from East Africa, but perhaps also found in other regions.

australopithecines is cranial size. For all the measurable *H. habilis* skulls, the estimated average cranial capacity is 631 cm³ compared to 520 cm³ for all measurable robust australopithecines and 442 cm³ for the less robust species (McHenry, 1988) (see Box 10–2). *Homo habilis*, therefore, shows an increase in cranial size of about 20 percent over the larger of the australopithecines and an even greater increase over some of the smaller-brained forms (from South Africa, discussed shortly). In their initial description of *H. habilis*, Leakey and his associates also pointed to differences from australopithecines in cranial shape and in tooth proportions (larger front teeth relative to back teeth and narrower premolars).

The naming of this fossil material as *Homo habilis* ("handy man") was meaningful from two perspectives. First of all, Leakey inferred that members of this group were the early Olduvai toolmakers. If true, how do we account for a robust australopithecine like "Zinj" lying in the middle of the largest excavated area known at Olduvai? What was he doing there? Leakey suggested that he was the remains of a *habilis* meal! Excepting those instances where cut marks are left behind (see pp. 220–221), we must point out again that there is no clear way archaeologically to establish the validity of such a claim. However, the debate over this assertion serves to demonstrate that cultural factors as well as physical morphology must be considered in the interpretation of hominids as biocultural organisms. Secondly, and most significantly, by calling this group *Homo*, Leakey was arguing for at least *two separate branches* of hominid evolution in the Plio-Pleistocene. Clearly, only one could be on the main branch eventually leading to *Homo sapiens*. By labeling this new group *Homo* rather than *Australopithecus*, Leakey was guessing that he had found our ancestors.

Because the initial evidence was so fragmentary, most paleoanthropologists were reluctant to accept *H. habilis* as a valid taxon distinct from *all* australopithecines. Later discoveries, especially from Lake Turkana, of better-preserved fossil material have shed further light on early *Homo* in the Plio-Pleistocene. The most important of this additional material is a nearly complete cranium (ER 1470) discovered at Koobi Fora (Fig. 10–17). With a cranial capacity of 775 cm³, this individual is well outside the known range for australopithecines and actually overlaps the lower boundary for *Homo erectus*. In addition, the shape of the skull vault is in many respects unlike that of australopithecines. However, the face is still quite robust (Walker, 1976), and the fragments of tooth crowns that are preserved indicate that the back teeth in this individual were quite large. Dating of the Koobi Fora early *Homo* material places it contemporaneous with the Olduvai remains, that is, about 1.8–1.6 m.y.a.

On the basis of evidence from Olduvai and particularly from Koobi Fora, we can reasonably postulate that one or more species of early *Homo* were present in East Africa probably by 2.4 m.y.a., developing in parallel with at least one line of australopithecines (Fig. 10–18). These two hominid lines lived contemporaneously for a minimum of 1 million years, after which the australopithecine lineage apparently disappeared forever. At the same time, probably the early *Homo* line was evolving into a later form, *Homo erectus*, which in turn developed into *H. sapiens*.

Central Africa

In 1995, another new early hominid discovery was announced from a rather surprising location—Chad, in central Africa (Brunet et al., 1995) (see Fig. 10–6). From an area called the Bahr el Ghazal (Arabic for "River of the Gazelles"), a partial hominid mandible was discovered in association with faunal remains tentatively dated to 3.5–3.0 m.y.a. (Further confirmation will have to await chronometric dating, assuming that appropriate materials become available.) The preliminary analysis suggests that this fossil is an australopithecine with closest affinities to *A. afarensis*. What makes this find remarkable is its geographical location, more than 1,500 miles west of the previously established range of early hominids!

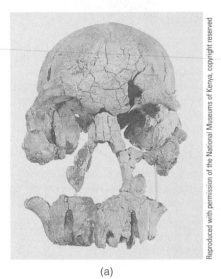

(a)

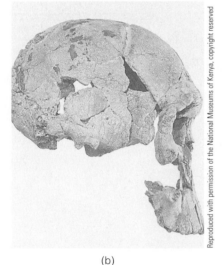

(b)

FIGURE 10–17
A nearly complete early *Homo* cranium from East Lake Turkana (ER 1470), one of the most important single fossil hominid discoveries from East Africa.

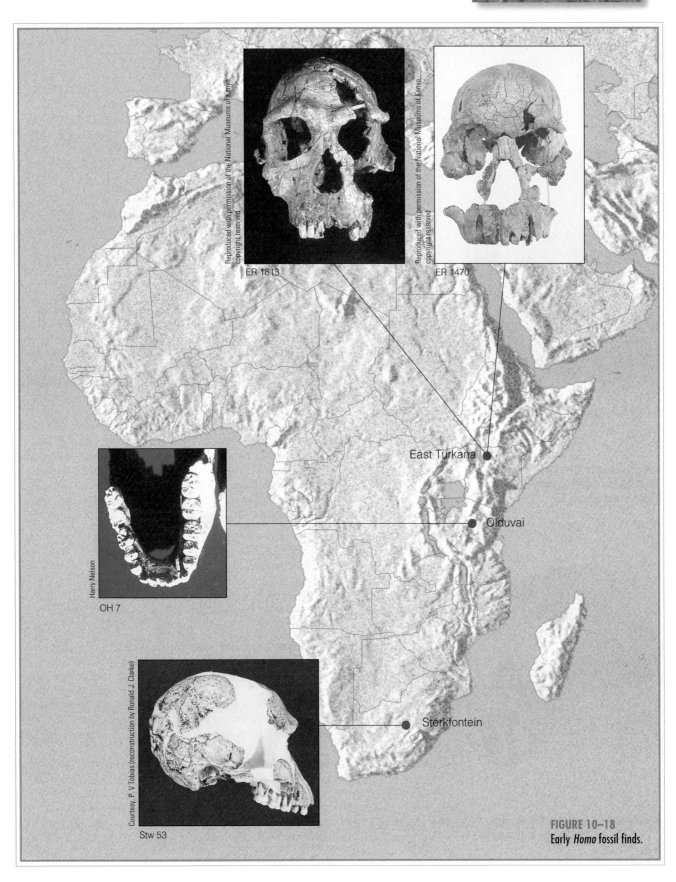

ER 1813

ER 1470

East Turkana

Olduvai

OH 7

Sterkfontein

Stw 53

FIGURE 10–18
Early *Homo* fossil finds.

South African Sites

Earliest Discoveries

The first quarter of the twentieth century saw the discipline of paleoanthropology in its scientific infancy. Informed opinions considered the likely origins of the human family to be in Asia, where fossil forms of a primitive kind of *Homo* had been found in Indonesia in the 1890s. Europe was also considered a center of hominid evolution, for spectacular discoveries there of archaic *Homo sapiens* (including the famous Neandertals) and millions of stone tools had come to light, particularly in the early 1900s.

Few scholars would have given much credence to Darwin's prediction:

> In each region of the world the living mammals are closely related to the extinct species of the same region. It is, therefore, probable that Africa was formally inhabited by extinct apes closely allied to the gorilla and chimpanzee, and as these two species are now man's nearest allies, it is somewhat more probable that our early progenitors lived on the African continent than elsewhere. (Darwin, *The Descent of Man*, 1871)

Moreover, it would be many more decades before the East African discoveries would come to light. It was in such an atmosphere of preconceived biases that the discoveries of a young Australian-born anatomist were to jolt the foundations of the scientific community in the 1920s. Raymond Dart (Fig. 10–19) arrived in South Africa in 1923 at the age of 30 to take up a teaching position in Johannesburg. Fresh from his evolution-oriented training in England, Dart had developed a keen interest in human evolution. Consequently, he was well prepared when startling new evidence began to appear at his very doorstep.

The first clue came in 1924, when Dart received a shipment of fossils from the commercial limeworks quarry at Taung (200 miles southwest of Johannesburg). He immediately recognized something that was quite unusual, a natural **endocast** of a higher primate. The endocast fit into another limestone block containing the fossilized front portion of the skull, face, and lower jaw (Fig. 10–20). However, these were difficult to see clearly, for the bone was hardened into a cemented limestone matrix. Dart patiently chiseled away for weeks, later describing the task:

> No diamond cutter ever worked more lovingly or with such care on a precious jewel—nor, I am sure, with such inadequate tools. But on the seventy-third day, December 23, the rock parted. I could view the face from the front, although the right side was still imbedded. . . . What emerged was a baby's face, an infant with a full set of milk teeth and its permanent molars just in the process of erupting. I doubt if there was any parent prouder of his offspring than I was of my Taung baby on that Christmas. (Dart, 1959, p. 10)

As indicated by the formation and eruption of the teeth, the Taung child was probably about three to four years old. Interestingly, the rate of development of this and many other Plio-Pleistocene hominids was more like that of apes than of modern *Homo* (Bromage and Dean, 1985). Dart's initial impression that this form was a hominoid was confirmed when he could observe the face and teeth more clearly. However, as it turned out, it took considerably more effort before the teeth could be seen completely, since Dart worked for four years to separate the upper and lower jaws.

But Dart was convinced long before he had an unimpeded view of the dentition that this discovery was a remarkable one, an early hominoid from South Africa. The question was, What kind of hominoid? Dart realized that it was extremely improbable that this specimen could have been a forest ape, for South Africa has had a relatively dry climate for millions of years. Even though the climate at Taung may not have been as dry as Dart initially speculated (Butzer, 1974), it was still a very unlikely spot to find an ape!

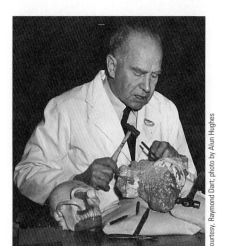

FIGURE 10-19
Raymond Dart, shown working in his laboratory.

Courtesy, Raymond Dart; photo by Alun Hughes

Endocast
A solid impression of the inside of the skull, often preserving details relating to the size and surface features of the brain.

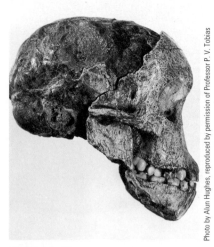

FIGURE 10–20
The Taung child discovered in 1924. The endocast is in back, with the fossilized bone mandible and face in front.

Photo by Alun Hughes, reproduced by permission of Professor P. V. Tobias

If not an ape, then what was it? Features of the skull and teeth of this small child held clues that Dart seized on almost immediately. The entrance of the spinal cord into the brain (the *foramen magnum* at the base of the skull; see Fig. 10–8) was farther forward in the Taung skull than in modern great apes, though not as much as in modern humans. From this fact Dart concluded that the head was balanced *above* the spine, indicating erect posture. In addition, the slant of the forehead was not as receding as in apes, the milk canines were exceedingly small, and the newly erupted permanent molars were very large, broad teeth. In all these respects, the Taung fossil was more akin to hominids than to apes. There was, however, a disturbing feature that was to confuse many scientists for several years: The brain was quite small. More recent studies have estimated the Taung child's brain size at approximately 405 cm^3 (which translates to a full adult estimate of 440 cm^3), not very large (for a hominid) when compared to modern great apes (see Box 10–2).

The estimated cranial capacity of the Taung fossil falls within the range of modern great apes, and gorillas actually average about 10 percent greater. It must, however, be remembered that gorillas are very large animals, whereas the Taung specimen derives from a population where adults may have averaged less than 80 pounds. Since brain size is partially correlated with body size, comparing such differently sized animals is unjustified. A more meaningful comparison would be with the bonobo (*Pan paniscus*), whose body weight is comparable. Bonobos have adult cranial capacities averaging 356 cm^3 for males and 329 cm^3 for females, and thus the Taung child, versus a *comparably sized* ape, displays a 25 percent increase in cranial capacity.

Despite the relatively small size of the brain, Dart saw that it was no ape. Realizing the immense importance of his findings, Dart promptly reported them in the British scientific weekly *Nature* on February 7, 1925—a bold venture, since Dart, only 32, was presumptuously proposing a whole new view of human evolution. The small-brained Taung child was christened by Dart ***Australopithecus africanus*** (southern ape of Africa), which he saw as a kind of halfway "missing link" between modern apes and humans. This concept of a single "missing link" was a fallacious one, but Dart correctly emphasized the hominid-like features of the fossil.

Not all scientists were ready for such a theory from such an "unlikely" place. Hence, Dart's report was received with indifference, disbelief, and even caustic scorn. Dart realized that more complete remains were needed. The skeptical world would not accept the evidence of one partial immature individual, no matter how suggestive the clues. Most scientists in the 1920s regarded this little Taung child as an interesting aberrant form of ape. Clearly, more fossil evidence was needed, particularly adult crania (since these would show more diagnostic features). Not an experienced fossil hunter himself, Dart sought further assistance in the search for more australopithecines.

Further Discoveries of South African Hominids

Soon after publication of his controversial theories, Dart found a strong ally in Robert Broom (Fig. 10–21). A Scottish physician and part-time paleontologist, Broom's credentials as a fossil hunter had been established earlier with his highly successful paleontological work on early mammal-like reptiles in South Africa.

Although interested, Broom was unable to participate actively in the search for additional australopithecines until 1936. From two of Dart's students, Broom learned of another commercial limeworks site, called **Sterkfontein**, not far from Johannesburg. Here, as at Taung, the quarrying involved blasting out large sections with dynamite, leaving piles of debris that often contained fossilized remains. Accordingly, Broom asked the quarry manager to keep his eyes open for fossils, and when Broom returned to the site in August 1936, the manager asked, "Is this what you are looking for?" Indeed it was, for Broom held in his hand the endocast of an adult australopithecine—exactly what he had set out to find! Looking further over the scattered debris, Broom was able to find most of the rest of the skull of the same individual.

Australopithecus africanus
(os-tral-oh-pith´-e-kus af-ri-kan´-us)

FIGURE 10–21
Robert Broom.

Sterkfontein
(sterk´-fon-tane)

Swartkrans
(swart´-kranz)

 See Virtual Lab 8, section I, for a discussion of South African hominids.

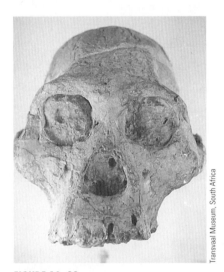

FIGURE 10–22
A gracile australopithecine cranium from Sterkfontein (Sts 5). Discovered in 1947, this specimen is the best-preserved gracile skull yet found in South Africa.

Such remarkable success, just a few months after beginning his search, was not the end of Broom's luck, for his magical touch was to continue unabated for several more years. In the 1930s and 1940s, Broom discovered two further hominid sites, including **Swartkrans**, the most prolific of all South African Plio-Pleistocene locales (and it has since yielded hundreds of fossils). In the 1940s, Raymond Dart discovered another hominid site, bringing the total to five.

Numerous extremely important discoveries came from these additional sites, discoveries that would eventually swing the tide of intellectual thought to the views that Dart expressed back in 1925. Particularly important was a nearly complete cranium and pelvis, both found at Sterkfontein in 1947. As the number of discoveries accumulated, it became increasingly difficult to simply write the australopithecines off as aberrant apes.

By 1949, at least 30 hominid individuals were represented from five South African sites, and leading scientists were coming to accept the australopithecines as hominids. With this acceptance also came the necessary recognition that hominid brains had their greatest expansion *after* earlier changes in teeth and locomotor systems. In other words, once again we see that the rate of evolution in one functional system of the body varies from that of other systems, thus displaying the *mosaic* nature of human evolution.

Since the 1950s, exploration of the South African hominid sites has continued, and numerous important discoveries were made in the 1970s and 1980s. The most spectacular new find was made in 1998 at Sterkfontein, where the remains of a virtually complete australopithecine skeleton were found by Ron Clarke and his associates from the University of Witwatersrand. Most of the remains are still embedded in the surrounding limestone matrix and may require years for removal, cleaning, and reconstruction.

As we will discuss in more detail shortly, dating of all the South African Plio-Pleistocene sites has proved most difficult; estimates for the Sterkfontein australopithecine skeleton are between 3.6 and 2.5 m.y.a. Even before the remains have been fully excavated, this is still recognized as an unusual and highly significant find. Because such complete individuals are so rare in the hominid fossil record, this discovery has tremendous potential to shed more light on the precise nature of early hominid locomotion. For example, will the rest of the skeleton confirm what foot bones of the same individual have implied regarding arboreal climbing in this bipedal hominid (see p. 226)? Moreover, relative proportions of brain size compared to body size, better estimates of overall body size, relative proportions of the limbs, and much more can be more accurately assessed from such a completely preserved skeleton.

Review of Hominids from South Africa

The Plio-Pleistocene hominid discoveries from South Africa are most significant. First, they were the initial hominid discoveries in Africa and helped point the way to later finds in East Africa. Second, morphology of the South African hominids shows broad similarities to the forms in East Africa, but with several distinctive features, which argues for separation at least at the species level. Finally, there is a large assemblage of hominid fossils from South Africa, and exciting discoveries are still being made (Fig. 10–22).

Further discoveries are also coming from entirely new sites. In the 1990s, the site known as Drimolen was found in South Africa, very near to Sterkfontein and Swartkrans (Keyser, 2000). While only provisionally published thus far, we do know that up to 80 specimens have been recovered—including the most complete *Australopithecus* cranium found anywhere in Africa.

A truly remarkable collection of early hominids, the remains from South Africa exceed 1,500 (counting all teeth as separate items), and the number of individuals is now more than 200. From an evolutionary point of view, the most meaningful remains are those of the pelvis, which now include portions of nine ossa coxae (see

p. 223). Remains of the pelvis are so important because, better than any other area of the body, this structure displays the unique requirements of a bipedal animal (as in modern humans *and* in our hominid forebears).

"Robust" Australopithecines   In addition to the discoveries of *A. aethiopicus* and *A. boisei* in East Africa, there are also numerous finds of robust australopithecines in South Africa. Like their East African cousins, the South African robust forms also have small cranial capacities. (The only measurable specimen equals 530 cm^3; the Drimolen cranium is smaller and might come from a female, but no cranial measurements have as yet been published.) They also possess large broad faces and very large premolars and molars (although not as massive as in East Africa). Owing to the differences in dental proportions, as well as important differences in facial architecture (Rak, 1983), most researchers now agree that there is a species-level difference between the later East African robust variety (*A. boisei*) and the South African group (*A. robustus*).

Despite these differences, all members of the robust lineage appear to be specialized for a diet made up of hard food items, such as seeds and nuts. For many years, paleoanthropologists (e.g., Robinson, 1972) had speculated that robust australopithecines concentrated their diet on heavier vegetable foods than those seen in the diet of other early hominids. More recent research that included examining microscopic polishes and scratches on the teeth (Kay and Grine, 1988) has confirmed this view.

"Gracile" Australopithecines   Another variety of australopithecine (also small-brained, but not as large-toothed as the robust varieties) is known from Africa. However, while the robust lineage is represented in both East and South Africa, this other (gracile) australopithecine form is known only from the southern part of the continent. First named *A. africanus* by Dart for the single individual at Taung, this australopithecine is also found at other sites, especially Sterkfontein (Fig. 10–23).

Traditionally, it had been thought that there was a significant variation in body size between the gracile and robust forms. But as mentioned earlier and shown in Table 10–3, there is not much difference in body size among the australopithecines. In fact, most of the differences between the robust and gracile forms are found in the face and dentition.

The facial structure of the gracile australopithecines is more lightly built and somewhat dish-shaped compared to the more vertical configuration seen in robust specimens. As we noted earlier, in robust individuals, a raised ridge along the midline of the skull is occasionally observed. Indeed, at Sterkfontein, among the larger individuals (males?), a hint of such a sagittal crest is also seen. This structure provides additional attachment area for the large temporal muscle, which is the primary muscle operating the massive jaw below. Such a structure is also seen in some

TABLE 10–3   Estimated Body Weights and Stature in Plio-Pleistocene Hominids

	Body Weight		Stature	
	Male	**Female**	**Male**	**Female**
A. afarensis	45 kg (99 lb)	29 kg (64 lb)	151 cm (59 in.)	105 cm (41 in.)
A. africanus	41 kg (90 lb)	30 kg (65 lb)	138 cm (54 in.)	115 cm (45 in.)
A. robustus	40 kg (88 lb)	32 kg (70 lb)	132 cm (52 in.)	110 cm (43 in.)
A. boisei	49 kg (108 lb)	34 kg (75 lb)	137 cm (54 in.)	124 cm (49 in.)
H. habilis	52 kg (114 lb)	32 kg (70 lb)	157 cm (62 in.)	125 cm (49 in.)

Source: After McHenry, 1992.

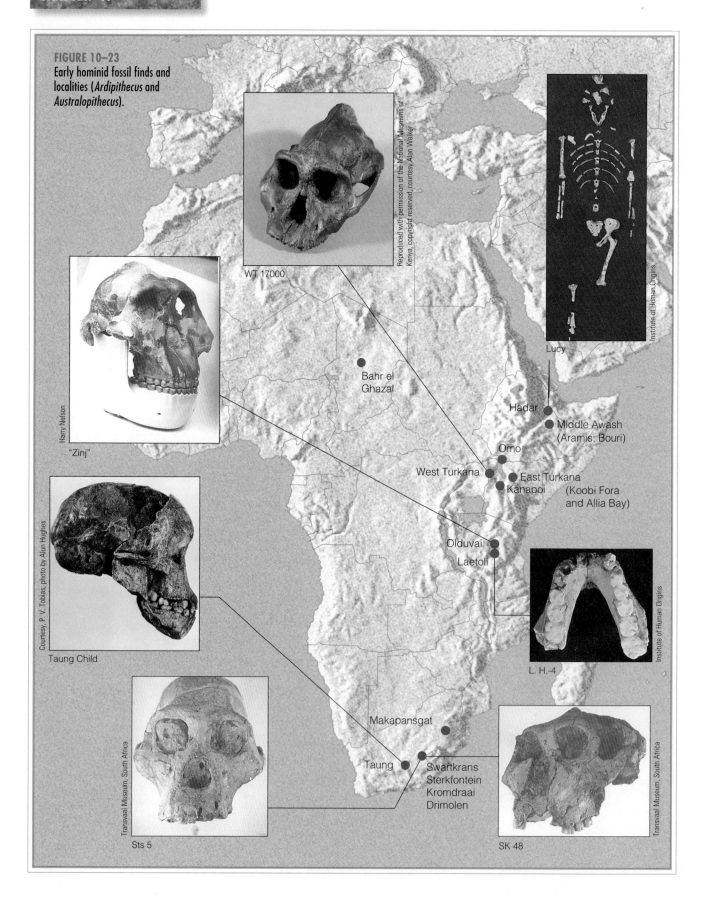

FIGURE 10–23
Early hominid fossil finds and localities (*Ardipithecus* and *Australopithecus*).

WT 17000

Reproduced with permission of the National Museums of Kenya, copyright reserved, courtesy Alan Walker

Lucy

Institute of Human Origins

Harry Nelson

"Zinj"

Courtesy, P. V. Tobias; photo by Alun Hughes

Taung Child

Transvaal Museum, South Africa

Sts 5

Bahr el Ghazal

Hadar

Middle Awash (Aramis; Bouri)

Omo

West Turkana

East Turkana

Kanapoi

(Koobi Fora and Allia Bay)

Olduvai

Laetoli

L. H.-4

Institute of Human Origins

Makapansgat

Taung

Swartkrans
Sterkfontein
Kromdraai
Drimolen

SK 48

Transvaal Museum, South Africa

modern apes, especially male gorillas and orangutans; however, in most australopithecines, the temporal muscle acts most efficiently on the back of the mouth and is therefore not functionally equivalent to the pattern seen in great apes, where the emphasis is more on the front teeth (Fig 10–24).

The most distinctive difference observed between gracile and robust australopithecines is in the dentition. Compared to modern humans, they both have relatively large teeth, which are, however, definitely hominid in pattern. In fact, more emphasis is on the typical back-tooth grinding complex among these early forms than is seen in modern humans; therefore, if anything, australopithecines are "hyperhominid" in their dentition. (In other words, they are dentally more *derived* than are modern humans.) Robust forms emphasize this trend to an extreme degree, showing deep jaws and much-enlarged back teeth, particularly the molars, leaving little room in the front of the mouth for the anterior teeth (incisors and canines). Conversely, the gracile australopithecines have proportionately larger front teeth compared to the size of their back teeth. The contrast is seen most clearly in the relative size of the canine compared to the first premolar: In robust individuals, the first premolar is clearly a much larger tooth than the small canine (about twice as large), whereas in gracile specimens, it only averages about 20 percent larger than the fairly good-sized canine (Howells, 1973).

These differences in the relative proportions of the teeth and jaws best define a gracile, as compared to a robust, australopithecine. In fact, most of the differences in skull shape we have discussed can be directly attributed to contrasting jaw function in the two forms. Both the sagittal crest and broad vertical face of the robust form are related to the muscles and biomechanical requirements of the heavy back-tooth chewing adaptation seen in this animal.

Early *Homo* in South Africa   As in East Africa, early members of the genus *Homo* have also been found in South Africa, apparently living contemporaneously with australopithecines. At both Sterkfontein and Swartkrans, and perhaps Drimolen as well, fragmentary remains have been recognized as most likely belonging to *Homo*. In fact, Ron Clarke (1985) has shown that the key fossil of early *Homo* from Sterkfontein (Stw 53) is nearly identical to the OH 24 *Homo habilis* cranium from Olduvai.

However, a problem with both OH 24 and Stw 53 is that while most experts agree that they belong to the genus *Homo*, there is considerable disagreement as to whether they should be included in the species *habilis*. The relationships of the Plio-Pleistocene fossil hominids to one another and the difficulties of such genus and species interpretation will be discussed in the following sections. A time line for all the Plio-Pleistocene sites discussed in the text is shown in Figure 10–25.

Geology and Dating Problems in South Africa

While the geological and archaeological context in East Africa is often straightforward, the six South African early hominid sites are much more complex geologically. All were discovered by commercial quarrying activity, which greatly disrupted the geological picture and, in the case of Taung, completely destroyed the site.

The hominid remains are found with thousands of other fossilized bones embedded in limestone cliffs, caves, fissures, and sinkholes. The limestone was formed by millions of generations of shells of marine organisms during the Precambrian—more than 2 billion years ago—when South Africa was submerged under a shallow sea. Once deposited, the limestones were cut through by percolating groundwater from below and rainwater from above, forming a maze of caves and fissures often connected to the surface by narrow shafts. Through these vertical shafts and horizontal cave openings, bones either fell or were carried in, where they conglomerated with sand, pebbles, and soil into a cementlike matrix called *breccia*.

As the cave fissures filled in, they were constantly subjected to further erosion forces from above and below, so that caves would be partially filled, then closed to

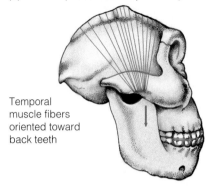

(a) Hominid (robust australopithecine)

Temporal muscle fibers oriented toward back teeth

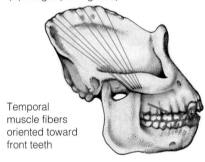

(b) Pongid (male gorilla)

Temporal muscle fibers oriented toward front teeth

FIGURE 10–24
Sagittal crests and temporal muscle orientations. Hominid compared to pongid. (Line of greatest muscle force is shown in red.)

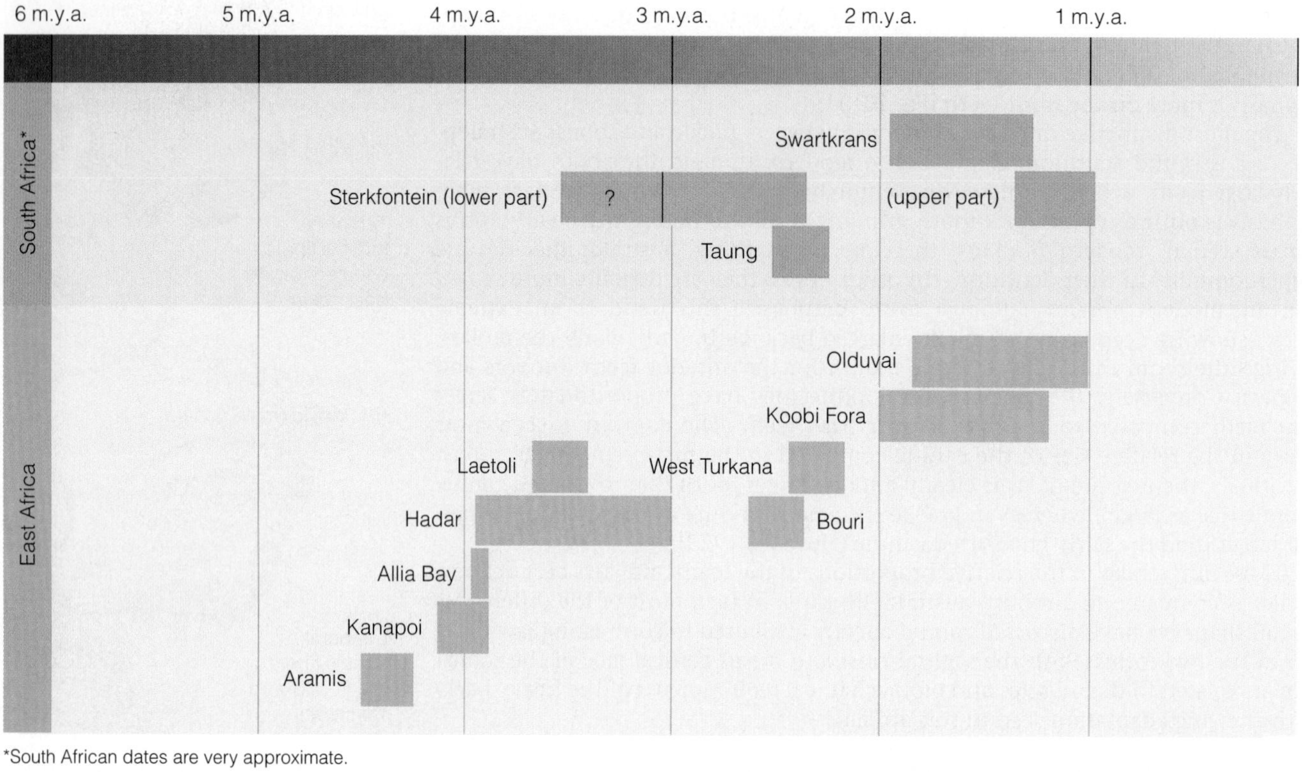

*South African dates are very approximate.

FIGURE 10–25

Time line of major Plio-Pleistocene hominid sites. Note that many dates are approximations. Question marks indicate those estimates that are most tentative.

the surface for a considerable time, then reopened again to commence accumulation thousands of years later. All this activity yields an incredibly complex geological situation that can be worked out only after the most detailed kind of paleoecological analysis.

Since bones accumulated in these caves and fissures largely by accidental processes, it seems likely that none of the South African australopithecine sites are *primary* hominid localities. In other words, unlike the East African sites, these are not areas where hominids organized activities, scavenged food, and so on.

Just how did all the fossilized bone accumulate, and, most particularly, what were the ancient hominids doing there? In the case of Swartkrans and Sterkfontein, the bones probably accumulated through the combined activities of carnivorous leopards, saber-toothed cats, and hyenas (Fig. 10–26). Moreover, the unexpectedly high proportion of primate (baboon and hominid) remains suggests that these localities were the location (or very near the location) of primate sleeping sites, thus providing ready primate prey for various predators (Brain, 1981).

Raymond Dart argued enthusiastically for an alternative explanation, suggesting that the hominids regularly used bone, tooth, and horn remains as tools, which he called the **osteodontokeratic** culture complex. Analogies with the food habits of modern African foragers indicate that the bone accumulation may be accounted for simply by hominid and carnivore eating practices.

Owing to the complex geological picture, as well as lack of appropriate material such as volcanic deposits for chronometric techniques, dating the South African early hominid sites has posed tremendous problems. Without chronometric dating, the best that can be done is to correlate the faunal sequences in South Africa with areas in East Africa where dates are better known (this approach is called biostratigraphy; see p. 211). Faunal sequencing of this sort on pigs, bovids such as antelope, and Old World monkeys has provided the following tenuous chronology:

Osteodontokeratic
(*osteo*, meaning "bone," *donto*, meaning "tooth," and *keratic*, meaning "horn")

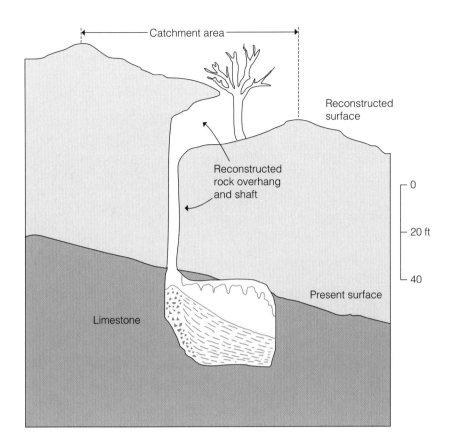

FIGURE 10–26
Swartkrans, geological section. The upper (reconstructed) part has been removed by erosion since the accumulation of the fossil-bearing deposit. (After Brain, 1970.)

Location	Age
Swartkrans	1 m.y.
Taung	2 m.y.
Sterkfontein	3 m.y.

Attempts at paleomagnetic dating (see p. 211) suggest an age of 3.3–2.8 m.y.a. for the oldest South African hominid (Brock et al., 1977), thus pushing the estimates to the extreme limits of those provided by biostratigraphy. In fact, some researchers believe that the paleomagnetic results are ambiguous and continue to "put their money" on the biostratigraphic data, especially those dates determined by analysis of pig and monkey fossils. From such consideration, they place the oldest South African early hominid sites at perhaps as much as half a million years later (i.e., around 2.5 m.y.a.) (White et al., 1981). This is crucial, since it places *all* the South African hominids after *Australopithecus afarensis* in East Africa (Fig. 10–27). Recent excavations at Sterkfontein have suggested that the earliest hominids *may* come from levels as early as 3.5 m.y.a. (Clarke and Tobias, 1995). However, this date, which would be as early as *A. afarensis* in East Africa, has not yet been corroborated.

Interpretations: What Does It All Mean?

By this time, it may seem that anthropologists have an almost perverse fascination in finding small scraps buried in the ground and then assigning them confusing numbers and taxonomic labels impossible to remember. We must realize that the collection of all the basic fossil data is the foundation of human evolutionary research. Without fossils, our speculations would be completely hollow. Several

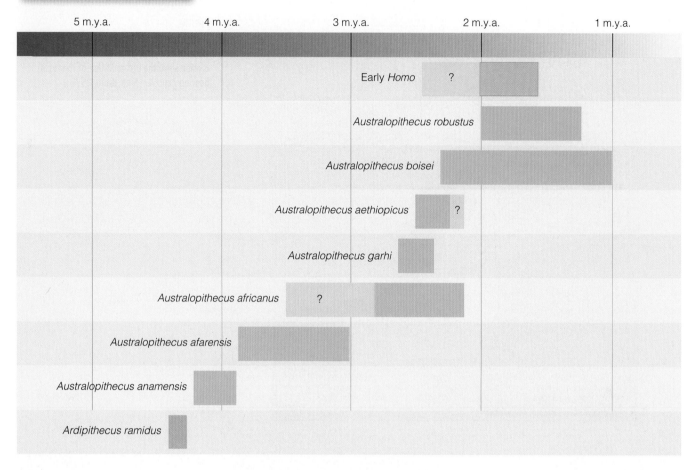

Early *Homo* ?

Australopithecus robustus

Australopithecus boisei

Australopithecus aethiopicus ?

Australopithecus garhi

Australopithecus africanus ?

Australopithecus afarensis

Australopithecus anamensis

Ardipithecus ramidus

FIGURE 10–27
Time line of Plio-Pleistocene hominids. Note that most dates are approximations. Question marks indicate those estimates that are most tentative.

A. africanus   *A. boisei*

Early *Homo*

FIGURE 10–29
Phylogenetic interpretation. Early *Homo* is generically distinct from australopithecines.

large, ongoing paleoanthropological projects discussed in Chapter 9 are now collecting additional data in an attempt to answer some of the more perplexing questions about our evolutionary history.

The numbering of specimens, which may at times seem somewhat confusing, is an attempt to keep the designations neutral and to make reference to each individual fossil as clear as possible. The formal naming of finds as *Australopithecus*, *Homo habilis*, or *Homo erectus* should come much later, since it involves a lengthy series of complex interpretations. Assigning generic and specific names to fossil finds is more than just a convenience; when we attach a particular label, such as *A. boisei*, to a particular fossil, we should be fully aware of the biological implications of such an interpretation.

Even more basic to our understanding of human evolution, the use of taxonomic nomenclature involves interpretations of fossil relationships. For example, the two fossils "Zinj" and ER 406 (Fig. 10–28) are both usually called *A. boisei*. What we are saying here is that they are both members of one interbreeding species. These two fossils can now be compared with others, like Sts 5 from Sterkfontein (see Fig. 10–22), which is usually called *A. africanus*. What we are implying now is that "Zinj" and ER 406 are more closely related to each other than *either* is to Sts 5. Furthermore, that Sts 5 (*A. africanus*) populations were incapable of successfully interbreeding with *A. boisei* populations is a direct biological inference of this nomenclature.

We can carry the level of interpretation even further. For example, fossils such as ER 1470 (see Fig. 10–17) are called early *Homo* (*Homo habilis*). We are now making a genus-level distinction, and two basic biological implications are involved:

1. *A. africanus* (Sts 5) and *A. boisei* ("Zinj" and ER 406) are more closely related to each other than either is to ER 1470 (Fig. 10–29).

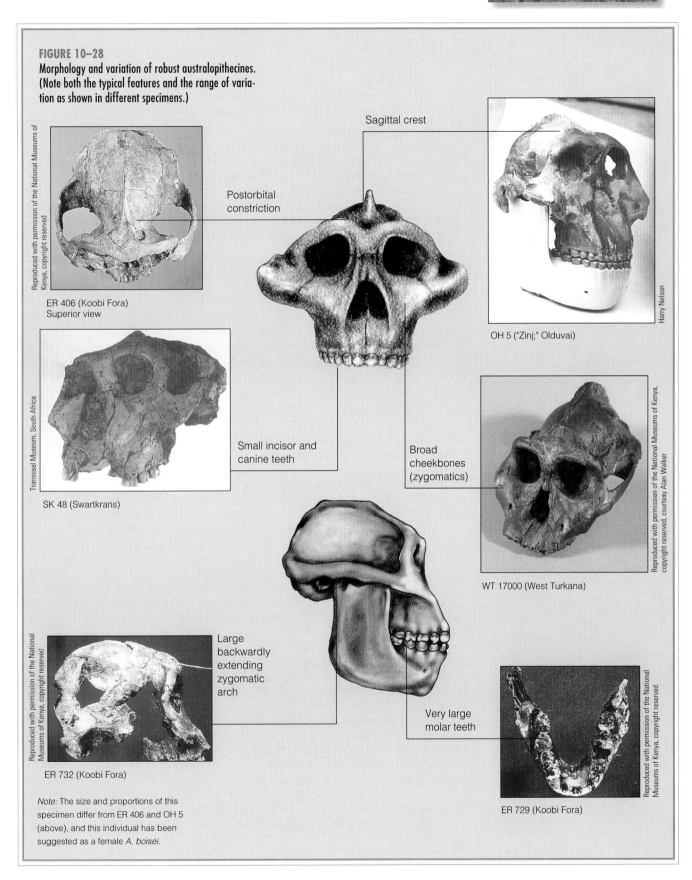

FIGURE 10–28

Morphology and variation of robust australopithecines. (Note both the typical features and the range of variation as shown in different specimens.)

Sagittal crest

Postorbital constriction

ER 406 (Koobi Fora)
Superior view

OH 5 ("Zinj;" Olduvai)

SK 48 (Swartkrans)

Small incisor and canine teeth

Broad cheekbones (zygomatics)

WT 17000 (West Turkana)

Large backwardly extending zygomatic arch

Very large molar teeth

ER 732 (Koobi Fora)

ER 729 (Koobi Fora)

Note: The size and proportions of this specimen differ from ER 406 and OH 5 (above), and this individual has been suggested as a female *A. boisei.*

2. The distinction between the groups reflects a basic difference in adaptive level (see Chapter 8).

From the time that fossil sites are first located to the eventual interpretation of hominid evolutionary events, several steps are necessary. Ideally, they should follow a logical order, for if interpretations are made too hastily, they confuse important issues for many years. Here is a reasonable sequence:

1. Selecting and surveying sites
2. Excavating sites and recovering fossil hominids
3. Designating individual finds with specimen numbers for clear reference
4. Cleaning, preparing, studying, and describing fossils
5. Comparing with other fossil material—in chronological framework if possible
6. Comparing fossil variation with known ranges of variation in closely related groups of living primates and analyzing ancestral and derived characteristics
7. Assigning taxonomic names to fossil material

The task of interpretation is still not complete, for what we really want to know in the long run is what happened to the populations represented by the fossil remains. Indeed, in looking at the fossil hominid record, we are looking for our ancestors. In the process of eventually determining those populations that are our most likely antecedents, we may conclude that some hominids are on evolutionary side branches. If this conclusion is accurate, those hominids necessarily must have become extinct. It is both interesting and relevant to us as hominids to try to find out what influenced some earlier members of our family to continue evolving while others died out.

Continuing Uncertainties—Taxonomic Issues

As previously discussed, paleoanthropologists are crucially concerned with making biological interpretations of variation found in the hominid fossil record. Most especially, researchers endeavor to assign extinct forms to particular genera and species. We saw that for the diverse array of Miocene hominoids, the evolutionary picture is exceptionally complex. As new finds accumulate, there is continued uncertainty even as to family assignment, to say nothing of genus and species!

For the Plio-Pleistocene, the situation is considerably clearer. First, there is a larger fossil sample from a more restricted geographical area (South and East Africa) and from a more concentrated time period (spanning 3.4 million years, from 4.4 to 1 m.y.a.). Second, more complete specimens exist (e.g., Lucy), and we thus have good evidence for most parts of the body. Accordingly, there is considerable consensus on several basic aspects of evolutionary development during the Plio-Pleistocene. Researchers agree unanimously that these forms are hominids (members of the family Hominidae). And as support for this point, all these forms are seen as habitual, well-adapted bipeds, committed at least in part to a terrestrial niche. Moreover, researchers generally agree as to genus-level assignments for most of the forms (although *Ardipithecus* has been so recently named as to not yet be fully evaluated and accepted, and there is also some disagreement regarding how to group the robust australopithecines).

As for species-level designations, little consensus can be found. Indeed, as new fossils have been discovered (e.g., the "black skull"), the picture seems to muddy further. Once again, we are faced with a complex evolutionary process. In attempts to deal with it, we impose varying degrees of simplicity. In so doing, we hope that the evolutionary processes will become clearer—not just for introductory students, but for professional paleoanthropologists and textbook authors as well! Nevertheless, evolution is not a simple process, and disputes and disagreements are bound to arise, especially in making such fine-tuned interpretations as species-level designations.

Consider the following ongoing topics of interest and occasional disagreement among paleoanthropologists dealing with Plio-Pleistocene hominids. You should realize, however, that such continued debate is at the heart of scientific endeavor; indeed, it provides a major stimulus for further research. Here we raise questions regarding five areas of taxonomic interpretation. In general, there is still reasonably strong agreement on these points, and we follow, where possible, the current consensus as reflected in recent publications (Grine, 1988a; Klein, 1989; Conroy, 1997; Fleagle, 1999).

1. *Is* Ardipithecus *a hominid? If so, is* Ardipithecus *really generically distinct from* Australopithecus*?*
   Only tentative clues from the cranium and upper limb have thus far suggested that the 4.4-million-year-old fossils from Aramis were bipedal. Descriptions of the more complete skeleton (including a pelvis) have not yet been published. However, from what is known and what has been initially reported, it appears that these forms were bipedal and thus should (provisionally) be classified as hominids. Much more detailed analysis will need to be completed before it can be concluded how habitual and obligate the bipedal adaptation was. Also uncertain is the genus status of these new finds. Again, from what is known, especially of the dentition (showing thin enamel on the back teeth), the Aramis finds do look quite different from *any* known *Australopithecus* species.

2. *How many species are there at Hadar and Laetoli (i.e., is* Australopithecus afarensis *one species)?*
   Some paleoanthropologists argue that what has been described as a single species (especially regarding the large Hadar sample) actually represents at least two separate species (taxa). However, it is clear that all australopithecines were highly variable, and thus the pattern seen at Hadar might well represent a single, highly dimorphic species. Most scholars accept this interpretation, and it is best, for the moment, to follow this more conservative view. As a matter of good paleontological practice, it is desirable not to overly "split" fossil samples until compelling evidence is presented.

3. *Are* Australopithecus anamensis *and* Australopithecus garhi *separate species from* Australopithecus afarensis*?*
   The fossil discoveries of *A. anamensis* have thus far been quite fragmentary. When we compare them with the much better known *A. afarensis* materials, the anatomical differences in the Allia Bay and Kanapoi specimens are by no means striking. Likewise, the newly discovered materials from Bouri (*A. garhi*) are still provisionally assigned to a new species. Thus, until more complete remains are discovered, it is best to be cautious and regard the new species designations (*Australopithecus anamensis* and *A. garhi*) as a tentative hypothesis and one requiring further confirmation.

4. *How many genera of australopithecines are there?*
   Many years ago, a plethora of genera was suggested by Robert Broom and others. However, in the 1960s and 1970s, most researchers agreed to "lump" all these forms into *Australopithecus*. With the discovery of early members of the genus *Homo* in the 1960s (and its general recognition in the 1970s), most researchers also recognized the presence of our genus in the Plio-Pleistocene as well (Fig. 10–30).
   In the last decade, there has been an increasing tendency to resplit some of the australopithecines. Recognizing that the robust group (*aethiopicus, boisei,*

FIGURE 10–30
Plio-Pleistocene hominids.

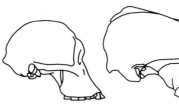

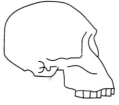

A. afarensis   A. robustus   A. africanus   A. boisei   Early *Homo*

and *robustus*) forms a distinct evolutionary lineage (clade), many researchers (Grine, 1988a; Wood et al., 1994) have argued that the generic term *Paranthropus* should be used to set these robust forms apart from *Australopithecus* (now used in the strict sense).

We agree that there are adequate grounds to make a genus-level distinction, given the evolutionary distinctiveness of the robust clade as well as its apparent adaptive uniqueness (see Fig 10–28). However, for *closely related taxa*, such as we are dealing with here, making this type of interpretation is largely arbitrary. (See discussion, pp. 197–198.) The single genus *Australopithecus* has been used for four decades in the wider sense (to include all robust forms), and because it simplifies terminology, we follow the current consensus and continue the traditional usage—*Australopithecus* for all small-brained Plio-Pleistocene hominids with large, thickly enameled teeth (particularly molars) and including all five recognized species: *A. afarensis, A. aethiopicus, A. africanus, A. robustus,* and *A. boisei.*

5. ***How many species of early* Homo *existed?***
Here is another species-level type of interpretation that is unlikely to be resolved soon. Yet, as it strikes closer to home (our own genus) than the issue for robust australopithecines, the current debate is generating more heat.

Whether we find resolution or not, the *form* of the conflicting views is instructive. The main issue is again interpreting whether variation is *inter-* or *intraspecific*. For those anthropologists who include all the early *Homo* remains from Africa within *one* species (e.g., Tobias, 1991), the considerable variation is thought largely to be due to sexual dimorphism. However, many other researchers (a growing consensus, in fact) see too much variation among the specimens to be explained as part of just one species (even a highly variable one). These paleoanthropologists (Lieberman et al., 1988; Wood, 1992a) thus argue that there was *more than one species* of early *Homo*.* We agree that more than one species is probably represented, but for simplicity suggest referring to all the specimens as "early *Homo*."

Putting It All Together

The interpretation of our paleontological past in terms of which fossils are related to other fossils and how they are all related to modern humans is usually shown diagrammatically in the form of a **phylogeny**. Such a diagram is a family tree of fossil evolution. (Note that strict practioners of cladistics prefer to use cladograms; see pp. 178–182.) This kind of interpretation is the eventual goal of evolutionary studies, but it is the final goal, only after adequate data are available to understand what is going on.

Another, more basic way to handle these data is to divide the fossil material into subsets. This avoids (for the moment) what are still problematic phylogenetic relationships. Accordingly, for the Plio-Pleistocene hominid material from Africa, we can divide the data into four broad groupings:

Set I. Basal hominids (4.4 m.y.a.)   The earliest (and most primitive) collection of remains that have been classified as hominids are those from Aramis. These fossils have, for the moment, been assigned to *Ardipithecus ramidus* and are hence provisionally interpreted as being generically distinct from all the other Plio-Pleistocene forms (listed in sets II–IV). Analysis thus far indicates that these forms were likely bipedal, but with a primitive dentition. Brain size of *A. ramidus* is not yet known, but was almost certainly quite small.

Set II. Early, primitive *Australopithecus* (4.2–3.0 m.y.a.)   This grouping comprises one well-known species, *A. afarensis*, especially well documented at

Phylogeny
A schematic representation showing ancestor-descendant relationships, usually in a chronological framework.

---

*The species names *Homo habilis* and *Homo rudolfensis* are the ones most commonly used for designating two different species of early *Homo*.

Laetoli and Hadar. Slightly earlier, closely related forms (perhaps representing a distinct second species) come from two other sites and are provisionally called "*Australopithecus anamensis.*" Best known from analysis of the *A. afarensis* material, these hominids are characterized by a small brain, large teeth (front and back), and a bipedal gait (probably still allowing for considerable climbing).

Set III. Later, more derived *Australopithecus* (2.5–1.4 m.y.a.; possibly as early as 3.5 m.y.a.)   This group is composed of numerous species. (Most experts recognize at least three; some subdivide this material into five or more species.) Remains have come from several sites in both South and East Africa. All of these forms have very large back teeth and do not show appreciable brain enlargement (i.e., encephalization) compared to *A. afarensis.*

Set IV. Early *Homo* (2.4–1.8 m.y.a.)   The best known specimens are from East Africa (East Turkana and Olduvai), but early remains of *Homo* have also been found in South Africa (Sterkfontein and possibly Swartkrans and Drimolen). This group is composed of possibly just one, but probably more than one, species. Early *Homo* is characterized (compared to *Australopithecus*) by greater encephalization, altered cranial shape, and smaller (especially molars) and narrower (especially premolars) teeth.

Although hominid fossil evidence has accumulated in great abundance, the fact that so much of the material has been discovered so recently makes any firm judgments concerning the route of human evolution premature. However, paleoanthropologists are certainly not deterred from making their "best guesses," and diverse hypotheses have abounded in recent years. The vast majority of more than 300 fossils from East Africa is still in the descriptive and early analytical stages. At this time, the construction of phylogenies of human evolution is analogous to building a house with only a partial blueprint. We are not even sure how many rooms there are! Until the existing fossil evidence has been adequately studied, to say nothing about possible new finds, speculative hypotheses must be viewed with a critical eye.

In Figure 10–31, we present several phylogenies representing different and opposing views of hominid evolution. We suggest that you not attempt to memorize them, for they *all* could be out of date by the time you read this book. It will prove more profitable to look at each one and assess the biological implications involved. Also, note which groups are on the "main line" of human evolution (the one including *Homo sapiens*) and which are placed on extinct side branches.

Interpreting the Interpretations

All the schemes in Figure 10–31 postdate 1979, when *A. afarensis* was first suggested as the most likely common ancestor of all later hominids (Johanson and White, 1979). Since the early 1980s, most paleoanthropologists have accepted this view. One exception is shown in phylogeny B (after Senut and Tardieu, 1985), but this position—based on the premise that *A. afarensis* is actually more than one species—has not been generally supported.

We have not included evolutionary schemes prior to 1979, as they do not account for the crucial discoveries at Hadar and Laetoli of *Australopithecus afarensis.* These now-outdated models frequently postulated *A. africanus* as the common ancestor of later *Australopithecus* (robust varieties) and early *Homo.* In modified form, this view is still continued in some respects (see phylogeny C). Yet another new, and potentially highly significant, discovery was announced in 2001: a quite complete cranium from West Lake Turkana, dated to about 3.5–3.0 m.y.a. This specimen, although distorted, appears to combine a small brain and a primitive cranial vault with a more derived vertical face. This unusual morphology has led Meave Leakey and colleagues to propose an entirely new genus (*Kenyanthropus*) of early hominid (Leakey, et al., 2001).

Probably the most intractable problems for interpretation of early hominid evolution involve what to do with *A. aethiopicus* and *A. africanus.* Carefully look at

PHYLOGENY A
A. afarensis common ancestor theory
(after Johanson and White, 1979)

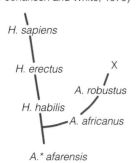

Note: Afarensis postulated as common
ancestor to all Plio-Pleistocene hominids.

PHYLOGENY B
Multiple lineage early divergence
(after Senut and Tardieu, 1985)

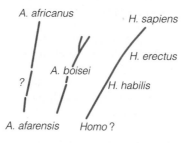

Note: Major split occurs before A. afarensis.
Possible multiple lineages in Plio-Pleistocene.

PHYLOGENY C
A. africanus common ancestor theory
(after Skelton et al., 1986)

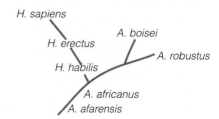

Note: Major split occurs after A. africanus.
Therefore, A. africanus is seen as still in our
lineage as well as that of more derived
australopithecines.

PHYLOGENY D
Early robust lineage
(after Delson, 1986, 1987; Grine, 1993)

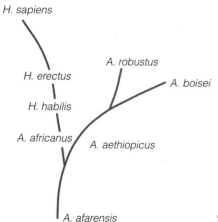

PHYLOGENY E
Ardipithecus as probable root species for later hominids (and also incorporating other
recent modifications) (after Skelton and McHenry, 1992; Wolpoff, 1999)

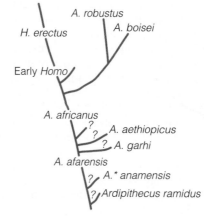

* For genus designation, the "A" in all phylogenies refers to Australopithecus.

FIGURE 10–31
Phylogenies of hominid evolution.

the different evolutionary reconstructions to see how various researchers deal with these complicated issues. Finally, the newest finds from Aramis (*Ardipithecus*), northern Kenya (*Australopithecus anamensis*), and Ethiopia (*A. garhi*) will need to be incorporated into these schemes. Phylogeny E is an initial attempt to do so, but only points up how frequently hominid evolutionary interpretations need to be reevaluated and substantially revised.

SUMMARY

After so much detail relating to hominid evolution in the Plio-Pleistocene, you may feel frustrated by what must seem to be endlessly changing and conflicting interpretations. However, after 75 years of discoveries of early hominids in Africa, there are several general points on which most researchers agree:

1. *A. afarensis* is the earliest hominid at present with substantial definite supporting evidence. It is possible, however, that *Ardipithecus* will soon supplant *A. afarensis* for this status of earliest definite hominid.
2. *A. afarensis*, as defined, probably represents only one species.
3. *A. afarensis* is probably ancestral to all later hominids (or is very closely related to the species that is).

4. *A. aethiopicus* is ancestral solely to the "robust" group (clade), linking it with earlier *afarensis* as well as with one (or both) later robust species.

5. All australopithecines were extinct by 1 m.y.a. (or shortly before).

6. All australopithecine species (presumably early *Homo* as well) were highly variable, showing extreme sexual dimorphism.

7. Since there is so much intraspecific variation, on average there was not much difference in body size among australopithecine species.

8. *A. africanus* was probably not the last common ancestor of the robust lineage *and* genus *Homo*. That is, phylogeny C is probably not entirely correct. Indeed, the robust "lineage" may actually be more than one group, or clade. As phylogeny E suggests, *A. aethiopicus* may have diverged earlier, prior to *A. africanus*.

9. All forms (*Australopithecus* and early *Homo*) were small-brained (as compared to later species of the genus *Homo*); nevertheless, all early hominids are more encephalized than apes of comparable body size.

10. Most forms (including some members of early *Homo*) had large back teeth.

11. There was substantial parallelism (homoplasy) in physical traits among early hominid lineages.

12. Given the current state of knowledge, there are several equally supportable phylogenies. In fact, in a recent publication, three leading researchers (Bill Kimbel, Tim White, and Don Johanson, 1988) make this point; moreover, they note that of four possible phylogenetic reconstructions they present (various modifications of phylogenies D and E), they have not reached agreement among themselves as to which is the most likely.

As this list makes clear, we have come a long way in reaching an understanding of Plio-Pleistocene hominid evolution. Nevertheless, a truly complete understanding is not at hand. Such is the stuff of science!

QUESTIONS FOR REVIEW

1. In East Africa, all the early hominid sites are found along the Rift Valley. Why is this significant?

2. (a) Why is postcranial evidence (particularly the lower limb) so crucial in showing the australopithecines as definite hominids? (b) What particular aspects of the australopithecine pelvis and lower limb are hominid-like?

3. In what ways are the remains of *Ardipithecus ramidus* and *Australopithecus anamensis* primitive? How do we know that these forms are hominids?

4. Why are some Plio-Pleistocene hominids from East Africa called "early *Homo*" (or *H. habilis*)? What does this imply for the evolutionary relationships of the australopithecines?

5. What kinds of dating techniques have been used in South Africa?

6. Why is the dating control better in East Africa than in South Africa?

7. Discuss the first thing you would do if you found an early hominid fossil and were responsible for its formal description and publication. What would you include in your publication?

8. Discuss two current disputes regarding taxonomic issues concerning early hominids. Try to give support for alternative positions.

9. Why would one use the taxonomic term *Paranthropus* in contrast to *Australopithecus*?

10. What is a phylogeny? Construct one for early hominids (4.4–1 m.y.a.). Make sure you can describe what conclusions your scheme makes. Also, try to defend it.

11. Discuss at least two alternative ways that *A. africanus* is currently incorporated into phylogenetic schemes.

12. What are the most recently discovered of the Plio-Pleistocene hominid materials, and how are they, for the moment, incorporated into a phylogenetic scheme? How secure do you think this interpretation is?

SUGGESTED FURTHER READING

Conroy, Glenn C. 1997. *Reconstructing Human Origins. A Modern Synthesis*. New York: Norton.

Corruccini, Robert S., and Russel L. Ciochon (eds.). 1994. *Integrative Paths to the Past: Paleoanthropology Advances in Honor of F. Clark Howell*. Englewood Cliffs, NJ: Prentice Hall.

Delson, Eric (ed.). 1985. *Ancestors: The Hard Evidence*. New York: Liss.

Grine, Fred (ed.). 1988. *Evolutionary History of the Robust Australopithecines*. New York: de Gruyter.

Rak, Yoel. 1983. *The Australopithecine Face*. New York: Academic Press.

Wolpoff, Milford H. 1999. *Paleoanthropology*. 2nd ed. Boston: McGraw-Hill.

RESOURCES ON THE INTERNET

 Wadsworth Anthropology Resource Center
http://anthropology.wadsworth.com

The companion website for this text includes a range of enrichment material focused on the chapter's topic. While online you can enhance your understanding of the chapter by exploring one of the several additional Internet Exercises, by researching topics, and by accessing full articles on InfoTrac College Edition. You can also reinforce the concepts by taking online practice exams.

Internet Exercises

Search the Internet for information regarding one of the very earliest hominid sites, Aramis, Kanapoi, or Allia Bay. What information have you learned that supplements the material in the textbook? Also, search the news sites including ScienceDaily (http://www.sciencedaily.com). What new information has come out regarding these sites or any other early hominid sites since this text was written?

 InfoTrac College Edition
http://www.infotrac-college.com/wadsworth

Review the Plio-Pleistocene hominid sites mentioned in the text. Can you find research about any of these sites on InfoTrac College Edition? (Hint: use PowerTrac.) What was found at these sites? To what taxon or taxa are these finds attributed?

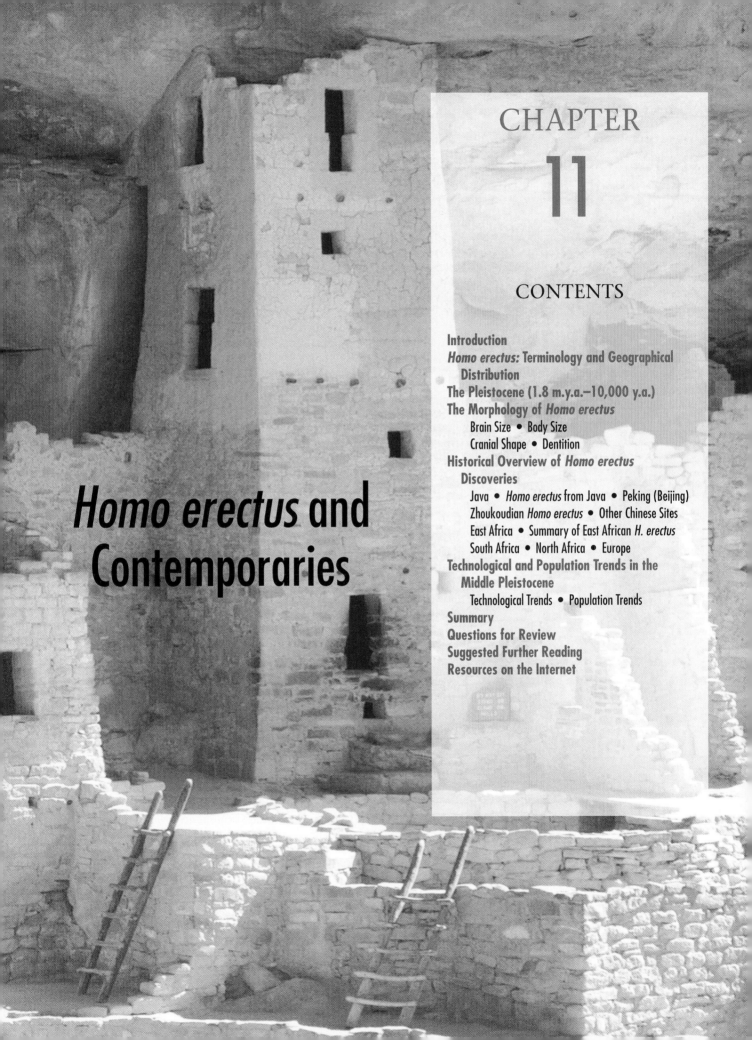

CHAPTER

11

CONTENTS

Homo erectus and
Contemporaries

See the following section of the CD-ROM for topics covered in this chapter: Virtual Lab 10.

Introduction

In Chapter 10, we traced the earliest evidence of hominid evolution by reviewing the abundant fossil material from Africa that documents the origins of *Australopithecus* and *Homo* during the Pliocene and early Pleistocene. In this chapter, we take up what might be called the next stage of hominid evolution, the appearance and dispersal of *Homo erectus* (see Fig. 11–2 on pages 260–261).

Homo erectus was a widely distributed species and was in fact the first hominid (for which we have definite evidence) to have migrated out of Africa and to have inhabited vast new regions of the Old World. Moreover, as a species, *H. erectus* existed over an exceptionally long time, spanning well over 1 million years! If one judges species success by longevity, *H. erectus* appears to be the most successful hominid that has ever existed. How can we explain the remarkable success of this species?

In this chapter, we discuss many of the physical changes that characterized *H. erectus*, especially as compared to what came before (early *Homo*) and after (*Homo sapiens*). Certainly, some of the physical alterations, such as increased brain size, larger body size, and dental modifications, help account for the success of *H. erectus*. But that is not the whole story. As we have emphasized, hominid evolution has long been characterized by a biocultural interaction. Thus, it is only through explaining the behavioral capacities of *Homo erectus* (in concert with morphological change) that we can understand the success of this hominid species. For this reason, we also highlight some of the abundant archaeological evidence and related biocultural reconstructions that have so long occupied and fascinated paleoanthropologists.

Homo erectus: Terminology and Geographical Distribution

The discoveries of fossils now referred to as *H. erectus* go back to the nineteenth century. Later in this chapter, we will discuss in some detail the historical background of these earliest discoveries in Java and the somewhat later discoveries in China. From this work, as well as presumably related finds in Europe and North Africa, a variety of taxonomic names were suggested. The most significant of these earlier terms were *Pithecanthropus* (for the Javanese remains) and *Sinanthropus* (for the fossils from northern China). In fact, you may still see these terms in older sources or occasionally used colloquially and thus placed in quotation marks (e.g., "Pithecanthropus").

It is important to realize that taxonomic *splitting* (which this terminology reflects) was quite common in the early years of paleoanthropology. Only after World War II and with the incorporation of the Modern Synthesis (see p. 70) into paleontology did more systematic biological thinking come to the fore. Following this trend, in the early 1950s all the material previously referred to as "Pithecanthropus," "Sinanthropus," and so forth, was included in a single species of genus *Homo*—*H. erectus*. This reclassification proved to be a most significant development on two counts:

1. It reflected the incorporation of modern evolutionary thinking into hominid paleontology.
2. The simplification in terminology, based as it was on sound biological principles, refocused research away from endless arguments regarding classification to broader populational, behavioral, and ecological considerations.

Discoveries in the last few decades have established *well-dated* finds of *H. erectus* in East Africa from geological contexts chronometrically dated as old as 1.8 m.y.a. In addition, new dates first published in 1994 by geologists from the Berkeley Geochronology Laboratory (Swisher et al., 1994) have suggested that two localities in Java are as old as those in East Africa (with dates of 1.8 and 1.6 m.y.a.). These early dates have come as somewhat of a surprise to many paleoanthropologists, but as you will see, there is now growing evidence for an early dispersal of hominids outside of Africa—that is, one *well before* 1 m.y.a.

Current interpretations thus view the first hominid dispersal out of Africa as occurring between 1.5 and 2 m.y.a. A likely route would have taken these hominids through southwestern Asia, and there are some intriguing hints from the Ubeidiya site in Israel that this route was indeed exploited quite early on. The most conclusive evidence from Ubeidiya is archaeological, including a number of stone tools dated (by paleomagnetism and faunal correlation) to 1.4–1.3 m.y.a. In addition, there are some fragmentary hominid remains, including cranial pieces and two teeth. Unfortunately, the association of these hominid remains with the tools at a date prior to 1 m.y.a. is uncertain. Consequently, there is not yet *definitive* fossil evidence of *H. erectus* (or a close relative) from Southwest Asia. Nevertheless, the Ubeidiya archaeological discoveries are highly suggestive and fit with the overall emerging pattern of an early hominid dispersal from Africa.

More than likely, these first continental migrants were members of *H. erectus* or a group very closely related to *H. erectus* (although an earlier dispersal of a more primitive member of genus *Homo* cannot be ruled out). What the current evidence most economically suggests is that *Homo erectus* migrated out of East Africa, eventually to occupy South and North Africa, southern and northeastern Asia, and perhaps Europe as well. A recent, not yet fully described hominid mandible from the Dmanisi site in the Republic of Georgia has been provisionally dated to 1.8–1.6 m.y.a. (Fig. 11–1). In other words, if this as yet unconfirmed date should prove accurate, this fossil would be as early as any *H. erectus* discovery in Java and about as old as East African remains as well! Another new find pushing back the antiquity of hominids in Europe has come from the 500,000-year-old Boxgrove site in southern England, where a hominid tibia (shinbone) was unearthed in 1994. And still another recent find (1994), from the Ceprano site in central Italy, may be the best evidence yet of *H. erectus* in Europe (Ascenzi et al., 1996). Provisional dating of a partial cranium from this important site suggests a date greater than 700,000 years ago. The primary researchers, as well as Rightmire (1998), conclude that cranial morphology places this specimen quite close to *H. erectus*.

Finally, some other fossil remains from Spain, also discovered in 1994 and announced in 1995, may well be the oldest hominids yet found in western Europe (see Fig. 11–2 for locations of these hominid sites). From the Gran Dolina site in the highly productive Atapuerca region of northern Spain, where numerous, somewhat more recent hominid fossils have also been discovered (discussed in Chapter 12), several fragments of at least four individuals have been found (Carbonell et al., 1995). The dating, based on paleomagnetic determinations (see p. 211), places the Gran Dolina hominids at approximately 780,000 y.a.* (Parés and Pérez-González, 1995). If this dating is further corroborated, these early Spanish finds would be *at least* 250,000 years older than any other hominid yet discovered in western Europe. Because all the 36 pieces thus far identified are quite fragmentary, the taxonomic assignment of these fossils still remains problematic. Initial analysis, however, suggests that most of the European fossils are *not H. erectus*. Whether any of these early European hominids, except perhaps for the Ceprano cranium, belong within the species *Homo erectus* thus still remains to be determined.

The dispersal of *Homo erectus* from Africa was influenced by climate, topography, water boundaries, and access to food and other resources. Paleoenvironmental reconstructions are thus of crucial importance in understanding the expansion of *H. erectus* to so many parts of the Old World. The long temporal span of *H. erectus* begins very early in the **Pleistocene** and extends to fairly late in that geological epoch. To comprehend the world of *Homo erectus*, we must understand how environments shifted during the Pleistocene.

*y.a. stands for "years ago."

 See Virtual Lab 10 for an interactive map showing the distribution of *Homo erectus*.

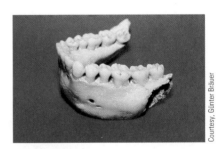

Courtesy, Günter Bräuer

FIGURE 11–1
Dmanisi mandible.

Pleistocene
The epoch of the Cenozoic from 1.8 m.y.a. until 10,000 y.a. Frequently referred to as the Ice Age, this epoch is associated with continental glaciations in northern latitudes.

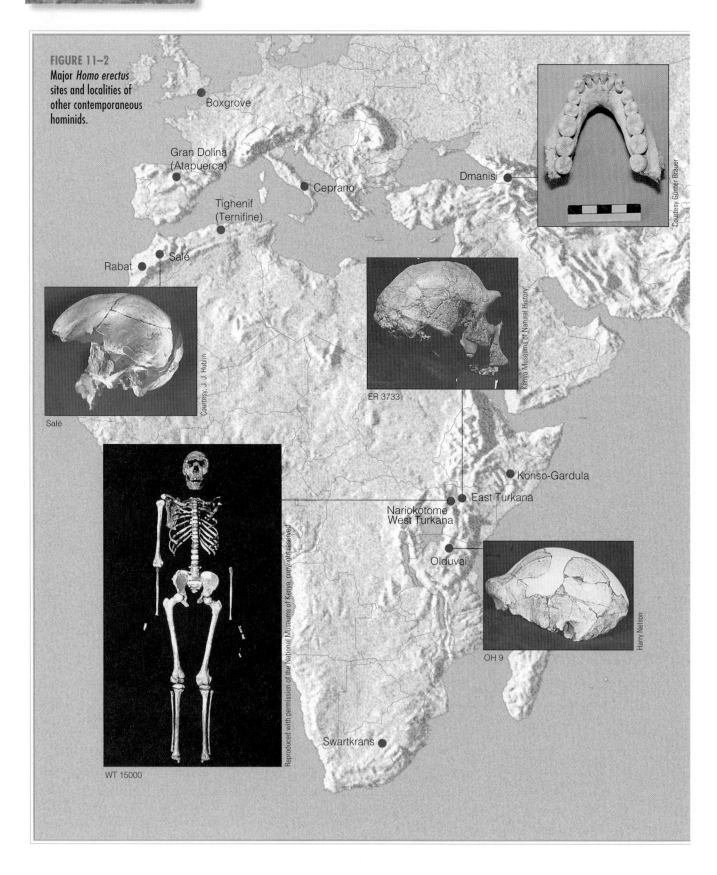

FIGURE 11–2
Major *Homo erectus* sites and localities of other contemporaneous hominids.

Boxgrove

Gran Dolina (Atapuerca)

Ceprano

Tighenif (Ternifine)

Salé

Rabat

Salé

Courtesy, J. J. Hublin

Dmanisi

Courtesy Günter Bräuer

ER 3733

Kenya Museums of Natural History

Konso-Gardula

East Turkana

Nariokotome West Turkana

Olduvai

OH 9

Harry Nelson

Swartkrans

WT 15000

Reproduced with permission of the National Museums of Kenya, copyright reserved

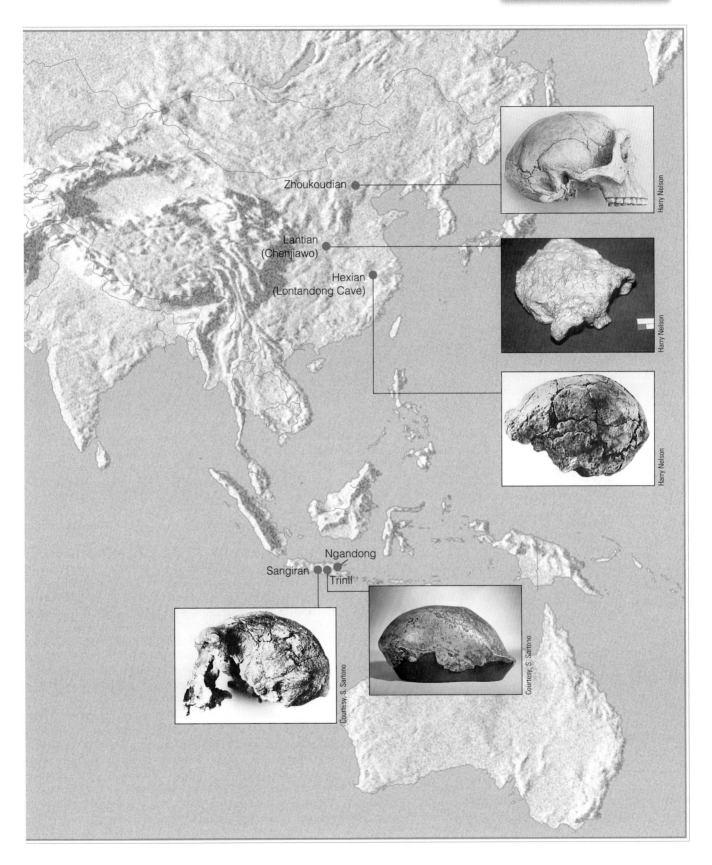

Zhoukoudian

Lantian
(Chenjiawo)

Hexian
(Lontandong Cave)

Harry Nelson

Harry Nelson

Harry Nelson

Ngandong

Sangiran

Trinil

Courtesy, S. Sartono

Courtesy, S. Sartono

The Pleistocene (1.8 m.y.a.–10,000 y.a.)

During much of the Pleistocene (also known as the Age of Glaciers or Ice Age), large areas of the Northern Hemisphere were covered with enormous masses of ice, which advanced and retreated as the temperature fell and rose. An early classification of glacial (and interglacial) Europe divided the Pleistocene into four major glacial periods. However, climatic conditions varied in different areas of Europe, and distinctive glacial periods are also now known for the North Sea, England, and eastern Europe, not to mention Asia and North America. New dating techniques have revealed a much more complex account of glacial advance and retreat, and the many oscillations of cold and warm temperatures during the Pleistocene affected both plants and animals: "The Pleistocene record shows that there were about 15 major cold periods and 50 minor advances during its [more than] 1.5-m.y. duration, or one major cold period every 100,000 years" (Tattersal et al., 1988, p. 230).

The Pleistocene, which lasted more than 1.75 million years, was a significant period in hominid evolutionary history and encompassed the appearance and disappearance of *Homo erectus*. By the end of the Pleistocene, modern humans had already appeared, dependence on culture had dramatically increased, and domestication of plants and animals—one of the great cultural revolutions of human history—was either about to commence or had already begun. Given this background on the time span in which *H. erectus* evolved and lived, let us examine more closely this predecessor of *H. sapiens*.

The Morphology of *Homo erectus*

Brain Size

Homo erectus differs in several respects from both early *Homo* and *Homo sapiens*. The most obvious feature is cranial size (which, of course, is closely related to brain size). Early *Homo* had cranial capacities ranging from as small as 500 cm³ to as large as 800 cm³. *H. erectus*, on the other hand, shows considerable brain enlargement, with a cranial capacity of 750 to 1,250 cm³ (with a mean of approximately 900 cm³). However, in making such comparisons, we must bear in mind two key questions: What is the comparative sample, and what were the overall body sizes of the species being compared?

In relation to the first question, you should recall that many scholars are now convinced that there was more than one species of early *Homo* in East Africa around 2 m.y.a. If so, only one of these could have been ancestral to *H. erectus*. (Indeed, it is possible that neither species gave rise to *H. erectus* and that perhaps we have yet to find direct evidence of the ancestral species.) Taking a more optimistic view that at least one of these fossil groups is a likely ancestor of later hominids, the question still remains—which one? If we choose the smaller-bodied sample of early *Homo* as our presumed ancestral group, then *H. erectus* shows as much as a 40 percent increase in cranial capacity. However, if the comparative sample is the larger-bodied group of early *Homo* (as exemplified by skull 1470, from East Turkana), then *H. erectus* shows a 25 percent increase in cranial capacity.

As we previously discussed, brain size is closely tied to overall body size (a relationship termed *encephalization*). We have made a point of the increase in *H. erectus* brain size; however, it must be realized that *H. erectus* was also considerably larger overall than earlier members of the genus *Homo*. In fact, when *H. erectus* is compared with the larger-bodied early *Homo* sample, *relative* brain size is about the same (Walker, 1991). Furthermore, when considering the relative brain size of *H. erectus* in comparison with *H. sapiens*, it is seen that *H. erectus* was considerably less encephalized than later members of the genus *Homo*.

CHAPTER 11

Body Size

As we have just mentioned, another feature displayed by *H. erectus*, compared to earlier hominids, is a dramatic increase in body size. For several decades, little was known of the postcranial skeleton of *H. erectus*. However, with the discovery of a nearly complete skeleton in 1984 from **Nariokotome** (on the west side of Lake Turkana in Kenya) and its detailed analysis (Walker and Leakey, 1993), the data base is now much improved. From this specimen (and from less complete individuals at other sites), some *Homo erectus* adults are estimated to have weighed well over 100 pounds, with an average adult stature of about 5 feet 6 inches (McHenry, 1992; Ruff and Walker, 1993). Another point to keep in mind is that *Homo erectus* was quite sexually dimorphic—at least as indicated by the East African specimens. Thus, for male adult body size, weight and stature in some individuals may have been considerably greater than the average figures just mentioned. In fact, it is estimated that if the Nariokotome boy had survived, he would have attained an adult stature of over 6 feet (Walker, 1993).

Associated with the large stature (and explaining the significant increase in body weight) is also a dramatic increase in robusticity. In fact, this characteristic of very heavy body build was to dominate hominid evolution not just during *H. erectus* times, but through the long transitional era of archaic *Homo sapiens* as well. Only with the appearance of anatomically modern *H. sapiens* do we see a more gracile skeletal structure, which is still characteristic of most modern populations.

Cranial Shape

The cranium of *Homo erectus* displays a highly distinctive shape, partly as a result of increased brain size, but probably more correlated with significant body size (robusticity). The ramifications of this heavily built cranium are reflected in thick cranial bone (most notably in Asian specimens) and large browridges (supraorbital tori) in the front of the skull and a projecting **nuchal torus** at the rear (Fig. 11–3 on page 264).

The vault is long and low, receding back from the large browridges with little forehead development. Moreover, the cranium is wider at the base compared with earlier *or* later species of genus *Homo*. The maximum breadth is below the ear opening, giving a pentagonal contour to the cranium (when viewed from behind). In contrast, both early *Homo* crania and *H. sapiens* crania have more vertical sides, and the maximum width is *above* the ear openings.

Dentition

The dentition of *Homo erectus* is much like that of *Homo sapiens*, but the earlier species exhibits somewhat larger teeth. However, compared with early *Homo*, *H. erectus* does show some dental reduction.

Another interesting feature of the dentition of some *H. erectus* specimens is seen in the incisor teeth. On the back (lingual) surfaces, the teeth are scooped out in appearance, forming a surface reminiscent of a shovel. Accordingly, such teeth are referred to as "shovel-shaped" incisors, and they are also found in several modern human populations (Fig. 11–4). It has been suggested that teeth shaped in this manner are an adaptation in hunter-gatherers for processing foods, a contention not yet proved (or really even framed in a testable manner). One thing does seem likely: Shovel-shaped incisors are probably an ancestral feature of the species *H. erectus*, as the phenomenon has been found not just in the Chinese specimens, but also in the early individual from Nariokotome.

Nariokotome
(nar´-ee-oh-ko´-tow-may)

Nuchal torus
(nuke´-ul, pertaining to the neck)
A projection of bone in the back of the cranium where neck muscles attach, used to hold up the head. The nuchal torus is a distinctive feature of *H. erectus*.

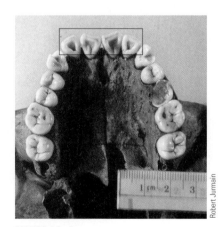

FIGURE 11–4
Shovel-shaped incisors, shown here in a modern *Homo sapiens* individual.

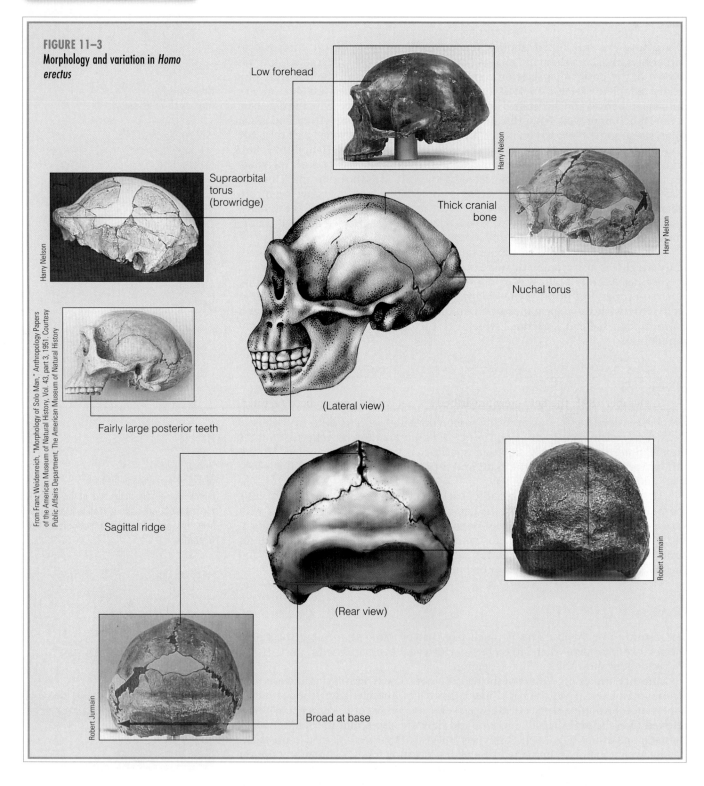

FIGURE 11–3

Morphology and variation in *Homo erectus*

Low forehead

Supraorbital torus (browridge)

Thick cranial bone

Nuchal torus

Harry Nelson

Harry Nelson

Harry Nelson

From Franz Weidenreich, "Morphology of Solo Man," Anthropology Papers of the American Museum of Natural History, Vol. 43, part 3, 1951. Courtesy Public Affairs Department, The American Museum of Natural History

Fairly large posterior teeth

(Lateral view)

Sagittal ridge

Robert Jurmain

(Rear view)

Broad at base

Robert Jurmain

Historical Overview of *Homo erectus* Discoveries

In our discussion of Plio-Pleistocene hominids, we traced the evolutionary developments in *chronological* order, that is, discussing the oldest specimens first. Here we take a different approach and discuss the finds in the order in which they were discovered. We believe that this approach is useful, as the discoveries cover a broad range of time—indeed, almost the entire history of paleoanthropology. Given this relatively long history of scientific discovery, the later finds were assessed in the light of earlier ones (and thus can still be best understood within a historical context).

Java

Dutch anatomist Eugene Dubois (1858–1940) (Fig. 11–5) was the first scientist to deliberately design a research plan that would take him from his anatomy lab to where fossil bones might be buried. Up until this time, embryology and comparative anatomy were considered the proper methods of studying humans and their ancestry, and the research was done in the laboratory. Dubois changed all this.

The latter half of the nineteenth century was a period of intellectual excitement. In Europe, Darwin's *On the Origin of Species* (published in 1859) provoked scientists as well as educated laypeople to take opposing sides, often with heated emotion. In 1856, an unusual skull had been recovered near Düsseldorf, Germany. This specimen is now known as Neandertal, but when a description of it was published, scientific opinion was again divided, and feelings ran high.

This stimulating intellectual climate surrounded the youthful Eugene Dubois, who left Holland for Sumatra in 1887 to search for, as he phrased it, "the missing link." Dubois went to work immediately and soon unearthed a variety of animal bones, including orangutan, gibbon, and several other mammalian species. However, his successes soon diminished, and in 1890 he switched his fieldwork to the banks of the Solo River near the town of Trinil, on the neighboring island of Java.

In October 1891, the field crew unearthed a skullcap that was to become internationally famous. The following year, a human femur was recovered about 15 yards upstream in what Dubois claimed was the same level as the skullcap. Dubois assumed that the skullcap (with a cranial capacity of slightly over 900 cm^3) and the femur belonged to the same individual.

After studying these discoveries for a few years, Dubois startled the world in 1894 with a paper provocatively titled *"Pithecanthropus erectus*, A Manlike Species of Transitional Anthropoid from Java.*"* In 1895, Dubois returned to Europe, where his paper had received strong criticism. He countered the criticism by elaborating the points briefly covered in his original paper. He also brought along the actual fossil material, which gave scientists an opportunity to examine the evidence. As a result, many opponents became more sympathetic to his views.

However, to this day, questions about the finds remain: Does the femur really belong with the skullcap? Did the field crew dig through several layers, thus mixing the remains? Moreover, some anthropologists think that the Trinil femur is relatively recent and representative of modern *H. sapiens*, not *H. erectus*.

Despite the still-unanswered questions, there is general acceptance that Dubois was correct in identifying the skull as representing a previously undescribed species; that his estimates of cranial capacity were reasonably accurate; that *"Pithecanthropus erectus,"* or *H. erectus* as we call it today, is the ancestor of *H. sapiens*; and that bipedalism preceded enlargement of the brain.

By 1930, the controversy had faded, especially in the light of important new discoveries near Peking (Beijing), China, in the late 1920s (discussed shortly). Similarities between the Beijing skulls and Dubois' *"Pithecanthropus"* were obvious, and scientists pointed out that the Java form was not an "apeman," as Dubois contended, but rather was closely related to modern *Homo sapiens*.

One might expect that Dubois would welcome the finds from China and the support they provided for the human status of *"Pithecanthropus,"* but Dubois would have none of it. He refused to recognize any connection between Beijing and Java and described the Beijing fossils as "a degenerate Neanderthaler" (von Koenigswald, 1956, p. 55). He also refused to accept the classification of *"Pithecanthropus"* in the same species with later finds from Java.

FIGURE 11–5
Eugene Dubois, discoverer of the first *H. erectus* fossil to be found.

FIGURE 11–6
Rear view of a Ngandong skull. Note that the cranial walls slope downward and outward (or upward and inward), with the widest breadth low on the cranium, giving it a pentagonal form.

Courtesy, S. Sartono

Zhoukoudian
(zhoh´-koh-dee´-en)

The New York Academy of Medicine Library

FIGURE 11–7
Davidson Black, responsible for the first study of the Zhoukoudian fossils.

Homo erectus from Java

Six sites in eastern Java have yielded all the *H. erectus* fossil remains found to date on that island. The dating of these fossils has been hampered by the complex nature of Javanese geology. It has been generally accepted that most of the fossils belong in the Middle Pleistocene and are less than 800,000 years old. However, as we noted earlier, new dating estimates have suggested one find (from Modjokerto) to be close to 1.8 m.y.a. and another fossil from the main site of Sangiran to be approximately 1.6 m.y.a.

At Sangiran, where the remains of at least five individuals have been excavated, the cranial capacities of the fossils range from 813 cm³ to 1,059 cm³. Another site called Ngandong has also been fruitful, yielding the remains of 12 crania (Fig. 11–6). The dating here is also confusing, but the Upper Pleistocene has been suggested, which may explain the larger cranial measurements of the Ngandong individuals as well as features that are more modern than those found on other Javanese crania. Newly published dates for the Ngandong site are very recent, remarkably so, in fact. Using two specialized dating techniques (discussed in Chapter 13; see p. 321), Swisher and colleagues from the Berkeley Geochronology Laboratory have determined from animal bones found at the site (and presumably associated with the hominids) a date ranging from about 50,000 years ago to as recently as 25,000 years ago (Swisher et al., 1996). If these dates are further confirmed, it would show a *very* late survival of *Homo erectus* in Java, long after they had disappeared elsewhere. They would thus be contemporary with *Homo sapiens*—which, by this time, had expanded widely in the Old World (see Chapter 12).

We cannot say much about the *H. erectus* way of life in Java. Very few artifacts have been found, and those have come mainly from river terraces, not from primary sites: "On Java there is still not a single site where artifacts can be associated with *H. erectus*" (Bartstra, 1982, p. 319).

Peking (Beijing)

The story of Peking *H. erectus* is another saga filled with excitement, hard work, luck, and misfortune. Europeans had known for a long time that "dragon bones," used by the Chinese as medicine and aphrodisiacs, were actually ancient mammal bones. In 1917, the Geological Survey of China decided to find the sites where these dragon bones were collected by local inhabitants and sold to apothecary shops. In 1921 a Swedish geologist, J. Gunnar Andersson, was told of a potentially fruitful fossil site in an abandoned quarry near the village of **Zhoukoudian**. A villager showed Andersson's team a fissure in the limestone wall, and within a few minutes they found the jaw of a pig: "That evening we went home with rosy dreams of great discoveries" (Andersson, 1934, pp. 97–98).

A young Chinese geologist, Pei Wenshong, took over the excavation in 1929 and began digging out the sediment in one branch of the lower cave, where he found one of the most remarkable fossil skulls to be recovered up to that time. One of the Chinese workers tells the story:

> We had got down about 30 meters deep. . . . It was there the skull-cap was sighted, half of it embedded in loose earth, the other in hard clay. The sun had almost set . . . . The team debated whether to take it out right away or to wait until the next day when they could see better. The agonizing suspense of a whole day was felt to be too much to bear, so they decided to go on. (Jia, 1975, pp. 12–13)

Pei brought the skull to anatomist Davidson Black (Fig 11–7). Because the fossil was embedded in hard limestone, it took Black four months of hard, steady work to free it from its tough matrix. The result was worth the labor. The skull, that of a juvenile, was thick, low, and relatively small, but in Black's mind there was no doubt it belonged to an early hominid. The response to this discovery, quite unlike that which greeted Dubois almost 40 years earlier, was immediate and enthusiastically favorable.

Franz Weidenreich (Fig 11–8), a distinguished anatomist well known for his work on European fossil hominids, succeeded Black. After Japan invaded China in 1933, Weidenreich decided to move the fossils from Beijing to prevent them from falling into the hands of the Japanese. Weidenreich left China in 1941, taking excellent prepared casts, photographs, and drawings of the fossil material with him. After he left, the bones were packed, and arrangements were made for the U.S. Marine Corps in Beijing to take them to the United States. The bones never reached the United States, and they have never been found. To this day, no one knows what happened to them, and their location remains a mystery.

Zhoukoudian *Homo erectus*

In their recent book (1990), Jia and Huang list the total fossil remains of *H. erectus* unearthed at the Zhoukoudian Cave as of 1982 (Fig. 11–9):

14 skullcaps (only 6 relatively complete) (Fig. 11–10)
6 facial bones (including maxillae, palates, and zygomatic bone fragments)
15 mandibles (mostly one side, only one nearly complete, many fragments)
122 isolated teeth
38 teeth rooted in jaws
3 humeri (upper arm bones, only 1 well preserved, the rest in fragments)
1 clavicle (both ends absent)
1 lunate (wrist bone)
7 femurs (only 1 well preserved)
1 tibia (shinbone, fragmentary)
(and over 100,000 artifacts)

These remains belong to upward of 40 male and female adults and children and constitute a considerable amount of evidence, the largest number of *H. erectus* specimens found at any one site. With the meticulous work by Weidenreich, the Zhoukoudian fossils have led to a good overall picture of the eastern *H. erectus* of China.

Peking *H. erectus*, like that from Java, possesses typical *H. erectus* features, including the supraorbital torus in front and the nuchal torus behind; also, the skull is keeled by a sagittal ridge, the face protrudes, the incisors are shoveled, and the molars contain large pulp cavities. Again, like the Javanese forms, the skull shows the greatest breadth near the bottom. (These similarities were recognized long ago by Black and Weidenreich.)

FIGURE 11–8
Franz Weidenreich.

 See Virtual Lab 10, section I, for a 3-D animation of a Zhoukoudian cranium.

FIGURE 11–9
Zhoukoudian Cave. The grid on the wall was drawn for purposes of excavation. The entrance to the cave can be seen near the grid.

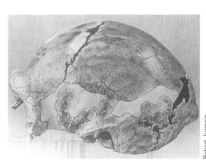

FIGURE 11–10
H. erectus (cast of specimen from Zhoukoudian). From this view, the supraorbital torus, low vault of the skull, and nuchal torus can clearly be seen.

Cultural Remains   More than 100,000 artifacts have been recovered from this vast site that was occupied intermittently for almost 250,000 years. According to the Chinese (Wu and Lin, 1983, p.86), Zhoukoudian "is one of the sites with the longest history of habitation by man or his ancestors." The occupation of the site has been divided into three cultural stages:

Earliest Stage (460,000–420,000 y.a.)*   The tools are large, close to a pound in weight, and made of soft stone, such as sandstone.

Middle Stage (370,000–350,000 y.a.)   Tools become smaller and lighter (under a pound), and these smaller tools comprise approximately two-thirds of the sample.

Final Stage (300,000–230,000 y.a.)   Tools are still small, and the tool materials are of better quality. The coarse quartz of the earlier periods is replaced by a finer quartz, sandstone tools have almost disappeared, and flint tools increase in frequency by as much as 30 percent.

The early tools are crude and shapeless but become more refined over time. Common tools at the site are choppers and chopping tools, but retouched flakes were fashioned into scrapers, points, burins, and awls (Fig 11–11).

The way of life at Zhoukoudian has traditionally been described as that of hunter-gatherers who killed deer and horses as well as other animals and gathered fruits, berries, and ostrich eggs. Fragments of charred ostrich eggshells, the abundant deposits of hackberry seeds unearthed in the cave, and the flourishing plant growth surrounding the cave all suggest that meat was supplemented by the gathering of herbs, wild fruits, tubers, and eggs. Layers of what has long thought to be ash in the cave, over 18 feet deep at one point, suggest to some researchers the use of fire by *H. erectus*; however, whether Beijing hominids could actually make fire is unknown (see below). Wu and Lin (1983, p. 94) state that "Peking Man was a cave dweller, a fire user, a deer hunter, a seed gatherer and a maker of specialized tools," but several questions about Zhoukoudian *H. erectus* remain unanswered.

Did *H. erectus* at Zhoukoudian use language? If by language we mean articulate speech, it is unlikely. Nevertheless, some scholars believe that speech originated early in hominid evolution; others argue that speech did not originate until up to 200,000 years later in the Upper Paleolithic, with the origin of anatomically modern humans (see Chapter 13). We agree with Dean Falk when she writes, "Unfortunately, what it is going to take to *settle* the debate about when language originated in hominids is a time machine. Until one becomes available, we can only speculate about this fascinating and important question" (1989, p. 141).

FIGURE 11–11
Chinese tools from Middle Pleistocene sites. (Adapted from Wu and Olsen, 1985.)

Quartzite chopper

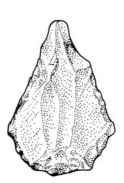
Flint point

Flint awl

Graver or burin

*These dates should be considered tentative until more precise chronometric techniques are available.

Did these hominids wear clothes? Almost surely clothing of some type, probably in the form of animal skins, was worn. Winters in Beijing are harsh today and appear to have been bitter during the Middle Pleistocene as well. Moreover, awls were found at Zhoukoudian, and one of the probable bone tools may be a needle.

What was the life span of *H. erectus* at Zhoukoudian? Apparently, not very long, and infant and childhood mortality was probably very high. Studies of the fossil remains reveal that almost 40 percent of the bones belong to individuals under the age of 14, and only 2.6 percent are estimated to be in the 50- to 60-year age-group (Jia, 1975).

This picture of Zhoukoudian life has more recently been challenged by several researchers. Lewis Binford and colleagues (Binford and Ho, 1985; Binford and Stone, 1986a, 1986b) reject the description of Beijing *H. erectus* as hunters and argue that the evidence clearly points to them as scavengers. As we saw in Chapter 9, the controversy of early hominids as hunters or scavengers has engaged the attention of paleoanthropologists, and the matter is not yet settled.

Using techniques of taphonomy (discussed in Chapter 9), Noel Boaz and colleagues have even questioned whether the *H. erectus* remains at Zhoukoudian represent evidence of hominid habitation of the cave. By carefully comparing types of and damage to the bones found at Zhoukoudian with that seen in contemporary carnivore dens, Boaz and Ciochon (2001) have suggested that much of the materials in the cave likely accumulated through the activities of a giant extinct hyena. Indeed, they hypothesize that most of the *H. erectus* remains, too, are the food refuse of hyaenid meals!

Boaz and his associates do recognize that the tools in the cave and possibly cut marks on some of the animal bones do provide evidence of hominid activities at Zhoukoudian. They also recognize that more detailed analysis is required to test their hypotheses and to "determine the nature and scope" of the *H. erectus* presence at Zhoukoudian.

Probably the most intriguing archaeological aspect of the presumed hominid behavior at Zhoukoudian has been the long-held assumption that *H. erectus* deliberately utilized fire inside the cave. The technological control of fire was one of the major cultural breakthroughs of all prehistory. By providing warmth, a means of cooking, an aid to further modify tools, and so forth (see Box 11–1), controlled fire would have been a giant technological innovation. While some potential early African sites have been suggested as giving evidence of hominid control of fire, it has long been concluded that the first *definite* evidence of hominid fire use comes from Zhoukoudian.

Now, new evidence has radically altered this assumption. Much more detailed excavations at Zhoukoudian were carried out in 1996 and 1997 by biologist Steve Weiner and colleagues. These researchers also carefully analyzed the soil samples they collected for distinctive chemical signatures (which would show whether fire had occurred in the cave) (Weiner et al., 1998). Weiner and his colleagues found that only rarely was any burnt bone found associated with tools, and in most cases the burning appeared to have taken place *after* fossilization (i.e., they were not cooked). Moreover, the "ash" layers mentioned earlier are not ash at all, but rather naturally accumulated organic sediment. This last conclusion was derived from chemical testing showing no sign whatsoever of wood burning inside the cave. Finally, the "hearths" that have figured so prominently in archaeological reconstructions of the fire control at this site where apparently not hearths at all. They simply are round depressions formed in the past by water collecting when the cave was more open to the elements.

Indeed, another provisional interpretation of the cave's geology suggests that the cave did not open in the manner of habitation sites, but had access only through a vertical shaft, leading archaeologist Alison Brooks to remark, "It wouldn't have been a shelter, it would have been a trap" (quoted in Wuethrich, 1998).

These serious doubts regarding control of fire, coupled with the suggestive evidence of bone accumulation by carnivores, have led anthropologists Noel Boaz and Russell Ciochon to conclude, "Zhoukoudian cave was neither hearth nor home" (Boaz and Ciochon, 2001).

BOX 11–1 DIGGING DEEPER

The Control of Fire

An important distinction exists between the *making* of fire and the *use* of fire captured from natural sources. Some very ancient methods that could have been used deliberately to make fire might have included striking hard rocks together or rubbing wood together to create sparks through friction. Without such technological innovations, earlier hominids would have been limited to obtaining and transporting fire from natural sources, such as lightning strikes and geothermal localities.

The archaeological evidence, however, may never be sufficiently complete to allow this distinction to be made with much precision. Nevertheless, *at minimum*, the consistent use of fire would have been a major technological breakthrough and could have had potentially marked influence on hominid biological evolution as well. For example, as a result of cooking, food items would have been more tender; thus, chewing stresses would have been reduced, perhaps leading to selection for reduced size of the dentition.

It is possible that australopithecines took advantage of and used naturally occurring fire, but the evidence relating to the use of fire is not always easy to interpret. At open-air sites, for example, remains suggesting an association between hominids and burning may be found. However, ashes may already have been blown away, and stones and bones blackened by fire could be the result of a natural brush fire, as could charcoal and baked earth. Furthermore, remains found on the surface of a site might be the result of a natural fire that occurred long after the hominids had left.

There are several possible advantages that controlled use of fire may have provided to earlier hominids, including:

1. Warmth
2. Cooking meat and/or plant foods, thus breaking down fibers and, in the case of many plants, neutralizing toxins
3. Fire-hardening wood, such as the end of a spear
4. Facilitating the predictable flaking of certain stone materials, thus aiding in the production of stone tools
5. Chasing competing predators (such as bears) from caves and keeping dangerous animals at bay
6. Providing illumination in caves and, more fundamentally, extending usable light into the night

This last implication of human control of fire may have had a profound effect on human sleep cycles and with it alterations in activity patterns, neurological functioning, and hormonal balance. In fact, recent experiments have suggested that humans still today can readily (and comfortably) adjust to "natural" light/dark cycles with periods of inactivity of up to 14 hours (thus simulating winter conditions *prior* to the systematic control of fire).

Other Chinese Sites

More work has been done at Zhoukoudian than at any other Chinese site. Nevertheless, there are other hominid sites worth noting. Three of the more important sites, besides Zhoukoudian, are Chenjiawo and Gongwangling (both in Lantian County and sometimes referred to as Lantian) and Longtandong Cave in Hexian County (often referred to as the Hexian find) (Table 11–1).

At Chenjiawo, an almost complete mandible containing several teeth was found in 1963. It is quite similar to those from Zhoukoudian but has been provisionally dated at about 650,000 y.a. If the dating is correct, this specimen would be older than the Beijing material. The following year, a partial cranium was discovered at Gongwangling, not far from Chenjiawo. Provisionally dated to as much as 1.15 m.y.a. (Etler and Tianyuan, 1994), the Gongwangling specimen may be the oldest Chinese *Homo erectus* fossil yet known.

Perhaps the most significant find was made in 1980 at Longtandong Cave, where remains of several individuals were recovered. One of the specimens is a well-

Since controlling fire is so important to humans, it would be useful to know who tamed the wild flames and when, where, and how they did it. With that knowledge we could learn much more about the culture of our ancient ancestors and their evolution. Archaeologists are not certain who the first fire makers were. Two of the earliest presumed examples of fire use come from Africa, and both have been suggested as indicating deliberate hominid pyrotechnics *prior* to 1 m.y.a. First, at Chesowanja in southern Kenya, patches of burned clay dated at 1.4 m.y.a. were found in association with stone tools. John Gowlett and his colleague, Jack Harris, have suggested that the burned clay is the residue of ancient campfires. Second, recent excavations from upper levels at Swartkrans in South Africa by C. K. Brain and Andrew Sillen have recovered many pieces of burnt bone, again in association with stone tools dated at 1.3–1 m.y.a. (For a further discussion of Swartkrans, see pp. 242–247.) Both of these possible occurrences of hominid control of fire in Africa are thought to be associated with *Homo erectus*. However, neither of the early African contexts has yet to fully convince other experts.

True caves* may be a more probable source for finding human-made fire, because caves, except at the entrance, are damp, very dark, and impossible for habitation without light. Also, by the time humans began to occupy caves, they may have invented a method of making fire. It is possible, of course, to carry a natural fire into a cave, which is another snag in determining whether the fire was deliberately made or natural.

Probably the most famous cave site is Zhoukoudian (discussed in this chapter), where both Chinese and Western archaeologists have been working for more than 70 years. Evidence of supposed fire is abundant, but the evidence (such as charred animal bones, layers of ash, charcoal, and burned stone artifacts) has led to differing interpretations by archaeologists (see discussion in text).

There appears to be evidence of fire at other open *H. erectus* sites in China and several caves in Europe, provisionally dated to about 300,000 years ago. They have yielded evidence of fire possibly made by archaic *H. sapiens*. But again, not all archaeologists are persuaded that humans were responsible.

Other prehistorians are sure that Neandertals (discussed in Chapter 12), who built hearths, were the first to make fire toward the end of the Middle Pleistocene (circa 125,000 y.a.). A deliberately built hearth is probably the best evidence for human-controlled fire. Ancient hearths are usually built with stone cobbles arranged in a circular or oval shape to constrain the fire. The presence of numerous hearths at a site (like finding a box of matches near a fire) tends to serve as proof that the fires were probably started by humans. It is the absence of identifiable hearths that is so troublesome at the older sites and which immediately signals a doubt that the fire was made (or even systematically used) by hominids. It will take the development of carefully constructed interpretive techniques to overcome the difficulties of solving the case of the first significant controllers of fire.

*Swartkrans was not a cave during the time of hominid archaeological accumulation, but has been shown to have been a natural fissure into which animals and other objects fell.

preserved cranium (with a cranial capacity of about 1,025 cm^3) lacking much of its base. Dated roughly at 250,000 y.a., it is not surprising that this Hexian cranium displays several advanced features. The cranial constriction, for example, is not as pronounced as in earlier forms, and certain temporal and occipital characteristics are "best compared with the later forms of *H. erectus* at Zhoukoudian" (Wu and Dong, 1985, p. 87).

In June 1993, Li Tianyuan and Dennis Etler reported that two relatively complete skulls were discovered in 1989 at a hominid site in Yunxian County. The date given for the site is 350,000 y.a., which, if correct, would make these the most complete crania of this great antiquity in China (Fig 11–12).

The Yunxian crania are both large and robust, considerably exceeding in size those from Zhoukoudian. In general, the Yunxian individuals fit within *Homo erectus*, but in the facial region especially they also show some interesting advanced features. A few of these features suggest to some scholars "a mid-facial morphology similar to that of modern Asians" (Etler and Tianyuan, 1994, p. 668).

TABLE 11–1 *H. erectus* Fossils from China

Designation	Site	Age* (Years Ago)	Material	Cranial Capacity (cm3)	Year Found	Remarks
Hexian	Longtandong Cave, Anhui	250,000	Calvarium, skull fragments, mandible fragments, isolated teeth	1,025	1980–81	First skull found in southern or southwest China
Zhoukoudian (Peking)	Zhoukoudian Cave, Beijing	500,000–200,000	5 adult crania, skull fragments, facial bones, isolated teeth, postcranial pieces (40+ individuals)	850–1,225; avg: 1,010	1927–ongoing	Most famous fossils in China and some of the most famous in the world
Yunxian	Longgudong Cave, Hubei	?500,000	Isolated teeth		1976–82	
Yunxian	Quyuanhekou	350,000	2 mostly complete (but crushed) crania	Undetermined	1989	The most complete crania from China, but still requiring much restoration
Lantian	Chenjiawo, Lantian	650,000	Mandible		1963	Old female
Lantian	Gongwangling, Lantian	1,150,000–800,000	Calvarium, facial bones	780	1964	Female over 30; most ancient *H. erectus* found so far in China

Sources: Atlas of Primitive Man in China (1980); Lisowski, 1984; Pope, 1984; Wu and Dong, 1985; Etler and Tianyuan, 1994.

*These are best estimates; authorities differ.

Unfortunately, both skulls are still covered with a hard calcareous matrix, and critics argue that until the skulls are cleaned and the crushed parts properly put together, it is too early to make accurate assessments. In any case, these Yunxian crania will ultimately provide considerable data to help clarify hominid evolution in China and perhaps elsewhere in the Old World as well.

A number of archaeological sites have been excavated in China, and early stone tools have been found in numerous locations in widely separated areas. At present, there is little reason to believe that *H. erectus* culture in these provinces differed much from that described at Zhoukoudian.

The Asian crania from both Java and China are mainly Middle Pleistocene fossils and share many similar features, which may be explained by *H. erectus* migration from Java to China about 800,000 years ago. African *H. erectus* forms are generally older than most Asian forms and are not as similar to them as Asian forms (i.e., from Java and China) are to each other.

FIGURE 11–12

(a) EV 9002 (Yunxian, China). The skull is in better shape than its companion, and its lateral view clearly displays features characteristic of *H. erectus*: flattened vault, receding forehead (frontal bone), angulated occiput, and supraorbital torus. (b) EV 9001 (Yunxian). Unfortunately, the skull was crushed, but it preserves some lateral facial structures absent in EV 9002.

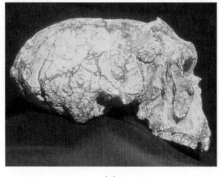

(a)

(b)

East Africa

Olduvai   Back in 1960, Louis Leakey unearthed a fossil skull at Olduvai (OH 9) that he identified as *H. erectus*. Skull OH 9 from Upper Bed II is dated at 1.4 m.y.a. and preserves a massive cranium but is faceless except for a bit of nose below the supraorbital torus. Estimated at 1,067 cm^3, the cranial capacity of OH 9 is the largest of all the African *Homo erectus* specimens. The browridge is huge, the largest known for any hominid in both thickness and projection, but the vault walls are thin. This latter characteristic of fairly thin cranial vault bones is seen in most east African *H. erectus* specimens, and in this respect, they differ from Asian *H. erectus* (in which cranial vaults are thick).

East Turkana   Some 400 miles north of Olduvai Gorge, on the northern boundary of Kenya, is Lake Turkana. Explored by Richard Leakey and colleagues since 1969, the eastern shore of the lake has been a virtual gold mine for australopithecine, early *Homo*, and *H. erectus* fossil remains.

The most significant *H. erectus* discovery from East Turkana is ER 3733, an almost complete skull lacking a mandible (Fig. 11–13). Discovered in 1974, the specimen has been given a firm date of close to 1.8 m.y.a. The cranial capacity is estimated at 848 cm^3, at the lower end of the range for *H. erectus*, but this is not surprising considering its early date. The cranium generally resembles Asian *H. erectus* in many features (but with some important differences, discussed shortly).

Not many tools have been found at *H. erectus* sites in East Turkana. Oldowan types of flakes, cobbles, and core tools have been found, and the introduction of **Acheulian** tools about 1.4 m.y.a. replaced the Oldowan tradition.

West Turkana*   In August 1984, Kamoya Kimeu (see p. 282), a member of Richard Leakey's team, further added to his reputation as an outstanding fossil hunter when he discovered a small piece of skull near the base camp on the west side of Lake Turkana. Leakey and his colleague, Alan Walker of Pennsylvania State University, excavated the site known as Nariokotome in 1984 and again in 1985 (see Box 11–2 on p. 274).

The dig was a resounding success. The workers unearthed the most complete *H. erectus* skeleton yet found (Fig. 11–14). Known properly as WT 15000, the all but complete skeleton includes facial bones and most of the postcranial bones, a rare finding indeed for *H. erectus*, since these particular elements are scarce at other *H. erectus* sites.

Another remarkable feature of the find is its age. Its dating is based on the chronometric dates of the geological formation in which the site is located and is set at about 1.6 million years. The skeleton is that of a boy about 12 years of age and 5 feet 3 inches tall. Had he grown to maturity, his height, it is estimated, would have been more than 6 feet, taller than *H. erectus* was heretofore thought to have been. The postcranial bones appear to be quite similar, though not identical, to those of modern humans. The cranial capacity of WT 15000 is estimated at 880 cm^3; brain growth was nearly complete, and it is estimated that the boy's adult cranial capacity would have been approximately 909 cm^3 (Begun and Walker, 1993).

Ethiopia   In southern Ethiopia, the 1991 Paleoanthropological Inventory of Ethiopia team of international scientists discovered a site, Konso-Gardula (KGA), containing a remarkable abundance of Acheulian tools, a hominid upper third molar, and an almost complete mandible with several cheek teeth. Both specimens are attributed to *H. erectus* "because they lack specialized characteristics of robust *Australopithecus*" (Asfaw et al., 1992).

The mandible is robust and is dated to about 1.3 m.y.a. The Acheulian stone tools, mainly bifaces and picks, are made of quartz, quartzite, and volcanic rock.

---

*WT is the symbol for West Turkana, that is, the west side of Lake Turkana. The east side is designated by ER—East Rudolf. Rudolf was the former name of the lake. (See p. 236.)

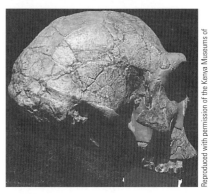

FIGURE 11–13
ER 3733, the most complete East Turkana *H. erectus* cranium.

Reproduced with permission of the Kenya Museums of Natural History

Acheulian
(ash'-oo-lay-en) Pertaining to a stone tool industry of the Lower and Middle Pleistocene characterized by a large proportion of bifacial tools (flaked on both sides). Acheulian tool kits are very common in Africa, southwest Asia, and western Europe, but are nearly absent elsewhere. (Also spelled "Acheulean.")

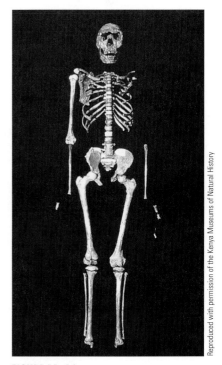

Reproduced with permission of the Kenya Museums of Natural History

FIGURE 11–14
WT 15000 from Nariokotome, Kenya: the most complete *H. erectus* specimen yet found.

BOX 11-2   DIGGING DEEPER

The Nariokotome Skeleton— A Boy for All Seasons

The discovery of the spectacularly well-preserved skeleton from Nariokotome on the west side of Lake Turkana has allowed considerable new insight into key anatomical features of *Homo erectus*. Since its recovery in 1984 and 1985, detailed studies have been undertaken, and recent publication of the results (Walker, 1993; Walker and Leakey, 1993) have allowed some initial conclusions to be drawn. Moreover, the extraordinary quality of the remains has also allowed anthropologists to speculate on some major behavioral traits of *H. erectus* in Africa (and, more generally, of the entire species).

The remains comprise an almost complete skeleton, lacking only most of the small bones of the hands and feet and the unfused ends of long bones. This degree of preservation is remarkable, and this individual is the most complete skeleton of *any* fossil hominid yet found from before about 100,000 y.a. (after which deliberate burial facilitated much improved preservation). This superior preservation may well have been aided by rapid sedimentation in what is thought to have been an ancient shallow swamp. Once the individual died, his skeleton would have been quickly covered up, but some disturbance and breakage nevertheless did occur—from chewing by catfish, but most especially from trampling by large animals wading in the swamp 1.6 m.y.a.

As we have discussed, the individual was not fully grown when he died. His age (11 to 13 years—Walker, 1993) is determined by the stage of dental eruption (his permanent canines are not yet erupted) and by union of the ends of long bones. Moreover, as we have noted, this young *Homo erectus* male was quite tall (5 feet 3 inches), and using modern growth curve approximations, his adult stature would have been over 6 feet had he lived to full maturity.

More than simply tall, the body proportions of this boy's skeleton are intriguing. Reconstructions suggest that he had a linear build with long appendages, thus conforming to predictions of *Allen's rule* for inhabitants of hot climates (see Chapter 5). Further extrapolating from this observation, Alan Walker also suggests that *H. erectus* must have had a high sweating capacity to dissipate heat (in the modern human fashion). (See pp. 97–98 for a discussion of heat adaptation in humans.)

The boy's limb proportions suggest a quite warm mean annual temperature (90°F/30°C) in East Africa 1.6 m.y.a. Paleoecological reconstructions confirm this estimate of tropical conditions (much like the climate today in northern Kenya).

Another fascinating anatomical clue is seen in the beautifully preserved vertebrae. The opening through which the spinal cord passes (the neural canal; see Appendix A) is quite small in the thoracic elements. The possible behavioral corollaries of this reduced canal (as compared to modern *H. sapiens*) are also intriguing. Ann MacLarnan (1993) has proposed that the reduced canal argues for reduced size of the spinal cord, which in turn may suggest less control of the muscles between the ribs (the intercostals). One major function of these muscles is the precise control of breathing during human speech. From these data and inferences, Alan Walker has concluded that the Nariokotome youth (and *H. erectus* in general) was not fully capable of human articulate speech. (As an argument regarding language potential, this conclusion will no doubt spark considerable debate.)

A final interesting feature can be seen in the pelvis of this adolescent skeleton. It is very narrow and is thus correlated with a narrow bony birth canal. Walker (1993) again draws a behavioral inference from this anatomical feature. He estimates that a newborn with a cranial capacity no greater than a mere 200 cm^3 could have passed through this pelvis. As we showed elsewhere, the adult cranial capacity estimate for this individual was slightly greater than 900 cm^3—thus arguing for significant postnatal growth of the brain (exceeding 75 percent of its eventual size, again mirroring the modern human pattern). Walker speculates that this slow neural expansion (compared to other primates) leads to delayed development of motor skills and thus a prolonged period of infant/child dependency (what Walker terms "secondary altriciality"). Of course, as with other speculative behavioral scenarios, critics will no doubt find holes in this reconstruction. One point you should immediately note is that this specimen is the immature pelvis of a male. Thus, the crucial dimensions of an adult female *H. erectus* pelvis remain unknown. Nevertheless, they could not have departed too dramatically from the dimensions seen at Nariokotome—unless one accepts an extreme degree of sexual dimorphism in this species.

Summary of East African *H. erectus*

The *Homo erectus* remains from East Africa show several differences from the fossil samples from Java and China. The African specimens (as exemplified by ER 3733, presumably a female, and WT 15000, presumably a male) are not as strongly buttressed in the cranium (by supraorbital or nuchal tori) and do not have such thick cranial bones as seen in Asian representatives of *H. erectus*. These differences, as well as others observed in the postcranial skeleton, have so impressed some researchers that they in fact argue for a *separate* species status for the African *H. erectus* remains (as distinct from the Asian samples). Bernard Wood, the leading proponent of this view, has suggested that the name *Homo ergaster* be used for the African remains; *H. erectus* would then be reserved solely for the Asian material (Wood, 1991). In addition, the very early dates now postulated for the dispersal of *H. erectus* into Asia (Java) would argue for a more than 1-million-year separate history for Asian and African populations.

Nevertheless, this species division has not been generally accepted, and the current consensus (reflected in this text) is to continue to refer to all these hominids as *Homo erectus* (Kramer, 1993; Conroy, 1997; Rightmire, 1998). As with the Plio-Pleistocene samples, we accordingly will have to accommodate a considerable degree of intraspecific variation within this species. Wood has concluded, regarding variation within such a broadly defined *H. erectus* species, "It is a species which manifestly embraces an unusually wide degree of variation in both the cranium and postcranial skeleton" (Wood, 1992a, p. 329).

South Africa

A mandible was found among fossil remains collected at Swartkrans in South Africa in the 1940s and 1950s. This specimen, SK 15, was originally assigned to "*Telanthropus capensis*," but is now placed within the genus *Homo* (there is, however, disagreement about its species designation). Rightmire (1990) suggests that it may be linked with *Homo erectus*, but others are not certain. If it is *H. erectus*, it would demonstrate that *H. erectus* inhabited South Africa as well as the other regions documented by other more complete fossil finds.

North Africa

With evidence from China and Java, it appears clear that *H. erectus* populations, with superior tools and weapons and presumably greater intelligence than their predecessors, had vastly expanded their habitat beyond that of early hominids. The earliest evidence for *H. erectus*, 1.8–1.6 m.y.a., comes from East Africa and Java and about 1 million years later in China. Early dispersal of *H. erectus* to Europe (prior to 1 m.y.a.) may also have occurred. It is not surprising, therefore, that *H. erectus* migrations would have taken them to northwest Africa as well.

North African remains, consisting almost entirely of mandibles (or mandible fragments) and a partial parietal bone, have been found at Ternifine (now Tighenif), Algeria, and in Morocco, at Sidi Abderrahman and Thomas Quarries. The three Ternifine mandibles and the parietal fragment are quite robust and have been dated to about 700,000 y.a. The Moroccan material is not as robust as Ternifine and may be a bit younger, at 500,000 years. In addition, an interesting cranium was found in a quarry north of Salé, in Morocco. The walls of the skull vault are thick, and several other features resemble those of *H. erectus*. Some features suggest that Salé is *H. sapiens*, but a date of 400,000 y.a. and an estimated cranial capacity of about 900 cm^3 throw doubt on that interpretation.

Europe

The situation in Europe during the Pleistocene appears especially complex. With accumulating evidence suggesting dispersal of the first hominids to Europe in the Lower Pleistocene (i.e., prior to 700,000 y.a.), there is a growing realization that some of the earliest European hominids should perhaps be included within the species *H. erectus* (particularly the remains from Dmanisi and Ceprano, since the morphology of these specimens suggests at least a provisional assignment to *H. erectus*; see p. 259). The remains from Atapuerca, in Spain (Gran Dolina site), are not as clearly similar to *Homo erectus*, and Spanish researchers have suggested placing them in a completely different species of hominid ("*Homo antecessor*"). Clearly, such an interpretation will require considerably more evaluation (and verification) before it can become widely accepted. We should note that all of this early Pleistocene European fossil material is both fragmentary and quite recently discovered. Thus, all current interpretations are, for the moment, both tentative and controversial.

After about 400,000 y.a., the European fossil hominid record becomes increasingly abundant. Nevertheless, interpretations relating to the proper taxonomic assessment of many of these remains have been debated, in some cases for decades. In recent years, several of these somewhat later (i.e., Middle Pleistocene) specimens have been placed within a grouping of early *Homo sapiens* referred to as "archaic *Homo sapiens*." Needless to say, not everyone agrees. These enigmatic archaic *H. sapiens* specimens are discussed in Chapter 12. A time line for the *H. erectus* discoveries discussed in this chapter as well as other finds of more uncertain status is shown in Figure 11–15.

Technological and Population Trends in the Middle Pleistocene

Technological Trends

Many researchers have noted the remarkable stasis of the physical and cultural characteristics of *Homo erectus* populations, which seemed to change so little in the more than 1.5 million years of their existence. There is, however, dispute on this point. Some scholars (Rightmire, 1981) see almost no detectable changes in cranial dimensions over more than 1 million years of *H. erectus* evolution. Other paleoanthropologists (e.g., Wolpoff, 1984), who use different methodologies to date and subdivide their samples, draw a different conclusion, seeing some significant long-term morphological trends. Accepting a moderate position, we can postulate that there were some changes: The brain of later *H. erectus* was somewhat larger, the nose more protrusive, and the body not as robust as in earlier forms. Moreover, there were modifications in stone tool technology.

Expansion of the brain presumably enabled *H. erectus* to develop a more sophisticated tool kit than seen among earlier hominids. The important change in this kit was a core worked on both sides, called a *biface* (known widely as a hand axe or cleaver; Fig 11–16). The biface had a flatter core than the roundish earlier Oldowan pebble tool. And, probably even more important, this *core* tool was obviously a target design, that is, the main goal of the toolmaker. This greater focus and increased control enabled the stoneknapper to produce sharper, straighter edges, resulting in a more efficient implement. This Acheulian stone tool became standardized as the basic *H. erectus* all-purpose tool (with only minor modification) for more than a million years. It served to cut, scrape, pound, dig, and more—a most useful tool that has been found in Africa, parts of Asia, and later in western Europe. It should also be noted that Acheulian tool kits also included several types of small tools (Fig. 11–17).

For many years, it has been thought that a cultural "divide" separated the Old World—with Acheulian technology found *only* in Africa, southwest Asia, and western Europe, but not elsewhere (i.e., absent in eastern Europe and most of Asia). However, newly reported excavations from more than 20 sites in the Bose Basin of southern China have forced reevaluation of this hypothesis (Yamei et al., 2000).

As noted, the most distinctive tools of the Acheulian are bifaces, and they are the very tools thought lacking throughout most of the Pleistocene in eastern Europe and most of Asia. The new archaeological assemblages from southern China

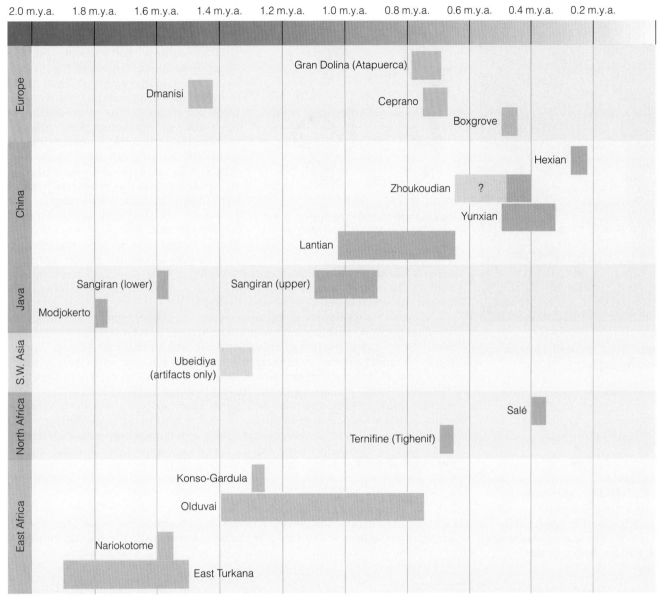

Note: Most dates are only imprecise estimates. However, the dates from East African sites are chronometrically determined and are thus much more secure. In addition, the early dates from Java are also radiometric and are gaining wide acceptance, although some researchers (e.g., Wolpoff, 1999) suggest that they are not secure and may be later than shown.

are securely dated at abut 800,000 y.a. and contain numerous bifaces, very similar to contemporaneous Acheulian bifaces from Africa (see Figures 11–16 and 11–18b). It now appears likely that cultural traditions relating to stone tool technology were largely equivalent over the *full* geographical range of *H. erectus* and contemporaries.

While geographical distinctions are not so obvious, temporal changes in tool technology are evident. In early days, toolmakers employed a stone hammer (simply an ovoid-shaped stone about the size of an egg or a bit larger) to remove flakes from the core, thus leaving deep scars. Later, they used other materials, such as wood and bone. They learned to use these new materials as soft hammers, which gave them more control over flaking, thus leaving shallow scars, sharper edges, and a more symmetrical form. Toward the end of the Acheulian industry, toolmakers blocked out a core with stone hammers and then switched to wood or bone for refining the edges. This technique produced more elegant-appearing and pear-shaped implements.

FIGURE 11–15
Time line for *Homo erectus* discoveries and other contemporary hominids. Note that most dates are approximations.

FIGURE 11–16
Acheulian biface ("hand axe"), a basic tool of the Acheulian tradition.

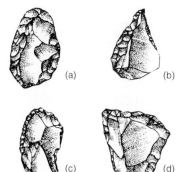

FIGURE 11–17
Small tools of the Acheulian industry. (a) Side scraper. (b) Point. (c) End scraper. (d) Burin.

Evidence of butchering is widespread at *H. erectus* sites, and in the past, such evidence has been cited in arguments for consistent hunting. For example, at the Olorgesailie site in Kenya (see Fig. 11–18), dated at approximately 800,000 y.a., thousands of Acheulian hand axes have been recovered in association with remains of large animals, including giant baboons (now extinct). However, the assumption of consistent hunting has been challenged, especially by archaeologists who argue that the evidence does not prove the hunting hypothesis. Instead, they suggest that *H. erectus* was primarily a scavenger, a hypothesis that also has not yet been proved conclusively. We thus discuss *H. erectus* as a potential hunter *and* scavenger. It is crucial to remember, too, that *gathering* of wild plant foods was also practiced by *H. erectus* groups. Indeed, probably a majority of the calories they consumed came from such gathering activities.

Moreover, as we have seen, the mere *presence* of animal bones at archaeological sites does not prove that hominids were killing animals or even necessarily exploiting meat. Indeed, as was the case in the earlier South African sites (discussed in Chapter 10), the hominid remains themselves may have been the meal refuse of large carnivores! Thus, in making interpretations of early hominid sites, we must consider a variety of alternatives. As Stanford University archaeologist Richard Klein has concluded regarding Middle Pleistocene sites, the interpretations are far from clear: "In sum, the available data do not allow us to isolate the relative roles of humans, carnivores, and factors such as starvation, accidents, and stream action in creating bone assemblages. . . . Certainly, as presently understood, the sites do not tell us how successful or effective *Homo erectus* was at obtaining meat" (1989, p. 221).

Population Trends

One of the fascinating qualities of *H. erectus* was a penchant for travel. From the relatively close confines of East Africa, *H. erectus* dispersed widely in the Old World. By

FIGURE 11–18
(a) A Middle Pleistocene butchering site at Olorgesailie, Kenya, excavated by Louis and Mary Leakey, who had the catwalk built for observers. (b) A close-up of the Acheulian tools, mainly hand axes, found at the site.

(a)

(b)

the time *H. sapiens* appeared a million or more years later, *H. erectus* had migrated to South and North Africa. And even earlier, some groups had moved from Africa to Asia and perhaps to Europe as well.

The life of hunter-scavengers (and still, no doubt, *primarily* gatherers) was nomadic, and the woodland and savanna that covered the southern tier of Asia would have been an excellent environment for *H. erectus* (as it was similar to the econiche of their African ancestors). As the population grew, small groups budded off and moved on to find their own resource areas. This process, repeated again and again, led *H. erectus* east, crossing to Java, arriving there, it seems, as early as the most ancient known sites in East Africa itself.

Once in Java, it had been assumed that *H. erectus* would have found it impossible to venture farther south or east, since during the Pleistocene, deep water channels presumably separated Java completely from more southerly islands and Australia. However, recent reinterpretation (and firmer chronometric dates) of stone tools found on the island of Flores, 375 miles east of Java, has prompted some paleoanthropologists to reconsider this assumption (Gibbons, 1998). With a suggested date of 750,000 y.a. for these tools, it raises a most unexpected possibility: Could ancient *H. erectus* at this *very* early period construct ocean-going vessels (rafts?) that could navigate over deep, fast-moving waters?

While initial dating of the Flores stone materials appears reasonably good, the conclusion that the finds *prove* such seemingly advanced capabilities for *H. erectus* is not yet generally accepted. A number of troublesome issues remain to be resolved, the first being whether the lithic materials from Flores are *deliberate* tools or are simply naturally fractured rock. This latter possibility would argue against *H. erectus* (or any other hominid) having expanded south or east beyond Java at such an early date. Of course, the most unambiguous evidence would be fossil discoveries of *H. erectus* itself.

When we look back at the evolution of *H. erectus*, we realize how significant this early human's achievements were. It was *H. erectus* who increased in body size with more efficient bipedalism; who embraced culture wholeheartedly as a strategy of adaptation; whose brain was reshaped and increased in size to within *H. sapiens* range; who became a more efficient scavenger and likely hunter with greater dependence on meat; and who apparently established more permanent bases. In short, it was *H. erectus*, committed to a cultural way of life, who transformed hominid evolution to human evolution; or as Foley states, "The appearance and expansion of *H. erectus* represented a major change in adaptive strategy that influenced the subsequent process and pattern of human evolution" (1991, p. 425).

SUMMARY

Homo erectus remains are found in geological contexts dating from about 1.8 million to about 200,000 years ago (and perhaps much later), a period of more than 1.5 million years. The first finds were made by Dubois in Java, and later discoveries came from China and Africa. Differences from early *Homo* are notable in *H. erectus'* larger brain, taller stature, robust build, and changes in facial structure and cranial buttressing.

The long period of *H. erectus'* existence was marked by a remarkably uniform technology over space and time. Nevertheless, compared to earlier hominids, *H. erectus* and contemporaries introduced more sophisticated tools and probably ate novel and/or differently processed foods, using these new tools and at later sites perhaps fire as well. They were also able to move into different environments and successfully adapt to new conditions.

It is generally assumed that some *H. erectus* populations evolved to *H. sapiens*, since many fossils, such as Ngandong (and others discussed in Chapter 12), display both *H. erectus* and *H. sapiens* features. There remain questions about *H. erectus* behavior (e.g., did they hunt?) and about evolution to *H. sapiens* (was it gradual or rapid, and which *H. erectus* populations contributed genes to *H. sapiens*?). The search for answers continues.

QUESTIONS FOR REVIEW

1. Describe the Pleistocene in terms of (a) relationship to glacial sequences and (b) the dating of fossil hominids.
2. Describe *Homo erectus*. How is *H. erectus* anatomically different from early *Homo*? From *H. sapiens*?
3. In what areas of the world have *Homo erectus* fossils been found?
4. In comparing *H. erectus* with earlier hominids, why is it important to specify which comparative sample is being used?
5. What was the intellectual climate in Europe in the latter half of the nineteenth century, especially concerning human evolution?
6. Why do you think there was so much opposition to Dubois' interpretation of the hominid fossils he found in Java?
7. Why do you think Zhoukoudian *H. erectus* was enthusiastically accepted, whereas the Javanese fossils were not?
8. Describe the way of life of *H. erectus* at Zhoukoudian as depicted by earlier researchers. What disagreements have been voiced about this conjecture?
9. *H. erectus* has been called the first human. Why?
10. What is the *H. erectus* evidence from Africa, and what questions of human evolution does the evidence raise?
11. Can you suggest any reason why the earliest remains of *H. erectus* have come from East Africa?
12. *H. erectus* migrated to various points in Africa and vast distances to eastern Asia and elsewhere. What does this tell you about the species?
13. What kinds of stone tools have been found at *H. erectus* sites?

SUGGESTED FURTHER READING

Day, Michael. 1986. *Guide to Fossil Man.* Chicago: University of Chicago Press.
Lewin, Roger. 1998. *Principles of Human Evolution: A Core Textbook.* New York: Blackwell Science.
Rightmire, G. P. 1990. *The Evolution of* Homo erectus. New York: Cambridge University Press.
Shapiro, Harry L. 1980. *Peking Man.* New York: Simon & Schuster.
Walker, Alan, and Richard Leakey (eds). 1993. *The Nariokotome* Homo erectus *Skeleton.* Cambridge, MA: Harvard University Press.
Wolpoff, Milford. 1984. "Evolution in *Homo erectus*: The Question of Stasis." *Paleobiology* 10: 389–406.

RESOURCES ON THE INTERNET

 Wadsworth Anthropology Resource Center
http://anthropology.wadsworth.com

The companion website for this text includes a range of enrichment material focused on the chapter's topic. While online you can enhance your understanding of the chapter by exploring one of the several additional Internet Exercises, by researching topics, and by accessing full articles on InfoTrac College Edition. You can also reinforce the concepts by taking online practice exams.

Internet Exercises

Visit The Evidence for Human Evolution in China (**http://www.cruzio.com/ ~cscp/index.htm**). There is a great deal of information on this site about *Homo erectus* and early *Homo sapiens* in China. Go to the Interactive Timeline to view summary evidence for human evolution in China. You can click on any of the individual pictures to get more information on that specimen. Choose one feature of morphology—brain size, cranial shape, facial shape, dentition, etc.—and go through the time line. Write a short paper on how that feature of the anatomy changes through time, based on the evidence presented here.

InfoTrac College Edition

http://www.infotrac-college.com/wadsworth

Using PowerTrac search InfoTrac College Edition for news on *Homo erectus*. Choose one story, read, and write a page about the contribution of this piece of research to what we know about early hominid evolution. Does this article provide any information that differs from that in the textbook? If so, write a summary of these differences.

PHOTO ESSAY

Paleoanthropology

As we discussed throughout Chapters 9 through 11, paleoanthropology is a multidisciplinary science, drawing on the skills of many experts. Because sites are often found in remote, largely inaccessible locales, their discovery has traditionally been arduous and time-consuming. In the last decade, however, sophisticated use of satellite imaging has greatly aided the search for likely new areas containing evidence of human origins.

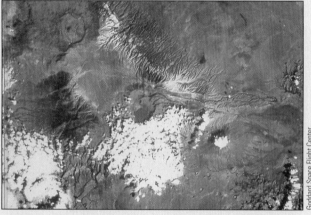

FIGURE 1
A satellite photo of geological exposures in northern Tanzania, near Olduvai Gorge. The mountainous regions are part of the escarpment of the Rift Valley. The lake has formed inside a volcanic crater.

FIGURE 2
The field camp at Hadar, in Ethiopia. A paleoanthropological project requires a large crew, all of whom must be supplied with food, water, and other basics. Members of the local Afar tribe, who serve as guards, are shown in the foreground.

FIGURE 3
The Kenyan field crew at Lake Turkana, Kenya. Kamoya Kimeu (driving) has probably been the most successful fossil discoverer in East Africa, responsible for dozens of discoveries.

FIGURE 4
Archaeologist Erella Hovers, during a recent field season at Hadar, carefully examines the surface of the AL 333 site. Up to 13 hominid individuals were discovered here in 1975. Work at this site is aimed at recovering more fragments of these individuals.

After a potentially productive region has been identified, many long hours of ground surveying are required to find the fossils themselves. In most cases, and with any good fortune at all, numerous remains of nonhominid animals (such as elephant, pig, and antelope) will be found. However, the discovery of hominid fossils themselves is always a problematic undertaking. Thus, a truly successful paleoanthropological project

FIGURE 5
When large areas of geological exposures are surveyed, geological and paleontological localities are mapped.

FIGURE 6
If an area is surveyed and any fossils are seen on the surface, very precise searching is done.

FIGURE 7
It takes a well-trained eye to locate fossils eroding out of old land surfaces. Shown here is part of a hominid maxilla (upper jaw) found at Olduvai in 1987.

Paleoanthropology (continued)

(i.e., one that attracts public attention and funding) requires not just good science, but a considerable degree of luck as well.

Fossils are most often found scattered on the ground surface as they erode out from sediments (through the combined action of wind, rain, and gravity). When fossils are located, their precise position is recorded.

FIGURE 8
As fragments of a hominid find are collected, each location where a piece is discovered is marked with a flag. Here, Yoel Rak of Tel Aviv University and the Institute of Human Origins flags the precise location for each fragment of the *Australopithecus afarensis* cranium discovered at Hadar in 1992.

Institute of Human Origins, photo by Don Johanson

FIGURE 9
Even the most careful searching and hand sifting cannot locate all the fragments of a fossil. To retrieve the very small fragments, the surrounding soil is screened through a fine mesh and then sifted through again by hand.

Institute of Human Origins, photo by Don Johanson

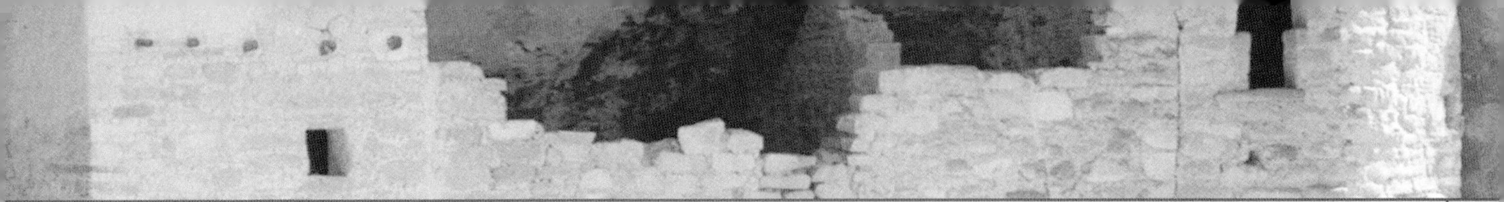

In addition to recovering fossils, paleoanthropologists also collect varied geological and pollen samples (for dating and paleoecological reconstruction).

The fossils frequently are found heavily encrusted in hard rock (called matrix) and thus require enormous effort in their cleaning and reconstruction (i.e., putting the fragments back together).

FIGURE 10
Techniques for recording the position of materials (artifacts and fossils) at a site, shown here being used at Olduvai Gorge. The grid to the left is divided into 10 cm squares to record horizontal position, and the triangular apparatus to the right is used to determine vertical position.

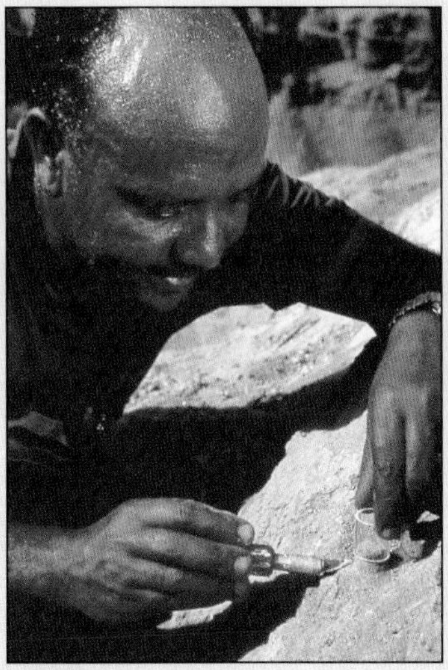

FIGURE 11
Geological samples are recovered along with the fossils. Here, Ethiopian field member, Michael Tesfaye, precisely excavates a sample of sediment to be used later for paleomagnetic analysis.

FIGURE 12
In some cases, fossils are found completely embedded in surrounding matrix, and great effort and skill are required to remove the fossil fragments from the rock. This specimen comes from Sterkfontein, in South Africa, where fossils are embedded in a limestone matrix called breccia.

Paleoanthropology (continued)

Once the field season ends, materials are brought back and distributed to various laboratories for specialized analysis. Experts in different fields study the materials in the hope of obtaining valuable data, including chronometric dating and geological context, as well as paleontological and palynological information. This painstaking work can take several years.

FIGURE 13
Dating is a key aspect of paleoanthropological interpretation. The Berkeley Geochronology Laboratory (formerly part of the Institute of Human Origins) has provided many of the chronometric dates using K/Ar or ^{39}Ar/^{40}Ar dating (e.g., the new *H. erectus* dates from Indonesia discussed in Chapter 11).

Institute of Human Origins, photo by Nanci Kahn

FIGURE 14
To facilitate further study and to provide precise replicas to other scholars (as well as to universities for demonstration specimens in classes), original hominid fossils are made into casts. The casting laboratory at the Kenya Museums of Natural History has provided a large number of high-quality casts to researchers and universities throughout the world.

Robert Jurmain

CHAPTER

12

CONTENTS

Neandertals and Other Archaic *Homo sapiens*

See the following sections of the CD-ROM for topics covered in this chapter: Virtual Lab 10, section I, and Virtual Lab 11.

Archaic *H. sapiens*
Earlier forms of *Homo sapiens* (including Neandertals) from the Old World that differ from *H. erectus* but lack the full set of characteristics diagnostic of modern *H. sapiens*.

Anatomically modern *H. sapiens*
All modern humans and some fossil forms, perhaps dating as early as 200,000 y.a.; defined by a set of derived characteristics, including cranial architecture and lack of skeletal robusticity; usually classified at the subspecies level as *Homo sapiens sapiens*.

Introduction

In Chapter 11, we saw that *H. erectus* was present in Africa approximately 1.8 m.y.a. and also in Java at about this same time. Except for new finds at Dmanisi, in the Republic of Georgia, and at Ceprano, in Italy, we also noted that *H. erectus* fossils thus far are very scarce in Europe, although several routes could easily have provided access. A major difficulty in accurately assessing finds is that a number of fossils from Europe—as well as Africa, China, and Java—display *both H. erectus* and *H. sapiens* features.

These particular forms, possibly representing some of the earliest members of our species, fall into the latter half of the Middle Pleistocene, from about 400,000 to 130,000 years ago, and are often referred to as **archaic *H. sapiens***. The designation *H. sapiens* is used because the appearance of some derived sapiens traits suggests that these hominids are transitional forms. In most cases, these early archaic *H. sapiens* specimens also retain some *H. erectus* features mixed with those derived features that distinguish them as *H. sapiens*. However, as they do not possess the full suite of derived characteristics diagnostic of **anatomically modern *H. sapiens***, we classify them as archaic forms of our species. In general, we see in several different areas of the Old World through time a morphological trend from groups with more obvious *H. erectus* features to later populations displaying more diagnostic *H. sapiens* features.

When we speak of evolutionary trends and transitions from one species to another—for example, from *H. erectus* to *H. sapiens*—we do not wish to imply that such changes were in any way inevitable. In fact, most *H. erectus* populations never evolved into anything else. *Some* populations of *H. erectus* did apparently undergo slow evolutionary changes, and thus, some populations of what we call archaic *H. sapiens* emerge as transitional forms. In turn, *some* of these archaic *H. sapiens* populations suggest evolutionary change in the direction of anatomically modern *H. sapiens*.

In this chapter, we attempt, where the data permit, to focus on those populations that provide clues regarding patterns of hominid evolutionary change. We would like to ascertain *where* such transformations took place, *when* they occurred, and *what* the adaptive stimuli were (both cultural and biological) that urged the process along.

There are still significant gaps in the fossil data, and we certainly do not have a complete record of all the transitional stages; nor are we ever likely to possess anything approaching such a complete record. What we will do in this chapter is to paint the evolution of later hominids in fairly broad strokes to show the general trends.

Early Archaic *H. sapiens*

Many early archaic forms show morphological changes compared with *H. erectus*. These derived changes are reflected in brain expansion; increased parietal breadth (the basal portion of the skull is no longer the widest area, and therefore, the shape of the skull as seen from the rear is no longer pentagonal); some decrease in the size of the molars; and general decrease in cranial and postcranial robusticity.

A difficulty of major significance concerns exactly how to classify all this Middle Pleistocene hominid material. Here we take a conservative taxonomic approach and classify *all* of the specimens (as archaic forms) within the species *Homo sapiens*. However, a growing number of paleoanthropologists (e.g., Stringer, 1995; Larick and Ciochon, 1996; Rightmire, 1998) disagree with this interpretation and prefer to classify most, if not all, of the individuals into other species of the genus *Homo*. In this view, some of the earlier archaic forms could be ancestral to modern humans, but the later ones most likely would not be. As in other debates of this nature discussed in previous chapters, the essential issue concerns interpretation of intra- as compared to interspecific variation. We will return to this crucial topic at the end of this chapter.

A further complication in understanding archaic *H. sapiens* is that there is considerable variation both within and between samples of these hominids. Moreover, they are geographically very widely dispersed. In fact, archaic *H. sapiens* fossils have been found on the three continents of Africa, Asia, and Europe. In Europe, the well-known Neandertals are included in this category. (Neandertals are not found anywhere *except* Europe and western Asia.)

Africa

In Africa, archaic *H. sapiens* fossils have been found at several sites (Figs. 12–1 and 12–2). One of the best known is Broken Hill (Kabwe). At this site in Zambia, a complete cranium, together with other cranial and postcranial elements belonging to several individuals, was discovered.

In this and other African early archaic specimens, a mixture of older and more recent traits can be seen. The skull's massive supraorbital torus (one of the largest of any hominid), low vault, and prominent occipital torus recall those of *H. erectus*. On the other hand, the occipital region is less angulated, the cranial vault bones are thinner, and the cranial base is essentially modern. Dating estimates of Broken Hill and most of the other early archaic *H. sapiens* specimens from Africa have ranged throughout the Middle and Upper Pleistocene, but recent estimates have given dates for most of the localities in the range of 150,000–125,000 y.a.

A total of eight other archaic *H. sapiens* crania from South and East Africa also show a combination of *H. erectus* and *H. sapiens* characteristics, and they are all mentioned in the literature as being similar to Broken Hill. The most important of these African finds come from the sites of Florisbad and Elandsfontein in South Africa, Laetoli in Tanzania, and Bodo in Ethiopia (see Fig. 12–2). The general similarities in all these African archaic *H. sapiens* fossils may signify a fairly close genetic relationship of hominids from East and South Africa. It is also possible—although it seems most unlikely—that several populations were evolving in a somewhat similar way from *H. erectus* to a more *H. sapiens*-looking morphology.

We should point out that the evolutionary path of these hominids did not take a Neandertal turn. It seems that there were no Neandertals in Africa—nor were there any in the Far East (Table 12–1 on p. 292).

Asia

China Like their counterparts in Europe and Africa, Chinese archaic *H. sapiens** specimens also display both earlier and later characteristics. Chinese paleoanthropologists suggest that archaic *H. sapiens* traits, such as a sagittal ridge (see p. 264) and flattened nasal bones, are shared with *H. erectus*, especially those specimens from Zhoukoudian. They also point out that some of these features can be found in modern *H. sapiens* in China today, indicating substantial genetic continuity. That is, some Chinese researchers have argued that anatomically modern Chinese did not evolve from *H. sapiens* in either Europe or Africa, evolving instead specifically in China from a separate *H. erectus* lineage.

That such regional evolution occurred in many areas of the world or, alternatively, that anatomically modern migrants from Africa displaced local populations is the subject of a major ongoing debate in paleoanthropology. This important controversy will be the central focus of the next chapter.

Dali, the most complete skull of the late Middle or early Upper Pleistocene fossils in China, displays *H. erectus* and *H. sapiens* traits, but it is clearly classified as early *H. sapiens* (despite its relatively small cranial capacity of 1,120 cm³). Several other Chinese specimens also reflect both earlier and later traits and are placed in the same category as Dali. In addition, the more recently discovered (1984) partial skeleton from Jinniushan, in northeast China, has been given a provisional date of 200,000 y.a. (Tiemel et al., 1994). The cranial capacity is fairly large (approximately 1,260 cm³), and the walls of the braincase are thin—both modern features and quite unexpected in an individual this ancient (if the dating estimate does indeed hold up).

FIGURE 12–1
Broken Hill (Kabwe). Note the very heavy supraorbital torus.

---

*Chinese anthropologists prefer the term "early *Homo sapiens*" instead of "archaic *H. sapiens*."

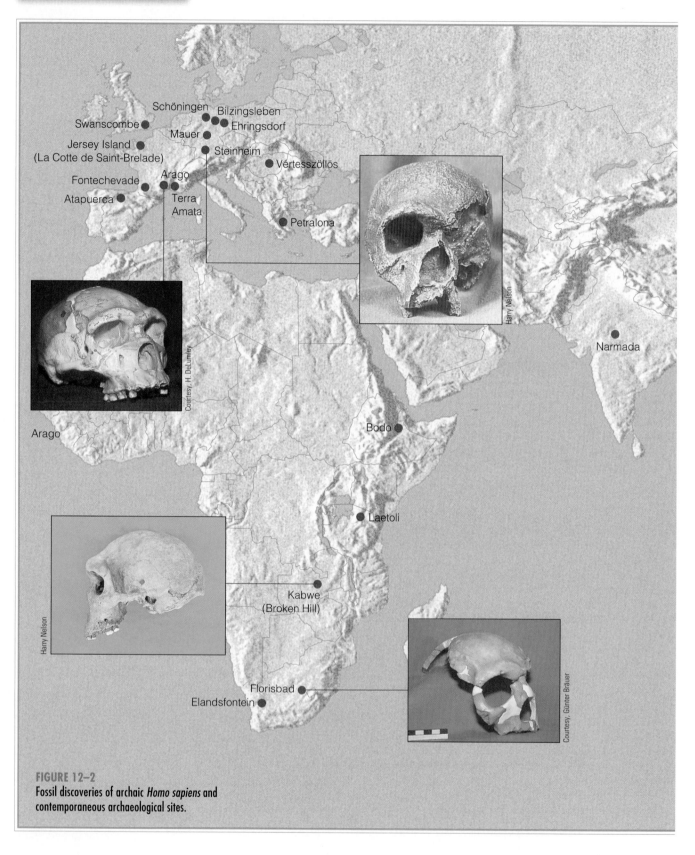

FIGURE 12–2
Fossil discoveries of archaic *Homo sapiens* and
contemporaneous archaeological sites.

Jinniushan

Dali

Maba

Courtesy, Xinzhi Wu

TABLE 12–1   A Partial List of Archaic *Homo sapiens* (Outside of Europe)

Name	Site	Date*	Human Remains	Associated Finds	Cranial Capacity (cm³)	Comments
Africa						
Bodo	Awash River Valley, Ethiopia	Middle Pleistocene (600,000 y.a.?)	Incomplete skull, part of braincase	Acheulian artifacts, animal bones	1,300	Resembles Broken Hill; first evidence of scalping
Broken Hill (Kabwe)	Cave deposits near Kabwe, Zambia	Late Middle Pleistocene; (130,000 y.a. or older)	Nearly complete cranium, cranial fragments of second individual, miscellaneous postcranial bones	Animal bones and artifacts in cave, but relationship to human remains unknown	1,280	Massive browridge, low vault, prominent occipital torus; cranial capacity within range of modern *H. sapiens*
China						
Dali	Shaanxi Province, north China	Late Middle Pleistocene (230,000–180,000 y.a.)	Nearly complete skull	Flake tools, animal bones	1,120–1,200	Robust supra-orbital ridge, low vault, retreating forehead, canine fossa
Jinniushan	Liaoning Province, northeast China	Late Middle Pleistocene (200,000 y.a.)	Partial skeleton, including a cranium	Flake tools	1,260	Thin cranial bones
Maba	Cave near Maba village, Guangdong Province, south China	Early Upper Pleistocene (140,000–120,000 y.a.)	Incomplete skull of middle-aged male	Animal bones	Insufficient remains for measurement	Receding forehead, modest keel on frontal bone

*Also see Figure 12–3.

India   In 1982, a partial skull was discovered in the Narmada Valley, in central India. Associated with this fossil were various hand axes, cleavers, flakes, and choppers. This Narmada specimen has been dated as Middle Pleistocene with a probable cranial capacity within the range of 1,155 to 1,421 cm³. K. A. R. Kennedy (1991), who made a recent study of the fossil, suggests that Narmada should be viewed as an early example of *H. sapiens*.

Europe

Various attempts have been made to organize European archaic *H. sapiens* of the Middle and early Upper Pleistocene in the time range of 400,000–150,000 y.a. (Fig. 12–3). Because in many cases definite dates or adequate remains (or both) are lacking, it is difficult to be certain which fossils belong where in the evolutionary sequence. As already noted, what we find in Europe are fossils, such as those in Africa and China, whose features resemble both *H. erectus* and *H. sapiens*. You should further note that the earliest fossil finds from Europe (including those from Boxgrove in England and Atapuerca in Spain, discussed in Chapter 11) already show some of these transitional features.

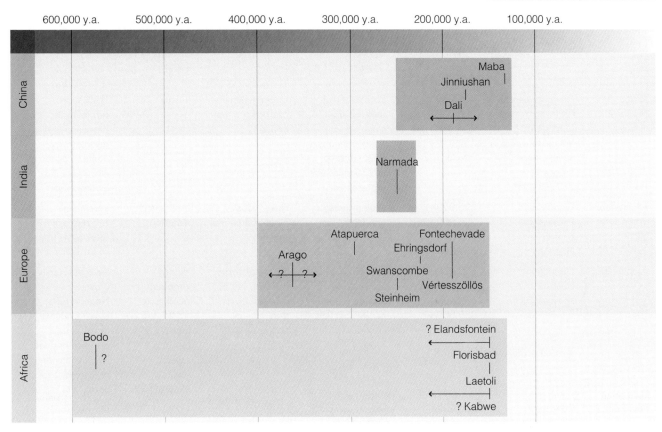

The earliest archaic *H. sapiens* representatives from Europe show some resemblance to *H. erectus* in the robusticity of the mandible, thick cranial bones, pronounced occipital torus, heavy supraorbital torus, receding frontal bone, greatest parietal breadth near the base of the skull, and large teeth. (They, of course, also have one or more *H. sapiens* characteristics.) Examples of these early archaic forms from Europe include fossils from Steinheim, Swanscombe, and Vértesszöllös (see Fig. 12–2). Later European archaic representatives also possess some *H. erectus* characteristics, but they also have one or more of the following traits: larger cranial capacity, more rounded occipital area, parietal expansion, and reduced tooth size (Table 12–2).

The later group, essentially from the later half of the Middle Pleistocene, overlaps to some extent with the earlier group. From an evolutionary point of view, this later group may have evolved from the earlier one, and since many of these individuals display traits unique to Neandertals, they may in turn have given rise to the Neandertals. Examples of this somewhat later European transitional group include specimens from Fontechevade (France) and Ehringsdorf (Germany), as well as recent discoveries from Atapuerca, in northern Spain, in the same region as the recently discovered more ancient remains discussed in Chapter 11. This last site (called Sima de los Huesos), dated to approximately 300,000 y.a., has yielded the largest sample yet of archaic *Homo sapiens* from anywhere in the world and includes the remains of at least 32 individuals (among which are several excellently preserved crania) (Arsuaga et al., 1993, 1997; Kunzig, 1997). Excavations continue at this remarkable site, where bones have somehow accumulated within a deep chamber inside a cave. There are also large numbers of carnivore remains (bear, fox), but these fossils are generally in separate locations from where the hominids were found. From initial descriptions, the hominid morphology has been interpreted as showing several indications of an early Neandertal-like pattern (arching browridges, projecting midface, and other features) (Rightmire, 1998).

FIGURE 12–3
Time line of early archaic *Homo sapiens*. Note that most dates are approximations. Question marks indicate those estimates that are most tentative.

TABLE 12–2 Archaic *Homo sapiens* in Europe*

Name	Site	Date*	Human Remains	Associated Finds	Cranial Capacity (cm3)	Comments
Arago (Tautavel)	Cave site near Tautavel, Verdouble Valley, Pyrenees, southeastern France	400,000–300,000 y.a.; date uncertain	Face; parietal perhaps from same person; many cranial fragments; up to 23 individuals represented	Upper Acheulian artifacts, animal bones	1,150	Thick supra-orbital torus, pronounced alveolar prognathism; parietal resembles Swanscombe
Bilzingsleben	Quarry at Bilzingsleben, near Erfurt, Germany	425,000–200,000 y.a., probably 280,000 y.a.	Skull fragments and teeth	Flake industry, plant and animal remains	Insufficient material	Resembles *H. erectus* in some features
Atapuerca	Sima de los Huesos, northern Spain	320,000–190,000 y.a., probably 300,000 y.a.	Minimum of 32 individuals, including some nearly complete crania	Many carnivore remains, but at different levels from human remains	Highly variable; small indiv., 1,125; larger indiv., 1,390 (probably reflects sexual dimorphism)	Several resemblances to Neandertals; oldest evidence of deliberate disposal of dead; largest sample of archaic *H. sapiens* at any site
Petralona	Cave near Petralona, Khalkidhiki, northeastern Greece	300,000–200,000 y.a.; date uncertain	Nearly complete skull	None	1,190–1,220	Mosaic; some bones resemble Neandertal, Broken Hill, and *H. erectus*
Steinheim	Gravel pit at Steinheim, Germany	Mindel-Riss Interglacial—300,000–250,000 y.a.; date uncertain	Nearly complete skull, lacking mandible	No artifacts, some animal bones	1,100	Pronounced supraorbital torus, frontal low, occipital rounded
Swanscombe	Swanscombe, Kent, England	Mindel-Riss Interglacial—300,000–250,000 y.a.; date uncertain	Occipital and parietals	Middle Acheulian artifacts, animal bones	1,325 (estimate)	Bones thick like *H. erectus*; occipital resembles Neandertal
Ehringsdorf	Fossil quarry; travertine deposits, eastern Germany	245,000–190,000 y.a.	Minimum of 9 individuals, including partial cranium	Mousterian artifacts	1,450	Resembles Neandertals in some respects
Vértesszöllös	Near village of Vértesszöllös, 30 miles west of Budapest, Hungary	210,000–160,000 y.a.; date uncertain	Adult occipital bone, fragments of infant teeth	Flake and pebble tools, animal bones	1,115–1,434 (estimate)	Occipital thick (*H. erectus* trait), but size and angulation suggest *H. sapiens*

*Also see Figure 12–3.

A Review of Middle Pleistocene Evolution (circa 400,000–125,000 y.a.)

Like the *erectus/sapiens* mix in Africa and China, the fossils from Europe also exhibit a mosaic of traits from both species (Fig. 12–4). However, it is important to note that the fossils from each continent differ; that is, the mosaic Chinese forms are not the same as those from Africa or Europe. Some European fossils, assumed to be earlier, are more robust and possess more similarities to *H. erectus* than to modern *H. sapiens*. The later Middle Pleistocene European fossils appear to be more Neandertal-like, but the uncertainty of dates prevents a clear scenario of the Middle Pleistocene evolutionary sequence.

The physical differences from *H. erectus* are not extraordinary. Bones remain thick, the supraorbital torus is prominent, and vault height shows little increase. There is, however, a definite increase in brain size and a change in the shape of the skull from pentagonal to globular as seen from the rear. There is also a trend, especially with the later Middle Pleistocene forms, toward less occipital angulation. It is interesting to note that in Europe, the changes move toward a Neandertal *H. sapiens* pattern, but in Africa and Asia, toward modern *H. sapiens*.

Middle Pleistocene Culture

The Acheulian technology of *H. erectus* carried over into the Middle Pleistocene with relatively little change until near the end of the period, when it became slightly more sophisticated. Bone, a very useful tool material, apparently went practically unused by archaic *H. sapiens*. Stone flake tools similar to those of the earlier era persisted, perhaps in greater variety. Archaic *H. sapiens* in Africa and Europe invented a method—the Levallois technique (Fig. 12–5)—for controlling flake size and shape. Requiring several coordinated steps, this was no mean feat and suggests to many scholars increased cognitive abilities in late archaic *H. sapiens* compared to earlier archaic forms.

(a)

(b)

FIGURE 12–4

Cast of an archaic *Homo sapiens* skull from Germany (Steinheim). (a) Frontal view showing damaged skull. (b) Basal view showing how the foramen magnum was enlarged, apparently for removal of the brain, perhaps for dietary or ritualistic purposes.

Nodule

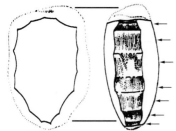

The nodule is chipped
on the perimeter.

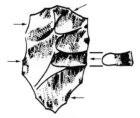

Flakes are radially
removed from top surface.

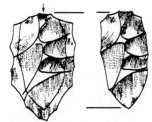

A final blow at one end
removes a large flake.

FIGURE 12–5
The Levallois technique.

Interpretation of the distribution of artifacts during the later Middle Pleistocene has generated considerable discussion among archaeologists. We have noted (in Chapter 11) that there is a general geographical distribution characteristic of the Lower Pleistocene, with bifaces (mostly hand axes) found quite often at sites in Africa, but only rarely at sites in most of Asia, and not at all among the rich assemblage at Zhoukoudian (see p. 268). Moreover, where hand axes proliferate, the stone tool industry is referred to as Acheulian, while at localities without hand axes, various other terms are used (e.g., "chopper/chopping tool"—a misnomer, since most of the tools are actually flakes).

Acheulian assemblages have been found at many African sites as well as numerous European ones (e.g., Swanscombe in England and Arago in France). Nevertheless, the broad geographical distribution of what we call Acheulian should not blind us to the considerable intraregional diversity in stone tool industries. For example, while a variety of European sites do show a typical Acheulian complex, rich in bifacial hand axes and cleavers, other contemporaneous ones—for example, Bilzingsleben in Germany and Vértesszöllös in Hungary—do not. At these latter two sites, a variety of small retouched flake tools and flaked pebbles of various sizes were found, but no hand axes.

It thus appears that different stone tool industries coexisted in some areas for long periods. Various explanations (Villa, 1983) have been offered to account for this apparent diversity: (1) The tool industries were produced by different peoples (i.e., different cultures, perhaps hominids that also differed biologically); (2) the tool industries represent different types of activities carried out at separate locales; (3) the presence (or absence) of specific tool types—bifaces—represents the availability (or unavailability) of appropriate local stone resources.

Archaic *H. sapiens* populations continued to live both in caves and in open-air sites, but may have increased their use of caves. Did archaic *H. sapiens* control fire? Klein (1989, p. 255) suggests that these hominids did. He writes that there was a "concentration of burnt bones in depressions 50–60 cm across at Vértesszöllös" and that "fossil hearths have also been identified at Bilzingsleben and in several French caves that were probably occupied by early *H. sapiens.*" Chinese archaeologists insist that many Middle Pleistocene sites in China contain evidence of human-controlled fire. However, not everyone is convinced.

That archaic *H. sapiens* built temporary structures is revealed by concentrations of bones, stones, and artifacts at several sites. Here, they manufactured artifacts and exploited the area for food. The stones may have been used to support the sides of a shelter.

In the Lazaret Cave in the city of Nice, in southern France, a shelter about 36 feet by 11 feet was built against the cave wall, and skins probably were hung over a framework of poles as walls for the shelter. The base was supported by rocks and large bones, and inside the shelter were two hearths. The hearth charcoal suggests that the hominid occupants used slow-burning oak and boxwood, which produced easy-to-rekindle embers. Very little stone waste was found inside the shelter, suggesting that they manufactured tools outside, perhaps because there was more light.

Archaeological evidence clearly alludes to the utilization of many different food sources, such as fruits, vegetables, seeds, nuts, and bird eggs, each in its own season. Marine life was also exploited. From Lazaret and Orgnac (southern France) comes evidence of freshwater fishing for trout, perch, and carp. The most detailed reconstruction of Middle Pleistocene life in Europe, however, comes from evidence at Terra Amata, on the southern coast of France (de Lumley and de Lumley, 1973; Villa, 1983). From this site has come fascinating evidence relating to short-term, seasonal visits by archaic *H. sapiens* groups, who built flimsy shelters (Fig. 12–6), gathered plants, exploited marine resources, and possibly hunted medium-sized and large mammals.

The hunting capabilities of these early members of *H. sapiens*, as for earlier hominids, remain open to dispute. What seems clear is that the evidence does not yet unambiguously establish widely practiced advanced abilities. In earlier professional discussions (as well as in earlier editions of our texts), archaeological evidence from Terra Amata (in France) and Torralba and Ambrona (in Spain) was used to argue for significantly advanced hunting skills for archaic *H. sapiens* in Europe. However, reconstruction of these sites by Richard Klein and others has now cast doubt on those prior conclusions. Once again, we see that application of scientific rigor (which is simply good critical thinking) makes us question assumptions. And in so doing, we frequently must conclude that other less dramatic (and less romantic) explanations fit the evidence as well as or better than those based on initial imaginative scenarios.

A possible exception to the current, much more conservative view of the hunting skills of archaic *H. sapiens* comes from an archaeological site excavated on the Channel Island of Jersey off the west coast of France (see Fig. 12–2). In a cave site called La Cotte de Saint-Brelade, many skeletal remains of large mammals (mammoth and woolly rhinoceros) were found in association with stone flakes. Unlike the remains from the sites mentioned earlier, the animals sampled at La Cotte de Saint-Brelade represent primarily subadults and adults in prime age (*not* what one would expect in naturally occurring accumulations). Moreover, the preserved elements also exhibit the kind of damage that further suggests hominid activities. Directly killing such large animals may not have been within the capabilities of the hominids (archaic *H. sapiens*?) who occupied this site. Thus, K. Scott, who led the excavations, has suggested that these early hominids may have driven their prey off a nearby cliff, bringing certain prized parts back to the cave for further butchering (Scott, 1980).

Another recent and exceptional find is also challenging assumptions regarding hunting capabilities of archaic *H. sapiens* in Europe. From the site of Schöningen in Germany, three remarkably well-preserved wooden spears were discovered in 1995 (Thieme, 1997). As we have noted before, fragile organic remains (such as wood) can rarely be preserved more than a few hundred years; yet these beautifully crafted implements are provisionally dated to 380,000–400,000 y.a.! Beyond this surprisingly ancient date, the spears are intriguing on a variety of other counts. Firstly, they are all large (about 6 feet long), very finely made, selected from hard spruce wood, and expertly balanced. Each spear would have required considerable planning, time, and skill to manufacture. Further, the weapons were most likely used as throwing spears, presumably to hunt large animals. Of interest in this context, bones of numerous horses were also recovered at Schöningen. Archaeologist Hartmut Thieme has thus concluded that "the spears strongly suggest that systematic hunting, involving foresight, planning and the use of appropriate technology, was part of the behavioural repertoire of pre-modern hominids" (1997, p. 807). Therefore, as with the remains from La Cotte de Saint-Brelade, these extraordinary spears from Schöningen make a strong case for advanced hunting skills, practiced by at least some archaic *Homo sapiens* populations.

As documented by the fossil hominid remains as well as artifactual evidence from archaeological sites, the long period of transitional hominids in Europe was to continue well into the Upper Pleistocene (after 125,000 y.a.). However, the evolution of archaic *H. sapiens* was to take a unique turn with the appearance and expansion of the Neandertals.

Neandertals: Late Archaic *H. sapiens* (130,000–35,000 y.a.)

Since their discovery more than a century ago, the Neandertals have haunted the best-laid theories of paleoanthropologists. They fit into the general scheme of human evolution, and yet they are misfits. Classified as *H. sapiens*, they are like us and yet different. It is not an easy task to put them in their place.*

---

*Homo sapiens neanderthalensis is the subspecific designation for Neandertals, although not all paleoanthropologists agree with this terminology. (The subspecies for anatomically modern *H. sapiens* is designated as *Homo sapiens sapiens*.) *Thal,* meaning "valley," is the old spelling and is kept in the species designation (the "h" was always silent and not pronounced). The modern spelling is *tal* and is now used this way in Germany; we shall adhere to contemporary usage in the text with the spelling *Neandertal.*

While Neandertal fossil remains have been found at dates approaching 130,000 y.a., in the following discussion of Neandertals, we refer to those populations that lived especially during the last glaciation, which began about 75,000 y.a. and ended about 10,000 y.a. (Fig. 12–6). We should also note that the evolutionary roots of Neandertals apparently reach quite far back in western Europe, as evidenced by the 300,000 y.a. remains from Sima de los Huesos, Atapuerca, in northern Spain. The majority of fossils have been found in Europe, where they have been most studied, and our description of Neandertals is based primarily on those specimens from western Europe, who are usually called *classic* Neandertals. Not all Neandertals—

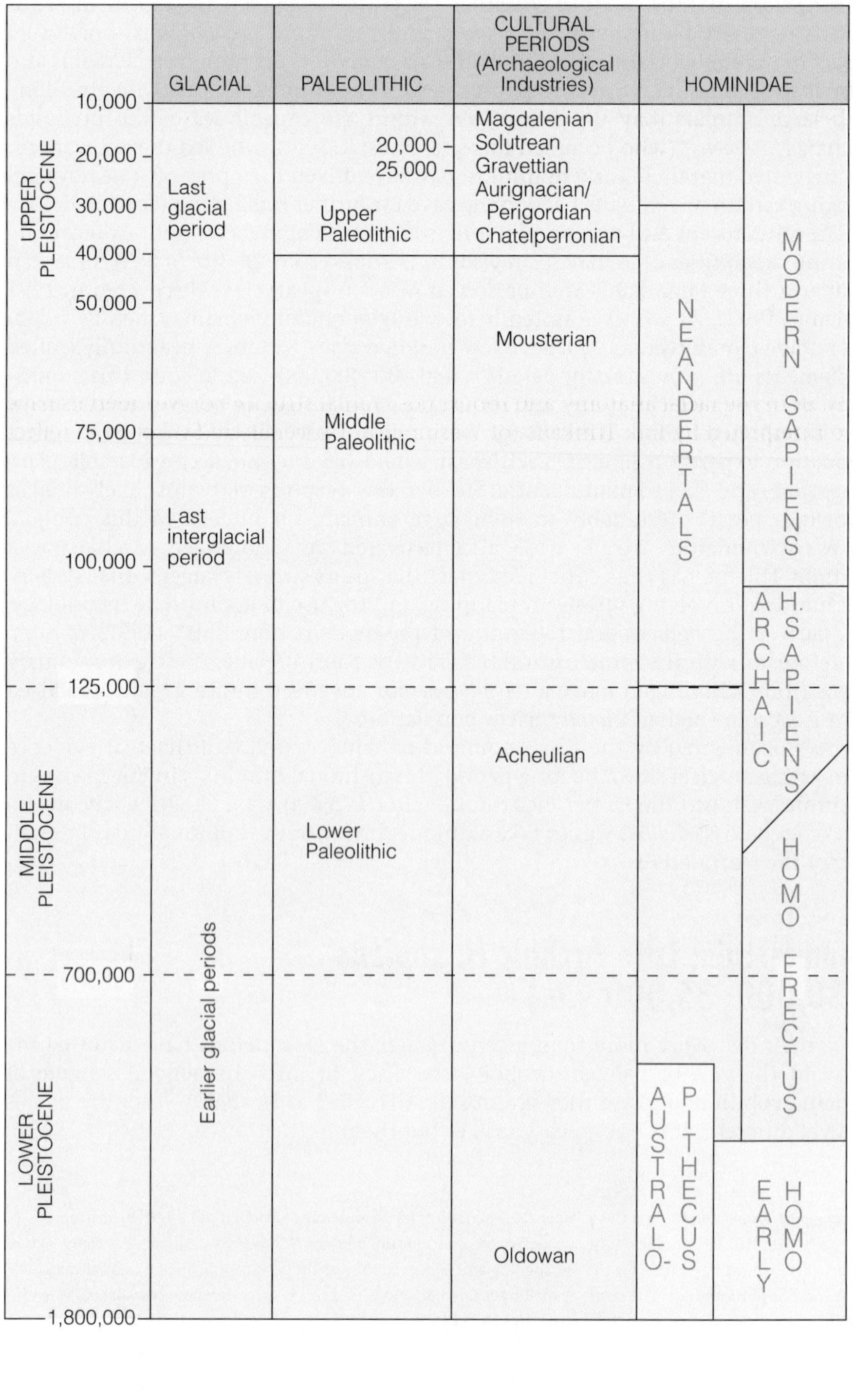

FIGURE 12–6

Correlation of Pleistocene subdivisions with archaeological industries and hominids. Note that the geological divisions are separate and different from the archaeological stages (e.g., Upper Pleistocene is *not* synonymous with Upper Paleolithic).

	GLACIAL	PALEOLITHIC	CULTURAL PERIODS (Archaeological Industries)	HOMINIDAE	
UPPER PLEISTOCENE — 10,000 — 20,000 — 30,000 — 40,000 — 50,000 — 75,000 — 100,000	Last glacial period	Upper Paleolithic	20,000 — 25,000 — Magdalenian Solutrean Gravettian Aurignacian/ Perigordian Chatelperronian	N E A N D E R T A L S	M O D E R N
		Middle Paleolithic	Mousterian		S A P I E N S
	Last interglacial period				
— 125,000				A R C H A I C	H. S A P I E N S
MIDDLE PLEISTOCENE — 700,000	Earlier glacial periods	Lower Paleolithic	Acheulian		H O M O E R E C T U S
LOWER PLEISTOCENE — 1,800,000			Oldowan	A U S T R A L O- P I T H E C U S	E A R L Y H O M O

including others from eastern Europe and western Asia and those from the interglacial that preceded the last glacial—entirely conform to our description of the classic morphology. They tend to be less robust, perhaps because the climate in which they lived was not as cold as western Europe during the last glaciation.

One striking feature of Neandertals is brain size, which in these hominids actually was larger than that of *H. sapiens* today. The average for contemporary *H. sapiens* is between 1,300 and 1,400 cm³, while for Neandertals it was 1,520 cm³. The larger size may be associated with the metabolic efficiency of a larger brain in cold weather. The Inuit (Eskimo) brain also averages larger than that of other modern human populations (about the size of the Neandertal brain). It should also be pointed out that the larger brain size in both archaic and contemporary *Homo sapiens* in populations adapted to *cold* climates is partially correlated with larger body size, which has also evolved among these groups (see Chapter 5).

The classic Neandertal cranium is large, long, low, and bulging at the sides. Viewed from the side, the posterior portion of the occipital bone is somewhat bun-shaped, but the marked occipital angle typical of many *H. erectus* crania is absent. The forehead rises more vertically than that of *H. erectus*, and the browridges arch over the orbits instead of forming a straight bar (Fig. 12–7).

Compared with anatomically modern humans, the Neandertal face stands out. It projects almost as if it were pulled forward. This feature can be seen when the distance of the nose and teeth from the eye orbits is compared with that of modern *H. sapiens*. Postcranially, Neandertals were very robust, barrel-chested, and powerfully muscled. This robust skeletal structure, in fact, dominates hominid evolution from *H. erectus* through archaic *H. sapiens*. Nevertheless, the Neandertals appear particularly robust, with shorter limbs than seen in most modern *H. sapiens* populations. Both the facial anatomy and robust postcranial structure of Neandertals have been interpreted by Erik Trinkaus (of Washington University in St. Louis) to reflect adaptation to rigorous living in a cold climate.

For about 100,000 years, Neandertals lived in Europe and western Asia (Fig. 12–10 on pp. 302–303), and their coming and going has raised more questions and controversies than perhaps any other hominid group. Neandertal forebears date back to the later archaic *H. sapiens*. But these were transitional forms, and it is not until the last interglacial that Neandertals were fully recognizable.

Neandertal takes its name from the Neander Valley, near Düsseldorf, Germany. In 1856, workmen quarrying limestone caves in the valley came across some fossilized bones. The owner of the quarry believed them to be bear and gave them to a natural science teacher, who realized that they were not the remains of a cave bear, but rather the remains of an ancient human. Exactly what the bones represented became a *cause célèbre* for many years, and the fate of "Neandertal Man," as the bones were named, hung in the balance until later finds provided more evidence.

What swung the balance in favor of accepting the Neander Valley specimen as a genuine hominid fossil were other nineteenth-century finds similar to it. What is more important, the additional fossil remains brought home the realization that a form of human different from nineteenth-century Europeans had in fact once existed.

France and Spain

One of the most important Neandertal discoveries was made in 1908 at La Chapelle-aux-Saints in southwestern France. A nearly complete skeleton was found buried in a shallow grave in a **flexed** position, with several fragments of nonhuman long bones placed over the head, and over them, a bison leg. Around the body were flint tools and broken animal bones.

The skeleton was turned over for study to a well-known French paleontologist, Marcellin Boule, who published his analysis in three copious volumes. Boule depicted the La Chapelle Neandertal as a brutish, bent-kneed, not fully erect biped. As a result of this exaggerated interpretation, some scholars, and certainly the general public, concluded that all Neandertals were highly primitive creatures.

See Virtual Lab 10, section I, for a discussion of Neandertals.

Flexed
The position of the body in a bent orientation, with the arms and legs drawn up to the chest.

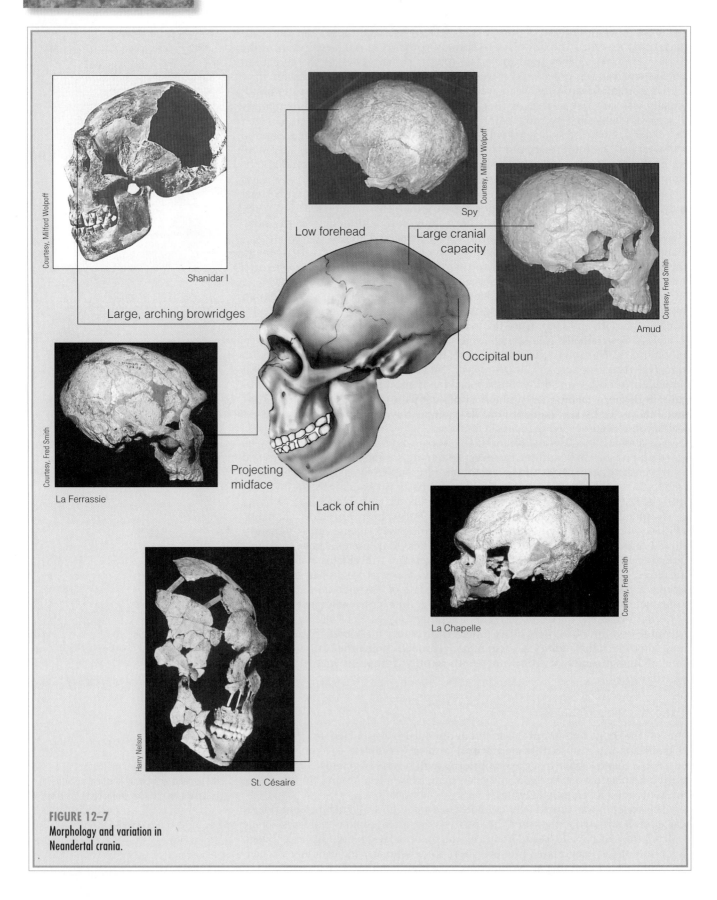

Low forehead

Large cranial capacity

Large, arching browridges

Occipital bun

Projecting midface

Lack of chin

Shanidar I

Spy

Amud

La Ferrassie

La Chapelle

St. Césaire

Courtesy, Milford Wolpoff

Courtesy, Milford Wolpoff

Courtesy, Fred Smith

Courtesy, Fred Smith

Courtesy, Fred Smith

Harry Nelson

FIGURE 12–7
Morphology and variation in
Neandertal crania.

Why did Boule draw these conclusions from the La Chapelle skeleton? Apparently, he misconstrued Neandertal posture owing to the presence of spinal osteoarthritis in this older male. In addition, and probably more important, Boule and his contemporaries found it difficult to accept fully as a human ancestor an individual who appeared to depart from the modern pattern.

The skull of this male, who was possibly at least 40 years of age when he died, is very large, with a cranial capacity of 1,620 cm³. As is typical for western European "classic" forms, the vault is low and long, the supraorbital ridges are immense, with the typical Neandertal arched shape, the forehead is low and retreating, and the face is long and projecting. The back of the skull is protuberant and bun-shaped (Figs. 12–7 and 12–8).

La Chapelle, however, is not a typical Neandertal, but an unusually robust male that "evidently represents an extreme in the Neandertal range of variation" (Brace et al., 1979, p. 117). Unfortunately, this skeleton, which Boule claimed did not even walk completely erect, was widely accepted as "Mr. Neandertal." But not all Neandertal materials express the suite of "classic Neandertal" traits to the degree seen in La Chapelle.

Another Neandertal site excavated recently in southern France has revealed further fascinating details relating to Neandertal behavior. From the 100,000- to 120,000-year-old Moula-Guercy cave site, Alban Defleur, Tim White, and colleagues have analyzed 78 broken hominid fragments representing probably six individuals (Defleur et al., 1999). The intriguing aspect of these remains concerns *how* they were broken. Detailed analysis of cut marks, pits, scars, and other features clearly suggests that the Neandertal individuals were *processed*—that is, they "were defleshed and disarticulated. After this, the marrow cavity was exposed by a hammer-on-anvil technique" (Defleur et al., 1999, p. 131). Moreover, the non-human bones at this site, especially the deer remains, were processed in an identical fashion. In other words, the Moula-Guercy Neandertals provide the best-documented evidence thus far of Neandertal *cannibalism*.

Some of the most recent of the western European Neandertals come from St. Césaire in southwestern France and are dated at about 35,000 y.a. (Fig. 12–9). The bones were recovered from a bed including discarded chipped blades, hand axes, and other stone tools of an **Upper Paleolithic** tool industry associated with Neandertals. Another site, Zafarraya Cave in southern Spain, may provide yet a more recent time range for Neandertal occupation in Europe. During the 1980s and 1990s, a few pieces of hominid individuals were found at Zafarraya that have been interpreted as Neandertal in morphology. What is most interesting, however, is the *date* (as determined by radiocarbon dating; see Chapter 14) suggested for the site. French archaeologist Jean-Jacques Hublin, who has excavated the site, asserts that the date is close to 29,000 y.a.—a full 6,000 years later than St. Césaire.

Another site, also recently redated, is apparently about the same age as Zafarraya, but it is located in central Europe. Recent recalibration by radiocarbon dating has indicated that the later Neandertal levels at Vindija, in Croatia (discussed shortly), are about 28,000 to 29,000 years old (Smith et al., 1999). If one of these dates is further confirmed, then either Zafarraya or Vindija would gain the distinction of having the most recent Neandertals thus far discovered.

Yet a more recent site in Portugal has recently been interpreted as showing hybridization between Neandertals and modern *Homo sapiens*. (We will discuss this intriguing suggestion in more detail in Chapter 13.)

The St. Césaire, Zafarraya, and Vindija sites are fascinating for several reasons. Anatomically modern humans were living in central and western Europe by about 35,000 y.a. or a bit earlier. Therefore, it is possible that Neandertals and modern *H. sapiens* were living in close proximity for several thousand years. How did these two groups interact? Evidence from a number of French sites (Harrold, 1989) indicates that Neandertals borrowed technological methods and tools (such as blades) from the anatomically modern populations and thereby modified their own tools,

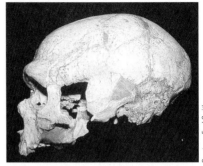

FIGURE 12–8
La Chapelle-aux-Saints. Note the occipital bun, projecting face, and low vault.

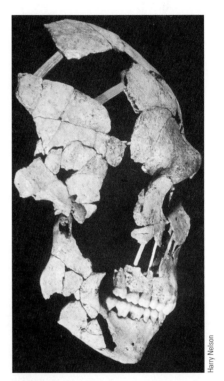

FIGURE 12–9
St. Césaire, among the "last" Neandertals.

Upper Paleolithic
A cultural period usually associated with early modern humans (but also found with Neandertals) and distinguished by technological innovation in various stone tool industries. Best known from western Europe, similar industries are also known from central and eastern Europe and Africa.

301

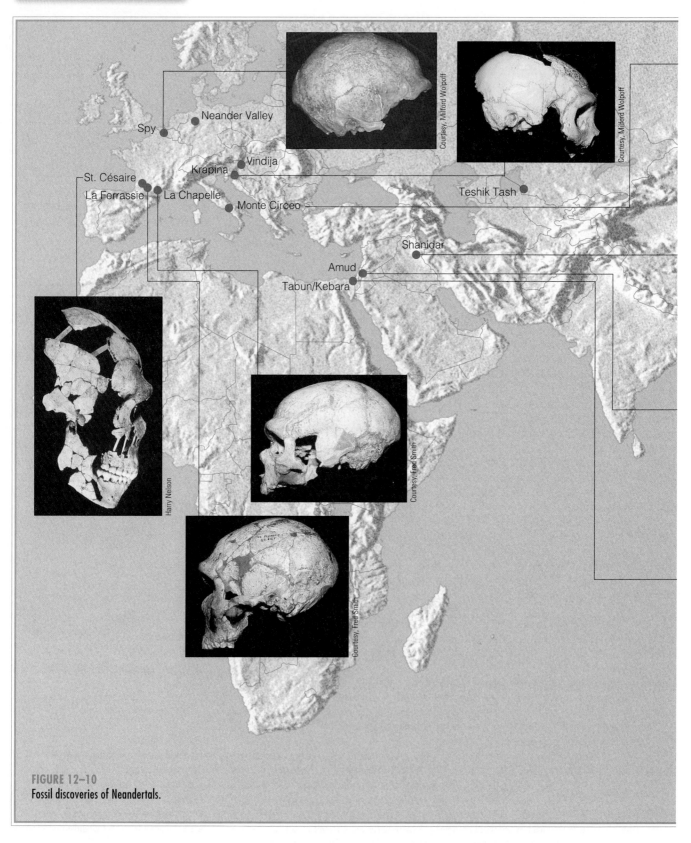

FIGURE 12–10
Fossil discoveries of Neandertals.

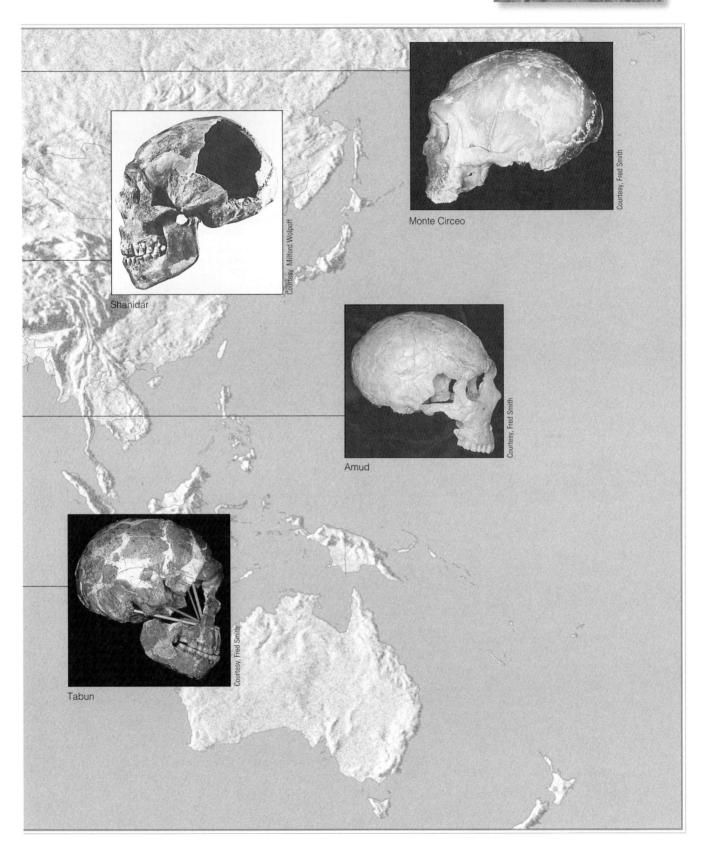

Shanidar

Courtesy, Milford Wolpoff

Monte Circeo

Courtesy, Fred Smith

Amud

Courtesy, Fred Smith

Tabun

Courtesy, Fred Smith

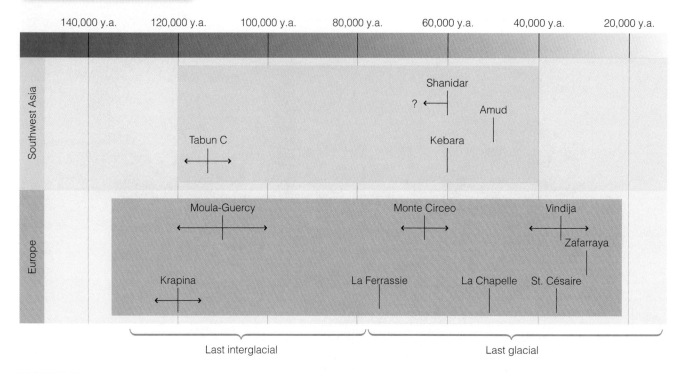

FIGURE 12–11
Time line for Neandertal (*Homo sapiens neanderthalensis*) fossil discoveries.

Chatelperronian
Pertaining to an Upper Paleolithic tool industry found in France and Spain, containing blade tools and associated with Neandertals.

creating a new industry, the **Chatelperronian**. However, such an example of cultural diffusion does not specify *how* the diffusion took place. Did the Neandertals become assimilated into modern populations? Did the two groups interbreed? It would also be interesting to know more precisely how long the coexistence of Neandertals and modern *H. sapiens* lasted.* No one knows the answers to these questions, but it has been suggested that an average annual difference of 2 percent mortality between the two populations (i.e., modern *H. sapiens* lived longer than Neandertals) would have resulted in the extinction of the Neandertals in approximately 1,000 years (Zubrow, 1989).

It should be noted that not all paleoanthropologists agree with the notion of the coexistence of Neandertals and Upper Paleolithic modern humans. For example, in a recent paper, David Frayer of the University of Kansas states: "There is still *no human fossil evidence* which supports the coexistence of Neanderthal and Upper Paleolithic forms in Europe" (emphasis added) (1992, p. 9). That is, despite the indications of cultural diffusion noted here, no European site has yet produced directly associated remains of *both* types of humans.

Central Europe

There are quite a few other European classic Neandertals, including significant finds in central Europe. At Krapina, Croatia, an abundance of bones (1,000 fragments representing up to 70 individuals) and 1,000 stone tools or flakes have been recovered (Trinkaus and Shipman, 1992). Krapina is an old site, perhaps the earliest showing the full "classic" Neandertal morphology, dating back to the last interglacial (estimated at 130,000–110,000 y.a.). Moreover, despite the relatively early date, the characteristic Neandertal features of the Krapina specimens (although less robust) are similar to the western European finds (Fig. 12–12). Krapina is also important as an intentional burial site, one of the oldest on record.

Another interesting site in central Europe is Vindija, about 30 miles from Krapina. The site is an excellent source of faunal, cultural, and hominid materials

---

*For a fictionalized account of the meeting between Neandertals and anatomically modern humans, see Bjorn Kurten's *Dance of the Tiger. A Novel of the Ice Age.* Another novel on the subject is Jean M. Auel's *Clan of the Cave Bear.* Several movies and a recent *Discovery Channel* production have also been made on this theme.

stratified in *sequence* throughout much of the Upper Pleistocene. Neandertal fossils consisting of some 35 specimens are dated between about 42,000 and 28,000 y.a. (the latter date would be among the most recent of all Neandertal discoveries). Even though some of their features approach the morphology of early modern south-central European *H. sapiens*, the overall pattern is definitely Neandertal. However, these modified Neandertal features, such as smaller browridges and slight chin development, may also be seen as an evolutionary trend toward modern *H. sapiens*.

Fred Smith, of Northern Illinois University, takes the view that variation in Vindija cranial features points to a trend continuing on to the later anatomically modern specimens found in the upper levels of the cave. Does Vindija support the proposition that the origin of *H. sapiens* could have occurred here in central Europe? Smith does not insist on this interpretation and suggests that anatomically modern *Homo sapiens* could have come from elsewhere. But he does believe that there is at least some morphological and genetic continuity between the samples found in the lower and upper levels of the cave.

Western Asia

Israel   In addition to European Neandertals, there are numerous important discoveries from southwest Asia. Several specimens from Israel display some modern features and are less robust than the classic Neandertals of Europe, but again the overall pattern is Neandertal. The best known of these discoveries is from Tabun (Mugharet-et-Tabun, "Cave of the Oven") at Mt. Carmel, a short drive south from Haifa (Fig. 12–13). Tabun, excavated in the early 1930s, yielded a female skeleton, recently dated by thermoluminescence (TL) at about 120,000–110,000 y.a. If this dating proves accurate, it places the Tabun find as clearly contemporary with early modern *H. sapiens* found in nearby caves. (TL dating is discussed on p. 321.)

A more recent Neandertal burial, a male discovered in 1983, comes from Kebara, a neighboring cave of Tabun at Mt. Carmel. Although the skeleton is incomplete—the cranium and much of the lower limbs are missing—the pelvis, dated to 60,000 y.a., is the most complete Neandertal pelvis so far recovered. Also recovered at Kebara is a hyoid bone, the first from a Neandertal, and this find is especially important from the point of view of reconstructing language capabilities.*

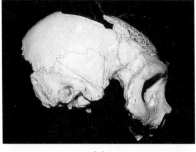

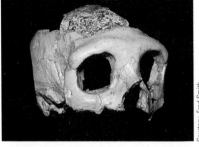

(a)

(b)

FIGURE 12–12
Krapina C. (a) Lateral view showing characteristic Neandertal traits. (b) Three-quarters view.

FIGURE 12–13
Excavation of the Tabun Cave, Mt. Carmel, Israel.

---

*The Kebara hyoid is identical to that of modern humans, suggesting that Neandertals did not differ from *H. sapiens sapiens* in this key element.

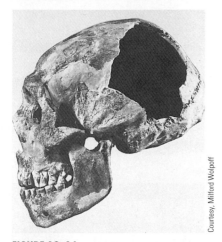

Courtesy, Milford Wolpoff

FIGURE 12–14
Shanidar 1. Does he represent an example of Neandertal compassion for the disabled?

Iraq   A most remarkable site is Shanidar, in the Zagros Mountains of northeastern Iraq, where partial skeletons of nine individuals—males and females, seven adults and two infants—were found, four of them deliberately buried. One of the more interesting individuals is Shanidar 1, a male who lived to be approximately 30 to 45 years old, a considerable age for a prehistoric human (Fig. 12–14). His stature is estimated at 5 feet 7 inches, with a cranial capacity of 1,600 cm^3. This individual shows several fascinating features:

> There had been a crushing blow to the left side of the head, fracturing the eye socket, displacing the left eye, and probably causing blindness on that side. He also sustained a massive blow to the right side of the body that so badly damaged the right arm that it became withered and useless; the bones of the shoulder blade, collar bone, and upper arm are much smaller and thinner than those on the left. The right lower arm and hand are missing, probably not because of poor preservation . . . but because they either atrophied and dropped off or because they were amputated. (Trinkaus and Shipman, 1992, p. 340)

In addition to these injuries, there was damage to the lower right leg (including a healed fracture of a foot bone). The right knee and left leg show signs of pathological involvement, and these changes to the limbs and foot may have left this man with a limping gait.

How such a person could perform normal obligations and customs is difficult to imagine. However, both Ralph Solecki, who supervised the work at Shanidar Cave, and Erik Trinkaus, who has carefully studied the Shanidar remains, believe that to survive, he must have been helped by others: "A one-armed, partially blind, crippled man could have made no pretense of hunting or gathering his own food. That he survived for years after his trauma was a testament to Neandertal compassion and humanity" (Trinkaus and Shipman, 1992, p. 341).*

Central Asia

Uzbekistan   About 1,600 miles east of Shanidar in Uzbekistan, in a cave at Teshik-Tash, is the easternmost Neandertal discovery. The skeleton is that of a nine-year-old boy who appears to have been deliberately buried. It was reported that he was surrounded by five pairs of wild goat horns, suggesting a burial ritual or perhaps a religious cult, but owing to inadequate published documentation of the excavation, this interpretation has been seriously questioned. The Teshik-Tash individual, like some specimens from Croatia and southwest Asia, also shows a mixture of Neandertal traits (heavy browridges and occipital bun) and modern traits (high vault and definite signs of a chin).

As noted, the Teshik-Tash site represents the easternmost location presently established for Neandertals. Thus, based on current evidence, it is clear that the geographical distribution of the Neandertals extended from France eastward to central Asia, a distance of about 4,000 miles.

Culture of Neandertals

Neandertals, who lived in the cultural period known as the Middle Paleolithic, are usually associated with the **Mousterian** industry (although the Mousterian industry is not always associated with Neandertals). In the early part of the last glacial period, Mousterian culture extended across Europe and North Africa into the former Soviet Union, Israel, Iran, and as far east as Uzbekistan and perhaps even China. Moreover, in Africa, the contemporaneous Middle Stone Age industry is broadly similar to the Mousterian.

Mousterian
Pertaining to the stone tool industry associated with Neandertals and some modern *H. sapiens* groups; also called Middle Paleolithic. This industry is characterized by a larger proportion of flake tools than is found in Acheulian tool kits.

---

*K. A. Dettwyler (1991) asserts that Shanidar 1 could have survived without assistance and that there is no solid evidence that compassion explains this individual's survival.

Technology

Neandertals improved on previous prepared-core techniques (i.e., the Levallois) by inventing a new variation. They trimmed a flint nodule around the edges to form a disk-shaped core. Each time they struck the edge, they produced a flake, continuing this way until the core became too small and was discarded. Thus, the Neandertals were able to obtain more flakes per core than their predecessors. They then trimmed (retouched) the flakes into various forms, such as scrapers, points, and knives (Fig.12–15).

Neandertal craftspeople elaborated and diversified traditional methods, and there is some indication of development in the specialization of tools used in skin and meat preparation, hunting, woodworking, and hafting. There is, however, still nearly a complete absence of bone tools, in strong contrast to the succeeding cultural period, the Upper Paleolithic. Nevertheless, Neandertals advanced their technology, which tended to be similar in basic tool types over considerable geographical distances, far beyond that of *H. erectus*. It is quite possible that their modifications in technology helped provide a basis for the remarkable changes of the Upper Paleolithic (discussed in the next chapter).

Settlements

People of the Mousterian culture lived in a variety of open sites, caves, and rock shelters. Living in the open on the cold tundra suggests the building of structures, and there is some evidence of such structures (although the last glaciation must have destroyed many open sites). At the site of Moldova, in the Ukraine (now an independent state and neighbor of Russia), archaeologists found traces of an oval ring of mammoth bones enclosing an area of about 26 by 16 feet and which may have been used to weigh down the skin walls of a temporary hut or tent. Inside the ring are traces of a number of hearths, hundreds of tools, thousands of waste flakes, and many bone fragments, quite possibly derived from animals brought back for consumption.

Evidence of life in caves is abundant. Windbreaks of poles and skin were probably erected at the cave mouth for protection against severe weather. Fire was in general use by this time and was no doubt used for cooking, warmth, light, and keeping predators at bay.

How large were Neandertal settlements, and were they permanent or temporary? These questions are not yet answered, but Binford (1981) suggests that the settlements were used repeatedly for short-term occupation.

Subsistence

Neandertals were successful hunters, as the abundant remains of animal bones at their sites demonstrate. But while it is clear that Neandertals could hunt large mammals, they may not have been as efficient at this task as were Upper Paleolithic hunters. Inferring from his detailed work in the Middle East, Harvard anthropologist Ofer Bar-Yosef (1994) has concluded that only after the beginning of the Upper Paleolithic was the spear-thrower, or atlatl (see p. 331), invented. Moreover, shortly thereafter, the bow and arrow may have greatly facilitated efficiency (and safety) in hunting large mammals. Lacking such long-distance weaponry, and thus mostly limited to close-proximity spears, Neandertals may have been more prone to serious injury—a hypothesis recently given some intriguing support by paleoanthropologists Thomas Berger and Erik Trinkaus. Berger and Trinkaus (1995) analyzed the pattern of trauma (particularly fractures) in Neandertals and compared it with that seen in contemporary human samples. Interestingly, the pattern in Neandertals—especially the relatively high proportion of head and neck injuries—matched most closely to that seen in contemporary rodeo performers. Berger and Trinkaus thus conclude, "The similarity to the rodeo distribution suggests frequent close encounters with large ungulates unkindly disposed to the humans involved" (Berger and Trinkaus, 1995, p. 841).

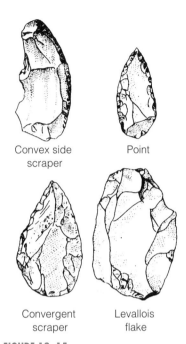

Convex side scraper   Point

Convergent scraper   Levallois flake

FIGURE 12–15
Mousterian tools. (After Bordes.)

See Virtual Lab 11 for a discussion of dietary reconstruction.

Meat was, of course, not the only component of Neandertal diet. Evidence (from Shanidar, for example) indicates that Neandertals gathered as well, consuming berries, nuts, and other plants.

It is assumed that in the bitter cold of the last glacial period, Neandertals wore clothing, and they probably had developed methods of curing skins. But since there is no evidence of sewing equipment, the clothing was probably of simple design, perhaps something like a poncho.

We know much more of European Middle Paleolithic culture than of any prior period, as it has been studied longer by more scholars. In recent years, however, Africa has been a target not only of physical anthropologists (as we have seen copiously documented in earlier chapters), but also of archaeologists, who have added considerably to our knowledge of African Pleistocene hominid history. In many instances, the technology and assumed cultural adaptations were similar in Africa to those in Europe and southwest Asia. We will see in the next chapter that the African technological achievements also kept pace with (or even preceded) those in western Europe.

Symbolic Behavior

There are a variety of hypotheses concerning the speech capacities of Neandertals. Many of these views are highly contradictory, with some scholars arguing that Neandertals were incapable of human speech. Nevertheless, the current consensus is that Neandertals were capable of articulate speech, even perhaps fully competent in the range of sounds produced by modern humans. However, this conclusion is not to argue that because Neandertals *could* speak, they necessarily had the same language capacities as modern *Homo sapiens*. A major contemporary focus among paleoanthropologists is the apparently sudden expansion of modern *H. sapiens* (discussed in Chapter 13) and various explanations for the success of this group. Moreover, at the same time we are explaining how and why *H. sapiens sapiens* expanded its geographical range, we are left with the further problem of explaining what happened to the Neandertals. In making these types of interpretations, a growing number of paleoanthropologists suggest that *behavioral* differences are the key.

Upper Paleolithic *H. sapiens* is hypothesized to have possessed some significant behavioral advantages that Neandertals (and other archaic *H. sapiens*) lacked. Was it some kind of new and expanded ability to symbolize, communicate, organize social activities, elaborate technology, obtain a wider range of food resources, or care for the sick or injured, or was it some other factor? Were there, compared with *H. sapiens sapiens*, neurological differences that limited the Neandertals and thus contributed to their demise?

The direct anatomical evidence derived from Neandertal fossils is not especially helpful in specifically answering these questions. Ralph Holloway (1985) has maintained that Neandertal brains (at least as far as the fossil evidence suggests) do not differ significantly from that of modern *H. sapiens*. Moreover, Neandertal vocal tracts and other morphological features, compared with our own, do not appear seriously to have limited them. Furthermore, a recent study of the size of a small opening in the base of the skull (the hypoglossal canal; see Figure A–4 in Appendix A) has shed new insight on Neandertal speech capabilities. Richard Kay, Matt Cartmill, and Michelle Balow of Duke University measured the size of this canal in a variety of fossil hominids as well as in modern humans and great apes (Kay et al., 1998). The size of the hypoglossal canal may be particularly significant to speech production, since the main nerve supply for the tongue passes through this opening. The Duke researchers found that Neandertals (and other archaic *H. sapiens*) had hypoglossal canals as large as those seen in modern humans, arguing that Neandertal speech capabilities would not have been hampered in this respect. Interestingly, however, in earlier hominids (*Australopithecus* and early *Homo*), the hypoglossal canal was much smaller—in fact, similar in size to that seen in chimpanzees. Another recent study (DeGusta et al., 1999), however, has cast considerable doubt on all these assertions (see p. 340).

Most of the reservations about advanced cognitive abilities in Neandertals have come from archaeological data. Interpretation of Neandertal sites, when compared with succeeding Upper Paleolithic sites (especially as documented in western Europe), have led to several intriguing contrasts, as shown in Table 12–3.

On the basis of this type of behavioral and anatomical evidence, Neandertals in recent years have increasingly been viewed as an evolutionary dead end. Whether their disappearance and ultimate replacement by anatomically modern Upper Paleolithic peoples (with their presumably "superior" culture) was solely the result of cultural differences or was also influenced by biological variation cannot at present be determined.

Burials

It has been known for some time that Neandertals deliberately buried their dead. Indeed, the spectacular discoveries at La Chapelle, Shanidar, and elsewhere were the direct results of ancient burial, thus facilitating much more complete preservation. Such deliberate burial treatment extends back at least 90,000 years at Tabun. Moreover, some form of consistent "disposal" of the dead (but not necessarily below-ground burial) is evidenced at Atapuerca, Spain, where at least 32 individuals

TABLE 12–3 Cultural Contrasts* Between Neandertals and Upper Paleolithic *Homo sapiens sapiens*

Neandertals	Upper Paleolithic *H. sapiens sapiens*
Tool Technology	
Numerous flake tools; few, however, apparently for highly specialized functions; use of bone, antler, or ivory very rare; relatively few tools with more than one or two parts	Many more varieties of stone tools; many apparently for specialized functions; frequent use of bone, antler, and ivory; many more tools comprised of two or more component parts
Hunting Efficiency and Weapons	
No long-distance hunting weapons; close-proximity weapons used (thus, more likelihood of injury)	Use of spear-thrower and bow and arrow; wider range of social contacts, perhaps permitting larger, more organized hunting parties (including game drives)
Stone Material Transport	
Stone materials transported only short distances—just "a few kilometers" (Klein, 1989)	Stone tool raw materials transported over much longer distances, implying wider social networks and perhaps trade
Art	
Artwork uncommon; usually small; probably mostly of a personal nature; some items perhaps misinterpreted as "art"; others may be intrusive from overlying Upper Paleolithic contexts; cave art absent	Artwork much more common, including transportable objects as well as elaborate cave art; well executed, using a variety of materials and techniques; stylistic sophistication
Burial	
Deliberate burial at several sites; graves unelaborated; graves frequently lack artifacts	Burials much more complex, frequently including both tools and remains of animals

*The contrasts are more apparent in some areas (particularly western Europe) than others (eastern Europe, Near East). Elsewhere (Africa, eastern Asia), where there were no Neandertals, the cultural situation is quite different (see p. 336). Moreover, even in western Europe, the cultural transformations were not necessarily abrupt, but may have developed more gradually from Mousterian to Upper Paleolithic times. For example, Straus (1995) argues that many of the Upper Paleolithic features were not consistently manifested until after 20,000 y.a.

comprising more than 700 fossilized elements were found in a cave at the end of a deep vertical shaft. From the nature of the site and the accumulation of hominid remains, Spanish researchers are convinced that the site demonstrates some form of human activity involving deliberate disposal of the dead (Arsuaga et al., 1997).

The provisional 300,000-year-old age for Atapuerca suggests that Neandertals (more precisely, their immediate precursors) were, by the Middle Pleistocene, handling their dead in special ways, a behavior thought previously to have emerged only much later (in the Upper Pleistocene). And, apparently as far as current data indicate, this practice is seen in western European contexts well before it appears in Africa or in eastern Asia. For example, in the archaic *H. sapiens* sites at Laetoli, Kabwe, and Florisbad (discussed earlier), deliberate disposal of the dead is not documented. Nor is it seen in African early modern sites (e.g., Klasies River Mouth, dated at 120,000–100,000 y.a.; see p. 321).

Nevertheless, in later contexts (after 35,000 y.a.) in Europe, where anatomically modern *H. sapiens* (*H. sapiens sapiens*) remains are found in clear burial contexts, their treatment is considerably more complex than is seen in Neandertal burials. In these later (Upper Paleolithic) sites, grave goods, including bone and stone tools as well as animal bones, are found more consistently and in greater concentrations. Because many Neandertal sites were excavated in the nineteenth or early twentieth century, before the development of more rigorous archaeological methods, there are questions regarding numerous purported burials. Nevertheless, the evidence seems quite clear that deliberate burial was practiced at La Chapelle, La Ferrassie (eight graves), Tabun, Amud, Kebara, Shanidar, and Teshik-Tash (as well as at several other localities, especially in France). Moreover, in many instances, the *position* of the body was deliberately modified and placed in the grave in a flexed posture (see p. 299). Such a flexed position has been found in 16 of the 20 best-documented Neandertal burial contexts (Klein, 1989).

Finally, the placement of supposed grave goods in burials, including stone tools, animal bones (such as cave bear), and even arrangements of flowers, together with stone slabs on top of the burials, have all been postulated as further evidence of Neandertal symbolic behavior. However, in many instances, again due to poor excavation documentation, these assertions are questionable. Placement of stone tools, for example, is occasionally seen, but apparently was not done consistently. In those 33 Neandertal burials for which adequate data exist, only 14 show definite association of stone tools and/or animal bones with the deceased (Klein, 1989). It is not until the next cultural period, the Upper Paleolithic, that we see a major behavioral shift, as demonstrated in more elaborate burials and development of art.

Genetic Evidence

As a result of the revolutionary advances in molecular biology (discussed in Chapter 3), fascinating new avenues of research have become possible in the study of earlier hominids. The extraction, amplification, and sequencing of ancient DNA from contexts spanning the last 10,000 years or so are now becoming fairly commonplace (e.g., the analysis of DNA from the 5,000-year-old "Iceman" found in the Italian Alps).

Finding usable DNA in yet more ancient remains is much more difficult because the material has become more mineralized, obliterating organic components, including (usually) the DNA. Nevertheless, in the past few years, very exciting results have been announced relating to DNA found in two different Neandertal fossils. The first of these comes from the original Neander Valley specimen, and analysis was completed in 1997 (Krings et al., 1997); the second comes from Mezmaiskaya Cave, in the Caucasus region of Russia, and results were published in 2000 (Ovchinnikov et al., 2000). In both cases, the individuals are by far the oldest hominid remains from which DNA has been recovered. The Neander Valley fossil is estimated at 70,000 years old, and the Mezmaiskaya material is securely dated (by radiocarbon) at 29,000 y.a. (Note: This places the latter among the most recent of all Neandertal discoveries.)

The technique used in the study of both Neandertal fossils involved the extraction of mitochondrial DNA (mtDNA), amplification by PCR (see p. 61), and nucleotide sequencing of portions of the molecule. Results from the two specimens show that they are both genetically more different from contemporary *Homo sapiens* populations than these latter populations are from each other (about three times as much). Extrapolating from these comparative data, Krings and colleagues (1997) have hypothesized that the Neandertal lineage separated from that of modern *H. sapiens* ancestors between 690,000 and 550,000 years ago.

The intriguing hypothesis, however, has not been fully confirmed and is most certainly not accepted by all paleoanthropologists. It is still not clear how rapidly mtDNA evolves, nor is it obvious how genetically different we should *expect* ancient hominids to be compared to us. (In other words, at present, we cannot rule out evolutionary relationships on the basis of available genetic evidence.) Nevertheless, such data probably offer the best hope of ultimately untangling the place of Neandertals in human evolution—and perhaps even of understanding something of their fate.

Evolutionary Trends in the Genus *Homo*

To understand the evolution of the various forms of *Homo sapiens* discussed in this chapter, it is useful to briefly review general trends of evolution in the genus *Homo* over the last 2 million years. In doing so, we see that at least three major *transitions* have taken place. Paleoanthropologists are keenly interested in interpreting the nature of these transitions, as they inform us directly regarding human origins. In addition, such investigations contribute to a broader understanding of the mechanics of the evolutionary process—at both the micro- and macroevolutionary levels.

The first transition of note was from early *Homo* to *Homo erectus*. This transition was apparently geographically restricted to Africa and appears to have been quite rapid (lasting 200,000 years at most, perhaps considerably less). It is important to recall that such a transition by no means implies that all early *Homo* groups actually evolved into *H. erectus*. In fact, many paleoanthropologists (part of a growing consensus) suggest that there was more than one species of early *Homo*. Clearly, only one could be ancestral to *H. erectus*. Even more to the point, only *some* populations of this one species would have been part of the genetic transformation (speciation) that produced *Homo erectus*.

The second transition is more complex and is the main topic of this chapter. It is the gradual change in populations of *H. erectus* grading into early *H. sapiens* forms—what we have termed archaic *H. sapiens*. This transition was not geographically restricted, as there is evidence of archaic *H. sapiens* widespread in the Old World (in East and South Africa, in China, India, and Java, and in Europe). Moreover, the transition appears not to have been rapid, but rather quite slow and uneven in pace from area to area. The complexity of this evolutionary transition creates ambiguities for our interpretations and resulting classifications.

For example, in Chapter 11, we included the Ngandong (Solo) material from Java within *Homo erectus*. However, there are several derived features in many of these specimens that suggest, alternatively, that they could be assigned to *Homo sapiens*. The dating (just recently indicating a date of only 29,000 y.a.) would argue that if this is a *H. erectus* group, it is a *very* late remnant, probably isolated *H. erectus* population surviving in southern Asia long after archaic *H. sapiens* populations were expanding elsewhere. Whatever the interpretation of Ngandong—either as a late *H. erectus* or as a quite primitive (i.e., not particularly derived) archaic *H. sapiens*—the conclusion is actually quite arbitrary (after all, the evolutionary process is continuous). We, by the nature of our classifications, have to draw the line *somewhere*.

Another important ramification of such considerations relates to understanding the nature of the *erectus/sapiens* transition itself. In Java, the transition (with late-persisting *H. erectus* genetic components) appears to have been slower than, for example, in southern Africa or in Europe. Nowhere, however, does this transition appear to have been as rapid as that which originally produced *H. erectus*. Why should this be so? To answer this question, we must refer back to basic evolutionary mechanisms (discussed in Chapters 3 and 4). First, the environments certainly differed from one region of the Old World to another during the time period 350,000–100,000 y.a. And recall that by the beginning of this time period, *H. erectus* populations had been long established in eastern and southern Asia, in North and East Africa, and in Europe. Clearly, we would not expect the same environmental conditions in northeast China as we would in Indonesia. Accordingly, natural selection could well have played a *differential* role, influencing the frequencies of alternative alleles in different populations in a pattern similar (but more intensive) to that seen in environmental adaptations of contemporary populations (see Chapter 5).

Second, many of these populations (in Java, southernmost Africa, and glacial Europe) could have been isolated and thus probably quite small. Genetic drift, therefore, also would have played a role in influencing the pace of evolutionary change. Third, advance or retreat of barriers, such as water boundaries or glacial ice sheets, would dramatically have affected migration routes.

Thus, it should hardly come as a surprise that some populations of *H. erectus* evolved at different rates and in slightly different directions from others. Some limited migration almost certainly occurred among the various populations. With sufficient gene flow, the spread of those few genetic modifications that distinguish the earliest *H. sapiens* eventually did become incorporated into widely separated populations. This, however, was a long, slow, inherently uneven process.

What, then, of the third transition within the genus *Homo*? This is the transition from archaic *H. sapiens* to anatomically modern *H. sapiens*—and it was considerably *faster* than the transition we have just discussed. How quickly anatomically modern forms evolved and exactly *where* this happened is a subject of much contemporary debate—and is the main topic of the next chapter.

Taxonomic Issues

As we discussed in Chapter 11, (and briefly at the beginning of this chapter), there is considerable debate regarding how to classify much of the *Homo* fossil material prior to 35,000 years ago. Our view, followed throughout the discussions in Chapters 10 through 12, proposes a minimum number of species and thus interprets the evolutionary processes influencing the genus *Homo* in a fairly straightforward manner.

However, this interpretation might well be *too* simplistic, and certainly, many paleoanthropologists now suggest much more diversity and complexity in the evolution of our genus. Accordingly, several new species of *Homo* have been proposed. In this text, we have classified the *Homo* fossil materials into three recognized species: *H. habilis*, *H. erectus*, and *H. sapiens*. We further noted that *H. habilis* might well be only one of two species of what we collectively called "early *Homo*." Moreover, in this chapter we made a clear distinction between archaic forms of *H. sapiens* and anatomically modern forms (*H. sapiens sapiens*). A diagrammatic phylogeny representing this interpretation is shown in Figure 12–16a.

Remember, however, that this is a conservative interpretation, implying a minimum amount of species diversity. This scheme is just about as simple as most paleoanthropologists are willing to consider seriously. Yet, there is another view, proposed by Milford Wolpoff of the University of Michigan, which is even more simple (Fig. 12–16b). Wolpoff argues that subsequent to early *Homo*, only one species (*H. sapiens*) should be recognized. In other words, Professor Wolpoff sinks *H. erectus* into *H. sapiens*. Given the significant anatomical (and probably behavioral) differences between *H. erectus* and *H. sapiens*, Wolpoff's suggestion has not received much support from other paleoanthropologists (see particularly the discussion in Rightmire, 1998).

At the other end of the spectrum are views expressed by a number of researchers who subdivide the *Homo* material into a variety of species. In fact, at every major stage of the evolution of *Homo* over the last 2 million years, some professional opinion has argued seriously for more than one species. First, as noted in Chapter 10 (p. 252), early *Homo* is now frequently subdivided into two different

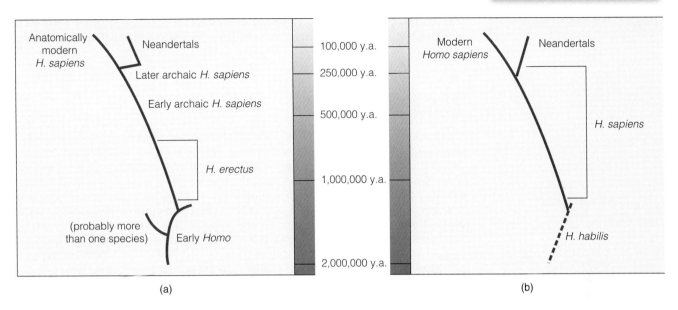

(a)

(b)

species (usually named *H. habilis* and *H. rudolfensis*). Second, as briefly discussed in Chapter 11, what is usually called *H. erectus* is also partitioned into two species (*H. erectus* and *H. ergaster*, the latter referring solely to African specimens). And third (and most relevant to the present discussion), various forms of archaic *H. sapiens* have been assigned by other paleoanthropologists to two or three additional species of *Homo* (some researchers think even more species might be represented).

The major issues relating to these interpretations (and consequent classifications) of what we have termed "archaic *Homo sapiens*" are as follows:

1. The classification of individual fossils into "archaic *Homo sapiens*" is viewed by many as imprecise, since this is an ill-defined evolutionary group (and one quite geographically widespread). At minimum, many researchers have urged a more precise anatomical definition of exactly what "archaic *Homo sapiens*" means.

2. Several early archaic specimens are interpreted by paleoanthropologists as showing derived features different from *Homo sapiens*. These fossils come from Africa and Europe (e.g., Kabwe, Mauer) and are now often classified as *Homo heidelbergensis*.

3. Neandertals are also viewed by numerous researchers as representing a distinct species, what is called *Homo neanderthalensis*. In prior discussions, we have interpreted the variation as representing intraspecific differences; this alternative view argues for a greater degree of interspecific variability (with the inference that fertile interbreeding between Neandertals and *H. sapiens* would not have been possible).

Figure 12–17 shows a phylogeny incorporating these more complex, multiple-species interpretations and suggesting possible evolutionary relationships. For an introductory course,

FIGURE 12–16

(a) Phylogeny showing evolution of genus *Homo*, as discussed in the text. Only very modest species diversity is implied. (Contrast with Figure 12–17.) (b) Highly simplified view of evolution of genus *Homo* with minimal species diversity. (After Wolpoff, 1999.)

FIGURE 12–17

Phylogeny showing multiple species of genus *Homo* with considerable species diversity represented.

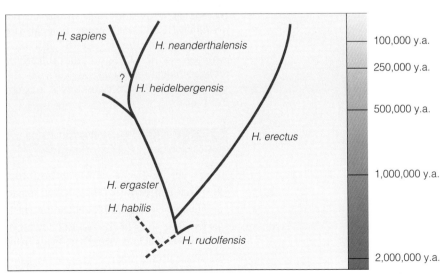

it is less important to memorize all the species names than to recognize what such interpretations imply about the evolutionary process—and what these differing views suggest about our origins.

SUMMARY

During the Middle Pleistocene, significant changes occurred in *H. erectus* morphology. The changes, especially in cranial traits, led scientists to assign a new species designation to these forms (*Homo sapiens*). Because they exhibited a mosaic of *H. erectus* and *H. sapiens* characteristics, the name archaic *H. sapiens* is used to indicate that they were forms transitional between *H. erectus* and anatomically modern humans. Some archaic *H. sapiens* populations possessed more derived modern traits than others, and these populations are sometimes referred to as later archaic *H. sapiens* or early *H. sapiens sapiens*. It has been suggested that some later European archaic forms were directly ancestral to Neandertals.

In addition to morphological changes among archaic forms, there were cultural developments as well. Archaic *H. sapiens* invented new kinds of tools and tool-making techniques, exploited new foods, built more complex shelters, probably controlled fire, and may have used some form of speech.

In western Europe, archaic *H. sapiens* developed into a unique form—classic Neandertals—who apparently migrated from Europe to the Near East and then even further into Asia. Neandertals were physically robust and muscular, different from both early archaic forms and modern *H. sapiens*. Their culture was more complex than earlier archaic cultures, and it appears that in Europe and the Near East, they lived in areas also inhabited by modern *H. sapiens*. Whether modern forms in these areas evolved directly from Neandertals or migrated from Africa (or the Near East) and ultimately replaced Neandertals is one of the important issues currently being debated by paleoanthropologists.

Finally, we would emphasize that Neandertals and all humans on earth today belong to the same species, *H. sapiens*. There are physical differences between these forms, of course, and for that reason Neandertals are assigned to the subspecies *H. sapiens neanderthalensis* and anatomically modern forms to the subspecies *H. sapiens sapiens*.

We should point out that this assignment of a *separate* subspecies for the Neandertals emphasizes some notable degrees of variation; that is, Neandertals are viewed as more different from *any* modern group of *H. sapiens* than these groups differ from one another. Some scholars would even more dramatically emphasize this variation and thus assign Neandertals to a separate species from *Homo sapiens*. In this view, Neandertals would be placed in the separate species *Homo neanderthalensis*. Likewise, many paleoanthropologists would also subdivide what we call "early archaic *H. sapiens*" into another species. The behavioral differences between Neandertals and anatomically modern *H. sapiens*, as interpreted from the archaeological record, are also discussed. These differences are emphasized by those scholars who view Neandertals as an evolutionary dead end.

QUESTIONS FOR REVIEW

1. In what respect does *H. sapiens* (broadly defined) contrast with *H. erectus*?
2. What is meant by "archaic" *H. sapiens*?
3. How does archaic *H. sapiens* contrast with anatomically modern *H. sapiens*?
4. In what areas of the world have archaic *H. sapiens* specimens been discovered? Compare and contrast the finds from two separate areas.
5. What do we mean when we say that archaic *H. sapiens* specimens are transitional?

6. Why have Neandertals been depicted (by the popular press and others) as being primitive? Do you agree with this interpretation? Why or why not?

7. In what general areas of the world have Neandertal fossil remains been discovered?

8. What evidence suggests that Neandertals deliberately buried their dead? What interpretations do such treatment of the dead suggest to you?

9. What physical characteristics distinguish the Neandertals from anatomically modern *Homo sapiens*?

10. What behavioral characteristics distinguish Neandertal culture from that of the Upper Paleolithic?

11. What two major transitions within the genus *Homo* have been discussed in this chapter and in Chapter 11? Compare these transitions for geographical distribution as well as for aspects of evolutionary pace.

12. Discuss why some paleoanthropologists subdivide the archaic *H. sapiens* material into more than one species. What does this interpretation imply biologically?

SUGGESTED FURTHER READING

Mellars, Paul. 1995. *The Neanderthal Legacy. An Archaeological Perspective from Western Europe.* Princeton, NJ: Princeton University Press.

Shreeve, James. 1995. *The Neandertal Enigma.* New York: Morrow.

Stiner, Mary C. 1995. *Honor Among Thieves. A Zooarchaeological Study of Neandertal Ecology.* Princeton, NJ: Princeton University Press.

Stringer, Christopher, and Clive Gamble. 1993. *In Search of the Neanderthals.* New York: Thames and Hudson.

Trinkaus, Erik, and Pat Shipman. 1993. *The Neandertals: Changing the Image of Mankind.* New York: Knopf.

RESOURCES ON THE INTERNET

 ### Wadsworth Anthropology Resource Center
http://anthropology.wadsworth.com

The companion website for this text includes a range of enrichment material focused on the chapter's topic. While online you can enhance your understanding of the chapter by exploring one of the several additional Internet Exercises, by researching topics, and by accessing full articles on InfoTrac College Edition. You can also reinforce the concepts by taking online practice exams.

Internet Exercises

Use your search engine to find articles pertaining to the Neandertals. Specifically, look for information regarding the evidence that Neandertals continued to exist later than previously believed. If you have difficulties finding such information, try www.archaeology.org but we encourage you to look for other Web sites as well.

 ### InfoTrac College Edition
http://www.infotrac-college.com/wadsworth

Using PowerTrac search for the subject *Neanderthal* (InfoTrac College Edition spells Neandertal with the *h*, the older spelling—using the newer spelling will pull up fewer references). How many articles or abstracts did you find? Read at least one article and discuss how it relates to material in Chapter 12.

CHAPTER

13

CONTENTS

Homo
sapiens sapiens

Introduction

In this chapter, we discuss anatomically modern humans, taxonomically known as *Homo sapiens sapiens*. As we discussed in Chapter 12, in some areas evolutionary developments produced early archaic *H. sapiens* populations exhibiting a mosaic of *H. erectus* and *H. sapiens* traits. In some regions, the trend emphasizing *H. sapiens* characteristics continued, and possibly as early as 200,000 y.a., transitional forms (between early archaic and anatomically modern forms) appeared in Africa. Given the nature of the evidence and ongoing ambiguities in dating, it is not possible to say exactly when anatomically modern *H. sapiens* first appeared. However, the transition and certainly the wide dispersal of *H. sapiens sapiens* in the Old World appear to have been relatively rapid evolutionary events. Thus, we can ask several basic questions:

1. *When* (approximately) did *H. sapiens sapiens* first appear?
2. *Where* did the transition take place? Did it occur in just one region or in several?
3. *What* was the pace of evolutionary change? How quickly did the transition occur?
4. *How* did the dispersal of *H. sapiens sapiens* to other areas of the Old World (outside that of origin) take place?

These questions concerning the origins and early dispersal of *Homo sapiens sapiens* continue to fuel much controversy among paleoanthropologists. And it is no wonder, for members of early *Homo sapiens sapiens* are our *direct* kin and are thus closely related to all contemporary humans. They were much like us skeletally, genetically, and (most likely) behaviorally as well. In fact, it is the various hypotheses relating to the behavioral capacities of our most immediate predecessors that have most fired the imagination of scientists and laypeople alike. In every major respect, these are the first hominids that we can confidently refer to as "fully human."

In this chapter, we will also discuss archaeological evidence from the Upper *Paleolithic* (see p. 301). This evidence will allow us to better understand technological and social developments during the period when modern humans arose and quickly came to dominate the planet.

The evolutionary story of *Homo sapiens sapiens* is really a biological autobiography of us all. It is a story that still has many unanswered questions; but several theories have been proposed that seek to organize the diverse information that is presently available.

The Origin and Dispersal of *Homo sapiens sapiens* (Anatomically Modern Human Beings)

There are two major theories that attempt to organize and explain modern human origins: the complete replacement model and the regional continuity model. These two views are quite distinct and in some ways diametrically opposed to each other. Moreover, the popular press has further contributed to a wide and incorrect perception of irreconcilable argument on these points by "opposing" scientists. Indeed, there is a third theory, which we call the partial replacement model, that is a compromise hypothesis incorporating some aspects of the two major theories. Because so much of our contemporary view of modern human origins is driven by the debates linked to these differing theories, let us begin by briefly reviewing each. We will then turn to the fossil evidence itself to see what it can contribute to resolving the questions we have posed.

See the following sections of the CD-ROM for topics covered in this chapter: Virtual Lab 11, section IV, and Virtual Lab 12, sections I and II.

See Virtual Lab 12, section II, for a discussion of the Complete Replacement Theory.

The Complete Replacement Model (Recent African Evolution)

The complete replacement model, developed by British paleoanthropologists Christopher Stringer and Peter Andrews (1988), is based on the origin of modern humans in Africa and later replacement of populations in Europe and Asia (Fig. 13–1). In brief, this theory proposes that anatomically modern populations arose in Africa within the last 200,000 years, then migrated from Africa, completely *replacing* populations in Europe and Asia. This model does not take into account any transition from archaic *H. sapiens* to modern *H. sapiens* anywhere in the world except Africa. A critical deduction of the Stringer and Andrews theory is that it considers the appearance of anatomically modern humans as a biological speciation event. Thus, in this view there could be no admixture of migrating African modern *H. sapiens* with local populations because the African modern humans were a *biologically* different species. In a taxonomic context, all of the "archaic *H. sapiens*" populations outside Africa would, in this view, be classified as belonging to different species of *Homo* (e.g., the Neandertals would be classified as *H. neanderthalensis*; see p. 313 for further discussion). While this speciation explanation fits nicely with, and in fact helps explain, *complete* replacement, Stringer has more recently stated that he is not dogmatic regarding this issue. Thus, he suggests that there may have been potential for interbreeding, but he argues that very little apparently took place.

A crucial source of supporting evidence for the African origin hypothesis (and complete replacement elsewhere) has come from genetic data obtained from living peoples. Underlying this approach is the assumption that genetic patterning seen in contemporary populations will provide clues to relationships and origins of ancient *Homo sapiens*. However, as with numerous prior attempts to evaluate such patterning from more traditional data on human polymorphisms (e.g., ABO, HLA—see Chapter 4), the obstacles are enormous.

A recent innovation uses genetic sequencing data derived directly from DNA. The most promising application has come not from the DNA within the nucleus, but from DNA found in the cytoplasm—that is, mitochondrial DNA (mtDNA; see Chapter 3). You may recall that mitochondria are organelles found in the cell, but outside the nucleus. They contain a set of DNA, dissimilar from nuclear DNA, inherited only through the mother. Thus, mtDNA does not undergo the genetic recombination that occurs in nuclear DNA during meiosis.

Using mtDNA gathered from a number of different populations, scientists at the University of California, Berkeley, constructed "trees" (something like a family tree) that, they claimed, demonstrated that the entire population of the world today descended from a single African lineage. However, the methodology of these molecular biologists has been faulted. Using the same mtDNA material, other scientists constructed many trees that differed from those of the Berkeley group, and some of them are *without African roots* (i.e., the same data can be used statistically to show that *H. sapiens* arose in Asia, *not* in Africa).

This question of the applicability of the mtDNA evidence continues to generate considerable disagreement. Paleoanthropologist Robert Corruccini of Southern Illinois University has been unimpressed with the entire approach, stating that "critical shortcomings of molecular population genetic assumptions and of analysis . . . render any mtDNA conclusions virtually useless to ruminations about human evolution" (Corruccini, 1994, p. 698). Likewise, Glenn Conroy (1997) has critiqued many of the oversimplifications inherent in the genetic data and consequent interpretations. However, molecular anthropologist Mark Stoneking of Pennsylvania State University (and one of the founders of this approach) remains much more confident in the general reliability of the mtDNA results, especially as they show a much greater diversity among contemporary African groups as compared to other world populations. Stoneking thus concludes: "Because non-African populations that predate the mtDNA ancestor apparently did not contribute mtDNAs to contemporary human populations, it follows that the spread of modern populations was accomplished with little or no admixture with resident non-African populations. If it were otherwise, there should be evidence of much more divergent mtDNA types in contemporary human populations" (Stoneking, 1993, pp. 66–67).

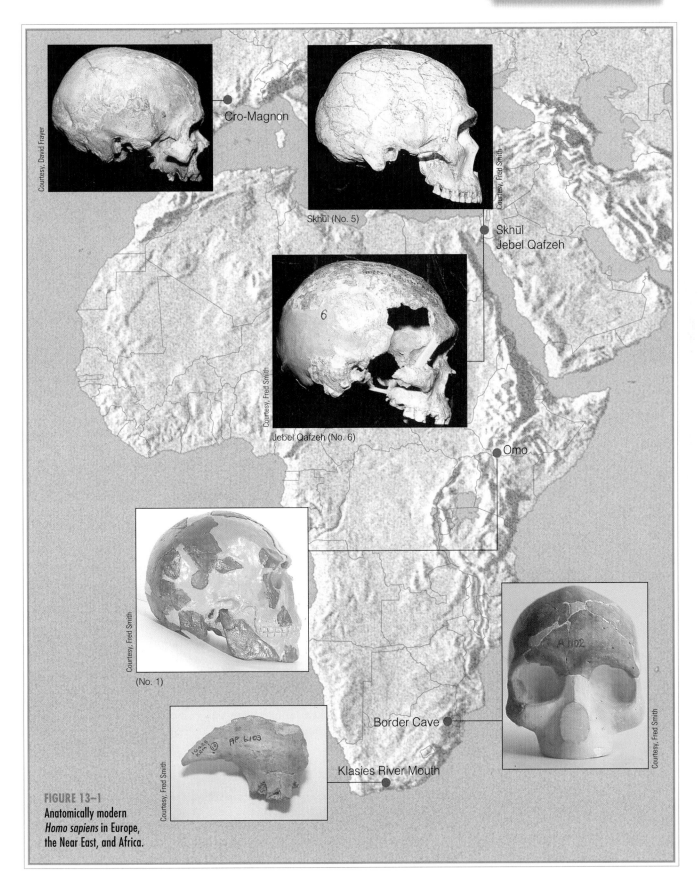

Cro-Magnon

Skhūl (No. 5)

Skhūl
Jebel Qafzeh

Jebel Qafzeh (No. 6)

Omo

(No. 1)

Border Cave

Klasies River Mouth

FIGURE 13–1
Anatomically modern
Homo sapiens in Europe,
the Near East, and Africa.

Recently, some further genetic data have helped bolster some of the main tenets of the complete replacement model. A team of Yale, Harvard, and University of Chicago researchers (Dorit et al., 1995) has investigated variation in the Y chromosome, finding *much* less variation in humans than in other primates. And another group of Yale researchers (Tishkoff et al., 1996), looking at DNA sequences on chromosome 12, again found much more variation among contemporary Africans than is seen in all the remainder of the world combined. Finally, the recent reports of the distinctive nature of Neandertal mtDNA (see p. 310) also argue that substantial replacement took place. Nevertheless, some geneticists find the results unconvincing (e.g., Ayala, 1995; Templeton, 1996), and many paleoanthropologists (agreeing with the views expressed by Corruccini and Conroy) are extremely skeptical of the main conclusions derived from the genetic data (see Box 13–1 on p. 324 for further discussion).

The Partial Replacement Model

The partial replacement model also begins with African early archaic *H. sapiens*. Later, also in Africa, anatomically modern *H. sapiens* populations first evolved. This theory, proposed by Günter Bräuer of the University of Hamburg, postulates the earliest dates for African modern *Homo sapiens* at over 100,000 y.a. Bräuer sees the initial dispersal of *H. sapiens sapiens* out of South Africa as significantly influenced by shifting environmental conditions and thus as a gradual process. Moving into Eurasia, modern humans hybridized, probably to a limited degree, with resident archaic groups and eventually replaced them. The disappearance of archaic humans was therefore due to both hybridization and replacement and was a gradual and complex process. This model includes components of regional continuity, hybridization, and replacement, with the emphasis on replacement.

The Regional Continuity Model (Multiregional Evolution)

The regional continuity model is most closely associated with paleoanthropologist Milford Wolpoff of the University of Michigan and his associates (Thorne and Wolpoff, 1992; Wolpoff et al., 1994). These researchers suggest that local populations (not all, of course) in Europe, Asia, and Africa continued their indigenous evolutionary development from archaic *H. sapiens* to anatomically modern humans. A question immediately arises: How is it possible for different local populations around the globe to evolve with such similar morphology? In other words, how could anatomically modern humans arise separately in different continents and end up physically (and genetically) so similar? The multiregional model explains this phenomenon by (1) denying that the earliest modern *H. sapiens* populations originated *exclusively* in Africa and challenging the notion of complete replacement and (2) asserting that some gene flow (migration) between archaic populations was extremely likely, and consequently, modern humans cannot be considered a species separate from archaic forms.

Through gene flow and local selection, according to the multiregional hypothesis, local populations would *not* have evolved totally independently from one another, and such mixing would have "prevented speciation between the regional lineages and thus maintained human beings as a *single*, although obviously *polytypic* (see p. 90), species throughout the Pleistocene" (Smith et al., 1989).

The Earliest *Homo sapiens sapiens* Discoveries

Current evidence strongly indicates that the earliest modern *H. sapiens* fossils come from Africa, but not everyone agrees on the dates or designations or precisely which specimens are the modern and which are the archaic forms. With this cautionary note, we continue our discussion, but there undoubtedly will be corrections as more evidence is gathered.

Africa

In Africa, several early fossil finds have been interpreted as fully anatomically modern forms (see Fig. 13–1). These specimens come from the Klasies River Mouth on the south coast (which could be the earliest find), Border Cave slightly to the north, and Omo Kibish 1 in southern Ethiopia. With the use of relatively new techniques, all three sites have been dated to about 120,000–80,000 y.a. The original geological context at Border Cave is uncertain, and the fossils may be younger than at the other two sites (see Table 13–1 and Fig. 13–5). Some paleoanthropologists consider these fossils to be the earliest known anatomically modern humans. Problems with dating, context, and differing interpretations of the evidence have led other paleoanthropologists to question whether the *earliest* modern forms (Fig. 13–2) really did evolve in Africa. Other modern *H. sapiens* individuals, possibly older than these Africans, have been found in the Near East.

The Near East

In Israel, early modern *H. sapiens* fossils (the remains of at least 10 individuals) were found in the Skhūl Cave at Mt. Carmel (Figs. 13–3 and 13–4a), very near the Neandertal site of Tabun. Also from Israel, the Qafzeh Cave has yielded the remains of at least 20 individuals (Fig. 13–4b). Although their overall configuration is definitely modern, some specimens show certain archaic (i.e., Neandertal) features. Skhūl has been dated to about 115,000 y.a., and Qafzeh has been placed around 100,000 y.a. (Bar-Yosef, 1993, 1994) (Fig. 13–5 on p. 326).

Such early dates for modern specimens pose some problems for those advocating local replacement (the multiregional model). How early do archaic *H. sapiens* populations (Neandertals) appear in the Near East? A recent chronometric calibration for the Tabun Cave suggests a date as early as 120,000 y.a. Neandertals thus may *slightly* precede modern forms in the Near East, but there would appear to be

TABLE 13–1   Additional Techniques for Dating Middle and Upper Pleistocene Sites

Technique	Physical Basis	Examples of Use
Uranium series dating	Radioactive decay of short-lived uranium isotopes	To date limestone formations (e.g., stalagmites) and ancient ostrich eggshells; to estimate age of Jinniushan site in China and Ngandong site in Java, both corroborated by ESR dates
Thermoluminescence (TL) dating*	Accumulation of trapped electrons within certain crystals released during heating	To date ancient flint tools (either deliberately or accidentally heated); to provide key dates for the Qafzeh site
Electron spin resonance (ESR) dating	Measurement (counting) of accumulated trapped electrons	To date dental enamel; to corroborate dating of Qafzeh, Skhūl, and Tabun sites in Israel, Ngandong site in Java, and Klasies River Mouth and Border Cave sites in South Africa

*TL is also used in more recent archaeological contexts; see Chapter 14.

Source: Cook et al., 1984; Aiken et al., 1993.

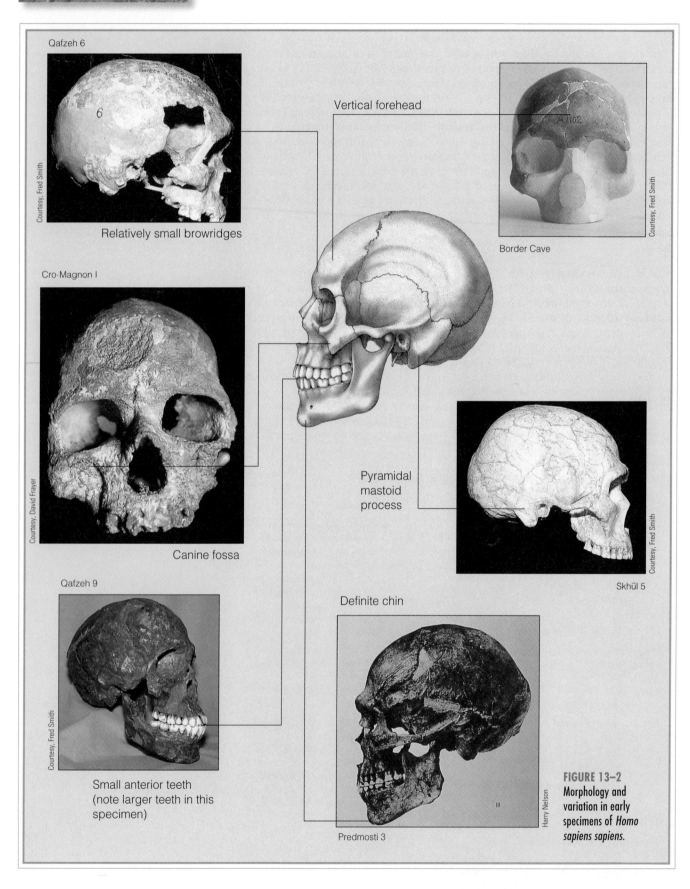

Qafzeh 6

6

Relatively small browridges

Courtesy, Fred Smith

Vertical forehead

Border Cave

Courtesy, Fred Smith

Cro-Magnon I

Courtesy, David Frayer

Canine fossa

Pyramidal
mastoid
process

Skhūl 5

Courtesy, Fred Smith

Qafzeh 9

Courtesy, Fred Smith

Small anterior teeth
(note larger teeth in this
specimen)

Definite chin

Predmosti 3

Harry Nelson

FIGURE 13–2
Morphology and
variation in early
specimens of *Homo
sapiens sapiens*.

(a)

(b)

FIGURE 13–3
(a) Mt. Carmel, studded with caves, was home to *H. sapiens sapiens* at Skhūl (and to Neandertals at Tabun and Kebara). (b) Skhūl Cave.

considerable overlap in the timing of occupation by these different *H. sapiens* forms. And recall, the modern site at Mt. Carmel (Skhūl) is very near the Neandertal site (Tabun). Clearly, the dynamics of *Homo sapiens* evolution in the Near East are highly complex, and no simple model may explain later hominid evolution adequately.

Central Europe

Central Europe has been a source of many fossil finds, including numerous fairly early anatomically modern *H. sapiens*. At several sites, it appears that some fossils display both Neandertal and modern features, which supports the regional continuity hypothesis (from Neandertal to modern). Some genetic continuity from earlier (Neandertal) to later (modern *Homo sapiens*) populations was perhaps the case at Vindija in Croatia, where typical Neandertals were found in earlier contexts (see p. 304).

FIGURE 13–4
(a) Skhūl 5. (b) Qafzeh 6. These specimens from Israel are thought to be representatives of early modern *Homo sapiens*. The vault height, forehead, and lack of prognathism are modern traits.

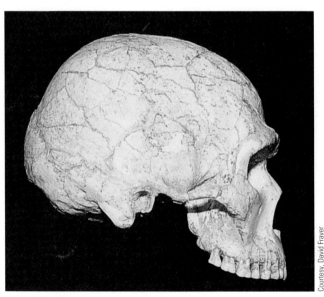

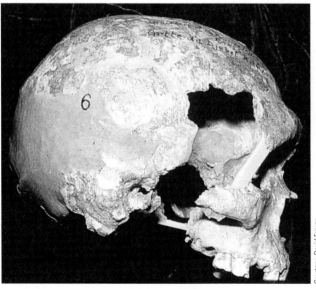

(a)

(b)

BOX 13–1   DIGGING DEEPER

The Garden of Eden Hypothesis

Gathering samples of mtDNA from placentas of women whose ancestors lived in Africa, Asia, Europe, Australia, and New Guinea, biologists Allan Wilson, Rebecca Cann, and Mark Stoneking, from the University of California, Berkeley, postulated a distinctive genetic pattern for each area. They then compared the diversity of the various patterns (Cann et al., 1987).

They found the greatest variation among Africans and therefore postulated Africa to have been the home of the oldest human populations (the assumption is that the longer the time, the greater the accumulation of genetic variation). They also found that the African variants contained only African mtDNA, whereas those from other areas all included at least one African component. Therefore, the biologists concluded, there must have been a migration initially from Africa, ultimately to all other inhabited areas of the world. By counting the number of genetic mutations and applying the *rate* of mutation, Rebecca Cann and her associates calculated a date for the origin of anatomically modern humans: between 285,000 and 143,000 years ago—in other words, an average estimate of about 200,000 years ago. Indeed, a further contention of the mtDNA researchers is that the pattern of variation argues that all modern humans shared in common a single African female lineage that lived sometime during this time range. Thus was born the popularized concept of "mitochondrial Eve."

Not all scientists, by any means, agree with this scenario. The estimated rate of mutations may be incorrect, and therefore, the proposed date of migration out of Africa would also be in error. Secondly, differing population size in Africa, compared to elsewhere, would complicate interpretations (Relethford and Harpending, 1994). Also, secondary migration, outside

Africa, could disrupt the direct inheritance of the African maternal line. Even more troubling are the inherent biases in the statistical technique used to identify the primary population relationships ("trees"). Recent reanalyses of the data suggest that the situation is not nearly as clear-cut as originally believed.

Scrutiny of the mitochondrial DNA–based model of modern human origins came when the approach was attempted by other laboratories using similar techniques and statistical treatments. In February 1992, three different papers were published by different teams of researchers, all of which severely challenged the main tenets of the hypotheses as proposed by Wilson, Cann, and Stoneking. The most serious error was a failure to recognize how many *equally valid* results could be deduced statistically from the *same set* of original data. In science, as we have remarked before, beyond the data themselves, the methodological treatments (especially statistical models) greatly influence both the nature and *confidence limits* of the results.

The central conclusion that Africa alone was the *sole* source of modern humans could still be correct. Yet, now it had to be admitted that dozens (indeed, thousands) of other equally probable renditions could be derived from the supposedly unambiguous mitochondrial data. Thus, barely a few months after the original researchers had proposed their most systematic statement of their hypotheses, the entire perspective (especially its statistical implications) was shaken to its very foundations—and, in many people's eyes, falsified altogether.

An interesting twist regarding this entire reassessment is that the team from Pennsylvania State University that challenged the initial results was joined in its critique by Mark Stoneking, one of the original

---

Smith (1984) offers another example of local continuity from Mladeč, in the Czech Republic. Among the earlier European modern *H. sapiens* fossils, dated to about 33,000 y.a., the Mladeč crania display a great deal of variation, probably in part due to sexual dimorphism. Although each of the crania (except for one of the females) displays a prominent supraorbital torus, it is reduced from the typical Neandertal pattern. Even though there is some suggestion of continuity from Neandertals to modern humans, Smith is certain that, given certain anatomical features, the Mladeč remains are best classified as *H. sapiens sapiens*. Reduced mid-

formulators of the now-questioned hypothesis. A viable scientific perspective, so well illustrated here, is that new approaches (or refined applications) often necessitate reevaluation of prior hypotheses. It takes both objectivity and courage to admit miscalculations. By so doing, an even more permanent and positive legacy helps contain the inherent personal biases that sometimes have so divided the study of human origins.

On the basis of these new studies, many have proclaimed that mitochondrial Eve is dead—and perhaps the complete replacement hypothesis with her. As could be expected, the proponents of the African origin view are not yet ready to bury Eve or significantly alter their confidence in the complete replacement hypothesis.

As the debate continues, new lines of evidence and new techniques are being pursued: more ways to sequence both mitochondrial and nuclear DNA; more complete evidence of human polymorphisms; genetic sequence data for the Y chromosome; and, it is hoped, more reliable statistical techniques to interpret these complex data. The new data for the Y chromosome are particularly interesting. Since the Y chromosome is inherited *paternally* (and thus also is *not* recombined), its pattern of genetic diversity makes for an excellent complement to the maternally inherited mtDNA. Biologist Robert Dorit of Yale University, along with his team of researchers, sequenced a portion of the Y chromosome. Surprisingly, they found absolutely *no* variation in this region, but did see much more Y chromosome variation in great apes (chimpanzees, gorillas, orangutans). Dorit suggests that this lack of variation indicates a recent origin for *Homo sapiens*. He notes at the same time, however, that "the lack of variation in the Y chromosome regions we examined also makes it impossible for us to reconstruct the geographic location of the last common ancestor" (Henahan, 1995).

Further evidence along these lines has come from another group of Yale biologists led by Sarah Tishkoff (Tishkoff et al., 1996). Tishkoff and her colleagues have been investigating genetic patterns within nuclear DNA (their research target is a region on chromosome 12). Assembling a very large sample of data (1,600 individuals from 42 populations), Tishkoff and her team found by far the most variation among contemporary Africans. (Of 24 possible variants, 21 of these were found in Africa; Europe and the Middle East displayed only 3; Asia, the Pacific Islands, and the New World together displayed a mere 2.) Tishkoff draws the same conclusion as that proposed by both the mtDNA and the Y chromosome researchers—that all modern humans are the result of a single recent evolutionary event. (Tishkoff, in fact, places the date at 100,000–70,000 y.a., even more recent than that suggested by the mtDNA evidence.) Moreover, the results from the chromosome 12 DNA polymorphisms, like those relating to mtDNA, suggest that Africa was the geographical source for all modern humans.

What can we then conclude? Results are still tentative, but various studies are now corroborating one another. First, we can conclude that *Homo sapiens* is not a very genetically variable species; indeed, genetically, we are quite a homogeneous lot (a point we emphasized in Chapter 5). By some estimates, comparisons with other primates suggest that human mtDNA is only about 1/40 to 1/50 as variable as the mtDNA of chimpanzees (Cann et al., 1994)! Does human genetic homogeneity imply a *recent origin* for all *H. sapiens sapiens*? Perhaps. At the least, these increasingly consistent genetic data argue that it is unlikely that the present genetic patterning in *H. sapiens* can be traced back to the early dispersal of *H. erectus* out of Africa (circa 1.8 m.y.a.). It would appear that there must have been one or more later dispersals as well. But how much later? The broadest time limits so far indicated by various genetic techniques would suggest a time frame in the range of 850,000–100,000 y.a. (with the greatest probabilities between 450,000 and 100,000 y.a.). If you were inclined to make a wager on the probabilities of the time of the last major dispersal of hominids, somewhere in this latter range looks like a good bet.

facial projection, a higher forehead, and postcranial elements "are clearly modern *H. sapiens* in morphology and not specifically Neandertal-like in a single feature" (Smith, 1984, p. 174).

Western Europe

This area of the world and its fossils have received the greatest paleoanthropological attention for several reasons, one of which is probably serendipity. Over the last

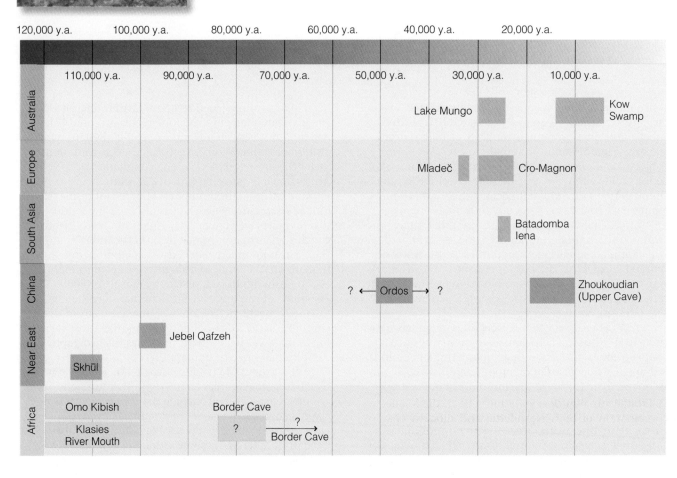

FIGURE 13–5

Time line of *Homo sapiens sapiens* discoveries. Note that most dates are approximations. Question marks indicate those estimates that are most tentative.

Cro-Magnon
(crow man´yon)

Aurignacian
Pertaining to an Upper Paleolithic stone tool industry in Europe beginning at about 40,000 y.a.

century and a half, many of the scholars interested in this kind of research happened to live in western Europe, and the southern region of France happened to be a fossil treasure trove. Also, early on, discovering and learning about human ancestors caught the curiosity and pride of the local population.

Because of this scholarly interest beginning back in the nineteenth century, a great deal of data accumulated, with little reliable comparative information available from elsewhere in the world. Consequently, theories of human evolution were based almost exclusively on the western European material. It has only been in recent years, with growing evidence from other areas of the world and with the application of new dating techniques, that recent human evolutionary dynamics have been seriously considered on a worldwide basis.

There are many anatomically modern human fossils from western Europe going back 40,000 years or more, but by far the best-known sample of western European *H. sapiens* is from the **Cro-Magnon** site. A total of eight individuals were discovered in 1868 in a rock shelter in the village of Les Eyzies, in the Dordogne region of southern France (Gambier, 1989).

Associated with an **Aurignacian** tool assemblage, an Upper Paleolithic industry, the Cro-Magnon materials, dated at 30,000 y.a., represent the earliest of France's anatomically modern humans. The so-called "Old Man" (Cro-Magnon I) became the archetype for what was once termed the Cro-Magnon, or Upper Paleolithic, "race" of Europe (Fig.13–6). Actually, of course, there is no such race, and Cro-Magnon I is not typical of Upper Paleolithic western Europeans, and not even all that similar to the other two male skulls that were found at the site.

Considered together, the male crania reflect a mixture of modern and archaic traits. Cro-Magnon I is the most gracile of the three—the supraorbital tori of the

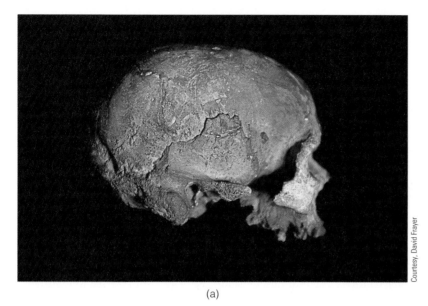

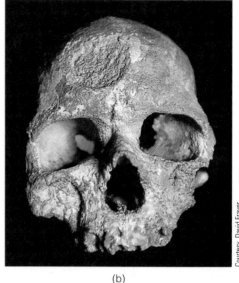

(a)   (b)

FIGURE 13–6
Cro-Magnon I (France). In this specimen, modern traits are quite clear. (a) Lateral view. (b) Frontal view. (Courtesy of David Frayer.)

other two males, for example, are more robust. The most modern-looking is the female cranium, the appearance of which may be a function of sexual dimorphism.

The question of whether continuous local evolution produced anatomically modern groups directly from Neandertals in some regions of Eurasia is far from settled. From central Europe, variation seen in the Mladeč and Vindija fossils indicate a combination of both Neandertal and modern characteristics and may suggest gene flow between the two different *H. sapiens* groups. However, tracing such relatively minor genetic changes—considering the ever-present problems of dating, lack of fossils, and fragmented fossil finds—has proved extremely difficult.

However, a newly discovered child's skeleton from Portugal has provided some of the best evidence yet of possible hybridization between Neandertals and anatomically modern *H. sapiens*. This important new hominid discovery from the Abrigo do Lagar Velho site in central western Portugal was excavated in late 1998 and is dated to 24,500 y.a. (i.e., at least 5,000 years *later* than the last clearly Neandertal find). Associated with an Upper Paleolithic industry (see p. 328) and interred with red ocher and pierced shell is a fairly complete skeleton of a four-year-old child (Duarte et al., 1999). Cidália Duarte, Erik Trinkaus, and colleagues, who have studied the remains, found a highly mixed set of anatomical features. Many characteristics (of the teeth, lower jaw, and pelvis) were like those seen in anatomically modern humans. Yet, several other features (lack of chin, limb proportions, muscle insertions) were more similar to Neandertals. The authors thus conclude, "The presence of such admixture suggests the hypothesis of variable admixture between early modern humans dispersing into Europe and local Neandertal populations" (Duarte et al., 1999, p. 7608). These researchers thus argue that this new evidence provides strong support for the partial replacement model while seriously weakening the complete replacement model. However, the evidence from one child's skeleton—while intriguing—is certainly not going to convince everyone!

Asia

There are six early anatomically modern human localities in China, the most significant of which are Upper Cave at Zhoukoudian and Ordos. The fossils from these sites are all fully modern, and most are considered to be of quite late Upper Pleistocene age. Upper Cave at Zhoukoudian has been dated to between 18,000 and 10,000 y.a. The Ordos find was discovered at Dagouwan, Inner Mongolia, and may be the oldest anatomically modern material from China, perhaps dating to 50,000 y.a. or more (Etler, personal communication) (see Fig. 13–5).

See Virtual Lab 12, section I, for a discussion of the transformations in physical characteristics that accompanied the evolution of modern *Homo sapiens*.

In addition, the Jinniushan skeleton discussed in Chapter 12 (see p. 289) has been suggested by some researchers (Tiemel et al., 1994) as hinting at modern features in China as early as 200,000 y.a. If this date (as early as that proposed for direct antecedents of modern *H. sapiens* in Africa) should prove accurate, it would cast doubt on the complete replacement model. Indeed, quite opposed to the complete replacement model and more in support of regional continuity, many Chinese paleoanthropologists see a continuous evolution from Chinese *H. erectus* to archaic *H. sapiens* to anatomically modern humans. This view is supported by Wolpoff, who mentions that materials from Upper Cave at Zhoukoudian "have a number of features that are characteristically regional" and that these features are definitely not African (1989, p. 83).*

In addition to the well-known finds from China, anatomically modern remains have also been discovered in southern Asia. At Batadomba Iena, in southern Sri Lanka, modern *Homo sapiens* finds have been dated to 25,500 y.a. (Kennedy and Deraniyagala, 1989).

Australia

During glacial times, the Indonesian islands were joined to the Asian mainland, but Australia was not. It is likely that by 50,000 y.a., Sahul—the area including New Guinea and Australia—was inhabited by modern humans. Bamboo rafts may have been the means of crossing the sea between islands, which would not have been a simple exercise. Just where the future Australians came from is unknown, but Borneo, Java, and New Guinea have all been suggested.

Archaeological sites in Australia have been dated to at least 55,000 y.a. (Roberts et al., 1990), but the oldest human fossils themselves have been dated to about 30,000 y.a. These oldest Australians are from Lake Mungo, where the remains of two burials (one individual was first cremated) date to 25,000 y.a. and at least 30,000 y.a. (Fig. 13–8 on the following page). The crania are rather gracile with, for example, only moderate development of the supraorbital torus.

Unlike these more gracile early Australian forms are the Kow Swamp people, who are thought to have lived between about 14,000 and 9,000 years ago (Fig. 13–7). The presence of certain archaic traits, such as receding foreheads, heavy supraorbital tori, and thick bones, are difficult to explain, since these features contrast with the postcranial anatomy, which matches that of recent native Australians.

Technology and Art in the Upper Paleolithic

Europe

The cultural period known as the Upper Paleolithic began in western Europe approximately 40,000 years ago (Fig. 13–9). Upper Paleolithic cultures are usually divided into five different industries based on stone tool technologies: (1) Chatelperronian, (2) Aurignacian, (3) Gravettian, (4) Solutrean, and (5) Magdalenian. Major environmental shifts were also apparent during this period. During the last glacial period, at about 30,000 y.a., a warming trend lasting several thousand years partially melted the glacial ice. The result was that much of Eurasia was covered by tundra and steppe, a vast area of treeless country dotted with lakes and marshes. In many areas in the north, permafrost prevented the growth of trees but permitted the growth, in the short summers, of flowering plants, mosses, and other kinds of vegetation. This vegetation served as an enormous pasture for herbivorous animals, large and small, and carnivorous animals fed off the herbivores. It was a hunter's paradise, with millions of animals dispersed

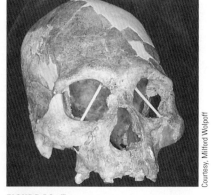

FIGURE 13–7
Kow Swamp (Australia). Note the considerable robusticity in this relatively late Australian *Homo sapiens sapiens* cranium.

Courtesy, Milford Wolpoff

---

*Wolpoff's statement supports his regional continuity hypothesis. His reference to Africa is a criticism of the complete replacement hypothesis.

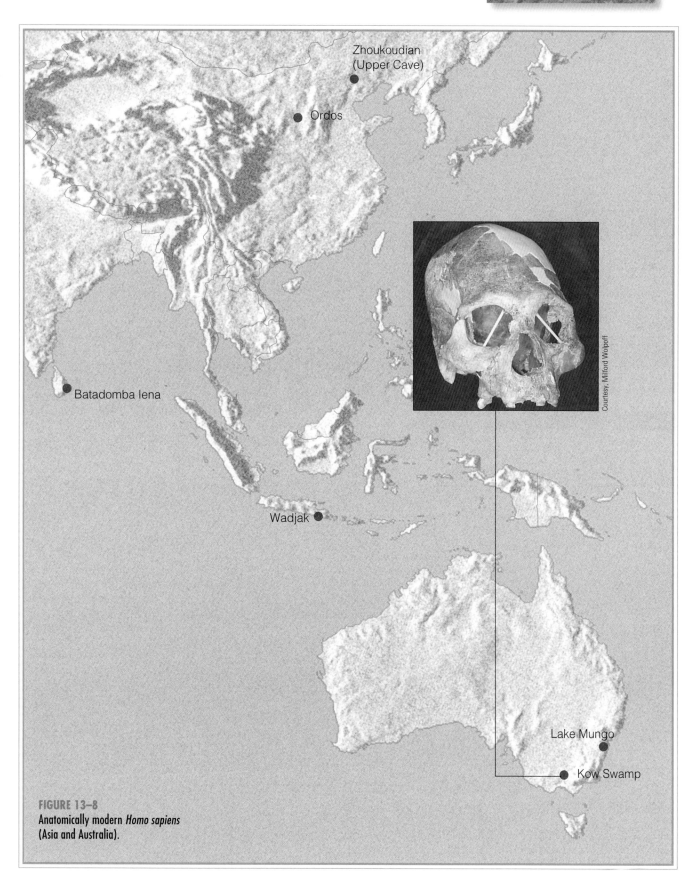

Courtesy, Milford Wolpoff

FIGURE 13–8
Anatomically modern *Homo sapiens*
(Asia and Australia).

GLACIAL	UPPER PALEOLITHIC (beginnings)	CULTURAL PERIODS
W Ü R M	17,000 –	Magdalenian
	21,000 –	Solutrean
	27,000 –	Gravettian
	33,000 –	Aurignacian Chatelperronian
	Middle Paleolithic	Mousterian

FIGURE 13–9
Cultural periods of the European Upper Paleolithic and their approximate beginning dates.

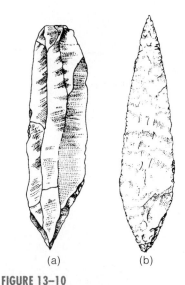

(a)   (b)

FIGURE 13–10
(a) Burin. A very common Upper Paleolithic tool. (b) Solutrean blade. This is the best-known work of the Solutrean tradition. Solutrean stonework is considered the most highly developed of any Upper Paleolithic industry.

Magdalenian
Pertaining to the final phase (stone tool industry) of the Upper Paleolithic in Europe.

Burins
Small, chisel-like tools (with a pointed end) thought to have been used to engrave bone, antler, ivory, or wood.

across expanses of tundra and grassland, from Spain through Europe and into the Russian steppes.

Large herds of reindeer roamed the tundra and steppes along with mammoths, bison, horses, and a host of smaller animals that served as a bountiful source of food. In addition, humans exploited fish and fowl systematically for the first time, especially along the southern tier of Europe. It was a time of relative affluence, and ultimately Upper Paleolithic people spread out over Europe, living in caves and open-air camps and building large shelters. Large dwellings with storage pits have been excavated in the former Soviet Union, with archaeological evidence of social status distinctions (Soffer, 1985). During this period, either western Europe or perhaps portions of Africa achieved the highest population density in human history up to that time.

In Eurasia, cultural innovations allowed humans for the first time to occupy easternmost Europe and northern Asia. In these areas, even during glacial warming stages, winters would have been long and harsh. Human groups were able to tolerate these environments probably because of better constructed structures as well as warmer, better fitting *sewn* clothing. The evidence for wide use of such tailored clothing comes from many sites and includes pointed stone tools such as awls and (by at least 19,000 y.a.) bone needles as well. Especially noteworthy is the clear evidence of the residues of clothing (including what has been interpreted as a cap, a shirt, a jacket, trousers, and moccasins) in graves at the 22,000-year-old Sungir site, located not far from Moscow (Klein, 1989).

Humans and other animals in the midlatitudes of Eurasia had to cope with shifts in climatic conditions, some of which were quite rapid. For example, at 20,000 y.a. another climatic "pulse" caused the weather to become noticeably colder in Europe and Asia as the continental glaciations reached their maximum extent for this entire glacial period (called the Würm in Eurasia). Meanwhile, the southern continents, too, experienced widespread climatic effects. Notably, in Africa around 20,000 y.a. it became significantly wetter, thus permitting reoccupation of areas in the north and south that had previously been abandoned.

As a variety of organisms attempted to adapt to these changing conditions, *Homo sapiens* had a major advantage: the elaboration of an increasingly sophisticated technology (and probably other components of culture as well). Indeed, probably one of the greatest challenges facing numerous late Pleistocene mammals was the ever more dangerously equipped humans—a trend that has continued to modern times.

The Upper Paleolithic was an age of technological innovation and can be compared to the past few hundred years in our recent history of amazing technological change after centuries of relative inertia. Anatomically modern humans of the Upper Paleolithic not only invented new and specialized tools (Fig. 13–10), but, as we have seen, also greatly increased the use of, and probably experimented with, new materials, such as bone, ivory, and antler.

Solutrean tools are good examples of Upper Paleolithic skill and perhaps aesthetic appreciation as well (Fig. 13–10b). In this lithic (stone) tradition, stoneknapping developed to the finest degree ever known. Using a pressure-flaking technique (see p. 351), the artist/technicians made beautiful parallel-flaked lance heads, expertly flaked on both surfaces, with such delicate points that they can be considered works of art that quite possibly never served, or were intended to serve, a utilitarian purpose.

The last stage of the Upper Paleolithic, known as the **Magdalenian**, saw even more advances in technology. The spear-thrower (Fig. 13–11), a wooden or bone hooked rod (called an *atlatl*), acted to extend the hunter's arm, thus enhancing the force and distance of a spear throw. For catching salmon and other fish, the barbed harpoon is a clever example of the craftsperson's skill. There is also evidence that the bow and arrow may have been used for the first time during this period. The introduction of the punch technique (Fig. 13–12) provided an abundance of standardized stone blades that could be fashioned into **burins** (see Fig. 13–10a) for

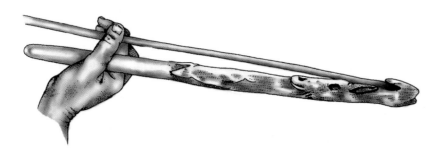

FIGURE 13–11
Spear-thrower (atlatl). Note the carving.

working wood, bone, and antler; borers for drilling holes in skins, bones, and shells; and blades for knives with serrated or notched edges for scraping wooden shafts into a variety of tools.

The elaboration of many more specialized tools by Upper Paleolithic peoples probably made more resources available to them and may also have had an impact on the biology of these populations. C. Loring Brace of the University of Michigan has suggested that with more efficient tools used for food processing, anatomically modern *H. sapiens* would not have required the large front teeth (incisors) seen in earlier populations. With relaxed selection pressures (no longer favoring large anterior teeth), incorporation of random mutations would through time lead to reduction of dental size and accompanying facial features. In particular, the lower face became less prognathic (as compared to archaic specimens) and thus produced the concavity of the cheekbones called a *canine fossa* (see Fig. 13–2). Moreover, as the dental-bearing portion of the lower jaw regressed, the buttressing below would have become modified into *a chin*, that distinctive feature seen in anatomically modern *H. sapiens*.

In addition to their reputation as hunters, western Europeans of the Upper Paleolithic are even better known for their symbolic representation, what has

See Virtual Lab 11, section IV, for a discussion of blade manufacture.

FIGURE 13–12
The punch blade technique.

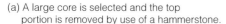

(a) A large core is selected and the top portion is removed by use of a hammerstone.

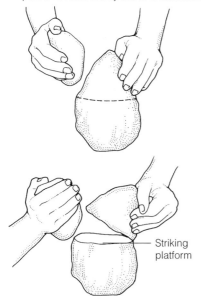

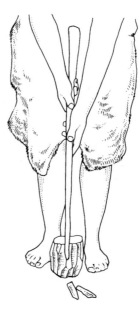

(b) The objective is to create a flat surface called a striking platform.

Striking platform

(c) Next, the core is struck by use of a hammer and punch (made of bone or antler) to remove the long narrow flakes (called blades).

(d) Or the blades can be removed by pressure flaking.

(e) The result is the production of highly consistent sharp blades, which can be used, as is, as knives; or they can be further modified (retouched) to make a variety of other tools (such as burins, scrapers, and awls).

331

commonly been called "art." Certainly, in the famous caves of France and Spain (discussed below), we easily relate to an aesthetic property of the images—one that *may* have been intended by the people who created them. But here we cannot be certain. Our own cultural perspectives create labels (and categories) such as "art," which in itself *assumes* aesthetic intent. While such a cultural orientation is obviously a recognizable part of Western culture, many other contemporary peoples would not relate to this concept within their own cultural context. Furthermore, prehistoric peoples during the Upper Paleolithic did not necessarily create their symbols as true artistic representations. Rather, these representations may have served a variety of quite utilitarian and/or social functions—as do contemporary highway signs or logos on a company's letterhead. Would we call these symbols art?

Given these uncertainties, archaeologist Margaret Conkey of the University of California, Berkeley, refers to Upper Paleolithic cave paintings, sculptures, engravings, and so forth, as "visual and material imagery" (Conkey, 1987, p. 423). We will continue to use the term *art* to describe many of these prehistoric representations, but you should recognize that we do so mainly as a cultural convention—and perhaps a limiting one.

Moreover, the time depth for these prehistoric forms of symbolic imagery is quite long, encompassing the entire Upper Paleolithic (from at least 35,000 to 10,000 y.a.). Over this time span there is considerable variability in style, medium, content, and no doubt meaning as well. In addition, there is an extremely wide geographical distribution of symbolic images, best known from many parts of Europe, but now also well documented from Siberia, North Africa, South Africa, and Australia. Given the 25,000-year time depth of what we call "Paleolithic art" and its nearly worldwide distribution, there is indeed marked variability in expression.

In addition to cave art, there are numerous examples of small sculptures excavated from sites in western, central, and eastern Europe. Beyond these quite well-known figurines, there are numerous other examples of what is frequently termed "portable art," including elaborate engravings on tools and tool handles (Fig. 13–13). Such symbolism can be found in many parts of Europe and was already well established early in the Aurignacian (by 33,000 y.a.). Innovations in symbolic representations also benefited from, and probably further stimulated, technological advances. New methods of mixing pigments and applying them were important in rendering painted or drawn images. Bone and ivory carving and engraving were made easier with the use of special stone tools (see Fig. 13–10). At two sites in the Czech Republic, Dolni Vestonice and Predmosti (both dated at 27,000 y.a.), small animal figures were fashioned from fired clay—the first documented use of ceramic technology anywhere (and preceding later pottery invention by more than 15,000 years!).

Female figurines, popularly known as "Venuses," were sculpted not only in western Europe, but in central and eastern Europe and Siberia as well. Some of these figures were realistically carved, and the faces appear to be modeled after actual women (Fig. 13–14). Other figurines may seem grotesque, with sexual characteristics exaggerated, perhaps for fertility or other ritual purposes (Fig. 13–15).

It is, however, during the final phases of the Upper Paleolithic, particularly during the Magdalenian, that European prehistoric art reached its climax. Cave art is now known from more than 150 separate sites, the vast majority from southwest-

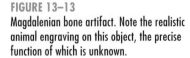

FIGURE 13–13
Magdalenian bone artifact. Note the realistic animal engraving on this object, the precise function of which is unknown.

(a)

(b)

FIGURE 13–14
Venus of Brassempouy. Upper Paleolithic artists were capable of portraying human realism (shown here) as well as symbolism (depicted in Fig. 13–15). (a) Frontal view. (b) Lateral view.

ern France and northern Spain. Apparently, in other areas the rendering of such images did not take place in deep caves. Peoples in central Europe, China, Africa, and elsewhere certainly may have painted or carved representations on rockfaces in the open, but these images long since would have eroded. Thus, it is fortuitous that the people of at least one of the many sophisticated cultures of the Upper Paleolithic chose to journey belowground to create their artwork, preserving it not just for their immediate descendants, but for us as well.

In Lascaux Cave of southern France, immense wild bulls dominate what is called the Great Hall of Bulls, and horses, deer, and other animals adorn the walls in black, red, and yellow, drawn with remarkable skill. In addition to the famous cave of Lascaux, there is equally exemplary art from Altamira Cave in Spain. Indeed, discovered in 1879, Altamira was the first example of advanced cave art recorded in Europe. Filling the walls and ceiling of the cave are superb portrayals of bison in red and black, the "artist" taking advantage of bulges to give a sense of relief to the paintings. The cave is a treasure of beautiful art whose meaning has never been satisfactorily explained. It could have been religious or magical, a form of visual communication, or art for the sake of beauty.

Yet another spectacular example of cave art from western Europe was discovered in late 1994. On December 24, a team of three French cave explorers chanced upon a fabulous discovery in the valley of the Ardèche at Combe d'Arc. Inside the cave, called the Grotte Chauvet after one of its discoverers, preserved unseen for perhaps 30,000 years are many hundreds of images, including stylized dots, stenciled human handprints, and, most dramatically, hundreds of animal representations. Included are depictions of such typical Paleolithic subjects as bison, horse, ibex, auroch, deer, and mammoth (Fig. 13–16). But quite surprisingly, there are also numerous images of animals rarely portrayed elsewhere—such as rhino, lion, and bear. Three animals seen at Grotte Chauvet—a panther, a hyena, and an owl—have never before been documented at cave sites (Fig. 13–17). The artwork, at least after provisional study, seems to consistently repeat several stylistic conventions, causing French researchers to suggest that the images all may have been produced by the same artist. Provisional dating has placed the paintings during the Aurignacian (perhaps more than 30,000 y.a.), and thus Grotte Chauvet may be considerably earlier than the Magdalenian sites of Lascaux and Altamira. The cave was found as Paleolithic peoples had left it, and the initial discoverers, as well as archaeologists, have been careful not to disturb the remains. Among the archaeological traces

FIGURE 13–15
Venus of Willendorf, Austria. (*Note:* This figure is among the most exaggerated and should be compared with Fig. 13–14.)

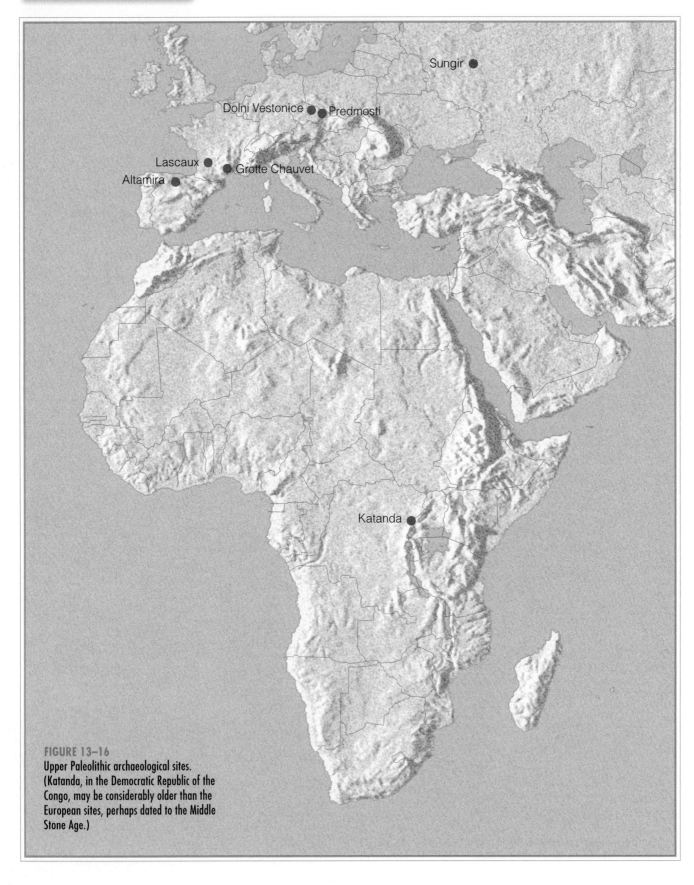

FIGURE 13–16
Upper Paleolithic archaeological sites. (Katanda, in the Democratic Republic of the Congo, may be considerably older than the European sites, perhaps dated to the Middle Stone Age.)

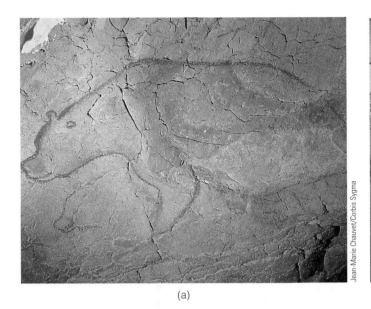

(a)

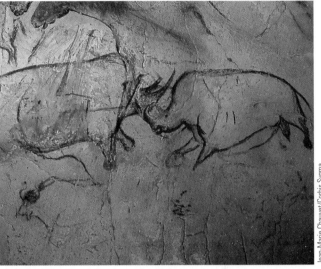

(b)

Jean-Marie Chauvet/Corbis Sygma

Jean-Marie Chauvet/Corbis Sygma

already noted are dozens of footprints on the cave floor, produced by bears as well as by humans. We do not know yet how far the cave extends or what crucial artifactual remains lie along the floor.

A familiar motif seen at Grotte Chauvet and elsewhere is the representation of human hands, usually in the form of outlines. Apparently, the technique used was to liquefy the pigment and blow it onto a hand held flat against the cave wall. At one site in France, at least 159 such hand outlines were found (Leroi-Gourhan, 1986). Another stylistic innovation was the partial sculpting of a rock face—in what is called bas-relief (a technique used much later, for example, by the ancient Greeks at the Parthenon). Attaining depths up to 6 inches, some of the Paleolithic sculptures were quite dramatic and were attempted on a fairly grand scale. In one rock shelter in southwest France, several animals (including mountain goats, bison, reindeer, and horses) and one human figure were depicted in bas-relief. Interestingly, these representations were carved in an area also used as a living site—quite distinct from the special-purpose contexts in the deep cave locations. These bas-reliefs were executed throughout the Magdalenian, always in areas immediately adjacent to those of human habitation.

Strikingly, subject matter seems to differ by location and type of art motif. In portable art, common themes are horses and reindeer as well as stylized human figures; rarely are bison represented. However, in cave contexts, bison and horses are frequently seen, but almost never do we see reindeer (although in Europe, reindeer were probably the most common meat source). Cave artists were thought heretofore to have depicted carnivores only rarely, but the new finds at Grotte Chauvet give us a further perspective on the richness *and* diversity of Paleolithic art.

Ever since ancient art was discovered, attempts have been made to interpret the sculptures, paintings, and other graphic material found in caves or on rocks and tools at open-air archaeological sites. One of the early explanations of Upper Paleolithic art emphasized the relationship of paintings to hunting. Hunting rituals were viewed as a kind of imitative magic that would increase prey animal populations or help hunters successfully find and kill their quarry. As new hypotheses were published, their applicability and deficiencies were discussed. When many of these new hypotheses faded, others were expounded, and the cycle of new hypotheses followed by critiques continued.

Among these hypotheses, the association of religious ritual and magic is still considered viable because of the importance of hunting in the Upper Paleolithic. Nevertheless, other ideas about these graphics have been widely discussed, including

FIGURE 13–17
Cave art from Grotte Chauvet, France.
(a) Bear. (b) Aurochs and rhinoceros.

the viewing of Upper Paleolithic art from a male/female perspective and the consideration of a prevalent dots-and-lines motif as a notational system associated with language, writing, or a calendar (Marshack, 1972). Other perspectives and ongoing questions include why certain areas of caves were used for painting, but not other, similar areas; why certain animals were painted, but not others; why males were painted singly or in groups, but women only in groups; why males were painted near animals, but women never were; and why groups of animals were painted in the most acoustically resonant areas. (Were rituals perhaps performed in areas of the cave with the best acoustic properties?) It should be noted that given the time depth, different contexts, and variable styles of symbolic representations, no *single* explanation regarding their meaning is likely to prove adequate. As one expert has concluded, "It is clear that there can no longer be a single 'meaning' to account for the thousands of images, media, contexts, and uses of what we lump under the term 'paleolithic art'" (Conkey, 1987, p. 414).

A recent explanation for the florescence of cave art in certain areas has been suggested by archaeologists Clive Gamble (1991) and Lawrence Straus (1993), who point to the severe climatic conditions during the maximum (coldest interval) of the last glacial, around 20,000–18,000 y.a. It was during this period in southwestern France and northern Spain that most of the cave art was created. Straus notes that wherever there are clusters of living sites, there are cave art sanctuaries and residential sites with abundant mobile art objects. The caves could have been meeting places for local bands of people and locations for group activities. Bands could share hunting techniques and knowledge, and paintings and engravings served as "encoded information" that could be passed on across generations. Such information, Straus argues, would have been crucial for dealing with the severe conditions of the last glacial period.

Africa

Early accomplishments in rock art, perhaps as early as in Europe, are seen in southern Africa (Namibia), where a site containing such art is dated between 28,000 and 19,000 y.a. In addition, evidence of portable personal adornment is seen as early as 38,000 y.a. in the form of beads fashioned from ostrich eggshells.

In terms of stone tool technology, microliths (thumbnail-sized stone flakes hafted to make knives, saws, etc.) and blades characterize Late Stone Age* African industries. There was also considerable use of bone and antler in central Africa, perhaps some of it quite early. Recent excavations in the Katanda area of the eastern portion of the Democratic Republic of the Congo have shown remarkable development of bone craftwork. In fact, preliminary reports by Alison Brooks of George Washington University and John Yellen of the National Science Foundation have demonstrated that these technological achievements rival those of the more renowned European Upper Paleolithic (Yellen et al., 1995).

The most important artifacts discovered at Katanda are a dozen intricately made bone tools excavated from three sites along the Semiliki River (not far from Lake Rutanzige—formerly, Lake Edward) (see Fig. 13–16). These tools, made from the ribs or long bone splinters of large mammals, apparently were first ground to flatten and sharpen them, and then some were apparently precisely pressure-flaked to produce a row of barbs. In form these tools are similar to what have been called "harpoons" from the later Upper Paleolithic of Europe (Magdalenian, circa 15,000 y.a.). Their function in Africa, as well, is thought to have been for spearing fish, which archaeological remains indicate were quite large (catfish weighing up to 150 pounds!). In addition, a few carved bone rings with no barbs were also discovered, but their intended function (if indeed they were meant to have a utilitarian function at all) remains elusive.

The dating of the Katanda sites is crucial for drawing useful comparisons with the European Upper Paleolithic. However, the bone used for the tools retained no

---

*The Late Stone Age in Africa is equivalent to the Upper Paleolithic in Eurasia.

measurable nitrogen and thus proved unsuitable for radiocarbon dating (perhaps it was too old and beyond the range of this technique). As a result, the other techniques now used for this time range—thermoluminescence, electron spin resonance, and uranium series dating (see p. 321)—were all applied. The results proved consistent, indicating dates between 180,000 and 75,000 y.a.*

However, there remain some difficulties in establishing the clear association of the bone implements with the materials that have supplied the chronometric age estimates. Indeed, Richard Klein, a coauthor of one of the initial reports (Brooks et al., 1995), does not accept the suggested great antiquity for these finds and believes they may be much younger. Nevertheless, if the early age estimates should hold up, we once again will look *first* to Africa as the crucial source area for human origins—not just for biological aspects, but for cultural aspects as well.

Summary of Upper Paleolithic Culture

As we look back at the Upper Paleolithic, we can see it as the culmination of 2 million years of cultural development. Change proceeded incredibly slowly for most of the Pleistocene, but as cultural traditions and materials accumulated and the brain (and, we assume, intelligence) expanded and reorganized, the rate of change quickened.

Cultural evolution continued with the appearance of early archaic *H. sapiens* and moved a bit faster with later archaic *H. sapiens*. Neandertals in Eurasia and their contemporaries elsewhere added deliberate burials, technological innovations, and much more.

Building on existing cultures, late Pleistocene populations attained sophisticated cultural and material heights in a seemingly short (by previous standards) burst of exciting activity. In Europe and central Africa particularly, there seem to have been dramatic cultural innovations that saw big game hunting, potent new weapons (including harpoons, spear-throwers, and possibly the bow and arrow), body ornaments, needles, "tailored" clothing, and burials with elaborate grave goods (the latter might indicate some sort of status hierarchy).

This dynamic age was doomed, or so it appears, by the climatic changes of about 10,000 y.a. As the temperature slowly rose and the glaciers retreated, animal and plant species were seriously impacted, and humans were thus affected as well. As traditional prey animals were depleted or disappeared altogether, other means of obtaining food were sought.

Grinding hard seeds or roots became important, and as familiarity with plant propagation increased, domestication of plants and animals developed. Dependence on domestication became critical, and with it came permanent settlements, new technology, and more complex social organization. The development of these revolutionary new technologies and their global ramifications will be the topic of the remainder of this text.

SUMMARY

The date and location of the origin of anatomically modern human beings have been the subjects of a fierce debate for the past decade, and the end is not in sight. One hypothesis (complete replacement) claims that anatomically modern forms first evolved in Africa more than 100,000 y.a. and then, migrating out of Africa, completely replaced archaic *H. sapiens* in the rest of the world. Another school (regional continuity) takes a diametrically different view and maintains that in various geographical regions of the world, local groups of archaic *H. sapiens* evolved directly to anatomically modern humans. A third hypothesis (partial replacement)

---

*If these dates prove accurate, Katanda would actually be earlier than Late Stone Age (and thus be referrable to the Middle Stone Age).

takes a somewhat middle position, suggesting an African origin but also accepting some later hybridization outside of Africa.

The Upper Paleolithic was an age of extraordinary innovation and achievement in technology and art. Many new and complex tools were introduced, and their production indicates fine skill in working wood, bone, and antler. Cave art in France and Spain displays the masterful ability of Upper Paleolithic painters, and beautiful sculptures have been found at many European sites. Sophisticated symbolic representations have also been found in Africa and elsewhere. Upper Paleolithic *Homo sapiens* displayed amazing development in a relatively short period of time. The culture produced during this period led the way to still newer and more complex cultural techniques and methods.

QUESTIONS FOR REVIEW

1. What characteristics define anatomically modern *H. sapiens*?
2. How do the characteristics of modern *H. sapiens* compare with those of archaic *H. sapiens*?
3. What are the three major theories that seek to explain the origin and dispersal of *Homo sapiens sapiens*? Compare and critically discuss these three views.
4. How have data from mitochondrial DNA been used to support an African origin of *H. sapiens sapiens*? What other genetic data have recently been analyzed, and how do they accord with the mtDNA results?
5. Discuss (and compare) the early evidence of anatomically modern humans from two different regions.
6. It is said that the Upper Paleolithic was a time of technological innovation. Support this statement with specific evidence, and compare the Upper Paleolithic with cultural data from earlier in the Pleistocene.
7. From which regions has cave art, dating to the Upper Pleistocene, been discovered? Particularly for the cave art of Europe, what explanations of its meaning have been proposed?

SUGGESTED FURTHER READING

Aitken, M. J., C. B. Stringer, and P. A. Mellars (eds.). 1993. *The Origin of Modern Humans and the Impact of Chronometric Dating.* Princeton, NJ: Princeton University Press.

Klein, Richard. 1999. *The Human Career: Human Biological and Cultural Origins.* 2nd ed. Chicago: University of Chicago Press.

Nitecki, Matthew H., and Doris V. Nitecki (eds.). 1994. *Origins of Anatomically Modern Humans.* New York: Plenum.

Smith, Fred, and Frank Spencer (eds.). 1984. *The Origin of Modern Humans.* New York: Liss.

Wolpoff, Milford. 1999. *Paleoanthropology.* 2nd ed. New York: McGraw-Hill.

RESOURCES ON THE INTERNET

 Wadsworth Anthropology Resource Center
http://anthropology.wadsworth.com

The companion website for this text includes a range of enrichment material focused on the chapter's topic. While online you can enhance your understanding of the chapter by exploring one of the several additional Internet Exercises, by researching topics, and by accessing full articles on InfoTrac College Edition. You can also reinforce the concepts by taking online practice exams.

Internet Exercises

Some of the most recently discovered cave paintings are those at Grotte Chauvet in France. These paintings were completed between 30,000 and 32,000 years ago. Visit the site on the Web at **http://www.france.diplomatie.fr/label_france/ENGLISH/ SCIENCES/CHAUVET/cha.html**, or use your search engine to find sites for either *Grotte Chauvet* or *Lascaux Cave*. Another suggestion is: *Prehistoric France*. Examine the photographs of the cave paintings and read the text. What is portrayed in the pictures? What do you think might have motivated the people to make the images? What do you think they were trying to communicate?

InfoTrac College Edition
http://www.infotrac-college.com/wadsworth

Use PowerTrac to search for *Upper Paleolithic*. This should pull up several references from which you should choose at least two that deal with topics not covered in detail in Chapter 13. After reading these articles, make a list of facts you found particularly interesting. Did these articles change your views of how humans lived during the Upper Paleolithic? If so, how?

The Evolution of Language

One of the most distinctive behavioral attributes of all modern humans is our advanced ability to use highly sophisticated symbolic language. Indeed, it would be impossible to imagine human social relationships or human culture without language.

When did language evolve? First, we should define what we mean by *full* human language. As we discussed in Chapter 7 (see pp. 164–168), nonhuman primates have shown some elements of language. For example, some chimpanzees, gorillas, and bonobos display abilities to manipulate symbols and a rudimentary understanding of grammar. Nevertheless, the full complement of skills displayed by humans includes the extensive use of arbitrary symbols, sophisticated grammar, and a complex *open* system of communication (see p. 165).

Most scholars are comfortable attributing such equivalent skills to early members of *H. sapiens sapiens*, as early as 200,000–100,000 years ago. In fact, several researchers hypothesize that the elaborate technology and artistic achievements, as well as the rapid dispersal of anatomically modern humans, were directly a result of behavioral advantages—particularly full language capabilities. This rapid expansion of presumably culturally sophisticated modern *H. sapiens* (and the consequent disappearance of other hominids) has sometimes been termed "the human revolution."

Of course, this hypothesis does not deny that earlier hominids had some form of complex communication; almost everyone agrees that even the earliest hominids did (at least as complex as that seen in living apes). What is not generally agreed upon is just when the full complement of human language capacity *first* emerged. Indeed, the controversy relating to this process will continue to ferment, since there is no clear answer to the question. The available evidence is not sufficient to establish clearly the language capabilities of any fossil hominid. We have discussed in Chapter 7 that there are neurological foundations for language and that these features relate more to brain reorganization than to simple increase in brain size. Moreover, as far as *spoken* language is concerned, during hominid evolution there were also physiological alterations of the vocal tract (in particular, a lower position of the larynx as compared to other primates).

Yet, we have no complete record of fossil hominid brains or their vocal tracts. We do have *endocasts* (see p. 240), which preserve a few external features of the brain. For example, there are several preserved endocasts of australopithecines from South Africa. However, the information is incomplete and thus subject to varying interpretations. (For example, did these hominids possess language? If not, what form of communication did they display?) Evidence from the vocal tract is even more elusive.

In such an atmosphere of fragmentary data, a variety of conflicting hypotheses have been proposed. Some paleoanthropologists argue that early australopithecines (3 m.y.a.) had language. Others think that such capabilities were first displayed by early *Homo* (perhaps 2 m.y.a.). Still others suggest that language did not emerge fully until the time of *Homo erectus* (2–1 m.y.a.), or perhaps it was archaic forms of *H. sapiens* (such as the Neandertals) who first displayed such skills. And finally, a number of researchers assert that language first developed *only* with the appearance of *H. sapiens sapiens*.

Because the question of language evolution is so fundamental to understanding human evolution (indeed, what it *means* to be human), a variety of creative techniques have been applied to assess the (limited) evidence that is available. We have already mentioned the analysis of endocasts. Other researchers have suggested that the size of the vertebral canal in the thoracic region of the spine might be related to precise muscle control of breathing and thus an indicator of certain language skills. This conclusion was drawn from features of the *H. erectus* skeleton from Nariokotome (see p. 274). Lastly, and perhaps most informative of all, other paleoanthropologists have recently presented provisional data on the size of the hypoglossal canal at the base of the cranium (the size of the canal is thought to reflect the degree of neurological control of the tongue). As we noted earlier (see p. 308), investigators have so far suggested that australopithecines and early *Homo* (with small canals) did not have full articulate language, but that archaic *H. sapiens* (Neandertals) and early *H. sapiens sapiens* probably did (these latter showing canals as large as those of contemporary people).

Subsequent to the initial suggestion that size of the hypoglossal canal might reflect speech capabilities (Kay et al., 1998), the hypothesis has been further tested using a much wider sample of nonhuman primates, fossil hominids, and modern humans (DeGusta et al., 1999). These new data do *not* confirm the hypothesis and in fact seriously question it. For example, many nonhuman primates have hypoglossal canals as large as humans; similarly, some early hominids (members of *Australopithecus*) also have canals as large as contemporary humans. Perhaps even more revealing, the size of the canal, as shown in dissections of human cadavers, does not appear correlated with the size of the (hypoglossal) nerve running through it. Further studies might help resolve some of these issues, but, for the moment, the initial hypothesis concerning the utility of hypoglossal canal size for estimating speech abilities has been seriously weakened.

A final line of inquiry has also focused on language (i.e., speech) by reconstructing in various fossil hominids the presumed position of the larynx within the vocal tract. As first proposed by Lieberman and Crelin (Lieberman and Crelin, 1971; Lieberman, 1992) and more recently by Laitman (Laitman et al., 1993), it is argued that Neandertals and other members of archaic *H. sapiens* could not articulate full speech, since the larynx would have been positioned higher in the throat than is seen in *H. sapiens sapiens*. This inference is based on indirect reconstruction of the vocal tract from the contours of the cranial base. Again, the evidence is far from unambiguous, and interpretations are often varied (and contentious; see, for example, Falk, 1975; Frayer, 1993). Given these uncertainties, most paleoanthropologists have been reluctant to conclude exactly what *speech* capabilities Neandertals had. The most *direct* evidence was discovered in 1983 and includes an adult Neandertal *hyoid bone* (from Kebara Cave in Israel; see p. 305). This important structure, which supports the larynx, is identical in this Neandertal to that seen in modern humans. Given this information, it would be most imprudent to argue that Neandertals could not articulate full human speech. Nevertheless, simply because Neandertals *could* speak in a fully articulate manner does not necessarily argue that they communicated with the entire array of contemporary human symbolic language. We have noted in Chapter 12 several probable behavioral contrasts of Neandertals with Upper Paleolithic *H. sapiens sapiens*. Was language ability among these contrasts and perhaps the most important difference? Do more advanced language capabilities help explain the rapid success of modern humans in displacing other hominids? Does language, then, mostly account for the human revolution? Surely, these are fascinating and important questions. Perhaps someday we will be able to answer them in a comprehensive, scientifically rigorous manner.

Critical Thinking Questions

1. What is meant by human language? How does it differ from communication seen in great apes?

2. What direct evidence (fossil and archaeological) is used to suggest that early hominids had language capabilities? How sufficient is this evidence?

3. What kind of evidence would convince you that an earlier hominid (Neandertals, for example) did or did not possess language?

Sources

Falk, Dean. 1975. "Comparative Anatomy of the Larynx in Man and the Chimpanzee: Implications for Language in Neandertal." *American Journal of Physical Anthropology* 43: 123–132.

Frayer, D. W. 1993. "On Neanderthal Crania and Speech: Response to Lieberman." *Current Anthropology* 34: 721.

Kay, R. F., M. Cartmill, and M. Balow. 1998. "The Hypoglossal Canal and the Origins of Human Vocal Behavior" (abstract). *American Journal of Physical Anthropology, Supplement* 26: 137.

Laitman, J. T., J. S. Reidenberg, D. R. Friedland, et al. 1993. "Neandertal Upper Respiratory Specializations and Their Effect upon Respiration and Speech" (abstract). *American Journal of Physical Anthropology* 16: 129.

Lieberman, Phillip. 1992. "On Neanderthal Speech and Neanderthal Extinction." *Current Anthropology* 33: 409–410.

Lieberman, P., and E. S. Crelin. 1971. "On the Speech of Neanderthal Man." *Linguistic Inquiries* 2: 203–222.

MacLarnon, Ann. 1993. "The Vertebral Canal of KNM-WT 15000 and the Evolution of the Spinal Cord and Other Canal Contents." In A. Walker and R. E. Leakey (eds.), *The Nariokotome* Homo erectus *Skeleton.* Cambridge: Harvard University Press, pp. 359–390.

CHAPTER

14

CONTENTS

Understanding the Past: Archaeological Approaches

Introduction

Having traced the evolutionary development of our primate and hominid ancestors in Chapters 8 through 11, and after considering archaic and early modern *Homo sapiens* in the last two chapters, we devote the remainder of this text to the later members of our own subspecies, *Homo sapiens sapiens*.

It would be impossible in the remaining chapters to catalog everything of interest concerning our species that has occurred even since the end of the Paleolithic. Instead, we will focus on several major themes. The present chapter focuses on the methods of archaeology, the scientific study of the past, which is the sole source of our information about prehistory. Next, Chapter 15 will follow the archaeological clues used in tracing the expansion of humans into the vast uninhabited American continents. The same chapter concludes with an overview of the advanced food-collecting strategies that developed in some Old World and New World societies after the end of the last ice age. From there, Chapter 16 continues the theme with a treatment of one of humankind's most significant achievements, the ability to produce food through domestication and agriculture. Finally, Chapters 17 and 18 deal with the subsequent rise of early civilizations, first in the Old World and then in the New. These advanced cultures were a prelude to modern society.

By this point in our study, it must be increasingly clear that our species no longer functions as just another element of the natural ecosystem, as our earliest primate forebears surely did. The dynamic interaction between our human biology (big brain, upright posture, manual dexterity, capacity for speech, etc.) and our distinctive human cultural behaviors (e.g., sophisticated technology, complex social systems, means of communication), which we have termed *biocultural evolution*, set our species on a unique trajectory. Compared to our ancestors, modern *Homo* has come to exhibit infinitely greater behavioral and cultural complexity, as well as more intricate relationships with the natural and social environments, including the ability of the species to radically modify its own surroundings.

Most people find the study of our ancestors a compelling and fascinating topic. We are, after all, the living descendants of these earlier people, and their cultural activities have contributed immeasurably to our modern lifeways. Armed with a range of research skills, an array of technical equipment, and an immense curiosity, archaeologists, paleoanthropologists, and researchers in related disciplines devote their energies to learning all they can about our ancient predecessors throughout the world, from the earliest hominids to more recent *Homo sapiens*. In this chapter, we examine some of the basic techniques that archaeologists use to uncover and assess information about human prehistory.

Archaeology and the Study of Prehistory

Archaeology is a set of scientific methods applied to the study of the human past. To investigate the earliest hominids, archaeologists generally combine forces with physical anthropologists and geologists in an endeavor called *paleoanthropology* (see Chapter 9). Archaeologists researching anatomically modern Holocene humans and their cultures employ basically the same techniques of excavation and analysis used by archaeologists and paleoanthropologists on early hominid sites in the Old World, with modifications as circumstances require and permit. Of course, most of the methods used for dating the early Plio-Pleistocene hominid sites are not applicable to the sites of later prehistory, and the reverse is also true (see p. 208 and following discussion).

The evidence patiently accumulated through decades of paleoanthropological excavation and analysis still affords us only fleeting glimpses of our Plio-Pleistocene ancestors. The meticulous long-term projects at Olduvai, East and West Turkana, Hadar, and other notable locations associated with these early hominids have yielded many important discoveries. Even so, the sum of our knowledge about the most ancient humans leaves many important questions unanswered, because their sites tend to be both scarce and small, with few preserved physical or cultural remains.

Over the last 12,000 years or so, as anatomically modern human beings have become much more numerous, they have occupied most of the earth's surface, and their cultural activities have left extensive and enduring traces. Understandably, the Holocene record of our species is more accessible than that for any earlier epoch. Archaeologists have a wealth of sites and artifacts available for the study of *Homo sapiens*. Consequently, our picture of this later period tends to be somewhat clearer, though even here portions remain obscured. After all, prehistory, the long span for which we have no contemporary written accounts (writing dates back just a few thousand years, and in only a few places), is accessible to us only through archaeological research. Claims that special knowledge of the very distant past has been faithfully conveyed to the present through oral traditions are impossible to scientifically evaluate and so must be skeptically regarded. Thus, unless some tangible bit of evidence from prehistory has managed to survive the ages as a piece of the archaeological record and is then excavated and properly interpreted by archaeologists, we have no way of learning about something that happened in the unrecorded past, no matter how significant the event may have been. Indeed, much of what we would like to know about prehistory will always remain beyond our reach. For example, we cannot expect to learn any individual's name—or even what that individual's society may have called itself—solely from the data of prehistoric archaeology. Only the historical record of most recent times, which has been compiled by scholars with access to written documentation, can provide such information.

Still, archaeology offers a direct way to learn about many aspects of the past, with or without the assistance of written documentation. In fact, since all individuals are likely to contribute something (if only their trash!) to the archaeological record during their lifetimes, the past as revealed through archaeology is less likely than the historical record to be biased in favor of the powerful and the literate.

Archaeological Research Objectives

Archaeology is generally acknowledged to have three objectives. The first objective is to *describe* the past. Our fundamental concerns here are to answer the essential questions who, when, and where. Archaeologists and physical anthropologists attempt to identify and characterize the peoples of the past from the scant physical evidence they left behind. Paleoanthropological research provides us with basic descriptions of the most remote hominids; we can sketch in further details for later *Homo*, with our view improving as we approach the present.

Our descriptive approach to the past must be set into a framework of time and place. Advances in archaeological dating techniques during the late twentieth century have provided us with a good sense of prehistoric chronology, allowing us to order the key events of the past and often assign actual date ranges. The cumulative efforts of researchers who have surveyed archaeological landscapes on a global scale provide an appreciation of the geography of the human past. Basic descriptive data of this type form the substance of many chapters in this text.

Archaeology's second objective is to *analyze and reconstruct* ancient lifeways. Using clues from recovered artifacts, features, sites, and contexts, archaeologists attempt to understand how people actually created and used those cultural products to interact with each other and their surroundings. What was the function of these tools? What did people eat at a certain time of the year? What goods did they obtain through trade? By paying close attention to the archaeological evidence itself, by collecting and studying previously ignored categories of data using a battery of impressive analytical techniques, and even by undertaking controlled experiments to replicate ancient technologies, modern archaeologists have gained insights into past behaviors.

Some people fault archaeology for its technological bias, suggesting that we talk more about ancient tools and structures than about the people who made them. This focus is difficult to avoid. Over time, the processes of weathering and decay eliminate all but the most durable materials from the archaeological record. Tools, especially those made from resistant substances such as stone, bone, or metal, may survive to be discovered; but direct evidence of kinship systems, social organization, or religion is very rarely preserved in tangible form, so we can say relatively little about these topics with much confidence.

Describing and interpreting the lives and activities of ancient societies from their meager enduring remains are not easy tasks, and most archaeological endeavor is directed toward those ends. However, a third objective of archaeological research is to *explain* how and why the past took place as it did. This is the ultimate goal and is also the hardest to attain. Even if we somehow succeeded in learning exactly what had occurred in some ancient time and place, we could never be certain of having sufficient understanding to evaluate all the circumstances and motives that led to that result. Thus, while we recognize that farmers in the Tigris-Euphrates valley began living together in cities by 5,500 y.a., explaining why they chose to do so is much more difficult. Nevertheless, on occasion archaeologists (and textbook authors) may give in to modest speculation about such matters (see Box 14–1).

BOX 14–1   DIGGING DEEPER

Mechanisms of Cultural Variation and Change

We have stressed that modern human beings are *biocultural* organisms, meaning that our biology and culture interact seamlessly to influence the course of our evolution. One clear advantage of cultural behavior is that it allows people to respond quickly to stimuli and it is also more versatile than biological evolution. Because people can so readily create new behaviors or easily modify old ones, the world's geographically dispersed societies display a wide range of cultural variation.

In their attempts to explain cultural variability and to account for the nature of cultural change, some archaeologists (following the lead of evolutionary biologists) view cultural variation and change as resulting from cultural factors that are comparable in their effect to those evolutionary factors that influence population genetics (see Chapter 4). Thus, prehistorians consider that several mechanisms of cultural variation and change may have a role in determining the course of cultural development:

- *Cultural drift* describes the imperfect transmission of cultural information from generation to generation or over increasing distances. Thus, minor *unintended* variations inevitably creep into hand-painted designs on clay pots or filter into the wording of a sacred chant, so that over time distinctive cultural varieties may evolve out of the original version.

- *Invention and innovation* represent sources of *intentional* variation. The invention of a new cultural item, whether a device for trapping birds or a novel projectile point style, represents a significant departure from the status quo. An innovation, on the other hand, may simply improve on or provide a new use for an existing element of culture, such as adding a grip to a digging stick so that it won't slip from the hand.

- *Cultural selection* is the process by which new cultural traits are either generally accepted or rejected. For example, a people may or may not adopt the new projectile point style, or they may make further innovations to improve its effectiveness. Obviously, cultural traits or objects that are advantageous and become popular tend to show up more often in the archaeological record.

- *Diffusion* describes the transmission of cultural objects or behaviors into new regions. Cultural traits may be carried by people as they migrate or go off to war, or they may be spread through trade or other means of contact and communication.

Piecing Together the Past

Everyone recognizes excavation as the most visible activity associated with archaeology and the one most central to discovery (Fig. 14–1). By literally digging into the past, archaeologists hope to gain direct access to actual products of human handiwork and cultural activity that have survived down to the present. Moreover, through excavation, we expect to find these materials in much the same relationship to one another as they had when they were components of a living society. Fieldwork is essential not only for generating new data from unexplored sites but also for rescuing and preserving archaeological resources from sites that may be threatened with destruction by nature or development.

Excavation is not the only method archaeologists use in attempting to learn about our ancestors, however. Several other approaches rely on the interpretation of nonexcavated sources of information, including written observations and interviews with recent or contemporary peoples and even replicative experiments carried out by archaeologists themselves.

Artifacts and Contexts

Two essential products—artifacts and contexts—result from an archaeological "dig" (and by-products, too—dirt, sweat, aching muscles, and plenty of paperwork among them!). The relationships between artifacts and contexts are most often observed on *sites*, which are the locations of past human activity where archaeologists concentrate their excavation efforts.

Artifacts are tangible objects; in fact, anything that was made or modified by people in the past qualifies as an artifact. It might be a stone tool or a sherd (fragment) of broken pottery or even an ancient chariot. (Nonportable creations, such as a trash pit, an irrigation canal, or a pyramid, which often are integral components of a site, can be considered artifacts, too, but archaeologists usually refer to them as **features**.)

Context describes the spatial and temporal associations between artifacts and/or features. What was the object's precise location, recorded from several coordinates so as to provide its three-dimensional position within the site? Was it associated somehow with any other artifact or feature? For example, was this projectile point

Features
Products of human activity that are usually integral to a site and therefore nonportable. Examples include fire hearths and foundations.

FIGURE 14–1
An archaeological excavation gets under way on an island in the Bahamas.

recovered from deep within a trash pit, found on the floor of a hunter's shelter, or lodged between the ribs of a large animal? Can we be certain that this apparent association was really contemporaneous and not the result of natural processes of erosion or mixing? You can appreciate that the context is just as important as the artifact itself in understanding the past, which is why archaeologists dig carefully and keep accurate records of all they uncover. The photo essay following Chapter 15 offers a comprehensive overview of standard archaeological field and laboratory approaches.

Certainly, some questions about the human past cannot be answered directly through excavation. Not every activity produces the kind of durable material remains that will long survive in the archaeological record as artifacts or features. Nor have archaeologists located every significant site where some piece of our human story might be added to the puzzle. Many sites remain unexcavated or undiscovered; countless others have been or are being destroyed by the actions of later humans. There is much about even the more recent periods that we do not yet know.

Ethnoarchaeology and Ethnographic Analogy

In addition to researching the artifacts and contexts discovered through site excavation, archaeologists who study prehistory sometimes seek to enhance their understanding and interpretations of ancient life by turning to **ethnoarchaeology** (sometimes called "living archaeology") and **ethnographic analogy**. Briefly, both ethnoarchaeology and ethnographic analogy examine contemporary small-scale societies to gain insights into past human behavior (Fig. 14–2).

An ethnoarchaeologist personally conducts in-depth cultural research among a living group, such as the !Kung San in southern Africa (Yellen, 1980), Australian aborigines (Gould, 1977; Meehan, 1982), or the Nunamiut peoples of the Alaskan Arctic (Binford, 1978). The researcher resides with and accompanies the people in their daily routines, closely observing their activities. Such studies yield detailed information about hunting or gathering, toolmaking, discard of debris, residence data, and the like. By being "on the scene" as modern tribal people are literally creating a site, the ethnoarchaeologist can better appreciate the comparable processes that formed the ancient archaeological record, at the same time becoming painfully aware of how much potential evidence simply decays and disappears between the time a site is created and the time an archaeologist may excavate it thousands or millions of years later. For just this reason, some archaeologists have even looked to contemporary American culture to see what they can learn by studying the relationship between a society and what it throws away (see Box 14–2).

Ethnoarchaeology
Approach used by archaeologists to gain insights into the past by studying contemporary people.

Ethnographic analogy
Proposing hypotheses to explain something about the past based on anthropological observations of living societies.

FIGURE 14–2
Ethnoarchaeological studies of contemporary !Kung lifeways have provided insights useful to archaeologists working on ancient sites.

Courtesy, John Yellen

BOX 14–2 ## DIGGING DEEPER

Reconstructing Cultural Behavior from Garbage

Most of what we find on archaeological sites represents the debris of earlier societies, the material that was discarded, lost, or simply abandoned. Archaeologists have always assumed that the study of refuse can reveal something about past cultural behavior. William L. Rathje, of the University of Arizona, put that assumption to the test when he began looking at garbage generated in modern-day Tucson and at landfills in other urban areas (Fig. 1). By demonstrating the archaeologist's ability to learn about our present culture through the study of modern refuse, he reinforces the claim that the past can be revealed through archaeology.

Over a three-year period, Rathje and his students sampled more than 1,000 households in Tucson and classified more than 70,000 items into some 200 categories of food and other household goods. Referring to census data as a control, the researchers correlated statistics on family size, income, and ethnicity with the representative garbage samples they had collected.

Results from the Tucson study revealed much about the society that produced, used, and finally discarded the materials. For example, evidence from garbage provided substantially different (and, no doubt, more accurate) information concerning alcohol consumption than people admitted to in questionnaire

FIGURE 1

A crew under the direction of archaeologist William L. Rathje employs a bucket auger to sample deep levels of the Fresh Kills landfill, on Staten Island. New York City's solid waste accumulated here at the rate of 14,000 tons per day before the dump reached its capacity and was closed in 2001.

surveys. It also demonstrated that middle-class households account for a higher percentage of wasted food (nearly 10 percent of the food purchased) than either the poor or the wealthy. Since the garbage data have been carefully sampled and quantified, we get an

Archaeologists may also interview modern tribal peoples or refer to studies of native cultures compiled by other anthropologists. Many traditional societies claim that their oral histories preserve information that has passed through countless generations. Archaeologists are interested in any insights that these sources may offer. Often, though, the generalized nature of traditional stories does not match the archaeologist's desire for detailed cultural data. But researchers who have consulted with modern Native Americans or Australians about the use or significance of individual artifacts or features found in archaeological contexts have at times benefited from their interpretations.

Western cultural anthropologists, or ethnographers, have been writing detailed studies of tribal societies for well over a century. These accounts, called ethnographies, are comprehensive narratives prepared by ethnographers who generally have resided in the culture for extended periods. Archaeologists find that many ethnographies contain useful discussions of material objects and their functions.

Any of these resources may assist archaeologists in finding parallels with prehistoric data and in devising appropriate hypotheses to account for archaeological observations. Working from the modern ethnographic examples, the archaeologist tests the premise that similar patterns encountered in the archaeological record

accurate idea of exactly how many usable items are thrown away. Despite the standard image of Americans as "conspicuous consumers," the archaeologists found few usable household items in garbage bags or trash dumps (Fig. 2). Instead, recycling furniture and appliances through yard sales and charities seems to be a common practice. Higher-income households do tend

Courtesy, William L. Rathje

FIGURE 2
Professor Rathje (right foreground) and his students screen material from the Fresh Kills landfill to search for small artifacts of modern American culture.

to replace items at a somewhat higher rate, thus replenishing the supply of goods entering the system.

This "archaeological" approach to modern garbage clarifies our understanding of contemporary cultural behavior and also supports the notion that we can study the past in similar ways. Rathje's work with garbage demonstrates that archaeological methods work especially well in conjunction with historical documentation to reveal new information about more recent periods, up to and including modern times. His studies also serve as a sobering reminder of the environmental consequences of our behavior as consumers and refuse producers.

Sources:

Lilienfeld, Robert M., and William L. Rathje. 1998. *Use Less Stuff: Environmental Solutions for Who We Really Are*. New York: Fawcett Books.

Rathje, William L. 1979. "Modern Material Culture Studies." *Advances in Archaeological Method and Theory* 2: 1–37.

Rathje, William L. 1991. "Once and Future Landfills." *National Geographic* 179(5): 116–134.

Rathje, William L., and Cullen Murphy. 2001. *Rubbish!: The Archaeology of Garbage*. Tucson: University of Arizona Press.

may have been produced in an analogous manner—hence, *ethnographic analogy*. We must be aware, however, that the activities of living groups may not be truly representative of past lifeways. Also, the greater the distance in time or place that separates the living society from the archaeological site, the less confidence one should have in drawing any analogies. The ideal situation is where one is studying the modern descendants of a group who lived in a similar manner in the same area in the not-too-distant past. Mindful of these considerations, archaeologists sometimes use such approaches to get beyond mere description, advancing to the interpretation and reconstruction of ancient lifeways.

Experimental Archaeology

Yet another way to gain a closer understanding of our ancestors is by learning how they made their tools and how they used them. It is, after all, the artifactual traces of prehistoric tools of stone (and, to a lesser degree, of bone) that constitute our primary information concerning early human behavior. Stone is by far the most common residue of prehistoric cultural behavior. Tons of stone debris litter archaeological sites worldwide. A casual walk along the bottom of Olduvai Gorge could well be interrupted every few seconds by tripping over prehistoric tools!

FIGURE 14–3
An archaeologist uses the skill of knapping to demonstrate ancient stone toolmaking techniques.

Experimental archaeologists
Researchers who replicate ancient toolmaking techniques and other procedures to test hypotheses about past activities.

Flake
Thin-edged fragment removed from a core.

Core
Stone reduced by flake removal and not necessarily a "tool" itself.

Knappers
Those who flake stone tools.

Direct percussion
Striking a core or flake with a hammerstone.

Microliths
(*micro*, meaning "small," and *lith*, meaning "stone") Small stone flakes or bladelets, punched from a core and used as cutting edges in tools and weapons; common Upper Paleolithic tool category.

But what do these artifacts tell us about our ancestors? How do we determine an artifact's original function? (After all, ancient artifacts are not found with identifying labels attached!) Learning how ancient people may have made and used an object is a worthy goal, one that would assist us in reconstructing past lifeways. In fact, contemporary **experimental archaeologists** have attempted to reconstruct prehistoric techniques of stone toolmaking, butchering, and so forth (Fig. 14–3). In this way, archaeologists are, in a sense, trying to re-create the past.

Stone Tool (Lithic) Technology   Products of prehistoric technology resulted from a limited range of natural materials and manufacturing procedures. The earliest hominid cultural inventions probably employed nondurable materials that did not survive archaeologically (such as a digging stick or an ostrich eggshell used as a watertight container). A basic human invention was the recognition that a stone can be fractured to produce sharp edges. Hominids in East Africa took this major cultural step more than 2.5 m.y.a. (see Chapter 9).

Stone tools were made by subtractive techniques. When struck properly, certain types of stone will fracture in a controlled way (Kooyman, 2000). The smaller piece struck off is called a **flake**, while the larger remaining chunk is called a **core** (Fig. 14–4). The obvious result is that both core and flake now possess sharp edges useful for cutting, sawing, or scraping. Some modern experimental archaeologists have acquired the skills to replicate these ancient practices using appropriate materials and methods, enabling them to reproduce facsimile tools to be compared with ancient specimens or used in performance tests (Whittaker, 1994).

For many years, it had been assumed that in the earliest known stone tool industry (i.e., the Oldowan), both core and flake tools were deliberately manufactured as final, desired products. Such core implements as "choppers," "polyhedrons," and "discoids" were thought to be central artifactual components of these early lithic assemblages (indeed, the Oldowan has often been described as a "chopping tool industry"). However, detailed reevaluation of these artifacts by Richard Potts of the Smithsonian Institution has thrown these traditional assumptions into doubt. From careful statistical analysis of the attributes of Oldowan artifacts from Bed I at Olduvai, Potts (1991, 1993) concluded that the so-called core tools were really not tools after all. He suggests rather that what early hominids were deliberately producing were flake tools, and the various stone nodule forms (discoids, polyhedrons, choppers, etc.) were simply "incidental stopping points in the process of removing flakes from cores" (Potts, 1993, p. 60).

Breaking rocks by bashing them together is one thing. Producing consistent results, even apparently simple flakes, is quite another. The object in making most stone tools, of course, is to produce a usable cutting surface. By reproducing results similar to those of earlier stoneworkers, experimental archaeologists can infer which kinds of techniques *might* have been employed. It takes much practice before modern stone **knappers** learn the intricacies of the type of rock to choose, the kind of hammer to employ, the angle and velocity with which to strike, and so on. Such experience allows us to appreciate how skilled in stoneworking our ancestors truly were.

Flakes can be removed from cores in a variety of ways. The nodules (now thought to be blanks) found in sites in Bed I at Olduvai (circa 1.85–1.2 m.y.a.) are flaked on one side only (i.e., *unifacially*). It is possible, although by no means easy, to produce such implements by hitting one stone—the hammerstone—against another—the core—in a method called **direct percussion** (Fig. 14–5).

In Bed IV sites at Olduvai (circa 400,000 y.a.), however, the majority of tools are flaked on both sides (i.e., *bifacially*) and have long sinuous edges. Such a result cannot be reproduced by direct percussion with just a hammerstone. The edges must have been straightened ("retouched") with a "soft" hammer, such as bone or antler.

To reproduce implements similar to those found in later stages of human cultural development, even more sophisticated techniques are required. Tools such as the delicate **microliths** found in the uppermost beds at Olduvai (circa 17,000 y.a.), the superb Solutrean blades from Europe (circa 20,000 y.a.)(Fig. 14–6), and the expertly crafted Folsom projectile points from the New World (circa 10,000 y.a.) (see

Core

Flake

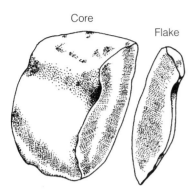

FIGURE 14–4
Core and flake.

FIGURE 14–5
Direct percussion, striking a core with a hammerstone to remove a flake.

FIGURE 14–6
Solutrean blades are considered the most highly developed form of Upper Paleolithic stonework.

Fig. 15–10b) all require a mastery of stone matched by only the most expert knappers today. Reproducing implements such as those mentioned above requires removal of extremely thin flakes, possible only through **pressure flaking**—using a pointed piece of bone, antler, or hard wood and pressing firmly against the stone (Fig. 14–7). In addition to using the several flaking techniques, later prehistoric toolmakers sometimes ground and polished the edges of their stone implements.

Once the tools are manufactured, the ways our ancestors used them can be inferred through further experimentation. For example, archaeologists from the Smithsonian Institution successfully butchered an entire elephant (which had died in a zoo) using stone tools they had flaked for that purpose. Others have cut down trees using stone axes, and many more have successfully tested stone spear and arrow points of their own making. But how can we be certain that ancient peoples actually used such objects in the same manner? Is there some way to verify the function of stone tools?

Ancient tools themselves may carry telltale signs of how they were used. In his graduate work at Oxford University, Lawrence Keeley performed a series of experiments in which he manufactured flint tools and then used them in diverse ways—whittling wood, cutting bone, cutting meat, and scraping skins (Keeley, 1980). Viewing those implements under a microscope at fairly high magnification (200×) revealed patterns of polishes, striations, and other kinds of **microwear**, damage that generally appears on the working edge of a tool (Fig. 14–8). What is most intriguing is that these patterns vary, depending on how the implement was used and which material was worked. For example, Keeley was able to distinguish among implements used on bone, antler, meat, plant materials, and hides. In the latter case, he was even able to determine if the hides were fresh or dried! In addition, orientations of microwear markings are also indicative of the ways in which the tool was used (e.g., for cutting or scraping). Evidence of microwear scars has been examined on even the extremely early hominid stone tools from Koobi Fora (East Lake Turkana), in Kenya (Keeley and Toth, 1981).

Working at much higher magnification (500× to 4,000×) using scanning electron microscopy (SEM), researchers have found that the working edges of stone implements sometimes retain plant fibers, hide or bone particles, and amino acids, as well as nonorganic residues, including **phytoliths**. Because fibers and phytoliths produced by different plant species are morphologically distinctive, there is good potential for identifying the botanical materials that came in contact with the tool during use. Stone flakes from the early Native American site at Monte Verde, Chile (see p. 382), seem to have been used for shaping wood, as indicated by the fibers adhering to their edges, and other tools were used for processing edible wild plants (Dillehay, 1997, p. 541). Such work is truly exciting: For the first time, we are able to make definite statements concerning the uses of ancient tools.

FIGURE 14–7
Pressure flaking, using an antler tip to press thin flakes from the edge of a stone tool.

Pressure flaking
A method of removing flakes from a core by pressing a pointed implement (e.g., bone or antler) against the stone.

Microwear
Polishes, striations, and other diagnostic microscopic changes on the edges of stone tools.

Phytoliths
(*phyto*, meaning "hidden," and *lith*, meaning "stone") Microscopic silica structures formed in the cells of many plants, particularly grasses.

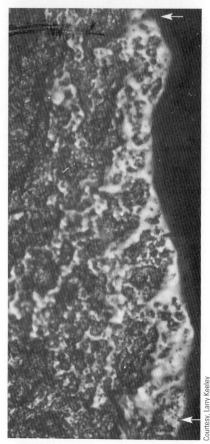

Courtesy, Larry Keeley

FIGURE 14–8
Microwear, shown here as the polish left on an experimental flint implement by scraping wood for 10 minutes, is seen in the bright, smooth areas. Dark, grainy areas are the unworn flint surface. Arrows indicate implement edge. (Magnification, 200×)

Stratigraphy
Study of the sequential layering of deposits.

Bone Research Experimental archaeologists are also interested in the ways bone is altered by humans and natural forces. Other scientists are vitally concerned with these matters as well. In fact, an entire new branch of paleoecology—*taphonomy*—is dedicated to researching the processes that influence bone deposition and preservation. In East African game parks and elsewhere, observations have been made on decaying animals to measure the effects of weathering, predator chewing, and trampling (Behrensmeyer et al., 1979). In an experiment conducted at the University of California, Berkeley, human bones were put into a running-water trough. Researchers observed how far different elements were transported and how much damage was done (Boaz and Behrensmeyer, 1976). Such information is useful in interpreting early hominid sites. For example, the distribution of hominid fossils at Olduvai suggests that less active water transport was prevalent there than in the Omo River valley.

Of primary concern to anthropologists is how to recognize and distinguish bone that has been altered by cultural processes, such as butchering, from bone that has simply undergone natural weathering or breakage due to animal activities. Detailed examination of the bones may provide evidence of damage inflicted by hominids, including cut marks and percussion marks left by stone tools. Great care must be taken to distinguish scars left on bone by carnivore or rodent gnawing, weathering processes, hoof marks, or even normal growth. High SEM magnification of a cut made by a stone tool may reveal a minutely striated and roughened groove scored into the bone's surface (Bunn, 1981; Potts and Shipman, 1981). A careful comparison with bones collected from predator dens and kills led Lewis Binford to conclude that animal predators and scavengers produced much, if not most, of the damage observed on animal bones found in the Olduvai sites (Binford, 1981). Some of the remaining damage probably represented tool marks, but he found that most appeared in the midshaft area of long bones, rather than at the joint ends, where butchering would have taken place. Binford concluded that the hominids who wielded the tools were not true hunters, but rather scavengers who arrived too late to either kill the game or butcher its carcass. Instead, with the aid of simple tools, they resorted to obtaining the hard-to-get marrow, probably the last edible morsels remaining (see Issue, Chapter 9, for further discussion).

Dating Prehistory

One of the essential considerations of archaeology and paleoanthropology is to place sites, fossils, and cultural artifacts into a chronological framework. In other words, we want to know how old they are.

There are two ways in which the question of age may be answered. We can say that fossil X lived before or after fossil Y, an example of *relative dating*. Or we can say that a particular fossil is *x* number of years old, a date determined by one of several *chronometric dating* techniques. Relative dating methods tell us merely that something is older or younger than something else, but not by how much. Chronometric dating (also known as *absolute dating*) estimates the age of a find in terms of calendar years. Chronometric dating techniques are not applicable to every site or discovery, especially those lacking materials suitable for dating, and so relative dating methods sometimes remain our best available source of information. Depending on the specific nature of the find or site, a paleontologist, geologist, paleoanthropologist, or archaeologist will select the most appropriate technique from a wide range of dating methods.

Relative Dating

The most basic method of relative dating is **stratigraphy**, one of the first techniques used by scholars (such as Charles Lyell and others) working with the vast period of geological time. Stratigraphy, in turn, is based on the *law of superposition*, which states that a lower stratum (layer) is older than a higher stratum. Given the fact that much of the earth's crust has been laid down by layer after layer of sedi-

William Turnbaugh

FIGURE 14–9
The Colorado River has cut through sedimentary rock layers and exposed the deep stratification of the Grand Canyon, in Arizona.

mentary rock, much like the layers of a cake (Fig. 14–9), stratigraphy has been a valuable aid in reconstructing the history of the earth and the life upon it. If, for example, a cranium is found at a depth of 15 feet and another cranium at 20 feet at the same site, we usually assume that the specimen discovered at 20 feet is older. We may not know the date (in years) of either one, but we would know that one is older (or younger) than the other. Although this may not satisfy our curiosity about the actual number of years involved, it would give some idea of the evolutionary changes in cranial morphology (structure), especially if a number of crania at different levels are found and compared.

Stratigraphic dating does, however, have a number of problems. Earth disturbances, such as volcanic activity, river activity, and mountain building, may shift strata and the objects within them, and the sequence of the material may be difficult or even impossible to reconstruct. Furthermore, the time period of a particular stratum—that is, the length of time it took to accumulate—is not possible to determine with much accuracy.

Closely connected to stratigraphic dating is the method called *biostratigraphy*, or *faunal correlation*, a dating technique employed in the Lower Pleistocene beds at Olduvai and other African sites. This technique is based on the regular evolutionary changes in well-known groups of mammals. Animals that have been widely used in biostratigraphic analysis in East and South Africa are fossil pigs (suids), elephants (proboscids), antelope (bovids), rodents, and carnivores. From areas where evolutionary sequences have been dated by chronometric means (such as potassium-argon dating, discussed shortly), approximate ages can be extrapolated to other lesser-known areas by noting which genera and species are present.

In a similar manner, **typological dating** applies to sequences of human cultural artifacts that exhibit stylistic trends through time. As with the evolution of biological species, most material objects that humans produce undergo stylistic change as basic inventions are modified and improved. For example, specific types of artifacts, such as projectile points, ceramic pots, and even stone wall construction, underwent sequential stages of development, just as automobiles, airplanes, and personal computers have in more recent times. By recognizing that certain characteristic attributes or modifications preceded or followed others, the archaeologist may arrange a series of artifacts in a sequence that puts each in its proper relative temporal position, from earliest to latest (Fig. 14–10).

Typological dating
Method of dating objects of unknown age by comparing their stylistic features to determine which object is older or newer.

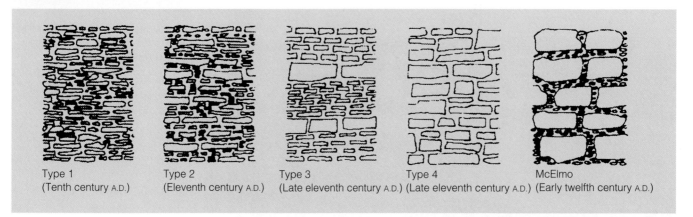

Type 1	Type 2	Type 3	Type 4	McElmo
(Tenth century A.D.)	(Eleventh century A.D.)	(Late eleventh century A.D.)	(Late eleventh century A.D.)	(Early twelfth century A.D.)

FIGURE 14-10
Typological dating of ancient stone masonry walls at Chaco Canyon, in New Mexico. The relative dating sequence shown is independently confirmed by chronometric dating techniques (dates shown in parentheses).

Seriation
Based on typological dating, a technique for putting groups of artifacts, or even sites containing such artifacts, into relative chronological order.

Fluorine analysis
A relative dating method that measures and compares the amounts of fluorine that bones have absorbed from groundwater during burial.

By expanding this typological approach from individual artifacts to entire sites or groups of sites in an area, we may be able to devise a relative chronology for a region through the use of **seriation** dating. The familiar Stone-Bronze-Iron Age sequence long recognized by prehistorians is a good example of seriation: Sites containing metal tools are generally more recent than those where only stone was used, and since bronze technology is known to have developed before iron making, sites containing bronze but no iron occupy an intermediate chronological position. Likewise, the presence of clay vessels of a specific form in a given site may allow researchers to place that site in a sequence relative to others containing only pots known to be of earlier or later styles. Using this approach, archaeologists working in the southwestern United States determined the correct sequence of ancient Pueblo Indian sites based on the presence or absence of pottery and a comparison of stylistic traits. Later, radiocarbon dating—a chronometric technique—confirmed this sequence. Unless we have some independent means of actually assigning chronometric dates to some or all of the artifacts in the series, we know only that certain types (and, by extension, the sites where they occur) are relatively older or younger than others.

Another method of relative dating is **fluorine analysis**, which applies only to bones (Oakley, 1963). Bones in the earth are exposed to the seepage of groundwater that often contains fluorine. The longer a bone lies in the earth, the more fluorine it will incorporate during the fossilization process. Therefore, bones deposited at the same time in the same location should contain the same amount of fluorine. The use of this technique by Kenneth Oakley of the British Museum in the early 1950s exposed the famous Piltdown (England) hoax by demonstrating that a human skull was considerably older than the jaw (ostensibly also human) found with it (Weiner, 1955). A discrepancy in fluorine content led Oakley and others to a closer examination of the bones, and they found that the jaw was not that of a hominid at all but of a young adult orangutan!

Unfortunately, fluorine is useful only with bones found at the same location. Because the amount of fluorine in groundwater is based on local conditions, it varies from place to place. Also, some groundwater may not contain any fluorine. For these reasons, comparing bones from different localities by fluorine analysis is impossible.

Chronometric Dating

It is impossible to calculate the actual age of a site's geological stratum and the objects in it using relative dating techniques. To determine the age in years, scientists have developed a variety of chronometric techniques based on the phenomenon of **radiometric decay**. The theory is quite simple: Certain radioactive isotopes of some elements are unstable, disintegrate, and form an isotopic variation of another element. Since the rate of disintegration follows a definite mathematical

Radiometric decay
A measure of the rate at which certain radioactive isotopes disintegrate.

pattern, the radioactive material forms an accurate geological time clock. By measuring the amount of disintegration in a particular sample, scientists can calculate the number of years it took for that amount of decay to accumulate. Some chronometric techniques are used for dating the immense geological age of the earth, but others may be applied to artifacts less than 1,000 years old. (For more on these techniques, see Lambert, 1997; Taylor and Aitken, 1997.)

A chronometric technique of great value to paleoanthropology is based on the radiometric decay of potassium-40 (^{40}K), which has a radiometric half-life of 1.3 billion years and produces argon-40 (^{40}Ar). The **potassium-argon (K/Ar) method** has been widely used in dating hominid materials in the 1- to 5-million-year range, especially in East Africa, where suitable potassium-enriched rock of volcanic origin is available. When the rock is in a molten state, argon, a gas, is driven off. As the rock cools and solidifies, potassium-40 continues to break down to argon, but now the gas is physically trapped in the cooled rock. To obtain the date of the rock, it is reheated and the escaping gas measured. It is important to note that organic material, such as bone, cannot be directly analyzed by this technique, but the rock matrix in which the bone is found can be. At Olduvai, K/Ar dating has given several reliable dates of the underlying basalt and several ash layers in Bed I, including the one associated with the *Zinjanthropus* cranium (now dated at 1.79 ± 0.03 m.y.a.). A variant of this technique, the argon-argon (^{39}Ar/^{40}Ar) method, has been used to date hominid localities in Java (see Chapter 11).

When dating relatively recent samples (from the perspective of a half-life of 1.3 billion years for K/Ar, *all* paleoanthropolgoical material is relatively recent), the amount of radiogenic argon (the argon produced by disintegration of a potassium isotope) is going to be exceedingly small. Experimental errors in measurement can therefore occur as well as the thorny problem of distinguishing the atmospheric argon normally clinging to the outside of the sample from the radiogenic argon. In addition, the initial sample may have been contaminated or argon leakage may have occurred while it lay buried. Due to these potential sources of error, K/Ar dating must be cross-checked using other independent methods.

Fission-track dating is one of the most important techniques for cross-checking K/Ar determinations. The key to fission-track dating is that uranium-238 (^{238}U) decays regularly by spontaneous fission. By counting the fraction of uranium atoms that have fissioned (shown as microscopic tracks caused by explosive fission of ^{238}U nuclei), we can ascertain the age of a mineral or natural glass sample (Fleischer and Hart, 1972). One of the earliest applications of this technique was on volcanic pumice from Olduvai, giving a date of 2.30 ±0.28 m.y.a.—in good accord with K/Ar dates.

Another important means of cross-checking dates is called **paleomagnetism**. This technique is based on the constantly shifting nature of the earth's magnetic pole. Of course, the earth's magnetic pole is now oriented in a northerly direction, but this has not always been the case. In fact, the orientation and intensity of the geomagnetic field have undergone numerous documented changes in the last few million years. From our present point of view, we call a northern orientation "normal" and a southern one "reversed." Major epochs (also called "chrons") of recent geomagnetic time are:

0.7 m.y.a.–present	Normal
2.6–0.7 m.y.a.	Reversed
3.4–2.6 m.y.a.	Normal
?–3.4 m.y.a.	Reversed

Paleomagnetic dating is accomplished by carefully taking samples of sediments that contain magnetically charged particles. Since these particles maintain the magnetic orientation they had when they were consolidated into rock (many thousands or millions of years ago), we have a kind of "fossil compass." Then the paleomagnetic sequence is compared against the K/Ar dates to check if they agree. Some complications may arise, for during an epoch, a relatively long period of time can occur when the geomagnetic orientation is the opposite of what is expected. For

Potassium-argon (K/Ar) method
Dating technique based on accumulation of argon-40 gas as a by-product of the radiometric decay of potassium-40 in volcanic materials; used especially for dating early hominid sites in East Africa.

Fission-track
Dating technique based on the natural radiometric decay (fission) of uranium-238 atoms, which leaves traces in certain geological materials.

Paleomagnetism
Dating method based on the earth's shifting magnetic pole.

FIGURE 14–11
Paleomagnetic sequences correlated for some East African sites—Olduvai, East Turkana, and Omo. (After Isaac, 1975.)

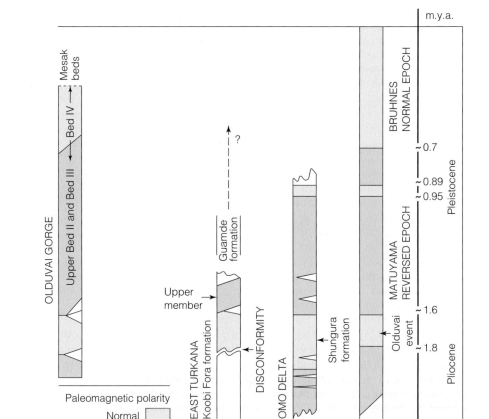

Radiocarbon dating
Method for determining the age of organic archaeological materials using the steady rate of isotope decay as a measure; also known as ^{14}C dating.

example, during the reversed epoch from 2.6 to 0.7 m.y.a. (the Matuyama epoch), there was an *event* lasting about 210,000 years when orientations were normal (Fig. 14–11). (Because this phenomenon was first conclusively demonstrated at Olduvai, it is appropriately called the *Olduvai event*.) However, once these oscillations in the geomagnetic pole are worked out, the sequence of paleomagnetic orientations can provide a valuable cross-check for K/Ar and fission-track age determinations.

The standard chronometric method for dating later prehistory is carbon-14 (^{14}C) dating, also known as **radiocarbon dating**. This technique has been used to date organic material from less than 1,000 years old to as old as 50,000 years or so, although the probability of error rises rapidly after 40,000 years. The ^{14}C technique is based on the following natural processes: Cosmic radiation enters the earth's atmosphere as nuclear particles, some of which react with nitrogen to produce small quantities of an unstable isotope of carbon, ^{14}C. This radioactive ^{14}C diffuses through the atmosphere, mixing with ordinary carbon-12 (^{12}C). Combined with oxygen (O_2) in the form of carbon dioxide (CO_2), carbon is taken up by plants during photosynthesis. Herbivorous animals absorb it by feeding on plants, and carnivores by feeding on herbivores. Thus, ^{14}C and ^{12}C are found in all living forms at a ratio that reflects the atmospheric proportion. Once an organism dies, it absorbs no more ^{14}C either through photosynthesis or in its diet. Without replacement, the ^{14}C atoms in the tissue continue to decay at a constant rate to nitrogen-14 (^{14}N) and a beta particle, while the ^{12}C remains stable. Thus, the $^{14}C/^{12}C$ ratio decreases steadily through time at a rate that can be measured precisely.

This technique is limited primarily to dating organic materials that were once alive and part of the carbon cycle. Carbon-14 has a radiometric half-life of 5,730 years, meaning it takes exactly 5,730 years for half the remaining ^{14}C to disintegrate. Let us say that charcoal, the remains of a campfire, is found at an archaeological site and analyzed for its $^{14}C/^{12}C$ ratio. First, the sample is carefully collected to avoid contamination. Using today's sophisticated technology, even tiny quantities of carbon—just a few milligrams—can be analyzed. In the laboratory, sensitive radiation detectors measure the residual ^{14}C (Fig. 14–12). Suppose the findings show that only 25 percent of the original ^{14}C remains, as indicated by the $^{14}C/^{12}C$ ratio. Since we know that it takes 5,730 years for half the original number of ^{14}C atoms to become ^{14}N and another 5,730 years for half the remaining ^{14}C to decay, the sample must be about 11,460 years old. Half the yet-remaining ^{14}C will disappear over the next 5,730 years (when the charcoal is 17,190 years old), leaving only 12.5 percent of the original amount. This process continues, and as you can estimate, there would be very little ^{14}C left after 40,000 years, when detection becomes difficult. Carbon-14 dates (and most other chronometric age determinations) are often cited with a plus or minus range; thus, the reading on the campfire charcoal might be expressed as 11,460 ±225, indicating a 67 percent chance that the actual date lies somewhere between 11,235 and 11,685 y.a. (see Box 14–3).

Some inorganic artifacts can be directly dated through the use of **thermoluminescence (TL)**. Used especially for dating ceramics, but also applied to clay cooking hearths and even burned flint tools and hearth stones on later hominid sites (see p. 321), this method, too, relies on the principle of radiometric decay. Clays used in making pottery invariably contain trace amounts of radioactive elements, such as uranium or thorium. As the potter fires the ware (or a campfire burns on a hearth), the rapid heating releases displaced beta particles trapped within the clay, which, as they escape, emit a dull glow known as thermoluminescence. Thereafter, radioactive decay resumes within the fired clay or stone, again building up electrons at a steady rate. To determine the age of an archaeological sample, the researcher must heat the sample to 500°C and measure its thermoluminescence; from that, the date can be calculated. TL is routinely used to authenticate fine ceramic vessels prized by

FIGURE 14–12
Technician in a modern radiocarbon dating laboratory.

Thermoluminiscence (TL)
(ther-mo-loo-min-ess'-ence) Technique for dating certain archaeological materials, such as ceramics, that release stored energy of radioactive decay as light upon heating.

BOX 14–3   DIGGING DEEPER

Chronometric Dating Estimates

Chronometric dates are usually determined after several archaeological or geological samples are tested. The dates that result from such testing are combined and expressed statistically. For example, say that five different ^{14}C samples are used to give the radiocarbon date 11,460 ± 225 years for a particular campfire feature. The individual results from each of the five samples were totaled together to give the average date (here, 11,460 years), and then the standard deviation was calculated (here, 225 years). The dating estimate is then reported as the mean, plus or minus (±) one standard deviation. Those

of you who have taken statistics realize that, assuming a normal distribution, 67 percent of the distribution of dates is included within one standard deviation (±) of the mean. Thus, the chronometric result, as shown in the reported range, is simply a probability statement that 67 percent of the dates from all samples tested fell within the range of dates from 11,235 to 11,685 years. You should carefully read chronometic dates and study the reported ranges. The smaller the range, the more likely that many samples were analyzed. Smaller ranges mean more precise estimates; better laboratory controls will also increase precision.

Understanding the Past: Archaeological Approaches

collectors and museums, and the technique has exposed many fake Greek and Maya vases displayed in prominent collections.

A chronometric dating technique that does not involve radioactive elements is **dendrochronology**, or dating by tree rings. Its use is limited to a few locales where ancient wood is commonly preserved, particularly the arid American Southwest and the bogs of western Europe. Because tree rings represent seasonal growth layers, the amount of new wood added each year depends directly on rainfall and other factors. The growth rings of an individual tree read like its biography, but its story may be read in either direction—from the beginning or from the end! If we know when the tree was cut and then count from the outer rings inward toward the center, we readily determine the year the tree began growing.

Moreover, we can also learn something about the changing environmental conditions that occurred during the tree's life span. Again counting back from the most recent ring, we may encounter thick layers of cells added during extended wet periods; these contrast with narrow rings laid down earlier during a few years of little precipitation. Usually, the pattern found in one tree—a few wide rings followed by a certain number of thin rings, succeeded in turn by more wide rings, and so forth—appears consistently throughout an entire region. These regional conditions, of course, affect all the trees whose life spans overlap, regardless of when they began growing. Thus, a certain six-year drought will be recorded by a narrow band of rings near the heart of a young seedling, whereas a tree that already has attained considerable age will be laying down those narrow rings over many earlier years' growth. The older tree may die first, thus ending its record shortly after the six-year drought; but the younger tree may survive for decades or centuries, continuing to add a long series of climate-induced growth rings.

By cutting or drawing core samples from living trees, recently dead trees, and successively older wood (including archaeological sources such as ancient house posts or beams), archaeologists obtain overlapping life histories of many trees. When compared, these life histories form an extensive record of tree-ring growth through many centuries. Remember, the archaeologist is mostly interested in determining precisely when a tree *stopped* growing and became part of a cultural process such as construction or cooking. As a result, a tree used as a beam in a prehistoric Southwestern structure may be dated to the very year in which it was felled (Fig. 14–13), for the distinctive pattern of its growth should exactly match some segment of the tree-ring record compiled for the region. Archaeologists studying the ceiling beams in the traditional homes still occupied by the Acoma people in northern New Mexico were able to precisely date construction undertaken in the mid-seventeenth century (Robinson, 1990). Wood from the commonly used pinyon pines and the long-lived Douglas fir trees, sequoia redwoods, and bristlecone pines of the American West, as well as preserved oak logs from western European bogs, afford archaeologists continuous regional tree-ring records extending back thousands of years.

But there is yet another dimension to tree-ring dating. By submitting wood taken from individual growth rings of known age to radiocarbon analysis, archaeologists have used dendrochronology to fine-tune ^{14}C technology by factoring out past fluctuations in the atmospheric production of the ^{14}C isotope over the past 9,800 years (the period for which tree-ring dates are available). They then use this factor to recalibrate the raw dates obtained by standard ^{14}C analyses, resulting in closer correspondence to actual calendar-year ages. Recently, by comparing ^{14}C dates obtained from coral reefs with dates on the same samples obtained using a uranium-thorium (^{234}U/^{230}Th) dating method, technicians have been able to adjust the radiocarbon calibration curve back to 23,700 years ago (Fiedel, 1999b).

Using a technique somewhat similar to dendrochronology, geoarchaeologists have devised **varve** chronologies for a few late Pleistocene and early Holocene sites in parts of northern Europe and North America. Meltwater runoff from ancient glaciers deposited a layer of silt in nearby lakes each summer, the thickness of this stratum fluctuating with seasonal conditions. More silt was laid down in warmer years, less during years with cooler summers. As with tree rings, the pattern of varve deposits

Dendrochronology
Archaeological dating technique based on the study of yearly growth rings in ancient wood.

William Turnbaugh

FIGURE 14–13
Doorway in White House Ruin, Canyon de Chelly, Arizona. Wooden beams and supports can be dated by dendrochronology. Archaeologists have removed a core sample from the left end of the lintel for dating.

Varve
Layer of silt deposited annually by a melting glacier; used as basis for archaeological dating in Europe.

from one lake to other nearby lakes may be compared, so that once a chronometric date is obtained for one set of varves, the calendar-year equivalents for others may be calculated from it. Nevertheless, this technique has only limited archaeological applications, because so few cultural sites are associated directly with varve deposits.

In some areas, including Egypt and Central America, the recorded calendar systems of ancient civilizations have been calibrated to our own, resulting in direct dating of some sites and inferential or cross-dating of others shown to be contemporaneous with them by the presence of distinctive artifacts. For example, firmly dated objects originating in the Nile valley and traded into the Aegean allow us to assign dates to the Mycenaean civilization (see Chapter 17). Obviously, this approach is of little use outside those regions having some connection with literate societies.

Since the advent of radiocarbon and other physicochemical dating techniques in the latter half of the twentieth century, the age of many archaeological finds has been proclaimed with some confidence. Although no other dating technique is as widely used as ^{14}C dating, each is an ingenious method with its own special applications. Still, none of these methods is truly precise, and each is beset with limitations and problems that must be carefully considered: What kinds of materials can be dated? What are the upper and lower age limits for this technique? Has the sample been properly collected? Is it of adequate size? Is there contamination? Any of these factors might introduce ambiguities into our so-called "absolute" dates, and as noted in Chapter 9, that is why more than one technique is often needed to confirm the dating at a site. No single technique is perfectly reliable by itself. However, the sources of error are different for each; therefore, cross-checking among several independent methods is the most reliable way of authenticating the chronology. Moreover, because it is both practical and advisable for the dating laboratory to analyze several samples of small size, some variation in results may be expected. Therefore, approximate dates are expressed as probability statements with a plus-or-minus factor.

The Archaeological Research Project

To the uninitiated, archaeology may appear to be a field whose principal reason for existence is to discover interesting and valuable objects that once were associated with ancient and exotic cultures. There were times when archaeology may have been, in fact, little more than a glorified treasure hunt. Modern archaeology, however, is a method of scientific investigation with the goal of learning about past humans and their behavior. An archaeologist may focus on one culture or time period or site, but ideally each individual project contributes to a broader understanding of what it means to be human.

Research Archaeology and Cultural Resource Management

Although pure research and the possibility of making exciting new discoveries about our predecessors remain justifiable incentives for doing archaeology, the endeavor also has its practical applications. In fact, much of the archaeological work done in the United States today is contracted by government agencies or corporations, who are required by law to minimize the impact of their proposed actions on the environment, including its cultural and archaeological components. Construction of highways and pipelines, as well as residential developments and shopping malls, continues to threaten archaeological resources at an alarming rate. **Cultural resource management (CRM)** is an outgrowth of these concerns. Archaeologists working in CRM are engaged to assess (and, when necessary, to devise ways to mitigate) potential damage to cultural resources.

Contract archaeologists working under CRM guidelines approach their work somewhat differently from many of their academic and museum colleagues, who may enjoy the luxury of picking and choosing the sites on which to investigate specific research topics. In contrast to this ideal, contract archaeologists more often work under adverse conditions in unfamiliar settings, face strict deadlines and

Cultural resource management (CRM)
Field of archaeological effort applied to the protection and salvage of archaeological sites from development and other forms of destruction.

Contract archaeologists
Researchers who are employed to carry out CRM projects.

budgetary constraints, and feel pressure from clients to complete the work with minimal disruption to their plans. Because the archaeological potential of the areas where they work is sometimes poorly known, these archaeologists must be fully prepared to deal with any and all kinds of evidence, ranging from scattered prehistoric artifacts to the complex features of abandoned nineteenth-century industrial sites. With its emphasis on flexibility, efficiency, and accountability, contract archaeology has become a distinct field, a business enterprise that provides professional, scientific expertise and service. And even though they may not always be able to tackle a contracted assignment as a well-defined research project, responsible CRM archaeologists must be thoroughly grounded in standard archaeological research techniques, while also possessing exceptional business and communication skills.

Designing a Research Program

Somewhat in contrast to most CRM projects, modern research archaeology is problem oriented, meaning that archaeologists are seeking answers to specific questions. Depending on the extent of previous work in an area, it might be possible to go beyond the basics of where and when: *Where* did people settle in this valley? *When* was this site occupied? As we have seen, archaeologists are ultimately interested in seeking explanations about the past: *Why* did farming develop in the Tehuacán Valley at such an early date? *How* did the impact of European exploration affect the balance of power among West African societies in the sixteenth century?

To address concerns such as these, archaeologists have adopted the general scientific method of *hypothesis testing*. Considerable background research is necessary, even before the archaeologist steps onto a site. Familiarity with all previous archaeological study of the question or region is essential, as is consultation with modern descendant populations and review of earlier ethnographic accounts that might provide clues to ancient lifeways. Long-term climatological data, knowledge of local flora and fauna, and an understanding of the regional geology all may have a bearing on the issue at hand and may assist the archaeologist in framing a reasonable hypothesis that can be examined and tested archaeologically. For example, after due consideration, an archaeologist in southwestern Colorado might formulate a working hypothesis like this one: *Overexploitation of their environment forced the people of Mesa Verde to abandon their sites in the late thirteenth century* A.D.

Once the problem has been defined and a hypothesis proposed, the archaeologist devises a **research design**, a specific strategy to test the hypothesis by collecting new data. Some practical concerns must be addressed at this point: Where might appropriate sites be sought? How can the essential resources—money, labor, equipment, lab space—be obtained? What formal permissions are needed? What specialists from other disciplines should be consulted? Only after these and other matters are settled is it finally time to head into the field.

Gathering the Data

As noted, contract archaeologists generally do not have an opportunity to pick and choose the sites they study, but must work within the specific area to be directly impacted by a proposed development. On the other hand, the research archaeologist may seek the right site (or portion of a site) that will yield pertinent information about the research question or hypothesis. To define a precise area for primary investigation, all archaeologists may choose from several survey and sampling strategies (Fig. 14–14):

- *Walkover survey.* Team members walk across the surface of potential sites, usually in a series of parallel transects, marking locations of all finds. Any concentration of artifacts or features may merit further investigation.
- *Simple random sampling.* A map of the study area is gridded into sampling units of standard size (10 m², 100 m²), and a predetermined

Research design
A plan of action for collecting and analyzing the data with which to test hypotheses.

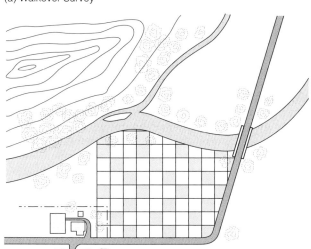

(a) Walkover Survey

(b) Simple Random Sampling

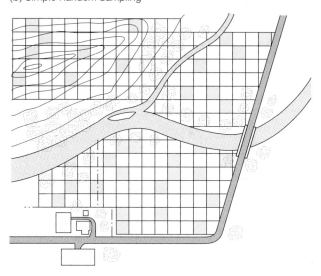

(c) Systematic Sampling

(d) Stratified Random Sampling

FIGURE 14–14
Survey and sampling techniques of the archaeologist.

percentage of these units (perhaps 10 or 20 percent) is selected randomly for collection or testing.

- *Systematic sampling.* A grid of the proposed study area is again used to guide the on-the-ground surveyors. This time, units are selected for examination in some systematic way—every tenth unit (for a 10 percent sample), every fifth unit (for a 20 percent sample), and so on. In surveying a narrow corridor, such as a pipeline route, a contract archaeologist may elect to place a shovel test pit at 10 m intervals.
- *Stratified random sampling.* If the archaeologist has some basis for differentiating the study area into distinct zones, he or she may then wish to randomly sample each zone separately to ensure that all are represented and examined for sites.

An advantage of using standardized survey and sampling techniques is that it becomes possible to use statistics and apply **probability** predictions with confidence. Nonprobabilistic techniques, such as intuition, informants, or even incantations, could be used to locate sites, of course, but such methods would not permit a researcher to make statistically valid statements about the representativeness of what has been found.

Probablility
The mathematical likelihood that a sampled data set is representative of the whole.

Single-component site
An archaeological site occupied by just one culture, usually for a relatively short period.

Stratum
(*pl.*, strata) A single layer of soil or rock; sometimes called a "level."

Horizontal excavation
Strategy for exposing a stratum to reveal a large area of a site.

Multicomponent sites
Archaeological sites that were periodically reused or occupied by successive cultures, often exhibiting a series of superimposed strata.

Vertical excavation
Strategy for digging multicomponent sites by opening pits or trenches that penetrate successive strata, or levels.

Provenience
The specific site location from which an artifact is recovered; may also refer to an artifact's cultural affiliation. *Provenance* is an alternate spelling.

FIGURE 14–15
A standard excavation unit, in this case an initial 2 × 2 m test pit to determine the site's stratigraphy. Each stratum is marked by pins.

Courtesy, Lena Sisco

For archaeologists engaged in CRM, archaeological sampling is of particular concern. The contract archaeologist must devise an effective sampling strategy that will result in a fair and cost-effective evaluation of any potentially significant cultural sites in the project area. Once in the field, a standard CRM procedure is to begin systematic shovel test pitting (using one of the previously mentioned approaches) to establish the presence of any sensitive spots. Subsequently, further field testing will be needed to determine the exact nature and size of any sites or features noted during the initial phase of the work. If any locations are deemed culturally significant, perhaps owing to their antiquity or special meaning for contemporary descendant populations, the contract archaeologist may recommend a full or partial excavation. Such a labor-intensive (and costly) strategy could be pursued if no alternative for preserving the site in place can be worked out in consultation with the client and other interested parties.

Excavation Excavation is the activity the general public most closely associates with archaeology. At one time, archaeologists routinely excavated entire sites, sometimes employing enormous numbers of untrained diggers. As noted, excavation is a labor-intensive activity, and as costs have risen and techniques have become more refined, large-scale excavation has become less common. Fortunately, probabilistic sampling and the use of innovative analytical techniques and interdisciplinary research efforts have largely eliminated the need for total site excavation. In fact, archaeologists prefer to preserve untouched portions of their sites for the benefit of future scientists, who may develop even better ways of extracting archaeological information. Thus, most excavation today is a sampling procedure.

Sites may be classified on the basis of their cultural histories. Was the site occupied for a long time or only briefly? The answer to this question often determines the techniques required to excavate the site. A **single-component site** was occupied by only one culture and usually for a relatively short period. Therefore, such sites generally produce only one cultural level, or **stratum**, in the otherwise natural stratification of the area. Using a **horizontal excavation** strategy to expose this stratum will reveal the pattern of relationships among artifacts and features across the site. On the other hand, **multicomponent sites** preserve evidence of several cultures (or perhaps a long-term occupation by one culture) and so produce successive levels, or strata, of cultural debris or overlapping features. A **vertical excavation** strategy would allow the archaeologist to examine each of these levels in turn, beginning with the top, or most recent. Often, the researcher will use limited vertical excavation—perhaps digging a test trench—to sample the site and understand its structure and formation before choosing to explore specific portions of it with horizontal excavation.

Archaeologists lay out their sites in a gridwork of squares, or excavation units, usually 1 or 2 m on a side (Fig. 14–15). These units are keyed to a central datum point or permanent marker. In this way, excavators can precisely locate the horizontal position of anything they find. By carefully noting the depth of the find as well, they can pinpoint its location in three dimensions (Fig. 14–16). This locational information is the artifact's **provenience**. It is faithfully mapped and recorded and will enable the archaeologist to reconstruct the context of the artifact after the fieldwork has ended.

On multicomponent sites, it is especially important that each stratum be recognized and individually excavated to keep the cultural materials from each component separate. At times, such a site may comprise a vertical stack of stratified levels, each readily distinguishable from the others. More often, though, the strata may be undulating, may disappear intermittently, or may have been thoroughly mixed by later rodent burrowing or activities such as plowing, laying foundations, or digging ditches (Fig. 14–17). Archaeologists use any and all

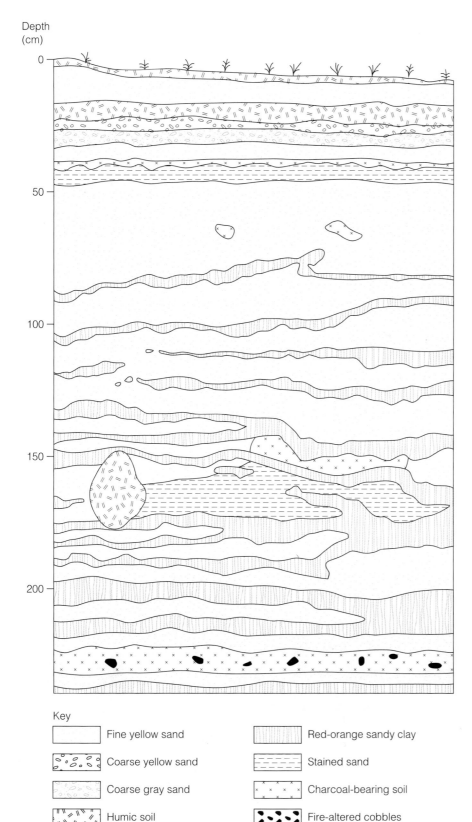

Depth (cm)

0

50

100

150

200

Stephanie M. Collins

FIGURE 14–16
Using plumb bob and tapes, archaeologists record the precise location of a stone feature found within the ruins of an ancient structure in Peru.

Key

Fine yellow sand	Red-orange sandy clay
Coarse yellow sand	Stained sand
Coarse gray sand	Charcoal-bearing soil
Humic soil	Fire-altered cobbles

FIGURE 14–17
Typical stratification of a deep site, such as this one in central Pennsylvania, exhibits alternating natural and cultural strata. (For a photographic view of this same excavation unit, see Figure 11 in the archaeology photo essay, p. 403.)

FIGURE 14–18
Using a Munsell soil color chart as a reference to describe an archaeological stratum on a Peruvian site by its characteristic color.

Stephanie M. Collins

of the following characteristics to distinguish one stratum from another: color, texture, artifact contents, degree of disturbance by earthworms or rodents, and even the variable sound of a trowel scraping across the soil (Fig. 14–18)!

Excavation is a meticulous process, and the most useful hand tools of the archaeologist reflect the delicacy of the operation: trowel, brushes, dental picks (Fig. 14–19). Keeping records is as important (and as time-consuming) as the digging itself. The archaeologist carefully notes the nature of each stratum, photographs the artifacts and features as they are uncovered, and records the exact location of each find (Fig. 14–20).

Naturally, the kinds of data recovered from a site will depend on several factors: past and recent site environment, earlier disturbance by people or animals, original nature of the site and its contents. During its period of occupation, a site represents an interplay between *additive* and *subtractive* processes: building versus destruction, growth versus decay. Once a site is finally abandoned, the subtractive processes are seldom interrupted. Organic matter decays, structures and other features become

FIGURE 14–19
A student excavator carefully scoops soil loosened by her trowel into containers that will be taken to be screened for small finds.

Stephanie M. Collins

Stephanie M. Collins

FIGURE 14–20
Photographing a newly excavated unit of a large structure. The painted rods provide scale.

Paul G. Richmond

disarranged, and weathering and breakdown proceed unchecked (Fig. 14–21). Depending on when the archaeologist breaks into this process and what recovery and conservation techniques are used, the site may yield much or only a little pertaining to the research topic.

It is the common goal of both the research archaeologist and the contract archaeologist to maximize the recovery of data, especially since a site can be excavated only once. To this end, a barrage of special equipment and techniques are routinely employed. For example, flecks of animal bone and microflakes from stone tools are caught in fine-mesh screens, while minute fragments of charcoal, seeds, and nut hulls are retrieved from **flotation** (wet-sieving) devices.

Materials recovered from a site undergo immediate processing. Artifacts are recorded and photographed even while they are in the ground. Once removed, everything is quickly bagged and tagged with provenience data, then forwarded to the field lab or on to specialists who will begin their detailed analyses (Fig. 14–22).

FIGURE 14–21
Tree roots grasp an 850-year-old Cambodian temple, dislodging its carved stones. When the tree dies, the walls will tumble.

Flotation
Technique for separating preserved organic material from other archaeological samples by water immersion.

Stephanie M. Collins

FIGURE 14–22
Specimens from this excavation unit have been bagged according to the types of material represented: bone, charcoal, shell, pottery, and miscellaneous small finds.

CHAPTER 14

Analyzing the Data

As we saw in our discussion of paleoanthropological research (see Table 9–1), archaeology today makes use of the expertise of numerous specialists from many disciplines. As a result, field archaeologists now recognize and collect many previously ignored kinds of data from their sites. Some of these materials will be studied in the archaeological laboratory, while others will be submitted to specialists in related fields (Banning, 2000).

Artifacts, the products of human cultural behavior, remain a primary focus of archaeological interest and study. More than anything else, these surviving objects reveal clues about ancient lifeways. In addition, a site may yield identifiable plant or animal remains that can inform archaeologists about diet or environmental conditions. Soil samples, too, yield evidence of past environments and human activity through analysis of composition and chemistry. And, of course, appropriate materials are collected for dating purposes. The archaeologist may then turn some of these finds over to colleagues who specialize in ceramic studies, lithic technology, archaeozoology, archaeobotany, or soil chemistry. Human bones discovered in burials and other features or in geological deposits would be analyzed by a physical anthropologist or osteologist (see the paleopathology photo essay, pp. 282–286). Few archaeologists can claim competence in working with more than one or two of these categories of material, which is why interdisciplinary research is so essential in the scientific study of the past. These various specialists, in turn, attempt to extract relevant cultural information from a systematic study of what is essentially ancient peoples' garbage.

After being cleaned and numbered, the artifacts themselves are sorted into significant groups for study and interpretation. The first divisions may simply separate ceramic from stone and organic objects. Artifacts are then further classified into archaeological **types**, categories of objects that share significant characteristics (Fig. 14–23):

- *Morphological types*. Here, basic shared attributes of size, shape, or color are recognized. This classification is purely descriptive and does not presume a specific purpose for the objects. Example: bifacially flaked stone disk.
- *Functional types*. This category focuses on artifacts for which evidence of use is preserved, such as a cooking vessel with food residue or an edge-worn flint blade. If function can be determined by objective means, it is proper to assign the artifact to a specific functional category. Examples: arrow point, hide scraper.
- *Temporal types*. Many categories of cultural artifacts undergo stylistic changes through time, making it possible to assign an example of a given type to a specific position in the stylistic sequence (see p. 353). A prehistoric artifact may be placed in its proper relative position in a series—a relative dating technique that allows one to say that this type is earlier or later than others in the sequence. A modern example: new models produced annually by car manufacturers.

Archaeologists devise typological categories so they can work with a manageable number of groupings of related or similar artifacts rather than countless individual specimens. Typology helps us note significant trends and associations that might otherwise be obscured by minor stylistic details and individual variations.

But, simply classifying artifacts into categories and types is scientifically insufficient if the ultimate goal of archaeology is to understand the past and its people. To that end, we attempt to elicit as much information as we can from the material objects that represent an extinct society.

Further insights may be gained in a number of ways. Close physical examination of the specimen is one approach. Earlier in this chapter, we saw that the surfaces of an artifact may exhibit signs of use that offer clues to its function. Recall that microwear evidence of an artifact's use may be visible if the working surface of

Types
In archaeology, categories of objects that share significant characteristics.

Morphological types

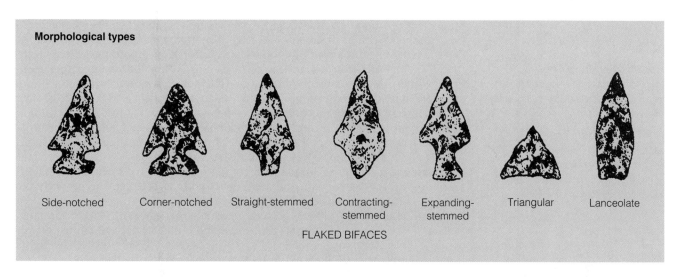

Side-notched · Corner-notched · Straight-stemmed · Contracting-stemmed · Expanding-stemmed · Triangular · Lanceolate

FLAKED BIFACES

Functional types

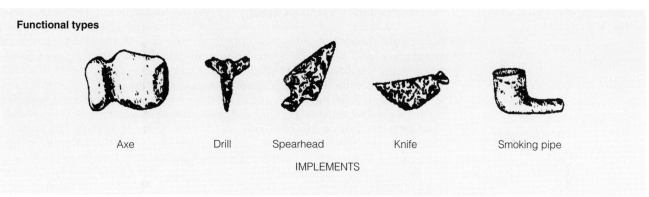

Axe · Drill · Spearhead · Knife · Smoking pipe

IMPLEMENTS

Temporal types

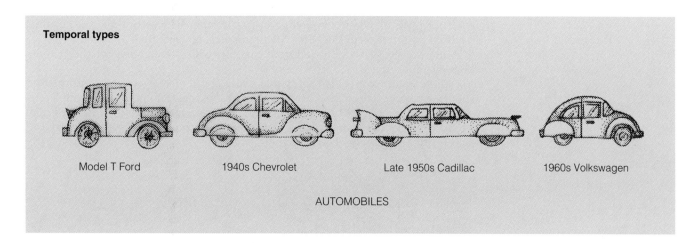

Model T Ford · 1940s Chevrolet · Late 1950s Cadillac · 1960s Volkswagen

AUTOMOBILES

the tool is examined under a powerful lens. Microwear analysis allows us to discriminate between similar-looking objects if, for example, one was used as a knife for shaving wood and another for slicing meat (Keeley, 1980; Dillehay, 1997). We also noted that modern experimental archaeologists have developed techniques to make and use replica tools and to simulate other activities that enable us to better appreciate ancient cultural practices.

FIGURE 14–23
Artifact typology.

Neutron activation analysis
Technique for determining the chemical composition of a material by irradiating it to identify its component elements.

X-ray fluorescence spectrometry
Technique for analyzing the chemical composition of a material by bombarding it with X-rays and then identifying individual elements by their distinctive afterglow.

Ecofacts
Natural objects or materials, such as seeds or animal bones, that are found in cultural contexts and that may indicate ancient diet or ecological relationships.

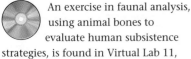
An exercise in faunal analysis, using animal bones to evaluate human subsistence strategies, is found in Virtual Lab 11, section V.

Sometimes the chemical analysis of artifactual materials provides information on ancient procurement activities or exchange routes. The chemical characterization of lithics (such as obsidian or steatite), clay pottery, and some metals can be determined using a variety of sophisticated laboratory procedures. These techniques include **neutron activation analysis** and **X-ray fluorescence spectrometry**, both of which involve the irradiation of the subject material so as to identify its component elements and measure their relative abundance. The results of such tests are extremely accurate compositional analyses, measured in parts per million or relative percentages. For instance, obsidian blades found in 2,000-year-old burial mounds in Ohio have a specific geochemical profile linking them to a quarry in what is now Yellowstone National Park, in Wyoming. In such cases, we can confidently ascribe the artifacts' lithic source to that specific quarry, since no other location is known to have the same mix of primary and trace elements in precisely the same proportions (Harbottle, 1982; Shackley, 1998).

Quite often, archaeologists recover materials that are not, strictly speaking, artifacts. When found in cultural contexts, natural objects such as animal or fish bones and plant parts are termed **ecofacts** (Fig. 14–24). Ecofacts aid archaeologists in identifying ancient food remains and in reconstructing the native ecology of a site and its vicinity. Preserved bones, teeth, and antlers from larger mammals may yield direct information about human diet and hunting or herding behavior. Using some of the techniques familiar to the physical anthropologist, archaeozoologists study faunal skeletal elements, not only to identify species, but also to determine the age, sex, and season of death for animals exploited by humans (O'Connor, 2000). Many sites also preserve the bones of small rodents, birds, and reptiles; fish bones and scales; mollusk shells; insect parts; and, on occasion, feathers or hairs. Some migratory mammal, bird, or fish species may have inhabited a site area during just a part of each year. Certain land snails tolerate only a narrow range of temperature and soil moisture conditions, so the presence of their shells is a sensitive indicator of the past environment. Bones and teeth may also be analyzed for their stable carbon isotope ratios, which reflect the kinds of plants consumed and therefore the general environmental conditions in which the animal lived (see pp. 214 and 420).

Likewise, archaeobotanists contribute their expertise to the study of ancient plant remains. Macrobotanical specimens, including preserved wood, charcoal, seeds, or nuts, may be recovered and directly compared with a modern regional study collection for identification. Microbotanical remains such as pollen or phytoliths must be tediously removed from carefully collected samples for study under high magnification.

In the hands of qualified specialists, ecofacts can yield a wealth of information about past environments and human cultural activities, telling us, for example, the seasons people occupied the site, the kinds of trees available for their fires, and when deer were hunted or shellfish gathered. (In Chapter 16, we examine what ecofacts reveal about the process of domestication.)

FIGURE 14–24
Examples of ecofacts.

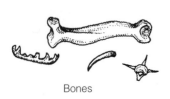

Bones

Shells

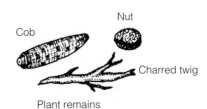

Cob

Nut

Charred twig

Plant remains

Pollen
(highly magnified)

Documenting the Results

Many seasons of fieldwork are sometimes necessary to produce enough data to address the investigator's original research questions. Moreover, every hour that each person spends in actual site excavation may later require at least several more hours away from the site devoted to processing artifacts or records or studying nonartifactual samples. The increasingly sophisticated analyses required by archaeologists often are available from only a small number of specialists or labs, so the time needed to process these samples may run into many months. When, at last, everything has been examined, considered, reexamined, and argued about, the time has come to synthesize the data into a comprehensive final report. Doing so obviously demands that the archaeologist be thoroughly conversant with the results of any specialist studies commissioned for the project.

In the end, documenting a research project and making its results available to colleagues, funding agencies, and the interested public is an important obligation. A "final" report should eventually be published for every project or site. Very likely, it will consist largely of basic descriptive data, hopefully balanced with a fair measure of analysis and some reconstructions of cultural behavior. It will probably include few ultimate explanations. By one measure, a fruitful archaeological project is one that has tested a hypothesis or two and shown it to be reasonable or not. Perhaps new questions will have arisen out of the work, which may in turn lead to new or more refined hypotheses to be tested on yet another site.

In view of the public funds invested in archaeology today, most researchers also recognize their obligation to make the results of their work more widely available. In addition to preparing professional publications and presentations, many archaeologists routinely provide press releases or even write their own articles for popular magazines to report the highlights of their work. Some significant artifacts may find their way into museum exhibits, but many more people today are likely to view a TV program featuring a photogenic site and its articulate excavator. Some archaeological projects even maintain active websites on the Internet, allowing visitors to take virtual site tours, read daily journal entries, and ask the researchers questions via the computer.

SUMMARY

In a sense, our view of the archaeological past is something like what we see out of the small passenger window of a jet cruising high above the continent. Much evidence of human activity may be apparent on the ground far below us—in the net of roadways, plowed fields, towns, and other large constructions. But the individuals who produced these patterns on the landscape are not usually visible to us from our high altitude. A cultural landscape without people does not tell the whole story. Still, by observing their handiwork, even at a distance, we can at least gain some insight to their society. In archaeology, it is *time* rather than space that separates us from those we study.

In this chapter, we have seen that archaeologists apply a battery of research techniques to discover, excavate, and evaluate sites, features, and artifacts associated with the expansion of anatomically modern humans and their subsequent activities in all regions of the globe. Essentially, all of these techniques are an attempt to "close the distance" between ourselves and our predecessors so that we might better understand their lives. In the absence of written records, archaeological research is our primary scientific approach to learning about the ancient past.

A fundamental goal of archaeology is to describe the past by placing people and cultures into a chronological framework. A number of scientific dating techniques aid archaeologists in developing a time frame for prehistory. A second important

research objective is to analyze and reconstruct ancient lifeways. Archaeologists have gathered clues from countless excavations, comparative cultural studies, and experimentation to help them interpret past lives. Ultimately, archaeologists hope to use the insights gained through careful fieldwork and data analysis to explain how and why the past took the course it did.

QUESTIONS FOR REVIEW

1. What are three primary research goals, or objectives, of archaeological research?
2. Why is excavation such an essential component of archaeological study?
3. What kinds of cultural information may not be represented by artifacts alone? How do archaeologists attempt to compensate for these shortcomings through approaches such as ethnoarchaeology and ethnographic analogy?
4. Explain the relationship between artifacts, features, sites, and context in archaeology.
5. Can you think of two or three good experimental archaeology projects? What specific hypotheses about ancient lifeways would each of these experiments be designed to test? How would you go about collecting and then interpreting the data?
6. What kinds of information may be obtained by closely examining the working edges of ancient stone tools?
7. Compare relative dating and chronometric dating. Name one or two examples of each, and briefly explain the principles by which the dates are determined.
8. What is the role of a "contract archaeologist" in modern American archaeology?
9. Compare horizontal excavation and vertical excavation strategies. Under what conditions would each be most appropriate?
10. Why are archaeologists so concerned with creating artifact typologies? What are three criteria that may be used to define major typological categories of artifacts?

SUGGESTED FURTHER READING

Banning, E. B. 2000. *The Archaeologist's Laboratory: The Analysis of Archaeological Data.* Norwell, MA: Kluwer Academic Publishers.

Hester, Thomas R., Harry J. Shafer, and Kenneth L. Feder. 1997. *Field Methods in Archaeology.* 7th ed. Mountain View, CA: Mayfield.

Hodder, Ian. 2001. *Archaeological Theory Today.* Cambridge, England: Polity Press.

Orton, Clive. 2000. *Sampling in Archaeology.* Cambridge Manuals in Archaeology. Cambridge, England: Cambridge University Press.

Rathje, William, and Cullen Murphy. 2001. *Rubbish!: The Archaeology of Garbage.* Tucson: University of Arizona Press.

Taylor, R. E., and Martin J. Aitken. 1997. *Chronometric Dating in Archaeology.* New York: Plenum.

RESOURCES ON THE INTERNET

Wadsworth Anthropology Resource Center
http://anthropology.wadsworth.com

The companion website for this text includes a range of enrichment material focused on the chapter's topic. While online you can enhance your understanding of the chapter by exploring one of the several additional Internet Exercises, by researching topics, and by accessing full articles on InfoTrac College Edition. You can also reinforce the concepts by taking online practice exams.

Internet Exercises

Archaeology is prominently represented on the Internet. Visit the website of the Society for American Archaeology (**http://www.saa.org**), the largest professional association of archaeologists working in the Western Hemisphere. Click on the heading "What is Archaeology?" and follow the link to "Archaeology & You," an online booklet. Read Chapter 2, "The Science of Archaeology," which briefly discusses several recent North American research projects. What factors did the archaeologists consider before deciding to excavate (and thereby at least partly destroy) the sites?

InfoTrac College Edition
http://www.infotrac-college.com/wadsworth

A subject search for *archaeological dating* should produce several dozen journal references. After reading the titles and evaluating several of the abstracts, select at least one article to read completely. Which dating technique was featured in this article? What kind of material was analyzed for dating pruposes? How were the dating results used in interpreting a site, artifacts, or physical remains? Did these results correspond well with other data from the site?

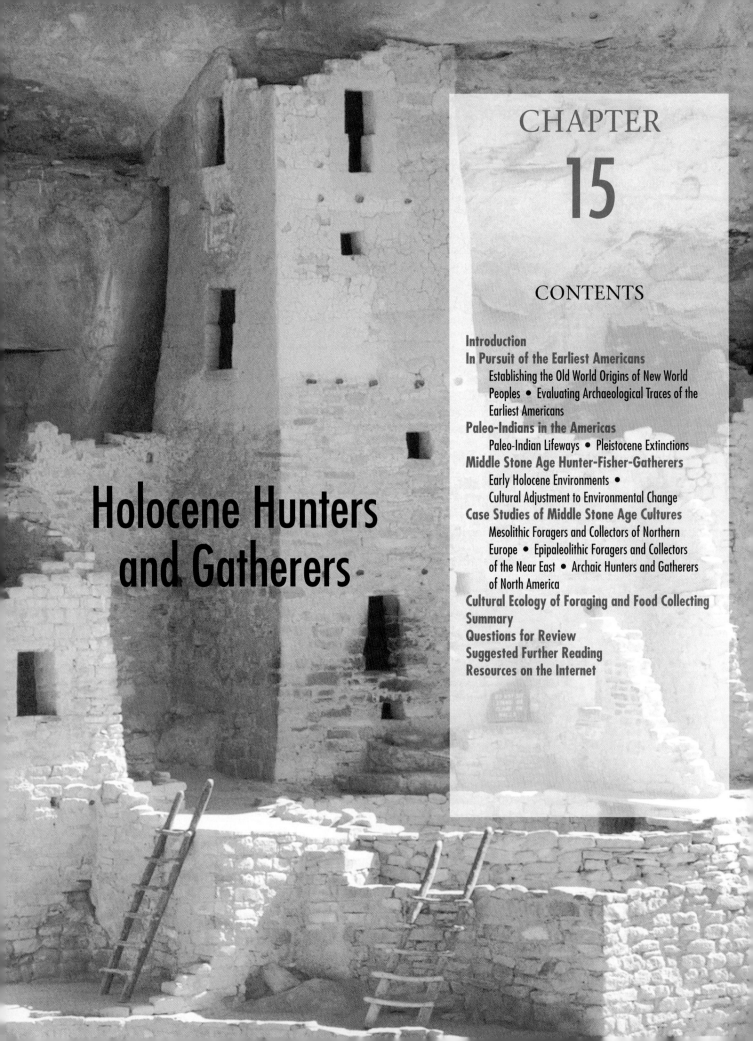

CHAPTER

15

Holocene Hunters and Gatherers

CONTENTS

Introduction

The story of primate evolution and hominid development, processes that took place largely in Africa and other regions of the Old World over millions of years, has dominated the earlier chapters of this text. Now we are coming down the home stretch and have yet to encounter any signs of the earliest Americans, first farmers, ancient Egyptians, and other great civilizations of "antiquity." But given our organization and focus, that is just as it should be. The events of recent prehistory—and the past 12,000 to 15,000 years definitely count as "recent," even in terms of the relatively modest time span of human evolution—will receive more than their proportionate share of space in our remaining pages (Fig. 15–1).

The dozen or so brief millennia since the end of the last Ice Age have been, by some measures, unlike any comparable period in human prehistory. The post-Pleistocene, or Holocene, epoch is associated with the final major geographical expansion of our species (into the Americas) and with a remarkably accelerated pace of cultural development worldwide. At the beginning of the Holocene, the world's modest human population of perhaps a few tens of millions sustained itself as it always had, by collecting food from the natural environment, living in small groups, constructing humble shelters, and making use of effective but simple equipment crafted from basic natural materials. Some 600 generations later, the species has attained a population of 6 billion, nearly all of whom regularly consume foods derived from a select inventory of domesticated plants and animals under human

FIGURE 15–1
Time line for Chapter 15.

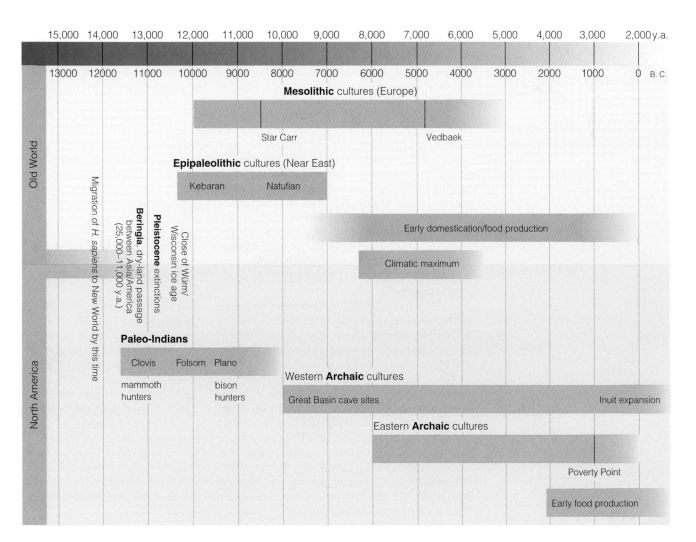

373

control. The world's surface has been transformed to accommodate our farms and cities and other cultural landscapes. Most of its natural resources, including even deeply buried ores, fossil fuels, and radioactive elements, are routinely processed into consumer products and industrial or military devices of remarkable ingenuity, most of which are distributed through our global economy. Humankind has plumbed the deepest seas and explored the solar system. And we have learned to write poetry—and college textbooks.

It is important to recall that these fundamental and far-reaching transformations are *not* primarily the result of human physical evolution, which has played a relatively insignificant role during the short span since the last Ice Age (see Chapters 4 and 5). Rather, the most radical developments affecting the human condition continue to be the consequences of our uniquely human *biocultural evolution*, for the most part stimulated by cultural innovations rather than genetic processes.

In this chapter, we examine the archaeological and biological clues relating to the origins of the first Americans and then review the evidence for their initial arrival date and subsequent cultural adjustments in their new homeland. We then focus on the development and consequences of a way of life that replaced specialized hunting with a broader-based hunting and gathering economy in both the Old World and the New.

In Pursuit of the Earliest Americans

A topic of perennial archaeological debate is the issue of *Homo sapiens* expansion into previously uninhabited regions of the globe during the late Pleistocene. Because the evolution of hominoids and hominids took place primarily in Africa and secondarily in Eurasia, we can be certain that the anatomically modern humans occupying Australia, the islands of the Pacific, and the Americas when European explorers *re*-discovered them just five centuries ago had been immigrants themselves at some much earlier time.

The close of the Würm ice age (called the **Wisconsin** ice age in North American terminology) after about 15,000 y.a. marked a divide in human prehistory. Certainly, other glacial periods had come and gone in the several million years during which humans evolved from ancestral primates. But continental glaciation primarily affected the higher latitudes, and since early hominids ranged the tropics, only the more subtle effects of the Pleistocene climate change reached them. By the time the most recent ice sheets were receding, anatomically modern human populations were expanding into the temperate regions, including many areas only recently vacated by the glaciers (see Chapter 13). Dealing with the unfamiliar conditions of these new environments necessitated rapid adjustments, which later *Homo* could accomplish effectively through culture change, rather than waiting for biological evolution to take its course over many generations.

The spread of people into the Western Hemisphere, in particular, represented a remarkable opportunity for a species that had until then been confined to the Old World. The American continents truly represented a "new world" to the first hunters to enter and explore their vastness shortly before the close of the Pleistocene ice age. With these steps into the Americas, the territorial range of *Homo sapiens* increased by 16 million square miles (41.4 million km^2), or 30 percent of the inhabitable globe. A virgin landscape teeming with animals that were unfamiliar with humans awaited these hardy, intelligent, well-armed hunters.

Most scientists agree that the first human population of the Americas arrived by way of Asia, though some deviate from this view (Verrengia, 1999; Parfit, 2000). And questions of how long ago and what kind of people they were are still hotly debated. Could there have been more than one migration? What kinds of cultural equipment did the newcomers bring with them? Who were the first Americans, and what do we know about them?

Wisconsin
Time of the last major glacial advance in North America; analogous to late Würm or Weichsel in the Old World.

Establishing the Old World Origins of New World Peoples

In tracing the earliest Americans back to their Old World origins, we consider three primary lines of evidence: geographical, cultural, and biological.

Both geographical circumstances and cultural traces point to an Asian origin for American Indians.* Any modern world map shows that the most direct approach to the Americas by land lies through northeastern Asia. During the ice ages, this route was even more convenient, as we shall see. Archaeology confirms that during the later phases of the Pleistocene, Upper Paleolithic hunters pursuing large herbivores with efficient stone- and bone-tipped weapons (and probably with the aid of domesticated dogs) filtered into the farthest reaches of Eurasia. Hunting bands stopped on the shores of Lake Baikal in southern Siberia after 25,000 y.a. and reached sites like Dyuktai Cave on the Aldan River in eastern Siberia by around 18,000 y.a. (Hoffecker et al., 1993). Their use of fire, tailored skin clothing, and shelters made from the hides and bones of butchered mammoths and other animals contributed to their survival in these bleak regions during the height of the last Ice Age (Soffer and Praslov, 1993). Culturally and geographically, these Asian hunters seem to have been poised to become the first Americans.

The latest era of continental glaciation (the Würm, or Wisconsin, stage) saw massive ice sheets blanketing much of the northern latitudes. At the same time—and for spans of thousands of years—northeastern Asia and Alaska remained linked by a wide "land bridge" (West and West, 1996). This connection was actually the exposed floor of the shallow Bering Sea. The land bridge formed during long periods of maximum glaciation, when the volume of water locked up in glacial ice sheets reduced worldwide sea levels by 300 to 400 feet (90 to 120 m). During this time, **Beringia**, as it is known, comprised a broad plain up to 1,300 miles (2,000 km) wide from north to south (Fig. 15–2). Ironically, its cold, dry arctic climate kept Beringia itself relatively ice-free, a windswept area of low relief covered with a scant vegetation of mosses, lichens, and sedges.

Despite its treeless and barren appearance, Beringia's dry steppes and **tundra** supported herds of grazing animals—and, very likely, the hunters who preyed on them. The region was, after all, an extension of the familiar landscape of northern Asia. It is possible that more than one group of people ventured across Beringia during the millennia when it bridged the continents. Perhaps they were merely following game or even purposefully seeking new hunting grounds. At the same time, a rich marine environment along Beringia's southern shoreline could have attracted exploring bands, some of whom may even have reached North America by following the coast in boats (Dixon, 2000). No matter what brought them here, they became the first humans in the Western Hemisphere.

Geologists have determined that except for short spans, the Bering passage was dry land between about 25,000 and 11,000 y.a. and for other extended periods even before that time (especially between 75,000 and 45,000 y.a.). The New World probably received its first human inhabitants during the later episode. Establishing a more precise entry date is crucial yet remains one of the nagging unsolved problems of American prehistory. If we speculate that people might have arrived much before about 35,000 y.a. (perhaps over the earlier land bridge), we would have to conclude that they were either *Homo sapiens* of an archaic physical type (such as Neandertal) or else among the earliest anatomically modern humans found outside Africa or southwest Asia. Though highly unlikely, it is at least conceivable that a small population of this type might have died out subsequently during latter stages of the Pleistocene, leaving few remains and no surviving progeny. However, no incontrovertible physical evidence supporting this scenario has been recognized.

Still, we must acknowledge that archaeological or physical data of any kind bearing directly on the earliest people to reach the New World are frustratingly

Beringia
(bare-in'-jya) The dry-land connection between Asia and America that existed periodically during the Ice Age.

Tundra
Treeless plains characterized by permafrost conditions that support the growth of shallow-rooted vegetation such as grasses and mosses.

American Indian, though obviously a misnomer, is a well-established term that is favored by many of the peoples to whom it refers, while others prefer *Native American*. We use both terms interchangeably here.

FIGURE 15–2
North America during the late Pleistocene ice age, about 18,000 y.a. Lower sea levels during times of maximum glaciation exposed Beringia and other parts of the continental margins. Note mountain glaciation and temporary lakes in the West and the location of a periodic "ice-free corridor" between the Cordilleran and Laurentian ice caps in western Canada.

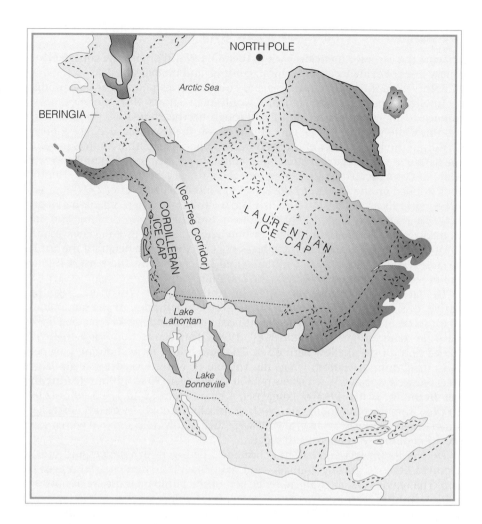

scarce. Well-documented skeletons are especially rare. The physical remains of fewer than two dozen North American individuals appear to date much before 9,500 y.a., by which time humans had certainly been present in the New World for millennia.* Ironically, just as advances in molecular biology (DNA) offer new possibilities for analyzing human remains, many of the ancient bones will be unavailable for further scientific study because they are being claimed by modern Native American communities under the terms of a 1990 federal law intended to protect Indian graves and funerary artifacts (Box 15–1). Several sets of ancient bones have already been reburied at the insistence of Indian groups, among them the 12,800-year-old partial skeleton of a young female discovered in a cave above the Snake River near Buhl, Idaho, who was one of the Americas' most senior citizens (Green et al., 1998).

These rare early finds afford us some valuable insights to ancient life and death. An examination of the Buhl bones prior to their reburial revealed the presence of interrupted-growth lines in a long bone and an enamel hypoplasia in a tooth, both suggesting that the woman experienced some metabolic stress in childhood, perhaps as the result of disease or seasonal food shortages (Green et al., 1998). And wrapped in fine matting, the partially desiccated body of a male who was in his early 40s when he died at Spirit Cave, Nevada, some 10,600 years ago exhibited a

---

*Dates cited in the sections dealing with early American prehistory in this chapter are based on a recently recalibrated radiocarbon (14C) chronology (Fiedel, 1999b) and have been adjusted to reflect calendar years before the present.

fractured skull and tooth abscesses as well as signs of back problems (Winslow and Wedding, 1997). Around the same time near Grimes Point rock-shelter, another Nevada site, a teenager died of his wounds after being stabbed in the chest with an obsidian blade that left slash marks and stone flakes embedded in one of his ribs (Owsley and Jantz, 2000). And a nearly complete skeleton washed out of the Columbia River in Washington state in 1996 dates to the same early period. Kennewick Man, as he is known to the media, also endured violent trauma and other health problems during his 40 or 50 years of life. His most intriguing injury is an old wound in his pelvis that had healed around a still-embedded stone spear point (Slayman, 1997). In addition, he had several badly healed ribs, fused neck vertebrae, and an infected head injury.

Physical anthropologists and archaeologists hoping to study the ancient and well-preserved skeleton of Kennewick Man have been frustrated by federal agencies acting in the interests of five local Indian tribes who claim the remains under NAGPRA. During lengthy and highly publicized legal disputes in federal courts over the status of the skeleton, Native Americans assert their rights to rebury their "ancestor," while many anthropologists argue that no biological or cultural connection between the 9,000-year-old remains and tribes currently living in the area can be scientifically established without further testing and analysis (Downey, 2000; Thomas, 2000).

Physical anthropologists who made the preliminary studies of Kennewick Man, the Spirit Cave mummy, and other early specimens have announced surprising interpretations based on this modest sample. Multivariate statistical analyses comparing a series of standard cranial measurements—including those that define overall skull size and proportion, shape of nasal opening, face width, and distance between the eyes—place the earliest known American remains outside the normal range of variation observed in modern populations (Owsley and Jantz, 2000). The more derived craniofacial morphological traits that characterize most modern Asian and American Indian populations appear to be absent in this early population. Instead, the archaeological examples display relatively small, narrow faces combined with long skulls. In living populations today, physical anthropologists note these generalized (nonderived) traits among the Ainu of Japan and some Pacific Islanders and Australians. Crania that more closely resemble those of modern Native Americans became prevalent only after about 7,000 y.a. (Owsley and Jantz, 2000; Steele, 2000).

There are, of course, no uniform biological "types" of human beings in the sense once assumed by traditional classifiers of race (see Chapter 5). Generalities regarding human variation must, given the nature of genetic recombination and the effects of environment and nutrition, be taken simply as that—generalities. Still, the lack of distinctive American Indian physical markers on the oldest skeletal specimens invites speculation as to how the early population of the Americas, as represented by these individuals, may be related to contemporary populations.

Assuming there *is* a relationship (as seems most likely), then possibly we are seeing the microevolutionary effects of natural selection, which may have operated with unusual rapidity as populations evolved under different selective stresses in dissimilar regions after the Ice Age. Or perhaps the observed differences are merely the cumulative result of random genetic drift during hundreds of generations of genetic isolation in these vast continents. Alternatively, gene flow may be the explanation if genetic exchanges between Asia and America continued periodically. On the other hand, it is possible that the earliest people to arrive left no modern descendant population in the Americas, having been absorbed or replaced altogether by later Asian immigrants exhibiting more derived traits.

Several other sources of biological data offer evidence bearing on American Indian origins. Comparing specific details of dental morphology for many Asian and Native American populations, physical anthropologist Christy Turner recognized that a so-named Sinodont (literally, "Chinese tooth") pattern is found widely among New World native peoples, but in the Old World it is common to only one area of northern China (Turner, 1987). A high incidence of shovel-shaped incisors

BOX 15–1   DIGGING DEEPER

NAGPRA and American Archaeology

In November 1990, Congress passed and President George Bush approved the Native American Graves Protection and Repatriation Act (P.L. 101–601), also known as NAGPRA. This federal law contains provisions restricting acquisition and ownership of Native American skeletal and artifactual materials by public institutions and, under some circumstances, by others. It also mandates the return, or repatriation, of human physical remains to lineal descendants, along with funerary artifacts and other objects that hold cultural, ceremonial, or religious significance for present-day Native American peoples. Many tribes are now actively pursuing their claims.

NAGPRA policies have a profound effect on archaeological and physical anthropological fieldwork, research, and museum activities. As provided for by the law, many Native American skeletal remains are being routinely removed from publicly funded American museums and reburied in native religious ceremonies. These actions have brought mixed responses from anthropologists. Some agree that returning all human remains, not just those for whom a connection with living groups can be established, is a proper and significant gesture that overrides any other considerations. Others express concern over the loss of a unique and irreplaceable scientific data base. After all, they argue, the study of collections of human skeletons of many eras, gathered from populations all over the world by archaeologists and physical anthropologists, has revealed much of what we know today about human genetic relationships and microevolution, ancient diseases and health, social structure and demography, and cultural customs. Innovative bioarchaeological techniques still in development promise further insights, but only if skeletal materials remain available for examination.

Among the thousands of skeletons that have been returned so far are several exceedingly rare specimens dating to the Paleo-Indian era, the bones of some of the earliest occupants of the Americas. Notwithstanding the impossibility of demonstrating direct lineal (biological) descent through 500 generations, native claims (usually based on oral tradition and geographical proximity to the finds) have prevailed over the protests of scientists, even with the most ancient examples. Currently, a group of anthropologists is asking a federal court to stop, or at least to delay, the U. S. government's plan to give up the well-preserved 9,300-year-old skeleton of Kennewick Man, dislodged by the Columbia River in 1996, to the Umatilla and other Indian tribes of Washington for reburial. This unique skeleton might shed light on the ancestry of the earliest people to reach the New World. Many scientists fear that a loss in this case could prevent any further studies of early American skeletons, now or in the future, no matter how ancient.

Those who regularly visit museums or work with collections of artifacts or skeletons are well aware of the changes brought about by NAGPRA. Visitors no longer find cases displaying skeletons and grave goods. Many other kinds of objects are being withdrawn from view, too. One example is the Iroquois "bushy head" mask, woven of braided cornhusks and modeled on wooden masks worn in traditional healing ceremonies (Fig. 1). Although most such masks were routinely made to be sold to tourists on the upstate New York reservations in the twentieth century, some traditionalists now regard all of them as "sacred" and therefore inappropriate for public exhibition. Some museums, concerned over potential offenses, are choosing to remove items of this type and replace them with

(see Fig. 11–4), distinctive roots on molar teeth, and a score of other dental diagnostics characterize the Sinodont groups, including nearly all American Indians. The Mongolian Chinese who shared these traits are related to those people who crossed Beringia some 14,000 years ago, in Turner's view. More than 20,000 years ago, he postulates, these populations had started out somewhere in southeast Asia.

We acknowledge that contemporary Asian and American Indian populations share many superficial physical similarities—for example, the texture, color, and distribution of head and body hair. But Native Americans also display distinctive variations that set them apart from other populations. The distribution pattern of ABO blood types (antigens) among living American Indians is one example.

displays of recent works by contemporary Native American artists.

Many institutions believe that they hold legal title to cultural items that anthropologists or travelers collected or purchased directly from natives decades ago. But even where a record of the transaction is preserved, the matter is not necessarily settled. Did the individual or group of tribal members who originally parted with the object really have a legitimate right to do so? Because many native societies apparently did not recognize the concept of private property, objects of significance might have been *communally* owned, and therefore no one person or group of persons could rightfully have disposed of them. A few museums have placed their older holdings off-limits, even to accredited researchers, pending eventual repatriation decisions.

Controversy over ownership of the past rages internationally, too, as many of the world's ethnic groups and nations seek to reclaim widely dispersed elements of their own heritage, including such prominent objects as the Elgin Marbles from the Parthenon in Athens, exhibited at the British Museum since 1816. International sanctions against trafficking in cultural antiquities have been in place for some time, but most properties in question were acquired long ago by collecting expeditions or under circumstances of colonialism or warfare.

In the United States, NAGPRA has provoked sharp debate over unresolved issues: Whose claim on the past—and, particularly, the objects of the past—is truly legitimate? Does any ethnically, religiously, or politically defined group have an *exclusive* right of possession or access to cultural materials? If so, under what circumstances, and how far back does this right extend?

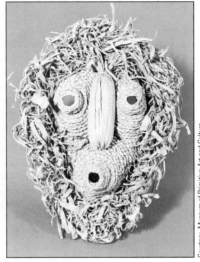

Courtesy, Museum of Primitive Art and Culture, Peace Dale, RI, photo by William Turnbaugh

FIGURE 1
Iroquois cornhusk mask, or "bushy head."

Sources:

American Association of Museums. 2000. *Implementing the Native American Graves Protection and Repatriation Act: Resource Report.* Washington, DC: American Association of Museums.

Messenger, Phyllis Mauch. 1989. *The Ethics of Collecting Cultural Property: Whose Culture? Whose Property?* Albuquerque, NM: University of New Mexico Press.

Mihesuah, Devon A. (ed.). 2000. *Repatriation Reader: Who Owns American Indian Remains?* Lincoln, NE: University of Nebraska Press.

"Native American Graves Protection and Repatriation Act." Public Law 101–601, November 16. 1990. Washington, DC: Government Printing Office.

Thomas, David Hurst. 2000. *Skull Wars: Kennewick Man, Archeology, and the Battle for Native American Identity.* New York: Basic Books.

Modern Indians of North and South America exhibit unusually high frequencies of the type O allele (80 to 100 percent), along with a near absence of several other blood group antigens (including A^2, B, and D) more commonly found in other populations (see Chapter 4).

This unique suite of specific traits shared by modern Native Americans surely reflects the limited variability of a small founding gene pool. (For a discussion of the founder effect, an example of genetic drift, see p. 73.) Recent analyses of mitochondrial DNA among contemporary Indian populations have led genetic researchers to suggest that just four or five maternal lineages contributed to the early peopling of the Americas (Schurr et al., 1990; Schurr, 2000). However, different

interpretations based on these findings have been offered. Some geneticists surmise that the present distribution pattern of mtDNA derived from these maternal lineages is consistent with the hypothesis that the New World's original inhabitants derived from a single northeastern Asian population of small size (Merriwether et al., 1995). Others, however, see in the same data a dramatically different scenario, wherein a number of migrant bands filtered out of different parts of Asia and into the New World as much as 40,000 to 20,000 y.a. (Schurr, 2000). Obviously, these widely divergent interpretations leave open the question of whether people entered the Americas only once or in several waves over time, but they do generally point back to Asia as the source of American Indian populations.

Genetic studies of proteins in human blood serum (Gm allotype) and of DNA taken from ancient but well-preserved human soft tissues found in 7,000-year-old waterlogged Florida sites and other locations are helping to calibrate the genetic "distances" within the New World native populations themselves (Suarez et al., 1985). Such studies attempt to measure and account for the observable physical variation among living Native American populations in body build, skin color, and the like, which probably resulted either from random genetic drift or from shifts in allele frequencies due to natural selection pressures affecting isolated populations within their local environments.

Linguistic evidence complements the physical studies in providing clues and a plausible chronological framework for three separate migratory "pulses." Linguists study relationships among modern American Indian languages to calculate the amount of divergence, or "drift" (linguistic, not genetic, in this case), they may have undergone from a common ancestral tongue (Greenberg, 1987; Ruhlen, 1994). Assuming a "normal" rate of drift, they then calculate the time needed to account for the observed differences. According to these reconstructions, the founding population of most of the living aboriginal groups of the New World arrived sometime after 18,000 y.a. Perhaps 9,000 y.a., hunters who became ancestral to the Athabaskan-speaking peoples of central Alaska, the Northwest Coast, and the Canadian interior made their appearance. Finally, about 6,000 y.a., according to linguists, Asian sea mammal hunters came to occupy the Arctic coasts and islands, establishing the distinctive Inuit/Eskimo and Aleut cultural traditions.

Evaluating Archaeological Traces of the Earliest Americans

Could people have lived in the Americas more than 15,000, 25,000, 50,000, even 250,000 y.a., as some allege? Archaeologists agree that American Indians originated in the Old World, yet they vary in their opinions about the date when people first arrived in the New World (Meltzer, 1993b; Dillehay, 2000). Most of the controversy focuses on the span between 25,000 and 13,500 y.a. The earlier date represents the time by which anatomically modern people first began to appear in those parts of Asia closest to North America. By the later date, verified sites associated with **Paleo-Indians** had been established in many parts of the Western Hemisphere. So the question is, Was there a *pre*-Paleo-Indian period in American prehistory?

One more factor must be considered with regard to dating the first passage into America. Even with the land bridge "open," extensive glaciers southeast of Beringia restricted access to the New World through most of the Pleistocene. The **Cordilleran** ice fields, extending through the mountains of western Canada and Alaska, and the vast **Laurentian** sheet, radiating from Hudson Bay across much of eastern Canada and the northeastern United States, coalesced as one massive flow during stages of maximum glaciation around 20,000 y.a. Only toward the close of the Pleistocene, about 15,000 y.a., did the edges of the ice sheets finally melt back from one another, allowing animals and possibly their hunters to gain entry to the south through an "ice-free corridor" along the eastern flank of the Canadian Rockies (Holmes, 1996). Whether, in fact, people followed this inland route is uncertain. So far, archaeologists have found no convincing sites in this passageway or elsewhere that they can confidently attribute to the initial immigrants. Silt and gravel borne by raging glacial meltwaters possibly erased most camp locations.

Paleo-Indians
(*paleo*, meaning "ancient") In the Americas, early big game hunting cultures, from about 14,000 y.a. to 8,000 y.a.

Cordilleran
(cor-dee-yair'-an) Pleistocene ice sheet originating in mountains of western North America.

Laurentian
(lah-ren'-shun) Pleistocene ice sheet centered in the Hudson Bay region and extending across much of eastern Canada and the northern United States.

Ancient sites along Beringia's shoreline, too, would have been inundated as rising seas once more submerged the land bridge after the Pleistocene. So even if people took a coastal route to the south instead of traveling through the interior, we have few prospects of finding actual traces of their journey.

What kind of archaeological evidence *does* survive from this early period of American prehistory? The answer to that question depends largely on how rigorously one evaluates the "evidence." For example, isolated artifacts, including stone choppers and large flake tools of simple form, are at times recovered from exposed surfaces and other undatable contexts in the Americas. They are sometimes proposed as evidence of a period predating the use of bifacial projectile points, which were common in North America by 13,500 y.a. If typologically primitive-looking finds cannot be securely dated, most (but not all) archaeologists regard them with justifiable caution. The appearance of great age or crude condition may be misleading and is all but impossible to verify without corroborating evidence. To be properly evaluated, an artifact has to meet several criteria: It must be unquestionably the product of human handiwork and must have been recovered from a geologically sealed and undisturbed context that can be dated reliably.

Most difficult to assess are some atypical sites that have been carefully excavated by honest researchers who believe that their work offers proof of great human antiquity in the New World. Currently, a number of sites fall into this disputed category (Fig. 15–3). Pedra Furada is a rock-shelter in northeastern Brazil where excavators

FIGURE 15–3
Location of some early New World sites. Excavations at Clovis and Folsom, in New Mexico, confirmed the presence of Paleo-Indians in the New World by 13,500 y.a., but finds and dates from many other locations shown here are still disputed.

found what they claim to be simple stone tools in association with charcoal hearths dating back 40,000 years (Guidon et al., 1996). Others who have examined these materials remain convinced that natural, rather than cultural, factors account for them (Lynch, 1990; Meltzer et al., 1994). A number of other Central and South American locations have been proposed as extremely early cultural sites in recent decades (Lynch, 1990; Parfit, 2000). Archaeologists have been uncertain how to evaluate most of them because the associated cultural materials are so typologically diverse and their contexts are frequently secondary, or mixed, geological deposits.

The United States, too, has its share of sites that defy easy explanation. At Pendejo Cave in southern New Mexico, excavators have discovered 16 friction skin prints impressed on fire-hardened clay nodules in three stratigraphic zones dated from 37,000 to 12,000 y.a. (Chrisman et al., 1996). Clear impressions of ridge patterns and even of sweat pores, visible under magnification, seem to confirm the palm prints and fingerprints as primate, and most likely human, but their origin and significance remain uncertain (Dincauze, 1997; Shaffer and Baker, 1997). Possible cultural materials from the same levels include charred wood, crude stone tools, and an extinct horse toe bone with what reportedly may be an embedded bone or stone point. Far to the east, archaeologists have retrieved unusual assemblages of stone cores, flakes, and tools from strata lying well beneath more typical Paleo-Indian components at the Cactus Hill site along the Nottoway River in southern Virginia and at the Topper site in Allendale County, South Carolina (Dixon, 2000). The unusually early radiocarbon dates associated with these materials (calibrated at 18,000 to 15,000 y.a.) are consistent with their stratigraphic position, but the evidence will require cautious review before these sites are generally accepted.

The scientific method is not a democratic process; we cannot simply dismiss (or side with) unpopular positions without assessing the evidence as it is presented. The burden of proof to substantiate claims of great antiquity must fall upon those who make them. Each allegation requires critical evaluation, a process that the general public sometimes perceives as unnecessarily conservative or obstructive. Dating results, archaeological contexts, and whether or not materials are of cultural origin must all be scrutinized and accepted before intense debate can resolve into consensus.

The evaluation process may take years. Consider, for example, the case of the Meadowcroft rock-shelter, near Pittsburgh, Pennsylvania. In a meticulous excavation over 25 years ago, archaeologists explored a deeply stratified site containing cultural levels dated between 19,000 and 14,000 y.a. by standard radiocarbon methods (Adovasio et al., 1990). Stratum IIa, from which the earliest dates derive, contained several prismatic blades, a retouched flake, a biface, and a knifelike implement (Fig. 15–4). None of the tools from this deep stratum is particularly distinctive, so it is difficult to assess technological relationships with other known assemblages. Despite lingering concern over the possibility that fossil carbon from nearby coal seams may have contaminated the carbon-dated samples, more archaeologists are coming to accept the Meadowcroft evidence because of the excavators' careful documentation and the coherence of the dated strata with one another.

Excavations at Monte Verde in southern Chile revealed another remarkable site of apparent pre-Paleo-Indian age (Dillehay, 1989, 1997). Here, remnants of the wooden foundations of a dozen rectangular huts were arranged back to back in a parallel row. The structures measured between 10 and 15 feet (3 and 4.5 m) on a side, and animal hides may have covered their sapling frameworks. Apart from the main cluster, a separate wishbone-shaped building contained stone tools and animal bones (Fig. 15–5). Numerous spheroids (possibly sling stones), flaked stone points, perforating tools, a wooden lance, digging sticks, mortars, and fire pits comprised the cultural equipment. Mastodon bones represented at least seven individuals, and remains of some 100 species of nuts, fruits, berries, wild tubers, and firewood testify to the major role of plants in subsistence activities at this site.

Monte Verde's excavator, Tom Dillehay, concludes that "the form and arrangement of the architecture and activity areas . . . reveal technological sophistication and a social and economic organization much more complex than previously suspected for a late Pleistocene culture of the New World" (Dillehay, 1989,

FIGURE 15–4
Knifelike implement from Stratum IIa at the Meadowcroft rock-shelter, in Pennsylvania.

FIGURE 15–5
This 14,800-year-old wishbone-shaped structure at Monte Verde, in Chile, had a sand and pebble foundation. Mastodon bones, hide, and flesh were preserved in association with this feature, along with 26 species of medicinal plants.

p. 2). And that startling complexity is one reason Monte Verde's early dates—about 14,800 years old, with a few features possibly much older—have been hotly debated. In 1997, a "jury" of archaeological specialists reviewed the findings one more time and agreed that the excavator's claims for Monte Verde had been substantiated. The broader implications for American prehistory are not yet fully apparent, though Monte Verde's South American location clearly hints that people may have crossed Beringia much earlier than most archaeologists previously considered. The site becomes the first in the New World to be recognized by the archaeological "establishment" as older than 13,500 years, but not everyone accepts the evidence as it has been presented, so the controversy continues (Meltzer et al., 1997; Fiedel, 1999a).

Paleo-Indians in the Americas

Archaeologists generally acknowledge the numerous sites from many regions of the Americas that date to shortly after about 13,500 y.a.—that is, during the final centuries of the Pleistocene. Specialists refer to this interval as the Paleo-Indian period. Evidence for a lifeway of mobile hunting and gathering comes from widely scattered locations, including a great many sites in the western United States (Fig. 15–6). The distinctive **fluted point** is the hallmark artifact of the Paleo-Indian period. Each face of a fluted point typically displays a groove (or "flute") resulting from the removal of a long channel flake, perhaps to facilitate a special hafting technique for securing the point to a shaft (Fig. 15–7). Other typical Paleo-Indian artifacts include a variety of stone cutting and scraping tools and, less commonly surviving, bone rods and points (Gramly, 1992).

Because certain allegedly ancient American sites lack the diagnostic fluted points that typify most standard Paleo-Indian locations, some archaeologists propose that those sites may pertain to an ancient pre-Paleo-Indian period, while others question the dating or even the authenticity of the sites themselves. However, a growing number of researchers theorize that the migrants who crossed Beringia included representatives of *two* contemporary northeastern Asian toolmaking traditions. The first created large bifacially flaked stone projectile points derived from Old World prototypes, particularly the thick, bifacial leaf-shaped points found on some Upper Paleolithic sites in easternmost Siberia. In the Nenana Valley near

Fluted point
A biface or projectile point having had long, thin flakes removed from each face to prepare the base for hafting, or attachment to a shaft.

FIGURE 15–6
North American Paleo-Indian and Archaic sites.

FIGURE 15–7
Clovis fluted points in simulated mountings.

Courtesy, Peter Storck, Royal Ontario Museum

Microblades
Tiny, parallel-sided flakes struck from a special core and mounted into tools as cutting edges; a type of microlith made by East Asians and some early American cultures.

Fairbanks, Alaska, some 13,800-year-old sites contain only unfluted bifacial points and scrapers. Much farther south, controversial sites like Meadowcroft, Cactus Hill, and Monte Verde also produced unfluted bifacial points (Adovasio, 1993). Thus, it appears that the fluted spear point may have been an innovation based on the bifacial point tradition and developed in the New World sometime after the initial Beringia crossing.

The second distinctive toolmaking tradition—based on **microblades** struck from wedge-shaped cores—prevailed across much of northeastern Asia around 14,000 y.a. (Grigor'ev, 1993). The sharp bits were probably set into bone or antler tips and handles to serve as points and knives. This microblade tradition was carried into the New World, too, but it does not seem to have spread as widely as the bifacial point tradition. Very early American sites containing wedge-shaped cores and microblades, as well as worked mammoth bone (but lacking bifacial points) occur in the vicinity of Old Crow in the Yukon Territory. In Alaska, bifacial points seldom appear together with microblades and wedge cores on the same sites. In fact, fluted points are altogether rare in that region.

Based on these distinctive technologies, it has been suggested that individual pioneering groups, or lineages, from Asia may have remained separate, perhaps even following different routes and developing different cultural adaptations as they expanded through the Americas. Descendants of the bifacial toolmakers, those who subsequently developed the fluted points, created the sites that most archaeologists recognize as Paleo-Indian.

Paleo-Indian Lifeways

Great uniformity in weaponry, hunting behavior, and early site contexts across the American continents argues for a fairly rapid spread of people throughout the New World during Paleo-Indian times, beginning about 13,500 y.a. Hunters wielding spears tipped with fishtail-shaped fluted points reached even the farthest extremes of South America and were already active around Fell's Cave, in Patagonia, by some 11,000 y.a. The wide distribution of the specialized fluted point sites implies that Paleo-Indians quickly made cultural adjustments as they dispersed through the varied environments of the New World during the terminal Pleistocene and early Holocene.

Of the sites associated with Paleo-Indians, the most impressive are the places where ancient hunters actually killed and butchered large herbivores, such as mammoth and giant bison (Figs. 15–8 and 15–9). At many of these kill sites, knives, scrapers, and the finely flaked fluted projectile points are directly associated with the animal bones.

North American archaeologists have identified a sequence of Paleo-Indian cultures in the western Plains and Southwest based on changing tool technology, chronology, and the primary prey species of each period. The centuries between about 13,500 and 13,000 y.a. was a time of hunters who employed **Clovis**-type fluted points (Fig. 15–10a; also see Fig. 15–7). On at least 20 western sites, including Colby, in Wyoming, and Naco and Lehner, in southern Arizona, their spear tips lie embedded in mammoth remains (Fig. 15–11). Similar points from northern Alaska retain residues that have been biochemically identified as mammoth red blood cells and hemoglobin crystals (Loy and Dixon, 1998). Meat—but not all of it from mammoths—was certainly a major component in the diet of early Americans. Isotopic analysis of Buhl Woman's bone collagen indicates that her diet was largely game and fish, much of it probably preserved by sun-drying or smoking. The heavy wear on her teeth suggests that she regularly ingested grit in her food, probably the residue of grinding stones used to pulverize the dried meat (Green et al., 1998).

Fluted projectile points are also found throughout eastern North America. Though the damp, acid soils of that region seldom preserve animal bone, evidence indicates a varied Paleo-Indian diet here, too. Clovis points littered the Vail site, an ancient caribou-hunting camp in northern Maine (Gramly, 1982). A mixed subsistence of smaller game, fish, and gathered plants apparently supplied the Paleo-Indians at the Shawnee-Minisink site in eastern Pennsylvania (McNett, 1985). Acquiring such resources surely involved the use of a variety of equipment made from perishable materials, such as nets and baskets, but only the stone spear tips survive on most Paleo-Indian sites. Farther to the south, submerged locations in Florida, including Little Salt Spring and Warm Mineral Spring in Sarasota County, held the remains of giant sloths, mammoths, bison, and huge land tortoises, as well as bones of smaller animals and plant remains, all exhibiting evidence of human exploitation.

Excavations along the lower Amazon in northern Brazil provide further evidence for early alternatives to "standard" Paleo-Indian big game hunting practices (Roosevelt et al., 1996). Carbonized seeds, nuts, and faunal remains at Pedra Pintada Cave, in the Amazon

William Turnbaugh

FIGURE 15–8
The largest American woolly mammoths were over 13 feet (4 m) high at the shoulder, with long, downward curving tusks.

Clovis
Phase of North American prehistory, 13,500–13,000 y.a. in the West, during which short-fluted projectile points were used in hunting mammoths.

FIGURE 15–9
Giant Pleistocene long-horned bison were hunted by Paleo-Indians.

William Turnbaugh

FIGURE 15–10
Major types of North American Paleo-Indian projectile points. (a) Clovis. (b) Folsom. (c) Plano. (d) Dalton (length 2.4 inches).

(a)   (b)   (c)   (d)

William Turnbaugh

Folsom
Phase of southern Great Plains prehistory, around 12,500 y.a., during which long-fluted projectile points were used for bison hunting.

Plano
Great Plains bison-hunting culture of 11,000–9,000 y.a., which employed narrow, unfluted points.

FIGURE 15–11
Partially articulated remains of three mammoths, one of several bone piles that probably represent Paleo-Indian meat caches at the Colby site, in Wyoming.

Reproduced with permission from George C. Frison, *Prehistoric Hunters of the High Plains*, New York: Academic Press, Copyright 1978

basin, indicate a broad-based food-collecting, fishing, and small game hunting routine in the tropical rain forest around 12,000 y.a., at a time when hunters elsewhere in South America were in pursuit of much larger prey. Paleo-Indian big game hunters concentrated along the Pacific slope of the Andes, where mastodons, horses, and sloths comprised an important part of their diet, though deer, camelids, and smaller animals and tuberous roots were consumed, too (Lynch, 1983).

These varied data help to balance the view of Paleo-Indians as strictly big game hunters by demonstrating that their subsistence activities were flexible enough to accommodate the very considerable climatic and geographical diversity they encountered throughout America at the end of the Pleistocene.

We have seen that Clovis-tipped spears armed the mammoth hunters of the North American Plains. Then, about 12,500 y.a., some of those pursuing large animals in the American West devised a modified style of fluted point, named **Folsom** for the type site in New Mexico (Fig. 15–10b). Smaller and thinner than Clovis points, but with a proportionally larger central flute, Folsom points are associated exclusively with the bones of the now-extinct giant long-horned bison (Figs. 15–9 and 15–12).

In turn, Folsom points shortly gave way to a long sequence of new point forms—a variety of unfluted but slender and finely parallel-flaked projectile heads collectively called **Plano** (Fig. 15–10c), which came into general use throughout the West even as modern-day *Bison bison* was supplanting its larger Pleistocene relatives. At some Great Plains sites, like Olsen-Chubbuck and Jones-Miller in Colorado, an effective technique of bison hunting was for hunters to stampede the animals into dry stream beds or over cliffs, then to quickly dispatch those that survived the fall (Wheat, 1972; Frison, 1978). Remember, the horse had not yet been introduced onto the Plains (the Spanish brought them in the sixteenth century), so these early bison hunters were strictly pedestrians!

Again, sites in the East exhibit a degree of regional variation, where the later Paleo-Indians employed still other types of projectile points, such as the Dalton variety (Fig. 15–10d). Poor bone preservation generally leaves us with little direct information about their hunting techniques or favored prey in this region, though deer were probably becoming common by this time as oak forests expanded over much of the eastern United States.

Pleistocene Extinctions

Circumstantial evidence like that found mainly in the American West, where bones of the large herbivores are more often preserved in undeniable association with the weapons used to kill them, leads some researchers to blame Paleo-Indian hunters for the extinction of North American Pleistocene **megafauna**—animals over 100 pounds (44 kg), including the mammoth, mastodon, giant bison, horse, camel, and ground sloth (Fig. 15–13). Paul S. Martin (1967, 1982, 1999) has been especially fervent in asserting that overhunting by a rapidly expanding human population resulted in the swift extermination of these animals throughout the New World around 13,000 y.a. He points out that over half of the large mammal species found in the Americas when humans first arrived were gone within just a few centuries, especially those whose habits and habitats would have made them most vulnerable to the hunters. Martin recognizes a comparable extinction event with the peopling of Australia tens of thousands of years earlier, when most of that continent's native fauna died off. African and Eurasian species were less affected, he argues, because of long coexistence with humans and familiarity with their hunting behaviors.

The evidence does seem persuasive, but the issue is complex. First, the dramatic nature of the Paleo-Indian kill sites should not lead us to overemphasize big game hunting as an aspect of their life and economy (Meltzer, 1993a). As we have seen, recent excavations demonstrate that the same people often exploited a diverse range of plant and animal foods within their environments, and Paleo-Indian groups may have killed big animals only rarely. Some species, like the giant ground sloth of the southwestern United States, seem not to have been hunted in that area at all, yet became extinct there, too. Paleo-Indian lifeways shared much with the late Upper Paleolithic hunting cultures of the Old World, from which they surely derived. But the notion of an exclusive specialization on big game has become

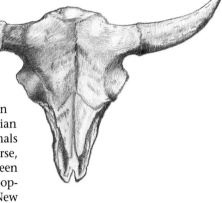

FIGURE 15–12
The horn cores on this Pleistocene bison skull from Wyoming span 33 inches (83 cm).

Megafauna
Literally, "large animals," those weighing over 100 pounds (44 kg).

FIGURE 15–13
Molar teeth of mastodon (left) and mammoth (right). Mastodons browsed on evergreen branches; mammoths grazed on low vegetation. The New World's earliest hunters preyed on both animals and may have contributed to their extinction.

William Turnbaugh

difficult to sustain, given present evidence for the varied adaptations of America's first human inhabitants.

Others note that major climate changes of any type may sever the ecological connections that bind plant and animal species into an interdependent community and thereby provoke rapid and wholesale extinctions (Lundelius and Graham, 1999). Geoarchaeologists recognize that late Pleistocene extinctions and the expansion of Paleo-Indian hunters coincided with a time of widespread drought that was immediately followed by rapidly plunging temperatures. This so-called Younger Dryas climatic event, a return to near-glacial conditions, persisted for 1,500 years, from 13,000 to 11,500 y.a. (Fiedel, 1999b). Perhaps humans took advantage of animals drawn to shrinking water holes before further climate changes finished the job (Haynes, 1993, 1999).

Biologists remind us that species extinction is an ongoing process, one that may result from many factors, including predator-prey imbalance, climate change, ecological disruption, and even disease pathogens. The degree of human involvement in these earlier New World extinctions remains an unresolved though intriguing issue.

Middle Stone Age Hunter-Fisher-Gatherers

Across North America and Eurasia, gradual warming conditions during the transition from the late Pleistocene to the early Holocene had profound ecological effects that extended well beyond the waning glaciers. Much of the Northern Hemisphere experienced radical environmental change, leaving only the polar regions and Greenland with permanent ice caps today. Climatic fluctuations, the redistribution or even extinction of many plant and animal species, and the reshaping of coastlines as glacial meltwaters flowed to the sea all entailed consequences that affected many of the world's human inhabitants. When we examine the archaeological record, we can see that people devised new technologies and economic patterns to adjust to their changing world.

Early Holocene Environments

In the Old World, much as in America, major changes in climate, landscape, flora, and fauna accompanied the end of the Pleistocene ice age. Of course, dramatically higher temperatures—an increase of perhaps 20°F (almost 7°C) in July—rapidly wasted the glaciers. As they receded to higher latitudes, the great northern ice sheets left behind thick mantles of broken and pulverized rock, or **till**. Wind and water sorted this debris, and powerful currents moved it along redefined stream drainages. Swollen rivers disgorged their meltwater upon reaching the seas. Eventually, by 5,000 y.a., sea levels had risen as much as 400 feet (120 m), drowning the broad coastal plains and flooding into inlets to shape the continental margins we recognize today. By then, overflow from the rising Mediterranean had spilled into a low-lying basin to create the Black Sea, and the North and Baltic seas now separated England and Scandinavia from the rest of Europe.

As deglaciation proceeded, the major biotic zones expanded northward, so that areas once covered by ice were clothed successively in tundra, grassland, fir and spruce forests, pine, then mixed deciduous forests (Delcourt and Delcourt, 1991). Likewise, temperate animals displaced their arctic counterparts. Grazers like the musk ox and caribou, or reindeer, which had ranged over open tundra or grasslands, made way for browsing species, such as moose and white-tailed deer, which fed on leaves and the tender twigs of forest plants (Fig. 15–14). Meanwhile, the annual mean summer temperatures continued to climb toward the local **climatic maximum**, attained between 8,000 and 6,000 y.a. in many areas. By then, July temperatures averaged as much as 5°F higher than at present. Lakes that had formed during the Ice Age as a result of increased precipitation in nonglaciated areas of the American West, southwest Asia (the Near East), and Africa now evap-

FIGURE 15–14
Skeleton of the extinct Irish elk, a relative of the American moose.

Till
Glacial waste, consisting of mixed rock particles that range in size from clay, silt, and sand to boulders, strewn across landscapes once covered by ice sheets.

Climatic maximum
Episode of higher average annual temperatures that affected much of the globe for several millennia after the final Wisconsin/Würm glaciation; also known as the *altithermal* in the western United States or *hypsithermal* in the East.

orated under more arid conditions, bringing great ecological changes to those regions, too.

These geoclimatic transformations most directly affected the temperate latitudes, including northern and central Europe and the northern parts of America. They were sufficient to alter conditions of life for flora and fauna by creating new econiches for some species and pushing others toward extinction. We cannot measure precisely how these shifting natural conditions may have affected human populations, although they surely did.

Cultural Adjustment to Environmental Change

Environmental readjustments were the natural consequences of climatic change. While they occurred relatively quickly on a geological time scale, we should recognize that most such changes probably spanned many human generations. Their impact was cumulative, and in time, the redistribution of living plant and animal species, plus variations in local topography, drainage, and exposure, resulted in a virtual mosaic of new econiches, some of which invited human exploitation and settlement.

Cultures in both hemispheres kept pace with these changes by adjusting their ways of coping with local conditions. Distinctive climatic and cultural circumstances pertained in different regions. Recognizing this variability, archaeologists have devised specific terms to designate the early and middle Holocene cultures that turned to an intensive hunting, fishing, and gathering routine in response to post-Pleistocene conditions. The term **Mesolithic** (literally, "middle stone") describes primarily the cultures of northern and western Europe. These hunter-fisher-gatherers adapted to an environment with a relatively low carrying capacity for humans. **Epipaleolithic** ("after old stone") pertains to the Near East, a region with a relatively higher carrying capacity. New World archaeologists customarily use the term **Archaic** ("ancient"), which is broadly applied to North America's Middle Stone Age cultures.

Of importance here is the fact that people in temperate latitudes now extracted their livelihood from a range of local resources by both hunting and gathering. Of course, the relative role of each of these subsistence activities varied from region to region, and even from season to season within a given area. In some places, the focus on different food sources, particularly more plants, fish, shellfish, birds, and smaller mammals, corresponded to a lesser emphasis on pursuing larger wide-ranging herbivores. What accounts for this shift? First, many former prey animals were by now extinct or—like the reindeer—locally unobtainable, having followed their receding habitat north with the waning ice sheets. Additionally, one way to accommodate human population growth was to broaden the definition of "food" by exploiting more species.

New habitats and less familiar species presented both challenges and opportunities. The invention and use of an array of new tools and weapons promoted greater efficiency in utilizing these diverse resources. Mesolithic and Archaic people commonly crafted not only stone, but also bone, antler, and leather, as well as bark and other plant materials (Clark, 1967; Bordaz, 1970). Hunters invented several **composite** tools (Fig. 15–15). The bow and arrow and the harpoon are examples: Each consists of a blade or point, a foreshaft, a main shaft, bindings, and other parts expertly combined into a sophisticated weapon system. Tough antlers of the European red deer and elk (equivalent to the American elk and moose, respectively) saw use as picks in quarrying flint for the production of chipped or polished stone tools.

With the spread of forests, wood became readily available. It replaced animal bones, tallow, and herbivore dung as the primary fuel and served well for house posts, spear shafts, bowls, and countless smaller items. Wooden dugout canoes and skin-covered boats aided in navigating streams and crossing larger bodies of water. Middle Stone Age people caught large quantities of fish in nets, woven basketry

Mesolithic
(*meso*, meaning "middle," and *lith*, meaning "stone") Middle Stone Age; period of foragers, especially in northwestern Europe.

Epipaleolithic
(*epi*, meaning "after") Term used primarily in reference to the Near East, designating the time of Middle Stone Age foragers and collectors.

Archaic
Cultural stage of hunting and gathering after the end of the Wisconsin ice age in North America; equivalent to the Mesolithic in the Old World.

Composite
Made of several parts.

Courtesy, Museum of Primitive Art and Culture, Peace Dale, RI, photo by William Turnbaugh

FIGURE 15–15
European Mesolithic stone axe in its antler sleeve, shaped to fit into the socket of a missing wooden handle.

FIGURE 15–16
A Mesolithic forager uses a basket or bag to collect honey from a nest of wild bees in this painting on a rock-shelter wall in southeastern Spain.

Foraging
The process of locating food while moving across the landscape; a standard strategy of some hunters and gatherers.

Nomadism
Free-wandering lifeway, most often practiced by herders, who follow their animals.

Seasonality and scheduling
Technique of hunters and gatherers to maximize subsistence by relocating in accord with the availability of key resources at specific times and places throughout the year.

Food collecting
Strategy developed by hunters and gatherers to take advantage of highly seasonal wild resources by storing surpluses for later use.

traps, and brushwood or stone fish dams designed to obstruct the mouths of small tidal streams. They extracted the honey of wild bees from hollow trees with the aid of axes and containers (Fig. 15–16).

Foragers and Collectors Given the environmental complexity of the temperate regions in the Holocene, including a diversity of potentially exploitable plants and animals, hunting and gathering techniques applied in one region were not always effective in another. Under the general description of "hunting and gathering," anthropologists recognize a range of subsistence strategies used by Middle Stone Age people as well as their more recent counterparts (Kelly, 1995).

At one end of this spectrum is **foraging**, which implies a daily food quest where people seek whatever resources are then available and consume them almost immediately. The necessity of moving from one resource area to another kept foraging groups highly mobile. (The often misused term **nomadism**—meaning a more or less *random* wandering existence—cannot properly be applied to most hunting and gathering groups, who usually followed a predictable annual cycle.) Middle Stone Age foragers developed an intimate knowledge of their local environment and its assets. They invented specialized equipment to take advantage of a broad spectrum of terrestrial and aquatic plant and animal species.

In foraging, anyone—young or old, male or female—might contribute to the general food supply by taking up whatever resources are at hand. Still, not everything that *can* be eaten *will* be eaten, even in the harshest environment. Humans tend to be selective about their menu. Preferred foods are usually those that are most readily available, easily collected and processed, tasty, and nutritious. Thus, while the twentieth-century San people of the Kalahari Desert in southwestern Africa regarded about 80 local plants as edible, they relied on only about a dozen of them as primary foods (A. Smith et al., 2000). The rest were used infrequently, yet could serve as a "cushion" in tough times.

Particularly in regions with only minor seasonal fluctuations in wild food supplies, foraging held prospects for good returns. Jochim (1976, 1998) estimated that foraging activities could maintain a stable population density of about one person per 4 square miles (10 km²) in some regions. More territory might be required to sustain people in less favorable situations or where continuing environmental fluctuations influenced the composition and predictability of animal and plant communities or the stability of estuaries and coastlines.

In areas where dramatic seasonal variations in rainfall or temperature affected resource availability, day-to-day foraging might not always yield a stable diet. Human population density and equilibrium could be maintained only if the group adopted an alternative strategy. Familiarity with their environment enabled people to predict when specific resources should reach peak productivity or desirability. By making well-informed decisions, hunters and gatherers scheduled their movements so as to arrive on the scene at the optimum time for obtaining a particularly important food. This concept of **seasonality and scheduling**, or optimal foraging, is a key to understanding a lifeway based on **food collecting**.

Compared with foragers, food collectors relied more intensively on a few seasonally abundant resources. Collectors usually took greater advantage of temporary surpluses by developing specialized processing and storage technologies, which allowed them to balance out fluctuations and to remain longer in one place. Migratory fish might be split and cured; nuts or seeds could be parched, packed into baskets, and stored in dry caves. Archaeologists find capacious storage pits, drying racks, and evidence of other processing activities on collectors' sites.

Foraging and collecting are not either/or categories, but rather two ends of a continuum. Foragers might occasionally gather and set aside a supply of a favorite food for later use, while collectors would enjoy an impromptu treat of wild honey to vary their dried fish diet. In truth, most societies combined aspects of both foraging and collecting as they met their daily needs, while also adjusting to environmental circumstances.

Case Studies of Middle Stone Age Cultures

While mid-Holocene human population densities may have declined after the Ice Age in a few areas owing to inadequate resources (as in the northern coniferous forests), other regions with higher carrying capacities supported steady population growth. In both situations, as natural food resources came under increasing pressure, foragers and food collectors in several regions came up with ways of teasing more from their environments.

Mesolithic Foragers and Collectors of Northern Europe

People colonized Europe's northern reaches within centuries after the glacial ice withdrew (Jochim, 1998). Rising waters already had reclaimed the continental shelf and its shallow basins, flooding the North and Baltic Seas and the English Channel. On land, temperate plant and animal species succeeded their Ice Age counterparts. Across northwestern Europe, as grasses and then forests invaded the open landscape, red deer, elk, and **aurochs** replaced the reindeer, horse, and bison of Pleistocene times. Human hunters, armed with efficient weapons, accommodated themselves to the relatively low carrying capacity of these northern regions (where plant foods, at least, were seasonally scarce) by eating more animal protein.

Aurochs
European wild oxen, ancestral to domesticated cattle.

Star Carr, near Scarborough, in Yorkshire, England (Fig. 15–17), provides clues to the early ecology and foraging economy practiced by northern Mesolithic peoples some 10,500 y.a. Periodically over several centuries, the lakeshore site served as a temporary hunting camp, where aurochs, deer, elk, and wild pigs were regularly pursued (Clark, 1972, 1979). Because deer grow and shed their antlers annually, on a species-specific cycle, the several stages of antler development on deer killed at Star Carr indicate that hunters visited the site throughout the year, though they used it most intensively in spring and summer (Mellars and Dark, 1999).

Even basic hunters and foragers sometimes modified the environment for their own purposes. At Star Carr, people used stone axes and adzes in felling numerous birch trees to construct platforms and trackways over the marsh. In spring, they burned off the reeds along the lake margin to open the view and probably also to induce new growth to attract game. Hunters employed long wooden arrows tipped by *microliths*—small flint blades of geometric shape—set into slots along the end of the shaft and held in place by resin. An extremely effective weapon, the bow had been used in Europe even before the end of the Ice Age. Domesticated dogs probably aided in the hunt at Star Carr, as well. Barbed bone and antler spear points, butchering implements, and stone *burin* blades for working antler were common artifacts.

FIGURE 15–17
Mesolithic sites of northern Europe mentioned in the text.

Along the coasts of northern Europe, the British Isles, and even the Mediterranean, later Mesolithic groups came to rely increasingly on coastal and near-shore marine resources (Smith, 1998). Their favored site locations, sometimes marked by great shell heaps called **middens**, offered a combination of land and sea resources that encouraged year-round residence based on food collecting. By about 6,800 y.a., the area around Vedbaek, near Copenhagen, Denmark, was occupied on a more or less permanent basis. More than 60 species representing every econiche between the forest and the coast appeared on the Mesolithic menu at this site (Price and Petersen, 1987). The impressive size of some middens—the countless shells of oysters, mussels, periwinkles, and scallops piled along the shore—should not disguise the fact that one red deer carcass may represent the caloric equivalent of 50,000 oysters (Bailey, 1975). Nevertheless, for at least some Mesolithic foragers, shellfish provided a readily available alternative source of protein, probably exploited primarily in the spring when their normal fare of fish, sea mammals, and birds was in shortest supply (Erlandson, 1988). This supplement could have encouraged people to remain longer in one location.

Middens
Refuse disposal areas marking hunter-gatherer campsites.

FIGURE 15–18
Epipaleolithic sites in the Levant region of the Near East.

Transhumance
Seasonal migration from one resource zone to another, especially between highlands and lowlands.

Natufian
A food-collecting culture that established sedentary settlements in parts of the Near East after 12,000 y.a.

Dental caries
Tooth decay; cavities.

Epipaleolithic Foragers and Collectors of the Near East

Star Carr and other sites of northwestern Europe represent one end of a spectrum of Middle Stone Age lifeways in the Old World. In those regions, plant foods were scarce for much of each year, and foragers sustained themselves by relying mostly on hunting or fishing. Farther south, in central and southern Europe and the Near East (areas never covered by ice sheets, even during maximum glacial periods), the natural carrying capacity of the environment was generally higher. People in these regions tended to rely more heavily on wild plant resources, supplemented by animal protein. These distinctions in climate and culture justify the use of the separate term *Epipaleolithic* to distinguish the Middle Stone Age of the Near East and adjacent parts of southwest Asia (Fig. 15–18). For the most part, Epipaleolithic subsistence strategies resulted merely in more efficient foraging. But in a few locations, food-collecting strategies were already taking people imperceptibly toward an entirely new economic threshold—the development of food production (see next chapter).

For the moment, let us consider the transition from foraging to food collecting in the Levant region, in what is today Israel and Lebanon. A foraging culture known to archaeologists as the Kebaran had occupied this region for millennia. Many Kebaran groups had adopted a strategy of **transhumance**, a specific seasonality and scheduling technique whereby people divided their activities between resource zones at different elevations. The Kebarans harvested seeds of wild cereal grasses in the lowlands from fall through springtime. In summer, they made extended forays into the sparsely wooded uplands to hunt and to gather nuts.

Between 12,000 and 11,000 y.a., a moderating climate associated with the waning Pleistocene took effect in the arid lands bordering the eastern Mediterranean. As both temperatures and precipitation increased, the range of native lowland cereal grasses expanded into the higher forested zones (Henry, 1989). Convenient access to both cereals and nuts in the same locale encouraged Kebaran foragers to shift to a collecting strategy. As these groups began to concentrate on locally abundant, storable wild produce, they abandoned their mobility and made other cultural adjustments that left visible traces in the archaeological record. These changes included construction of larger and more permanent habitations, routine use of heavy seed-processing equipment and other nonportable items, creation of art objects, establishment of cemeteries, and a five- or tenfold increase in population, accompanied by signs of social ranking (Henry, 1989).

Because of such dramatic discontinuities, archaeologists apply a new label to the culture of these more sedentary collectors, identifying it as **Natufian** (Belfer-Cohen, 1991). Natufian subsistence depended heavily on nuts, the seeds of wild cereal grasses, and the gazelle, a kind of antelope (Bar-Yosef, 1987; Henry, 1989). Ancient gazelle-hunting practices are revealed through a study of tooth eruption and wear patterns on animal teeth recovered from Natufian sites (Legge and Rowley-Conwy, 1987). Analysis describes a nonselective population structure of newborns, yearlings, and adults, suggesting that the dominant hunting method was to surround or ambush an entire herd soon after the females gave birth to their young, probably in late April or early May.

Gazelle horn sickles with inset flint blades frequently appear on Natufian sites, along with an abundance of grinding stones and mortars (Fig. 15–19). Small clusters of semipermanent pit houses with stone foundations, often in close association with cemeteries, such as those excavated at 'Ain Mallaha, Hayonim, and Nahal Oren in Israel, and Abu Hureyra in Syria (Moore, 2000), confirm the Natufians' reliance on local species without moving from place to place. These finds, as well as an increase in human **dental caries** (i.e., tooth decay), *hypoplasias* (interrupted enamel formation), periodontal disease, and an overall reduction in tooth size in Natufian skeletons, all testify to the fact that starchy cereal grains figured prominently in their diet (P. Smith et al., 1984). The Natufians provide an instructive case study of an Epipaleolithic shift in subsistence economy from simple foraging to more complex food collecting. We shall further consider the consequences of this transition in the next chapter.

Archaic Hunters and Gatherers of North America

In most regions of North America, big game hunting steadily diminished as Middle Stone Age, or *Archaic*, societies exploited new options in their much-altered environments. Even the venerable bison-hunting tradition on the Plains barely persisted through several millennia of increasing aridity until a more favorable rainfall pattern finally restored the grasslands and the bow and arrow made hunters more effective around 2,000 y.a. Elsewhere, productive environments provided Archaic foragers with more substantial resources. Along the continental margins, as rising sea levels encroached onto the former Atlantic coastal plain, the developing estuaries fostered stocks of fish and shellfish and harbored migratory fowl, all of which Archaic people now exploited with an array of new collection devices, fishing equipment, dugout boats, traps, and nets specifically designed for those purposes. Expansive nut forests across much of the eastern continental interior likewise offered rich gathering opportunities.

Though these resources might be locally abundant, nearly all were highly seasonal. Adjusting to the rhythm of the annual fluctuations, many Archaic people moved beyond simple foraging strategies, which exploited a broad range of natural produce on a day-to-day basis. Instead, they scheduled subsistence activities to coincide with the annual sequence of particularly productive resources at specific locations within their territories. Seasonality and scheduling, or optimal foraging, encouraged food collection and storage for later use. Gradually, most Archaic groups developed a more **central-based wandering** pattern, at least compared to their wide-ranging Paleo-Indian predecessors. Collectors carried out their activities within smaller circumscribed territories and acquired through exchange with neighbors or more distant groups whatever might be lacking locally. Especially in temperate regions, efficient exploitation of edible nuts, deer, fish, shellfish, and other forest and riverine products was enhanced by new storage techniques and regional exchange networks. Increased site density and size beginning around 6,000 y.a. reflected local population growth in a number of regions. Archaic societies now began to exhibit signs of more complex sociopolitical organization, religious ceremonialism, and economic interdependence.

Cultural regionalism accelerated during Archaic times within localized resource zones. Not only culturally, but linguistically and probably even genetically, Archaic societies gradually diversified into increasingly distinctive local societies.

Archaic Cultures of Western America   Arid rock-shelters in the **Great Basin**, a harsh expanse between the Rocky Mountains and the Sierra Nevadas, preserve material evidence of desert Archaic lifeways (D'Azevedo, 1986). Hunting weapons, milling stones, twined and coiled basketry, nets, mats, feather robe fragments, fiber sandals and hide moccasins, bone tools, and even gaming pieces sealed in deeply stratified sites such as Gatecliff Shelter and Lovelock Cave, in Nevada, and Danger Cave, in Utah, illuminate nearly 10 millennia of hunting and gathering (Fig. 15–20). **Coprolites** (desiccated human feces) occasionally found in these deposits contain seeds, insect exoskeletons, and often the tiny scales and bones of fish, small rodents, and amphibians and thus provide direct evidence of diet and health (Reinhard and Bryant, 1992). Freshwater and brackish marshes were focal points for many subsistence activities—sources of fish, migratory fowl, plant foods, and raw materials during half the year—but upland resources such as pine nuts and game were critical, too. Larger animals might be taken occasionally, though smaller prey such as jackrabbits and ducks and the seasonal medley of seed-bearing plants afforded these foragers their most reliable diet. Success in this environment was a direct measure of cultural flexibility (Fig. 15–21).

Prehistoric societies throughout California's varied environments likewise sustained themselves without agriculture until the Gold Rush of the nineteenth century brought an influx of Euro-Americans. Rich oak forests fed much of the region's human and animal population. Foragers and collectors routinely ranged across several productive resource zones, from seacoast to interior valleys. Typical California societies, such as the Chumash of the Santa Barbara coast and Channel Islands,

FIGURE 15–19
Reconstruction of a Natufian gazelle horn reaping knife with inset flint blades.

Central-based wandering
A strategy of some food collectors, who work out of a long-term base camp.

Great Basin
Rugged, dry plateau between the mountains of California and Utah, comprising Nevada, western Utah, and southern Oregon and Idaho.

Coprolites
Preserved fecal material, which can be studied for what the contents reveal about diet and health.

FIGURE 15–20
Danger Cave, in Utah.

Totem
An animal or being associated with a kin-group and used for social identification; also, a carved pole representing these beings.

Potlatch
Ceremonial feasting and gift-giving event among Northwest Coast Indians.

obtained substantial harvests of acorns and deer meat in the fall, supplemented by migratory fish, small game, and plants throughout the year (Glassow, 1996). Collected wild resources sustained permanent villages of up to 1,000 occupants. The Chumash were the latest descendants of a long sequence of southern California hunting and gathering cultures that archaeologists have traced back more than 8,000 years (Moratto, 1984). As environmental fluctuations and population changes necessitated adjustments among coastal and terrestrial resources, Archaic Californians at times ate more fish and shellfish, then more sea mammals or deer, and later more acorns and smaller animal species.

Archaeological and cultural studies along the northwestern coast of the United States and Canada have delineated other impressive nonfarming societies whose economies also centered around collecting rich and diverse sea and forest resources. Inhabitants of this region exploited several species of salmon as the fish passed upriver from the sea to spawn each spring or fall. Berries and wild game such as bear and deer were locally plentiful; oily candlefish, halibut, and whales could be captured with the aid of nets, traps, large seaworthy canoes, and other well-crafted gear. Excavations at Ozette, on Washington's Olympic Peninsula, revealed a prosperous Nootka whaling community buried in a mud slide 250 years ago (Samuels, 1991).

By historical times along the northwestern coast, clan-based lineages resided in permanent coastal communities of sturdy plank-built cedar houses, guarded by carved cedar **totem** poles proclaiming their owners' genealogical heritage (Fig. 15–22). They vied with one another for social status by staging elaborate public functions (now generally known as the **potlatch**) in which quantities of smoked salmon, fish or whale oil, dried berries, cedar bark blankets, and other valuables were bestowed upon guests (Jonaitas, 1988). There are archaeological signs that these practices may be quite ancient, with substantial houses, status artifacts, and evidence of warfare dating back some 2,500 years (Ames and Maschner, 1999). While a successful potlatch earned prestige for the hosts and incurred obligations to be repaid in the future, it also served larger purposes. By fostering a network of mutual reciprocity that created both sociopolitical and economic alliances, this ritualized redistribution system ensured a wider availability of the region's dispersed resources, enabling highly organized sedentary communities to prosper without relying on domesticated crops.

Western Arctic Archaic bands pursued coastal sea mammals or else combined inland caribou hunting with fishing; their diet included virtually no vegetation (McGhee, 1996). Beginning about 2,500 y.a., Thule (Inuit/Eskimo) hunters

FIGURE 15–21
The arid Great Basin of the American West supported foraging cultures for thousands of years.

expanded eastward across the Arctic with the aid of a highly specialized tool kit that included effective toggling harpoons for securing sea mammals; blubber lamps for light, cooking, and warmth; and sledges and *kayaks* (skin boats) for transportation on frozen land or sea.

Archaic Cultures of Eastern America   Locally varied environments across eastern North America supported a range of Archaic cultures after about 6,000 y.a. (Snow, 1980). A general warming and drying trend lasting several thousand years promoted deciduous forest growth as far north as the Great Lakes. Archaic societies exploited the temperate oak-chestnut forests and rivers of the Northeast and Appalachians. Nuts of many kinds comprised an important staple for these forest groups. Acorn, chestnut, black walnut, butternut, hickory, and beechnut represent plentiful foods that are both nutritious and palatable, rich in fats and oils. Some nuts were prepared by parching or roasting, others by crushing and boiling into soups; leaching in hot water neutralized the toxic tannic acids found in acorns. Whitetail deer and black bear provided meat, hides for clothing, and bone and antler for toolmaking. Migratory fowl, wild turkey, fish, and small mammals, along with berries and seeds, also contributed to the diet.

Elsewhere in the East, some coastal Archaic groups from Massachusetts to Labrador used canoes to hunt sea mammals and swordfish with bone-bladed harpoons in summer, then relied on caribou and salmon the rest of the year. North of the St. Lawrence river, other Archaic bands dispersed widely through the sparse boreal forests, hunting caribou or moose, fishing, and trapping. Around the Great Lakes, seasonally mobile foragers employed an extensive array of equipment to fish, hunt, and gather. This region's so-called *Old Copper Culture* hammered natural copper nuggets found along Lake Superior's shores into tools and ornaments intended primarily as burial offerings and for exchange, the first use of metal in North America. The productive valleys of the midcontinent, where a nexus of great rivers join the Mississippi, supported a riverine focus. Favored sites in this region attained substantial size and were occupied for many generations, some—such as Eva and Rose Island, in Tennessee, and Koster, in southern Illinois—for thousands of years.

Eastern Archaic groups at times reinforced their claims to homelands by laying out cemeteries for their dead or by erecting earthwork mounds. These activities imply an emerging social differentiation within some of the preagricultural Archaic societies as well as a degree of sedentism. Archaeologists studying more than 1,000 Archaic burials at Indian Knoll, Kentucky, found possible status indicators reflected in the distribution of grave goods. Though two-thirds of the graves contained no offerings at all, certain females and children had been given disproportionate shares; only a few males were selected to receive tools and weapons (Rothschild, 1979).

Archaic people in the lower Missississippi valley began raising monumental earthworks beginning as early as 5,500 y.a. Mound building required communal effort and planning. Near Monroe, Louisiana, Watson Brake is a roughly oval embankment enclosing a space averaging 750 feet (225 m) across and capped by about a dozen individual mounds up to 24 feet (7 m) in height (Saunders et al., 1997). Not far to the east, Poverty Point's elaborate 3,500-year-old complex of six concentric semicircular ridges and several conical mounds covers a full square mile (2.6 km²) (Gibson, 2001). That hunters and gatherers chose to invest their energies in creating these and dozens of other impressive structures suggests highly developed Archaic social organization and ritualism, though their precise meaning remains unclear.

William Turnbaugh

FIGURE 15–22
Northwest Coast food collectors erected totem poles at their permanent villages.

Cultural Ecology of Foraging and Food Collecting

We have seen that in North America, as in the Old World, Holocene hunters and gatherers routinely adjusted to post-Pleistocene conditions through their cultural behavior, including subsistence practices and diet. Climate and resources seldom remain stable for long, so cultural flexibility was a key to successfully exploiting a

changing environment. Small, mobile bands of foragers, whose diets varied in accordance with locally available, seasonal resources, represented the basic cultural adaptation in meeting human subsistence needs. Relying exclusively on fluctuating natural food resources to meet its daily requirements tended to limit a population's potential for growth. Consequently, many foraging groups maintained very low population densities, a result that could be accomplished by strictly limiting birthrates (even through infanticide) or else by periodically splitting off into separate bands. Alternatively, foragers might try to accommodate population growth by expanding their territory (not usually practical or even possible in already occupied areas) or by more intensively exploiting the available resources. The latter was most often achieved through food collecting. (Recall that foraging and food collecting are not exclusive of each other; groups seldom practice one strategy exclusively, often incorporating elements of the other at the same time.)

We saw that in contrast to foragers, food collectors tend to focus on just a few primary seasonal resources, which in turn may encourage them to establish long-term residence in one area. Thus, long-term village sites, along with storage facilities, midden accumulations, cemeteries, and mounds, are archaeological clues indicating a shift from foraging to food collecting.

That change of focus clearly involved a new way of connecting with the environment as well. One consequence of food collection is that a people's reliance on one or just a few species may begin to act as a selection factor, with the result that the exploited plants or animals eventually exhibit changes in behavior, distribution, size, or other traits, reflecting human-induced preferences. Indeed, rather than promoting a steady-state system wherein natural products were used and maintained with little notable change over long periods, the activities of some advanced food collectors seem to have precipitated some destabilizing ecological consequences.

For example, as people took a more active role in manipulating the landscape to enhance favored species, they might have created forest clearings or eliminated competing animals or "weed" plants; or they might have intentionally introduced wild food species into new areas as they expanded. At times, as among the Natufians in the Near East, these intensive exploitation patterns greatly altered the overall relationship between people and their environment, promoting further changes in their society as well as in the resources they targeted. Thus, we see larger populations drawn to certain prime areas, where intergroup competition would be inevitable and where selection pressures on resources could become significant. In some instances, the changes brought about by advanced food collectors were actually a prelude to food production, the focus of the next chapter.

SUMMARY

By the early to middle Holocene, anatomically modern *Homo sapiens* had expanded into all the inhabitable regions of the globe, including the American continents. Most current evidence suggests that people initially arrived in the New World via a land connection with northeastern Asia sometime after about 15,000 y.a. The scarcity of skeletal and cultural materials surviving from the earliest stages of New World prehistory has encouraged much speculation about American Indian origins. Nevertheless, available cultural and biological traces clearly link the first Americans with their Asian roots. Specific similarities in material culture and hunting behaviors connect the widespread Paleo-Indian culture of North and South America to several earlier Upper Paleolithic locations in Siberia.

Defined biological traits relate early American populations to northeastern Asian ancestors, probably through one or more small founding populations comprised of members of just a few ancestral lineages that migrated across Beringia and subsequently expanded into vast and geographically diverse regions, where considerable microevolution ensued.

By about 12,000 y.a., after the close of the Pleistocene ice age, significant geo-climatic changes had altered the configuration of the landscape and of the animal and plant communities across much of the Northern Hemisphere, including North America and Eurasia. Global warming during the early Holocene promoted the expansion of temperate grasslands and forest succession in formerly glaciated areas. At the same time, many large mammal species became extinct, particularly in North America, where human hunters may have been involved.

Under Holocene conditions, Middle Stone Age societies in Europe, the Near East, and North America became increasingly proficient at gaining their livelihoods within more diverse environmental niches. Generalized hunting-gathering-fishing economies promoted long-term cultural stability for many foragers, such as the Mesolithic hunters of Star Carr and the Archaic peoples of California, the Great Basin, and the eastern American woodlands, who exploited their environments' varied resources at relatively low levels of intensity. Especially in regions with great seasonal resource fluctuations, experiencing intensely dry or cold months, people tended to settle on a few more productive species, which were collected in quantity and stored. As a rule, food collectors became less mobile and more sedentary than foragers, sometimes (like the Natufians of the Near East) establishing permanent settlements from which they exploited their resources with ever greater efficiency.

Middle Stone Age foragers and collectors occupied a chronological position between Paleolithic hunters and Neolithic farmers. Indeed, through their activities, certain advanced food collectors probably contributed to some of the cultural, environmental, and evolutionary circumstances that fostered the development of food production in some regions. Still, we must emphasize that individual Mesolithic and Archaic societies rarely *chose* to make the transition to agriculture.

The remaining chapters of this text are organized around two primary cultural developments associated with humans in the later Holocene period: first, the process of food production, and second, the rise of civilizations. Much of what we associate with modern humanity is linked to one or both of these central driving forces.

QUESTIONS FOR REVIEW

1. What are some of the significant environmental changes associated with the end of the Pleistocene? Which of these changes would have most affected humans?
2. Where was Beringia? How did it form, and why is it significant with respect to early American prehistory?
3. Discuss some of the specific biological and cultural clues that point to an Asian ancestry for the earliest American populations.
4. Evaluate some of the evidence cited in support of an alleged pre-Paleo-Indian period of New World prehistory.
5. How does the archaeological evidence pertaining to the Paleo-Indians bias our view of them as big game hunters?
6. Is there sufficient archaeological evidence to implicate Paleo-Indians in the extinction of Pleistocene animals? Discuss.
7. Contrast Middle Stone Age adaptations of northern Europe, as represented at Star Carr and Vedbaek, with those of the Near East, as represented by the Kebarans and Natufians in the Levant.
8. What differentiates food collecting from foraging? What are some of the economic and biocultural implications of each of these subsistence strategies?
9. What is the significance of the term *Archaic* as it pertains to American prehistory? What corresponding terminology is used for the Old World?
10. What evidence supports the view that a way of life based on hunting, gathering, and/or fishing may have been adequate and even satisfying for its practitioners, contrary to popular misconceptions?

SUGGESTED FURTHER READING

Fagan, Brian M. 2000. *Ancient North America*. 3rd ed. New York: Thames and Hudson.

Kelly, Robert L. 1995. *The Foraging Spectrum: Diversity in Hunter-Gatherer Lifeways*. Washington, DC: Smithsonian Institution Press.

Lee, Richard B., and Richard H. Daly (eds.). 1999. *The Cambridge Encyclopedia of Hunters and Gatherers*. New York: Cambridge University Press.

Phillips, James L., and Ofer Bar-Yosef. 2000. *The Prehistory of the Levant—A Reader*. Norwell, MA: Kluwer Academic Publications.

Smith, Christopher. 1998. *Late Stone Age Hunters of the British Isles*. London: Routledge.

Thomas, David Hurst. 2000. *Skull Wars: Kennewick Man, Archeology, and the Battle for Native American Identity*. New York: Basic Books.

RESOURCES ON THE INTERNET

 ### Wadsworth Anthropology Resource Center
http://anthropology.wadsworth.com

The companion website for this text includes a range of enrichment material focused on the chapter's topic. While online you can enhance your understanding of the chapter by exploring one of the several additional Internet Exercises, by researching topics, and by accessing full articles on InfoTrac College Edition. You can also reinforce the concepts by taking online practice exams.

Internet Exercises

The controversy over the Kennewick skeletal remains stems from the federal Native American Graves Protection and Repatriation Act (NAGPRA) of 1990. Visit the National NAGPRA Database (**http://www.cast.uark.edu/other/nps/nagpra**), which provides access to the text of NAGPRA and other related documents. Consult the section on "Kennewick Man Documents." Summarize the latest legal developments in this case.

 ### InfoTrac College Edition
http://www.infotrac-college.com/wadsworth

Foraging or food collecting were standard occupations in every human society until food production gradually replaced those activities. In a few regions, hunters and gatherers maintained their traditional cultures into the twentieth century. Conduct a keyword search for *hunting and gathering* to find current references on this topic in InfoTrac College Edition. Select an article or two that present research on one individual hunting and gathering society, either ancient or more recent. How does that society compare to one of those featured in this chapter, perhaps the Natufians or the people of Star Carr?

Archaeology: Methods and Practice

Our understanding of the human cultural past, especially of that long span before the invention of writing, is based on archaeological research. The ultimate source of the archaeological data on which our reconstructions of past lifeways are based is the cultural material lost or abandoned by earlier societies. These products generally are known as *artifacts*.

The locations where past human activities took place are called *sites*, and once discovered, they may become the focus of modern archaeological activity.

FIGURE 1

Archaeologists are testing for possible sites in an area about to be destroyed by construction. To standardize their search, they excavate small exploratory test pits at 10 m intervals along survey lines that crisscross the impacted zone.

FIGURE 2

Generally, one partner excavates while another screens the soil and searches for telltale evidence of previous human activity—ceramic fragments, stone flakes, bits of food bone, charcoal, etc.

Archaeology: Methods and Practice (continued)

FIGURE 3a
Some technologically sophisticated approaches offer the possibility of finding sites even before digging. A team conducts an electrical resistance survey to locate buried foundations at a military site. Filled pits, cellar holes, walls, and similar features disrupt the conductivity of electricity through soil. Undisturbed soil generally is more conductive.

William Turnbaugh

FIGURE 3b
Variations in the strength of an electrical current sent between successive pairs of probes indicate disturbed areas. With enough readings, the operators will be able to devise a contour map of resistance and suggest the most fruitful areas to excavate.

William Turnbaugh

William Turnbaugh

FIGURE 4
Buried metallic objects on late prehistoric or more recent sites may be located in a more direct manner by using a metal detector. The archaeologist flags every spot that produces a strong signal and then returns to properly excavate in the vicinity of any promising concentrations.

Once located, a site may be excavated if it is endangered by development or if it seems likely to provide some answers to important research questions. When possible, projects are conducted when the soil is damp and soft, so that subtle differences in coloration and texture are not missed. Digging is only a small part of what archaeology is all about, but most archaeologists admit that fieldwork is a lot of fun, despite the fact that it can also be hard labor.

FIGURE 5

On large sites, archaeologists often excavate a gridwork of square units, each carefully laid out and mapped with the aid of standard surveying equipment. In this way, the exact location of every find can be measured and mapped accurately for future reference. At this Ohio site, the archaeologist has chosen to retain thin walls between individual units. The walls (or *balks*) provide a profile view of the successive strata through which the excavators have dug.

FIGURE 6

Excavators appreciate the shade while working on a large barracks at a military post in western Nebraska. The deeper pits were dug to explore a partial cellar under the building.

FIGURE 7

This crew is comprised of one or two professional archaeologists along with students and adult volunteers. Most archaeological excavation is accomplished with simple hand tools such as trowels. Measuring tapes and clipboards are kept at the ready for recording the location of any finds as well as pertinent observations.

Archaeology: Methods and Practice (continued)

Courtesy, The Museum of Primitive Art and Culture, Peace Dale, RI

FIGURE 8
As soil from each excavation unit is removed, it is put into containers, then screened to remove any objects at first overlooked by the excavator. Fine mesh, no larger than $1/4$ inch, is used so that even the smallest traces can be recovered. Any artifacts found in the screening will be bagged and labeled.

Courtesy, The Museum of Primitive Art and Culture, Peace Dale, RI

FIGURE 9
It takes a close look to find the smallest flakes of flint or bits of pottery among the rootlets left on the screen.

William Turnbaugh

William Turnbaugh

FIGURE 10
The world in general may be looking for a better mousetrap, but archaeologists have always dreamed of mechanical inventions that would ease the labor of excavation. Gayle Carlson, archaeologist for the Nebraska Historical

Society, rigged up an agricultural seed separator as a motorized screen (left). The portion that does not drop through the initial screening is gathered (right), taken to the scale to be weighed, and then examined by hand.

Many sites were occupied over long spans of time—hundreds or even thousands of years. In these cases, archaeologists may encounter a number of stratified levels, or *strata*, overlying one another. Each stratum represents a different time period or cultural event, so all must be excavated and examined individually.

FIGURE 11
This site along the Susquehanna River in Pennsylvania was subject to frequent floods, which periodically buried the ground surface where prehistoric Indians lived and worked. The tagged strata represent cultural levels; the intervening strata are flood deposits. This profile represents 6,000 years of cultural and natural stratification.

FIGURE 12
Here is a most unusual archaeological site. This early hominid site, at Ubeidiya, in the Jordan valley of Israel dates to around 1.3 m.y.a. Since that time, geological forces have raised the once-horizontal strata nearly on edge. Archaeologists perch on ladders to excavate and map the successive living floors, but otherwise the process remains essentially the same.

FIGURE 13
Single-component sites are those that have only one stratum associated with cultural activity. Archaeologists can conveniently strip away the overburden and thereby expose a large area of the site at once.

Archaeology: Methods and Practice (continued)

FIGURE 14

At times, individual well-defined *features*, rather than entire sites, may be excavated. A colonial house foundation, partial cellar hole, cistern, and other related components are being uncovered and mapped in a wooded area of New England. Root cutters and poison ivy medications are essential equipment under these conditions!

William Turnbaugh

FIGURE 15

Here, excavators are clearing and preparing to map an oval house feature with a central firepit on a prehistoric American Indian site in Pennsylvania. The stakes represent the locations of individual wooden posts that have long since decayed and left only dark stains in the soil. The white markers indicate corners of excavation units and will aid in mapping.

William Turnbaugh

FIGURE 16

Drawing upon archaeological research and tribal ingenuity, modern descendants of New England's aboriginal people construct a traditional-style round house, or *wigwam*, at Plimoth Plantation, Massachusetts. Saplings set into the ground, bent and lashed together, provide a framework for the house, which will be lined and covered with water-deflecting reed matting.

William Turnbaugh

FIGURE 17

A time-lapse series illustrates the excavation of a foundation and filled cellar hole on an early-nineteenth-century military site near Boston. The central brickwork represents support for fireplaces and chimney. The unexcavated strip preserves the stratigraphic profile through the feature. The work required several weeks.

William Turnbaugh

William Turnbaugh

William Turnbaugh

William Turnbaugh

William Turnbaugh

Archaeology: Methods and Practice (continued)

Fieldwork is only a small part of an archaeologist's activity. Even before the excavation is done, the archaeological lab is bustling. During excavations, each day's finds need to be processed as they arrive, so that the work of analysis can get under way without delay. Study of artifacts, soil, and other ecological samples, as well as record keeping, photography, and report writing, will often go on for months after the site has been closed.

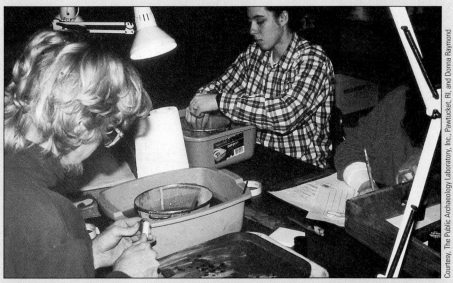

Courtesy, The Public Archaeology Laboratory, Inc., Pawtucket, RI, and Donna Raymond

FIGURE 18
Artifacts from each excavation unit are kept separate from all others as they are washed, then numbered in permanent ink and immediately cataloged to prevent any mix-up.

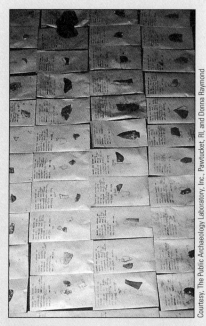

Courtesy, The Public Archaeology Laboratory, Inc., Pawtucket, RI, and Donna Raymond

FIGURE 19
Diagnostic artifacts from one excavation are laid out in the lab so that archaeologists can begin to get a "feel" for what the site has produced. The major task ahead is to make sense of all the data (from many different sources) bearing on the project.

Courtesy, The Public Archaeology Laboratory, Inc., Pawtucket, RI, and Donna Raymond

William Turnbaugh

FIGURE 20
Photography helps document important finds. (Left) Early prehistoric Paleo-Indian and Archaic period projectile points. (Right) Armaments and insignia from a Revolutionary War battle site.

FIGURE 21

A scientist scans materials recovered by *flotation*. When the contents of features such as garbage pits or fireplaces are dumped into a vat of agitated water, soil and stones drop to the bottom while the lighter organic components float to the top. Retrieved and dried, they are scrutinized for identifiable plant elements or small animal bones, which provide clues to ancient diet and environment.

FIGURE 22

Excavated materials, including artifacts, flotation samples, and soil samples, are systematically stored on metal shelving for future reference and study. Site maps and all other excavation records are retained as well, for they are an equally important product of the fieldwork.

FIGURE 23

The capability of data storage and retrieval made possible by computers has been of great assistance to archaeologists. It is not uncommon for a site to yield more than a million objects to be cataloged and kept track of. Artifact catalog information and field notes can be combined and stored with other data on the computer. Some large projects use computers in the field to monitor the flow of artifacts and other information coming from the site.

FIGURE 24

Computer graphics offer archaeologists innovative ways to work with and represent their data.

Archaeology: Methods and Practice (continued)

Make no mistake about it. The human past is an endangered resource. The documentation for more than 99 percent of our species' existence is accessible only through archaeological research. The pace of modern development is relentlessly erasing that record in many quarters of the globe, including the United States. Legislation in this and a few other countries only recently has been aimed at slowing the alarming loss of our cultural heritage.

FIGURE 25
In an effort to rescue information that would otherwise be lost forever, archaeologists are now granted access to some sites before they are destroyed. Cultural Resource Management (CRM) is a federal policy that has given rise to "contract archaeology," so called because independent and university-affiliated archaeological firms and organizations are awarded contracts to carry out specific research activities prior to construction.

Courtesy, The Public Archaeology Laboratory, Inc., Pawtucket, RI, and Donna Raymond

William Turnbaugh

FIGURE 26
Must we sacrifice our past for our future?

CHAPTER

16

Food Production: A Biocultural Revolution

CONTENTS

Introduction

The record of humankind during the Holocene reinforces the concept of modern *Homo sapiens sapiens* as a biocultural organism. The pace of change affecting our species has accelerated dramatically in just the past 10,000 years or so. In this period, human cultural activity has accounted for an increasing proportion of the observed change. By making cultural choices and devising new cultural solutions to age-old problems, humans have succeeded in mitigating some of the processes that operate in the "natural" world, attempting to turn them to our own advantage, or at least to minimize their negative effects. The consequences of cultural behavior not only affect the natural world, but invariably manifest themselves through human biology as well.

Two of the most profound and far-reaching developments of later prehistory are the shift to food production and the emergence of large-scale complex societies. The topics of this chapter—the record of plant and animal domestication and the associated spread of farming, as well as their relationship to the emergence of early civilizations in several regions of the globe—have been the subject of intensive archaeological research. These processes stimulated massive biocultural consequences that have affected our species, and our world, ever since (Fig. 16–1).

FIGURE 16–1
Time line for Chapter 16.

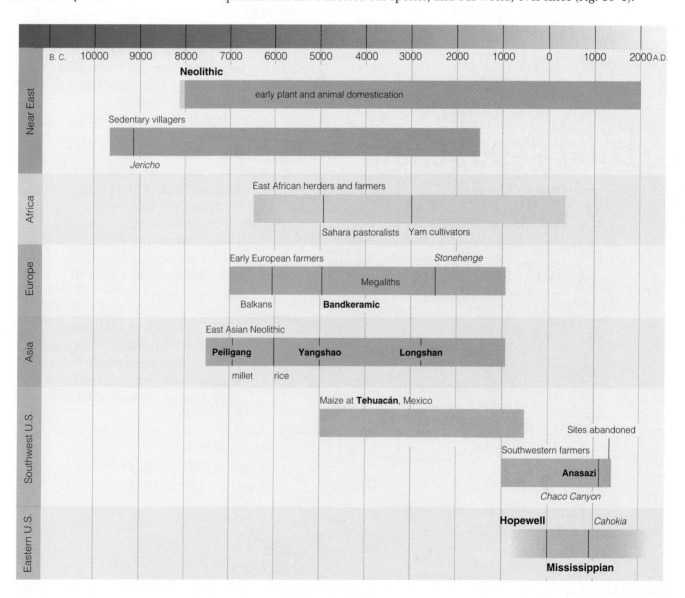

The Neolithic Revolution

V. Gordon Childe, an influential prehistorian and scholar, proposed the term **Neolithic Revolution** to acknowledge the fundamental significance of the changes brought about by food production (Childe, 1951). While hunters and gatherers had collected whatever foods nature made available, farmers in effect employed nature to produce only those crops and animals that humans had selected for their own exclusive purposes.

Beyond primary domestication and farming, **Neolithic** activities stimulated other far-reaching consequences, including new settlement patterns, new technologies, and profound biocultural effects. The emergence of food production eventually transformed most human societies either directly or indirectly and, in the process, brought about dramatic changes in the natural realm as well. The world has been a very different place ever since agriculture.

Childe recognized that maintaining fields and herds demanded a long-term commitment from early farmers. Obliged to stay in one area to oversee their crops, Neolithic people became more or less settled, or *sedentary*. As storable harvests gradually supported larger and more permanent communities, towns and cities developed in a few areas. Within these larger settlements, fewer people were directly involved in food production, allowing for cultural tasks to be redefined. For example, craft **specialization** fostered many of the technological advances of the Neolithic. Such activities as cloth making, pottery production, and metallurgy are multistage processes that can be accomplished most efficiently when skilled specialists work cooperatively.

Decades after Childe's original study, archaeologists still accept his general characterization of the Neolithic Revolution, but later research enables us to refine some of the specifics. For example, we now recognize that sedentism actually *preceded* farming in certain locations where permanent settlements were sustained solely by gathering and hunting or fishing. In Chapter 15, we noted that the Chumash Indians of southern California and the Natufian food collectors of the Near East, among others, established sizable villages. It has even been suggested that sedentism may sometimes *stimulate* food production, rather than the other way around.

We also now realize that the Neolithic lifeway evolved independently in separate areas of the world. Archaeologists see most regional Neolithic developments as the culmination of local cultural sequences rather than the result of **diffusion**, or spreading, from a single Near Eastern center. The Neolithic was truly revolutionary, but in an even broader sense than Childe envisioned.

In the following discussion, we examine the beginnings of domestication and farming by considering evidence drawn from around the globe. Although the process everywhere shared many similarities and produced equally dramatic consequences, archaeologists working in the Americas rarely apply the term *Neolithic* to studies of New World farmers, but instead use regional terminology (such as *Formative* or *Preclassic* in Mesoamerica and *Woodland* or *Mississippian* in eastern North America).

Why and How Did Domestication and Agriculture Occur?

Scholars once hoped to pin down the very place where some genius had first planted a seed or harnessed an animal. By now, we understand that ancient people who knew the natural world so intimately were both intelligent and observant enough to recognize the role of seeds in plant reproduction long before they finally turned to farming as a way of life just a few thousand years ago. So, you may ask, what took them so long to become farmers? From the perspective of our modern cultivated world, we may find it hard to accept that earlier peoples did not generally aspire to be farmers and that many no doubt resisted the "opportunity" for as long as possible! In recent centuries, the expansion of European culture was resisted by many hunter-gatherer societies. From the Sioux of the American Plains to the

Neolithic Revolution
Childe's term for the far-reaching consequences of food production.

Neolithic
(*neo*, meaning "new," and *lith*, meaning "stone") New Stone Age; period of farmers.

Specialization
Economic system that allows individuals to devote full time to certain occupations.

Diffusion
The idea that widely distributed cultural traits originated in a single center and were spread from one group to another through contact or exchange.

Hadza of East Africa, hunters and gatherers vigorously rebuffed the efforts of missionaries and government agencies to convert them into farmers. Farming was not an inevitable development, nor does it necessarily represent a better way of life than the alternatives. Perhaps a more pertinent question would be, What advantages did some groups seek in eventually turning to agriculture? Or did most adopt this mode of life not so much out of choice, but because they were forced into farming for some reason?

Ironically, although farming did not get started in a big way until later, it was the foragers and food collectors of the Mesolithic period who actually initiated the critical processes and even developed many of the innovations we usually credit to the Neolithic cultural period. In essence, the lifestyle of some hunter-gatherers anticipated many of the developments generally associated with farmers. The people whom archaeologists consider Neolithic were mostly the *recipients* of the domesticated species and agricultural ways from their predecessors.

Defining Agriculture and Domestication

At the outset, we must differentiate between two distinct though commonly associated terms, **domestication** and **agriculture** (Rindos, 1984). Domestication implies an interdependency between humans and one or more selected plant or animal species. Remember, domestication is really an evolutionary process, not an event. Domestication entails the *genetic* transformation of a wild species, resulting from long-term selection and biocultural feedback involving a living resource and the people who make use of it. Through artificial selection (i.e., selective breeding) or other ways of interfering (intentionally or not) with a species' natural processes, humans have induced changes resulting in new or enhanced characteristics deemed useful or desirable. Agriculture is a *cultural* activity, the propagation and exploitation of domesticated plants and/or animals by humans. Agriculture in its broad sense includes all the activities associated with both crop farming and animal herding. Together, these associated concepts are at the foundation of Neolithic lifeways.

Of course, people have sometimes gained control over selected plants and animals for purposes other than food. Some cultures have raised birds and animals solely for ritual offerings or ornamental use. Indians of Mexico and the American Southwest reared colorful parrots for their bright plumage, and Peruvian natives herded alpaca camelids primarily for their wool. Medicinal herbs, attractive flowers, and fibrous plants have also served nonfood uses. Our focus here, however, is on the shift to food production. The truly critical question we must answer is, Why did farming become an irresistible strategy at any given place and time?

Most hypotheses that account for farming point to resource imbalances brought on by climate change and/or human population growth. In these approaches, the central argument is that if the available natural food supply is no longer adequate to feed its numbers, a society must maintain itself by reducing its population, by extending its territory, or by making more intensive use of its environment. Farming, of course, represents a more intensive use of the environment. Through their efforts, farmers attempt to secure for themselves a greater proportion of the land's **carrying capacity** by harnessing more of its energy for the production of crops or animals that will feed people.

Environmental Explanations

The environment is often credited with stimulating the shift to farming. Environment does play a crucial role in farming, so one must consider what effect the climate and natural setting may have had on early agriculture. Childe himself conjectured that radical climate change at the end of the Ice Age increased Europe's rainfall while bringing widespread desiccation to southwestern Asia and North Africa (Childe, 1928, 1934). Humans, animals, and vegetation in the drought areas concentrated into shrinking zones around a few permanent water sources. At these **oases**, Childe hypothesized, intensive interaction between humans and certain

Domestication
A state of interdependence between humans and selected plant or animal species. Intense selection activity induces permanent genetic change, enhancing a species' value to humans.

Agriculture
Cultural activities associated with planting, herding, and processing domesticated species.

Carrying capacity
The population that the environment can sustain.

Oases (*sing.*, oasis)
Permanent springs or water holes in an arid region.

other plant and animal species resulted in domestication of some species, including wheat, barley, sheep, and goats, which people then began to use to their advantage.

Today, notions of *environmental determinism*, which propose that human actions are primarily responsive to and driven by natural conditions, enjoy little support. We now recognize that humans usually find a range of prospects in almost any environment (Fig. 16–2). In extreme situations, the choices may be more limited, but human/nature interactions always reflect cultural and historical factors. What a culture is already familiar with and has done in the past often guides its actions more than environmental factors alone. Thus, for example, a desert region might sustain opportunistic foragers, nomadic pastoralists, farmers using special deep-planting procedures, or even lawn-mowing suburbanites willing to pay for piped-in water! The relationship between people and environment is seldom unidirectional.

Although pollen and sediment profiles now confirm that at least some of the climatic changes hypothesized by Childe actually occurred in parts of the Near East prior to Neolithic times and so may have had a role in fostering new relationships between humans and other species in this marginal environment (Henry, 1989; Wright, 1993), the matter is not so simple. In places like the Near East, climate change that resulted in diminished or redistributed resource abundance did not directly force people into farming, though it may have limited their choices so that farming became one of the more reasonable options. On the other hand, we now suspect that the arid conditions familiar to us today may be as much a *result* as a cause of Neolithic activities in the region. That is, the ecologically disruptive activities of farmers and herd animals during the Neolithic period itself actually contributed to the destructive process of **desertification**. Their plowed fields exposed soil to wind erosion and evaporation, while the irrigation demands of their crops lowered the water table. And overgrazing herbivores rapidly reduced the vegetation that holds moisture and binds soil, thus destroying the fragile margin between grassland and desert. As you can see, these human/nature relationships are complex and dynamic.

Desertification
Any process resulting in the formation or growth of deserts.

Demographic Explanations

Population pressure as the prime stimulus for agriculture is the central theme of another set of explanatory models (Boserup, 1965; Flannery, 1973; Cohen, 1977; Binford, 1983). **Demographic** explanations share the premise that societies

Demographic
Pertaining to the size or rate of increase of human populations.

FIGURE 16–2
Farming is possible even in a desert if a culture devises special techniques for coping with the environment. Hopi farmers of Arizona plant a drought-resistant strain of maize deep into sand dunes where moisture lingers.

William Turnbaugh

Horticulture
Farming method in which only hand tools are used; typical of most early Neolithic societies.

committed themselves to farming only when no acceptable alternatives remained sufficient to feed a human population that had outgrown the carrying capacity of its natural environment. For one reason or another, population control or territorial expansion may not have been feasible or desirable choices. In other words, people faced a "prehistoric food crisis" (Cohen, 1977). Concentrated in a restricted territory or faced with the sudden failure of a once-reliable resource, food collectors might take up **horticulture** or herding to enhance the productivity or distribution of a natural species.

Binford's (1983) "packing model" develops one such scenario involving demographic stress. As modern climatic and biotic conditions became established in the early Holocene, people soon occupied every prime ecological niche in the temperate regions of Eurasia. Foraging areas became confined as territories filled, leading to crowded conditions ("packing") and overexploitation of the most desirable primary resources, especially meat. Forced to make more intensive use of smaller segments of habitat, people applied their Mesolithic technology to a broader range of species, including smaller animals and plants. A few of these resources proved more reliable than others, so they soon received greater attention. For example, collecting seeds became a more intensive and efficient activity, as indicated by the use of special sickles, basketry containers, and processing tools found on many Mesolithic sites.

If the population continued to grow or people tried to expand their territory, their only choice would be to move into the marginal zones at the edges of the optimal, resource-rich areas (Flannery, 1973). Because population stress would again quickly reach critical levels in these marginal environments where resources were already sparse, perhaps it was here that domesticated plants were initially developed. To feed itself, the expanding population might have attempted to reproduce artificially some of the resources they knew from their homeland.

This explanation assumes that the native range of the wild plants that were brought to domestication was very localized, but such may not have been the case (Dennell, 1983; Whittle, 1985). A more general objection to this line of argument is that prehistoric population levels probably never reached (let alone exceeded) the natural carrying capacity of their environments, so population pressure alone is unlikely to account for agriculture's invention. Instead, some archaeologists contend, social factors other than population growth may have pushed societies to come up with more food, perhaps to be used in enhancing group or individual status through competitive feasting, tribute payments, or offerings to the deities (Price, 1995). Such purposes would have required quantities of food well in excess of that which could be readily obtained from natural sources.

Ecological Explanations

By now, you may appreciate the difficulty of separating the issue of *why* people turned to farming from the question of *how* domestication came about. Obviously, these are not separate matters at all. Ecology is the study of organisms in their habitats, including their relations with other species and their surroundings. Ecological perspectives on the origins of domestication and agriculture recognize these interconnections and so offer more comprehensive explanations than the single-cause ideas we have just considered. Ecological theories generally acknowledge that human subsistence practices operated as an agency of natural selection (Rindos, 1984). That is, in attempting to increase their harvests from certain wild plants, collectors modified the very species they used. As the traits that improved a plant's advantages to humans became apparent, people made the effort to cultivate it, and farming followed.

In our discussion of foragers and food collectors in Chapter 15, we saw that the exploitation of specific productive localities within their overall territory led some hunter-gatherers to an increasing reliance on selected food resources. Ironically, some of our most important domesticates today originally held a low status in the diet as wild foods. Many were small, hard seeds and were generally reserved for use as secondary or emergency food sources. Given their choice, people everywhere prefer to eat fruit and meat (Yudkin, 1969). Yet, grains and roots tended to become increasingly important in the human diet (supplemented wherever possible by available animal or fish protein)—and not only when the more desirable foods were in short supply. Why?

As potential domesticates, such plants shared some important qualities in that they do well in disturbed ground, grow in dense concentrations, respond to human manipulation and selection, and represent storable forms of protein or carbohydrate (Flannery, 1968, 1973). Thus, food collectors were attracted to plants whose concentrated growth pattern contributed to easier and larger harvests that could be readily stored, especially if they were relatively tasty and nutritious. Those criteria put several species of wild cereal grasses high on the bill of fare across most of the dry temperate regions, including wheat, barley, and oats in the Near East, rice in Asia, millet in Asia and Africa, and maize (corn) in Mexico. In the temperate forests, nut trees of many varieties found a comparable role, including oak, walnut, hickory, chestnut, beech, and certain kinds of pines. A few other plants, especially legumes and roots, filled in the menu here and there.

People sought to make more intensive and efficient use of these and other plant resources with new food-collecting strategies, including specialized gathering, processing, and storage devices. To take advantage of hard mesquite beans and pine nuts, for instance, Archaic-period Native Americans in Nevada employed carrying baskets, milling stones, parching trays, and grass-lined pits dug into dry rockshelters (Thomas, 1985). As food collectors focused on specific resources and used more specialized technology to increase their harvests, their activities sometimes altered the plants themselves or the habitats in which they grew.

This new relationship may be recognized as an example of **symbiosis**, a mutually beneficial association between members of different species. The concept of domestication—humanly induced genetic change in a natural species—as a kind of symbiotic relationship is at the heart of the ecological approach to explaining domestication.

Let us consider an Old World example. As Epipaleolithic gatherers in the Levant region of the Near East harvested the natural stands of wild cereal grasses such as wheat or barley, their movements would cause many of the ripened seedheads to shatter spontaneously, with considerable loss of grain. Each time they used a gazelle horn sickle to cut through a stalk, some of the seeds would fall to the ground. This normal process of seed dispersal is a function of the **rachis**, a short connector linking each seed to the primary stalk (Fig. 16–3). While the embryonic seed develops, the rachis serves as an umbilical that conveys the nutrients to be stored and later used by the germinating seed. Once the seed has attained its full development on the stalk, the rachis normally becomes dry and brittle, enabling the seed to easily break away.

Even without human interference, wild cereal grasses tended to be particularly susceptible to natural genetic modification (much more so than, say, nut trees), since the plants grew together in dense patches, were highly *polytypic*, and were quick to reproduce. In essence, a stand of wild grasses was like an enormous genetic laboratory. The normal range of genetic variability among the grasses included some plants with slightly larger seeds and others with tougher or more flexible rachis segments, meaning that their seedheads would be slightly less prone to shattering. As people worked through the stands, seeds from these genetic variants would end up in the gathering baskets slightly more often. Later, as the gatherers carried their baskets to camp, stored or processed the grain, or moved from place to place, a disproportionate number of the seeds they dropped, defecated, or perhaps even scattered purposely in likely growing areas would carry the flexible-rachis allele. (So, too, with the larger seeds preferred by the collectors.) As these genetic variants became isolated from the general wild population, each subsequent harvest would advance the "selection" process in favor of the same desirable traits.

Hence, human manipulation became an evolutionary force in modifying the species, a process Darwin labeled "unconscious selection." People did not have to be aware of genetic principles to act as effective agents of evolution. And where

Symbiosis
(*syn*, meaning "together," and *bios*, meaning "life") Mutually advantageous association of two different organisms; also known as *mutualism*.

Rachis
The short stem by which an individual seed attaches to the main stalk of a plant as it develops.

William Turnbaugh

FIGURE 16–3
In seedheads of wild cereal grasses, individual grains are linked together by a flexible jointed stem, or *rachis*, as they develop. At maturity, the rachis disarticulates and the seeds scatter. In domesticated forms, the rachis remains supple, keeping the seedhead intact until harvested by humans.

desirable traits could be readily discerned—larger grain size, fuller seedheads, earlier maturity, and so forth—human choice would even more predictably and consistently favor the preferred characteristics. The result within just a few seasons might be a significant shift in allele frequencies—that is, *evolution*—resulting from classic Darwinian selection processes, in this case the consequence of long-term pressure by gatherers, who consistently selected for those traits that improved the plant's productivity and quality.

From Collecting to Cultivating

Adopting evolutionary ecology as our preferred explanation, we now consider why and how food collectors became farmers. Of course, the rate of divergent evolution away from the wild ancestral forms of a plant (or animal) species will accelerate as people continue to exercise control through selecting for genetically based characteristics they find desirable. To continue with our example of Old World cereals such as barley and wheat, the human-influenced varieties typically came to average more grains per seedhead than their wild relatives. The rachis became less brittle in domesticated forms, making it easier for groups to harvest the grain with less loss because the seedhead no longer shattered to disperse its own seed. At the same time, individual seed coats or husks (glumes) became less tough, making them easier to process or digest. Many of these changes obviously would have proved harmful to the plant under natural conditions. Frequently, a consequence of domestication is that the plant species becomes dependent on humans to disperse its seeds. After all, symbiosis is a mutual, two-way relationship.

Whenever favorable plant traits developed, foragers could be expected to respond to these improvements by quickly adjusting their collecting behavior to take fullest advantage, thus stimulating further genetic changes in the subject plants and eventually producing a **cultigen**, or domesticate, under human control. Again, these "unconscious," or "artificial" (as opposed to "natural," in Darwin's terminology) selection pressures constitute an evolutionary force in their own right. As continuous selection and isolation from other plants of the same species continued to favor desirable genetic variants, the steps to full domestication would have been small ones.

Likewise, the steps between advanced foraging or food collecting and early agriculture were also small ones. It usually is impossible to determine archaeologically when harvesting activities may have expanded to include the deliberate scattering of selected wild seeds in new environments or the elimination of competing plants by "weeding" or even burning over a forest clearing. As they intensified their focus on wheat and barley in the Near East (or on species such as maize or runner beans in Mexico), hunter-gatherers finally abandoned the rhythm of their traditional food-collecting schedules and further committed themselves to increasing the productivity of these plants through cultivation.

Archaeological Evidence for Domestication and Agriculture

Agriculture is arguably the most far-reaching "invention" our species can claim. No other has had such a profound biocultural impact. The accumulated archaeological evidence reveals that humans *independently* domesticated local species and developed agriculture in several geographically separate regions relatively soon after the Ice Age ended (see Box 16–1). Domestication and farming got under way in both southwestern and southeastern Asia well before 10,000 y.a. and began several thousand years later in the Americas.

We need to point out that the domestication of a local species or two would not always trigger the enormous biocultural consequences we usually associate with the Neolithic period. In fact, most altered species retained only local significance. In the eastern woodlands of the United States, food collectors brought a number of small-seeded species under domestication; yet the wild forest products obtained by hunting and gathering retained their primary importance for many centuries until more

Cultigen
A plant that is wholly dependent on humans; a domesticate.

BOX 16–1

DIGGING DEEPER

What's to Eat?

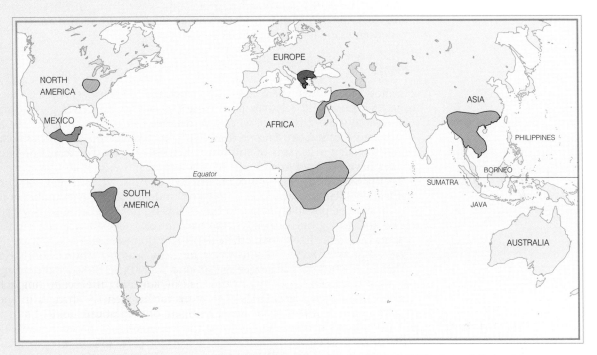

Origin and Approximate Dates of Domestication for Selected Plants and Animals

Asia

Banana *(Musa)*, 2,000 y.a.
Chicken *(Gallus)*, 8,000 y.a.
Millet *(Setaria)*, 9,000 y.a.
Orange *(Citrus)*, 2,000 y.a.
Peach *(Prunus)*, 6,000 y.a.
Rice *(Oryza)*, 7,000 y.a.
Soybean *(Glycine)*, 3,000 y.a.

Southwest Asia/Near East

Apple *(Malus)*, 3,000 y.a.
Barley *(Hordeum)*, 10,500 y.a.
Cattle *(Bos)*, 9,000 y.a.
Chickpea *(Cicer)*, 8,000 y.a.
Date *(Phoenix)*, 4,500 y.a.
Goat *(Capra)*, 10,500 y.a.
Horse *(Equus)*, 6,000 y.a.
Lentil *(Lens)*, 10,000 y.a.
Pea *(Pisum)*, 8,500 y.a.
Pig *(Sus)*, 9,500 y.a.
Pistachio *(Pistacea)*, ?
Sheep *(Ovis)*, 10,000 y.a.
Wheat *(Triticum)*, 10,500 y.a.

Mediterranean

Asparagus *(Asparagus)*, 2,200 y.a.
Broccoli *(Broccoli)*, 1,900 y.a.
Cabbage *(Brassica)*, 2,000 y.a.
Grape *(Vitus)*, 6,000 y.a.

Lettuce *(Lactuca)*, 6,500 y.a.
Olive *(Olea)*, 5,000 y.a.
Pear *(Pyrus)*, 2,500 y.a.
Rabbit *(Oryctolagus)*, 3,000 y.a.

Africa

Coffee *(Coffea)*, ?
Millet *(Pennisetum)*, 4,000 y.a.
Muskmelon *(Cucumis)*, 5,000 y.a.
Sorghum *(Sorghum)*, 4,500 y.a.
Watermelon *(Citrullus)*, 4,000 y.a.
Yam *(Dioscorea)*, ?

North America

Goosefoot *(Chenopodium)*, 3,000 y.a.
Gourd *(Cucurbita)*, 5,000 y.a.
Marsh elder *(Iva)*, 3,000 y.a.
Sunflower *(Helianthus)*, 3,000 y.a.

Mexico/Central America

Amaranth *(Amaranthus)*, 6,000 y.a.
Avocado *(Persea)*, 2,500 y.a.
Cacao *(Theobroma)*, 1,500 y.a.
Chili pepper *(Capsicum)*, 5,500 y.a.
Common bean *(Phaseolus)*, 7,000 y.a.
Maize *(Zea mays)*, 4,500 y.a.
Squash *(Cucurbita)*, 7,500 y.a.
Tomato *(Lycopersicon)*, ?
Turkey *(Agriocharis)*, 2,300 y.a.

South America

Cashew *(Anacardium)*, ?
Chili pepper *(Capsicum)*, 4,500 y.a.
Coca *(Erythroxylon)*, ?
Guinea pig *(Cavia)*, 4,000 y.a.
Lima bean *(Phaseolus)*, 7,000 y.a.
Llama *(Lama)*, 7,000 y.a.
Manioc *(Manihot)*, 4,200 y.a.
Muscovy duck *(Cairina)*, 3,000 y.a.
Papaya *(Carica)*, ?
Peanut *(Arachis)*, 4,000 y.a.
Pineapple *(Ananas)*, ?
Potato *(Solanum)*, 4,000 y.a.
Quinoa *(Chenopodium)*, 3,500 y.a.
Sweet potato *(Ipomoea)*, 4,500 y.a.
Tobacco *(Nicotiana)*, ?

Sources:
Harlan, Jack R. 1992. *Crops and Man.* 2nd ed. Madison, WI: American Society of Agronomy/Crop Science Society of America.
Roaf, Michael. 1996. *Cultural Atlas of Mesopotamia and the Ancient Near East.* New York: Facts on File.
Sauer, Jonathan D. 1994. *Historical Geography of Crop Plants: A Selected Roster.* Boca Raton, FL: CRC Press.

productive varieties of maize reached that area. The prehistoric yam cultivators of sub-Saharan Africa serve as a similar example.

In most regions, a fully developed Neolithic phase did not begin until people were exploiting a mosaic of plants (and sometimes animals, too) from different locations, brought together in various combinations to meet several cultural requirements: nutrition, palatability, hardiness, yield, processing, and storage. Thus, in the Near East, an agricultural complex consisting of wheat, barley, sheep, and goats proved to be an irresistible alternative to foraging and was adopted widely and rapidly after about 10,000 y.a.

Plants

In most of the areas where agriculture emerged, early farmers relied on local plant species whose wild relatives grew close by. Old World cereal grasses, including barley and some varieties of wheat, were native throughout the Near East and perhaps into southeastern Europe (Dennell, 1983). Wild varieties of these plants still flourish today over parts of this range. Therefore, barley or wheat domestication could have occurred in any part of this region, possibly more than once. Such is also the case with maize and beans in Mexico. Thus, we conclude that domestication and agriculture were likely "invented" independently in a number of regions.

It may be possible to explain these separate but parallel processes from a cultural and ecological perspective. We have already seen that certain kinds of wild plants were more likely than others to become domesticated. Many of these species tend to grow in regions where a very long dry season follows a short wet period (Harlan, 1992). After the last ice age, around 10,000 y.a., these conditions pertained around the Mediterranean basin and the hilly areas of the Near East and in the dry forests and savanna grasslands of portions of sub-Saharan Africa, India, southern California, southern Mexico, and eastern and western South America.

Documenting the actual domestication of individual species is greatly impeded by the low survival rate of archaeobotanical evidence. To date, the best archaeological data on the shift toward food production have come from sites located in arid regions of both hemispheres, where organic remains are most often available. Did the initial steps toward farming really take place in such seemingly marginal agricultural situations, or are dry areas merely better environments for preservation? Many researchers remain convinced that most of our significant food plants originated in the dry temperate environments and that their domestication probably occurred there also. Not all archaeobotanists agree, arguing instead that early domesticated forms may have been introduced from other, more humid environments, where preservation is poor and research has been limited.

Advances in archaeobotanical research are forcing significant revisions in our theories of early farming. Although most plant materials (even those not consumed by people or animals) are fragile and subject to rapid decay, ancient plant remains are at times recovered from archaeological contexts, even in unlikely environments. Today's excavators more carefully sample cultural features in search of *ecofacts* (see Chapter 14). *Flotation* techniques are used to separate and recover the smallest bits of organic material from filled pits and other features (see Box 16–2). Actual seeds or other identifiable plant parts (stems, cobs, rinds, hulls) are preserved occasionally by charring or carbonization or by being buried in waterlogged sites. Rarely, the impressions of individual grains that once adhered to wet plaster, mud brick, or pottery surfaces may remain. Microscopic **pollen** and *phytoliths* (see p. 351) can survive even where seeds and other plant parts do not, at times preserved as residues on the cutting edges of ancient stone tools, inside pottery containers, and among other debris in refuse pits (Piperno, 1988; Traverse, 1988). Likewise, starch grains, fats, and amino acids may remain on the surfaces of scrapers, bowls, smoking pipes, kettles, and the like. No wonder archaeologists are becoming reluctant to clean artifacts just removed from the ground!

Studies of such microbotanical traces in Panama and elsewhere south of Mexico have begun to alter our perception of New World domestication (Piperno

Pollen
Microscopic male gametes produced by flowering plants.

BOX 16-2   DIGGING DEEPER

What Archaeologists Can Learn from Dead Plants

Archaeologists have come to recognize that evidence once overlooked can open new vistas on the past. Despite their relative rarity, small size, fragility, and perishability, plant remains occasionally show up around ancient dwelling sites. Usually they are found in a carbonized state, the result of being burned in a garbage pit or house or granary fire or simply overcooked (Fig. 1). More rarely, uncharred plant parts may be preserved in extremely arid environments, such as deserts or Egyptian tombs. To recover and study these materials requires specialized procedures and knowledge. *Archaeobotany* is a cross-disciplinary study practiced by a growing number of specialists.

The most effective way to extract delicate carbonized plant remains from features such as pits or refuse heaps is to process the excavated soil by *flotation*. In this procedure, a quantity of excavated material is dumped into a container of water and agitated briefly, separating the heavier particles of rock and soil from the lighter organic fragments, such as charcoal, which rise to the surface. These organic fragments are skimmed off, allowed to dry, and then examined under a microscope. Separating and identifying minute fragments of ancient carbonized plants is a most tedious task, but archaeobotanists are making important contributions to our understanding of early farming.

Recognizing which plant species may be represented by charred fragments is yet another challenge. Even with well-preserved grains, distinguishing among the several types of cereals grown in the Near East or Egypt can be frustrating. Researchers are making progress in using DNA analyses and other chemical tests to identify individual species from archaeological sources.

Ancient agricultural practices may be revealed through the careful study of plant remains. Of course, these preserved materials offer the most direct evidence for the location of farming areas and the precise nature of the crops being harvested. But they also provide insights of other kinds. For example, the presence of perennial and biennial weed seeds in an ancient agricultural context suggests that each year's farming activities only minimally disturbed the soil; perhaps a digging stick, hoe, or simple scratch plow was used. If, on the other hand, seeds of annual weeds predominate, the use of a mold board plow (one that turns over the soil as it cuts through) may be indicated.

Working with such subtle and fragmentary evidence, archaeobotanical sleuths are also uncovering

clues to the later steps of harvesting, processing, storage, and use of plant foods by ancient cultures. Harvesting techniques also produce distinctive kinds of archaeobotanical evidence. If, for instance, cereal grasses were harvested selectively by plucking the ears or beating the seedheads, then there should be little evidence of stems or stalks or other extraneous material in archaeological contexts. Most often, however, crops were cut with sickles or even uprooted and then processed. These techniques produced a wider range of plant parts. Pulling plants up from the roots or cutting them off close to the base of the stalk yields stems and leaves that later must be separated from the seeds and then used either as animal forage or bedding or simply discarded. Moreover, these less discriminate harvesting methods inadvertently picked up elements of weed plants that grew in the fields alongside the crops. Thus, the presence of seeds or stems of certain low-growing weedy plants (such as knotweed, or *Polygonum*) indicates that the crop was gathered close to the ground. Alternatively, crops cut "high on the straw" would be mixed only with top parts of tall free-standing weeds (such as cockle, or *Agrostemma*). A high percentage of weed contamination in archaeobotanical samples from ancient Egypt implies that their grain fields were infested with competing plant species. However, "weeds" do reduce soil erosion and water loss and may be used later as fuel or livestock fodder, so perhaps the Egyptians intentionally left them undisturbed.

Reprinted by permission from "Use of Barley in the Egyptian Late Paleolithic," by F. Wendorf, et al., from *Science*, vol. 205, pp. 1,341–1,347, September 1979. Copyright September 1979 by the American Association for the Advancement of Science.

FIGURE 1
Carbonized grain of domesticated barley from the Nile valley.

Sources:

Hillman, Gordon. 1981. "Reconstructing Crop Husbandry Practices from Charred Remains of Crops," in *Farming Practice in British Prehistory*, Roger Mercer, ed., pp. 123–163. Edinburgh: Edinburgh University Press.

Murray, Mary Anne. 1998. "Cereal Production and Processing," in *Ancient Egyptian Materials and Technologies*, Paul T. Nicholson and Ian Shaw, eds. New York: Cambridge University Press.

Pearsall, Deborah M. 2000. *Paleoethnobotany: A Handbook of Procedures*. 2nd ed. San Diego, CA: Academic Press.

Van Zeist, W., and W. A. Casparie (eds.). 1988. *Plants and Ancient Man: Studies in Palaeoethnobotany*. Rotterdam, Netherlands: Balkema.

Manioc
Cassava, a starchy edible root crop of the tropics.

Tehuacán Valley
(tay-wah-kahn') A dry highland region on the boundary of the states of Puebla and Oaxaca in southern Mexico.

and Pearsall, 1998). They reveal that root crops like **manioc** (*Manihot* sp., also known as cassava) and other tubers were important in the diet of early tropical farmers well before seed crops like maize arrived on the scene. These studies also indicate that primitive varieties of maize, and probably beans as well, were introduced here long before they reached highland areas, like Mexico's dry **Tehuacán Valley**, where macrobotanical remains are most commonly encountered.

As we saw in Chapter 9, some domesticated species leave biochemical traces in those who consume them. Because plants of temperate and tropical regions evolved with slightly different processes for photosynthesis, their chemical compositions vary in the ratio of carbon-13 to "ordinary" carbon-12. This distinctive chemical profile gets passed along the food chain, and the bones of the human skeleton may provide evidence of dietary change. For example, their lower ^{13}C levels reveal that females at Grasshopper Pueblo, in east-central Arizona, consumed mostly the local plants they gathered, while their male relatives at first enjoyed more maize, a plant higher in ^{13}C. Later, maize became a staple in everyone's diet at Grasshopper, resulting in equivalent carbon isotopes in males and females (Ezzo, 1993).

Other biochemical analyses, using different elemental isotopes, have been devised to assess overall diet—not necessarily just the domesticated portions—from individual skeletons. (One drawback of performing these tests is that they destroy part of the specimen.) A higher ratio of nitrogen-15 to nitrogen-14 (^{15}N/^{14}N), for instance, corresponds to a greater seafood component (Schoeninger et al., 1983); and a higher strontium-to-calcium (Sr/Ca) ratio reflects the larger contribution of plant foods versus meat in the diet (Schoeninger, 1981). Other chemicals taken up by bones may inform us about ancient lifeways. For example, lead is a trace element found in unusually high concentration in Romans who drank wine stored in lead containers. The interplay among culture and diet and biology is, of course, a prime example of biocultural evolution. But to put it more simply, "You are what you eat."

Nonhuman Animals

The process of animal domestication differed from plant domestication to a degree and probably varied even from one faunal species to another. For example, the dog appears to have been the first domesticated animal, and wolflike canids may have accompanied even late Ice Age hunters (Olsen, 1985). The dog's relationship with humans differed (and still does) from that of most subsequently domesticated species. Valued less for its meat or hide, its primary role was most likely as a ferocious hunting weapon under at least a modicum of human control and direction. As other animals were domesticated, the dog's behavior had to be modified still further for service as a herder and later as an occasional transporter of possessions (in the Arctic and among the American Plains Indians). But the burial of a puppy with a Natufian person who died some 10,000 y.a. in the Near East suggests that dogs may have earned a role as pets very early (Davis and Valla, 1978).

Most other domesticated animals were maintained solely for their meat at first. Richard J. Harrison's (1985) insightful analysis of faunal collections from Neolithic sites in Spain and Portugal concluded that meat remained the primary product up until about 4,000 y.a., when subsequent changes in herd composition (age and sex ratios), slaughter patterns, and popularity of certain breeds all point to new uses for some livestock. Oxen pulled plows, horses provided transport, cattle and goats contributed milk products, and sheep were raised for wool. Animal waste became fertilizer in agricultural areas. Leather, horn, and bone—and even social status for the animals' owners—were other valued by-products. (In much the same way, recent East African cattle herders appreciate their animals as much more than packages of beefsteak, for a sizable herd testifies to a man's standing and may be used to fulfill social obligations such as bridewealth payments.)

Of course, animals are more mobile than plants and no less mobile than the early people pursuing them. Therefore, it is unlikely that hunters could have promoted useful genetic changes in wild animals merely by trying to restrict their movements or by selective hunting alone. Perhaps, by simultaneously destroying wild predators and reducing the number of competing herbivores, humans became surrogate protectors of the herds, though this arrangement would not have had the genetic impact of actual domestication.

Animals such as gazelle or reindeer might be managed to a degree in the wild state, possibly by establishing a "rapport" with the herds and encouraging them to graze in cleared areas in the winter or by restricting hunting activities to a few quick raids, during which the herd might be selectively harvested or thinned. Culling out all nonbreeding males, for example, would not limit the potential for herd expansion, nor would it much affect the population genetics. Epipaleolithic Natufians in the Near East were once thought to have managed wild gazelle in this manner (Legge, 1972), but reexamination of the faunal remains casts their gazelle hunting in a very different light, implying the use of large-scale surrounds or ambush techniques to nonselectively kill entire herds at once (Legge and Rowley-Conwy, 1987). This drastic approach would suppress the animal population for years. Obviously, true domestication, involving further genetic changes, must have been reached by other steps.

We once again emphasize that domestication is not an event, but a process. As such, it is nearly impossible to say precisely when a plant or animal species has been domesticated, for the process involves much more than an indication of "tameness" in the presence of humans. More significant are the changes in allele frequencies that result from selective breeding and isolation from wild relatives. People perhaps began with young animals spared by hunters for that purpose or, in the case of large and dangerous species such as the ancestral aurochs cattle, individuals of exceptional docility or smaller size (Fagan, 1993). Maintained in captivity, these animals could be selectively bred for desirable traits, such as more meat, fat, wool, or strength. (Captive animals not suitable for breeding represented meat on the hoof, a convenient method of storing food against spoilage or future want.) Once early farmers were consistently selecting breeding stock according to some criteria and succeeding in perpetuating those characteristics through subsequent generations, then domestication (i.e., evolution) clearly had occurred.

Overall, not many wild mammal species attained domestication. Those most amenable to domestication are animals that form hierarchical herds, are not prone to flee on the least provocation, and are not strongly territorial (Diamond, 1989). In other words, animals who will tolerate and transfer their allegiance to human surrogates make the best potential domesticates. A number of large Eurasian mammals met these specifications, allowing cultures of Asia, Europe, and Africa to rely on sheep and goats, pigs, cattle, and horses (listed here in approximately their order of domestication), as well as water buffalo, camels, reindeer, and a few other regionally significant species (see Box 16–1 on p. 417).

Even fewer New World herd animals were capable of being domesticated. Aside from two South American camelids—the llama and the alpaca—no large American mammal was brought fully under human control (Fig. 16–4). Dogs had probably accompanied the first people into the New World. Other domesticates—the guinea pig and Muscovy duck in western South America, turkeys in Mexico—were small in size and of minor importance beyond their localized distribution areas. None of these animals was suitable for transporting or pulling heavy loads (llamas balk at carrying more than about 100 pounds, and Plains Indian dogs dragged only small bundles), so the people of the New World continued to bear their own burdens, till their fields by hand, and hunt and fight on foot until the introduction of the Old World's livestock in the 1500s.

FIGURE 16–4
Peoples of highland South America bred the llama primarily as a source of wool and, to a limited extent, to transport loads.

William Turnbaugh

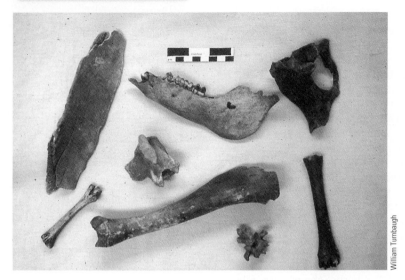

William Turnbaugh

FIGURE 16–5
Faunal remains of domesticated cattle, pigs, and fowl from an archaeological site.

Archaeological evidence of nonhuman animal domestication is subtle and difficult to assess from the bones themselves (Fig. 16–5). For most species, no significant increase in body size occurred, and early domesticated cattle, sheep, and goats are actually smaller than their wild relatives. Osteological comparisons between wild and domestic members of the same species disclose only relatively minor differences in skeletal morphology (Herre, 1969). For example, the bony horn cores of domestic goats display a somewhat flattened cross section when compared with their wild antecedents, and domesticated pigs exhibit a shortening of the maxilla in relation to the mandible.

Archaeozoologists also examine changes in prehistoric herd demography to document domestication. The population curve for animals randomly hunted from a wild herd tends to reflect a normal distribution that approximates the overall age and sex ratio of the herd. On the other hand, a notable increase in the number of skeletal elements of, say, young adult rams found in kitchen refuse may indicate that humans were selecting those particular animals for slaughter while reserving most females and lambs for breeding purposes (Bokonyi, 1969). Such indicators are seldom definitive, however, unless very large samples of faunal remains confirm domestication.

Agricultural Societies of the Old World

As noted, independent invention best accounts for the diversity of domesticates and the distinctiveness of Neolithic lifeways in the Far East, Southeast Asia, India, sub-Saharan Africa, the Near East, and the Americas. Moreover, we now recognize that many wild species, such as wheat and sheep, probably occupied more extensive natural ranges in the early Holocene and may in fact have undergone local domestication more than a few times.

However, the *diffusion*, or spread, of Neolithic lifeways from place to place cannot be discounted entirely. As we shall see, in at least some areas—southeastern Europe, for example—colonizing farmers appear to have brought their domesticates and their culture with them as they migrated into new territories searching for suitable farmland. Neolithic practices also spread through secondary contact as people on the margins of established farming societies acquired certain traits and passed them along to cultures yet further removed. Seeds and animals often must have become commodities in prehistoric exchange networks, just as did the Spanish horses obtained by Native Americans in the sixteenth century. Perhaps marriage partners from other groups introduced their in-laws to the new ways. We should bear in mind that each archaeological event is unique in its own way. "One-size-fits-all" explanations are rarely adequate, even if the results amount to much the same end product—in this case, the expansion of Neolithic lifeways.

With that point in mind, it is time to consider a sampling of Neolithic societies from around the world to get some idea of the variations on this common theme.

Near Eastern Farmers

Neolithic lifeways and their consequences appeared throughout the Near East and adjacent areas, but not necessarily because farming was a superior way of life. As we saw in Chapter 15, Middle Stone Age hunting and gathering cultures such as the Natufians apparently undertook the first steps, though perhaps inadvertently, toward agriculture in the Near East (Fig. 16–6). At Kebara and El Wad, stone-bladed sickles aided in harvesting the ancestral varieties of wheat and barley, wild grasses

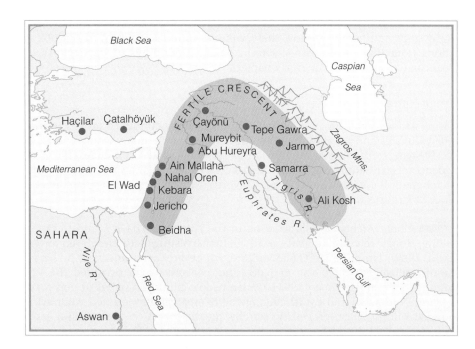

FIGURE 16–6
Early Neolithic sites of the Fertile Crescent.

native to the region (Henry, 1989). This technique, more efficient than plucking seeds by hand, netted greater yields during a short harvest period and so encouraged a dependency on grains that could be stored conveniently for weeks or months. The process of genetic selection that we have considered as the basis for plant domestication must have been well under way by this time.

The Natufians adopted farming to augment food supplies for their rapidly growing population at a time when natural subsistence resources were again in decline. The warming trends that initially had created optimal conditions for upland cereal and nut crops continued for several more centuries, leaving much of the Levant parched (Henry, 1989). Natufians then abandoned many upland sites, retreating to the lower stream valleys. There, in an effort to replicate the once-productive natural environments of the highlands, some groups established new stands of cereal grasses by dispersing seeds in favorable areas along the streams near their villages (Bar-Yosef, 1998). Thus, in this case at least, it appears that stresses associated with a destabilized population/resource balance stimulated the agricultural response.

These food collectors and earliest farmers established the first permanent sedentary communities in the Near East. Drawn by an ever-flowing spring in an otherwise arid region, settlers at a site known today as Jericho, near the biblical city of that name in the lower Jordan River valley, and at other Natufian sites, such as Ain Mallaha and Nahal Oren, in Israel, built their round stone or mud-brick houses some 11,500 y.a. Though of more substantial materials, in form these structures closely resembled the temporary huts of the region's earlier hunters and gatherers. Numerous grinding stones and clay-lined pits testify to the significance of cereal grains (Moore, 1985; Bar-Yosef, 1987). Still, the seeds of wild cereals, fruits, nuts, and the meat of wild game long remained an important component of the diet.

By some 9,000 y.a., sedentary villagers across a broad arc from the Red Sea to western Iran (sometimes known as the Fertile Crescent) engaged in wheat and barley agriculture and sheep and goat herding. Among these communities were Abu Hureyra and Mureybit, in Syria, and Ali Kosh on the Deh Luran plain of Iran (Hole et al., 1969; Moore, 1985). There, Neolithic families resided in adjacent multiroom rectangular houses, in contrast to the compounds of individual small, round shelters commonly built by Epipaleolithic collectors and the early Jericho settlers. Flannery (1972) believes that this change in residence pattern signals a shift toward

more economically and socially cohesive communities. Comprised of extended-family and multifamily groups, these villagers differed radically in outlook and actions from their predecessors. Herein lie the beginnings of the region's later urbanism (considered in the next chapter).

African Farmers

Tracing Africa's Neolithic past is challenging, given the continent's vast size and its varied climates and vegetation zones. Moreover, because many tropical foods lack woody stems or durable seeds, they are poorly represented at archaeological sites; evidence of agriculture based on these kinds of products awaits more intensive microbotanical studies. Arid sections of North Africa have yielded some direct evidence of farming and herding.

Northern Africa Archaeologists working in the Nile valley have found sickles and milling stones relating to early wild grain–harvesting activities (Wendorf and Schild, 1989). The so-called Qadan culture, whose sites are found near present-day Aswan, probably typified the Epipaleolithic collectors who occupied the valley around 8,000 y.a. (Hoffman, 1991). Qadan people employed spears or nets for taking large Nile perch and catfish. Along the riverbanks they hunted wildfowl and gathered wild produce, processing starchy aquatic tubers on their milling stones. They also stalked the adjacent grasslands for gazelle and other game and may have begun the process of domesticating wild cattle (Wendorf and Schild, 1994). Given the wealth of naturally occurring resources along the Nile, this foraging and collecting way of life might have continued indefinitely. So why did farming develop here at all?

Geologists and paleoecologists recognize that shifting rainfall patterns have affected North Africa since the late Pleistocene. Long-term cycles brought increased precipitation, which broadened the Nile and its valley and gave the river a predictable seasonal rhythm. Rains falling on its tropical headwaters, thousands of miles to the south, caused the river to overflow its downstream channels by late summer, flooding the low-lying basins of northern Egypt for about three months annually. Although desiccation followed, the flood-deposited silt grew lush with wild grasses through the following season. Periodically, however, extended drought episodes intervened to narrow the river's life-giving flow.

The expansive area west of the Nile, known today as the Sahara, was particularly susceptible to these fluctuations. The Sahara was a fragile environment, always marginal for humans. Down to 11,000 y.a., this arid region was uninviting even to hunters and gatherers. Then, a period of increased rainfall created shallow lakes and streams that nurtured the grasslands, attracting game animals and humans. Between 8,800 and 7,700 y.a., a diversified hunting, fishing, and foraging existence in the Sahara was interrupted by several dry periods, after which rainfall again increased somewhat. Still, conditions for subsistence remained marginal. By about 7,000 y.a., people in the Sahara devised a strategy of nomadic pastoralism, allowing their herds of sheep, goats, and possibly cattle to act as ecological intermediaries by converting tough grasses into meat and by-products useful to humans (Wendorf and Schild, 1994). Shortly thereafter, around 6,000 y.a., further deterioration of the region's climate, and possibly overgrazing, forced the herders and their animals to seek greener pastures closer to the river (Williams, 1984; Harlan, 1992; A. Smith, 1992).

As drought parched the adjacent areas, the narrowing Nile valley attracted more settlers. Wild resources were now insufficient to feed the growing sedentary population, and even the local domesticates that had been casually cultivated on the floodplain gave way to more productive cereals—the domesticated wheat and barley that had been brought under human control elsewhere by people like the Natufians.

Farmers gradually made the river's rhythm their own. Communities of reed-mat or mud-brick houses appeared across the Nile delta and along its banks. Basket-lined storage pits or granaries, milling stones, and sickles indicate a heavy reliance

FIGURE 16–7
Pearl millet, one of several varieties of millet grown in Africa and Asia.

U.S. Department of Agriculture

on grain. Pottery vessels of river clay, linen woven from flax fibers, flint tools, and occasional hammered copper items were produced locally. These ordinary Neolithic beginnings laid the foundation for the remarkable Egyptian civilization, to be considered in Chapter 17.

Outside the Nile valley, cattle herding took priority over farming in much of East Africa, where conditions were generally not suitable for cultivation.

Sub-Saharan Africa Limited evidence from archaeology and linguistic studies hints that hunters and gatherers in several other parts of Africa experimented with local **cultivars**. For example, mobile foragers and semisedentary fishers of tropical Africa practiced yam horticulture in clearings and along river margins by at least 5,000 y.a. (Clark, 1976; Ehret, 1984). The starchy wild tubers were pried out with digging sticks and carried away for cooking. As an added bonus, if the leafy tops or cuttings of the largest roots were pressed into the soil at the edge of the camp clearing, the yams would regenerate into an informal garden.

In these tropical regions, the standard Near Eastern cereals tended to rot, so African farmers developed comparable domesticates from local cereal grasses, including local varieties of **millet** (Fig. 16–7) and **sorghum**, which they successfully grew along the margins of the rain forest and the savanna grasslands (Sauer, 1994).

More dramatic shifts in sub-Saharan subsistence followed the introduction and spread of different Neolithic crops. Tropical plants from Southeast Asia reached Africa with Polynesian voyagers crossing the Indian Ocean to Madagascar about 2,000 y.a. (Murdock, 1959; Harlan, 1992). These new products spread quickly to the interior, where people throughout the rain forest zone adopted bananas, **taro**, and Asian yams. Bantu-speaking peoples, native to west-central Africa, relied on these productive new crops to support their rapid expansion through central and southern Africa (Phillipson, 1984). Driving herds of domestic goats and cattle and acquiring the technology of ironworking as they moved southeastward through central Africa (Van Noten and Raymaekers, 1987), the Bantu easily overwhelmed most hunting and gathering groups. With iron tools and weapons, they carved out gardens and maintained large semipermanent villages, and today, their numerous descendants live in eastern, southern, and southwestern Africa (Fig. 16–8).

Asian Farmers

Several centers of domestication in southern and eastern Asia gave rise to separate Neolithic traditions based on the propagation of productive local plant and animal species. The exploitation of these resources spread widely and in turn heralded further economic and social changes associated with the rise of early civilizations in these regions (see Chapter 17).

Southern Asia Excavations at **Mehrgarh** in central Pakistan have illuminated Neolithic beginnings on the Indian subcontinent (Jarrige and Meadow, 1980; Allchin and Allchin, 1982). Located at the edge of a high plain west of the broad Indus valley (Fig. 16–9), the site's lower levels, dating between 8,000 and 6,000 y.a., reveal the trend toward dietary specialization that accompanied the domestication of local plant and animal species. Early on, both wild and domesticated varieties of barley and wheat were harvested, among other native plants. Mehrgarh's archaeological deposits also include bones of many local herbivores: water buffalo, gazelle, swamp deer, goats, sheep, pigs, cattle, and even elephants.

By 6,000 y.a., the cultivated cereals prevailed, along with just three animal species—domestic sheep, goats, and cattle. Researchers believe that this early Neolithic phase at Mehrgarh represents a transition from seminomadic herding to a more sedentary existence that became the basis for later urban development in the Indus valley. Other planned settlements boasting multiroom mud-brick dwellings and granaries soon appeared in the region, supported by a productive agriculture and bustling trade in copper, turquoise, shells, and cotton.

Cultivars
Wild plants fostered by human efforts to make them more productive.

Millet
Small-grained cereal grass native to Asia and Africa.

Sorghum
Cereal grass with a sweet juicy stalk.

Taro
Species of tropical plant with an edible starchy root.

FIGURE 16–8
Bantu expansion in Africa.

Mehrgarh
(may-er-gar') One of the earliest Neolithic settlements of southern Asia.

China Far to the east, village farmers of the Peiligang culture in northern China's central Huanghe (Yellow River) valley were already cultivating local varieties of millet by perhaps 9,000 y.a. (Chang, 1986; Barnes, 1992). River terrace deposits of deep **loess** soil ensured large yields and undoubtedly contributed to the growth of populous settlements during this and the succeeding Yangshao farming period around 2,000 years later (7,000 y.a.). Millet farming continued to be supplemented with domestic pigs and chickens and a variety of wild plants, fish, and animals. At the site of Ban Po, more than 100 pit houses centered around a plaza and its communal house (see Fig. 16–9). Cemeteries and pottery kilns typically adjoined the residential portion of Yangshao villages. Jade carving, painted ceramics of tripod form, silkworm cultivation, and elite burials anticipated some of the hallmarks of the later Neolithic, or Longshan, period (beginning 4,700 y.a.).

In warmer and wetter central and southern China, rice agriculture supported substantial permanent villages, especially along the Yangzi River. Researchers now believe that food collectors were gathering this productive grain in southern China more than 11,000 y.a. and that it was being grown in the Yangzi delta by 8,500 y.a. (Normille, 1997; Crawford and Shen, 1998). Cultivators introduced rice into Southeast Asia over the next several thousand years, bringing settled village life and domesticated cattle, pigs, and dogs to locations such as Ban Chiang and Non Nok Tha. High yields and the varied conditions under which rice could be grown made it the basis for sustained population growth in many parts of this region (Higham and Lu, 1998).

European Farmers

Farmers in southeastern Europe already were tilling the Balkan Peninsula by about 8,000 y.a. at Argissa and Nea Nikomedeia, both in Greece (Fig. 16–10). Most archaeologists propose that these initial farming cultures of southeastern Europe were established by colonists filtering in from the Near East and that agriculture was *adopted* rather than invented in Europe (Whittle, 1985). This diffusionist view accounts for the seemingly sudden appearance of fully domesticated sheep, goats, wheat, and barley in the Balkans, along with a host of specific Near Eastern cultural traits, including structured settlements, burial practices, clay figurines, painted pottery, and specific flaked stone forms (Tringham, 1971). Cultivated cereals and domesticated animals were in use from Turkey to Iraq at least a millenium earlier

Loess

(luss) Fine-grained soil composed of glacially pulverized rock, deposited by the wind.

FIGURE 16–9
Early farming in Asia.

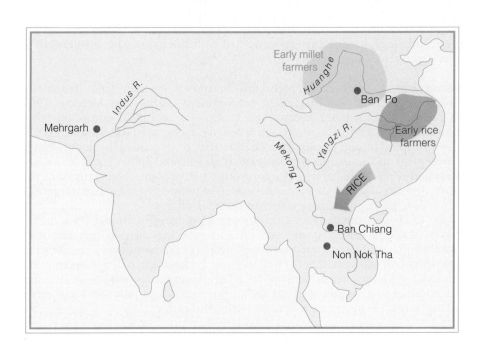

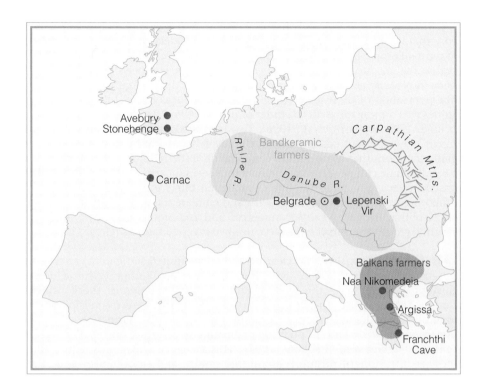

FIGURE 16–10
Early Neolithic sites of Europe.

than in Europe, and compact clusters of houses typified the Near Eastern agricultural communities long before similar settlements showed up in the Balkans alongside the other traits associated with early farming. In sum, many European cultural elements could be interpreted as extensions of Near Eastern Neolithic culture.

Still, not everyone agrees that the earliest European agriculture derived from southwest Asia. European sites such as Franchthi Cave, in Greece, and Lepenski Vir, on the Danube in present-day Serbia, provide evidence that people in these areas may have been moving independently toward food production by concentrating on local cereal grasses, legumes, and large herbivores as early as 10,000 y.a. In fact, the earliest known domesticated cattle found anywhere are at Argissa, in Greece, by 8,000 y.a. and may represent a locally developed species (Whittle, 1985). Dennell (1983), for one, believes that indigenous domestication of local plant and animal species, supplemented later by more productive strains of wheat obtained through exchange, transformed native societies in southeastern Europe with *no* influx of colonists from the Near East or elsewhere. The origin of Europe's first farmers remains an unresolved question.

Neolithic lifeways transformed other parts of Europe somewhat later than in the Balkans, and the source of these changes has also generated debate. Beginning around 7,000 y.a., farming village sites littered with linear-decorated pottery, or **bandkeramic** (Fig. 16–11), appeared across central and (still later) northern regions of the continent (Bogucki, 1988). Bandkeramic culture farmers sought deep, well-drained **alluvial** and loess soils located along the Danube, the Rhine, and their tributaries. Here they cultivated cereals and legumes, raised cattle and pigs, and collected wild hazelnuts (Whittle, 1985; Howell, 1987). Their settlements consisted of sturdy timber-framed structures averaging 100 feet (30 m) long, with some up to 150 feet (45 m). These longhouses sheltered extended families and perhaps also served as barns for storing harvested crops or for harboring animals. Wooden fences barred livestock from planted fields during the growing season, then, following the harvest, confined them in the field so that their manure could restore soil nutrients. The fertility of loess soils could be maintained for relatively long periods with simple manuring and crop rotation, and fixed-plot farming on rich alluvium could sustain permanent settlements for up to 500 years (Whittle, 1985; Howell, 1987).

FIGURE 16–11
Bandkeramic jar.

Bandkeramic
Literally, "lined pottery," referring to a Neolithic ceramic ware widely encountered in central Europe and to the culture that produced it.

Alluvial
Deposited by streams, usually during flood stages.

Food Production: A Biocultural Revolution

Geneticists have analyzed modern human DNA evidence to investigate the theory that the Bandkeramic culture represented outsiders who brought agriculture into central Europe. Bryan Sykes and his team interpret mtDNA comparisons to suggest that the ancestors of most northern and western European populations were already in place by about 13,000 y.a., near the end of the Ice Age. About 20 percent of the population of these areas share mtDNA sequences that exhibit Near Eastern affinities that appear to be on the order of just 6,000 to 10,000 years old (Powledge and Rose, 1996; Richards et al., 1996). Two identified mtDNA clusters within this segment may represent descendants of the distinctive early Neolithic ceramic and farming traditions that characterized central and southern Europe, one of which was the Bandkeramic culture. The mtDNA data thus seem most consistent with a limited migration scenario: A small Neolithic population filters into a region, whereupon neighboring peoples soon exchange with and emulate them, until all are sharing a basic Neolithic lifeway. Neolithic resources and techniques may then diffuse to Mesolithic groups in contact with these newly converted farmers (Gregg, 1988).

Megalith Makers   Extensive land clearing and concentrated settlements after 6,000 y.a. heralded the expansion of agriculture into western Europe (Whittle, 1985). Prehistoric farmers along the western and northern margins of the continent, including Spain, France, the British Isles, and Denmark, were responsible for an intriguing archaeological enigma. Communities of Neolithic farmers pooled their energies to erect thousands of puzzling prehistoric structures known collectively as **megaliths** (Service and Bradbery, 1997). This category encompasses individual stones set into upright position, megalithic tombs, and stone circles and alignments, including such famous and complex formations as Stonehenge and Avebury, in England, and Carnac, in France (Figs. 16–12 and 16–13).

Although speculation on the meaning of the megaliths abounds (Chippindale, 1994), one recurring notion identifies many megaliths as astronomical observatories used by ancient priests to accurately predict solstices and eclipses. Most archaeologists remain skeptical of these explanations, but agree that the monuments must have been inspired by some type of religious fervor or social initiative.

Burial chambers or tombs, constructed of earth and sometimes covering stone-built crypts, were raised during the earliest phases of the megalith-building era, beginning more than 6,000 y.a. and continuing through the next two millennia. Whereas the purpose of the tombs may appear obvious at first glance, their underlying social significance is more subtle. Although the mounds contained collective burials, not everyone was entitled to this special interment. Even the larger structures—up to 265 feet (80 m) in diameter and 50 feet (15 m) high—held relatively few inhumations, some with offerings of pottery and jewelry. Here, then, are indications of social differentiation among the earliest farmers of western Europe.

Why were these special and very conspicuous burial chambers erected? Certainly, their construction required the concerted effort of many cooperating individuals, and no doubt, the project would be directed by someone of authority. Again, we see evidence of social complexity. Perhaps the resulting mound became a prominent focal point for the people who erected it, a monument to the lineage buried within it. Possibly the structure served as a permanent marker of that group's territory. Howell (1987) senses an increasing regionalization and competition in the megalith-building era. He notes that villages were established in more defensible locations and their occupants sought protec-

Megaliths
(*mega*, meaning "large," and *lith*, meaning "stone") Monumental structures made of very large stones, characteristic of western Europe during the early Neolithic.

FIGURE 16–12
Stonehenge was built in several stages between 4,800 and 3,300 y.a.

George Gerster/Photo Researchers, Inc.

Harry Nelson

FIGURE 16–13
Some of Stonehenge's *trilithon* ("three-stone") units remain standing. The large uprights weigh up to 40 tons (36,000 kg).

tion behind heavy wooden palisades, some of which exhibit attack scars. With the best farmlands already occupied, population pressure and/or climatic deterioration would have made conflict over resources inevitable.

During the course of the Neolithic period in western Europe, down to about 4,000 y.a., megalithic constructions of increasing size and complexity dotted the landscape. Colin Renfrew (1983), studying megaliths in southern England, calculated that a typical burial mound of early Neolithic times required the effort of perhaps 20 people working for 50 days. Clusters of these tombs in a given area most often seem to be associated, in turn, with a large circular earthwork enclosure, perhaps a central gathering place for people from several local communities. Digging the concentric ditches and raising the surrounding embankments for these central monuments consumed an estimated 100,000 hours of labor, enough to keep 250 people busy for 40 days. Perhaps the work was undertaken during the fallow season, when farmers were able to leave their fields.

More impressive yet, megalithic projects of even grander scale marked the later Neolithic period. Renfrew figured that the most ambitious monuments, such as Stonehenge, represent tens of millions of hours of labor expended during periodic construction phases over the course of centuries. Some of these activities involved transporting enormous stones over substantial distances by land and sea. Despite long interest in them, the enigmatic megaliths have not yet yielded all their secrets.

Early Farmers in the Americas

Whereas Old World Neolithic cultures generally relied on agricultural practices that linked domesticated cereal grasses together with herd animals, the farmers of the Americas focused almost exclusively on plant resources. Most of these plants had very limited ranges, but one important cereal grass—maize, or corn—came to dominate prehistoric Native American agriculture nearly everywhere it could possibly be grown (Fig. 16–14).

Cereal grasses suitable for domestication were abundant on several continents, but the people of the Old World brought more of those species under control. The explanation may be found in the different harvesting techniques practiced by Middle Stone Age gatherers (Wilke et al., 1972). We have seen (see p. 415) that in the Near East (and also in northern Africa and Australia), collectors harvested grasses by cutting the stalks below the seedheads with a reaping knife. Individual plants with nonshattering seedheads (due to their more flexible rachis) tended to be favored in this operation, and as that trait became dominant in the population, the

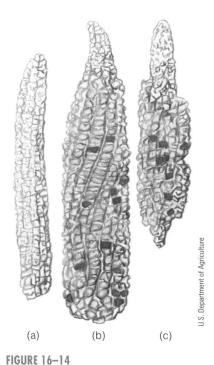

U.S. Department of Agriculture

(a)   (b)   (c)

FIGURE 16–14
Maize, or Indian corn. (a) Cob from prehistoric Arizona site. (b) Ear of nineteenth-century Pueblo Indian corn. (c) Corn from early site in Peru. Length of (b) is 6.75 inches (17 cm).

variety became more dependent on humans to disperse its seeds; in other words, it was domesticated. Native Americans, on the other hand, tended to harvest their wild grasses by beating the seedheads with a stick, loosening the seeds into a collecting basket. Here, readily shattering seedheads remained advantageous, and so the trait persisted and the species "avoided" domestication. With the exception of maize, whose wild ancestor was perhaps at first used in a different manner, human cultural behavior did not induce the same genetic transformations in American grasses as in the Old World.

New World Domesticates

Considered together, the products of New World farmers constitute a remarkable roster of familiar plants. To maize must be added white potatoes, sweet potatoes, yams, manioc, many varieties of beans, peanuts, sunflowers, and **quinoa** (*Chenopodium* sp.) as important staple foods. Supplemental vegetables and fruits included sweet peppers, hot chili peppers, tomatoes, squashes, and pumpkins, along with pineapples, papayas, avocados, guavas, and passion fruit. Vanilla and chocolate came from American tree beans. Tobacco, coca, and peyote were major stimulants, and a host of other American plant domesticates had medicinal, utilitarian, or ornamental uses long before the arrival of the Europeans. The principal New World domesticates were developed in several locations in Mexico and in South America, but the use of a few of these plants eventually spread well beyond those regional centers of domestication.

Aside from the dog, which probably accompanied the first humans across Beringia, domesticated animals had a relatively minor role in the Americas, as noted earlier (see p. 421). The llama and alpaca—long-haired relatives of the camel, found in highland South America, were the only large domesticated species (Kent, 1987). (Remember, horses were by now extinct in the New World, but would be reintroduced to the Americas by early-sixteenth-century Spanish explorers.)

Mexican Farmers

Of the more than 100 New World plant species fully domesticated by the aboriginal peoples of the Americas, maize (a grass), beans (legumes), and squashes (cucurbits) ultimately attained the widest prehistoric significance for food purposes. Ancient use of this important set of crops has been documented in the states of **Oaxaca** and **Tamaulipas**, and especially in the Tehuacán Valley of Puebla, southeast of Mexico City. Archaeologist Richard MacNeish led an exemplary interdisciplinary study in this arid highland valley in the 1960s, where archaeology, botany, and paleoecology shed light on early phases of New World agriculture (Byers, 1967; MacNeish et al., 1972; MacNeish 1978).

Investigators initially hypothesized that Tehuacán was at the very center of domestication, but most now agree that the ancient 2-inch corn cobs from San Marcos Cave represent an intermediate variety of maize developed elsewhere. In fact, the Tehuacán sites lie somewhat beyond the natural range of the variety of wild grass, **teosinte** (*Zea* sp.), that most archaeobotanists consider ancestral to maize (Beadle, 1980; Benz and Iltis, 1990; Piperno and Pearsall, 1998). Its source area was probably somewhere in the humid lowlands of southern or western Mexico, where teosinte and wild beans flourish even today.

Teosinte, which bears a few hard seed kernels on tiny "spikelets" growing from its multiple stalks, was probably just one of many wild plants that attracted local food collectors. Its young, green seeds were sweet and edible, as were the tender stems; mature seeds could either be ground or "popped" with heat and eaten. To promote teosinte, people may have scattered its seeds, transplanted young stalks to favorable locations, or reduced competition from other less desirable plants by burning or "weeding." Doing so may have inadvertently altered the genetic makeup of the plants by allowing them to cross-pollinate with other varieties.

Quinoa
(keen-wah') Seed-bearing member of the genus *Chenopodium*, cultivated by early Peruvians.

Oaxaca
(wah-ha'-kah) A southern Mexican state bordering the Pacific Ocean.

Tamaulipas
(tah-mah-leep'-ahs) A Mexican state located on the Gulf Coast south of Texas.

Teosinte
A native grass of southern Mexico, believed to be ancestral to maize.

DNA studies suggest that very few genetic loci control the features that distinguish teosinte from domestic maize (Doebley, 1994). Mutation of teosinte produced a variant having softer naked kernels arranged around a spike or cob encased in a single papery husk. Further artificial (human-induced) selection favored these heritable genetic changes, which became "fixed" when people carried the new varieties beyond teosinte's natural range, perhaps to Tehuacán. Thus resulted the first in a series of domesticated forms of maize, a cultigen having much larger, more numerous, and more easily collected and processed kernels, as well as being dependent on human assistance for detaching and dispersing its seeds. Today's many varieties of maize, or corn, make it one of the world's primary staples.

Other plants were coming under cultivation in southern Mexico around the same time, including several kinds of beans, squashes, gourds, chili peppers, avocados, and cactus fruit (Flannery, 1986; B. Smith, 1997). At least some of these plants also originated in the lowlands at some earlier time and distance from their first recognized use at Tehuacán (Piperno and Pearsall, 1998). Domesticated seeds of pumpkinlike squashes excavated at Guilá Naquitz cave in Oaxaca proved to be nearly 10,000 years old, some 5,000 years earlier than the oldest known maize.

Modern nutritionists recognize that maize and beans contain complementary amino acids, which, when consumed together, form a "complete" protein that can be synthesized effectively by the body, thereby reducing the nutritional need for meat (see pp. 107–108). Those who consume only one or the other type of seed do not obtain this beneficial effect and so are not as well nourished. These two American plants, in tandem, contributed more than others and may have encouraged some groups to take further steps toward full agriculture.

Earlier we suggested that people often postpone a major commitment to farming until a suitable mix of crops is available to meet their needs. How quickly did people in places like Tehuacán come to rely on food production? Based on the archaeobotanical fragments preserved in the excavated caves, MacNeish concluded (1964, 1967) that even with the availability of domesticated maize, beans, and other plants, agricultural products only gradually came to contribute even one-third of the diet. By getting involved in horticulture, these food collectors at first probably reaped no significant increases in *productivity*, yet may have benefited from greater *predictability*, with the seeds or dried flesh of domesticates available to equalize resources in leaner times (Wills, 1989).

The tiny maize cobs from Tehuacán, recently submitted to an improved ^{14}C technique, yield dates of only 4,700–4,500 y.a., much later than the 7,000 years at first indicated by standard carbon dating (Fritz, 1994). But bioarchaeological evidence—from bones of the ancient residents themselves—indicates that maize did play a role in the diet much earlier. In a very small sample of human skeletons from Tehuacán sites dating between 8,000 and 1,000 y.a., stable ^{13}C/^{12}C isotope ratios suggest reliance on maize by as early as 6,500 y.a. (Farnsworth et al., 1985)—that is, 2,000 years prior to the oldest cobs recovered so far at Tehuacán.

South American Farmers

Research into the history of domestication and agriculture in South America is in progress, with several major issues at question. First, what were the relative roles of maritime resources and agricultural products throughout prehistory on the continent's west coast? Second, to what extent did Mexican crops, particularly maize, contribute to South American agriculture? Finally, what was the nature of Amazonian agriculture in eastern South America?

Sediment cores and other geomorphological evidence indicate that the periodic climatic phenomenon known as **El Niño** became established between about 7,000 and 5,000 y.a. in the Pacific (Sandweiss et al., 1996). El Niño events are triggered when a persistent trough of atmospheric low pressure forces warm equatorial waters southward along South America's west coast, partially displacing the northward flow of deep cold currents. El Niño typically disrupts the maritime food chain and dramatically disturbs precipitation patterns over land, bringing excess rainfall

El Niño
Periodic climatic instability, related to temporary warming of Pacific Ocean waters, which may influence storm patterns and precipitation for several years.

and flooding to some areas, drought to others. El Niño returns every four years or so, on average, and some episodes are more severe or last longer than others.

Early farming in coastal Peru seems to relate somewhat to the El Niño pattern (Piperno and Pearsall, 1998). At Paloma (Chilca), a short distance south of present-day Lima, summer fishing expeditions had extended into year-round reliance on large and small fish species, shellfish, sea mammals, turtles, and sea birds. Midden contents, analyses of coprolites, and high strontium levels in human skeletons confirm the nearly exclusive role of sea resources by 5,000 y.a. (Moseley, 1992). Then the fishers began experimenting with nonlocal plant crops: bottle gourds for carrying water and a few squashes and beans for food. By about 4,500 y.a., they had taken up small-scale horticulture in nearby river valleys, growing cotton for nets and cloth and, significantly, adding at least 10 more edible plants to supplement their predominantly seafood diet. While they would maintain their basic maritime focus for centuries to come, coastal Peruvians may have decided that a greater variety of foods would help to minimize the periodic shortfalls in sea resources that they could expect with most El Niño events every few years.

The intercontinental dispersal or exchange of American cultigens is a topic of active archaeobotanical research and debate (B. Smith, 1995; Piperno and Pearsall, 1998). Maize may have reached coastal South America not long after its domestication in southern Mexico (Fig. 16–15). Preserved botanical elements, maize motifs

FIGURE 16–15
Early farming in the Americas, showing the spread of maize agriculture (purple).

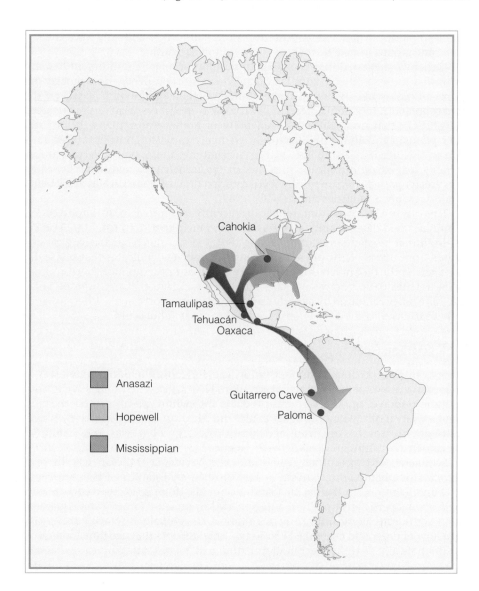

on pottery, and even the impression of a kernel on a vessel, as well as an increase in grinding stones and human dental caries, attest to the early presence of maize in this region. Maize eventually attained great importance among all the native cultures of western South America. Sixteenth-century Spanish chroniclers noted that highly varied races of maize accommodated Peru's demanding climatic and topographical diversity from sea level to 6,500 ft (2,000 m), with potatoes taking over at higher elevations. Developed through careful selection and hybridization, each of these varieties probably derived from a common ancestral form of Mexican maize.

Plant cultivation had gotten under way in a few highland areas of South America before 7,500 y.a. Nonfood species useful for fiber, containers, tool shafts, bedding, and medicines were tended even more often than edible plants around Guitarrero Cave in the Andes Mountains (Lynch, 1980). Native tree fruits, broad lima beans, small-seeded quinoa, and several starchy tubers were among the local food crops grown here (Lynch, 1980, 1983). One of these ancient root crops, the white potato, when eventually adopted into northern European agriculture and cuisine, became today's familiar mashed, fried, boiled, and baked mainstay.

Other native South American cultigens were developed in the tropical forests on the eastern slopes of the Andes or in the humid Amazon basin to the east. Roots of manioc shrubs and sweet potatoes became the dietary staples in the eastern lowlands, supplying abundant carbohydrate energy, but little else. Peanuts added some protein and fats to the starchy diet, but fish and insects remained essential food resources for most of the natives of Amazonia, whose gardens alone generally could not sustain them entirely.

Farmers of the Southwestern United States

Maize, beans, and squash seeds up to 3,000 years old are preserved on several Archaic sites in the southwestern United States (Simmons, 1986; Tagg, 1996). Introduced to the region possibly much earlier by farmers expanding northward in search of suitable planting areas, the domesticates came under increasing selection pressure as societies ever farther from the southern Mexican source area adopted them. Climatic conditions associated with higher latitudes and elevations shortened the growing season for these Mexican imports and thus slowed or limited agricultural expansion in some regions.

The maize-beans-squash complex gradually gained precedence over hunting and gathering in the American Southwest. Between 2,300 and 1,300 y.a., reliance on these domesticated products promoted increased population density and overall cultural elaboration, resulting in the emergence of several distinctive prehistoric cultural traditions in the Southwest (Fig. 16–16). Each of these regional traditions is distinguished on the basis of its cultural traits, including pottery styles, architecture, religious ideas, and sociopolitical organization (Plog, 1997).

The **Hohokam** of southern Arizona were growing both food and cotton by 1,500 y.a. and perhaps much earlier, irrigating their gardens through an extensive system of hand-dug channels that conveyed water from the Gila River or its tributaries. Architecture and artifacts on large Hohokam sites by around 1,000 y.a., such as Las Colinas and Snaketown, near Phoenix, reveal links to Mexican centers of domestication and culture. They include ball courts and platform mounds, as well as copper bells, parrot feathers, stone mirrors, and other Mesoamerican products (Haury, 1976). The Hohokam crafted human figurines and shell and turquoise ornaments in sufficient quantities for trade (Crown, 1991). The Casas Grandes district of northern Chihuahua, Mexico, may have served as a major exchange corridor between Mesoamerica and the Southwest (DiPeso, 1974). But whether the Hohokam maintained direct contact with Mexican civilizations or simply participated in the diffusion of ideas and products passed along trade routes is a matter for debate.

The **Mogollon**, whose prehistoric culture straddled southern New Mexico and Arizona, dwelt in pit houses until about A.D. 1000. Around that time, they began to construct aboveground room blocks and to create boldly painted black-on-white pottery in imitation of their northern neighbors. Archaeological traces of the

Hohokam
(ho-ho-kahm') Prehistoric farming culture of southern Arizona.

Mogollon
(mo-go-yohn') Prehistoric village culture of northern Mexico and southern Arizona/New Mexico.

FIGURE 16–16
Village farming cultures of the American Southwest, showing trade routes (red) and sites mentioned in the text.

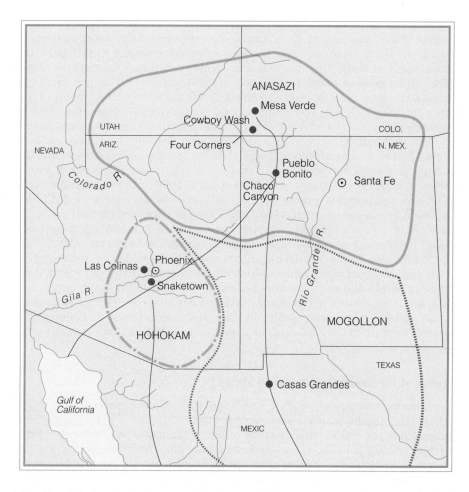

Anasazi
(an-ah-saw'-zee) Ancient culture of the south-western United States, associated with preserved cliff dwellings and masonry pueblo sites.

Pueblos
Spanish term for "town," referring to multiroom residence structures built by village farmers in the American Southwest; also refers collectively to the several cultures that built and lived in such villages.

Kivas
Underground chambers or rooms used for gatherings and ceremonies by pueblo dwellers.

Mogollon faded a century or more before Europeans arrived in the mid-1500s, perhaps as its people drifted southward into Mexico.

In the Four Corners region to the north, prehistoric farmers known to archaeologists as the **Anasazi** built impressive prehistoric masonry villages and towns, called **pueblos**, beginning around A.D. 900. Their scale, picturesque settings, and excellent preservation place some Anasazi sites among the most famous archaeological locations in the United States, including Chaco Canyon, New Mexico, and the so-called cliff dwellings of Mesa Verde, Colorado. Anasazi towns consisted of multiroom, multistory residential and storage structures and usually included underground ceremonial chambers, called **kivas**. Their compact sites were situated with good access to the limited agricultural lands and scarce water supply of this high and arid region.

Chaco Canyon, with a dozen large pueblos, served as a trade and religious center connected by nearly 1,000 miles (about 1,700 km) of radiating foot roads to as many as 80 far-flung villages (Judge, 1984; Wicklein, 1994). Pueblo Bonito (Figs. 16–17 and 16–18), the primary town of Chaco Canyon, was a multistory, D-shaped building of some 600 rooms, built in stages between A.D. 900 and 1125. Its sandstone walls incorporated some 200,000 wooden beams and rafters carried from distant mountains, making Pueblo Bonito the largest building in America until the first modern skyscrapers of just a century ago. Although its many rooms could have held 2,000 people or more, they appear to have had only intermittent use, perhaps as temporary quarters, as workshops, or for storage (Sebastian, 1992; Wicklein, 1994). Huge kivas accommodated participants and observers at major ceremonies. Trace-element analysis indicates that turquoise mined in the vicinity of present-day Santa Fe was cut into beads and carvings at Chaco Canyon before being sent on toward Mexico (Harbottle and Weigand, 1992).

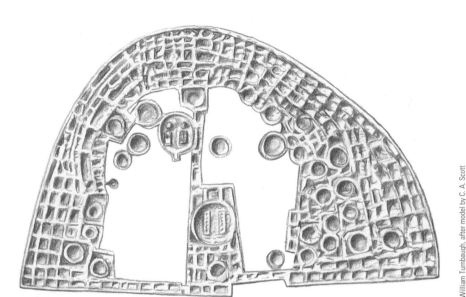

William Turnbaugh, after model by C. A. Scott

FIGURE 16–17
Plan view of Pueblo Bonito, the largest structure in Chaco Canyon, showing living and storage rooms and round ceremonial chambers, or kivas. The central kiva is about 65 feet (20 m) in diameter.

The phenomenal rise of the Chaco town sites and related villages represents a relatively brief aberration, probably nourished by a period of increased rainfall and sustained by social factors such as political or religious ideology, trade, and internal strife. A growing body of evidence points to Chaco-era warfare and terrorism among the Anasazi, extending even to cannibalism. Christy Turner, of Arizona State University, and others recognize patterns of cut marks, deliberate breakage, burning, and "pot polish" on victims' bones from dozens of sites where residents met a violent death (White, 1992; Turner and Turner, 1999). And recent biochemical analyses of residues in cooking vessels and a human coprolite recovered from a feature in a destroyed house at Cowboy Wash, Colorado, identified traces of human myoglobin from heart or muscle tissue (Marlar and Marlar, 2000). In accounting for the violence, different researchers have cited starvation, ritual executions, or the actions of a Mexican warrior cult (Kantner, 1999). These disturbing activities declined with the abandonment of Chaco (and eventually most other large pueblos in the region) beginning in the mid-1100s.

William Turnbaugh

FIGURE 16–18
Ruins of Anasazi rooms and kivas at Pueblo Bonito, Chaco Canyon, New Mexico.

FIGURE 16-19
Cliff Palace was the largest of the pueblos built by Anasazi farmers living at Mesa Verde, Colorado, about 800 y.a.

William Turnbaugh

By then, shifting precipitation patterns associated with a general warming period were leaving marginal zones of the Southwest, especially the Colorado Plateau, without adequate rainfall to grow maize (Cordell, 1998). As the drought worsened through the late 1200s, Anasazi town folk persisted in a few places like Mesa Verde (Fig. 16–19), where they built their communities into easily defended niches in the precipitous cliffs and tilled their fields on the canyon rim by day. By A.D. 1300, even Mesa Verde stood empty; the Anasazi of the Four Corners had dispersed toward the south and Southeast to become the people known today as Hopi, Zuni, and the Rio Grande Puebloans.

Farmers of Eastern North America

Aboriginal peoples of eastern North America, once thought to have lived without agriculture until maize arrived in that area, had in fact developed an independent center of domestication and cultivation. Small gourds, apparently native to the region and not derived from Mesoamerican species, were widely cultivated by Archaic hunters and gatherers more than 5,000 y.a., probably for use as fishing net floats rather than food (Fritz, 1999). Several other local plants—marsh elder or sumpweed, sunflower, and goosefoot (*Chenopodium* sp.)—are associated with ancient campsites and shell heaps along major river floodplains, where about 3,000 y.a. people maintained "incidental gardens" of plants selected to complement rather than replace foraging activities (B. Smith, 1985, 1989, 1995). In the next millenium, several more native species were added to the inventory: knotweed, maygrass, and little barley. Stone agricultural hoes began to appear on sites in the Illinois River valley at about the same time (Odell, 1998).

Harvesting and processing these weedy, small-seeded species was labor intensive and probably could have done little more than supplement a diet of wild foods. Nevertheless, the river valleys of the Southeast and the rich forests covering much of the Northeast, as well as the broken prairies of the Midwest, clearly provided adequate returns to support a degree of cultural elaboration even without maize agriculture. For example, the widespread practice of mound building and associated rituals pertaining to death and burial began long before any reliance on maize. We have seen that Archaic food collectors sometimes constructed mounds, possibly to stake territorial claims (see Chapter 15).

FIGURE 16–20
Cross section and floor of a 2,000-year-old Hopewell burial mound in Ohio. Cremated human bones and offerings deposited in a mica-lined burial chamber were covered with several layers of earth.

More elaborate rituals centering on mound building culminated about 2,000 y.a. in the **Hopewell** interaction sphere (Struever, 1964). Well-organized local groups throughout the midcontinent constructed earthen burial mounds of impressive size and participated in exchanges of ritual goods and ideological concepts that found expression in elaborate burials and socially valued grave offerings, including ornate smoking pipes, natural copper and stone ornaments, river pearls, and mineral pigments (Fig. 16–20). These mounds commemorated the prominent individuals buried within them, perhaps lineage leaders or others who earned special standing in the community through their deeds or ceremonial roles.

Only after 1,200 y.a. in the Southeast and around 800 y.a. in the Northeast did new varieties of maize and the introduction of domesticated beans support a more productive agriculture (B. Smith, 1992; Hart and Scarry, 1999). Even then, wild nuts, seeds, fish, and game retained their primary place in the diet of many groups. But in the broad river valleys of the Southeast, maize farming may have supported the remarkable culture called **Mississippian** (Fig. 16–21). Reaching its apex about 800 y.a., the Mississippian was a structured society, ruled by powerful chiefs who relied on elaborate rituals and displays of valued symbols to enhance their privileged positions. Populations and ceremonial centers throughout the region were linked by exchanges of symbolic copper, shell, pottery, and stone items, as well as a common focus on the construction of impressive earthen mounds. Most of these structures served the living as temple and residence platforms, while the elite dead and their elaborate offerings, including human sacrifices, were sometimes interred within other mounds.

The Mississippian site of Cahokia, located below the junction of the Missouri and Mississippi Rivers near St. Louis, boasted some 120 platform, conical, and ridgetop mounds (Pauketat and Emerson, 1997; Young and Fowler, 2000). The primary earthwork was Monks Mound (Fig. 16–22), as long as three football fields and as high as a 10-story building—the largest prehistoric structure north of Mexico. Undoubtedly the center of a great chiefdom, Cahokia's homes and garden plots spread over 6 square miles (15 km²) beyond the log stockade that enclosed the central mounds and elite living area (Fig. 16–23). Fields of maize, squash, and pumpkins extending along the river floodplain provided the harvest for innumerable storage pits and granaries (Iseminger, 1996).

Hopewell
A culture centered in southern Ohio between 2,100 and 1,700 y.a., but influencing a much wider region through trade and the spread of a cult centered on burial ritualism.

Mississippian
A southeastern United States mound-building culture that flourished from 1,100 to 500 y.a.

FIGURE 16–21
Flint hoe blade used by Mississippian farmers.

FIGURE 16–22
View of Monks Mound, part of the Cahokia group of Mississippian mounds near East St. Louis, Illinois. Built in late prehistoric times, it is about 1,000 feet (300 m) long and 100 feet (30 m) high.

Among other New World societies, farming had not yet attained much importance even by the time Europeans were arriving with their own ways of life and their Old World domesticates (Brown, 1994). In fact, throughout much of the far West, the far North, and most of South America, hunting, fishing, and gathering remained the principal means of making a living (Fig. 16–24). This persistence may be explained in part because the more productive American domesticates, those native to warm temperate zones, could be introduced and maintained in other geographical settings only with sustained effort. Yet, it was not always a matter of whether farming was possible; often it was also a matter of choice. Maize was far from an ideal crop, even where it could be grown most readily. Old World domesticated cereal grasses, including wheat, barley, oats, rye, millet, and rice, grew in dense stands that were harvested readily with a sickle and cleaned by threshing and winnowing. Maize, the primary New World cereal grass, required more space per plant and more moisture during its long growing season, and it was far more difficult to harvest and process by hand.

What is more, the products of agriculture were seldom superior in nutritional value to a mixed diet obtained through foraging. Maize itself is deficient in lysine (an amino acid) and niacin and contains a chemical that may promote iron-deficiency anemia. Similarly, peoples of the Amazon basin in South America, who domesticated manioc, sweet potatoes, and other starchy root crops before 1,500 y.a., found that these foods supplied bulk and carbohydrates, but little protein—a deficiency overcome by continued reliance on hunting, fishing, and gathering.

FIGURE 16–23
Reconstructed Mississippian farmstead at Cahokia.

Biocultural Consequences of Food Production

Domestication and agriculture were the driving forces of the Neolithic Revolution, but we have seen that the impact of Neolithic lifeways went far beyond subsistence. While accepting the advantages of today's more or less reliable food supply, we may take little notice of agriculture's liabilities. As an adaptive mechanism, the Neolithic way of life has been a mixed blessing for humankind, one that has promoted dramatic worldwide population growth and brought us a number of social, environmental, and health-related problems. Moreover, agricultural activities require long periods of toil. One thing is certain: People did not invent agriculture in response to a desire for more leisure, better health, and longer life. Those consequences, where they have occurred at all, were a very long time in coming. One writer bluntly refers to agriculture as "the worst mistake in the history of the human race" (Diamond, 1987). After reading the following sections, see if you agree with his assessment.

Increased Population Density and Permanent Settlements

Some theorize that population growth initiated the agricultural response; others see it happening the other way around. But there is no question that population size and density both tended to increase as farming activities produced larger and more predictable yields. People clustered into permanent villages and towns surrounded by fields and pastures. Sedentary living permitted closer birth spacing, since mothers no longer lugged infants from site to site, and the availability of soft cereals for infant food allowed for earlier weaning. Potentially, therefore, a woman might bear more children. It is not surprising that even very early Neolithic settlements, such as Jericho, in the Jordan River valley, and Çatalhöyük, in Turkey, quickly reached considerable size. Today's world population, sustained largely by the same set of Neolithic domesticates, has attained 6 billion people and shows few signs of slowing (Fig. 16–25).

New Technologies

Changes in material culture accompanied food production and the development of permanent settlements. For example, Neolithic people soon replaced most of their basketry and skin containers with bulkier but more versatile ceramic vessels. Their

FIGURE 16–24
Yahgan hunter of Cape Horn, South America, late nineteenth century.

Julian H. Steward, ed. *Handbook of South American Indians*, Vol. 1, plate 36. Washington, DC: U.S. Government Printing Office.

FIGURE 16–25
World population growth.

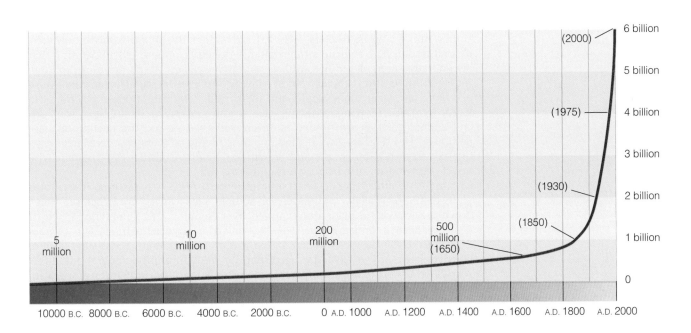

439

FIGURE 16–26
Prehistoric decorated pottery vessel from Arizona.

Courtesy, Museum of Primitive Art and Culture, Peace Dale, RI, photo by William Turnbaugh

pottery (Fig. 16–26) made simmering and boiling more practical, more readily converting grains into digestible foods. They used looms to weave cloth from the wool and plant fibers that replaced wild animal skins. Where durability was required, as in grinding slabs and axeheads, stone persisted for a time as the material of choice.

Eventually, as harvests increased, some food-producing communities could support and in turn benefit from nonfarmers who engaged in specialized crafts, exchanging the products of their skill for food grown by others. Thus, for example, the use of copper in the Near East expanded once people were able to devote the necessary effort to refining and processing the ore into a variety of metallic implements and ornaments. Specialization stimulated a proliferation of new inventions.

New Economic and Social Relations

Occasionally, farmers (or their leaders) found themselves with a food surplus in the form of stored grain or herds of animals. These products could be used to level out shortages in subsequent seasons. Often, excess production served as a kind of capital, or wealth, that fostered new socioeconomic transactions. Thus, the ability to redistribute food and other goods collected from the populace empowered Mississippian chieftains. And in Mesopotamia, barter and exchange flourished, as did credit, or lending against future productivity. (A need for accurate accounts inspired early writing here in the form of symbols pressed into clay tablets; see Issue, Chapter 17.)

Because farmland itself was a source of potential capital in later, highly developed Neolithic societies, its possession at times became the basis for a new social order that discriminated between landowners and tenant farmers. Such was the case especially where the society had invested in extensive land improvement, such as irrigation projects. In Egypt, for example, the ruler asserted claims over much of the arable land and its produce. Peasants worked the land but yielded the harvest to those in charge, who might then redistribute it throughout the society in proportion to social position rather than need.

As agricultural techniques and resulting harvests continued to improve, additional segments of the population were relieved of the obligation of producing food and came to fill specialized roles as priests, merchants, crafters, administrators, and the like. A social and economic hierarchy of productive peasants, nonfarming specialists of many kinds, and a tiny but dominant elite emerged in a few Neolithic state societies, or civilizations.

Environmental Changes

Unlike hunters and gatherers, who extracted their livelihood from the available natural resources, Neolithic farmers altered the environment by substituting their own domesticated plants and animals for native species. We do not mean to imply that all hunters and gatherers had been dedicated conservationists; but their numbers were few, their tools simple, and their needs relatively modest. On the other hand, Neolithic plowing, terracing, clear-cutting of forests, draining of wetlands, and animal grazing contributed to severe soil erosion and the decline of many natural species (Fig. 16–27). At the same time, many of these practices encouraged the growth of noxious weeds and presented new opportunities for crop-damaging insect pests and malaria-bearing mosquitoes.

Intensive agriculture depleted soil nutrients, especially potassium. In the lower Tigris-Euphrates valley, high levels of soluble salts carried by irrigation waters slowly poisoned the fields once farmed by Ubaidians and Sumerians. In North Africa, Neolithic herders allowed their animals to overgraze the fragile Sahara grasslands, furthering the development of the world's largest desert. These early farming practices left many areas so damaged that they remain unproductive thousands of years later. Unfortunately, comparable processes (such as burning forests for grazing lands) continue at an accelerated pace into our present day, hastening environmental degradation on a global scale and threatening the long-term food supply.

FIGURE 16–27
The Inka terraces, in Peru, required intensive effort to modify mountain land for farming.

Diminished Diversity

Some foragers selected from hundreds of wild species for food and other purposes as they moved from camp to camp throughout the year. The strategy of most Neolithic societies differed in that they emphasized only a small number of domesticated crops and animal species and had little interest in maintaining native flora and fauna. Through selective breeding practices, people sought to enhance the traits they valued in their domesticates (thicker wool or body fat, greater milk production, more and larger seeds, etc.) while strictly limiting random variability. These experiments resulted in genetically homogeneous strains.

Today, the earth's human population still relies primarily on the seeds of just a half-dozen grasses (wheat, barley, oats, rice, millet, maize), several root crops (potatoes, yams, manioc), and a few domesticated fowl and mammals (in addition to fish) for sustenance. Their relative genetic homogeneity renders these species highly susceptible to disease, drought, and pests. Agricultural scientists are attempting to forestall potential disaster by reestablishing some genetic diversity in these plants and animals through the controlled introduction of heterogenous (usually "wild") strains. A few farmers have realized the benefits of multicropping, interspersing different kinds of crops in a single agricultural plot. Combining grains, root crops, fruit trees, herbs, and plants used for fiber or tools mimics the natural species diversity and reduces soil depletion and insect infestation.

Role of Science and Religion

Prescribed rites, sanctions, and shrines ensured bountiful harvests and other supernatural blessings for Neolithic farmers. This statement is not to imply that prefarming peoples ignored the supernatural realm. But because of differences in population size and organization, farmers tended to make more impressive, permanent monuments to their beliefs and sometimes afforded practitioners the opportunity to engage full-time in religious specialties. In some cultures, early "sciences" were contemplated and practiced by a select group of priestly scholars. Disciplines such as botany, zoology, astronomy, meteorology, and mathematics trace their origins back to ancient attempts to improve agricultural techniques, to predict or ameliorate the weather, and to divide land.

Cultural Competition and Change

Neolithic societies often ran on a collision course with their nonfarming neighbors. Expanding agriculturists displaced hunter-gatherers or even eradicated them altogether as a result of direct competition for suitable land or as a consequence of habitat changes brought on by farming activities. Some food producers involved their nonfarming neighbors in exchange networks, trading surplus products of agriculture, animal husbandry, or new technology for raw materials, wild produce, and even slaves (Gregg, 1988). In time, farmers came to prevail almost everywhere, except in those marginal areas where agriculture or herding were impractical. And even those locales came under siege as modern food-producing and industrialized societies competed for land and other resources in the diminished domains left to foragers. Today, the process is complete: Virtually none of the world's population survives primarily by hunting and gathering. For others, fishing remains a viable option to farming, although pressure on the world's fish stocks is increasing at an alarming rate.

Diet and Health

The diets of preagricultural humans, while perhaps high in animal protein, were typically low in fats, particularly saturated fats. Hunter-gatherer diets were also high in complex carbohydrates (including fiber), low in salt, and high in calcium. We do not need to be reminded that the diets of many modern populations (especially in the United States) have exactly the opposite configuration. There is very good evidence that many of today's diseases in industrialized countries are related to the lack of fit between contemporary human diets and the one with which we evolved (Eaton, Shostak, and Konner, 1988).

Many of our biological and behavioral characteristics evolved because in the past they contributed to adaptation. But today these same characteristics may be maladaptive. An example is our ability to store fat. This capability was an advantage in the past, when food availability often alternated between abundance and scarcity. Those who could store fat during times of abundance could draw on those stores during times of scarcity. Today, considering the number of disorders associated with obesity, what was formerly an advantageous ability to store extra fat has now turned into a liability. Our "feast or famine" biology is now incompatible with the constant feast many people indulge in today. The increasing incidence of adult-onset diabetes in the industrialized world is but one example of this discordance between our biology and our contemporary culture. Granted, all forms of diabetes have a strong genetic component; nevertheless, lifestyle, especially diet, plays a major role in the expression of the disease.

It is clear that both excesses and deficiencies of nutrients can cause health problems and interfere with growth and development. While obesity is a problem in some places, many other people in all parts of the world, both industrialized and developing, suffer from inadequate supplies of food of any quality. We read of thousands dying from starvation due to drought, warfare, or political instability. The Neolithic Revolution is partly responsible for some of the problems with food and health we see today. The blame must be placed not only on the narrowed food base that resulted from the emergence of agriculture, but also on the increase in human population that occurred when people began to settle in permanent villages and raise more children.

Disease Consequences Clearly, the results of food production have not been entirely beneficial. The connection between the shift to food production and the increase in disease has been a topic of particular interest to scholars. Working with archaeologists, physical anthropologists, through their analysis of human skeletal remains, can often provide insight into crucial biocultural processes in the past (see photo essay, pp. 113–118). Certain skeletal changes, most notably on the teeth, are seen consistently in early agricultural groups (Larsen, 1995). Indeed, the increased presence of caries ("cavities") is frequently used as a marker of a largely agricultural diet (i.e., one including increased amounts of carbohydrates, which promote dental decay).

There were, however, other more serious health consequences faced by early food producers. Some of these risks relate to increased exposure to previously rare (or unknown) diseases; others are a direct product of increased population density. One major contributor to heightened disease exposure came from close proximity of humans to domestic animals. Many pathogens (e.g., viruses, bacteria, intestinal parasites) can be transferred from nonhuman animals to humans. Diseases that can be transmitted to humans by other vertebrates (particularly mammals and birds) are called **zoonoses**. For example, rabies is carried by dogs, tetanus by horses, and influenza by pigs or poultry. Indeed, with respect to influenza, an outbreak in 1918–1919 of a variety of swine flu caused the most devastating worldwide epidemic in recorded history, killing more than 20 million people (Kiple, 1993). Every year we still hear of new outbreaks of other strains of swine or avian flu, often beginning in Asia. With more than 1 million international travelers daily, the infection can swiftly spread over the entire planet. Another disease initially transmitted to humans by another animal is HIV/AIDS, which recent evidence shows was derived from chimpanzees (most likely as people ate contaminated meat) (see p. 145).

Early farmers who grew crops and tended herds in ancient Mesopotamia, China, the Indus valley, and elsewhere in the Old World (but not to the same degree in the New World, where animal domestication was little practiced) faced equally dangerous health challenges. We noted in Chapter 4 how human cultural modification with slash-and-burn agriculture produced a more conducive environment for the spread of malaria. Another major human disease likely stimulated by the activities of food producers is tuberculosis.

The origin of tuberculosis in humans is not completely understood, but we do know that several wild animals harbor a form of the disease (seen in bison, moose, elk, deer, and domestic cattle). The tuberculosis variant called *bovine tuberculosis* can be transmitted from the animal host to a human though ingestion of infected meat or milk. Clearly, with the domestication of cattle (which, as we have shown, occurred in the Middle East by 8,000 y.a.), there was much greater exposure of humans to bovine tuberculosis, and it became considerably greater yet with the development of dairying (Sherratt, 1981). In its later stages, tuberculosis can produce distinctive skeletal changes, especially of the spine (see photo, p. 117). The earliest evidence of such skeletal involvement comes from Italy and is dated to nearly 6,000 y.a. (about the same time that dairying was invented in the Middle East) (Roberts and Manchester, 1997).

Tuberculosis in humans has clearly evolved over the last six millenia, and indeed, most humans today who are infected carry a related variety of *pulmonary tuberculosis* that can spread from person to person. The relationship of bovine tuberculosis to pulmonary tuberculosis is not clearly understood, but the latter may have evolved from the former. Moreover, this transformation seems to have occurred only *after* humans became agriculturists.

A number of other significant human diseases are associated with sedentism and increasing population size and density. Measles, for example, has been shown to require a very large population pool—in the thousands—to sustain itself long-term (Cohen, 1989). Thus, measles can be viewed as a condition that became prevalent only with the emergence of larger urban centers, making it a "disease of civilization." Likewise, cholera is most commonly found in urban contexts, where large numbers of people share a common (and contaminated) water source.

By dramatically changing their relationship to the environment, often inadvertently, humans have placed themselves at increased risk of contracting disease from a variety of other animals. Rats congregate around human habitations, especially where food is stored (e.g., grain bins) and where refuse accumulates. Bubonic plague (carried by fleas that live on rats) occasionally infects an unwary hunter or camper who comes into contact with a wild rodent. But its devastating spread in

Zoonoses (*sing.*, **zoonosis**)
Diseases transmissible to humans from other vertebrates.

medieval Europe was an epidemic among urban dwellers who lived in close proximity to a burgeoning rat population.

Humans also changed their habitation designs as they settled down in permanent villages and towns and later in cities. Permanent houses replaced temporary shelters, and these more enclosed structures promoted the spread of all airborne pathogens (including influenza, the common cold, and pulmonary tuberculosis). Moreover, as the residents heated their now-confined quarters with fire, they became ever more vulnerable to the harmful effects of wood smoke. As a result, respiratory diseases became more prevalent and more serious.

It is important to remember that the varied health consequences of food production, sedentism, population growth, and dense urban centers were not entirely negative. Indeed, as Cohen (1989) and others have noted, exposure to some other kinds of disease decreased with the development of agriculture. Moreover, once people settled down in one place, there was more opportunity for caring for the ill and thus better chances of recovery. Finally, as biological organisms, perhaps the most basic aspect of our human biological adaptation relates to reproductive success—and humans have certainly increased reproduction in the last few thousand years! For most of hominid history, our ancestors' reproductive capacity was not much different from that of our ape cousins. Thus, a woman giving birth every three or four years was probably typical of hominids up to just a few thousand years ago. With the ability to stay in one place and predict the availability of food resources, weaning could come much sooner and birth spacing could be dramatically reduced. Consequently, human populations began to expand, a trend that continues today unabated in most of the world. The relative benefits and costs of this development for human well-being are yet to be determined.

Clearly, the development of food production has been the most significant revolution in human history. The enduring legacy for the vast majority of people over the last several thousand years has been a saga of coping with the consequences, both culturally and biologically.

SUMMARY

This chapter has examined the record of plant and animal domestication and the origin of early agricultural societies. Archaeological site excavations, along with refined dating methods and the analytical techniques of archaeobotany and archaeozoology, have yielded a wealth of comparative data on Neolithic cultures in several regions of the globe. Even so, the answers to ultimate questions about how and why domestication and agriculture developed remain elusive.

The invention and widespread adoption of agriculture occurred within the past 10,000 years, during the early to mid-Holocene. This so-called Neolithic Revolution represents a major force in human biocultural evolution. As a species, our biology and our cultural behavior are inextricably linked. For example, many of the cultural activities associated with agriculture have actually stimulated further biological changes, such as the spread of the sickle-cell allele as an adaptive response to malaria, a disease harbored in tropical environments disturbed by farmers (see pp. 75–77).

With the ability to produce food and support larger populations, the pace of human affairs quickened dramatically in the social, political, and economic realms as well. One consequence of relying on agriculture was a society's basic need for large tracts of productive cropland and adequate water supplies. Maintaining access to these essential resources was critical to a farming culture's survival. Certainly, securing land and water and supporting the vital agricultural process itself were primary functions of any Neolithic society, large or small.

In a few areas of the world, the emergence of large-scale, complex societies followed quickly on the heels of the Neolithic Revolution. The next two chapters consider the development and course of some early civilizations founded on Neolithic food-producing economies in the Old World and in the Americas.

QUESTIONS FOR REVIEW

1. What was so "revolutionary" about the Neolithic?

2. Distinguish between domestication and agriculture.

3. Compare the environmental and demographic approaches to explaining why farming began.

4. How does the concept of symbiosis contribute to our understanding of the domestication process?

5. What are some of the characteristics that made certain wild plant species and certain wild animal species better candidates for domestication than others?

6. What kinds of archaeological indicators provide actual evidence for plant or animal domestication?

7. Who were the Natufians? How does their changing relationship with certain plant and animal species illustrate the shift from hunting and gathering to Neolithic subsistence?

8. What was the probable role of megaliths among the farmers of western Europe?

9. Why do you think maize and beans attained such importance among the New World's Neolithic peoples?

10. Evaluate several important consequences of food production, both positive and negative.

SUGGESTED FURTHER READING

Cohen, Mark N. 1977. *The Food Crisis in Prehistory*. New Haven, CT: Yale University Press.

Davis, Simon J. M. 1987. *The Archaeology of Animals*. New Haven, CT: Yale University Press.

Harlan, Jack R. 1992. *Crops and Man*. 2nd ed. Madison, WI: American Society of Agronomy/Crop Science Society of America.

Harris, David R. (ed.). 1996. *The Origins and Spread of Agriculture and Pastoralism in Eurasia*. Washington, DC: Smithsonian Institution Press.

Moore, Andrew, Gordon Hillman, and Anthony Legge. 2000. *Village on the Euphrates: The Excavation of Abu Hureyra*. New York: Oxford University Press.

Plog, Stephen. 1997. *Ancient Peoples of the American Southwest*. New York: Thames and Hudson.

Sauer, Jonathan D. 1994. *Historical Geography of Crop Plants*. Boca Raton, FL: CRC Press.

Smith, Bruce D. 1998. *The Emergence of Agriculture*. New York: Freeman.

Service, Alastair, and Jean Bradbery. 1997. *The Standing Stones of Europe: A Guide to the Great Megalithic Monuments*. Rev. ed. London: Weindenfeld and Nicolson.

Thorpe, I. J. J. 1996. *The Origins of Agriculture in Europe*. London: Routledge.

Zohary, Daniel, and Maria Hopf. 2000. *Domestication of Plants in the Old World: The Origin and Spread of Cultivated Plants in West Asia, Europe, and the Nile Valley*. 3rd ed. New York: Oxford University Press.

RESOURCES ON THE INTERNET

 Wadsworth Anthropology Resource Center

http://anthropology.wadsworth.com

The companion website for this text includes a range of enrichment material focused on the chapter's topic. While online you can enhance your understanding of the chapter by exploring one of the several additional Internet Exercises, by

researching topics, and by accessing full articles on InfoTrac College Edition. You can also reinforce the concepts by taking online practice exams.

Internet Exercises

Many plant species were domesticated during the Neolithic period, but not all of them have been as widely cultivated as wheat or maize. Today, some regional food plants are finding new markets and attaining broader popularity. Use your search engine to do a word search for either *manioc* or *quinoa*. After exploring some pertinent Web pages relating to either of these plants, what can you say about where and in what ways they are being used as food today?

 InfoTrac College Edition

http://www.infotrac-college.com/wadsworth

Neolithic is the keyword to search in InfoTrac College Edition to locate references to current articles on some of the economic, social, technological, dietary, health, and even religious consequences that accompanied or resulted from food production. Review the article titles to find several that relate to one particular geographic region. Read one or two of these articles and try to identify examples of major cultural changes brought about by Neolithic developments in that region.

CHAPTER

17

CONTENTS

The First Civilizations

Introduction

In many respects, the emergence of **civilizations** in several regions of the globe had an effect on humankind that was comparable to the revolutionary changes initiated by Neolithic food production. Like domestication and agriculture, civilization brought about entirely new and unanticipated relationships between human beings and their social and natural environments. Civilization, in effect, represents a *culturally constructed* adaptive mechanism, one that enables human societies to support their burgeoning populations by organizing and directing their energies to more effectively compete for resources (including land, food, and raw materials) and to achieve other socially valued goals. Those goals often brought individual civilizations into conflict with one another and frequently had far-reaching environmental consequences as well.

The appearance of the first civilizations signaled the climax of prehistory and laid the foundation for our modern historical era. By about 5,500 y.a. in the Old World and perhaps 2,000 years later in the Americas, a number of Neolithic agricultural societies were slowly transforming into civilizations (Fig. 17–1). Somewhat like the metamorphosis of a caterpillar into a butterfly, the processes that these societies underwent were subtle yet profound. This chapter examines the significance that archaeologists attach to the term *civilization* and then surveys some of the primary Old World civilizations (Fig. 17–2).

Considering Civilization

The term *civilization* is not, as many people think, just another word for *culture* or *society*. Archaeologists reserve the term to describe a select set of ancient **state-level societies** exhibiting distinctive characteristics. Ancient civilizations were much larger in scale than previous sociopolitical entities. Their populations—invariably nourished by Neolithic domesticates—were large (at least tens of thousands) and densely concentrated into a few substantial permanent settlements, usually cities. In these crowded settings, people were involved in new kinds of interactions that inevitably led to more complex relationships and linkages among the society's economic, social, and administrative dimensions.

One hallmark of the social complexity that characterized all civilizations was **social stratification**, which generally resulted in a class structure where the vast majority of people continued to work the land while a smaller number now served in specialized tasks of craft production, military service, trade, and religion. At the top of this social hierarchy were a few elite individuals who closely controlled access to the food and commodities produced by others and who made most of the essential decisions—usually with the proclaimed sanction of the society's gods and the assistance of a bureaucracy of lesser officials. Those in charge assumed many critical functions, including the capacity to create and enforce laws, levy and collect taxes, store and redistribute food and other basic goods, and defend or expand the state's boundaries.

Monumental construction projects, prescribed religions, glorification of leaders, and culturally distinctive forms of expression (through writing, art, and architecture) also characterized most early states.

Taken together, all these features describe what we mean by civilization.

Why Did Civilizations Form?

Accounting for how or why civilizations developed has proved a frustrating task. Archaeologists realize that the material artifacts and features they excavate and analyze are but imperfect reflections of once-thriving cultural systems. Extracting explanations of causality from buried assemblages of bricks, potsherds, and other debris might well be compared to studying a bowl of mixed fruit (or maybe just the

---

Civilizations
Large-scale, complexly organized societies associated with urbanism and sociopolitical territories known as states.

State-level societies
Civilizations; sociopolitical entities that control defined territories.

Social stratification
Class structure or hierarchy, usually based on political, economic, or social standing.

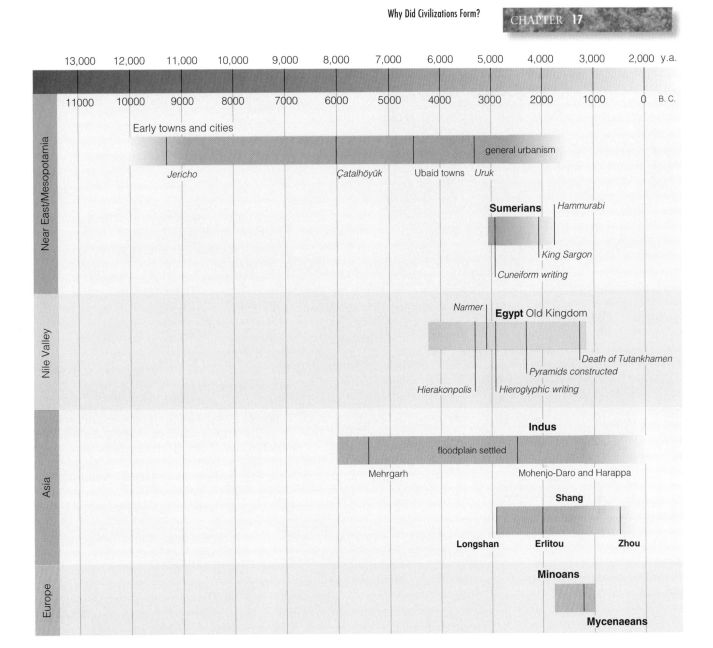

FIGURE 17–1
Time line for Chapter 17.

peels, pits, and cores) to understand how trees evolved. And yet, because archaeological artifacts once pertained to human cultural systems, we are confident that they can provide tangible clues to the nature of the early cultures and civilizations that produced them.

Decades ago, V. Gordon Childe enumerated the traits that he believed contributed to the evolution of early urban states. His long list reflects his appreciation of civilization as an outgrowth of increasing productivity, social complexity, and economic advantage (Childe, 1951, 1957). The use of writing, mathematics, animal-powered traction, wheeled carts, plows, irrigation, sailing boats, standard units of weight and measure, metallurgy, surplus production, and craft specialization all had a stimulating effect and were themselves products of changes initiated by earlier Neolithic activities, Childe argued. But Childe's recitation of material cultural inventions and equipment somehow failed to capture this central reality: A civilization is more than the sum of its parts.

FIGURE 17–2
Location of Old World civilizations
discussed in the text.

Mycenaean
Civilization

Minoan
Civilization

Sumerian
Civilization

Egypt

Indus Valley
Civilization

National Geographic Society

National Geographic Society

Walter H. Hodge, Peter Arnold, Inc.

Dallas and John Heaton, Westlight

National Geographic Society

Shang
Civilization

National Geographic Society

Moreover, Childe's trait list was not universally applicable. Though characterizing the Near Eastern civilizations with which he was most familiar, it did not describe American Indian societies such as the Maya and Inka,* which were clearly civilizations but had no use of sailing boats, animal traction, wheeled carts, and so on.

Prehistorians attempted to refine Childe's approach by singling out just the most essential qualities shared by *all* civilizations. Harvard anthropologist Clyde Kluckhohn proposed that civilizations are societies having (1) permanent towns with at least 5,000 residents, (2) record keeping, and (3) monumental ceremonial architecture (Kraeling and Adams, 1960). Note that each of these criteria is an outward indicator of a society's underlying complexity. Thus, if a culture is able to maintain thousands of people in a permanent town, then surely it is exercising some form of governance or administrative control based on something other than kinship—perhaps through the redistribution of goods and services. Record keeping (usually writing) manifests a need to maintain accurate accounts, ranging from inventories, economic reports, and tax tallies to law codes, histories, and literature. Large-scale construction activities for temples, pyramids, and other ceremonial architecture represent a society's surplus production capabilities, since such projects may not contribute to immediate and basic needs, like food, in the direct manner that digging an irrigation canal would. A culture that can afford the luxury of monumental structures demonstrates that it has attained a measure of success in supplying the needs of its population and in maintaining some control over it.

Still, descriptive approaches such as those of Childe and Kluckhohn remain inadequate because such lists fail to recognize the processes that account for *why* and *how* civilizations emerged in the first place. Stepping back from the sites and artifacts just a bit may give us a more holistic view of civilization. Certainly, we should recognize civilization as one of recent humankind's principal adaptive mechanisms—our *biocultural* response to dynamic environmental and social circumstances, including those resulting from food production (see pp. 439–444). We must, at the same time, acknowledge civilization as an innovation whose long-term consequences cannot yet be evaluated fully. Through their culture, a people may devise some appropriate response to a challenging situation and thereby extend their society's chances of survival and success—at least in the short run. Or they may make poor choices and have to suffer the lingering consequences. It is worth noting that *every* ancient civilization eventually failed. Although some were more durable than others, in the end, each proved to be maladapted.

Functionalist Explanations

For now, let us consider beginnings rather than endings. Some archaeologists believe that civilizations emerged in response to some pressing societal need. That is, civilization was invented to serve a specific purpose or function. For example, Karl Wittfogel's once-popular "hydraulic theory" suggested that civilizations generally emerged in arid regions, where small groups of elites assumed the authority to organize others into a workforce to build irrigation systems that would improve agricultural production (Wittfogel, 1957). Yet, the ancient Hohokam Indians along Arizona's Salt-Gila River created an extensive system of irrigation canals, section by section over a long time span, but did not develop many other traits associated with civilization. Similarly, local and small-scale irrigation works were established in central Mexico, coastal Peru, northern China, and the Indus River valley independently of any centralized political authority. Thus, a direct causal link between water control and civilized states is not convincingly demonstrated.

The formation of a large-scale and complexly organized society may have been an accommodation to rapid population growth brought about by agricultural prosperity. Or, conversely, perhaps it was a concentrated and hungry populace that

---

*This spelling (instead of "Inca") is now preferred, being more consistent with other terms in the Quechua language spoken by descendants of the native peoples of Peru.

prompted the intensification of farming activities in an attempt to increase crop yields (Boserup, 1965)? Have warfare and the need for common defense sometimes played a stimulating role (Carneiro, 1970)? Did religion or the vision of a theocratic leader give rise to civilization in some cases? Or, possibly, the new order served primarily to legitimize and protect the differential access to resources and wealth initiated by increased production and maintained by a self-interested elite (Harris, 1979).

These and other **functionalist** explanations have been tested against data from individual prehistoric societies, but few broadly applicable conclusions have emerged.

Systems Approach

The failure to identify civilization with a specific universal function leads other archaeologists to conclude that no single or prime factor invariably propels societies along a standard route to civilization. Acknowledging the relatively complex structure of all human societies, most anthropologists favor **multivariate** explanations to account for most kinds of culture change. They recognize that even the simplest cultural system is composed of interrelated components: technology, subsistence economy, social organization, beliefs and symbolic expression, and communication and exchange with other groups. Each of these elements is part of the culture's adaptive mechanism, the way a society organizes itself to deal with the world. Moreover, any change in the status quo, whether provoked internally (e.g., a new technological invention) or externally (e.g., a long drought or a war), requires a response from one or more of these components and thus stimulates a dynamic readjustment in all their interrelationships (Renfrew, 1972).

The following discussion adopts a systems approach to suggest how a complex state or civilization may develop. Though our starting point is basically Wittfogel's hydraulic theory, we go on to show how other changes are set in motion until the whole cultural system has evolved.

Suppose the members of a certain Neolithic community combined their efforts to increase their agricultural productivity, perhaps by digging irrigation canals. If the enterprise was to prove successful, the efforts of individual farmers had to be coordinated by managers able to convince people to pull together to meet a common goal. Eventually, as a result, the community occasionally produced harvests that exceeded the needs of the local population. Whether for reasons of coercion, cooperation, or merely convenience, the excess grain might have been stored in a communal granary, like those first seen in the Near East and Egypt after about 5,500 y.a. and later in the Indus valley, northern China, and elsewhere. In the hands of those responsible for its safekeeping and redistribution, the produce could become both a form of capital and a source of further control over the society. In times of general scarcity, or as a special inducement, grain could be redistributed to the populace at large or just to certain segments of it. Managers who oversaw the irrigated lands (or spiritual leaders taking some credit for the harvest) might claim a portion. Much of the grain might simply be retained as a form of taxation or temple tribute, to be used by those in charge. Producing food surpluses over several seasons could also stimulate a host of other developments: further population growth, trade with other societies, and, predictably, disproportionate accumulations of wealth, leading to social and economic stratification.

Yet another significant benefit of a secure food base might be the emergence of occupational specializations as alternatives to full-time farming for some individuals. The economies of even the most advanced Neolithic societies continued to be based primarily on domesticated plants and animals, of course. But specialized production by trained craftspersons who were not obliged to grow their own food made possible new kinds of products that supported nonsubsistence, or *market*, economies. Technological innovations and craft specializations created goods that could be consumed within the culture itself or, as was frequently the case, exchanged with other societies for comparable products or desirable raw materials.

Functionalist
Referring to explanations that account for a given development as a response to a specific need.

Multivariate
Involving more than one factor or variable.

An invention such as the potter's turntable, for example, which appeared in northern Mesopotamia around 5,500 y.a., revolutionized the craft of producing ceramic vessels while also provoking yet other changes. Fulfilling the wheel's mass production capabilities required the participation of many specialists (clay mixers, potters, glazers, kiln masters, merchants, accountants, and others). So long as a society's food supplies remained adequate, these specialists were exempted from the obligation of producing food and so could engage in their respective tasks on a full-time basis. Thus, an activity such as pottery making might contribute to a new order of social and economic relationships within the society. Each subsequent development would prompt yet other transformations, which together enhanced the society's complexity, moving it closer to the stage we recognize as civilization.

As with any other complex adaptive mechanism, civilization's effect on individuals was not uniformly beneficial. As Robert J. Wenke aptly observes, "We might suspect that the transition to social complexity was made in spite of its effect on the quality of life, and that its causes are not to be found in the choices of individuals or groups about how they want to live, but in the material factors of ecology, economics and technology" (1984, p. 200).

Cities and Civilizations

Ancient civilizations usually encompassed a hierarchy of settlement types. *Cities* were at the center of most ancient civilizations; in fact, many such societies initially developed around their urban centers. Commonly, one or more prominent cities dominated over a number of much smaller, dependent towns and villages in a region that also supported tiny farming hamlets. Only a few early civilizations—ancient Egypt and the New World's Inka are examples—sustained themselves without major cities as their focal points.

Cities are characterized by their sizable populations, of course, and also by social complexity, formal (nonkin) organization, and the concentration of specialized, nonagricultural roles (Redman, 1978). The city is the nucleus where production, trade, religion, and administrative activities converge. These central places usually proclaim their own importance by erecting prominent structures for ceremonial or other civic purposes.

Roots of Urbanism

The roots of urbanism seem to reach most deeply in the Near East, where a few ancient communities actually predated the Neolithic farming activities once assumed to be prerequisites for settled life (Fig. 17–3). In Chapter 15, we saw that sedentary settlements at times developed where native resources regularly produced predictable yields that could be stored for use throughout the year to sustain a stable population and so provide a practical alternative to seasonal migrations. Setting up residence close to valuable resources also helped ensure the group's continued access and control over them. These conditions occasionally prevailed among advanced foragers and food collectors, like the Natufians, who enjoyed a symbiotic relationship with selected local plant and animal species in the Levant.

Natufians or their contemporaries in the lower Jordan River valley had in fact established a permanent community of dome-shaped dwellings at Jericho centuries before its residents became fully reliant on farming (Kenyon, 1981). Though it never attained the size or status of a true city, early Jericho already anticipated some of the traits that would characterize later urban centers, including signs of social complexity. Before 10,000 y.a., Jericho participated in a regional exchange of salt, sulphur, shells, obsidian, and turquoise and used some of these products as offerings in the graves of certain individuals. More impressive were Jericho's remarkable construction features, clearly the products of organized communal effort. A massive stone wall 6 feet (1.8 m) thick, incorporating a 28-foot (8.5 m) stone tower with interior stairs, enclosed the settlement of several hundred modest houses. A deep trench, cut into the bedrock beyond the wall, afforded even greater security, but

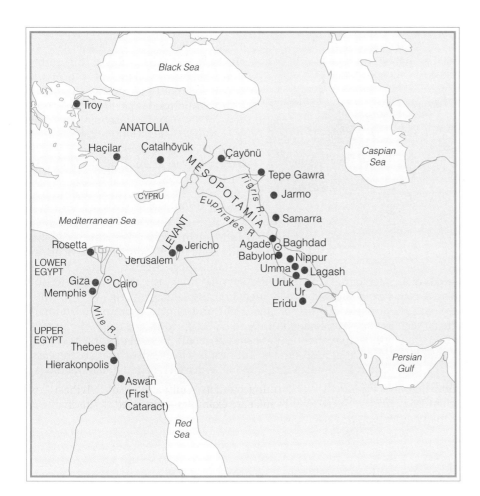

FIGURE 17–3
Sites associated with early civilizations in
Mesopotamia and the Nile valley.

against whom or what is uncertain. Viewed initially as fortifications against unknown human enemies, Jericho's wall and ditch may have been intended instead to divert mud flows brought on by severe erosion due to deforestation and poor farming practices in the vicinity (Bar-Yosef, 1986). The tower could have functioned either for defense or as a community shrine.

A 32-acre (13-hectare) site in south-central Turkey, **Çatalhöyük** was both larger and somewhat later than Jericho (Mellaart, 1975; Hodder, 1996). Çatalhöyük served as a trade and religious center some 8,000 y.a. during early Neolithic times. Its densely packed houses of timber and mud brick had only rooftop entrances; their painted plaster interiors included living and storage space, sleeping platforms, and hearths. The community's several thousand inhabitants farmed outside its walls or engaged in craft production within. Some residents exploited nearby sources of obsidian or volcanic glass to make beads, mirrors, and blades to be exported in exchange for raw materials and finished goods. The wealth that this trade generated apparently went in part to support religious activities in the numerous elaborately decorated shrines uncovered in the excavated portion of the site. Many of these shrines held representations of cattle, then only recently domesticated, as focal points for the worshipers.

Jericho and Çatalhöyük may be somewhat exceptional in that specialized trade or religious activities promoted their early development into relatively large and complex Neolithic communities. Even so, they were not truly cities, nor did they pertain to any larger cultural entity that could be described as a civilization. They simply surpassed in size and sophistication such contemporary settlements as Jarmo (Iraq), Çayönü (Turkey), and Haçilar (Turkey), which remained modest peasant villages. Despite their size and local prominence, they did not evolve into real urban centers of the kind associated with most ancient civilizations.

Çatalhöyük
(sha-tahl-hoo'-yook) Early Neolithic community in southern Anatolia, or Turkey.

The First Civilizations

William Turnbaugh

FIGURE 17–4
A small tell in the Jordan River valley.

Tells
Mounds of accumulated rubble representing the site of an ancient city. A tell differs in both scale and content from a *midden.*

FIGURE 17–5
A cross section through a tell at Harappa, India.

The earliest true city yet discovered is Uruk, in southern Iraq. Associated with the Sumerian civilization of the southern Tigris-Euphrates valley, the site of Uruk boasts remnants of massive mud-brick temples and residential areas that housed tens of thousands of people after 5,500 y.a. A number of other contemporary sites in northern Iraq and Syria, not yet excavated, indicate that urbanism was getting under way throughout that region in the late fourth millennium B.C. (about 5,200 y.a.).

In time, many of these early towns and urban centers of the Near East, including Uruk, and even Jericho and Çatalhöyük, became **tells**. Tells are mounds of archaeological rubble, built up of mud brick, ash, stone, and other accumulated debris from successive settlements on the same spot (Fig. 17–4). Some of these features attained the size of small hills and remain prominent landmarks. (Others, such as Old Jerusalem, continue to be occupied to this day.) As one might expect, the older components of these sites generally lie closer to the base of the tell, nearer the original ground surface. But neat layer-cake structures are the exception, since most tells accumulated in a sporadic manner as individual buildings or sections were erected or demolished (Fig. 17–5). In most other areas of the world, where people usually occupied more dispersed settlements, tells did not form.

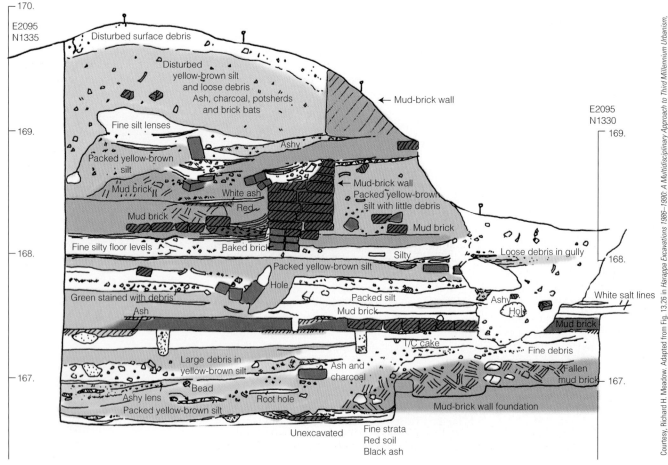

Courtesy, Richard H. Meadow. Adapted from Fig. 13.26 in *Harappa Excavations 1986–1990: A Multidisciplinary Approach to Third Millennium Urbanism,* Richard H. Meadow (ed.). *Monographs in World Archaeology,* No. 3., p. 220. Madison, WI: Prehistory Press, 1991.

Ancient Civilizations of the Old World

So seemingly familiar are the ancient Near Eastern civilizations—Egypt and Mesopotamia—that we instinctively use them as a standard against which to measure all others. It is inappropriate to do so, for the variety of advanced cultures in Asia, Africa, and the Americas defies easy comparison. Archaeologists recognize each of the world's early civilizations as unique, with individual cultural trajectories, distinctive accomplishments, and specific ways of confronting problems.

The survey of ancient civilizations that follows is not a random selection, nor is it a truly representative one. Our focus, for the most part, is on the premier civilizations to emerge in several major geographical regions of the Old World (American civilizations are covered in Chapter 18). The archaeological remains of these specific cultures have captured the general public's imagination and attracted the attention of scholars for many decades. Each left tantalizing traces of itself in the archaeological record, ranging from random assemblages of indecipherable written texts, in some instances, to the ruins of structures intended by their architects to be everlasting. The information amassed by numerous research expeditions to the valleys of the Tigris-Euphrates, Nile, Indus, and Huanghe has become the familiar fare of schoolrooms and travelogues. But do not let familiarity breed contempt, because these ancient societies are truly remarkable and they do merit our attention. Each one devised ways of grappling with the challenges presented by entirely new social, political, and economic circumstances. These societies pioneered achievements in technology, literacy, arts, and architecture. They invented religions and law codes and calendars. Their legacies have survived for millennia and may yet occasionally be recognized within the framework of our modern civilizations.

Mesopotamia

During the centuries after 8,000 y.a., pioneering farmers settled the vast alluvial plains bordering the lower Tigris and Euphrates Rivers, an area called **Mesopotamia** (see Fig. 17–3). These agriculturists shared the heritage of such early Neolithic communities as Jarmo in the Zagros foothills to the east and Çayönü at the edge of the Anatolian plateau (Nissen, 1988). Indeed, they were probably direct descendants of Samarran farmers, who had practiced small-scale irrigation agriculture along the edges of the central Tigris valley and obtained painted pottery and obsidian through trade with upland communities. Now advancing onto the southern plains, perhaps in search of vacant or more productive lands, these **Ubaid** farmers (as archaeologists refer to them) encountered great flood-prone streams bound only by immense mud flats and marshes.

The annual floods in this region began soon after the spring planting season, when young crops were particularly vulnerable. When the waters receded, a long, dry summer followed. At first, farmers cultivated only the well-drained rises above the river. But eventually they began the arduous task of redirecting the river's flow, even cutting through its banks to channel floodwater onto low-lying fields. Irrigation unlocked the fertility of the deep, stone-free silt that had accumulated on the floodplain for millennia. Barley was the Ubaidians' primary grain, but wheat and millet grew well, too, along with the date palm and vegetable crops. Their animals included pigs and several kinds of sheep. Domesticated donkeys and oxen performed heavy tasks. The abundant harvests, supplemented by fish and game, more than kept pace with the rapidly growing floodplain communities.

By around 6,500 y.a., Ubaid villagers were beginning to prosper in the southernmost Tigris-Euphrates valley (Lamberg-Karlovsky and Sabloff, 1995). A degree of cultural uniformity marked their settlements. Each of their more populous towns, such as Nippur, Eridu, and Uruk in the southern valley (see Fig. 17–3), centered around a platform-based temple; even the smaller communities had central shrines. Perhaps to acquire resources lacking in their new homeland, Ubaidians maintained contact with distant peoples through trade in decorated pottery, obsidian, ornamental stones, copper, and possibly grain. Archaeologists use chemical analyses of distinctive trace

Mesopotamia
(*meso*, meaning "middle," and *potamos*, meaning "river") Land between the Tigris and Euphrates Rivers, mostly included in modern-day Iraq.

Ubaid
(oo-bide') Early formative culture of Mesopotamia, 7,500–6,200 y.a.; predecessor to Sumerian civilization.

457

elements in raw materials and artifacts to track these exchanges throughout the region, from the Persian Gulf to the eastern Mediterranean (Roaf, 1996).

Important changes ushered in the late Ubaid period, around 5,500 y.a. The population of certain communities rapidly swelled into the thousands as people from outlying districts massed together. Expanding irrigation systems in the lower Tigris-Euphrates valley produced more food for the concentrated populace. Altering the riverine environment on this scale by digging drainage and irrigation channels was a daunting enterprise, one that could be accomplished only through organized communal effort, including a high degree of cooperation and direction. The activity transformed not only the landscape but undoubtedly the nature of the agricultural societies themselves.

What might these concentrated populations signify? Certainly, we are witnessing the birth of the first true cities. But what had stimulated their development? Perhaps intensified economic—or even military—rivalries in the region had forced populations to come together for protection (Adams, 1981). An alternative interpretation sees a more peaceful genesis, with urbanism an outgrowth of increased agricultural productivity and efficiency, which in turn fostered sociocultural changes (social stratification, craft specialization, commerce, etc.) within the urban setting. Whatever the reason, these trends were occurring simultaneously at a number of settlements along the lower Tigris-Euphrates valley as people flocked to the developing cities.

Sumerians   Over several centuries, Uruk's population expanded to perhaps as many as 50,000 people. Today, nearly 1.75 square miles (some 450 hectares) of dissolved brick foundations identify its site in southern Mesopotamia, 150 miles (240 km) southeast of modern Baghdad, Iraq (Nissen, 1988). The most ancient portions of Uruk reveal some features of the earliest city. Two massive temple complexes, built in stages and dedicated to the sun and to the goddess of love, probably served as focal points of political, religious, economic, and cultural activities. Inscribed clay tablets associated with these structures record that the temples distributed food and controlled nearby croplands. Growing social and religious complexity (including the rise of powerful kings and priests) kept pace with the physical growth of the city.

The developments associated with Uruk and the other urban centers were an immediate prelude and stimulus to a new order in southern Mesopotamia around 5,000 y.a. The inscribed tablets, teeming populations, and large-scale religious structures indicate that the essential elements of civilization had come together. Uruk ushered in the period of the first complex urban civilization, usually identified with a people called the Sumerians.

The region known as Sumer encompassed about a dozen largely autonomous political units, called **city-states**, in the southernmost Tigris-Euphrates valley. About the same number of Akkadian city-states hugged the river to the north, near present-day Baghdad. The Sumerians and their neighbors shared the world's first modern society between 4,900 and 4,350 y.a. Each Sumerian city-state incorporated a major population center—Ur, Lagash, Umma, Nippur, Eridu, and Uruk are examples—as well as some smaller satellite communities and, of course, a great deal of irrigated cropland. These city-states were controlled by hereditary kings, who often contested for dominance with their counterparts in neighboring cities.

Theirs was an urbanized and technologically accomplished culture, economically dependent on large-scale irrigation agriculture and specialized craft production (Kramer, 1963; Roaf, 1996). They were among the first to refine metals such as gold, silver, and copper and to make bronze alloys. Sophisticated architecture incorporated the true arch and the dome. Other practical innovations included the use of wheeled carts, draft animals, the plow, and sailing boats. Skilled crafters produced fine jewelry and textiles, while artists created sculpture and music. Sumerian merchants and administrators relied on written records and a counting system based on multiples of 6, which they also applied to measuring time and devising calendars. (Hence, buying a dozen doughnuts or counting minutes in our 24-hour day are modern reminders of ancient Sumerian numeration!) Their system of law

City-states
Autonomous sociopolitical units comprising an urban center and supporting territory.

became a basis for later legal codes, and Sumerian contributions to literature included many of the traditions subsequently gathered into the Old Testament.

The influence of these cities reached beyond Mesopotamia through exchange and perhaps even colonization. Excavations in northern Iraq, Turkey, and the Nile valley have revealed connections with Uruk through trade in prestige goods such as pottery, carved ivory, and lapis (Roaf, 1996). These valued products furnished the tombs of Sumerian elites in a society where social differentiation was becoming more pronounced.

Among the prerogatives of royalty was the right to burial in a lavish tomb. Sir Leonard Woolley's excavations of the 4,500-year-old royal tombs at Ur in the 1920s revealed that King Abargi and Queen Puabi were each accompanied in death by the men and women of their court, bedecked with precious jewelry as they composed themselves to be drugged and then sealed into the tomb. Rich offerings—ceremonial vessels, tools, musical instruments, and even chariots complete with their animals and human attendants—also were arranged within the burial pits (Woolley, 1929).

Mesopotamian citizens constructed brick walls around their city perimeters for security. The heart of each urban center was its sacred district, dominated by a grand temple and flanked by noble houses. In addition to a patron deity associated with each city, a pantheon of major and minor divinities received homage. Chief among them was Enlil, the air god. Like most Mesopotamian gods, Enlil exhibited remarkably human characteristics, taking a fatherly concern for mortals and their daily affairs, but also meting out punishment and misfortune. Some cities, like Ur, regularly augmented their shrines, eventually creating an impressive artificial mountain called a **ziggurat** (Fig. 17–6). Rising from an elevated platform roughly the size of a football field, these stepped temples were solidly built of millions of molded and baked mud bricks.

Ziggurat
Late Sumerian mud-brick temple-pyramid.

Outside the ceremonial district, narrow unpaved alleyways twisted through crowded residential precincts. Much like city dwellers everywhere, Sumerians endured social problems and pollution in their urban environment. The size and location of individual homes correlated with family wealth and position. Contemporary written accounts indicate that the populace comprised three general classes: nobility, commoners, and slaves. Numbered among the latter were formerly free citizens who had fallen on hard times and sold themselves into bondage, as well as captives taken in conflicts with neighboring city-states. Some of the commoners specialized in craft or merchant activities, but many were farmers with fields and herds just beyond the surrounding walls. The houses of all but the nobility were generally one story, with several rooms opening onto a central courtyard. Wall and

FIGURE 17–6
Reconstructed lower stage of the late Sumerian ziggurat at Ur.

National Geographic Society

FIGURE 17–7
This small Sumerian clay tablet (actual size) is a 4,000-year-old tax receipt with cuneiform impressions on both sides.

Cuneiform
(*cuneus*, meaning "wedge") Wedge-shaped writing of ancient Mesopotamia.

Gilgamesh
Semi-legendary king and culture hero of early Uruk, reputed to have had many marvelous adventures.

Hammurabi
(ham-oo-rah'-bee) Early Babylonian king, c. 1800–1750 B.C.

Nebuchadnezzar
(neh-boo-kud-neh'-zer) Late Babylonian king, c. 605–562 B.C.

Hierakonpolis
(high-rak-kon-po-lis) Important town and pottery production center of Upper Egypt.

floor coverings brightened the interiors, furnished with wooden tables, chairs, and beds and an assortment of household equipment for cooking and storage.

From our perspective, their writing system was perhaps the Sumerians' most significant invention, enabling us to discover more about them than their other artifacts and monuments could ever reveal. Literacy was a hard-won accomplishment. By about 5,000 y.a., the original pictographic form of Sumerian writing was evolving into a more flexible writing system utilizing hundreds of standardized signs. Highly trained scribes formed the characteristic wedge-shaped, or **cuneiform**, script by pressing a reed stylus onto damp clay pads; these tablets were then baked for preservation (Fig. 17–7). Ninety percent of early Sumerian writing concerned economic, legal, and administrative matters; like us, the Sumerians belonged to a complex and bureaucratic society. Later scribes recorded more historical and literary works, including several epic accounts featuring the adventures of **Gilgamesh**, an early Uruk king and culture hero reputed to have performed many amazing deeds in the face of overwhelming odds.

The loose conglomeration of Mesopotamian city-states faced hard times after around 4,500 y.a. Their long dependence on irrigation agriculture was slowly poisoning the fields that supported the large populations. Soluble mineral salts conveyed by irrigation water precipitated into the soil, destroying its fertility. Eroding silt threatened to choke off the canals themselves. Moreover, much of the energy of this early civilization was dissipated in fruitless internal competition. Clustered together in an area about the size of Vermont, the city-states of Sumer and neighboring Akkad, to the north, vied with one another for supremacy in commerce, prestige, and religion.

Finally, around 2334 B.C., a minor Akkadian official assumed the name Sargon of Agade and led armies from the north to victory in the Sumerian lands, thereby establishing the region's first consolidated empire. Military expansion led to economic, political, and linguistic dominance over a broad area. Under Sargon, his sons, and grandsons, the Akkadian state endured only a century before dissolving. But once initiated, the unification process continued on and off for many centuries in Mesopotamia, next under the kings of Ur and later (about 3,800 y.a.) under **Hammurabi** of Babylon, famed for his "eye for an eye" law code, among other accomplishments. Shortly thereafter, the ancient lands were incorporated into the realm of the Assyrians until 2,600 y.a., when a new Babylonian empire reclaimed dominance under King **Nebuchadnezzar**.

Egypt

The pyramids of Egypt remain unrivaled as the ancient world's most imposing monuments. They have adorned the banks of the Nile for so long that one can scarcely imagine a time when they had not yet taken form. Yet, as we have seen (in Chapter 16), Egyptian culture was rooted in the Nile valley long before the pyramids.

Archaeological evidence of these most ancient Nile cultures is rarely preserved in the unstable river floodplain (Trigger et al., 1983; Hays, 1984). Still, excavations reveal that the early farmers grew Near Eastern varieties of wheat and barley, as well as raising sheep and goats initially domesticated in the same region. Neolithic villages lined the great river's banks by 6,000 y.a. Even at this early stage, the settlements in the section of the valley known as Upper Egypt (just north of Aswan, the "First Cataract" of ancient times) contrasted somewhat with those in the delta region—Lower Egypt, close to the river's mouth. Archaeologists recognize a Mesopotamian influence at work among the Upper Egypt villagers, perhaps introduced through direct contact or by way of Palestinian traders (Hoffman, 1991). Mineral resources, especially gold, apparently drew outsiders to the region.

Increasing political and social cohesion gripped some of these Upper Egypt settlements as they coalesced into local chiefdoms around 5,300 y.a. Walls protected the towns of Naqada and **Hierakonpolis**, and well-stocked stone and brick tombs were a final measure of the social differentiation enjoyed by principal individuals (Wenke, 1990). Pottery making and trading became specialized economic enter-

prises (Fig. 17–8). Continuing contact with Mesopotamian cultures may have stimulated these developments, although no evidence of comparable Egyptian influence in the other direction is yet apparent.

In any event, during the next few centuries, this part of the Nile valley transformed rapidly. Historical tradition and textual evidence, including a relief-carved stone plaque from Hierakonpolis, record that one of Upper Egypt's early chiefs, taking the name Narmer, seized other communities of that region and successfully exerted his control over the delta villages in the north as well. This unification of Upper and Lower Egypt under Narmer, the traditional beginning of the First Dynasty of Egyptian civilization, dates to around 3000 B.C. (5,000 y.a.). The merger of Nile valley societies under one king marked an important milestone in the development of ancient Egypt by creating the world's first nation-state.

Following the initial unification period, a 425-year span known as Old Kingdom times (4,575–4,150 y.a.) represented the first full flowering of Nile valley civilization. The ruler, or **pharaoh**, was the supreme power of the society, and under his direction, Egypt became a wonder of the ancient world and a source of endless fascination for millennia to follow.

Egyptians soon adopted a complex pictographic script called **hieroglyphics**, a writing system that is Egyptian in form but probably Mesopotamian in inspiration. The earliest inscriptions are associated exclusively with the Egyptian royal court, as are other high-status products, such as cylinder seals, certain types of pottery, and specific artistic motifs and architectural techniques that also seem to be derived from beyond the Nile valley. Advanced methods of copper working came into use as well, including ore refining and alloying, casting, and hammering techniques. Some of these processes likewise were invented elsewhere. An important by-product of copper metallurgy was **faience**, an Egyptian innovation produced by fusing powdered quartz, soda ash, and copper ore in a kiln. The blue-green glassy substance, molded into beads or statuettes, became a popular trade item throughout the region (Friedman, 1998).

Early pharaohs were godlike kings who ruled with divine authority through a bureaucracy of priests and public officials. The pharaoh's power depended to a large degree on his assumed control over the annual Nile flood (Butzer, 1984), and throughout the course of Egypt's long history, pharaonic fortunes tended to fluctuate with the river's flow. Most Old Kingdom pharaohs maintained their royal courts at Memphis, about 15 miles south of present-day Cairo. In contrast to Mesopotamia, few urban centers emerged in the ancient Nile valley, and even the capital was of modest size. Egypt remained almost entirely an agrarian and rural culture, the vast majority of its citizenry comprising farmers and a few tradespersons engaged in their timeless routines (Aldred, 1998). Only in the immediate vicinity of Memphis and the sacred mortuary complexes along the Nile's west bank was Egypt's grandeur clearly evident.

The familiar Old Kingdom pyramids on the Nile's west bank at Giza evolved out of a tradition of royal tomb building that began at Hierakonpolis. In that early community, brick-lined burial pits were dug with adjoining chambers to stock the offerings for a deceased king's afterlife, and these rooms were then capped with a low, rectangular brick tomb (Lehner, 1997). The scale of these structures increased as successive rulers outdid their predecessors. The monumental pyramids best exemplify the pharaoh's absolute authority over the people and resources of his domain (Fig. 17–9). In a sense, these constructions were immense public works projects that served to solidify the power of the state while also glorifying the memory of individual rulers. Contrary to popular view, they were not built by slave labor, but by thousands of Egyptian farmers, put to work during the several months each year when the Nile floodwaters covered their fields.

In all, some 25 pyramids honored the Old Kingdom's elite (Lehner, 1997). The first stepped pyramids of stone were raised after 2630 B.C. (4,630 y.a.), and little more than a century later, the imposing tombs of Khufu and Khafra, Fourth Dynasty rulers, were among the last built in true pyramid form. Khufu's Great Pyramid is 765 feet (232 m) square at its base and 479 feet (146 m) in height, with

FIGURE 17–8
Decorated predynastic pottery jar, Nile valley.

After drawing by William Turnbaugh, based on specimen at Museum of Fine Arts, Boston

Pharaoh
Title of the king or ruler of ancient Egypt.

Hieroglyphics
(*hiero*, meaning "sacred," and *glyphein*, meaning "carving") The picture-writing of ancient Egypt.

Faience
(fay-ahnz') Glassy material, usually of blue-green color, shaped into beads, amulets, and figurines by ancient Egyptians.

FIGURE 17–9
Egyptian Old Kingdom pyramid and Sphinx at Giza.

2.3 million massive limestone blocks required in its construction. Although Khafra's tomb is about 20 percent smaller, he compensated by having a nearby rock outcrop carved with the likeness of his face on the body of a lion, today called the Great Sphinx (Hawass and Lehner, 1994). Pyramid building ceased soon after, during a time of political decentralization and greater local control over such practical programs as state irrigation works.

The Old Kingdom pyramids represented a remarkable engineering triumph and an enormous cultural achievement that has inspired subsequent civilizations (Fig. 17–10). Bear in mind that the stark structures we see along the Nile today were adjoined by extensive complexes of connecting causeways, shrines, altars, and storerooms filled with statuary and furnishings and ornamented with colorful

FIGURE 17–10
Ancient archaeological monuments inspire modern imitations, like this hotel and casino complex in Las Vegas, Nevada.

William Turnbaugh

FIGURE 17–11
Hieroglyphic inscriptions document this scene of a royal Egyptian hunting marsh birds from a papyrus boat.

friezes and carved stonework. The pyramids' slanting sides signified pathways to the sacred Sun. Worshipers flocked to them, paying reverence to the memory of the dead kings. The mortuary cult of the pharaohs absorbed a large share of the work and wealth of Egyptian society.

Later kings contented themselves with burial in smaller but nonetheless lavishly furnished tombs in a cramped desert valley below a natural pyramid-shaped mountain near Thebes (see Box 17–1 on p. 464). Discovered in the 1920s, the treasure-choked burial chamber of the young pharaoh **Tutankhamen**, who died more than 3,300 y.a. (circa 1323 B.C.) during New Kingdom times, is convincing evidence that dead royalty were not neglected even after the era of pyramids had passed (Carter and Mace, 1923). Near the same location, in 1995, archaeologist Kent Weeks discovered another impressive New Kingdom tomb. Although looted long ago, scores of rock-cut chambers prepared for many of the 52 sons of Ramesses II ("the Great") formed a vast underground mausoleum, now called KV5, that is now being systematically explored (Weeks, 1999).

Much of what we know of ancient Egypt's religion and rulers derives from the translation of countless hieroglyphic inscriptions (Fig. 17–11). The 1799 discovery at Rosetta, a small Nile delta town, of a 2.5-by-2.5-foot (76 cm) stone bearing an identical decree engraved in three scripts, including Greek and hieroglyphics, enabled the brilliant French linguist Jean-François Champollion to decipher the mysterious and complex writing after 20 years of effort (Fig. 17–12).

Egyptian hieroglyphics combine signs that represent ideas with others indicating sounds. Because hieroglyphics were used primarily in formal contexts (like Latin in more recent times), their translation tells us much about pharaohs and their concerns, revealing less about the commonplace events and people of the era. In fact, archaeologists can read disappointingly little about daily life in Egypt's Old Kingdom period outside the major administrative and mortuary centers, where tomb scenes occasionally portray peasants at work in their fields or winnowing or grinding grain. Happily, later periods of Egyptian society are more fully documented (Montet, 1981; Casson, 2001).

Although nothing surpassed the original glory of the Old Kingdom period, Egypt proved remarkably resilient through the centuries, surviving foreign invaders such as the Hyksos and Hittites of southwest Asia, as well as frequent episodes of internal misrule and rebellion. Its pharaohs enjoyed periods of resurgence and

Tutankhamen
(toot-en-cahm'-en) Egyptian pharaoh of the New Kingdom period, who died at age 19 in 1323 B.C.; informally known today as King Tut.

Courtesy, Bill Gamble, Ward's Scientific

FIGURE 17–12
The Rosetta Stone, as displayed in the British Museum in the nineteenth century.

BOX 17–1 DIGGING DEEPER

Discovering the Mummy's Secrets

Although mummies are most commonly associated with ancient Egypt, exceptionally dry, cold, or wet conditions have allowed human bodies to be preserved in many other areas. Corpses buried thousands of years ago in China's Tarim Basin, in the Atacama Desert of western South America, and within dry rock-shelters in the American Southwest are often in surprisingly good condition. Natural freeze-drying accounts for the remarkable preservation of children placed as sacrifices atop high peaks in the Peruvian Andes centuries ago. The frozen Siberia tundra entombs 2,400-year-old corpses of Scythian chieftains. A melting Alpine glacier recently freed the body of the "Ice Man," a middle-aged male who had died 5,300 years ago. Fully submerged in acidic, anaerobic (i.e., lacking oxygen) wetlands for two millennia, the many "bog bodies" of northwestern Europe represent victims of ritual sacrifice or execution.

Egypt's arid climate and the cultural practice of mummification preserved innumerable corpses in the cemeteries and tombs on the Nile's west bank, the traditional Land of the Dead. Simple burial in a shallow grave dug into dry sand desiccated the remains of most early Egyptians, but by Old Kingdom times, the bodies of royalty and high officials who were laid to rest in stone tombs or pyramids underwent a 70-day embalm-

ing process to prepare them for the afterlife. With most internal organs removed for separate processing, the body was packed in salts for six weeks, then artfully stuffed and wrapped with lengths of resin-soaked linen.

Early pharaohs took great wealth to their graves, so their pyramids were an obvious target for robbers. Attempting to thwart the thieves, New Kingdom pharaohs had themselves entombed in the desolate Valley of the Kings, near Thebes, the capital at that time (1560–1085 B.C., or 3,560–3,085 y.a.). Their corpses and offerings were secreted in chambers cut deep into the rock, then covered by sand. With the decline of the monarchy by the end of the New Kingdom period, tomb robbers were especially rampant, so high priests retrieved more than 50 royal mummies for safekeeping in two hidden caches. Their rediscovery a century ago brings us face to face with some important New Kingdom pharaohs, including Ramesses II ("the Great"), Amenhotep I, Thutmose I, Seti I, and many others.

Paleopathologists can learn a great deal from their encounters with mummies—Egyptian or otherwise. Nondestructive radiographic images of ancient mummies produced with standard X-rays or digitized CAT scans may reveal evidence of long-term health problems or trauma (such as fractures, healed or not), as well as

revival until, in a state of decline and defeated by the Persians (circa 2,500 y.a.), Egypt fell into the Greek sphere under Alexander the Great and eventually came under the rule of Rome.

The Indus Valley

As the first great pyramids rose beside the Nile, a collection of urban settlements that dotted a broad floodplain far to the east was forming into the Harappan, or Indus valley, civilization (Fig. 17–13 on p. 466). For seven centuries, beginning about 4,600 y.a. (2600–1900 B.C.), the banks of the Indus and its tributaries in present-day Pakistan and India supported at least five primary urban centers with populations each numbering in the tens of thousands (Kenoyer, 1998; Possehl, 1999; Meadow and Kenoyer, 2000). Many hundreds of smaller farming villages were socially and economically, if not politically, linked to these central places.

The people of the Indus were relative newcomers to the valley. As we saw in Chapter 16, their ancestors cultivated the higher valley margins to the west at sites like Mehrgarh by 8,000 y.a. Farming and herding, along with regional trade, had sustained village life from an early period in these uplands (Jarrige and Meadow, 1980). Around 5,300 y.a., farmers began to populate the Indus floodplain itself, pos-

medical treatments and other cultural practices. For example, the pharaohs Ramesses II and Amenhotep III suffered from severe dental disease (caries, abscesses, periodontal disease, tooth loss) and excessive tooth wear. Stages of dental eruption, fusion of long-bone epiphyses, and remodeling changes of the pubic symphyses provide estimates for age at death. A host of other factors may leave their marks on the skeleton beneath the mummy's skin: childhood illnesses or malnutrition (shown by X-ray imaging of Harris lines representing discontinuous growth periods), osteoarthritis, osteoporosis, iron-deficiency anemia, tuberculosis, cancer, venereal disease, and congenital or developmental malformations, among others.

A mummy's preserved soft tissues, including organs, may reveal further details about the individual's living conditions and health status. Video endoscopes—flexible fiber-optic devices—can be used to probe and photograph the body's internal passageways, and magnetic resonance imaging (MRI) provides nondestructive three-dimensional or cross-sectional views of the brain and other organs. Remarkably, tissue samples taken from New Kingdom mummies have been rehydrated, then studied in thin section under high magnification. These procedures have provided us with some interesting insights. For example, arteriosclerosis (hardening of the arteries) afflicted the pharaohs Ramesses and Merenptah. Moreover, carbon soot from fires and silica from blowing sand clogged the lungs of most ancient Egyptians, and intestinal parasites were common. DNA extracted from the royal mummies permits bioarchaeologists to verify individual identities and to confirm the recorded genealogies of these New Kingdom pharaohs. Analyses of stable carbon isotopes in mummified human tissue from northern Sudan indicate that Nile farmers in that region shifted from temperate grasses (wheat or barley) in favor of tropical millet or sorghum around A.D. 350. Other cultural practices are directly apparent on mummies, including the widespread use of tattoos as a form of body decoration in ancient Europe, Asia, the Pacific islands, and the Americas.

Sources:

Beckett, Ronald, Gerald Conlogue, and John Posh. 2000. "Picturing the Past." *Discovering Archaeology*, 2(5): 66–75.

Cockburn, Aidan, and Eve Cockburn. 1980. *Mummies, Disease, and Ancient Cultures*. New York: Cambridge University Press.

Ikram, Salima, and Aidan Dodson. 1998. *The Mummy in Ancient Egypt*. New York: Thames and Hudson.

van de Sande, Wijnand. 1996. *Through Nature to Eternity: The Bog Bodies of Northwest Europe*. Amsterdam: Batavian Lion International.

sibly seeking more productive cropland or better access to potential trade routes for valued copper, shell, and colorful stones. Occupying slight natural rises on the flat landscape at places like Kot Diji, they laid out fields for their vegetables, cereals, and cotton on the deep alluvium. As the new settlements grew, farmers cooperated in water management projects intended to provide irrigation for croplands and also reduce the effects of floods. They diverted part of the river's flow through irrigation sluices into their fields and constructed massive retaining walls or elevated platforms to repel its silty waters from their homes. Their work gained them a tentative control over the flood-prone stream.

A number of these settlements prospered and rapidly reached impressive size. By 4,600 y.a., several large urban centers hugged the river. Why had people accustomed to living in small farming communities congregated into these cities? Perhaps an increased threat of flooding along the river (brought on by extensive deforestation and other poor farming practices) simply forced people to come together in building and maintaining more levees and irrigation canals. An alternative hypothesis proposes trade as the "integrative force" behind Indus urbanization (Possehl, 1990). A few entrepreneurs may have fostered exchange between the valley settlements and the uplands, promoting resource development, craft specialization, and product distribution to stimulate and reap the economic benefits. As

The First Civilizations

FIGURE 17-13
Location of the Indus valley civilization.

commerce began to pay off, other changes, including urbanism and social stratification, further transformed Indus society. Once they had reached a critical mass, the cities continued to attract craftspeople, shopkeepers, and foreign traders.

As busy centers of craft production and trade, the cities prospered along the great river. Workshops in different neighborhoods turned out quantities of wheel-turned pottery, cut and polished stone beads and stamp seals, and molded figurines. Merchants' scales used standardized stone cubes of precise weight to facilitate exchange transactions. The Indus itself became a commercial highway for boats laden with goods moving up and down the river or destined for Persian Gulf ports. Carts, too, conveyed the colorfully dyed cotton cloth, pottery, carved stone, shell, ivory, and precious metal goods over land to Mesopotamia. For a time, a distant Harappan trade outpost was established near Sumerian Ur.

Thus far, archaeologists have carried out extensive excavations at only several of the major cities and a few of the smaller contemporary agricultural and pastoral villages (Fig. 17–14). The largest Indus sites excavated so far are Mohenjo-Daro and Harappa, which flourished between about 4,600 and 3,900 y.a. in present-day Pakistan. Raised on massive brick terraces above the river's flow, these cities were carefully planned, using grids of approximately 1,300 by 650 feet (400 by 200 m) for the residential blocks. Although these large sites certainly signify social complexity and central control, the Indus valley civilization lacks grand picturesque ruins of the type found in Egypt and Sumer. No sumptuous palaces or monumental religious structures here! Their absence may suggest a fundamental distinction of Harappan society, where glorification of individual rulers was less of a centralizing focus. At the same time, it is unlikely that economic and social power was more broadly shared here than in other civilizations. Indeed, the varied scale of residential architecture as well as the limited availability of valuable jewelry and personalized stamp seals reflects a definite social hierarchy. Still, Richard H. Meadow, who has been excavating at Harappa since 1987, describes this civilization as "an elaborate middle-class society" (Edwards, 2000, p. 116).

Both Mohenjo-Daro and Harappa encompassed a public district and several residential areas (Fig. 17–15). Mohenjo-Daro's "great bath" lies near what has been interpreted as that city's government center, a complex that also included elite residences and a large "assembly hall." The pool may have served worshipers for ritual cleansing. Close by was a capacious structure of uncertain function that some have interpreted as a granary, or grain storage facility. Farmers may have been obliged to contribute substantial portions of their harvests to help maintain the society. A

FIGURE 17-14
Excavated base of an outdoor baking oven from the Indus valley civilization, Lothal, India.

National Geographic Society

FIGURE 17-15
An excavated section of Mohenjo-Daro.

building of this type was found at Harappa, too. In other sections of both cities, the windowless walls of ordinary workers' homes of standard brick construction bordered unpaved avenues and alleys. More spacious multistoried houses with interior courtyards sheltered members of the privileged social classes. What has been proclaimed as the world's first efficient sewer system conveyed waste away from the densely packed dwellings, many of them equipped with indoor toilets and baths.

What might this culture have to say for itself? Unfortunately, the writing system, consisting of brief pictographic notations commonly found on seal stones and pottery, remains undeciphered (Parpola, 1994; Possehl, 1996).

The Indus civilization's decline seems to have been as rapid as its ascent. After little more than half a millennium, its major sites were virtually abandoned, although hundreds of smaller towns and villages outlasted them. In the absence of written records or any archaeological evidence for invasion or revolution, we are reduced to conjecture in accounting for this demise. Did competing trade routes bypass the Indus? Did the irrigation system fail or the river shift in its channel, either flooding the fields or leaving them parched? Was the society simply unable to maintain its urban centers? Floodwaters were a frequent threat; Mohenjo-Daro had been rebuilt perhaps 10 times before being given up to the Indus tide. All we know for sure is that in the end, the river that spawned the principal urban centers gradually reclaimed the surrounding fields and eventually the city sites themselves.

Northern China

As we saw in the previous chapter (see p. 426), the deep roots of China's early civilization were nurtured in the loess uplands and stark alluvial plains bordering the great rivers of the north. Specialized production and exchange of valued ritual goods came to characterize the prosperous farming societies along the central and lower Huanghe valley and brought about increased contact and perhaps even conflict among them. This phase of regional development and interaction continued during the later Neolithic, or Longshan, period, beginning about 4,800 y.a., and culminated in the formation of a distinctive Chinese culture that emphasized social ranking and ritualism, accompanied by persistent warfare (Chang, 1986).

In this Longshan period, the circulation of luxury products contributed to the concentration of wealth and the emergence of social hierarchies. Elite consumers supported such craft specialties as fine wheel-thrown pottery, jade carving, and a developing metal industry based on copper and (later) bronze production. Status differentiation is reflected in the range of burial treatments—from unusually lavish to mostly austere—accorded to individuals in the large Longshan cemeteries.

Erlitou
(err'-lee-too) Elaborate site in northern China associated with the earliest phase of civilization.

Xia
(shah) Semilegendary kingdom or dynasty of early China.

Divination
Foretelling the future.

Zhengzhou
(cheng-chew) Modern city of China associated with the site of the earliest Shang center.

Zhou
(chew) Chinese dynasty that followed Shang and ruled between 1122 and 221 B.C.

FIGURE 17–16
Centers of early Chinese civilization.

FIGURE 17–17
Cast bronze ritual vessel of the Shang dynasty.

Certain Longshan communities—or at least their central districts—were protected behind stout walls of stamped earth, compacted to the hardness of cement, more than 20 feet (6 m) high, 30 feet (9 m) thick, and up to 1 mile (1.6 km) in circumference. These enormous constructions obviously required a large supervised labor force. Numerous arrowheads testify to the prevalence of warfare. No clear explanations of these developments are yet possible.

Perhaps owing to their success in organizing and controlling communal agricultural efforts, or more directly through violence and coercion, local leaders who emerged in northern China over the next few centuries commanded the allegiance of ever-larger regions. The rising nobility assumed an ever more prominent role in the subsequent era of Chinese civilization.

Many Chinese archaeologists believe that **Erlitou** (Fig. 17–16), in Henan province, confirms the existence of the legendary **Xia** dynasty, proclaimed in myth as the dawn of Chinese civilization (Chang, 1980, 1986). The site displays evidence of increasing social complexity around 4,000 y.a. Here, for the first time, walled palaces set onto stamped earth foundations literally raised members of the royal household above all others. Valuable stone carvings and bronze and ceramic vessels figured in elaborate court ceremonies and rituals. Royal burials contrasted sharply with those of commoners, who were sometimes disposed of in rubbish pits.

Shang The subsequent Shang dynasty, beginning in the eighteenth century B.C. (3,750 y.a.), attained a level of sophistication in material culture, architecture, art styles, and writing that only a highly structured centralized society could achieve. Enduring for some six centuries, Shang is generally acknowledged as China's first civilization. While the large population of peasant farmers lived and labored as they always had, an elite and powerful ruling class, supported by slaves, specialized crafters, scribes, and other functionaries, topped the rigid social hierarchy.

The power and actions of Shang rulers were sometimes prescribed through the rite of **divination**, or prophecy. This practice was one of the original purposes for which writing was used in ancient China. Divination was performed by first inscribing a question on a specially prepared bone, such as an ox or deer scapula, or on turtle shells. Applying heat to the thin bones caused cracks to appear, whereupon the answer to the question could be "read." Divination was a vital activity to the Shang, and thousands of the marked bones survive as a unique historical archive that offers insights to early Chinese politics and society (Fitzgerald, 1978).

The primary center of the initial Shang period was on the banks of the Huanghe, near the modern city of **Zhengzhou**. Here, archaeologists revealed portions of a large walled precinct encompassing the residences of nobles and rulers as well as their temples and other ceremonial structures. Within sight of the high enclosure, extending in all directions for more than a mile (1.6 km), were clustered homes and specialized production areas. Among the latter were several bronze foundries, pottery kilns, and bone workshops.

Shang artisans created remarkable bronze work, particularly elaborate cauldrons cast in sectional molds (Fig. 17–17). Decorated with stylized animal motifs and worshipful inscriptions, the massive metal vessels were designed to hold ritual offerings of wine and food dedicated to ancestors and deities. They also served as prominent funerary items in the royal tombs, including about a dozen in the vicinity of the later Shang capital at Anyang (Chang, 1986). Digging each of these grave pits and its four ramped entryways probably occupied about 1,000 laborers for a week. In addition to the bronzes, lavish offerings of carved jade, horse-drawn chariots, and scores of human sacrificial victims accompanied the rulers in death. Only in much later times, as in the tomb of Qin emperor Shi Huangdi (died 2,200 y.a.) at Xian, were life-size clay sculptures of warriors and horses sometimes substituted for their living counterparts (Fig. 17–18).

The Shang kingdom appears to have been but one among several contentious feudal states in northern China. Despite their political competition, all shared a common culture, one that served as a foundation for most future developments in China. After the eclipse of the Shang state, successive **Zhou** rulers (1122–221 B.C.)

FIGURE 17–18
Some of the 8,000 clay warriors in the tomb of
Shi Huangdi.

FIGURE 17–19
Section of the Great Wall.

adopted and extended the social and cultural innovations introduced by their Shang predecessors. Much of China remained apportioned among competitive warlords until the Qin and Han dynasties (221 B.C.–A.D. 220), when this huge region was at last politically unified into a cohesive Chinese empire. Consolidated by Shi Huangdi, and protected from the outer world behind his 3,000-mile (5,000 km) Great Wall (Fig. 17–19), China in later times maintained many of the cultural traditions linking it to an ancient past.

The Mediterranean Realm

Compared to the ancient cultures of Egypt, Mesopotamia, and Asia, the Mediterranean societies of the second millennium B.C. were relatively late and less impressive in scale (Fig. 17–20). **Bronze Age** Minoans had a maritime orientation that kept them in contact with peoples bordering the eastern Mediterranean, including the venerable cultures of the Nile and the Fertile Crescent. Their contemporaries and successors, the Mycenaeans, developed the first civilization on the European mainland itself. Their special relevance to our discussion at this point is that these two cultures—Minoan and Mycenaean—bridged the old civilizations of the Near East and the formative societies of Neolithic Europe. In so doing, they helped set the course of modern Western civilization.

Minoans Neolithic farmers were the first to colonize Crete. Only with seaworthy boats could people reach this rugged caterpillar-shaped island in the eastern Mediterranean. Embarking from **Anatolia** about 8,000 y.a., the seafaring settlers transported their standard Neolithic cereals and livestock, but sheep, olives, grapes, and lentils were especially well adapted to Crete's mountainous semiarid terrain.

In time, a desire to exchange their surplus products promoted a lively internal trade among the scattered agricultural villages. These activities created new opportunities for economic and social advantage. Small kingdoms began to organize around thriving towns in several parts of the island. By 5,000 y.a., fine pottery,

Bronze Age
Period of early Old World civilizations associated with the widespread use of metal tools after 5,500 y.a.

Anatolia
Asia Minor; present-day Turkey.

FIGURE 17–20
Minoan and Mycenaean civilizations.

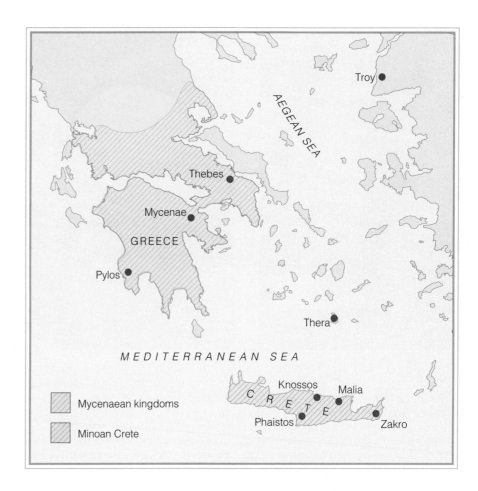

carved stamp seals, and circular stonework tombs distinguished a few of the island's most privileged inhabitants in life and death.

A growing appetite for locally unavailable status goods prompted the island's elite to look seaward. First with oar-propelled galleys, then sailing vessels, the Minoans of Crete mastered the sea lanes of the eastern Mediterranean. They plied among neighboring islands in the Aegean and on to Anatolia, the Nile delta, and the Levant, exchanging their foodstuffs, woolen cloth, pottery, and timber primarily for raw materials. At home in Crete, a host of specialized crafters converted these resources into luxury products. Attractively colored stones—carnelian, agate, sard, and jasper—became the carved stamp seals for impressing clay and other substances with an owner's personal mark. Copper and tin ores were smelted, alloyed, and cast into bronze weapons, armor, tools, and ornaments. Minoans also gained fame as skilled artisans in gold and silver. Elegant thin-walled pottery, stone vases and bowls, shell and ivory jewelry, and votive figurines emerged from their workshops. Some of these finished goods reentered the exchange network, while others remained in Crete to supply the wants of the growing Minoan elite.

The rapid transformation of Minoan society after 4,000 y.a. reflects this successful maritime trading activity (Hood, 1973; Castleden, 1990). Crete's coastal towns dominated the Mediterranean trade for the next five centuries. The prosperous communities expanded around multistoried temple-palaces and spacious homes that sheltered wealthy priest-kings and others of privileged status. **Knossos**, on the island's north face, had been one of the earliest settlements on Crete. Now it boasted a rambling temple-palace of more than a thousand rooms (Graham, 1987). (Though Knossos is the largest and most thoroughly explored, local centers dominated other sections of the island: Malia and Zakro to the east and Phaestos to the south.)

Knossos
Primary Minoan center, or regional capital; site of a huge temple-palace.

Walter H. Hodge, Peter Arnold, Inc.

FIGURE 17–21
Reconstruction of a Minoan palace room with frescoed walls, Knossos.

These immense structures were more than elite residences. They were the focus of Minoan life, the centers of its religion, economy, arts, crafts, and social hierarchy. Their balconies overlooked tiled courtyards, where religious ceremonies (including bloody sacrifices) took place. Within first-floor chambers, brightly frescoed walls revealed the Minoan love of art (Fig. 17–21). Painted scenes of commerce and exotic ports alternated with views of lush gardens, dancers and daring athletes, mythological landscapes, and imaginary creatures that captured a viewer's attention. In the buildings' workshops, artisans created delicate jewelry and elegant metal drinking vessels, while in other rooms, ranks of gaily decorated ceramic jars stored the valuable olive oil used for cooking, lighting, and food preservation. All these products would be redistributed within Minoan society or exported in trade. Scribes kept track of it all on carefully impressed clay tablets with symbols that remain to this day an undeciphered 70-character script known simply as *Linear A*. Finally, at the heart of the great building at Knossos lay a colonnaded chamber—the royal court with its carved gypsum throne.

The Minoan civilization of Crete was highly distinctive. Despite long contact with the Nile valley and the Near East, Minoans expressed their own cultural identity in every sphere, from art and architecture to statecraft and especially religion. Priestesses dominated the sacred realm, and Minoans worshiped a host of goddesses at modest hilltop shrines, sometimes tenanted by small figurines, including representations of a buxom young woman holding a serpent in each hand (Fig. 17–22). This so-called Snake Goddess may have been a fertility figure or earth mother. Her sister deities were associated with trees, caves, animals, and other phenomena. One more prominent character in the Minoan pantheon was the bull, sometimes an object of blood sacrifice but most often represented symbolically by the Minoan horn-shaped altar. In public rituals, daring young athletes performed somersaults over the back of a raging bull (Fig. 17–23). Later Greek mythology recalled the tale of the fierce half-man, half-bull Minotaur confined in the labyrinth by King Minos of Crete, from whom the civilization takes its modern name.

Once assumed to be peace-loving and gentle, this intriguing and colorful island civilization had its sinister side, too. Scenes of warfare do appear in some Minoan art, and their abundant bronze spears, daggers, swords, helmets, shields, and even chariots figured in combat on sea and land. Skeletal evidence confirms that animal and human sacrifices, and possibly even cannibalism, had a role in Minoan ritual (Castleden, 1990).

Human violence and natural catastrophe both may have contributed to the demise of Minoan civilization. Chronologies derived from cross-dated Minoan

After photograph of specimen in Herakleion Museum, Crete

FIGURE 17–22
Minoan snake goddess figurine, Knossos.

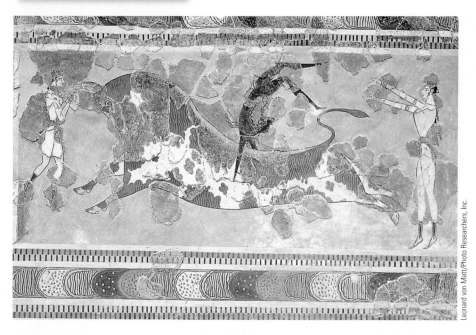

Leonard von Matt/Photo Researchers, Inc.

FIGURE 17–23
Minoan bull-jumping ceremony, depicted on the palace wall at Knossos.

National Geographic Society

FIGURE 17–24
Royal death mask of hammered gold from a Mycenaean shaft grave.

Megarons
Fortified palaces of Mycenaean kings.

pottery found in Egypt indicate that before 3,500 y.a. (about 1500 B.C.), a volcanic eruption claimed one-third of the island of Thera, a Minoan outpost 75 miles (120 km) off Crete's north coast, propelling volcanic ash and gases high into the atmosphere (Sigurdsson, 1999). Seawater churned into the volcano's gaping submarine crater, and devastating waves swept Crete's north shore. Even before this monumental explosion, severe tremors had driven Thera's occupants from their homes and may have wreaked heavy damage upon the great palaces and houses of Crete itself.

Thera's eruption caused extensive destruction, and while rebuilding took place at a few sites, including Knossos, the Minoans could not retain control of their Mediterranean trade routes owing to the loss of many ships. In the end, the great structure at Knossos, too, was abandoned, apparently after being burned by Mycenaean trespassers.

Mycenaeans Even as Minoan civilization reached its zenith, other Mediterranean societies were responding to the stimuli of contact and trade. One of these emerging cultures was the Mycenaean. Migrating from their Anatolian homeland, the people who came to be the Mycenaeans brought their proto-Greek language and basic Bronze Age culture into southeastern Europe about 4,200 y.a. Inspired by the Minoans, the newcomers were soon competing for a share of the lucrative sea trade by establishing an exchange network that included Cyprus, Egypt, Anatolia, and the central Mediterranean.

By 3,600 y.a., Mycenaeans already could afford to richly stock the deep "shaft graves" of their dead kings within their principal hilltop fortress-town of Mycenae in southern Greece (Fig. 17–24). The massive stonework protecting this citadel reflects the militarism that pervaded the Mycenaean world. Likewise, scenes engraved on finger rings, stamp seals, and gold-inlaid weapons characteristically exhibit combat themes. Much Mycenaean bronze work (their primary commercial product) took the form of daggers, swords, helmets, chariot components, and other armaments (Fig. 17–25). Mycenaean militarism flavors the epics of Homer, whose *Iliad* and *Odyssey* recount the long struggle with the rival city of Troy, on the Anatolian coast (modern Turkey) across the Aegean.

The extent to which Minoans and Mycenaeans competed or coexisted is not readily apparent. Yet, only after disaster eclipsed Knossos and the other Minoan centers did Mycenaeans dominate the Mediterranean, including Crete itself, for the next two centuries. They incorporated the Minoan palace-based economic system, written record keeping, and artistic and technical achievements into their own culture (Warren, 1989). Wealthy merchant-kings enjoyed the highest stations in Mycenaean society. Protected within the fortress walls, their colonnaded palaces, known as **megarons**, were virtual warehouses bulging with trade goods and imported luxuries. They were also the centers of craft production, where colorful stones and ivory were carved, and gold and bronze was worked into jewelry and weapons. The elite, local administrators, landholders, craftsworkers, peasants, and slaves participated in descending degree in the social and economic benefits of this stratified society, which was organized into small kingdoms centered around Mycenae, Pylos, and Thebes (see Fig. 17–20).

Their insatiable need for raw materials for armaments and socially valued status objects drew the Mycenaeans to distant Mediterranean and Near Eastern ports. One crucial resource was metal. The key to bronze making is the alloy added in small amounts to harden the copper. Arsenic may be used, but smiths who worked that substance rapidly experienced its lethal side effects. Tin, the preferred alloy, was very scarce. Mycenaean demand for it stimulated mining activities as far away as the Thames River valley near the future city of London, as well as in central Europe and the Near East. Another northern European resource from the far-off shores of the Baltic Sea also attracted the Mycenaeans: **amber**, or fossil pine resin, a translucent yellow-brown substance that may have fascinated the ancients because of its static electrical properties.

During the Mycenaean period, sailing ships plied the Mediterranean, conveying raw resources and finished products from port to port. The wreck of a merchant ship sunk off the southern coast of Turkey 3,300 y.a. preserves evidence of the extent of this international trade (Pulak, 1994). Its hold was laden with tons of copper ingots from Cyprus and smaller amounts of tin from Turkey, along with finished tools and weapons made by bronzesmiths in Mycenae, Egypt, and the Levant region. Baltic amber, wood and ivory from Africa, Egyptian amulets, Mesopotamian cylinder seals, colored glass stock, and foodstuffs crammed into Near Eastern pottery jars comprised other portions of the ill-fated cargo. Countless other merchant ships dispersed these kinds of goods around the eastern Mediterranean in Mycenaean times. Some products traveled further, filtering into the tribal societies of the European hinterlands (Harding, 1984; Bouzek, 1985). Just as their own exposure to Minoan trade and culture had earlier transformed the Mycenaeans, now the Mycenaeans themselves were making a similar, though indirect, impact on barbarian Europe (Piggott, 1965). Mycenaean overland supply routes served as cultural arteries, infusing the Europeans with new technologies and other far-reaching innovations.

While we cannot yet precisely delineate the later relationship between western Europeans and the Mediterranean world, we can detect that the Mycenaean sphere had begun to contract just before collapsing altogether. Had Europeans so quickly reached the point of seriously challenging Mycenaean trade and access to strategic resources? It seems doubtful. On the other hand, certain tribal peoples of the eastern Mediterranean, including some of Mycenae's near neighbors, appear to have become aggressive raiders. Late Egyptian texts make cryptic references to "sea people" and to "people of the north" who began to close in on the civilized world, armed with cutting and slashing swords.

Thus began an unsettled era, a time of troubles for many of the ancient societies that rimmed the Mediterranean. About 3,200 y.a., the principal Mycenaean cities were destroyed, their populations dispersed, their trade routes abandoned. From the Nile delta to Anatolia and Mesopotamia, invaders swept through the old kingdoms, creating chaos. In the wake of this destruction came a dark age, a period that is but sketchily known to European prehistorians. When the dust settled, centuries later, we find an Iron Age Europe peopled by Greeks, Etruscans, and Celts—the principals of a new era.

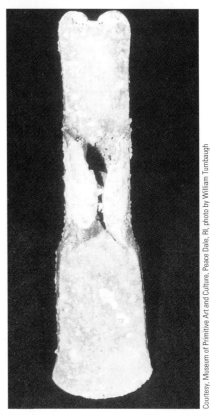

FIGURE 17–25
Bronze Age axe, or winged palstave.

Courtesy, Museum of Primitive Art and Culture, Peace Dale, RI, photo by William Turnbaugh

Amber
Fossil pine pitch or resin, long valued for jewelry or offerings.

SUMMARY

The pace of cultural change and elaboration accelerated during the mid-Holocene. It is noteworthy that the emergence of early civilizations followed directly on the achievement of sustainable food production in several regions. The primary civilizations of the Old World thrived particularly well on the alluvial plains of several major rivers. The earliest, the Sumerian civilization, emerged as a collection of city-states in the valley of the Tigris-Euphrates after 5,500 y.a. The formation of a unified Egyptian state occurred around 5,000 y.a. along the banks of the Nile, with the impressive cultural and architectural achievements of the Old Kingdom beginning several centuries later. Far to the east, urban commercial centers of the Harappan civilization dominated the Indus valley by about 4,500 y.a., and the Shang was one of a series of strongly hierarchical societies to emerge out of the advanced Neolithic farming cultures on the Huanghe floodplain by 3,750 y.a. Within the Mediterranean basin, two successive civilizations—the Minoan on the island of Crete (4,000–3,450 y.a.) and the Mycenaean on the Greek mainland (3,600–3,200 y.a.)—were associated with the expansion of early Bronze Age culture into Europe.

Archaeologists have had more than a little difficulty in trying to account for why and how civilizations developed out of Neolithic farming societies. They even have trouble coming up with a comprehensive definition of civilization, although many agree that the critical features of any civilization are its large scale and complexity and its interconnected social, political, and economic structures. Another characteristic of most early state-level societies was the use of writing. These features expressed themselves most clearly in the urban centers—cities—that characterized many, but not all, early civilizations. In managing and addressing the needs of their concentrated populations through the activities of formalized governmental, commercial, social, and religious institutions, cities represent a further stage of biocultural development. Humans, whose ancestral habitat generally supported relatively small groups of interactive fellow beings, have had to make significant adjustments in accommodating themselves to the unique environment of the urban society.

QUESTIONS FOR REVIEW

1. What are some of the problems that prehistorians encounter in trying to devise a universal definition of civilization?
2. List some of the essential differences between the lifeways of ancient village farmers and the residents of early urban communities. What are the social, economic, and political implications of city life?
3. Compare some of the hypotheses used to explain the rise of civilizations.
4. Where is Mesopotamia? Why does this region figure so prominently in our study of early civilizations?
5. Suggest why river valleys were the primary setting for so many early Old World civilizations.
6. Why is writing so closely associated with the rise of civilizations?
7. Although pyramid building was a relatively short-lived enterprise in ancient Egypt, the structures actually played multiple roles in the Old Kingdom period. What were some of these roles?
8. What kinds of comparable large-scale projects were organized by other civilizations, such as those in Mesopotamia, the Indus valley, and China? Why are such works so frequently associated with early civilizations?
9. Discuss some advantages and disadvantages the Minoans enjoyed as the first island-based civilization.
10. Explain how bronze technology stimulated cultural expansion and trade throughout the Mediterranean basin and Europe.

SUGGESTED FURTHER READING

Aldred, Cyril. 1998. *The Egyptians*. Rev. ed. New York: Thames and Hudson.

Allchin, Bridget, and Raymond Allchin. 1982. *The Rise of Civilization in India and Pakistan*. New York: Cambridge University Press.

Castleden, Rodney. 1990. *Minoans: Life in Bronze Age Crete*. London and New York: Routledge.

Chang, Kwang-chih. 1986. *The Archaeology of Ancient China*. 4th ed. New Haven, CT: Yale University Press.

Cohen, Mark N. 1989. *Health and the Rise of Civilization.* New Haven, CT: Yale University Press.

Dickinson, Oliver. 1994. *The Aegean Bronze Age.* New York: Cambridge University Press.

Fitton, J. Lesley. 1996. *The Discovery of the Greek Bronze Age.* Cambridge, MA: Harvard University Press.

Hoffman, Michael A. 1991. *Egypt before the Pharaohs.* Rev. ed. Austin, TX: University of Texas Press.

Kramer, Samuel N. 1963. *The Sumerians.* Chicago: University of Chicago Press.

Lamberg-Karlovsky, C. C., and Jeremy A. Sabloff. 1995. *Ancient Civilizations: The Near East and Mesoamerica.* 2nd ed. Prospect Heights, IL: Waveland Press.

Lehner, Mark. 1997. *The Complete Pyramids.* New York: Thames and Hudson.

Possehl, Gregory L. 1997. *Indus Age: The Beginnings.* Philadelphia: University of Pennsylvania Press.

Roaf, Michael. 1996. *Cultural Atlas of Mesopotamia and the Ancient Near East.* New York: Facts on File.

Warren, Peter. 1989. *The Aegean Civilizations.* New York: Bedrick.

RESOURCES ON THE INTERNET

Wadsworth Anthropology Resource Center
http://anthropology.wadsworth.com

The companion website for this text includes a range of enrichment material focused on the chapter's topic. While online you can enhance your understanding of the chapter by exploring one of the several additional Internet Exercises, by researching topics, and by accessing full articles on InfoTrac College Edition. You can also reinforce the concepts by taking online practice exams.

Internet Exercises

The Internet offers many sites relating to ancient civilizations. The Oriental Institute at the University of Chicago is one of the oldest and most highly respected research centers for the study of ancient Near Eastern cultures. Visit their site (**http://www.oi.uchicago.edu/OI/default.html**) and go to "Table of Contents," then click on either "Ancient Egypt" or "Mesopotamia." You will find a listing of recent and ongoing research projects. Read through the list of topics and explore some that are of interest to you. (Bear in mind that most are specialized or technical studies.) Specifically, how have the projects you read about made a contribution to ancient studies?

InfoTrac College Edition
http://www.infotrac-college.com/wadsworth

The region between the Tigris and Euphrates Rivers—ancient Mesopotamia—gave rise to the first true cities, the oldest writing, and the earliest formal civilization. Search under the keyword *Mesopotamia* to locate current references on this region (there should be several dozen). Take some time to look at each of the titles and read a few of the abstracts. What seems to be the focus of these reports—early writing, religion, art and architecture, ancient politics or economy, social structure? See if you can detect any current trends in Mesopotamian studies on the basis of this sample of recent publications. What topics seem to be getting the most attention?

Who Invented Writing?

Who invented the first writing? Like many questions of its type in archaeology, this one is not easily answered. Some might argue that the paintings that our Cro-Magnon relatives applied to cave walls in western Europe during the Upper Paleolithic between about 22,000 and 13,000 y.a. should be counted as writing (see Chapter 13). After all, Harvard University researcher Alexander Marshack and others have demonstrated that much of the cave art, as well as many small sculptural carvings and engraved bones and stones from the same period, surely were more than mere decorations. They were subject to manipulation and reworking and may have served in some symbolic way as reminders of significant or periodic events, including those associated with the annual progression of the seasons. However, a lack of standardized repetitive elements combined into meaningful patterns probably disqualifies this type of artwork as true writing. The magnificent and skillful renderings of Ice Age animals and other subjects may have conveyed significant meaning and perhaps even information to their late Stone Age viewers, but they probably were not "read" in the way that we

understand writing. Still, the distinctions tend to blur.

A more likely candidate for the world's earliest writing (or at least the source of its inspiration) may be the counting tokens of ancient Mesopotamia. Denise Schmandt-Besserat of the University of Texas, Austin, noted that small fired clay objects were common on many Neolithic sites in the upper valley of the Tigris-Euphrates and the adjacent Zagros Mountains. Represented in an array of geometric shapes—disks, spheres, cones, triangles, rectangles, tetrahedrons, ovoids, and others—these enigmatic objects, about the size of a fingernail, long puzzled archaeologists. They had been described as children's playthings, ornaments, "ritual objects." Schmandt-Besserat was struck by their wide distribution and persistent appearance on sites in the Fertile Crescent over thousands of years, with the earliest dating to 10,000 y.a. and great quantities coming from Jarmo and nearby Zagros Neolithic sites after about 8,500 y.a. She recognized that comparable clay geometrics had been used much later as counting tokens for tallying sheep, grain, and other products. Each distinctive shape represented a specific kind of agricultural or craft prod-

uct. At Nuzi, a 3,500-year-old site in Iraq, the tokens were found in conjunction with other types of Sumerian accounting records, which seemed to verify their purpose.

The most surprising and convincing connection between the tokens and early writing is that many of the token shapes subsequently were carried over onto the earliest Sumerian pictographic tablets, including those found at Uruk, as signs representing numerals, sheep, cow, dog, various types of containers, bread, wool, garment, bracelet, and so on. In essence, Schmandt-Besserat posits a translation of three-dimensional tokens into a two-dimensional script during the period of Sumerian development (later Ubaid and Uruk times, 5,500–5,100 y.a.) because of an increased need for efficient records and the availability of numerous new products. Where loose clay tokens representing a transaction once had been strung together or stored in a hollow clay container, now the diverse token shapes became individual symbols that could be recorded conveniently on wet clay tablets and baked for preservation.

These earliest accounting tablets were primarily pictographic, but before about 5,000 y.a., additional abstract signs were being devised to represent both concepts (ideograms) and sounds or syllables, resulting in a more comprehensive form of true writing. Eventually, the cuneiform ("wedge-shaped") writing of the Sumerians comprised hundreds of different signs, many somewhat comparable to a letter in an alphabet, while others represented individual words (logograms).

People of the Nile evidently received their first exposure to writing around 5,500 y.a. as they traded with Mesopotamia. The Egyptians adopted the concept of writing from this source but developed their own unique script. The famous hieroglyphics ("sacred carvings") of ancient Egypt retain a deceptively simple pictographic look, but really are both more syllabic and ideographic than they appear at first glance.

Writing in northern China already was well established more than 3,000 y.a., during the time of the late Shang civilization. A highly developed script of ideographic characters was inscribed on bone or bronze and also on less durable materials, such as wood, bamboo, and silk. The ultimate origins of Chinese writing may be traced back nearly 7,000 years to the early Neolithic Yangshao culture, where pottery vessels were marked with signs representing owners or makers.

Very few of the New World's aboriginal cultures employed writing. Sacred texts and calendars figure prominently only in several civilizations of Mesoamerica, particularly the Olmec, Zapotec, Maya, and Aztec. After about 2,500 y.a., calendrical notations in the form of hieroglyphic symbols representing both numerals and day names were carved onto stone monuments in southern Mexico. Within a few centuries, the Maya had elaborated their writing to include other ideograms and logograms, as well as signs standing for syllables and special emblem glyphs designating individual communities—some 800 different glyphs in all. With this advanced system, they recorded political and historical events and paid homage to their gods and kings.

And the rest, as they say, is *history*!

Sources

Chang, Kwang-chih. 1986. *The Archaeology of Ancient China*. 4th ed. New Haven, CT: Yale University Press.

Coe, Michael D. 1992. *Breaking the Maya Code*. New York: Thames and Hudson.

Marshack, Alexander. 1991. *The Roots of Civilization*. Rev. ed. Mount Kisco, NY: Moyer Bell.

Schmandt-Besserat, Denise. 1978. "The Earliest Precursor of Writing." *Scientific American* 238(6):50–59.

———. *Before Writing*. 1992. Austin, TX: University of Texas Press.

Critical Thinking Questions

1. Do you believe that Upper Paleolithic cave drawings should be considered a form of true writing? How would you distinguish writing from art as a form of communication?

2. Why do you think writing is almost universally associated with the advanced cultures we call civilization?

3. Is the invention of the primary forms of writing described in this Issue a sufficient basis for proclaiming the end of prehistory and the beginning of history? Why or why not?

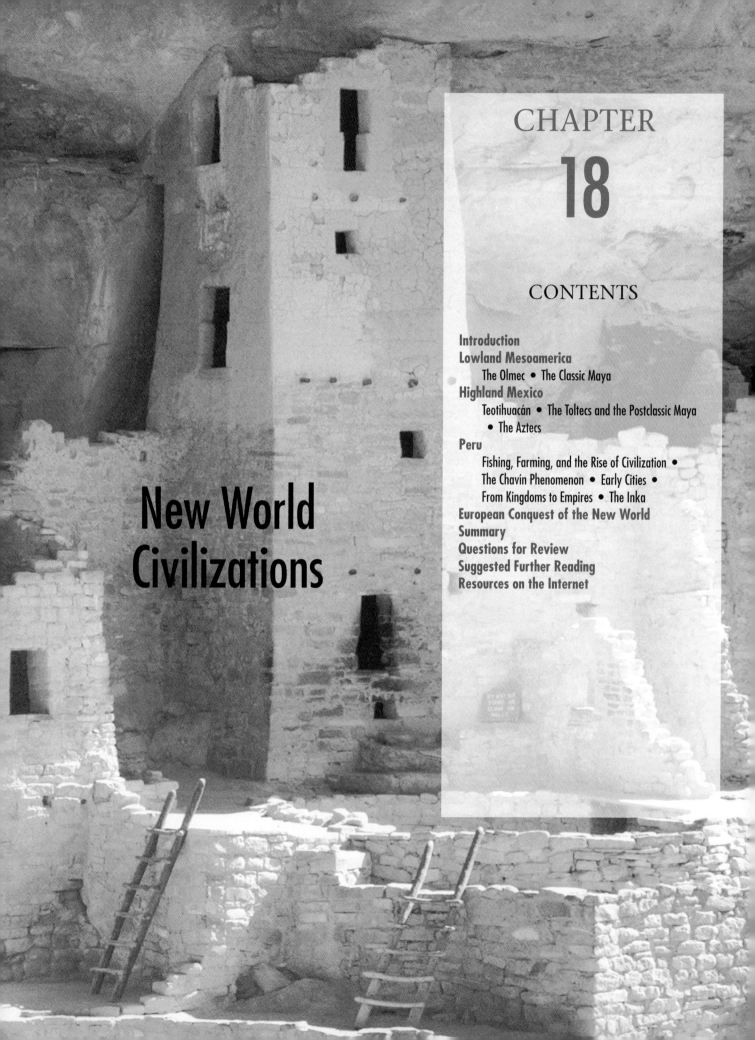

CHAPTER

18

New World Civilizations

CONTENTS

Introduction

In many of the regions where early farming prevailed in the Americas, the combination of maize, beans, and plants such as squash came to substitute for diets rich in animal protein. In time, these primary domesticates nourished large populations and formed the economic basis for social and political elaboration, culminating in the development of early civilizations in several areas of the New World (Fig. 18–1). The history of ancient America's most highly advanced cultures was closely intertwined with the progress of New World agriculture. Thus, the civilizations were concentrated around the hearths of domestication (Fig. 18–2).

Superficially, the high cultures of the New World are broadly comparable to those of the Old World. All shared some basic similarities: state economies based on agriculture and long-distance trade; powerful leaders and social stratification; human labor invested in large-scale constructions; public art styles; state religions; record keeping; and the prominent role of warfare.

Yet, there are significant points of contrast as well. For example, domesticated animals had only a minor status in New World agriculture; the technological role of metal was limited; and the wheel played no important function, nor did watercraft. These cultural differences should not be viewed as deficiencies, but rather as consequences of separate historical traditions. The peoples of the New World, too, devised remarkable and appropriate cultural responses to the environmental and social circumstances in which they lived. Still, history might have been written differently if both the Europeans and the aboriginal peoples of the Americas had possessed more similar technologies—or if neither had had them.

FIGURE 18–1
Time line for Chapter 18.

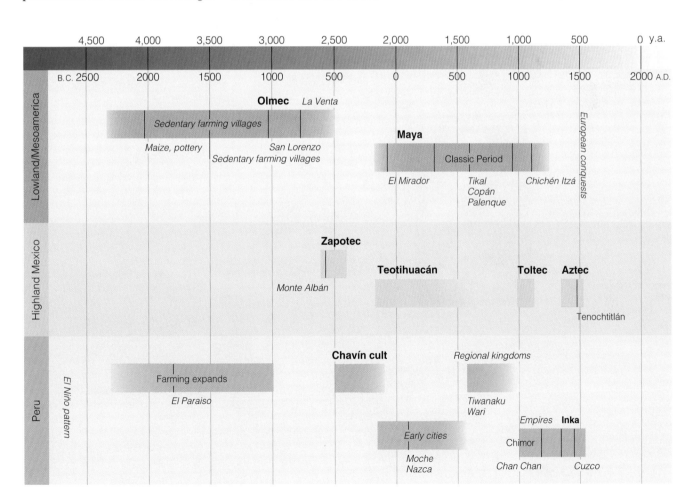

FIGURE 18–2
Location of ancient American civilizations discussed in the text.

Aztec

Teotihuacán

Monte Albán

Maya

Olmec

Chimu

Inka

Lowland Mesoamerica

Beginning around 4,000 y.a. and over the next several centuries, more productive varieties of maize and better storage techniques encouraged people in parts of **Mesoamerica** to settle close to their fields. One archaeological marker for this shift to more sedentary settlements is an abundance of pottery fragments, or *sherds*. While mobile foragers found little use for heavy, fragile clay containers, farmers preferred pottery for cooking and storage. Water and other products could be carried in them, and ceramic vessels could be placed directly over heat for as long as needed to convert starchy grains into a more digestible food. Thus, the distribution of pottery reflects the spread of village farming in Mesoamerica and elsewhere.

Mesoamerica
(*meso*, meaning "middle") Geographical and cultural region from southern Mexico through Panama; also known as Central America.

The Olmec

By some 3,500 y.a., sedentary farming villages dotted the lowlands of Mesoamerica. Maize grew exceptionally well in much of this subtropical environment, and increased yields stimulated and supported important cultural changes over the next few centuries. Among these major developments was the formation of local chiefdoms, whose archaeological hallmarks include prominent house sites, status or ritual objects, and other signs of social differentiation, especially in burial offerings.

Archaeologists have long been particularly interested in one of these formative societies, the **Olmec**, which achieved prominence in the riverine swamps along the southern Gulf Coast of Mexico from about 3,200 to 2,400 y.a. (Fig. 18–3). Their

Olmec
Culture in the Gulf Coast lowlands of Veracruz and Tabasco, Mexico, with a highly developed art style and social complexity; flourished from 3,200 to 2,400 y.a.

FIGURE 18–3
Mesoamerican archaeological sites mentioned in the text.

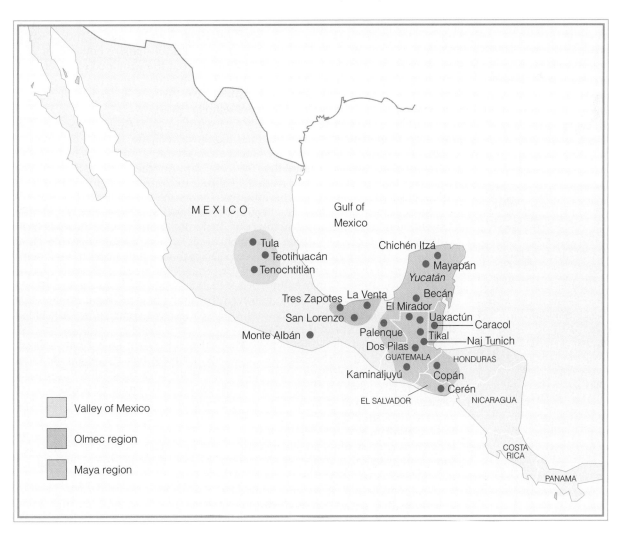

FIGURE 18–4
Olmec figure, carved from jade.

Ceremonial centers
Public spaces reserved for ritual activities, often dominated by special architecture and artwork.

Anthropomorphic
(*anthro*, meaning "man," and *morph*, meaning "shape") Having or being given humanlike characteristics.

FIGURE 18–5
Monumental Olmec head excavated at San Lorenzo, in Mexico.

highly distinctive art style and monumental constructions clearly set the Olmec apart from their other agrarian neighbors. So far, we cannot identify any precedents for most of these Olmec developments within the region. Though Olmec origins remain uncertain, its influence on later cultures is obvious. The Olmec anticipated, and may have inspired, a number of the features that characterized subsequent Mesoamerican civilizations. For example, the Olmec seem to have established the region's first **ceremonial centers** on a grand scale. They employed writing, in the form of hieroglyphic notations, and a calendar that would be adopted by their successors. The sacred ball game they created was still being played when the Spanish arrived.

The two best-known Olmec sites are the important ceremonial centers at San Lorenzo and La Venta. At both sites the natural landscapes were extensively modified (without the aid of domestic animals or machinery) to convert them into proper settings for impressive constructions and sculptures of ritual significance (Coe and Diehl, 1980; Coe, 1994). Alignments of earthen mounds enclose the wide courtyards, plazas, and even artificial ponds at San Lorenzo. A 100-foot-high (30 m) cone-shaped earthen pyramid distinguishes La Venta. Within and close to the sites themselves are hundreds of smaller earthen platforms that once supported homes and workshops.

Aside from their ceremonial architecture, the Olmec produced remarkable monumental sculptures and smaller, well-crafted carvings of jade and other attractive stones (Fig. 18–4). **Anthropomorphic** forms predominate, including some figurines and *bas-reliefs* that combine the features of humans with those of felines, probably jaguars. Olmec art and iconography are fascinating but poorly understood. Who or what did these anthropomorphic beings represent? Equally intriguing are the colossal Olmec heads, each of which seems to be an individualized portrait of a ruler in helmet-like headgear, carved from massive boulders of basalt weighing up to 20 tons. Archaeologists estimate that the sustained effort of 1,000-member crews were needed to drag and raft the boulders from the distant source area, some 60 miles (100 km) from the site (Lowe, 1989). Nine of these titanic likenesses have been found at San Lorenzo itself (Fig. 18–5).

Curiously, the Olmec intentionally buried caches of beads, as well as carved figurines and implements made from their highly valued jade. One pit offering at La Venta consisted of 460 green stone blocks arranged into a giant mosaic design and then buried at a depth of more than 20 feet (7 m). Another held an assemblage of small jade figures set into place so that all appear to confront one individual. Then, still in position, the group had been buried (Fig. 18–6).

Inexplicably, San Lorenzo's demise about 2,900 y.a. provoked the startling demolition of its artwork and architecture, including mutilation of the huge heads. With little evidence of outside interference, researchers assume that the Olmec inflicted most of the damage themselves, perhaps to save the images of their deified ancestors from dishonor (Weaver, 1993) or to mark the passing of some esteemed leader (Grove, 1984). Olmec culture persisted at La Venta down to about 2,400 y.a., when that site, too, was similarly destroyed. The final phase of Olmec is represented at the lesser-known site of Tres Zapotes, where a carved calendar stone has yielded a date equivalent to 31 B.C. (Coe, 1994).

In its heyday, Olmec influence extended eastward through Guatemala and westward into central Mexico, where carvings and paintings in the familiar Olmec style appear in graves, caves, and open sites (Sharer and Grove, 1989). Although some scholars have invoked models of empire and conquest to explain it, the Olmec presence in these areas more likely represents trade in objects of shared religious symbolism. Their own culture required quantities of raw materials, such as basalt, obsidian, and jade, available only in the distant highlands. In return, Olmec artists and crafters supplied clay figurines, ceramic vessels, stone masks and sculptures, and many other items, especially those of a ritual nature, to neighboring peoples (Stocker et al., 1980).

These exchanges may have stimulated the further growth of other regional chiefdoms that already were verging on civilization. For example, in the state of

Philip Drucker, Robert Squier, "Excavations at La Venta, Tabasco, 1955." Smithsonian Institution, Bureau of American Ethnology Bulletin 170, plate 20. Washington, DC: Government Printing Office, 1969.

FIGURE 18–6
Buried cache of small Olmec jade figurines found at La Venta, in Mexico.

Oaxaca in southern Mexico, the large Zapotec ceremonial center of Monte Albán, built after 2,400 y.a. into an artificially modified hill overlooking a fertile valley, shares some general similarities with Olmec sites (Marcus and Flannery, 1996). Zapotec hieroglyphic writing and calendar notations possibly owe their inspiration to Olmec precursors, as does its ritual ball court (Fig. 18–7). Some researchers see Olmec influence in the carving of some of the 300 stone slabs set up at Monte Albán, many depicting the naked, contorted bodies of defeated enemies or the elaborately costumed victors.

The Classic Maya

Another of the emerging Mesoamerican societies was the **Maya**. Analysis of pollen profiles obtained from swamps in the lowlands of eastern Mesoamerica indicates that the people who were directly ancestral to the Maya began practicing slash-and-burn maize farming in the region between 4,000 and 3,000 y.a. (Piperno and

Maya
Prehistoric Mesoamerican culture consisting of regional kingdoms and known for its art and architectural accomplishments from 1,800 to 1,100 y.a.

FIGURE 18–7
The ball court at Monte Albán, one of several types built by nearly all the major cultures of Mesoamerica.

Courtesy, Mark A. Gutchen

Pearsall, 1998). Fire assisted in opening clearings in the forest and reducing the vegetation to soluble ash, which served as fertilizer for crops. Some of the areas the farmers occupied, notably the scrublands of Yucatán and the Petén jungles farther south, were incapable of supporting an ever-increasing population that relied solely on shifting, slash-and-burn plots. To expand their food supply and obtain other essential products, the farmers resorted to more labor-intensive agricultural techniques, set up redistribution networks among their growing communities, and established trade connections with more distant societies.

To produce the bigger harvests that their population required, the Maya had to clear more and larger forest tracts. In low places, they dredged organic swamp muck to create ridged planting fields. Crucial materials that were lacking in most of the Maya homeland, especially suitable stone for making tools and milling slabs, could be obtained in exchange for commodities such as salt or the feathers of colorful jungle birds that were desired by highland groups.

What may have stirred a small-village farming culture into a civilization has long been debated. Some suggest that the stimulation to build ceremonial centers came in part from the Olmec, whose art, architecture, and rituals are reflected in some early Maya sites. Others suggest that Maya civilization resulted from an internal reorganization of Maya society itself. Most likely, the transformation from small-scale villages to a more integrated and locally centralized society may have begun as an adaptive strategy for supporting a growing population in an area of inadequate resources (Carneiro, 1970; Rathje, 1971; Adams, 1977). Establishing and maintaining new agricultural systems and commercial connections very likely could be accomplished only under the authority and oversight of strong or charismatic leaders.

In any event, by some 2,100 y.a., after centuries of development, the elements of Maya civilization were coming together. Control of trade routes or strategic waterways may have promoted the growth of the early preclassic center at El Mirador and subsequently at **Uaxactún** and **Tikal** (all in northern Guatemala; see Fig. 18–3). Here and elsewhere, Maya society came to be dominated increasingly by an elite social class (Fig. 18–8). A host of Maya kings, each claiming descent through royal lineages back to the gods themselves, held sway over the relatively modest regional kingdoms, or city-states, centered around elaborate ceremonial precincts. Under their patronage, writing, fine arts, and architecture flourished in the Maya lowlands, as did tactical warfare among the rival kingdoms. For seven centuries, from A.D. 200 to 900 (1,800 to 1,100 y.a.), the Maya experienced their own golden age, or classic period (Sharer, 1996; Coe, 1999).

The Maya are best known for their impressive classic-period ceremonial centers, Tikal, Copán (Honduras), and Palenque (Mexico) among them (Fig. 18–9). Such sites may have served as regional capitals, allied with small local centers in their respective areas (Marcus, 1993). Archaeologists historically have devoted much of their attention to these spectacular places. But their importance should be put into perspective. The more holistic approach of modern anthropological archaeology requires a fuller understanding of Maya culture than might be derived from their monumental constructions alone.

Estimates of overall population during the late classic period range widely, but perhaps 3 million Maya lived in the lowlands (Coe et al., 1986). As archaeologists focus more attention on individual households and villages where most Maya lived, they are reexamining the issue of Maya subsistence. Excavations at Cerén, El Salvador, provided important details (Sheets, 1994). Once a hamlet of mud-walled thatched huts, Cerén lay entombed for 1,400 years beneath 18 feet (5 m) of ash discharged from a nearby volcano. Remarkable traces of Maya peasant life survived, including a plentiful harvest of maize, beans, squash, tomatoes, and chilis stored in baskets and pots as when they came from adjacent garden plots.

According to one early estimate (Cowgill, 1962), shifting cultivation in this region provided for up to 200 people per square mile (2.6 km^2). Ancient Maya house platforms tend to appear throughout the jungle wherever maize might be grown by slash-and-burn agriculture. We now recognize that the Maya also

Uaxactún
(wash-akh-toon') Maya ceremonial center in Guatemala.

Tikal
(tee-kal') Principal Maya city and ceremonial center in Guatemala.

Courtesy, Mark A. Gutchen

FIGURE 18–8
Maya noble depicted in a limestone relief carving.

Courtesy, Mark A. Gutchen

FIGURE 18–9
The Temple of the Inscriptions at Palenque, in Mexico, served as the tomb of the important Maya ruler Pacal, who died in A.D. 683.

employed more intensive farming techniques for maximum production: raised or ridged fields in swampy zones; hillside terracing; irrigation and drainage; fertilization; and multiple cropping (Flannery, 1982). In addition, the Maya systematically hunted, fished, and collected wild plant foods.

These combined resources sustained the substantial Maya population, part of it nucleated around some 200 central places. Rural centers, having just one or two carved **stelae** (inscribed stone pillars) or a modest shrine maintained by nearby farmers, were subsidiary to regional centers, which were themselves under the domain of one of the primary centers (such as Copán or Tikal) at the top of the hierarchy. The largest settlements approached true cities in scale and function, providing a focus for sociopolitical activity, religious ceremonies, and commerce (Lucero, 1999). They served essentially as "capitals" of regional Maya kingdoms, despite their somewhat dispersed populace. Including the ruling elite and their retainers, crafters, other specialists, and farmers, some 27,000 people were attached to the important city of Copán, although two-thirds of them actually resided in farming compounds scattered through the Copán valley, within walking distance of the ceremonial center.

Formal, large-scale architecture dominated the greatest ceremonial centers. Tikal, with over 50,000 residents, boasted more than 3,000 structures in its core precinct alone. Most impressive were the stepped, limestone-sided pyramids capped with crested temples (Fig. 18–10). Facing across the broad stuccoed plazas were multiroomed "palaces" (presumably elite residences), generally a ritual ball court or two, and always a number of elaborately carved stelae (Figs. 18–11 and 18–12). Maya preferred to paint their structures in bold colors, so the overall effect must have been stunning. Other features might include graded causeways leading into the complex and masonry reservoirs for storing crucial runoff from tropical cloudbursts.

Stelae (*sing.,* stela)
(stee'-lee) Upright posts or stones, often bearing inscriptions.

FIGURE 18–10
One of several temple pyramids and numerous stelae at the Maya ceremonial center of Tikal, in Guatemala.

Courtesy, Mark A. Gutchen

FIGURE 18–11
This elaborately carved Maya stela at Copán, in Honduras, depicts King 18 Rabbit in ceremonial regalia.

FIGURE 18–12
Maya hieroglyphs on a stela at Copán record the date and purpose of its dedication.

Codices
(*sing.*, codex) Illustrated books.

Naj Tunich
(nah toon'-eesh) Maya sacred cave in Guatemala.

Courtesy, Mark A. Gutchen

Courtesy, Mark A. Gutchen

William Turnbaugh

FIGURE 18–13
This classic Maya cylindrical jar with bird motif and glyphs was used in ceremonies.

Scholars have made significant progress in interpreting the complex hieroglyphic inscriptions on Maya stelae, temples, and other monuments (Coe, 1992). Calendrical notations on the sculptures provide a precise chronology of major events in lowland Mesoamerica (see Box 18–1). For example, when the Maya calendar system is correlated with our own, the beginning of the classic period can be set in the year A.D. 199 (Freidel, et al., 1993). Many stelae proclaim the ancestry and noble deeds of actual Maya rulers, while others record significant historical occasions (Schele and Miller, 1986). These inscriptions provide direct insights to classic Maya sociopolitical organization, including the uneasy and frequently embattled relationships among leading ceremonial centers and their rival aristocracies (Schele and Freidel, 1990; Coe, 1992).

Religion entranced the Maya. Their architecture and art was dedicated to the veneration of divine kings and the worship of perhaps hundreds of major and minor deities (Fig. 18–13). Maya nobility included a priestly caste who carefully observed the sun, moon, and planet Venus; predicted the rains; prescribed the rituals; and performed the sacrifices. Most of the priestly lore and learning faithfully recorded in the Maya **codices**, or books, was lost when the Spanish burned the ancient texts during the conquest. But a number of sacred caves, like **Naj Tunich** in Guatemala, preserve some forgotten aspects of Maya religion. Within the dusky

BOX 18-1   DIGGING DEEPER

How to Count and Measure Time—The Maya Way

The Maya devised a number system that served primarily to record the passage of time. They reckoned time by reference to an intricate calendar with three distinct components. Their *long-count chronology* recorded the number of individual days that had passed since the beginning of the Maya universe (on August 11, 3114 B.C., by our own calendar); thus, for example, January 15 in A.D. 2003 is 1,868,735 days since the Maya zero date. This continuing sequence served as the formal measure of Maya chronology that was recorded on their monuments and stelae. Next, a 260-day *Sacred Round* counted 13 months, each 20 days in length, with each month-day combination holding religious significance. Finally, a *secular calendar* of 360 days—18 months of 20 days each—approximated the solar year, with a 5-day adjustment period added at the end. Every 52 years, or exactly 18,980 days, the Maya cycle of time began anew with the synchronization of both the secular and sacred calendars.

The Maya represented the numbers 1 through 19 by a simple bar-and-dot notation, wherein a dot equaled 1 and a bar had a value of 5. Note the use of the 0, a device not invented in Europe until the Middle Ages. Numbers larger than 19 were expressed as multiples of 20. The value of the number was determined by its position in a vertical column (much as the value of our numbers is indicated by their position relative to a decimal point). Thus, numbers in the first-place (lowest) position were multiplied by 1; those in the next higher position, by 20; in the third, by 360 (that is, 20 × 18—the number of days in the month multiplied by the number of months in the secular calendar); in the fourth, by 7,200 (20 × 360—the number of days in the month multiplied by the number of days in the secular year); in the fifth, by 144,000 (20 × 7,200); and so on.

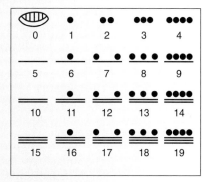

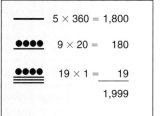

The number for 1,999

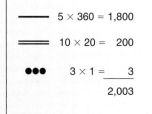

The number for 2,003

chambers archaeologists have come upon classic-period offerings, paintings that graphically depict ritual intercourse and self-mutilation, and the remains of young sacrificial victims (Brady and Stone, 1986).

Classic Maya Collapse   For several centuries, lowland Maya culture developed at an unabated pace, and ceremonial centers grew larger and more impressive. Yet despite appearances, all was not well. For 130 years (until A.D. 692), construction and expansion at the largest of these centers—Tikal—stalled dramatically. Archaeologists once blamed the hiatus on a breakdown in relations with highland

Mexico, but hieroglyphic translations tell of Tikal's defeat by Caracol, a second-order Maya center in Belize. Thus, the severed relations with this region must have been a result, not the cause, of Tikal's misfortunes.

From the end of this interruption until about A.D. 790, Maya civilization at first seemed reinvigorated, with unparalleled population growth and monumental development. However, a decline in classic Maya civilization rapidly encompassed all of southern lowland Mesoamerica and was essentially complete by A.D. 909, the generally accepted terminal date for the classic period. Maya artisans no longer turned out polychrome-decorated ceramics, nor did they carve and erect inscribed stelae. Ceremonial center construction ceased altogether, and nearly all major sites were abandoned. Maya culture in the heartland never regained its ancient glory.

The remarkable Maya collapse has intrigued scholars for decades. Archaeologists are not yet quite sure *what* happened, let alone *why* (Culbert, 1988). Proposed single-cause explanations have proved inadequate, among them devastation by hurricanes or earthquakes, extreme climatic fluctuations, insect infestations, epidemic diseases, malnutrition, overpopulation, an unbalanced male/female sex ratio, peasant revolts against the elite, and mass migrations. Some scholars have cited external factors, such as the breakdown of trade relations with the areas that supplied the resource-poor Maya or invasion by peoples from highland Mexico.

Many archaeologists are convinced that a tangle of ecological and social stresses must have brought about the Maya's rapid demise. To produce enough food for their own growing population as well as the surpluses needed for trade, the Maya may have overextended their agricultural capacity by cutting even more forest or perhaps by shortening the critical fallow period when fields are given a rest. Such procedures inevitably would have led to soil erosion and infertility, grass invasion, and poor harvests.

These ecological problems may have sparked internal conflict and even civil war. Some scholars postulate that political instability precipitated the collapse as Maya kings made aggressive moves to annex their neighbors' territories (Rice et al., 2001), as when Caracol dominated Tikal or when Copán's vigorous king, 18 Rabbit (see Fig. 18–11), lost his life at the hands of a neighboring ruler in A.D. 738. Archaeologists found vivid evidence of the effects of warfare—burned homes, fields, and ceremonial centers as well as the severed heads of male warriors—in a late classic site at Dos Pilas, in northern Guatemala (Demarest, 1993).

The consequences of this turmoil were primarily limited to the southern Maya region, where only much-reduced peasant populations remained in the vicinity of the silent centers. Some *northern* lowland sites actually expanded and continued to flourish for centuries as a comparatively modest and much modified postclassic Maya culture in Yucatán (Freidel and Sabloff, 1984).

Highland Mexico

The convergence of two mountain ranges in central Mexico forms a great highland of some 3,000 square miles (8,000 km^2), commonly known as the Valley of Mexico (see Fig. 18–3). Actually an elevated plateau rimmed by even higher volcanic peaks, with its rich agricultural soils watered by several rivers and with a large lake at its center, the broad basin served as a stage for the development of several important Mesoamerican civilizations. The earliest, **Teotihuacán**, was the first true city in the Americas.

Teotihuacán

The agricultural potential of Mexico's great central highland, with its deep soil and water resources, drew early farmers into the region's diverse landscapes. Some used stone axes and fire to open garden plots in the native oak and pine forests that clothed the marginal foothills. Others redirected the flow of streams or seeping springs to the roots of their maize plants. Among the marshes that obscured the shoreline of the brackish lake on the floor of the basin appeared fields of yet other

Teotihuacán
(tay-oh-tee-wah-cahn') The first city in the Western Hemisphere, located in central Mexico from 2,200–1,350 y.a.

kinds: raised ridges and dark beds of muck (known as **chinampas**) dredged from the lake bottom. Nearby, outcrops of volcanic obsidian, glassy and green, fostered stone toolmaking. Farming hamlets rapidly grew into villages and then coalesced into towns as agriculture and trade prospered within the basin.

Teotihuacán was one of these expanding communities by some 2,200 y.a. With its nearby fields nourished by a system of irrigation canals, Teotihuacán experienced especially rapid growth. Expert knappers monopolized its prime obsidian sources, gaining for the town a commodity much in demand everywhere. Trade in these sharp blades must have given Teotihuacán an "edge" over all other settlements. By 2,000 y.a., it had outpaced them and was showing no signs of slowing. In fact, Teotihuacán continued to expand for the next six centuries, becoming one of the world's largest cities in its time and the paramount urban center in the Western Hemisphere (Millon, 1988; Carlson, 1993).

At its height, after A.D. 600, the first true American city bustled with the activity of more than 125,000 residents, as well as buyers and sellers at its markets and visitors to its monumental shrines (Fig. 18–14). Somewhat in contrast to the Maya centers, Teotihuacán's layout appeared more orderly and its population more highly concentrated. Built on a grid pattern with a primary north-south axis, its avenues, plazas, major monuments, and homes alike—and even the San Juan River—were aligned to a master plan.

Teotihuacanos lived in some 2,000 residential compounds arranged into formal neighborhoods based on occupation or social class, ranging from trades workers to merchants, military officers, and even foreigners. Civic and religious leaders enjoyed more luxurious facilities in the central district (Millon, 1988). Artisans laboring in hundreds of individual household workshops specialized in producing ceramic vessels, obsidian blades, shell and jade carvings, fabrics, leather goods, and other practical or luxury items.

An impressive ceremonial center comprised the heart of the city. Imaginative Spanish explorers assigned the name Avenue of the Dead to the main thoroughfare extending northward 2.8 miles (4.5 km) to a massive structure, the Pyramid of the Moon. An even greater Pyramid of the Sun, its base equal to that of Khufu's pyramid in Egypt (though it rises only half as high), occupied a central position along the same avenue. Archaeologists have come to recognize that Teotihuacanos built this immense structure to resemble a sacred mountain, and they raised it directly over a natural cave that symbolized the entry to the underworld. Flanking the south end of the avenue, the Ciudadela was the administrative complex, and the Great Compound served as Teotihuacán's central marketplace.

Chinampas
(chee-nahm'-pahs) Productive fields created in wet environments by dredging lake bottom muck to form raised ridges or platforms.

FIGURE 18–14
Feathered Serpent figure on temple façade at Teotihuacán, in Mexico.

Courtesy, Mark A. Gutchen

Kaminaljuyú
(cam-en-awl-hoo-yoo') Site located at Guatemala City, contemporary with Olmec and also associated with classic Maya.

Teotihuacán's influence extended throughout Mexico's central region and well beyond. Its fine orange-slipped ceramics, architectural and artistic styles, and obsidian products appear at distant contemporary centers such as Monte Albán in Oaxaca; the Maya site of **Kaminaljuyú** in the Guatemalan highlands; and Tikal, Uaxactún, and Becán in the Maya lowlands (Berlo, 1992). Moreover, much of Mesoamerica became involved somehow in Teotihuacán's obsession with the planet Venus, whose movements through the heavens governed the timing of rituals and warfare (Carlson, 1991). Likewise, Teotihuacán's penchant for human sacrifice spread to every other dominant culture in the region right up to the time of the Spanish.

While either trade or military conquest might explain Teotihuacán's considerable influence, the nature of these contacts is not yet clear. In some manner, it appears, Maya history was closely linked with Teotihuacán's: The Maya classic period opened as Teotihuacán's expansion began; the Maya's decades of stagnation coincided with disrupted relations with the Mexican city; and the pinnacle of Maya achievement came only *after* the fall of Teotihuacán and the dispersal of its population and artisans (Diehl and Berlo, 1989). Enclaves of Maya and Oaxacans maintained long-term residence in Teotihuacán itself, and some Teotihuacanos lived in primary Maya centers, including Tikal. Even Yax K'uk' Mo', founder of Copan's 400-year ruling dynasty, was a Teotihuacano. Recent comparative studies of skeletons from these sites use differential strontium levels in bones and tooth enamel to distinguish recent migrants and long-term residents born elsewhere from the native-born population (Price, 2000). Because strontium levels in bedrock and soil vary regionally, the technique has also been used to trace the foreigners to their homelands.

Teotihuacán's brutal demise remains an archaeological mystery. After six remarkable centuries, the city's dominance beyond the Valley of Mexico clearly was waning. Internally, too, all was not well. Physical anthropologists who have examined human remains excavated from the site's later features recognize the common skeletal indicators of nutritional stress and disease as well as high infant mortality rates. Still, population levels remained stable for another century or so before declining rapidly.

Then, just about 1,350 y.a., the end came in flame and havoc (Millon, 1988). The entire ceremonial precinct blazed as temples were thrown down and their icons smashed (though residential areas remained unscathed). In the frenzy, some of the nobility were seized and dismembered, apparently by their own people. The destruction ended Teotihuacán's political and religious preeminence, and many of its residents scattered to other communities. The factors—whether internal or external—that precipitated the end of this first city of the Americas have yet to be determined.

The Toltecs and the Postclassic Maya

Teotihuacán's collapse left highland Mesoamerica devoid of its primary sociopolitical and religious center. Of the many peoples contending for control over the region during the next several centuries, the **Toltecs** eventually emerged as the most powerful. They established a capital at **Tula**, on the northern periphery of the Valley of Mexico some 40 miles (65 km) northwest of Teotihuacán. By the mid-tenth century A.D. (about 1,050 y.a.), the city, swollen with immigrants from the troubled region, had attained about half the size of Teotihuacán, with several pyramids and ball courts dominating its central plaza (Diehl, 1983).

Although its more modest ceremonial center scarcely rivaled those of classic times, Tula fulfilled its role as successor to Teotihuacán in another way: For a brief period, the Toltecs guided a commercial and military enterprise that expanded through trade and tribute networks, colonization efforts, and probably conquest (Davies, 1983; Healan, 1989). Toltec prestige reached in several directions. We even recognize their influence in the copper bells, ceremonial ball courts, and other exotic products on Hohokam sites in the American Southwest, from which the Toltecs acquired their valued blue turquoise stone, probably by way of long-distance exchanges (see p. 433).

Toltecs
Central Mexican highlands people who created a pre-Aztec empire with its capital at Tula in the Valley of Mexico.

Tula
(too'-la) Toltec capital in the Valley of Mexico; sometimes known as Tollan.

Within Mesoamerica, the Toltecs' association with the contemporary postclassic Maya site of **Chichén Itzá** in northern Yucatán is also intriguing. Separated by nearly 800 miles (1,275 km), Tula and Chichén Itzá nevertheless shared elements of art style as well as strikingly similar ball courts, skull racks, temple pyramids, and other public architecture. A cult of militarism and human sacrifice to the rain god Tlaloc pervaded both sites (Fig. 18–15).

Archaeologists are still debating the nature of this relationship. Many who once interpreted the evidence as an indication of Toltec military or political domination now suggest that members of the Mexican and Maya elites may have interacted more or less amiably during a period of extensive contact and trade between Yucatán and highland Mexico (Weaver, 1993). But others hold to the view that the Toltecs were masters of a dual empire, lording over the Maya from their second capital at Chichén Itzá (Coe et al., 1986). Despite research at some of Chichén's more interesting features, including the Sacred **Cenote**, or sacrificial pool, where offerings (including humans) were cast into the deep waters, no definitive clue to this puzzle has surfaced.

As Toltec power declined around 850 y.a., Chichén Itzá yielded its preeminence to Mayapán, a less flamboyant Maya trading center in northwestern Yucatán (Sabloff and Rathje, 1975). Within Mexico's central highlands, the Toltecs themselves confronted internal dissension and pressure on their frontiers before finally abandoning Tula, leaving its burned temples and palaces in rubble. By then, a prolonged drought was withering many of the farming communities in northern Mexico and the American Southwest, bringing streams of refugees into the Valley of Mexico and throwing the region into chaos once more.

The Aztecs

One of the groups that appeared on the scene at this juncture was the **Mexica**, better known historically as the **Aztecs** (Townsend, 1992). Impoverished and in search of a permanent homeland, like other people uprooted in this turbulent era, the Mexica encountered hostility in their wanderings and fought fiercely to gain a territory. Pushed from place to place, they finally settled a large, easily defended island near shallow Lake Texcoco's western shore, in the very heart of Mexico. From this more secure base they eventually won control of the entire region through strategic military alliances and brutal warfare.

The Aztecs, as they now called themselves, transformed their island into a remarkable capital they named **Tenochtitlán**. Tied to the mainland only by several narrow causeways, the city itself was sectioned by canals that encouraged canoe transport of goods and people. Its large central plaza encompassed palaces, administrative buildings, and a huge twin-towered temple pyramid for their gods. Between many of the canals, productive *chinampas* (today known as "floating gardens") yielded an abundance of agricultural foods throughout the year, including maize, beans, tomatoes, and chilis.

The Aztecs incorporated and built on many of the accomplishments of their Mesoamerican predecessors. Their calendar, for instance, was a modification of that employed by the Maya a thousand years earlier. Aztec religion, with its emphasis on the sun and on war and human sacrifice, derived from Toltec practices and, ultimately, from ancient Teotihuacán. The Aztecs also learned much about social and political organization and economic enterprise from their predecessors. They established a hereditary nobility of several ranks, including a royal lineage from which their highest leaders descended. Free commoners, comprising the vast majority of Aztec society, were organized into about 20 large kin-based groups to work their own communal lands, while slaves labored for the nobles.

More so than any of its predecessors, the Aztec domain was a consolidated and centralized state under the firm rule of a single leader (Clendinnen, 1991; Townsend, 1992). Using a well-trained military, political alliances, aggressive tax collectors, and a state-sponsored corps of professional traders, the Aztecs dominated neighboring peoples and extended their influence well beyond the Valley of

FIGURE 18–15
Toltec-style serpentine columns and votive figure, Temple of the Warriors, Chichén Itzá, Yucatán, Mexico.

Chichén Itzá
(chee-chen' eet-zah') Postclassic Maya site in Yucatán, strongly linked with the Toltecs of Mexico.

Cenote
(sen-o'-tay) Sinkhole, or collapsed cavern filled with water.

Mexica
(meh-shee'-ka) Original name by which the Aztecs were known before their rise to power.

Aztecs
Militaristic people who dominated the Valley of Mexico and surrounding area at the time of the European conquest.

Tenochtitlán
(tay-nosh-teet-lahn') Aztec capital, built on the future site of Mexico City.

FIGURE 18–16
Aztec rite of human sacrifice, depicted in a sixteenth-century chronicle.

Inka
People whose sophisticated culture dominated Peru at the time of the European arrival; also, the term for that people's highest ruler. (Sometimes spelled *Inca.*)

Mexico. Tribute in the form of maize, cotton cloth, colored stones, exotic feathers, gold, and slaves flowed into the capital. Many of the war captives seized by the Aztec army were reserved for the periodic bloody sacrifices to the Aztec gods (Fig. 18–16).

Until the arrival of the Spanish, Tenochtitlán remained a large and lively urban and religious center, the core of an empire of several million souls. With its magnificent public buildings, houses built over the water, and canoes crowding its canals, the Aztec city in 1519 reminded the Spanish conquistadors of Venice, Italy. One of the soldiers recalled that "so large a market place and so full of people, and so well regulated and arranged, (we) had never beheld before" (Diaz del Castillo, 1956, pp. 218–219). Yet, within a year, these same admirers had destroyed the remarkable city in their quest for wealth and territory. Some of its impressive ruins have been uncovered during subway construction beneath the streets of present-day Mexico City (Moctezuma, 1988), but few traces of Tenochtitlán remain visible aboveground.

Peru

The great **Inka** empire, when encountered by Europeans in the sixteenth century, extended over most of highland and coastal South America from Colombia to Argentina and Chile, including modern-day Peru. In many respects, the Inka civilization was the culmination of all that preceded it in western South America. Its foundations were rooted in the most ancient cultures of Peru, where sociopolitical complexity had developed in conjunction with an increasing proficiency in food production (Keatinge, 1988; Moseley, 1992; Bruhns, 1994).

On first view, Peru seems an unlikely region for nurturing agricultural civilizations (Fig. 18–17). Its Pacific shore forms a narrow coastal desert, a dry fringe of land broken at intervals by deeply entrenched river valleys slicing from the Andes to the ocean. The high mountains rise abruptly and dramatically behind the coastal plain, forming a rugged and snowcapped continental spine. These geographical contrasts figured prominently in Peru's prehistory (Bruhns, 1994). Indeed, the dynamic tension between coast and highlands—fishers and farmers—provides a key to understanding the region's cultural past.

We have seen that Paleo-Indians were active in South America at about the same time as others in western North America were pursuing late Pleistocene herbivores (see Chapter 15). The menagerie of fauna hunted by the southern Paleo-Indians ranged from mammoths and mastodons to giant ground sloths, horses, deer, camelids, and even ostrich-like rheas (Lynch, 1983). Preserved organic materials on the early sites of Monte Verde, in Chile, and Guitarrero Cave, Peru, hint at the important role of plants as well (see p. 382).

Because of Peru's topographic diversity, the natural distribution of food resources tended to correlate with elevation and also with the alternating wet and dry seasons. Some archaeologists have suggested that to effectively exploit a broad spectrum of species, generalized hunters and gatherers needed to move through a series of vertically stacked resource zones between coast and uplands, where various plants, animals, or seafoods were available at different times of the year (Lynch, 1980). We have previously referred to this food procurement strategy as *transhumance* (see p. 392). Other archaeologists, however, hypothesize that more intensive use of the varied microenvironments within a single resource zone would have been equally efficient (Keatinge, 1988).

Fishing, Farming, and the Rise of Civilization

The relative role of farming versus fishing in the development of Peruvian civilization has generated intense discussion (Moseley, 1975; Wilson, 1981; Bruhns, 1994), since most advanced societies elsewhere were generally agricultural. Archaeologist Michael Moseley points out that the deep, cold ocean currents off the Peruvian

FIGURE 18–17
Peruvian sites and locations mentioned in the text.

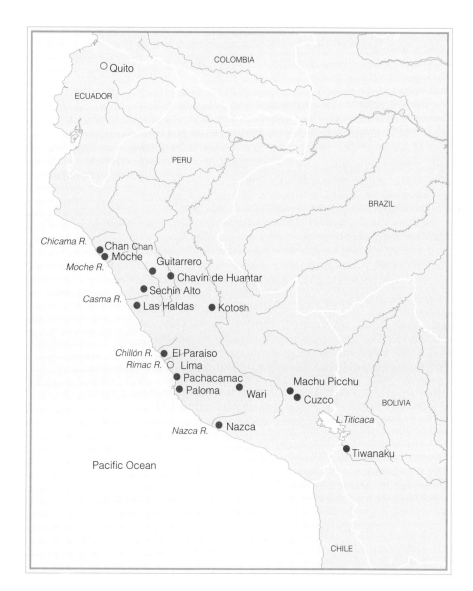

coast that create the richest fishing waters in the Western Hemisphere are also responsible for the onshore climatic conditions that make that same stretch of seacoast one of the world's driest deserts (Moseley, 1992, p. 102). Marine resources surely supported people in this region from the earliest period of human settlement. Before 5,000 y.a., at a time when farming was already under way in a few highland areas, coastal fishing populations had become permanent residents at sites such as Paloma (see p. 432). The productive fisheries may have delayed farming in this dry coastal region for some time, until the long-term effects of a stronger, recurrent El Niño pattern stimulated people to practice some provisional agriculture. These early farming enterprises near the coast involved simply planting seeds of squash, gourds, and beans in the damp beds of seasonal streams flowing down from the Andes.

After 4,000 y.a., more intensive farming activities spread widely in Peru, beginning in upland valleys and interior basins and finally reaching the lower coastal rivers. One key to this expansion was irrigation, which gave farmers the ability to deliver water to thirsty crops for a longer period each year by channeling streams onto adjacent lands. Another was hillside terracing, which gained farmers more space to grow crops. Creating irrigation canals and terraces required the coordinated

efforts of relatively large communal workforces, at least periodically. In return, these energy expenditures ensured significant agricultural payoffs.

Archaeological hallmarks associated with agricultural intensification in coastal Peru include pottery, artifacts associated with spinning and weaving, and especially large-scale architecture. But some archaeologists point out that farmers may not have been responsible for *all* the monumental constructions (Moseley, 1983, 1992). Located in the Chillón River valley on the central coast, the preagricultural site known as El Paraiso includes an impressive, U-shaped ceremonial complex of enormous masonry structures. As many as 1 million days of labor may have been spent in its creation. Building on such a massive scale is more typical of advanced farming communities; the relatively few permanent residents living around El Paraiso could not have built such large features on their own. Archaeologists suspect that villagers from a wide area may have cooperated in creating the monument, which perhaps served as a central place for farmers and fishers alike to gather and exchange products (Coe et al., 1986).

Whether spurred by a growing population, by failure of its fisheries, or both, eventually Peru's coastal region wholeheartedly committed to subsistence agriculture after about 3,800 y.a. This new emphasis on farming correlated with a population shift away from coastal fishing villages and up into river valleys such as the Chillón, Moche, and Rimac, where irrigation was feasible (see Fig. 18–17). Here, local communities organized themselves to excavate canals that would convey water to crops of maize, peanuts, and potatoes, plants originally domesticated in Mexico and the Andean highlands. Staples such as these made farming a worthwhile endeavor, especially given the periodic unreliability of coastal resources due to El Niño. The success of this initial farming period in the lowlands may be measured by the imposing size of ceremonial complexes, such as Sechín Alto on the Casma River, that mark more than two dozen coastal valleys and a number of upland sites in central and northern Peru.

El Paraiso, Sechín Alto, and other such sites are early examples of the "corporate construction" projects that became standard in Peru. Because the areas around these sites held few permanent residents, the huge U-shaped arrangements of temples, platforms, and courtyards—as well as irrigation networks, in many instances—must represent the labors of a large force of people drawn from the general vicinity and put to work under competent supervision. Clearly, sites of this kind were important ceremonial and perhaps market centers for several adjacent valleys (Pozorski and Pozorski, 1988).

By now you probably recognize that ceremonial centers and irrigation canals are the outward signs of underlying social processes. What inspired the collective efforts that produced the civic architecture and the defined art styles in Peru? Most archaeologists take these developments during the initial farming period to indicate greater social complexity as civil and/or religious leaders gained more authority. Under their direction, public energies were applied to large-scale projects. But what motivated individuals to participate in these collective enterprises? And what considerations guided their leaders? From where did they derive their persuasive or coercive powers? In Peru, as elsewhere, archaeologists have considered militarism, religion, and control of resources, among other motivating forces, in explaining the rise of civilizations, yet have come to few definite conclusions (e.g., Haas et al., 1987).

The Chavín Phenomenon

Around 2,500 y.a., the northern Peruvian highlands and coast were affiliated in a religious fervor that temporarily brought some degree of cultural unity to this broad region. The shared ideology was expressed especially through ritual art. **Chavín de Huantar**, an intriguing ceremonial center set in a high Andean valley, embodied this iconography in its most classic phase (Pozorski and Pozorski, 1987; Burger, 1992). Here, raised stone tiers flanked sunken courtyards where ceremonies took place in the shadow of an elaborate temple riddled by underground chambers and labyrinthine passageways. Anthropomorphic stone sculptures and other art at the

Chavín de Huantar
(cha-veen' day wahn'-tar) Prominent highland site associated with early ceremonial activities in Peru.

site combined human characteristics with the features of jaguars, snakes, birds of prey, and mythological beings.

While Chavín de Huantar itself may have served as a primary religious pilgrimage center—perhaps the seat of a respected *oracle*, or fortune-teller—the Chavín style was broadly disseminated throughout northern Peru. Contemporary sites shared elements of the distinctive art and architecture—and, presumably, ideology—during so-called early horizon times. Chavín motifs were reproduced most frequently on woven cotton and camelid wool textiles, but they also appeared on pottery, marine shell, and metal objects. The symbolism and artifacts conveyed prestige upon those who were privileged to acquire them. Thus, Chavín, perhaps much like the Olmec art of Mesoamerica, constituted an agent of widespread cultural change, at least on a stylistic and ideological level. By about 2,200 y.a., though, the appeal of Chavín had faded considerably.

Early Cities

The period just prior to 1,400 y.a. saw the founding and somewhat parallel development of regional kingdoms, or city-states, in the Moche valley on Peru's north coast and the Nazca valley in the south, and possibly at other as yet unexplored sites in between. The pace of construction of numerous pyramids, irrigation canals, and public buildings, as well as the production of specialized crafts, once again implies complex societies under effective management. Elaborate high-status burials and military symbolism, combined with some anthropomorphic artistic elements retained from the Chavín cult, hint at the nature of that control (Alva and Donnan, 1993).

Moche rulers consolidated their hold over neighboring valleys initially through warfare and then by greatly expanding irrigated agricultural lands in the conquered areas. Moche state religion prescribed periodic offerings of war captives in an elaborate and bloody ritual. Monumental constructions marking the ceremonial precincts near both the northern and southern coastal cities represented an impressive expenditure of each society's energy and resources. For example, Moche's **Huaca del Sol** (Pyramid of the Sun) incorporated some 100 million hand-formed bricks!

Artistic specialists at each center created remarkable objects that adhered to formally defined local styles. Most of these creations served the elite as status symbols in life and in death. Unique **polychrome** ceramic vessels modeled to represent portraits, buildings, everyday scenes, or imaginative fantasies were a Moche specialty (Fig. 18–18). Nazca pottery, too, had an appeal of its own, with brightly painted naturalistic and symbolic motifs. Metalsmiths hammered, alloyed, and cast breathtaking adornments, ceremonial weapons, and religious paraphernalia from precious gold, silver, and copper. (Unlike Old World societies, those in the Americas seldom employed metal for technological purposes, generally reserving it for ornamental use as a badge of social standing.)

The contents of excavated tombs of Moche warrior-priests rival those of the rulers of Egypt or Mesopotamia (Alva and Donnan, 1993). These high officials, both males and females, officiated over the human sacrifice ceremony. Upon their own deaths, they were dressed in the elaborate and distinctive regalia of their elevated position. Protected by dead attendants, llamas, and dogs, their tombs have yielded a trove of ceremonial accessories, including headdresses, earrings, necklaces, and blood-drinking goblets. In contrast, around Nazca, the prominent dead were customarily wrapped in yards of brilliantly dyed camelid wool textiles richly embroidered with stylized animals and humans and trophy heads reminiscent of the Chavín art style (Fig. 18–19).

The most mystifying feature of Nazca culture may be the radiating lines, geometric forms, and animal figures "drawn" in gigantic scale on the flat desert tableland of the south coast (Fig. 18–20). While the designs are fully visible only from the air and hence may not have been intended merely to amuse earthbound mortals, they certainly are not the work of ancient astronauts! The patterns were carefully laid out with the aid of wooden stakes and cordage, then simply swept clear of

Huaca del Sol
(wah'-ka dell sole) Massive adobe pyramid built at Moche, in northern Peru.

Polychrome
Many-colored.

William Turnbaugh

FIGURE 18–18
Moche portrait jar from northern Peru.

FIGURE 18–19
Detail of Paracas textile, Nazca region of southern Peru.

After photograph by William Turnbaugh

darkened surface stones to expose the lighter underlying soil (Aveni, 1986, 1990). Interpreted by some as appeals to the gods for water, many of the naturalistic motifs, including a fish, monkey, spider, birds, and plants, appear also on Nazca burial wrappings and decorated ceramic vessels. The much more numerous linear traces functioned as ceremonial pathways, some linking dispersed members of kin-groups to their family lands and others aligning with important streams, sacred mountains, pilgrimage sites, or even astronomical events (Aveni, 2000).

FIGURE 18–20
Nazca ground drawings as seen from the air include both zoomorphic and linear motifs. The monkey is longer than a football field.

Drawings by William Turnbaugh, from photographs

From Kingdoms to Empires

Archaeologists have noted that throughout the prehistory of western South America, highlands peoples tended to push "downward," toward the lowlands, as the early irrigation farmers apparently did. Coastal peoples spread laterally, often annexing adjacent coastal valleys, as did the Moche warriors. In either situation, the objective may have been to gain access to additional resource zones through what has been described as "vertical control" and "horizontal control" (Murra, 1972; Moseley, 1983). Overpopulation, resource depletion, and environmental degradation may have stimulated the intervals of aggressive expansionism recognized in ancient Peru. The result was a recurrent ebb and flow of sociopolitical integration; episodes of expansion and unification were invariably punctuated by periods of breakdown and regional isolation (Moseley, 1983).

Moche and Nazca influences had extended over the north and south coastal regions, respectively, before fading. Now, the southern highlands witnessed a renewed period of expansionism around 1,400 y.a. **Wari** (also spelled Huari) and **Tiwanaku** were well-organized highland capitals that used trade, control of food and labor resources, and military conquest to extend their interests from the Andes to the coast (Kolata, 1987). Religion, too, played an effective role in these enterprises. The prominent "staff god" deity shared by both kingdoms can be traced back to ancient Chavín iconography (Fig. 18–21). Wari's reach briefly extended over the northern highlands and much of coastal Peru, while Tiwanaku controlled the southern highlands for several centuries more.

Tiwanaku's 12,000-foot (3,600 m) altitude near the south shore of Lake Titicaca, in Bolivia (see Fig. 18–17), should have made farming a marginal activity there, threatened by frost and an unstable water supply. Undaunted, the people of the city and nearby communities altered their lakeshore environment, creating raised fields with elevated planting platforms in marshy areas and directing water through cultivated areas with aquaducts and canals. Based on these rediscovered principles, farming experiments conducted by archaeologist Alan Kolata proved so productive that modern growers are now adopting some of the ancient methods (Straughan, 1991).

The impetus toward unification of ever larger regions did not end with the highland kingdoms of Wari and Tiwanaku. In fact, Peru's north coast became the center of yet another episode of expansion beginning around 1,000 y.a. This **Chimor** kingdom of the north was rooted in the Moche valley, near the seat of the earlier city-state. The eroded mud-brick architecture of the Chimor capital, Chan Chan, still blankets several square miles of coastal desert there. Among the ruins are nearly a dozen walled compounds, each of which had served as a grand and secluded palace, storehouse, and tomb for the successive monarchs of the ruling lineages (Fig. 18–22). At the end of each reign, the ruler was interred in a burial platform amid prodigious wealth (and sometimes his harem of young women) and the compound was sealed. By contrast, the insubstantial quarters of tens of thousands of urban peasants once crammed the spaces below the massive walls (Moseley and Day, 1982).

The militaristic Chimor state extended its control along 620 miles (1,000 km) of the north coast and established regional administrative centers to watch over local populations and to coordinate agricultural terracing projects as well as road and canal construction, including a 40-mile (65 km) aquaduct to convey water from the Chicama River to the capital (Kus, 1984).

FIGURE 18–21
Staff god, Tiwanaku.

Wari
(wah'-ree) Capital of a regional kingdom in southern Peru.

Tiwanaku
(tee-wahn-ah'-koo) Capital of a regional kingdom near Lake Titicaca, in Bolivia.

Chimor
A powerful culture that dominated the northern Peruvian coast between about 1,000 and 500 y.a.

FIGURE 18–22
Aerial view of one of the royal enclosures at Chan Chan, the Chimor capital.

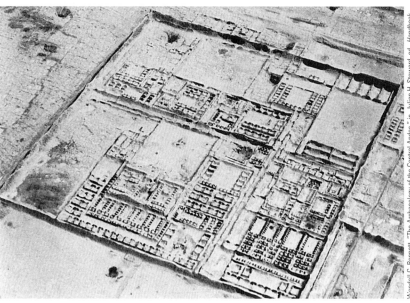

Cuzco
(coos'-co) Inka capital in the southern Peruvian highlands.

Sacsahuamán
(sak-sa-wah-mahn') Stone fortress and shrine overlooking Cuzco.

Huayna Capac
(why'-na kah'pak) Inka leader whose death precipitated civil war.

FIGURE 18-23
Inka stone walls of Sacsahuamán, near Cuzco, in Peru.

The Inka

The pattern of conquest and control set by Chimor was not ignored by their rivals and successors, the Inka, the last native empire builders of ancient Peru. Their minor highland society, centered around present-day **Cuzco**, gained rapid ascendancy over the southern highlands through bold military initiatives in the mid-fifteenth century A.D. (About 550 y.a.).

The aging Chimor kingdom itself succumbed to Inka conquests on the north coast about A.D. 1470, and within a decade the Inka were consolidating an imperial domain that extended over all of modern Peru and the adjacent region (Lanning, 1967; Mason, 1968). The Inka army played a major role in this enterprise, but equally important in maintaining the new state was an efficient administration that established communication and supply systems to hold the empire together. The absolute power of the divine ruler, or *Inka*, was effectively carried out by subordinates who oversaw tax collection, allotment of communal lands, resettlement of malcontents, and selection of the "chosen women" destined either for marriage to the nobles or for sacrifice to the gods. A key element of Inka success, however, was an enlightened tolerance for local ethnic and cultural diversity among their many subjects. Social, political, and religious customs that did not threaten Inka dominance were permitted to continue.

Rural Cuzco now served as capital of an empire of at least 6 million people and its rulers proclaimed it "the navel of the universe." But in contrast to the principal cities of most other American civilizations, the Inka's highland town retained its modest character. Cuzco itself comprised a relatively simple ceremonial center set amid residential areas. On an overlooking hill rose **Sacsahuamán** fortress, its massive mortarless walls formed by cyclopean stone blocks expertly dressed and fitted together without the aid of metal tools (Fig. 18–23). This distinctive architectural stonework appeared throughout the Inka realm in religious shrines, state warehouses, and administrative districts (Protzen, 1986).

Well-maintained roads led out of Cuzco to the four quarters of the Inka state (Hyslop, 1984; Morris, 1988). Crossing mountains, valleys, and deserts, some 18,750 miles (30,000 km) of paved ways tied the far-flung domain together, facilitating official communication by fleet-footed couriers, the deployment of army units, and royal processions. Way stations spaced along the primary routes offered comfort to official travelers.

Beyond Cuzco, the only sizable settlements were Pachacamac, a destination of religious pilgrims on Peru's north coast, and Quito, in Ecuador, established as a second capital by the Inka leader **Huayna Capac**. One of the most remarkable and pic-

Courtesy, Katherine Pomonis

FIGURE 18–24
Machu Picchu.

Courtesy, Carol Howell

turesque of Inka sites was the remote citadel of Machu Picchu, high above the upper reaches of the Urubamba River (Fig. 18–24). Situated to facilitate trade in jungle products from the east, the outpost also protected the capital and served as a seasonal retreat for the Inka aristocracy.

The Inka deliberately countered the development of major urban centers, fearing the possibility that large numbers of city dwellers might be a potential source of unrest. Resettlement programs dispersed larger communities in newly conquered areas so that the populace consisted almost entirely of rural peasants. Most grew maize, potatoes, quinoa, and other crops in irrigated alluvial valleys or on hillside terraces prepared by state-directed labor. Herders in the highlands tended flocks of domesticated llamas and alpacas, which supplied transport, dung for fuel, wool, objects of religious sacrifices, and food (although the only meat generally consumed by most people was the domesticated guinea pig, a small tailless rodent). Perhaps two-thirds of the produce was claimed by the state, much of it to be naturally freeze-dried in high-altitude warehouses and then eventually redistributed back to the citizens as they labored on roads and other state-sponsored civic projects. Despite its effective organization and precautions, the Inka empire lasted for only about 60 years. Its rapid demise, like that of the Aztecs in Mexico, was a consequence of unanticipated challenges from half a world away.

European Conquest of the New World

Just over 500 years have passed since a Genoese navigator, commissioned by the rulers of Spain to sail westward to the Orient, made his first landfall on a tiny island in the western Atlantic. By the beginning of the sixteenth century, within several

William Turnbaugh, from a private collection

FIGURE 18–25
Sixteenth-century woodblock print depicting an early encounter between Europeans and Native Americans.

Motecuhzoma Xocoyotzin
(mo-teh-ca-zooma' shoh-coh-yoh'-seen) Last Aztec ruler, also known as Moctezuma II, whose death at the hands of the Spanish precipitated the destruction of the Aztec empire.

Quetzalcoatl
(ket-sal'-kwat-el) Also known as the Feathered Serpent; a deity representing good, worshiped by Aztecs and possibly earlier at Teotihuacán.

years of this event, Europeans generally realized that Columbus had come upon a new world, rather than the new route to the East Indies that he and his sponsors had been seeking.

Most who had any direct interest in these matters at first expressed only bitter disappointment. But after disillusionment came a determination to make the most of the situation. Spanish, Portuguese, English, Dutch, and French parties set off, each to see what might be wrung from this "newe found land" that lay across the path to the exotic wealth of the Orient (Fig. 18–25). At the same time, all would be searching for any possible way over, around, or past the land they now called America.

Of course, no anthropologists were on hand in the 1500s to alert their contemporaries to the dramatic events that were rapidly unfolding not only in America but in Africa and Asia as well. Never before and never again would there be such a large-scale confrontation between peoples and cultures that had evolved in isolation over hundreds of generations. In any event, it is unlikely that the painful developments that followed could have been avoided, even if the situation had been more fully comprehended.

The Western Hemisphere was populated by tens of millions of people (Dobyns, 1966, estimates 100 million, but many believe that figure is far too high) who exhibited a remarkable range and richness of genetic, cultural, and linguistic variation. Small bands of hunters and fishers foraged the northernmost and southernmost extremes of the continents. Food collectors and horticulturalists shared most of the middle latitudes. A few agricultural chiefdoms maintained sway in southeastern North America, the Caribbean islands, and northern South America. But as many as a third of all the New World's peoples were subjects of one or the other of the native states that prevailed in highland Mexico and Peru in the early 1500s.

The Aztec and Inka empires comprised the nuclear civilizations of America. Each represented the culmination of many centuries of cultural tradition and development in its respective sphere. Both had reached an apex of achievement in every dimension—art, social organization, commerce, technology, learning, government, and religion. The Aztec and Inka states commanded the resources, talents, and vigor of vast territories. At the same time, their influence radiated into even larger regions of the two continents. These centers of wealth and power attracted the armored Europeans like a magnet.

The end for these native empires came with shocking swiftness. The two decades following 1520 saw both the Aztecs and the Inka and their domains fall into the hands of Spanish conquerors (Prescott, 1906). Leaving Cuba in 1517, Hernán Cortés and several hundred fellow adventurers pressed through the swampy lowlands of Veracruz and on to the central highlands of Mexico. There, in November 1519, the Aztec ruler **Motecuhzoma Xocoyotzin** (usually known as Moctezuma) received them with some justifiable suspicion. Cortés' arrival coincided remarkably with the divinely foretold return of the Aztec god **Quetzalcoatl**. But the Spaniards' obsession with gold and plunder seemed all too earthly. As Cortés and his soldiers entered Tenochtitlán, they compared it to the principal cities of Europe, which hardly surpassed the Aztec capital in size or grandeur. Their admiration notwithstanding, the newcomers resolved to seize Tenochtitlán. Almost immediately, Moctezuma found himself imprisoned and the Spanish in control. An uprising against the European invaders was quelled with the willing assistance of many thousands of the Aztecs' disenchanted neighbors and former subjects. By 1521, the Spanish were the uncontested successors to the great empire in the heartland of Mexico.

The conquest of Peru took much the same course barely a decade later. An expeditionary force of 180 Spanish soldiers led by Francisco Pizarro entered the Inka domain in 1532, just as **Atahuallpa** claimed victory in a bitter five-year struggle for succession to the throne of his father, Huayna Capac, who had died of European smallpox. Pizarro found many disappointed followers of Huascar, Atahuallpa's half-brother and rival for the throne, eager to assist in deposing the new Inka. Through treachery, the Spanish eliminated both contenders, but not until they first amassed a fabulous ransom in gold and silver from the unfortunate Atahuallpa, who was then put to death. Despite some native resistance following these events, the Spanish had firm control of Peru by 1538.

In one brief and tragic—yet remarkable—moment in history, the crowning achievements of half a world had been undone. Successive decades would witness the wholesale devastation of peoples and cultures that represented thousands of years of development and adaptation. The Spanish conquest proceeded outward from the Mexican and Peruvian centers while other Europeans began the process anew in more peripheral areas occupied by farming tribes and mobile foragers.

Armed conflict itself was relatively less destructive than the other cumulative effects of contact. Old World diseases against which native peoples had no natural antibodies—measles, smallpox, chicken pox, the "common" cold—often decimated populations well in advance of their first direct contact with the newcomers. Epidemics in many areas swept away perhaps 75 to 90 percent of the people within months, leaving survivors with little will or ability to resist further social and economic intrusions. Slavery took its toll as well; the skeletons of certain American Indians from this era exhibit the signs of heavy labor, malnutrition, and disease. Columbus himself enslaved local Indians to grow sugar on Caribbean islands, and by 1540, the native peoples of that region had died out entirely, necessitating the importation of black slaves from Africa to maintain the plantation system.

As colonizers invaded the lands they increasingly came to regard as their own, they brought with them the agricultural complexes, technological equipment, and social, economic, and religious philosophies that aided them in transforming much of the New World into a close approximation of the Old. The cost of the confrontation, in human, cultural, and ecological terms, was enormous; the foregone potential will be forever incalculable. The loss, if not the shame, is borne by all humankind.

Atahuallpa
(at-a-wall'-pah) Inka leader defeated by Pizarro.

SUMMARY

In Mesoamerica, cultivated crops—among which maize was primary—supported stable populations in some parts of the central highlands and along the southern Gulf of Mexico by about 4,000 y.a. In western South America, an area characterized by great topographic extremes, initial farming activities were complemented near the coast by fishing and in the highlands by maintaining flocks of camelids. These varied and productive resources served as the economic bases for a series of increasingly complex and sophisticated cultures in each of the regions considered here.

In time, a number of these societies attained the status of *civilization*. We have treated the Olmec and Maya in lowland Mesoamerica; Teotihuacán, Toltec, and Aztec in highland Mexico; and a 4,000-year sequence of increasingly integrated and expansive cultures in Peru, culminating in the Inka empire.

While there appear to have been some broad similarities in the major features of Old and New World development, especially regarding the connections between agriculture and civilization, the subtle but significant distinctions in these regions should not be overlooked. To mention only a few: American civilizations emerged in more ecologically diverse locations, relied very little on domesticated animals, wheels, or metal for technological purposes, and tended to "cycle" more rapidly from rise through decline. But again, these are broad statements.

Pre-Columbian transoceanic contact between the Old World and the Americas was (at most) minimal and probably nonexistent at least prior to the Viking explorations around a thousand years ago, in the considered opinion of most archaeologists. The effect of long-term isolation was a divergence between the populations of the two hemispheres, particularly in their cultures. With the confrontation of Old and New World peoples that took place during the Age of Exploration, biocultural isolation in these regions came to an end. So, very nearly, did the New World societies themselves.

QUESTIONS FOR REVIEW

1. Explain how the relatively resource-poor lowlands of Mesoamerica may have stimulated the development of such complex cultures as the Olmec and Maya.
2. What would a visitor expect to observe and experience at a major Maya center during the classic period?
3. What significance was attached to Maya stelae—by the Maya and by us?
4. Which great city flourished in the Valley of Mexico while the classic Maya dominated the lowlands? What evidence do we have for relations between these two regions?
5. Why do archaeologists find the relationship between Chichén Itzá and Tula so intriguing?
6. In what ways does it appear that Olmec and Chavín may have had a similar impact on their respective culture areas?
7. Explain how the prehistoric people of Peru were able to so successfully make use of the region's highly varied environmental zones.
8. The early coastal cities of Moche and Nazca in Peru have attracted much archaeological attention. What are some of the more remarkable accomplishments associated with these cities?
9. Review some of the historical parallels between the Aztec and Inka cultures.
10. Contrast the prehistoric civilizations of the New World with those of the Old World. How might some of these differences have contributed ultimately to the European conquest of the Americas?

SUGGESTED FURTHER READING

Boone, Elizabeth Hill. 1996. *The Aztec World*. Washington, DC: Smithsonian Institution Press.

Bruhns, Karen Olsen. 1994. *Ancient South America*. New York: Cambridge University Press.

Coe, Michael D. 1992. *Breaking the Maya Code*. New York: Thames and Hudson.

———. 1994. *Mexico*. 2nd ed. New York: Thames and Hudson.

Diaz del Castillo, Bernal. 1956. *The Discovery and Conquest of Mexico*. New York: Farrar, Straus and Cudahy.

Morris, Craig, and Adriana von Hagen. 1998. *The Cities of the Ancient Andes*. New York: Thames and Hudson.

Moseley, Michael E. 1992. *The Incas and Their Ancestors*. New York: Thames and Hudson.

Ramenofsky, Ann F. 1987. *Vectors of Death: The Archaeology of European Contact*. Albuquerque, NM: University of New Mexico Press.

Richardson, James, III. 1996. *People of the Andes*. Washington, DC: Smithsonian Institution Press.

Sharer, Robert J. 1996. *Daily Life in Maya Civilization*. Westport, CT: Greenwood Publishing.

Townsend, Richard. 1992. *The Aztecs*. New York: Thames and Hudson.

Weaver, Muriel Porter. 1993. *The Aztecs, Maya, and Their Predecessors: Archaeology of Mesoamerica*. 3rd ed. San Diego, CA: Academic Press.

RESOURCES ON THE INTERNET

Wadsworth Anthropology Resource Center
http://anthropology.wadsworth.com

The companion website for this text includes a range of enrichment material focused on the chapter's topic. While online you can enhance your understanding of the chapter by exploring one of the several additional Internet Exercises, by researching topics, and by accessing full articles on InfoTrac College Edition. You can also reinforce the concepts by taking online practice exams.

Internet Exercises

The Maya writing and calendar system has now been largely decoded. Visit Rabbit in the Moon (**www.halfmoon.org**) and after exploring this interesting website on the Maya language, click on "Mayan Calendar & Date Calculator." Then select "Mayan Date Calculator" to see how the Maya numeric system would represent any given date from A.D. 1903 to 2000. You can enter your own or a friend's birthday, for example, and see the unique combination of glyphs that indicate that specific day. If you like more of a challenge, click on "How to Write Your Name in Glyphs" and give it a try.

InfoTrac College Edition
http://www.infotrac-college.com/wadsworth

Much current archaeological research is focused on the pre-European civilizations of Mesoamerica and western South America. Use the InfoTrac College Edition to do a keyword search for at least two of the following: *Olmec, Maya* (also try *Mayan* and *ancient Maya*), *Teotihuacán, Aztec,* and *Inka* (try *Inca,* also). Evaluate the reference titles to be certain they pertain to an ancient society ("Maya" is popular as a personal name these days, and some commercial firms have adopted the names of these cultures, too.) Then, select and read an article that reports on a recent discovery relating to one of these cultures. How does this new information supplement the material presented in Chapter 18?

Epilogue: Our Biocultural Legacy

In this textbook, we have traced the human journey back to its beginnings close to 4 billion years ago, with the first origins of life on earth. From there, we briefly summarized early evolutionary history, documenting the first vertebrates and early mammals.

With the appearance and radiation of the first primates, more than 50 million years ago, our focus became much more thorough. The reason is obvious: Humans are primates, and our most immediate evolutionary history is as a primate. We have emphasized this *biological continuum* and have pointed out that human evolution is the product of the same evolutionary factors that affect all organisms.

We often hear claims that humans are *unique* for some type of physical trait or even more commonly argued, for some type of behavioral characteristic. However, when looking at the biological continuity that links our species with other life forms, and most especially with other primates, we see that this emphasis on uniqueness is frequently overstated—and is, more often than not, simply incorrect.

As we have said repeatedly, most, if not all, human physical and behavioral characteristics can also be seen to some degree in other primates. We have argued that the obvious way to understand those similarities that humans share with other primates (as well as any presumed differences) is to compare humans with our primate cousins. The vast number of similarities shared by human and nonhuman primates are both the result of and a testimony to our common evolutionary history. In other words, these commonalities reflect the biological continuum—one that obviously includes *Homo sapiens*.

Although a comprehension of human evolution is rooted in this *biological* continuity, the last few thousand years of human achievement reveal a seeming discontinuity. These very recent developments are *cultural* ones, and they have produced a dramatic impact worldwide. These profound cultural modifications came about mostly in the last 12,000 years—from an evolutionary perspective, just a flicker in time. The cause of such rapid changes in our own species, in our relationship with the environment, and in the ultimate fate of many other species was the development of agriculture.

The astounding swiftness of the transformations that have swept our planet in a mere 600 human generations has often been referred to as the agricultural revolution. Some researchers have criticized this terminology, since the first beginnings of domestication can be traced in some areas to well before 12,000 years ago. Nevertheless, once the momentum for change was established in widely scattered areas of the Old World as well as independently in the New World, the impact was swift, dramatic, and in many cases devastating. In all of human history, indeed of the entire record of the genus *Homo*, these agriculturally based modifications have produced the most profound cultural revolution known—and it is one that humanity is still inventing and with which we are still learning to cope. Humans have essentially transformed their population structure, altered their relationship with the environment, and ultimately reshaped the surface of the planet.

From a *Homo sapiens* population 12,000 years ago of probably no more than 5 million, the human population has grown to exceed 6 billion. In the history of life on earth, no animal of our body mass and physiological requirements has ever attained such numbers. In a strictly cultural sense, we could view these rapid developments and our ensuing increase in numbers as a form of "success."

Yet, we cannot forget the inevitable costs that came with this success—unforeseen and unwanted, but costs nevertheless. Indeed, for the first time in the 400,000-year record of our species, and perhaps for the first time in the history of life on earth, one species' actions are pushing thousands of other life forms to extinction—and at the same time producing an environment increasingly inhospitable to its own continued well-being.

If we appreciate that no other species has before unwittingly caused so much disruption, our species, at least, has the capacity to recognize the ramifications and to do something about them. This capability, the product of an expanded and elaborate primate brain, is yet another part of our legacy.

From the preceding paragraphs, you might infer that in recent history biology and culture have somehow become disjointed—but this view should not be taken too far. We are still biocultural beings. The mutual interaction of these joint factors is what produced us in the first place, gave us our current capabilities, and, to some extent, constrains our future options.

From the time an early hominid first learned to consistently remove flakes from stone nodules, our biology has been greatly influenced by our expanding cultural capabilities. But, our biology, in turn, has influenced, channeled, and set limits on these cultural processes. This biocultural interaction is a distinctive—indeed, crucial—aspect of hominid evolution, even if it is not entirely unique (as, for example, when compared with the biosocial evolution of other primates).

We think of ourselves as masters of our existence, but such arrogance is misplaced, perhaps even dangerous. We have said that we have become—albeit very recently—more dominant in numbers, biomass, and certainly environmental influence than has any other large animal. But you should pause and consider that bacteria have been the dominant life form on earth for more than 3 billion years—and still are, by almost any biological standard. When all is said and done, when no multicellular animals remain, the bacteria will endure. Such evolutionary observations are not really in dispute. They are offered here as a lesson in biological humility.

What then of the future? Our textbook has dwelt at length on where we have come from and how we have created the present dilemma. But where do we go from here? The answer to this question is, of course, less certain, and the cultural resolution is bound to engender debate over the imminent hard choices our species faces.

Remember, of course, that biological evolution is still occurring in *Homo sapiens*. In fact, the most apparent evolutionary shifts in the last few thousand years (e.g., changes in allele frequencies relating to the sickle-cell trait and lactose tolerance) have been pushed along by environmental modifications relating to agriculture and domestication. So, too, with the spread of all the major infectious diseases. But the environmental shifts associated with this largely cultural transformation have occurred at a pace that is far faster than biological evolution can match. Thus, while allele frequencies are surely still changing in varied human populations, these shifts are never going to respond fast enough to allow a functional adaptation to our transformed world. If there is a solution to the cultural dilemma we have created, it, too, must be cultural in nature.

We have noted one major ramification of our recent cultural success, that of enormous population expansion. Indeed, many scholars point to this change as the most pressing problem facing contemporary *Homo sapiens* because it influences so many other imminent issues: increased population density, poverty, the spread of infectious diseases, ethnic conflict, habitat destruction, widespread loss of biodiversity, pollution, and so on. If human beings, collectively through responsible political, economic, and social effort, do not stem the tide of increasing population size, then none of the other imminent problems are likely to be resolved. But the news is not all bad; some potentially hopeful trends are apparent, at least in some regions. For example, greater prosperity, self-determination, and the increased status of women have recently helped reduce birthrates in several parts of Asia and in Latin America (following trends already established some time ago in Europe, Japan, the United States, and elsewhere). Unfortunately, these encouraging patterns are not so evident in other parts of Asia (particularly south Asia) and most definitely not in most of sub-Saharan Africa.

What can be done? First, we should mention that while the central problem we face is an overwhelming multitude of people, this is not the *only* relevant issue. Almost as crucial is the amount of resources each of us consumes. It is very convenient for citizens of the United States or Australia, for example, to demand that something be done to limit population growth in the developing world (where, in fact, the vast majority of population growth is now occurring). But we must not forget that people in the industrialized, developed world continue to strain the earth's capacity to support its current population—and do so to a much greater extent than the billions of less fortunate souls in the developing world who live in poverty, scraping together and consuming the barest of resources. Ponder this: One resident of the United States is estimated to consume 400 times the amount of resources as does a resident of either the central African country of Rwanda or the south Asian nation of Bangladesh. Put another way, consider one good-sized American city—say, San Antonio (population 1.6 million). Given the resource demands of this typically affluent American urban area, it would take 80 Rwandas (population about 8 million) to consume the same amount of resources! Clearly, not all the answers are to be found by expecting sacrifices elsewhere. In fact, if any viable solutions are to emerge, sacrifices will have to come from all.

It is difficult to see from whence the political imperative will come, at least on an effective worldwide basis. Among the looming ecological disasters our planet faces is the greenhouse effect (caused by greenhouse gases, especially carbon dioxide, emitted as a product of industrialization). In 1997, a draft agreement (protocol) was reached in Kyoto, Japan, and was signed by more than 100 countries, including the United States. Before the ink was dry, there was heavy lobbying in the United States, which later resulted in a Sense of the Senate Resolution prohibiting any implementation without further concessions from developing countries (the resolution passed the U.S. Senate unanimously).

In 2000, another round of intense international negotiations took place to update and (at the insistence of the United States, Canada, Australia, and a few other countries) to amend the agreements reached at Kyoto. This time failure occurred at the international level. After days of often acrimonious debate, the conference broke up without any agreement. At this writing, further international talks are scheduled for later in 2001, but the political climate seems less favorable than in previous years. Realistically, the accords reached in Kyoto in 1997 seem doomed never to be implemented.

If the political will is lacking, what then of individual commitment? Again, it is easy to advocate sacrifice, but less pleasant to actually carry through. The authors of this text, the educators who have adopted it for their classes, and the many students who read these words are all consumers. Perhaps, some are more conspicuous than others, but all of us almost certainly devour resources at a level far above the world average. Should we ask the rest of the world to forfeit their share of resources so that we may continue our present lifestyle? Should we accept what seems inevitable—that any effort is futile? If so, we will simply perpetuate the problem and have to deal with the consequences later—or let our children and grandchildren deal with them.

As a last choice, we in the developed world, especially those in societies that have overconsumed in the past, could make a serious commitment to alter our lifestyles. Recognizing that the required changes will be painful and economically destabilizing, who is truly prepared to pursue this option?

Appendix A
Atlas of Primate Skeletal Anatomy

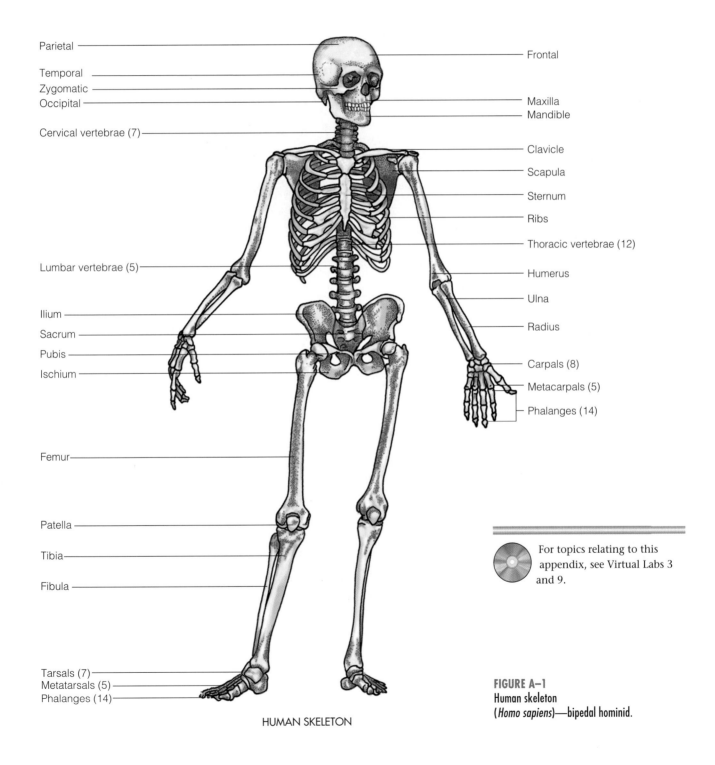

Parietal

Temporal
Zygomatic
Occipital

Cervical vertebrae (7)

Lumbar vertebrae (5)

Ilium
Sacrum
Pubis
Ischium

Femur

Patella

Tibia

Fibula

Tarsals (7)
Metatarsals (5)
Phalanges (14)

Frontal

Maxilla
Mandible

Clavicle

Scapula

Sternum

Ribs

Thoracic vertebrae (12)

Humerus

Ulna

Radius

Carpals (8)

Metacarpals (5)

Phalanges (14)

HUMAN SKELETON

For topics relating to this appendix, see Virtual Labs 3 and 9.

FIGURE A–1
Human skeleton
(*Homo sapiens*)—bipedal hominid.

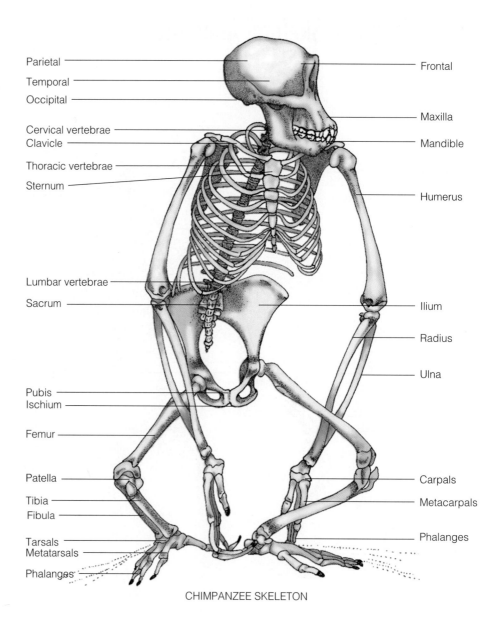

Parietal — Frontal

Temporal — Maxilla

Occipital — Mandible

Cervical vertebrae

Clavicle

Thoracic vertebrae — Humerus

Sternum

Lumbar vertebrae

Sacrum — Ilium

— Radius

— Ulna

Pubis

Ischium

Femur — Carpals

Patella — Metacarpals

Tibia

Fibula — Phalanges

Tarsals

Metatarsals

Phalanges

CHIMPANZEE SKELETON

FIGURE A–2
Chimpanzee skeleton (*Pan troglodytes*)—
knuckle-walking pongid.

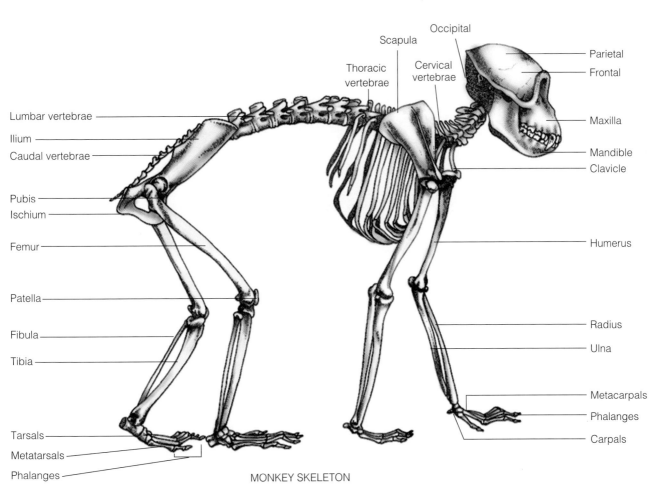

Occipital

Scapula

Thoracic
vertebrae

Cervical
vertebrae

Parietal

Frontal

Lumbar vertebrae

Ilium

Caudal vertebrae

Maxilla

Mandible

Clavicle

Pubis

Ischium

Femur

Humerus

Patella

Fibula

Tibia

Radius

Ulna

Metacarpals

Phalanges

Carpals

Tarsals

Metatarsals

Phalanges

MONKEY SKELETON

FIGURE A–3
Monkey skeleton (rhesus macaque; *Macaca
mulatta*)—a typical quadrupedal primate.

FIGURE A–4
Human cranium.
(continued on next page)

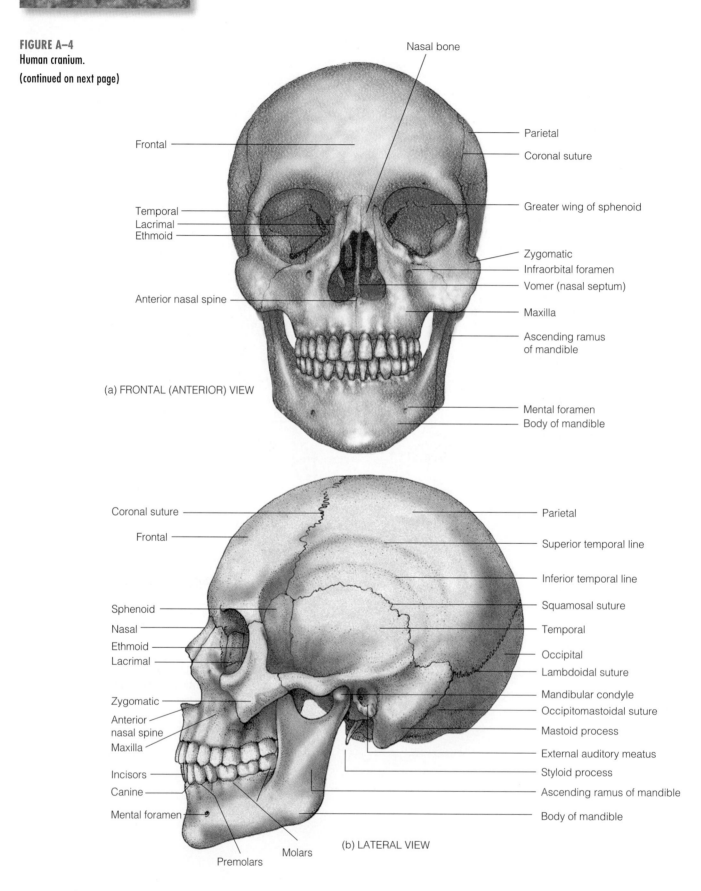

Nasal bone

Frontal

Parietal

Coronal suture

Greater wing of sphenoid

Temporal
Lacrimal
Ethmoid

Zygomatic

Infraorbital foramen

Vomer (nasal septum)

Anterior nasal spine

Maxilla

Ascending ramus
of mandible

(a) FRONTAL (ANTERIOR) VIEW

Mental foramen
Body of mandible

Coronal suture

Parietal

Frontal

Superior temporal line

Inferior temporal line

Sphenoid

Squamosal suture

Nasal

Temporal

Ethmoid

Lacrimal

Occipital

Lambdoidal suture

Zygomatic

Mandibular condyle

Anterior
nasal spine

Occipitomastoidal suture

Maxilla

Mastoid process

External auditory meatus

Incisors

Styloid process

Canine

Ascending ramus of mandible

Mental foramen

Body of mandible

Premolars

Molars

(b) LATERAL VIEW

FIGURE A–4
Human cranium. (continued)

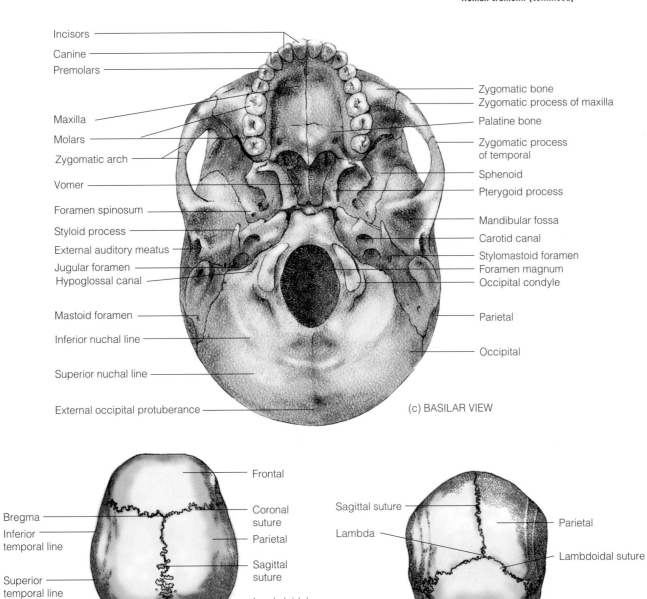

Incisors
Canine
Premolars

Maxilla
Molars
Zygomatic arch
Vomer
Foramen spinosum
Styloid process
External auditory meatus
Jugular foramen
Hypoglossal canal

Mastoid foramen
Inferior nuchal line
Superior nuchal line
External occipital protuberance

Zygomatic bone
Zygomatic process of maxilla
Palatine bone
Zygomatic process of temporal
Sphenoid
Pterygoid process
Mandibular fossa
Carotid canal
Stylomastoid foramen
Foramen magnum
Occipital condyle
Parietal
Occipital

(c) BASILAR VIEW

Frontal
Coronal suture
Parietal
Sagittal suture
Lambdoidal suture
Occipital

Bregma
Inferior temporal line
Superior temporal line

(d) SUPERIOR VIEW

Sagittal suture
Lambda
Occipital
Mastoid process

Parietal
Lambdoidal suture
Nuchal line

(e) REAR VIEW

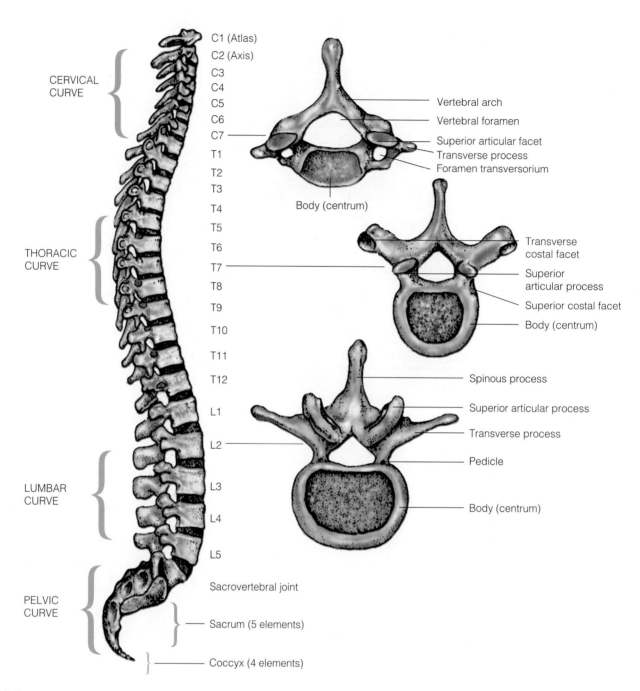

CERVICAL
CURVE

C1 (Atlas)
C2 (Axis)
C3
C4
C5
C6
C7
T1
T2
T3
T4
T5
T6
T7
T8
T9
T10
T11
T12
L1
L2
L3
L4
L5

THORACIC
CURVE

LUMBAR
CURVE

PELVIC
CURVE

Vertebral arch
Vertebral foramen
Superior articular facet
Transverse process
Foramen transversorium

Body (centrum)

Transverse
costal facet

Superior
articular process

Superior costal facet

Body (centrum)

Spinous process

Superior articular process

Transverse process

Pedicle

Body (centrum)

Sacrovertebral joint

Sacrum (5 elements)

Coccyx (4 elements)

FIGURE A–5
Human vertebral column (lateral view) and
representative cervical, thoracic, and lumbar
vertebrae (superior views).

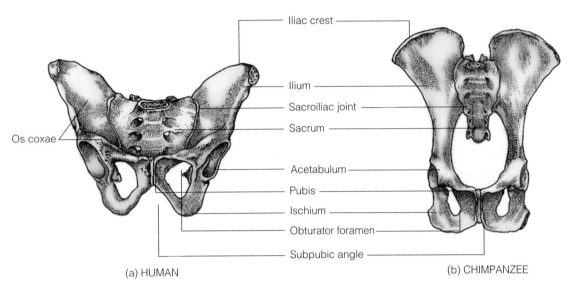

Iliac crest

Ilium

Sacroiliac joint

Sacrum

Os coxae

Acetabulum

Pubis

Ischium

Obturator foramen

Subpubic angle

(a) HUMAN

(b) CHIMPANZEE

FIGURE A–6
Pelvic girdles.

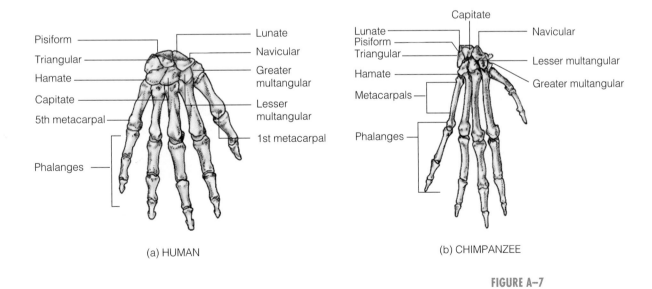

Pisiform

Triangular

Hamate

Capitate

5th metacarpal

Phalanges

Lunate

Navicular

Greater multangular

Lesser multangular

1st metacarpal

(a) HUMAN

Capitate

Lunate

Pisiform

Triangular

Hamate

Metacarpals

Phalanges

Navicular

Lesser multangular

Greater multangular

(b) CHIMPANZEE

FIGURE A–7
Hand anatomy.

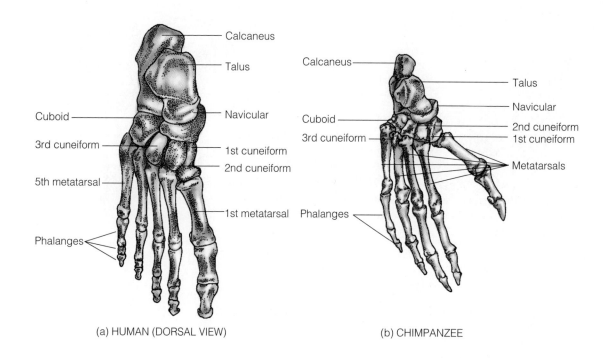

Calcaneus

Talus

Cuboid

Navicular

3rd cuneiform

1st cuneiform

2nd cuneiform

5th metatarsal

1st metatarsal

Phalanges

(a) HUMAN (DORSAL VIEW)

Calcaneus

Talus

Navicular

Cuboid

2nd cuneiform

3rd cuneiform

1st cuneiform

Metatarsals

Phalanges

(b) CHIMPANZEE

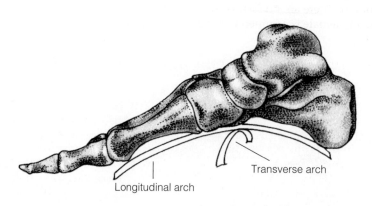

Transverse arch

Longitudinal arch

(c) HUMAN (MEDIAL VIEW)

FIGURE A–8
Foot (pedal) anatomy.

Appendix B
Population Genetics

As noted in Chapter 4, the basic approach in population genetics makes use of a mathematical model called the Hardy-Weinberg equilibrium equation. The Hardy-Weinberg theory of genetic equilibrium postulates a set of conditions in a population where *no* evolution occurs. In other words, none of the forces of evolution are acting, and all genes have an equal chance of recombining in each generation (i.e., there is random mating of individuals). More precisely, the hypothetical conditions that such a population would be *assumed* to meet are as follows:

1. The population is infinitely large. This condition eliminates the possibility of random genetic drift or changes in allele frequencies due to chance.
2. There is no mutation. Thus, no new alleles are being added by molecular changes in gametes.
3. There is no gene flow. There is no exchange of genes with other populations that can alter allele frequencies.
4. Natural selection is not operating. Specific alleles confer no advantage over others that might influence reproductive success.
5. Mating is random. There are no factors that influence who mates with whom. Thus, any female is assumed to have an equal chance of mating with any male.

If all these conditions are satisfied, allele frequencies will not change from one generation to the next (i.e., no evolution will take place), and a permanent equilibrium will be maintained as long as these conditions prevail. An evolutionary "barometer" is thus provided that may be used as a standard against which actual circumstances are compared. Similar to the way a typical barometer is standardized under known temperature and altitude conditions, the Hardy-Weinberg equilibrium is standardized under known evolutionary conditions.

Note that the idealized conditions that define the Hardy-Weinberg equilibrium are just that: an idealized, *hypothetical* state. In the real world, no actual population would fully meet any of these conditions. But do not be confused by this distinction. By explicitly defining the genetic distribution that would be *expected* if *no* evolutionary change were occurring (i.e., in equilibrium), we can compare the *observed* genetic distribution obtained from actual human populations. The evolutionary barometer is thus evaluated through comparison of these observed allele and genotype frequencies with those expected in the predefined equilibrium situation.

If the observed frequencies differ from those of the expected model, then we can say that evolution is taking place at the locus in question. The alternative, of course, is that the observed and expected frequencies do not differ sufficiently to state unambiguously that evolution is occurring at a locus in a population. Indeed, frequently this is the result that is obtained, and in such cases, population geneticists are unable to delineate evolutionary changes at the particular locus under study. Put another way, geneticists are unable to reject what statisticians call the *null hypothesis* (where "null" means nothing, a statistical condition of randomness).

The simplest situation applicable to a microevolutionary study is a genetic trait that follows a simple Mendelian pattern and has only two alleles (*A, a*). As you recall from earlier discussions, there are then only three possible genotypes: *AA, Aa, aa*. Proportions of these genotypes (*AA:Aa:aa*) are a function of the *allele frequencies* themselves (percentage of A and percentage of a). To provide uniformity for all genetic loci, a standard notation is employed to refer to these frequencies:

Frequency of dominant allele $(A) = p$
Frequency of recessive allele $(a) = q$

Since in this case there are only two alleles, their combined total frequency must represent all possibilities. In other words, the sum of their separate frequencies must be 1:

$$p \quad + \quad q = 1 \text{ (100\% of alleles at the locus in question)}$$

(Frequency of A alleles) — Frequency of a alleles)

To ascertain the expected proportions of genotypes, we compute the chances of the alleles combining with each other in all possible combinations. Remember, they all have an equal chance of combining, and no new alleles are being added.

These probabilities are a direct function of the frequency of the two alleles. The chances of all possible combinations occurring randomly can be simply shown as

$$
\begin{array}{r}
p + q \\
\times \quad p + q \\
\hline
pq + q^2 \\
p^2 + pq \\
\hline
p^2 + 2pq + q^2
\end{array}
$$

Mathematically, this is known as a binomial expansion and can also be shown as

$$(p + q)(p + q) = p^2 + 2pq + q^2$$

What we have just calculated is simply:

Allele Combination	Genotype Produced	Expected Proportion in Population
Chances of A combining with A	AA	$p \times p = p^2$
Chances of A combining with a;	Aa	$p \times q$
a combining with A	aA	$p \times q$ $= 2pq$
Chances of a combining with a	aa	$q \times q = q^2$

Thus, p^2 is the frequency of the AA genotype, $2pq$ is the frequency of the Aa genotype, and q^2 is the frequency of the aa genotype, where p is the frequency of the dominant allele and q is the frequency of the recessive allele in a population.

Calculating Allele Frequencies: An Example

How geneticists use the Hardy-Weinberg formula is best demonstrated through an example. Let us assume that a population contains 200 individuals, and we will use the *MN* blood group locus as the gene to be measured. This gene produces a blood group antigen—similar to *ABO*—located on red blood cells. Because the M and N alleles are codominant, we can ascertain everyone's phenotype by taking blood samples and observing reactions with specially prepared antisera. From the phenotypes, we can then directly calculate the *observed* allele frequencies. So let us proceed.

All 200 individuals are tested, and the results are shown in Table B–1. Although the match between observed and expected frequencies is not perfect, it is close enough statistically to satisfy equilibrium conditions. Since our population is not a large one, sampling may easily account for the small observed deviations. Our population is therefore probably in equilibrium (i.e., at this locus, it is not evolving). At the minimum, what we can say scientifically is that we cannot reject the *null hypothesis*.

TABLE B–1 Calculating Allele Frequencies in a Hypothetical Population

Observed Data

Genotype	Number of individuals*	Percent	Number of Alleles M	N		
MM	80	(40%)	160	0		
MN	80	(40%)	80	80		
NN	40	(20%)	0	80		
Totals	200	(100%)	240 +	160	=	400
		Proportion:	.6 +	.4	=	1

*Each individual has two alleles. Thus, a person who is MM contributes two M alleles to the total gene pool. A person who is MN contributes one M and one N. Two hundred individuals, then, have 400 alleles for the MN locus.

Observed Allele Frequencies

$M = .6(p)$
$N = .4(q)$ $\quad$ ($p + q$ should equal 1, and they do)

Expected Frequencies

What are the predicted genotypic proportions if genetic equilibrium (no evolution) applies to our population? We simply apply the Hardy-Weinberg formula: $p^2 + 2pq + q^2$.

$p2$	=	(.6)(.6)	=	.36
$2pq$	=	2(.6)(.4) = 2(.24)	=	.48
q^2	=	(.4)(.4)	=	.16
Total				1.00

There are three possible genotypes (MM, MN, NN), and the total of the relative proportions should equal 1; as you can see, they do.

Comparing Frequencies

How do the expected frequencies compare with the observed frequencies in our population?

	Expected Frequency	Expected Number of Individuals	Observed Frequency	Actual Number of Individuals with Each Genotype
MM	.36	72	.40	80
MN	.48	96	.40	80
NN	.16	32	.20	40

Glossary

Acclimatization Physiological response to changes in the environment that occurs during an individual's lifetime. Such responses may be short-term. The capacity for acclimatization may typify an entire population or species. This capacity is under genetic influence and thus is subject to evolutionary factors such as natural selection.

Acheulian (ash'-oo-lay-en) Pertaining to a stone tool industry of the Lower and Middle Pleistocene characterized by a large proportion of bifacial tools (flaked on both sides). Acheulian tool kits are very common in Africa, southwest Asia, and western Europe, but are nearly absent elsewhere. (Also spelled "Acheulean.")

Adaptation A physiological and/or behavioral adjustment made by organisms in response to environmental circumstances. Adaptations may be short-term or long-term, and strictly defined, they are the results of evolutionary factors, particularly natural selection.

Adaptive niche The entire way of life of an organism: where it lives, what it eats, how it gets food, how it avoids predators, etc.

Adaptive radiation The relatively rapid expansion and diversification of life forms into new ecological niches.

Adolescent growth spurt The period during adolescence in which well-nourished teens typically increase in stature at greater rates than at other points in the life cycle.

Affiliative Pertaining to amicable associations between individuals. Affiliative behaviors, such as grooming, reinforce social bonds and promote group cohesion.

Agriculture Cultural activities associated with planting, herding, and processing domesticated species.

Allele frequency The proportion of one allele to all alleles at a given locus in a population.

Alleles Alternate forms of a gene. Alleles occur at the same locus on paired chromosomes and thus govern the same trait. However, because they are different, their action may result in different expressions of that trait. The term *allele* is often used synonymously with *gene*.

Alluvial Deposited by streams, usually during flood stages.

Altruism Any behavior or act that benefits another individual but poses some potential risk or cost to oneself.

Amber Fossil pine pitch or resin, long valued for jewelry or offerings.

Amino acids Small molecules that are the components of proteins.

Analogies Similarities between organisms based strictly on common function with no assumed common evolutionary descent.

Anasazi (an-ah-saw'-zee) Ancient culture of the southwestern United States, associated with preserved cliff dwellings and masonry pueblo sites.

Anatolia Asia Minor; present-day Turkey.

Anatomically modern *H. sapiens* All modern humans and some fossil forms, perhaps dating as early as 200,000 y.a.; defined by a set of derived characteristics, including cranial architecture and lack of skeletal robusticity; usually classified at the subspecies level as *Homo sapiens sapiens*.

Ancestral (primitive) Referring to characters inherited by a group of organisms from a remote ancestor and thus not diagnostic of groups (lineages) branching subsequent to the time the character first appeared.

Anthropocentric Viewing nonhuman phenomena in terms of human experience and capabilities; emphasizing the importance of humans over everything else.

Anthropoids Members of a suborder of Primates, the *Anthropoidea* (pronounced "ann-throw-poid'-ee-uh"). Traditionally, the suborder includes monkeys, apes, and humans.

Anthropology The field of inquiry that studies human culture and evolutionary aspects of human biology; includes cultural anthropology, archaeology, linguistics, and physical anthropology.

Anthropometry Measurement of human body parts. When osteologists measure skeletal elements, the term *osteometry* is often used.

Anthropomorphic (*anthro*, meaning "man," and *morph*, meaning "shape") Having or being given humanlike characteristics.

Antigens Large molecules found on the surface of cells. Several different loci governing antigens on red and white blood cells are known. (Foreign antigens provoke an immune response in individuals.)

Arboreal Tree-living; adapted to life in the trees.

Arboreal hypothesis The traditional view that primate characteristics can be explained as a consequence of primate diversification into arboreal habitats.

Archaic Cultural stage of hunting and gathering after the end of the Wisconsin ice age in North America; equivalent to the Mesolithic in the Old World.

Archaic *H. sapiens* Earlier forms of *Homo sapiens* (including Neandertals) from the Old World that differ from *H. erectus* but lack the full set of characteristics diagnostic of modern *H. sapiens*.

Artifacts Objects or materials made or modified for use by hominids. The earliest artifacts are usually made of stone or, occasionally, bone.

Association What an archaeological trace is found with.

Atahuallpa (at-a-wall'-pah) Inka leader defeated by Pizarro.

Aurignacian Pertaining to an Upper Paleolithic stone tool industry in Europe beginning at about 40,000 y.a.

Aurochs   European wild oxen, ancestral to domesticated cattle.

Australopithecine   (os-tra-loh-pith´-e-seen) The colloquial name for members of the genus *Australopithecus*. The term was first used as a subfamily designation, but it is now most commonly used informally.

Australopithecus   An early hominid genus, known from the Plio-Pleistocene of Africa, characterized by bipedal locomotion, a relatively small brain, and large back teeth.

Autonomic   Pertaining to physiological responses not under voluntary control. An example in chimpanzees would be the erection of body hair during excitement. An example in humans is blushing. Both convey information regarding emotional states, but neither is a deliberate behavior, and communication is not intended.

Autosomes   All chromosomes except the sex chromosomes.

Aztecs   Militaristic people who dominated the Valley of Mexico and surrounding area at the time of European conquest.

Balanced polymorphism   The maintenance of two or more alleles in a population due to the selective advantage of the heterozygote.

Bandkeramic   Literally, "lined pottery," referring to a Neolithic ceramic ware widely encountered in Central Europe and to the culture that produced it.

Behavioral ecology   The study of the evolution of behavior, emphasizing the role of ecological factors as agents of natural selection. Behaviors and behavioral patterns have been selected for because they increase reproductive fitness in individuals (i.e., they are adaptive) in specific ecological contexts.

Beringia   (bare-in´-jya) The dry land connection between Asia and America that existed periodically during the Ice Age.

Binocular vision   Vision characterized by overlapping visual fields provided by forward-facing eyes; essential to depth perception.

Binomial nomenclature   (*Binomial* means "two names.") In taxonomy, the convention established by Carolus Linnaeus whereby genus and species names are used to refer to species. For example, *Homo sapiens* refers to human beings.

Biocultural evolution   The mutual, interactive evolution of human biology and culture; the concept that biology makes culture possible and that culture further influences the direction of biological evolution; a basic concept in understanding the unique components of human evolution.

Biological continuum   The fact that organisms are related through common ancestry and that behaviors and traits seen in one species are also seen in others to varying degrees. (When expressions of a phenomenon continuously grade into one another so that there are no discrete categories, they are said to exist on a continuum. For example, color is such a phenomenon.)

Biological determinism   The concept that various attributes and behaviors (e.g., intelligence, values, morals) are governed by biological (genetic) factors; the inaccurate association of various behavioral attributes with certain biological traits, such as skin color.

Brachiation   A form of locomotion in which the body is suspended beneath the hands and support is alternated from one forelimb to the other; arm swinging.

Brachycephalic   Having a broad head in which the width measures more than 80 percent of the length.

Breeding isolates   Populations that are clearly isolated geographically and/or socially from other breeding groups.

Bronze Age   Period of early Old World civilizations associated with the widespread use of metal tools after 5,500 y.a.

Burins   Small, chisel-like tools (with a pointed end) thought to have been used to engrave bone, antler, ivory, or wood.

Carrying capacity   The population that the environment can sustain.

Çatalhöyük   (sha-tahl-hoo´-yook) Early Neolithic community in southern Anatolia, or Turkey.

Catastrophism   The view that the earth's geological landscape is the result of violent cataclysmic events. This view was promoted by Cuvier, especially in opposition to Lamarck.

Cenote   (sen-o´-tay) Sinkhole, or collapsed cavern filled with water.

Central-based wandering   A strategy of some food collectors, who work out of a long-term base camp.

Centromere   The constricted portion of a chromosome. After replication, the two strands of a double-stranded chromosome are joined at the centromere.

Cercopithecines   (serk-oh-pith´-eh-seens) The subfamily of Old World monkeys that includes baboons, macaques, and guenons.

Ceremonial centers   Public spaces reserved for ritual activities, often dominated by special architecture and artwork.

Chatelperronian   Pertaining to an Upper Paleolithic tool industry found in France and Spain, containing blade tools and associated with Neandertals.

Chavín de Huantar   (cha-veen´ day wahn´-tar) Prominent highland site associated with early ceremonial activities in Peru.

Chichén Itzá   (chee-chen´ eet-zah´) Postclassic Maya site in Yucatán, strongly linked with the Toltecs of Mexico.

Chimor   A powerful culture that dominated the northern Peruvian coast between about 1,000 and 500 y.a.

Chinampas   (chee-nahm´-pahs) Productive fields created in wet environments by dredging lake bottom muck to form raised ridges or platforms.

Chordata   The phylum of the animal kingdom that includes vertebrates.

Chromosomes   Discrete structures composed of DNA and protein found only in the nuclei of cells. Chromosomes are visible only under magnification during certain stages of cell division.

City-states   Autonomous sociopolitical units comprising an urban center and supporting territory.

Civilizations   Large-scale, complexly organized societies; associated with urbanism and sociopolitical territories known as states.

Cladistics   An approach to classification that seeks to make rigorous evolutionary interpretations based solely on analysis of certain types of homologous (i.e., derived) characters.

Cladogram   A chart showing evolutionary relationships as determined by cladistic analysis. It is based solely on interpretation of shared derived characters. No time component is indicated, and ancestor-descendant relationships are *not* inferred.

Classification   In biology, the ordering of organisms into categories, such as phyla, orders, and families, to show evolutionary relationships.

Climatic maximum Episode of higher average annual temperatures that affected much of the globe for several millennia after the final Wisconsin/Würm glaciation; also known as the *altithermal* in the western United States or *hypsithermal* in the East.

Cline A gradient of genotypes (usually measured as allele frequencies) over geographical space; more exactly, the depiction of allele distribution produced by connecting points of equal frequency (as on a temperature map).

Clone An organism that is genetically identical to another organism. The term may also be used to refer to genetically identical DNA segments and molecules.

Clovis Phase of North American prehistory, 13,500-13,000 y.a. in the West, during which short-fluted projectile points were used in hunting mammoths.

Codices (*sing.*, codex) Illustrated books.

Codominance The expression of two alleles in heterozygotes. In this situation, neither is dominant or recessive, so that both influence the phenotype.

Colobines (kole´-uh-beans) The subfamily of Old World monkeys that includes the African colobus monkeys and Asian langurs.

Communication Any act that conveys information, in the form of a message, to another individual. Frequently, the result of communication is a change in the behavior of the recipient. Communication may not be deliberate but may be the result of involuntary processes or a secondary consequence of an intentional action.

Complementary Referring to the fact that DNA bases form base pairs in a precise manner. For example, adenine can bond only to thymine. These two bases are said to be *complementary* because one requires the other to form a complete DNA base pair.

Composite Made of several parts.

Context The environmental setting where an archaeological trace is found. *Primary* context is the setting in which the archaeological trace was originally deposited. A *secondary* context is one to which it has been moved (e.g., by the action of a stream).

Continental drift The movement of continents on sliding plates of the earth's surface. As a result, the positions of large landmasses have shifted dramatically during earth's history.

Continuum A set of relationships in which all components fall along a single integrated spectrum. All life reflects a single *biological* continuum.

Contract archaeologists Researchers who are employed to carry out CRM projects.

Coprolites Preserved fecal material, which can be studied for what the contents reveal about diet and health.

Cordilleran (cor-dee-yair´-an) Pleistocene ice sheet originating in mountains of western North America.

Core Stone reduced by flake removal, and not necessarily a "tool" itself.

Core area The portion of a home range containing the highest concentration of resources.

Crepuscular Active during the evening or dawn.

Cultigen A plant that is wholly dependent on humans; a domesticate.

Cultivars Wild plants fostered by human efforts to make them more productive.

Cultural Resource Management (CRM) Field of archaeological effort applied to the protection and salvage of archaeological sites from development and other forms of destruction.

Culture All aspects of human adaptation, including technology, traditions, language, and social roles. Culture is learned and transmitted from one generation to the next by nonbiological (i.e., not genetic) means.

Cuneiform (*cuneus*, meaning "wedge") Wedge-shaped writing of ancient Mesopotamia.

Cusps The elevated portions (bumps) on the chewing surfaces of premolar and molar teeth.

Cuzco (coos´-co) Inka capital in the southern Peruvian highlands.

Cytoplasm The portion of the cell contained within the cell membrane, excluding the nucleus. The cytoplasm consists of a semifluid material and contains numerous structures involved with cell function.

Data (*sing.*, datum) Facts from which conclusions can be drawn; scientific information.

Demographic Pertaining to the size or rate of increase of human populations.

Dendrochronology Archaeological dating technique based on study of yearly growth rings in ancient wood.

Dental caries Tooth decay; cavities.

Deoxyribonucleic acid (DNA) The double-stranded molecule that contains the genetic code. DNA is a main component of chromosomes.

Derived (modified) Referring to characters that are modified from the ancestral condition and thus *are* diagnostic of particular evolutionary lineages.

Desertification Any process resulting in the formation or growth of deserts.

Development Differentiation of cells into different types of tissues and their maturation.

Diffusion The idea that widely distributed cultural traits originated in a single center and were spread from one group to another through contact or exchange.

Direct percussion Striking a core or flake with a hammerstone.

Displays Sequences of repetitious behaviors that serve to communicate emotional states. Nonhuman primate displays are most frequently associated with reproductive or agonistic behavior.

Diurnal Active during the day.

Divination Foretelling the future.

Dolichocephalic Having a long, narrow head in which the width measures less than 75 percent of the length.

Domestication A state of interdependence between humans and selected plant or animal species. Intense selection activity induces permanent genetic change, enhancing species' value to humans.

Dominance hierarchies Systems of social organization wherein individuals within a group are ranked relative to one another. Higher-ranking individuals have greater access to preferred food items and mating partners than lower-ranking individuals. Dominance hierarchies have sometimes been referred to as "pecking orders."

Dominant Describing a trait governed by an allele that can be expressed in the presence of another, different allele (i.e., in heterozygotes). Dominant alleles prevent the expression of recessive alleles in heterozygotes. (This is the definition of *complete* dominance.)

Ecofacts   Natural objects or materials found in cultural contexts, such as seeds or animal bones, that may indicate ancient diet or ecological relationships.

Ecological   Pertaining to the relationship between organisms and all aspects of their environment (temperature, predators, other animals, vegetation, availability of food and water, types of food, and so on.)

Ecological niches   The positions of species within their physical and biological environments, together making up the *ecosystem*. A species' ecological niche is defined by such components as diet, terrain, vegetation, type of predators, relationships with other species, and activity patterns, and each niche is unique to a given species.

Ecology   Study of organisms in their habitats, including their relations with other species and their surroundings.

El Niño   Periodic climatic instability, related to temporary warming of Pacific Ocean waters, which may influence storm patterns and precipitation for several years.

Empirical   Relying on experiment or observation; from the Latin *empiricus*, meaning "experienced."

Endemically (endemic)   Continuously present in a population. With regard to disease, refers to populations in which there will always be some infected individuals.

Endocast   A solid impression of the inside of the skull, often preserving details relating to the size and surface features of the brain.

Endogamy   Mating with others from the same group.

Endothermic   (*endo*, meaning "within" or "internal") Able to maintain internal body temperature through the production of energy by means of metabolic processes within cells; characteristic feature of mammals, birds, and perhaps some dinosaurs.

Environmental determinism   An interpretation that links simple environmental changes directly to a major evolutionary shift in an organism. Such explanations tend to be extreme oversimplifications of the evolutionary process.

Enzymes   Specialized proteins that initiate and direct chemical reactions in the body.

Epipaleolithic   (*epi*, meaning "after") Term used primarily in Near East to designate time of Middle Stone Age foragers and collectors.

Epochs   Categories of the geological time scale; subdivisions of periods. In the Cenozoic, epochs include Paleocene, Eocene, Oligocene, Miocene, Pliocene (from the Tertiary), and the Pleistocene and Holocene (from the Quaternary).

Erlitou   (err'-lee-too) Elaborate site in northern China associated with the earliest phase of civilization.

Essential amino acids   The eight (nine for infants) amino acids that must be ingested by humans for normal growth and body maintenance. These include tryptophan, leucine, lysine, methionine, phenylalanine, isoleucine, valine, and threonine (plus histidine for infants).

Estrus   (ess´-truss) Period of sexual receptivity in female mammals (except humans), correlated with ovulation. When used as an adjective, the word is spelled "estrous."

Ethnoarchaeology   Approach used by archaeologists to gain insights into the past by studying contemporary people.

Ethnocentric   Viewing other cultures from the inherently biased perspective of one's own culture. Ethnocentrism often results in other cultures being seen as inferior to one's own.

Ethnographic analogy   Proposing hypotheses to explain something about the past, based on anthropological observations of living societies.

Ethnographies   Detailed descriptive studies of human societies. In cultural anthropology, *ethnography* is traditionally the study of a non-Western society.

Eugenics   The philosophy of "race improvement" through the forced sterilization of members of some groups and encouraged reproduction among others; an overly simplified, often racist view that is now discredited.

Evolution   A change in the genetic structure of a population. The term is also frequently used to refer to the appearance of a new species.

Evolutionary pulse theory   A view that postulates a correlation of periods of hominid diversification during the Pliocene and early Pleistocene with major shifts in several African mammalian species. These changes in mammalian evolution, in turn, are thought to be related to periodic episodes of aridity.

Evolutionary systematics   A traditional approach to classification (and evolutionary interpretation) in which presumed ancestors and descendants are traced in time by analysis of homologous characters.

Exogamy   Mating with individuals from other groups.

Experimental archaeologists   Researchers who replicate ancient toolmaking techniques and other procedures to test hypotheses about past activities.

Faience   (fay-ahnz') Glassy material, usually of blue-green color, shaped into beads, amulets, and figurines by ancient Egyptians.

Features   Products of human activity that are usually integral to a site and therefore nonportable; examples include fire hearths and foundations.

Fission-track   A dating technique based on the natural radiometric decay (fission) of uranium-238 atoms, which leaves traces in certain geological materials.

Fitness   Pertaining to natural selection, a measure of *relative* reproductive success of individuals. Fitness can be measured by an individual's genetic contribution to the next generation compared to that of others.

Fixity of species   The notion that species, once created, can never change; an idea diametrically opposed to theories of biological evolution.

Flake   Thin-edged fragment removed from a core.

Flexed   The position of the body in a bent orientation, with the arms and legs drawn up to the chest.

Flotation   Technique for separating preserved organic material from other archaeological samples by water immersion.

Fluorine analysis   A relative dating method which measures and compares the amounts of fluorine that bones have absorbed from groundwater during burial.

Fluted point   A biface or projectile point having had long, thin flakes removed from each face in order to prepare the base for hafting, or attachment to a shaft.

Folsom   Phase of southern Great Plains prehistory, around 12,500 y.a., during which long-fluted projectile points were used for bison hunting.

Food collecting   Strategy developed by hunters and gatherers to take advantage of highly seasonal wild resources by storing surpluses for later use.

521

Foraging The process of locating food while moving across the landscape; a standard strategy of some hunters and gatherers.

Foramen magnum The opening at the base of the skull through which the spinal cord passes as it enters the body to descend through the vertebral column. In quadrupeds, it is located more to the rear of the skull, while in bipeds, it is located farther beneath the skull.

Forensic anthropology An applied anthropological approach dealing with legal matters. Forensic anthropologists work with coroners and law enforcement agencies in the recovery, analysis, and identification of human remains.

Founder effect Also called the *Sewall-Wright effect*, a type of genetic drift in which allele frequencies are altered in small populations that are taken from, or are remnants of, larger populations.

Frugivorous (fru-give´-or-us) Having a diet composed primarily of fruit.

Functionalist Referring to explanations that account for a given development as a response to a specific need.

Gametes Reproductive cells (eggs and sperm in animals) developed from precursor cells in ovaries and testes.

Gene A sequence of DNA bases that specifies the order of amino acids in an entire protein or, in some cases, a portion of a protein. A gene may be made up of hundreds or thousands of DNA bases.

Gene flow The exchange of genes between populations; also called migration.

Gene pool The total complement of genes shared by reproductive members of a population.

Genetic drift Evolutionary changes—that is, changes in allele frequencies—produced by random factors. Genetic drift is a result of small population size.

Genetics The study of gene structure and action and of the patterns of inheritance of traits from parent to offspring. Genetic mechanisms are the underlying foundation for evolutionary change.

Genome The entire genetic makeup of an individual or species. In humans, it is estimated that each individual possesses approximately 3 billion DNA nucleotides.

Genotype The genetic makeup of an individual. Genotype can refer to an

organism's entire genetic makeup or to the alleles at a particular locus.

Genus A group of closely related species.

Geological time scale The organization of earth history into eras, periods, and epochs; commonly used by geologists and paleoanthropologists.

Gilgamesh Semi-legendary king and culture hero of early Uruk, reputed to have had many marvelous adventures.

Great Basin Rugged, dry plateau between the mountains of California and Utah, comprising Nevada, western Utah, and southern Oregon and Idaho.

Grooming Picking through fur to remove dirt, parasites, and other materials that may be present. Social grooming is common among primates and reinforces social relationships.

Growth Increase in mass or number of cells.

Hammurabi (ham-oo-rah´-bee) Early Babylonian king, c. 1800–1750 B.C.

Hardy-Weinberg equilibrium The mathematical relationship expressing—under ideal conditions—the predicted distribution of genes in populations; the central theorem of population genetics.

Hemoglobin A protein molecule that occurs in red blood cells and binds to oxygen molecules.

Heterodont Having different kinds of teeth; characteristic of mammals, whose teeth consist of incisors, canines, premolars, and molars.

Heterozygous Having different alleles at the same locus on members of a chromosome pair.

Hierakonpolis (high-rak-kon-po-lis) Important town and pottery production center of Upper Egypt.

Hieroglyphics (*hiero*, meaning "sacred," and *glyphein*, meaning "carving") The picture-writing of ancient Egypt.

Hohokam (ho-ho-kahm´) Prehistoric farming culture of southern Arizona.

Home range The entire area exploited by an animal or group of animals.

Homeostasis A condition of balance or stability within a biological system, maintained by the interaction of physiological mechanisms that compensate for changes (both external and internal).

Hominid Member of the family Hominidae, the classificatory group to which humans belong; also includes other, now extinct, bipedal relatives.

Hominoidea The formal designation for the superfamily of anthropoids that includes apes and humans.

Homo habilis (hab´-ih-liss) A species of early *Homo*, well known from East Africa, but perhaps also found in other regions.

Homologies Similarities between organisms based on descent from a common ancestor.

Homoplasy (*homo*, meaning "same," and *plasy*, meaning "growth") The separate evolutionary development of similar characteristics in different groups of organisms.

Homozygous Having the same allele at the same locus on both members of a chromosome pair.

Hopewell A culture centered in southern Ohio between 2,100 and 1,700 y.a., but influencing a much wider region through trade and the spread of a cult centered on burial ritualism.

Horizontal excavation A strategy for exposing a stratum in order to reveal a large area of a site.

Hormones Substances (usually proteins) that are produced by specialized cells and that travel to other parts of the body, where they influence chemical reactions and regulate various cellular functions.

Horticulture Farming method in which only hand tools are used; typical of most early Neolithic societies.

Huaca del Sol (wah´-ka dell sole) Massive adobe pyramid built at Moche, in northern Peru.

Huayna Capac (why´-na kah´pak) Inka leader whose death precipitated civil war.

Human Genome Project An international effort aimed at sequencing and mapping the entire human genome.

Hybrids Offspring of mixed ancestry; heterozygotes.

Hypothesis (*pl.*, **hypotheses**) A provisional explanation of a phenomenon. Hypotheses require verification.

Hypoxia Lack of oxygen. Hypoxia can refer to reduced amounts of available oxygen in the atmosphere (due to lowered barometric pressure) or to insufficient amounts of oxygen in the body.

Inka People whose sophisticated culture dominated Peru at the time of the European arrival; also, the term for that people's highest ruler. (Sometimes spelled *Inca*.)

Intelligence Mental capacity; ability to learn, reason, or comprehend and interpret information, facts, relationships, meanings, etc.; the capacity to solve problems, whether through the application of previously acquired knowledge or through insight.

Interspecific Between species; refers to variation beyond that seen within the same species to include additional aspects seen between two different species.

Intraspecific Within species; refers to variation seen within the same species.

Ischial callosities Patches of tough, hard skin on the buttocks of Old World monkeys and chimpanzees.

K-selected Pertaining to an adaptive strategy whereby individuals produce relatively few offspring, in whom they invest increased parental care. Although only a few infants are born, chances of survival are increased for each individual because of parental investments in time and energy. Examples of nonprimate K-selected species are birds and canids (e.g., wolves, coyotes, and dogs).

Kaminaljuyú (cam-en-awl-hoo-yoo') Site located at Guatemala City, contemporary with Olmec and also associated with classic Maya.

Kivas Underground chambers or rooms used for gatherings and ceremonies by pueblo dwellers.

Knappers Those who flake stone tools.

Knossos Primary Minoan center, or regional capital; site of a huge temple-palace.

Lactose intolerance The inability to digest fresh milk products; caused by the discontinued production of lactase, the enzyme that breaks down lactose (milk sugar).

Large-bodied hominoids Those hominoids including the great apes (orangutans, chimpanzees, gorillas) and hominids, as well as all ancestral forms back to the time of divergence from small-bodied hominoids (i.e., the gibbon lineage).

Laurentian (lah-ren'-shun) Pleistocene ice sheet centered in the Hudson Bay region and extending across much of eastern Canada and the northern United States.

Locus (*pl.*, **loci**) (lo´-kus, lo-sigh´) The position on a chromosome where a given gene occurs. The term is sometimes used interchangeably with *gene*.

Loess (luss) Fine-grained soil composed of glacially pulverized rock, deposited by the wind.

Macaques (muh-kaks´) Group of Old World monkeys comprising several species, including rhesus monkeys.

Macroevolution Large-scale evolutionary changes (especially speciation) that may require many hundreds of generations and are usually only detectable paleontologically (in the fossil record).

Magdalenian Pertaining to the final phase (stone tool industry) of the Upper Paleolithic in Europe.

Mammalia The technical term for the formal grouping (class) of mammals.

Manioc Cassava, a starchy edible root crop of the tropics.

Material culture The physical manifestations of human activities, such as tools, art, and structures. As the most durable aspects of culture, material remains make up the majority of archaeological evidence of past societies.

Maya Prehistoric Mesoamerican culture consisting of regional kingdoms and known for its art and architectual accomplishments from 1,800 to 1,100 y.a.

Megafauna Literally "large animals," those weighing over 100 pounds (44 kg).

Megaliths (*mega*, meaning "large," and *lith*, meaning "stone") Monumental structures made of very large stones, characteristic of western Europe during the early Neolithic.

Megarons Fortified palaces of Mycenaean kings.

Mehrgarh (may-er-gar') One of the earliest Neolithic settlements of southern Asia.

Meiosis Cell division in specialized cells in ovaries and testes. Meiosis involves two divisions and results in four daughter cells, each containing only half the original number of chromosomes. These cells can develop into gametes.

Mendelian traits Characteristics that are influenced by alleles at only one genetic locus. Examples include many blood types, such as ABO. Many genetic disorders, including sickle-cell anemia and Tay-Sachs disease, are also Mendelian traits.

Mesoamerica (*meso*, meaning "middle") Geographical and cultural region from southern Mexico through Panama; also known as Central America.

Mesolithic (*meso*, meaning "middle," and *lith*, meaning "stone") Middle Stone Age; period of foragers, especially in northwestern Europe.

Mesopotamia (*meso*, meaning "middle," and *potamos*, meaning "river") Land between the Tigris and Euphrates Rivers, mostly included in modern-day Iraq.

Metazoa Multicellular animals; a major division of the animal kingdom.

Mexica (meh-shee'-ka) Original name by which the Aztecs were known before their rise to power.

Microblades Tiny, parallel-sided flakes struck from a special core and mounted into tools as cutting edges; a type of microlith made by East Asians and some early American cultures.

Microevolution Small-scale evolutionary changes that occur over the span of a few generations and can therefore be detected in living populations.

Microliths (*micro*, meaning "small," and *lith*, meaning "stone") Small flakes or bladelets, punched from a core and used as cutting edges in tools and weapons; common Upper Paleolithic tool category.

Microwear Polishes, striations, and other diagnostic microscopic changes on the edges of stone tools.

Middens Refuse disposal areas marking hunter-gatherer campsites.

Midline An anatomical term referring to a hypothetical line that divides the body into right and left halves.

Millet Small-grained cereal grass native to Asia and Africa.

Mississippian A southeastern United States mound building culture that flourished from 1,100 to 500 y.a.

Mitochondria (sing., mitochondrion) (my´-tow-kond´-dree-uh) Structures contained within the cytoplasm of eukaryotic cells that convert energy, derived from nutrients, into a form that is used by the cell.

Mitochondrial DNA (mtDNA) DNA found in the mitochondria that is inherited through the maternal line.

Mitosis   Simple cell division; the process by which somatic cells divide to produce two identical daughter cells.

Mogollon   (mo-go-yohn') Prehistoric village culture of northern Mexico and southern Arizona/New Mexico.

Molecules   Structures made up of two or more atoms. Molecules can combine with other molecules to form more complex structures.

Monogenism   The theory that all human races are descended from one pair (Adam and Eve), but they differ from one another because they have occupied different habitats. This concept was an attempt to explain phenotypic variation between populations, but did not imply evolutionary change.

Morphological   Pertaining to the form and structure of organisms.

Morphology   The form (shape, size) of anatomical structures; can also refer to the entire organism.

Mosaic evolution   A pattern of evolution in which the rates of evolution in one functional system vary from those in other systems. For example, in hominid evolution, the dental system, locomotor system, and neurological system (especially the brain) all evolved at markedly different rates.

Motecuhzoma Xocoyotzin   (mo-teh-ca-zooma' shoh-coh-yoh'-seen) Last Aztec ruler, also known as Moctezuma II, whose death at the hands of the Spanish precipitated the destruction of the Aztec empire.

Mousterian   Pertaining to the stone tool industry associated with Neandertals and some modern *H. sapiens* groups; also called Middle Paleolithic. This industry is characterized by a larger proportion of flake tools than is found in Acheulian tool kits.

Multicomponent sites   Archaeological sites that were periodically reused or occupied by successive cultures, often exhibiting a series of superimposed strata.

Multivariate   Involving more than one factor or variable.

Mutation   A change in DNA. Technically, mutation refers to changes in DNA bases as well as changes in chromosome number and/or structure.

Naj Tunich   (nah toon'-eesh) Maya sacred cave, in Guatemala.

Natufian   A food-collecting culture that established sedentary settlements in parts of the Near East after 12,000 y.a.

Natural selection   The mechanism of evolutionary change first articulated by Charles Darwin; refers to genetic change, or to changes in the frequencies of certain traits in populations due to differential reproductive success between individuals.

Nebuchadnezzar   (neh-boo-kud-neh'-zer) Late Babylonian king, c. 605–562 B.C.

Neolithic   (*neo*, meaning "new," and *lith*, meaning "stone") New Stone Age; period of farmers.

Neolithic Revolution   Childe's term for the far-reaching consequences associated with food production.

Neutron activation analysis   A technique for determining the chemical composition of a material by irradiating it to identify its component elements.

Nocturnal   Active during the night.

Nomadism   Free-wandering lifeway, most often practiced by herders, who follow their animals.

Nuchal torus   (nuke´-ul, pertaining to the neck) A projection of bone in the back of the cranium where neck muscles attach, used to hold up the head. The nuchal torus is a distinctive feature of *H. erectus*.

Nucleotides   Basic units of the DNA molecule, composed of a sugar, a phosphate, and one of four DNA bases.

Nucleus   A structure (organelle) found in all eukaryotic cells. The nucleus contains chromosomes (nuclear DNA).

Oases (*sing.*, oasis)   Permanent springs or water holes in an arid region.

Oaxaca   (wah-ha'-kah) A southern Mexican state bordering the Pacific Ocean.

Olmec   Culture in the Gulf Coast lowlands of Veracruz and Tabasco, Mexico, with a highly developed art style and social complexity; flourished from 3,200 to 2,400 y.a.

Omnivorous   Having a diet consisting of many food types (i.e., plant materials, meat, and insects).

Osteodontokeratic   (*osteo*, meaning "bone," *donto*, meaning "tooth," and *keratic*, meaning "horn")

Osteology   The study of all aspects of the skeleton, including bone composition, growth, and response to disease and trauma. Human osteology focuses on the interpretation of the skeletal remains of past groups. The same techniques are used in paleoanthropology to study early hominids.

Paleoanthropology   The interdisciplinary approach to the study of earlier hominids—their chronology, physical structure, archaeological remains, habitats, etc.

Paleoecologists   (*paleo*, meaning "old," and *ecology*, meaning "environmental setting") Scientists who study ancient environments.

Paleo-Indians   (*paleo*, meaning "ancient") In the Americas, early big game hunting cultures, from about 14,000 y.a. to 8,000 y.a.

Paleomagnetism   Dating method based on the earth's shifting magnetic pole.

Paleontologists   Scientists whose study of ancient life forms is based on fossilized remains of extinct animals and plants.

Paleopathology   The branch of osteology that studies the traces of disease and injury in human skeletal (or, occasionally, mummified) remains.

Paleospecies   Species defined from fossil evidence, often covering a long time span.

Palynologists   Scientists who identify ancient plants from pollen samples unearthed at archaeological sites.

Pathogens   Substances or microorganisms, such as bacteria, fungi, or viruses, that cause disease.

Pellagra   Disease resulting from a dietary deficiency of niacin (vitamin B_3). Symptoms include dermatitis, diarrhea, dementia, and death (the "four Ds").

Pharaoh   Title of the king or ruler of ancient Egypt.

Phenotypes   The observable or detectable physical characteristics of an organism; the detectable expressions of genotypes.

Phenotypic ratio   The proportion of one phenotype to other phenotypes in a group of organisms. For example, Mendel observed that there were approximately three tall plants for every short plant in the F_2 generation. This is expressed as a phenotypic ratio of 3:1.

Phylogeny   A schematic representation showing ancestor-descendant relationships, usually in a chronological framework.

Phytoliths   (*phyto*, meaning "hidden," and *lith*, meaning "stone") Microscopic silica structures formed in the cells of many plants, particularly grasses.

Plano   Great Plains bison-hunting culture of 11,000-9,000 y.a., which employed narrow, unfluted points.

Plasticity The capacity to change; in a physiological context, the ability of systems or organisms to make alterations in order to respond to differing conditions.

Pleistocene The epoch of the Cenozoic from 1.8 m.y.a. until 10,000 y.a. Frequently referred to as the Ice Age, this epoch is associated with continental glaciations in northern latitudes.

Plio-Pleistocene Pertaining to the Pliocene and first half of the Pleistocene, a time range of 5–1 m.y.a. During this time period, the earliest fossil hominids have been found in Africa.

Pollen Microscopic male gametes produced by flowering plants.

Polyandry A mating system wherein a female continuously associates with more than one male (usually two or three) with whom she mates. Among nonhuman primates, this pattern is seen only in marmosets and tamarins.

Polychrome Many-colored.

Polygenic Referring to traits that are influenced by genes at two or more loci. Examples of such traits are stature, skin color, and eye color. Many polygenic traits are also influenced by environmental factors.

Polygenism A theory, opposed to monogenism, that states that human races are not all descended from Adam and Eve. Instead, there had been several original human pairs, each giving rise to a different group. Thus, human races were considered separate species.

Polymerase chain reaction (PCR) A method of producing copies of a DNA segment using the enzyme DNA polymerase.

Polymorphism A genetic trait (the locus governing the trait) with more than one allele in appreciable frequency (i.e., greater than 1 percent).

Polytypic Referring to species composed of populations that differ with regard to the expression of one or more traits.

Pongids Members of the family *Pongidae*, including orangutans, gorillas, chimpanzees, and bonobos.

Population Within a species, the community of individuals where mates are usually found.

Potassium-argon (K/Ar) method A dating technique based on accumulation of argon-40 gas as a by-product of the radiometric decay of potassium-40 in volcanic materials; used especially for dating early hominid sites in East Africa.

Potlatch Ceremonial feasting and gift-giving event among Northwest Coast Indians.

Prehensility Grasping, as by the hands and feet of primates.

Prehistory The several million years between the emergence of bipedal hominids and the availability of written records.

Pressure flaking A method of removing flakes from a core by pressing a pointed implement (e.g., bone or antler) against the stone.

Primate A member of the order of mammals Primates (pronounced "pry-may-tees"), which includes prosimians, monkeys, apes, and humans.

Primatologists Scientists who study the evolution, anatomy, and behavior of nonhuman primates. Those who study behavior in noncaptive animals are usually trained as physical anthropologists.

Primitive Referring to a trait or combination of traits present in an ancestral form.

Principle of independent assortment The distribution of one pair of alleles into gametes does not influence the distribution of another pair. The genes controlling different traits are inherited independently of one another.

Principle of segregation Genes (alleles) occur in pairs (because chromosomes occur in pairs). During gamete production, the members of each gene pair separate, so that each gamete contains one member of each pair. During fertilization, the full number of chromosomes is restored, and members of gene or allele pairs are reunited.

Probability The mathematical likelihood that a sampled data set is representative of the whole.

Prosimians Members of a suborder of Primates, the *Prosimii* (pronounced "pro-sim´-ee-eye"). Traditionally, the suborder includes lemurs, lorises, and tarsiers.

Protein synthesis The assembly of chains of amino acids into functional protein molecules. The process is directed by DNA.

Proteins Three-dimensional molecules that serve a wide variety of functions through their ability to bind to other molecules.

Provenience The specific site location from which an artifact is recovered; may also refer to an artifact's cultural affiliation. *Provenance* is an alternate spelling.

Pueblos Spanish term for "town," referring to multiroom residence structures built by village farmers in the American Southwest; also refers collectively to the several cultures that built and lived in such villages.

Punctuated equilibrium The concept that evolutionary change proceeds through long periods of stasis punctuated by rapid periods of change.

Quadrupedal Using all four limbs to support the body during locomotion; the basic mammalian (and primate) form of locomotion.

Quantitatively (quantitative) Pertaining to measurements of quantity and including such properties as size, number, and capacity. When data are quantified, they are expressed numerically and are capable of being tested statistically.

Quetzalcoatl (ket-sal´-kwat-el) Also known as the Feathered Serpent; a deity representing good, worshiped by Aztecs and possibly earlier at Teotihuacán.

Quinoa (keen-wah´) Seed-bearing member of the genus *Chenopodium*, cultivated by early Peruvians.

r-selected Pertaining to an adaptive strategy that emphasizes relatively large numbers of offspring and reduced parental care (compared to K-selected species). (*K-selection* and *r-selection* are relative terms; e.g., mice are r-selected compared to primates but K-selected compared to many fish species.)

Rachis The short stem by which an individual seed attaches to the main stalk of a plant as it develops.

Radiocarbon dating Method for determining the age of organic archaeological materials using the steady rate of isotope decay as a measure; also known as ^{14}C dating.

Radiometric decay A measure of the rate at which certain radioactive isotopes disintegrate.

Recessive Describing a trait that is not expressed in heterozygotes; also refers to the allele that governs the trait. For a recessive allele to be expressed, there must be two copies of the allele (i.e., the individual must be homozygous).

Recombination The exchange of DNA between paired chromosomes during meiosis; also called "crossing over."

Replicate   To duplicate. The DNA molecule is able to make copies of itself.

Reproductive strategies   The complex of behavioral patterns that contributes to individual reproductive success. The behaviors need not be deliberate, and they often vary considerably between males and females.

Reproductive success   The number of offspring an individual produces and rears to reproductive age; an individual's genetic contribution to the next generation as compared to the contributions of other individuals.

Research design   A plan of action for collecting and analyzing the data with which to test hypotheses.

Rhinarium   (rine-air´-ee-um) The moist, hairless pad at the end of the nose seen in most mammalian species. The rhinarium enhances an animal's ability to smell.

Ribonucleic acid (RNA)   A single-stranded molecule, similar in structure to DNA. The three forms of RNA are essential to protein synthesis.

Sacsahuaman   (sak-sa-wah-mahn´) Stone fortress and shrine overlooking Cuzco.

Sagittal crest   Raised ridge along the midline of the cranium where the temporal muscle (which closes the jaw) is attached.

Science   A body of knowledge gained through observation and experimentation; from the Latin *scientia*, meaning "knowledge."

Scientific method   A research method whereby a problem is identified, a hypothesis (or hypothetical explanation) is stated, and that hypothesis is tested through the collection and analysis of data. If the hypothesis is verified, it becomes a theory.

Scientific testing   The precise repetition of an experiment or expansion of observed data to provide verification; the procedure by which hypotheses and theories are verified, modified, or discarded.

Scurvy   A disease resulting from a dietary deficiency of vitamin C. It may result in anemia, poor bone growth, abnormal bleeding and bruising, and muscle pain.

Seasonality and scheduling   Technique of hunters and gatherers to maximize subsistence by relocating in accord with the availability of key resources at specific times and places throughout the year.

Sectorial   Adapted for cutting or shearing; among primates, refers to the compressed (side-to-side) first lower premolar, which functions as a shearing surface with the upper canine.

Selective pressures   Forces in the environment that influence reproductive success in individuals. In the example of the peppered moth, birds applied the selective pressure.

Seriation   Based on typological dating, a technique for putting groups of artifacts, or even sites containing such artifacts, into relative chronological order.

Sex chromosomes   The X and Y chromosomes.

Sexual dimorphism   Differences in physical characteristics between males and females of the same species. For example, humans are slightly sexually dimorphic for body size, with males being taller, on average, than females of the same population.

Sexual selection   A type of natural selection that operates on only one sex within a species. It is the result of competition for mates, and it can lead to sexual dimorphism with regard to one or more traits.

Single-component site   An archaeological site occupied by just one culture, usually for a relatively short period.

Site   A location of past human activity, often associated with artifacts and structures; also, a location of modern archaeological research.

Slash-and-burn agriculture   A traditional land-clearing practice whereby trees and vegetation are cut and burned. In many areas, fields were abandoned after a few years and clearing occurred elsewhere.

Social stratification   Class structure or hierarchy, usually based on political, economic, or social standing.

Social structure   The composition, size, and sex ratio of a group of animals. Social structures, in part, are the result of natural selection in specific habitats, and they function to guide individual interactions and social relationships.

Sociobiological   Pertaining to *sociobiology*, the study of the relationship between natural selection and behavior. Unlike the approach of behavioral ecology, sociobiological theory does not strongly emphasize ecological factors.

Somatic cells   Basically, all the cells in the body except those involved with reproduction.

Sorghum   Cereal grass with a sweet juicy stalk.

Specialization   Economic system that allows individuals to devote full time to certain occupations.

Specialized   Evolved for a particular function; usually refers to a specific trait (e.g., incisor teeth), but may also refer to the entire way of life of an organism.

Speciation   The process by which new species are produced from earlier ones; the most important mechanism of macroevolutionary change.

Species   A group of organisms that can interbreed to produce fertile offspring. Members of one species are reproductively isolated from all other species.

Stable carbon isotopes   Isotopes of carbon that are produced in plants in differing proportions, depending on environmental conditions. Through analyzing the proportions of the isotopes contained in fossil remains of animals (who ate the plants), it is possible to reconstruct aspects of ancient environments (particularly temperature and aridity).

State-level societies   Civilizations; sociopolitical entities that control defined territories.

Stelae (*sing.*, stela)   (stee´-lee) Upright posts or stones, often bearing inscriptions.

Stereoscopic vision   The condition whereby visual images are, to varying degrees, superimposed on one another. This provides for depth perception, or the perception of the external environment in three dimensions. Stereoscopic vision is partly a function of structures in the brain.

Stratigraphy   Study of the sequential layering of deposits.

Stratum (*pl.*, strata)   A single layer of soil or rock; sometimes called a "level."

Stress   In a physiological context, any factor that acts to disrupt homeostasis; more precisely, the body's response to any factor that threatens its ability to maintain homeostasis.

Symbiosis   (*syn*, meaning "together," and *bios*, meaning "life") Mutually advantageous association of two different organisms; also known as *mutualism*.

Tamaulipas   (tah-mah-leep´-ahs) A Mexican state located on the Gulf coast south of Texas.

Taphonomy   (*taphos*, meaning "dead") The study of how bones and other materials came to be buried in the earth and preserved as fossils. A taphonomist studies the processes of sedimentation, the action of streams, preservation properties of bone, and carnivore disturbance factors.

Taro   Species of tropical plant with an edible starchy root.

Taxonomy   The branch of science concerned with the rules of classifying organisms on the basis of evolutionary relationships.

Tehuacán Valley   (tay-wah-kahn') A dry highland region on the boundary of the states of Puebla and Oaxaca in southern Mexico.

Tells   Mounds of accumulated rubble representing the site of an ancient city. A tell differs in both scale and content from a *midden*.

Tenochtitlán   (tay-nosh-teet-lahn') Aztec capital, built on the future site of Mexico City.

Teosinte   A native grass of southern Mexico, believed to be ancestral to maize.

Teotihuacán   (tay-oh-tee-wah-cahn') The first city in the Western Hemisphere, located in central Mexico from 2,200–1,350 y.a.

Territories   Areas that will be aggressively protected against intrusion, particularly by other members of the same species.

Theory   A broad statement of scientific relationships or underlying principles that has been at least partially verified.

Thermoluminiscence   (ther-mo-loo-min-ess'-ence) Technique for dating certain archaeological materials, such as ceramics, which release stored energy of radioactive decay as light upon heating.

Theropods   Small- to medium-sized ground-living dinosaurs, dated to approximately 150 million years ago and thought to be related to birds.

Tikal   (tee-kal') Principal Maya city and ceremonial center, in Guatemala.

Till   Glacial waste, consisting of mixed rock particles that range in size from clay, silt, and sand, to boulders, strewn across landscapes once covered by ice sheets.

Tiwanaku   (tee-wahn-ah'-koo) Capital of a regional kingdom near Lake Titicaca, in Bolivia.

Toltecs   Central Mexican highlands people who created a pre-Aztec empire with its capital at Tula in the Valley of Mexico.

Totem   An animal or being associated with a kin-group and used for social identification; also, a carved pole representing these beings.

Transhumance   Seasonal migration from one resource zone to another, especially between highlands and lowlands.

Transmutation   The change of one species to another. The term *evolution* did not assume its current meaning until the late nineteenth century.

Tula   (too'-la) Toltec capital in the Valley of Mexico; sometimes known as Tollan.

Tundra   Treeless plains characterized by permafrost conditions that support the growth of shallow-rooted vegetation such as grasses and mosses.

Tutankhamen   (toot-en-cahm'-en) Egyptian pharaoh of the New Kingdom period, who died at age 19 in 1323 B.C.; informally known today as King Tut.

Types   In archaeology, categories of objects that share significant characteristics.

Typological dating   Method of dating objects of unknown age by comparing their stylistic features to determine which object is older or newer.

Uaxactún   (wash-akh-toon') Maya ceremonial center, in Guatemala.

Ubaid   (oo-bide') Early formative culture of Mesopotamia, 7,500–6,200 y.a.; predecessor to Sumerian civilization.

Uniformitarianism   The theory that the earth's features are the result of long-term processes that continue to operate in the present as they did in the past. Elaborated on by Lyell, this theory opposed catastrophism and provided for immense geological time.

Upper Paleolithic   A cultural period usually associated with early modern humans (but also found with Neandertals) and distinguished by technological innovation in various stone tool industries. Best known from western Europe, similar industries are also known from central and eastern Europe and Africa.

Variation   Inherited (i.e., genetically influenced) differences between individuals.

Varve   Layer of silt deposited annually by a melting glacier; used as basis for archaeological dating in Europe.

Vasoconstriction   Narrowing of blood vessels to reduce blood flow to the skin. Vasoconstriction is an involuntary response to cold and reduces heat loss at the skin's surface.

Vasodilation   Expansion of blood vessels, permitting increased blood flow to the skin. Vasodilation permits warming of the skin and also facilitates radiation of warmth as a means of cooling. Vasodilation is an involuntary response to warm temperatures, various drugs, and even emotional states (blushing).

Vectors   Agents that serve to transmit disease from one carrier to another. Mosquitoes are vectors for malaria, just as fleas are vectors for bubonic plague.

Vertebrates   Animals with bony backbones; includes fishes, amphibians, reptiles, birds, and mammals.

Vertical excavation   A strategy for digging multicomponent sites by opening pits or trenches that penetrate successive strata or levels.

Viviparous   Giving birth to live young.

Wari   (wah'-ree) Capital of a regional kingdom in southern Peru.

Wisconsin   Time of the last major glacial advance in North America; analogous to late Würm or Weichsel in the Old World.

Worldview   General cultural orientation or perspective shared by members of a society.

Xia   (shah) Semi-legendary kingdom or dynasty of early China.

X-ray fluorescence spectrometry   A technique for analyzing the chemical composition of a material by bombarding it with X-rays and then identifying individual elements by their distinctive afterglow.

Zhengzhou   (cheng-chew) Modern city of China, associated with the site of the earliest Shang center.

Zhou   (chew) Chinese dynasty that followed Shang and ruled between 1122 B.C. and 221 B.C.

Ziggurat   Late Sumerian mud-brick temple-pyramid.

Zoonoses (*sing.*, **zoonosis**)   Diseases transmissible to humans from other vertebrates.

Zygote   A cell formed by the union of an egg and a sperm cell. It contains the full complement of chromosomes (in humans, 46) and has the potential of developing into an entire organism.

Bibliography

Adams, Richard E. W.
   1977   *Prehistoric Mesoamerica*. Boston: Little, Brown.
Adams, Robert McC.
   1981   *Heartland of Cities*. Chicago: University of Chicago Press.
Adovasio, James M.
   1993   "The Ones That Will Not Go Away: A Biased View of
          Pre-Clovis Populations in the New World." *In:* Soffer
          and Praslov (eds.), q.v., pp. 199–218.
Adovasio, James M., J. Donahue, and Robert Stuckenrath
   1990   "The Meadowcroft Rockshelter Radiocarbon Chronology
          1975–1990." *American Antiquity*, **55**(2):348–354.
Aiello, L. C. and B. A. Wood
   1994   "Cranial Variables as Predictors of Hominine Body
          Mass." *American Journal of Physical Anthropology*,
          95:409–426.
Aitken, M. J., C. B. Stringer, and P. A. Mellars (eds.)
   1993   *The Origin of Modern Humans and the Impact of
          Chronometric Dating*. Princeton: NJ: Princeton
          University Press.
Aldred, Cyril
   1998   *The Egyptians*. (Rev. Ed.) New York: Thames & Hudson.
Allchin, Briget and Raymond Allchin
   1982   *The Rise of Civilization in India and Pakistan*. Cambridge:
          Cambridge University Press.
Altmann, S. A. and J. Altmann
   1970   *Baboon Ecology*. Chicago: University of Chicago Press.
Alva, Walter and Christopher Donnan
   1993   *Royal Tombs of Sipan*. Los Angeles: Fowler Museum
          of Cultural History, University of California, Los Angeles.
Ames, K. M. and Herbert D. Maschner
   1999   *Peoples of the Northwest Coast: Their Archaeology and
          Prehistory*. New York: Thames & Hudson.
Ammerman, A. J. and L. L. Cavalli-Sforza
   1984   *The Neolithic Transition and the Genetics of Populations in
          Europe*. Princeton: Princeton University Press.
Andersson, J. Gunnar
   1934   *Children of the Yellow Earth*. New York: Macmillan.
Arensburg, B., A. M. Tillier, et al.
   1989   "A Middle Paleolithic Human Hyoid Bone." *Nature*,
          338:758–760.
Aronson, J. L., R. C. Walter, and M. Taieb
   1983   "Correlation of Tulu Bor Tuff at Koobi Fora with the Sidi
          Hakoma Tuff at Hadar." *Nature*, **306**:209–210.
Arsuaga, Juan-Luis et al.
   1993   "Three New Human Skulls from the Sima de los Huesos
          Middle Pleistocene Site in Sierra de Atapuerca, Spain."
          Nature, **362**:534–537.
Arsuaga, J.L., I. Martinez, A. Garcia, et al.
   1997   "Sima de los Huesos (Sierra de Atapuerca, Spain). The
          Site." *Journal of Human Evolution*, **33**:109–127.
Ascenzi, A., I. Bidditu, P.F. Cassoli, et al.
   1996   "A Calvarium of Late *Homo erectus* from Ceprano, Italy."
          Journal of Human Evolution, **31**:409–423.

Asfaw, Berhane
   1992   "New Fossil Hominids from the Ethiopian Rift Valley
          and the Afar." Paper presented at the Annual Meeting,
          American Association of Physical Anthropologists.
Asfaw, Berhane et al.
   1992   "The Earliest Acheulian from Konso-Gardula." *Nature*,
          360:732–735.
   _____
   1995   "Three Seasons of Hominid Paleontology at Aramis,
          Ethiopia." Paper presented at the Paleoanthropology
          Society meetings, Oakland, CA, March 1995.
Asfaw, Berhane, Tim White, Owen Lovejoy, et al.
   1999   "*Australopithecus garhi*: A New Species of Early Hominid
          from Ethiopia." *Science*, **284**:629–635.
Aveni, Anthony F.
   1986   "The Nazca Lines: Patterns in the Desert." *Archaeology*,
          39(4):32–39.
   _____.
   2000   "Solving the Mystery of the Nazca Lines." *Archaeology*,
          53 (3): 26–35.
   _____ (ed.)
   1990   "The Lines of Nazca." *Memoirs of the American
          Philosophical Society, 183*.
Avery, O. T., MacLeod, C. M., and McCarty, M.
   1944   "Studies on the Chemical Nature of the Substance
          Inducing Transformation in Pneumococcal Types."
          Journal of Exploratory Medicine, **79**:137–158.
Ayala, Francisco
   1995   "The Myth of Eve: Molecular Biology and Human
          Origins." *Science*, **270**:1930–1936.

Bailey, G.
   1975   "The Role of Molluscs in Coastal Economies." *Journal of
          Archaeological Science*, **2**:45–62.
Balter, Michael
   1996   "Cave Structure Boosts Neandertal Image." *Science*,
          271:449.
Banning, E. B.
   2000   *The Archaeologist's Laboratory: The Analysis of
          Archaeological Data*. Norwell, MA: Kluwer Academic
          Publishers.
Barnes, G. L.
   1992   *China, Korea, and Japan: The Rise of Civilization in East
          Asia*. New York: Thames & Hudson.
Bartlett, Thad.Q., Robert W. Sussman, James M. Cheverud
   1993   "Infant Killing in Primates: A Review of Observed Cases
          with Specific References to the Sexual Selection
          Hypothesis." *American Anthropologist*, **95**(4):958–990.
Bartstra, Gert-Jan
   1982   "*Homo erectus erectus*: The Search for Artifacts." *Current
          Anthropology*, **23**(3):318–320.
Bar-Yosef, Ofer
   1986   "The Walls of Jericho: An Alternative Explanation."
          Current Anthropology, **27**:157–162.

1987 "Late Pleistocene Adaptations in the Levant." *In: The Pleistocene in the Old World: Regional Perspectives*, Olga Soffer (ed.), New York: Plenum, pp. 219–236.

1993 "The Role of Western Asia in Modern Human Origins." *In:* M. J. Aitken et al. (eds.), q.v., pp. 132–147.

1994 "The Contributions of Southwest Asia to the Study of the Origin of Modern Humans." *In: Origins of Anatomically Modern Humans*, M. H. Nitecki and D. V. Nitecki (eds.), New York: Plenum Press, pp. 23–66.

1998 "The Natufian Culture in the Levant, Threshold to the Origins of Agriculture." *Environmental Anthropology*, 6(5):159–177.

Beadle, George W.
1980 "The Ancestry of Corn." *Scientific American*, 242:112–119.

Bearder, Simon K.
1987 "Lorises, Bushbabies & Tarsiers: Diverse Societies in Solitary Foragers." *In:* Smuts et al., q.v., pp. 11–24.

Begun, D. and A. Walker
1993 "The Endocast." *In:* A. Walker and R. E. Leakey (eds.), q.v., pp. 326–358.

Behrensmeyer, A. K., D. Western, and D. E. Dechant Boaz
1979 "New Perspectives in Vertebrate Paleoecology from a Recent Bone Assemblage." *Paleobiology*, 5(1):12–21.

Belfer-Cohen, Anna
1991 "The Natufians in the Levant." *Annual Review of Anthropology*, 20:167–186.

Bell, Martin and Michael J. C. Walker
1992 *Late Quaternary Environmental Change*. New York: John Wiley and Sons

Benz, Bruce F. and Hugh H. Iltis
1990 "Studies in Archaeological Maize I: The 'Wild' Maize from San Marcos Cave Reexamined." *American Antiquity*, 55(3):500–511.

Berger, Thomas and Erik Trinkaus
1995 "Patterns of Trauma Among the Neandertals." *Journal of Archaeological Science*, 22:841–852.

Berlo, Janet (ed.)
1992 *Art, Ideology, and the City of Teotihuacán*. Washington, DC: Dumbarton Oaks.

Bermudez de Castro, J. M., J. L. Arsuaga, E. Carbonell, et al.
1997 "A Hominid from the Lower Pleistocene of Atapuerca, Spain: Possible Ancestor to Neandertals and Modern Humans." *Science*, 276:1392–1395.

Biasutti, R.
1951 *Rassa e Popoli della Terra*. Torino: Unione Tipografico Editria Torinese.

1959 *Razze e Popoli della Terra* (2nd Ed.). Torino: VTET.

Binford, Lewis R.
1978 *Nunamiut Ethnoarchaeology*. New York: Academic Press.

1981 *Bones. Ancient Men and Modern Myths*. New York: Academic Press.

1982 Comment on White's article, "Rethinking the Middle/Upper Paleolithic Transition." (*See* R. White, 1982, pp. 177–181).

1983 *In Pursuit of the Past*. New York: Thames & Hudson.

Binford, Lewis R. and Chuan Kun Ho
1985 "Taphonomy at a Distance: Zhoukoudian, 'The Cave Home of Beijing Man'?" *Current Anthropology*, 26:413–442.

Binford, Lewis R. and Nancy M. Stone
1986a "The Chinese Paleolithic: An Outsider's View." *AnthroQuest*, Fall 1986(1):14–20.

1986b "Zhoukoudian: A Closer Look." *Current Anthropology*, 27(5):453–475.

Birdsell, Joseph B.
1981 *Human Evolution* (3rd Ed.). Boston: Houghton Mifflin Co.

Blumenschine, Robert J.
1986 *Early Hominid Scavenging Opportunities*. Oxford: BAR International Series 283.

Boas, F.
1912 "Changes in the Bodily Form of Descendants of Immigrants." *American Anthropologist*, 14:530–562.

Boaz, N. T. and A. K.Behrensmeyer
1976 "Hominid Taphonomy: Transport of Human Skeletal Parts in an Artificial Fluviatile Environment." *American Journal of Physical Anthropology*, 45:56–60.

Boaz, Noel T. and Russell L. Ciochon
2001 "The Scavenging of Peking Man." *Natural History*, 110(2):46–51.

Boaz, N. T., F. C. Howell, and M. L. McCrossin
1982 "Faunal Age of the Usno, Shungura B and Hadar Formation, Ethiopia." *Nature*, 300:633–635.

Bodmer, Walter F.
1995 "Evolution and Function of the HLA Region." *Clinical Surveys*, 22:5–16.

Bodmer, Walter F. and Luigi L. Cavalli-Sforza
1976 *Genetics, Evolution, and Man*. San Francisco: W. H. Freeman and Company.

Boesch, C.
1994 "Hunting Strategies of Gombe and Tai Chimpanzees." *In:* Wrangham, R., W. C. McGrew, Frans B. M. de Waal, and Paul G. Heltne (eds.). *Chimpanzee Cultures*. Cambridge: Harvard University Press, pp.77–91.

Boesch, C. and H. Boesch
1989 "Hunting Behavior of Wild Chimpanzees in the Tai National Park." *American Journal of Physical Anthropology*, 78(4): 547–573.

1990 "Tool Use and Tool Making in Wild Chimpanzees." *Folia Primatologica*, 54:86–99.

Bogin, Barry
1988 *Patterns of Human Growth*. Cambridge: Cambridge University Press.

Bogucki, Peter
1988 *Forest Farmers and Stockherders: Early Agriculture and Its Consequences in North Central Europe*. Cambridge: Cambridge University Press.

Bokonyi, S.
1969 "Archaeological Problems and Methods of Recognizing Animal Domestication." *In: The Domestication and Exploitation of Plants and Animals*, P. J. Ucko and G. W. Dimbleby (eds.), Chicago: Aldine, pp. 207–218.

Boserup, Ester
1965 *The Conditions of Agricultural Growth*. Chicago: Aldine.

Bouzek, Jan
1985 "Relations between Barbarian Europe and the Aegean Civilizations." *Advances in World Archaeology*, 4:71–114.

Brace, C. Loring and Ashley Montagu
1977 *Human Evolution* (2nd Ed.). New York: Macmillan.

Brace, C. Loring, H. Nelson, and N. Korn
1979 *Atlas of Human Evolution* (2nd Ed.). New York: Holt, Rinehart & Winston.

Brady, James E. and Andrea Stone
1986 "Naj Tunich: Entrance to the Maya Underworld." *Archaeology*, 39(6):18–25.

Bromage, Timothy G. and Christopher Dean
1985   "Re-evaluation of the Age at Death of Immature Fossil Hominids." *Nature*, **317**:525–527.

Brooks, Alison et al.
1995   "Dating and Context of Three Middle Stone Age Sites with Bone Points in the Upper Semliki Valley, Zaire." *Science*, **268**:548–553.

Brown, F. H.
1982   "Tulu Bor Tuff at Koobi Fora Correlated with the Sidi Hakoma Tuff at Hadar." *Nature*, **300**:631–632.

Brown, Ian
1994   "Recent Trends in the Archaeology of the Southeastern United States." *Journal of Archaeological Research*, 2(1):45–111.

Brown, T. M. and K. D. Rose
1987   "Patterns of Dental Evolution in Early Eocene Anaptomorphine Primates Comomyidael from the Bighorn Basin, Wyoming." *Journal of Paleontology*, 61:1–62.

Brues, Alice M.
1990   *People and Races* (2nd Ed.). Prospect Heights, IL: Waveland Press.

Bruhns, Karen Olsen
1994   *Ancient South America*. Cambridge: Cambridge University Press.

Brunet, Michel et al.
1995   "The First Australopithecine 2,500 Kilometers West of the Rift Valley (Chad)." *Nature*, 378:273–274.

Bunn, Henry T.
1981   "Archaeological Evidence for Meat-eating by Plio-Pleistocene Hominids from Koobi Fora and Olduvai Gorge." *Nature*, 291:574–577.

Burger, Richard L.
1992   *Chavín and the Origins of Andean Civilizations*. New York: Thames & Hudson.

Butzer, Karl W.
1974   "Paleoecology of South African Australopithecines: Taung Revisited." *Current Anthropology*, **15**:367–382.

_____
1984   "Long-term Nile Flood Variation and Political Discontinuities in Pharaonic Egypt." *In*: Clark and Brandt (eds.), q.v., pp. 102–112.

Byers, Douglas S. (ed.)
1967   *The Prehistory of the Tehuacán Valley. Vol. 1: Economy and Subsistence*. Austin: University of Texas Press.

Carbonell, E. et al.
1995   "Lower Pleistocene Hominids and Artifacts from Atapuerca-TDG (Spain)." *Science*, 269:826–830.

Carlson, John B.
1991   "Venus-Regulated Warfare and Ritual Sacrifice in Mesoamerica: Teotihuacán and the Cacaxtla 'Star Wars' Connection." *University of Maryland Center for Archaeoastronomy Technical Publication*, 7.

_____
1993   "Rise and Fall of the City of Gods." *Archaeology*, 46(6):58–69.

Carneiro, Robert
1970   "A Theory of the Origin of the State." *Science*, 169:733–738.

Carrol, Robert L.
1988   *Vertebrate Paleontology and Evolution*. New York: W. H. Freeman and Co.

Carter, Howard and A. C. Mace
1923   *The Tomb of Tutankhamen*. London: Cassell and Co., Ltd.

Cartmill, Matt
1972   "Arboreal Adaptations and the Origin of the Order Primates." *In: The Functional and Evolutionary Biology of Primates*, R. H. Tuttle (ed.), Chicago: Aldine-Atherton, pp. 97–122.

_____
1974   "Rethinking Primate Origins." *Science*, **184**:436–443.

Casson, Lionel
2001   *Everyday Life in Ancient Egypt*. Baltimore: Johns Hopkins University Press.

Castleden, Rodney
1990   *Minoans: Life in Bronze Age Crete*. London and New York: Routledge.

Cavalli-Sforza, L. L., A. Piazza, P. Menozzi, and J. Mountain
1988   "Reconstruction of Human Evolution: Bringing Together Genetic, Archaeological, and Linguistic Data." *Proceedings of the National Academy of Sciences*, **85**:6002–6006.

Censky, E. J., K. Hodge and J. Dudley
1998   "Over-water Dispersal of Lizards due to Hurricanes." *Nature*, **395** (6702):556.

Chang, Kwang-chih
1980   *Shang Civilization*. New Haven: Yale University Press.

_____
1986   *The Archaeology of Ancient China* (4th Ed.). New Haven: Yale University Press.

Charteris, J., J. C. Wali, and J. W. Nottrodt
1981   "Functional Reconstruction of Gait from Pliocene Hominid Footprints at Laetoli, Northern Tanzania." *Nature*, **290**:496–498.

Cheney, D. L. and R. M. Seyfarth
1990   *How Monkeys See the World*. Chicago: Chicago University Press.

Childe, V. Gordon
1928   *The Most Ancient East*. London: Routledge and Kegan Paul.

_____
1934   *New Light on the Most Ancient East*. London: Kegan Paul, Trench, Trubner.

_____
1951   *Man Makes Himself* (Rev. Ed.). New York: New American Library.

_____
1957   *What Happened in History*. Baltimore: Pelican Books.

Chippindale, Christopher
1994   *Stonehenge Complete*. (Rev. ed.) New York: Thames & Hudson.

Chrisman, Donald, et al.
1996   "Late Pleistocene Human Friction Skin Prints from Pendejo Cave, New Mexico." *American Antiquity*, 61(2):357–376.

Ciochon, Russell L. and Robert S. Corruccini (eds.)
1983   *New Interpretations of Ape and Human Ancestry*. New York: Plenum Press.

Clark, J. Desmond
1976   "Prehistoric Populations and Resources Favoring Plant Domestication in Africa." *In: Origins of African Plant Domestication*, J. R. Harlan, J. DeWet, and A. Stemler (eds.), The Hague: Mouton, pp. 69–84.

Clark, J. Desmond and Steven A. Brandt (eds.)
1984   *From Hunters to Farmers*. Berkeley and Los Angeles: University of California Press.

Clark, Grahame
1967   *The Stone Age Hunters*. New York: McGraw-Hill.

_____
1972   *Star Carr: A Case Study of Bioarchaeology*. Reading, MA: Addison-Wesley.

1979   *Mesolithic Prelude*. Edinburgh: Edinburgh University Press.

Clark, W. E. LeGros
1971   *The Antecedents of Man* (3rd Ed.). New York: The New York Times Books.

Clarke, Ronald J. and Phillip V. Tobias
1995   "Sterkfontein Member 2 Foot Bones of the Oldest South African Hominid." *Science*, **269**:521–524.

Clendinnen, Inga
1991   *Aztecs*. Cambridge: Cambridge University Press.

Coe, Michael D.
1992   *Breaking the Maya Code*. New York: Thames & Hudson.

_____
1994   *Mexico: From the Olmecs to the Aztecs*. New York: Thames & Hudson.

_____
1999   *The Maya* (6th Ed.) New York: Thames & Hudson.

Coe, Michael D., Dean Snow, and Elizabeth Benson
1986   *Atlas of Ancient America*. New York: Facts on File Publications.

Cohen, Mark N.
1977   *The Food Crisis in Prehistory*. New Haven: Yale University Press.

_____
1989   *Health and the Rise of Civilization*. New Haven, CT: Yale University Press.

Cohen, Mark N. and George J. Armelagos (eds.)
1984   *Paleopathology at the Origins of Agriculture*. New York: Academic Press.

Colwell, Rita R.
1996   "Global Climate and Infectious Disease: The Cholera Paradigm." *Science*, **274**(5295):2025–2031.

Conkey, M.
1987   "New Approaches in the Search for Meaning? A Review of the Research in 'Paleolithic Art.'" *Journal of Field Archaeology*, **14**:413–430.

Conroy, Glenn C.
1997   *Reconstructing Human Origins. A Modern Synthesis*. New York: Norton.

Conroy, G. C., M. Pickford, B. Senut, J. van Couvering, and P. Mein
1992   "*Otavipithecus namibiensis,* First Miocene Hominoid from Southern Africa." *Nature*, **356**:144–148.

Cook, J., C. B. Stringer, A. Currant, H. P. Schwarcz, and A. G. Wintle
1982   "A Review of the Chronology of the European Middle Pleistocene Record." *Yearbook of Physical Anthropology*, **25**:19–65.

Coon, Carleton
1962   *The Origin of Races*. New York: Alfred A. Knopf.

Cordell, Linda S.
1998   *Prehistory of the Southwest*. (2nd Ed.) Orlando, FL: Academic Press.

Corruccini, R. S. and R. L. Ciochon (eds.)
1994   *Integrative Paths to the Past; Paleoanthropological Advances in Honor of F. Clark Howell*. Englewood Cliffs, NJ: Prentice-Hall.

Corruccini, Robert S.
1994   "Reaganomics and the Fate of the Progressive Neandertals." *In:* R.S. Corruccini and R. L. Ciochon (eds.), q.v., pp. 697–708.

Cowgill, Ursula M.
1962   "An Agricultural Study of the Southern Maya Lowlands." *American Anthropologist*, **64**:273–286.

Crawford, Gary W. and Chen Shen
1998   "The Origins of Rice Agriculture: Recent Progress in East Asia." *Antiquity*, **72**: 858–867.

Crown, Patricia L.
1991   "Hohokam: Current Views of Prehistory and the Regional System." *In: Chaco and Hohokam Prehistoric Regional Systems in the American Southwest*, Patricia L. Crown and W. James Judge (eds.), Santa Fe: School of American Research Press, pp. 135–157.

Culbert, T. Patrick
1985   "The Maya Enter History." *Natural History*, **94**(4):41–49.

_____
1988   "The Collapse of Classic Maya Civilization." *In: The Collapse of Ancient States and Civilizations*, N. Yoffee and G. Cowgill (eds.), Tucson: University of Arizona Press, pp. 69–101.

Cummings, Michael
1997   *Human Heredity. Principles and Issues*. (4th ed.) St Paul: West Publishing Co., Belmont, CA: West/Wadsworth.

Dalrymple, G. B.
1972   "Geomagnetic Reversals and North American Glaciations." *In: Calibration of Hominoid Evolution*, W. W. Bishop and J. A. Miller (eds.), Edinburgh: Scottish Academic Press, pp. 303–329.

Daniel, Glyn
1980   "Megalithic Monuments." *Scientific American*, **243**(7):15, 78–81.

Dart, Raymond
1959   *Adventures with the Missing Link*. New York: Harper & Brothers.

Darwin, Charles
1859   *On the Origin of Species*. A Facsimile of the First Edition. Cambridge, MA: Harvard University Press (1964).

_____
1871   *The Descent of Man and Selection in Relation to Sex*. Republished, 1981, Princeton: Princeton University Press.

Darwin, Francis (ed.)
1950   *The Life and Letters of Charles Darwin*. New York: Henry Schuman.

Davies, Nigel
1983   *The Ancient Kingdoms of Mexico*. New York: Penguin.

Davis, S. and F. R. Valla
1978   "Evidence for Domestication of the Dog 12,000 Years Ago in the Natufian of Israel." *Nature*, **276**:608–610.

Day, M. H. and E. H. Wickens
1980   "Laetoli Pliocene Hominid Footprints and Bipedalism." *Nature*, **286**:385–387.

D'Azevedo, Warren (ed.)
1986   *Handbook of North American Indians*, vol. 11: Great Basin. Washington, DC: Smithsonian Institution Press.

DeCastro, Jose, M. Bermudez, and M. E. Nicolas
1995   "Posterior Dental Size Reduction in Hominids: The Atapuerca Evidence." *American Journal of Physical Anthropology*, **96**:335–356.

Defleur, A., T. White, P. Valensi, et al.
1999   "Neanderthal Cannibalism at Moula-Guercy, Ardèche, France." *Science*, **286**:128–131.

DeGusta, D., W. H. Gilbert, and S. P. Turner
1999   "Hypoglossal Canal Size and Hominid Speech." *Proceedings of the National Academy of Sciences*, **96**:1800–1804.

Delcourt, Hazel R. and Paul A. Delcourt
1991   *Quaternary Ecology: A Paleoecological Perspective*. London: Chapman & Hall.

Delson, Eric
1987   "Evolution and Palaeobiology of Robust *Australopithecus*." *Nature*, **327**:654–655.

de Lumley, Henry and M. de Lumley
1973　"Pre-Neanderthal Human Remains from Arago Cave in Southeastern France." *Yearbook of Physical Anthropology*, **16**:162–168.

Demarest, Arthur A.
1993　"The Violent Saga of a Maya Kingdom." *National Geographic*, **183** (2): 95–111.

Dene, H. T., M. Goodman, and W. Prychodko
1976　"Immunodiffusion Evidence on the Phylogeny of the Primates." *In: Molecular Anthropology*, M. Goodman, R. E. Tashian, and J. H. Tashian (eds.), New York: Plenum Press, pp. 171–195.

Dennell, Robin
1983　*European Economic Prehistory: A New Approach*. New York: Academic Press.

Desmond, Adrian and James Moore
1991　*Darwin*. New York: Warner Books.

Dettwyler, K. A.
1991　"Can Paleopathology Provide Evidence for Compassion?" *American Journal of Physical Anthropology*, **84**:375–384.

de Waal, Frans B. M.
1999　"Cultural Primatology Comes of Age." *Nature*, **399**:635–636.

Diamond, Jared
1987　"The Worst Mistake in the History of the Human Race." *Discover*, **8**(5):64–66.

———
1989　"The Accidental Conqueror." *Discover*, **10**(12):71–76.

Diaz del Castillo, Bernal
1956　*The Discovery and Conquest of Mexico*. New York: Farrar, Straus & Cudahy.

Diehl, Richard
1983　*Tula: The Toltec Capital of Ancient Mexico*. New York: Thames & Hudson.

Diehl, Richard A. and Janet C. Berlo (eds.)
1989　*Mesoamerica after the Decline of Teotihuacán, A.D. 700–900*. Washington, DC: Dumbarton Oaks.

Dillehay, Thomas D.
1989　*Monte Verde: A Late Pleistocene Settlement in Chile, Vol. 1: Paleoenvironment and Site Context*. Washington, DC: Smithsonian Institution Press.

———
1997　*Monte Verde: A Late Pleistocene Settlement in Chile, Vol. 2: The Archaeological Content and Interpretation*. Washington, DC: Smithsonian Institution Press.

———
2000　*The Settlement of the Americas: A New Prehistory*. New York: Basic Books.

Dincauze, Dena
1997　"Regarding Pendejo Cave: Response to Chrisman et al." *American Antiquity*, **62**(3): 554–555.

DiPeso, Charles C.
1974　*Casas Grandes, A Fallen Trading Center of the Gran Chichimeca*. Flagstaff: Northland Press.

Dixon, E. James
2000　*Bones, Boats, and Bison: Archaeology and the First Colonization of Western North America*. Albuquerque: University of New Mexico.

Dobyns, Henry F.
1966　"Estimating Aboriginal American Population: An Appraisal of Techniques with a New Hemisphere Estimate." *Current Anthropology*, **7**:395–449.

Doebley, J.
1994　"Morphology, Molecules, and Maize." *In: Corn and Culture in the Prehistoric New World*, S. Johannessen and

C. A. Hastorf, (eds.), Boulder, CO: Westview Press, pp. 101–112.

Doran, Diane M. and Alastair McNeilage
1998　"Gorilla Ecology and Behavior." *Evolutionary Anthropology*, **6**(4):120–131.

Dorit, R. L., H. Akashi, and W. Gilbert
1995　"Absence of Polymorphism at the Zfy Locus on the Human Y Chromosome." *Science*, **268**:1183–1185.

Downey, Roger
2000　*Riddle of the Bones: Politics, Science, Race, and the Story of Kennewick Man*. New York: Copernicus.

Duarte, C., J. Maurício, P. B. Pettitt, et al.
1999　"The Early Upper Paleolithic Human Skeleton from the Abrigo do Lagar Velho (Portugal) and Modern Human Emergence in Iberia." *Proceedings of the National Academy of Sciences*, **96**:7604–7609.

Dunn, Frederick L.
1993　"Malaria." *In: The Cambridge World History of Human Disease*, Kenneth F. Kiple (ed.), Cambridge: Cambridge University Press, pp. 855–862.

Durham, William
1981　Paper presented to the Annual Meeting of the American Anthropological Association, Washington, D.C., Dec. 1980. Reported in *Science*, **211**:40.

Eaton, S. Boyd and Melvin Konner
1985　"Paleolithic Nutrition: A Consideration of Its Nature and Current Implications." *New England Journal of Medicine*, **312**:283–289.

Eaton, S. Boyd, Marjorie Shostak, and Melvin Konner
1988　*The Paleolithic Prescription*. New York: Harper & Row.

Edwards, Mike
2000　"Indus Civilization: Clues to an Ancient Puzzle." *National Geographic*, **197**(6):108–131.

Ehret, C.
1984　"Historical/Linguistic Evidence for Early African Food Production." *In:* J. D. Clark and S. A. Brandt (eds.), q.v., pp. 26–35.

Ehrlich, Paul R. and Anne H. Ehrlich
1990　*The Population Explosion*. New York: Simon & Schuster.

Eldredge, Niles
1977　"Punctuated Equilibria: The Tempo and Mode of Evolution Reconsidered." *Paleobiology*, **3**:115–151.

Erlandson, Jon M.
1988　"The Role of Shellfish in Prehistoric Economies: A Protein Perspective." *American Antiquity*, **53**:102–109.

Etler, Dennis A. and Li-Tianyuan
1994　"New Archaic Human Fossil Discoveries in China and Their Bearing on Hominid Species Definition During the Middle Pleistocene." *In:* R. Corruccini and R. Ciochon (eds.), q.v., pp. 639–675.

European Union GIS/Remote Sensing Expert Group
1997　*Fires in Indonesia, September 1997, a Report to the European Union*. Brussels, European Union.

Ezzo, Joseph A.
1993　"Human Adaptation at Grasshopper Pueblo, Arizona: Social and Ecological Perspectives." *International Monographs in Prehistory, Archaeological Series, 4*. Ann Arbor.

Fagan, Brian M.
1993　"Taming the Aurochs." *Archaeology*, **46**(5):14–17.

Falk, Dean
1980　"A Reanalysis of the South African Australopithecine Natural Endocasts." *American Journal of Physical Anthropology*, **53**:525–539.

1983   "The Taung Endocast: A Reply to Holloway." *American Journal of Physical Anthropology*, **60**:479–489.

1989   "Comments." *Current Anthropology*, **30**:141.

Farnsworth, Paul, et al.
1985   "A Re-evaluation of the Isotopic and Archaeological Reconstructions of Diet in the Tehuacán Valley." *American Antiquity*, **50**(1):102–116.

Fiedel, Stuart J.
1999a   "Artifact Provenience at Monte Verde: Confusion and Contradictions." *In:* "Special Report: Monte Verde Revisited," *Discovering Archaeology*, **1**(6):1–23 (separate insert).

1999b   "Older Than We Thought: Implications of Corrected Dates for Paleoindians." *American Antiquity*, **64**(1):95–116.

Fitzgerald, Patrick
1978   *Ancient China*. Oxford: Elsevier Phaidon.

Flannery, Kent V.
1968   "Archaeological Systems Theory and Early Mesoamerica." *In: Anthropological Archaeology in the Americas*, B. J. Meggers (ed.), Washington, DC: Anthropological Society of Washington, pp. 67–87.

1972   "The Origins of the Village As a Settlement Type in Mesoamerica and the Near East: A Comparative Study." *In: Man, Settlement and Urbanism*, P. J. Ucko, R. Tringham, and G. W. Dimbleby (eds.), London: Duckworth, pp. 23–53.

1973   "The Origins of Agriculture." *Annual Review of Anthropology*, **2**:217–310.

1986   *Guila Naquitz: Archaic Foraging and Early Agriculture in Oaxaca, Mexico*. New York: Academic Press.

Flannery, Kent V. (ed.)
1982   *Maya Subsistence: Studies in Memory of Dennis E. Puleston*. New York: Academic Press.

Fleagle, John
1983   "Locomotor Adaptations of Oligocene and Miocene Hominoids and their Phyletic Implications." *In:* R. L. Ciochon and R.S. Corruccini (eds.), q.v., pp. 301–324.

1988   *Primate Adaptation and Evolution*. New York: Academic Press.

1994   "Anthropoid Origins." *In:* R. S. Corruccini and R. L. Ciochon (eds.), q.v., pp. 17–35.

Fleischer, R. F. and H. R. Hart, Jr.
1972   "Fission Track Dating Techniques and Problems." *In: Calibration of Hominid Evolution*, W. W. Bishop and J. A. Miller (eds.). Edinburgh: Scottish Academic Press, pp. 135–170.

Foley, R. A.
1991   "How Many Species of Hominid Should There Be?" *Journal of Human Evolution*, **30**:413–427.

Foley, R. A. and M. M. Lahr
1992   "Beyond 'Out of Africa.'" *Journal of Human Evolution*, **22**:523–529.

Fossey, Dian
1983   *Gorillas in the Mist*. Boston: Houghton Mifflin.

Frayer, David
1992   "Evolution at the European Edge: Neanderthal and Upper Paleolithic Relationships." *Préhistoire Européenne*, **2**:9–69.

Freidel, David A. and Jeremy A. Sabloff
1984   *Cozumel: Late Maya Settlement Patterns*. New York: Academic Press.

Freidel, David, Linda Schele, and Joy Parker
1993   *Maya Cosmos: Three Thousand Years on the Shaman's Path*. New York: William R. Morrow.

Friedman, Florence Dunn (ed.) et al.
1998   *Gifts of the Nile: Ancient Egyptian Faience*. New York: Thames & Hudson.

Frisancho, A. Roberto
1993   *Human Adaptation and Accommodation*. Ann Arbor: University of Michigan Press.

Frison, George C.
1978   *Prehistoric Hunters of the High Plains*. New York: Academic Press.

Fritz, Gayle J.
1994   "Are the First American Farmers Getting Younger?" *Current Anthropology*, **35**(3):305–309.

1999   "Gender and the Early Cultivation of Gourds in Eastern North America." *American Antiquity*, **64**(3): 417-429.

Froelich, J. W.
1970   "Migration and Plasticity of Physique in the Japanese-Americans of Hawaii." *American Journal of Physical Anthropology*, **32**:429.

Gambier, Dominique
1989   "Fossil Hominids from the Early Upper Palaeolithic (Aurignacian) of France." *In:* Mellars and Stringer (eds.), q.v., pp. 194–211.

Gamble, C.
1991   "The Social Context for European Paleolithic Art." *Proceedings of the Prehistoric Society*, **57**:3–15.

Gao, Feng, Elizabeth Bailes, David L. Robertson, et al.
1999   "Origin of HIV-1 in the Chimpanzee *Pan troglodytes troglodytes*." *Nature*, **397**:436–441.

Gates, R. R.
1948   *Human Ancestry*. Cambridge: Harvard University. Press, p. 367.

Gebo, Daniel L., Marian Dagosto, K. Christopher Beard, and Tao Qi
2000   "The Smallest Primates." *Journal of Human Evolution*, **38**:585–594.

Gee, Henry
1996   "Box of Bones 'Clinches' Identity of Piltdown Palaeontology Hoaxer." *Nature*, **381**:261–262.

Gibbons, Anne
1998   "Ancient Tools Suggest *Homo erectus* was a Seafarer." Research News, *Science*, **279**:1635–1637.

Gibson, Jon L.
2001   *The Ancient Mounds of Poverty Point*. Gainesville, FL: University Press of Florida.

Gingerich, Phillip D.
1985   "Species in the Fossil Record: Concepts, Trends, and Transitions." *Paleobiology*, **11**:27–41.

Glassow, Michael A.
1996   *Purisimeño Chumash Prehistory*. New York: Harcourt Brace.

Goodall, A. G.
1977   "Feeding and Ranging Behaviour of a Mountain Gorilla Group, *Gorilla gorilla beringei* in the Tshibinda-Kahuze region (Zaire)." *In: Primate Ecology*, T. H. Clutton-Brock (ed.). London: Academic Press, pp. 450–479.

Goodall, Jane
1986   *The Chimpanzees of Gombe*. Cambridge: Harvard University Press.

1990   *Through a Window*. Boston: Houghton Mifflin.

Gossett, Thomas F.
1963 *Race, the History of an Idea in America.* Dallas: Southern Methodist University Press.

Gould, Richard A.
1977 "Puntutjarpa Rockshelter and the Australian Desert Culture." *Anthropological Papers of the American Museum of Natural History,* **54**(1).

Gould, Stephen Jay
1981 *The Mismeasure of Man.* New York: W. W. Norton.

_____
1987 *Time's Arrow Time's Cycle.* Cambridge: Harvard University Press.

Graham, J. Walter
1987 *The Palaces of Crete* (Rev. Ed.). Princeton: Princeton University Press.

Gramly, Richard Michael
1982 "The Vail Site: A Palaeo-Indian Encampment in Maine." *Bulletin of the Buffalo Society of Natural Sciences,* 30.

_____
1992 *Guide to the Palaeo-Indian Artifacts of North America.* (2nd Ed.) Buffalo, NY: Persimmon Press.

Green, T. J., B. Cochran, T. W. Fenton, et al.
1998 "The Buhl Burial: A Paleoindian Woman from Southern Idaho." *American Antiquity,* **43**(4):437–456.

Greenberg, Joseph
1987 *Language in the Americas.* Palo Alto: Stanford Univeristy Press.

Greene, John C.
1981 *Science, Ideology, and World View.* Berkeley: University of California Press.

Gregg, Susan Alling
1988 *Foragers and Farmers: Population Interaction and Agricultural Expansion in Prehistoric Europe.* Chicago: University of Chicago Press.

Grigor'ev, G. P.
1993 "The Kostenki-Avdeevo Archaeological Culture and the Willendorf-Pavlov-Kostenki-Avdeevo Cultural Unity." *In:* Soffer and Praslov (eds.), q.v., pp. 51–65.

Grine, Frederick E.
1993 "Australopithecine Taxonomy and Phylogeny: Historical Background and Recent Interpretation." *In: The Human Evolution Source Book,* R. L. Ciochon and J. G. Fleagle (eds.), Englewood Cliffs, N.J.: Prentice Hall, pp. 198–210.

_____ (ed.)
1988a *Evolutionary History of the "Robust" Australopithecines.* New York: Aldine de Gruyter.

_____
1988b "New Craniodental Fossils of *Paranthropus* from the Swartkrans Formation and Their Significance in "Robust" Australopithecine Evolution." *In:* F. E. Grine (ed.), q.v., pp. 223–243.

Grove, David C.
1984 *Chalcatzingo: Excavations on the Olmec Frontier.* New York: Thames & Hudson.

Guidon, N., A.-M. Pessis, Fabio Porenti, et al.
1996 "Nature and Age of the Deposits in Pedra Furada, Brazil: Reply to Meltzer, Adovasio, and Dillehay." *Antiquity,* **70**:408–421.

Haas, J. D., E. A. Frongillo, Jr., C. D. Stepick, J. L. Beard, and G. Hurtado
1980 "Altitude, Ethnic and Sex Difference in Birth Weight and Length in Bolivia." *Human Biology,* **52**:459–477.

Haas, Jonathan, Shelia Pozorski, and Thomas Pozorski (eds.)
1987 *The Origins and Development of the Andean State.* New York: Cambridge University Press.

Harbottle, Garman
1982 "Chemical Characterization in Archaeology." *In: Context for Prehistoric Exchange,* J. E. Ericson and T. K. Earle (eds.), New York: Academic Press, pp. 13–51.

Harbottle, Garman and Phil C. Weigand
1992 "Turquoise in Pre-Columbian America." *Scientific American,* **226**(2):78–85.

Harding, A. F.
1984 *The Mycenaeans and Europe.* New York: Academic Press.

Harlan, Jack R.
1992 *Crops and Man* (2nd Ed.). Madison, WI: American Society of Agronomy and Crop Science Society of America.

Harris, Marvin
1979 *Cultural Materialism: The Struggle for a Science of Culture.* New York: Vintage Press.

Harrison, Richard J.
1985 "The 'Policultivo Ganadero,' or Secondary Products Revolution in Spanish Agriculture, 5000–1000 B.C." *Proceedings of the Prehistoric Society,* **51**:75–102.

Harrold, Francis R.
1989 "Mousterian, Chatelperronian and Early Aurignacian in Western Europe: Continuity or Discontinuity." *In:* Mellars and Stringer, q.v., pp. 212–231.

Hart, John P. and C. Margaret Scarry
1999 "The Age of Common Beans (*Phaseolus vulgaris*) in the Northeastern United States." *American Antiquity,* **64**(4):653–658.

Hartl, Daniel
1983 *Human Genetics.* New York: Harper & Row.

Haury, Emil W.
1976 *The Hohokam, Desert Farmers and Craftsmen: Excavations at Snaketown, 1964–1965.* Tucson: University of Arizona Press.

Hawass, Zahi and Mark Lehner
1994 "The Sphinx: Who Built It, and Why?" *Archaeology,* **47**(5):30–41.

Hawkes, K., J. F. O'Connell, and N. G. Blurton Jones
1997 "Hadza Women's Time Allocation, Offspring Provisioning, and the Evolution of Long Postmenopausal Life Spans." *Current Anthropology,* **38**:551–577.

Haynes, C. Vance
1993 "Clovis-Folsom Geochronology and Climatic Change." *In:* Soffer and Praslov (eds.), q.v., pp. 219–236.

_____
1999 "Bad Weather and Good Hunters." *Discovering Archaeology,* **1**(5):52).

Hays, T. R.
1984 "A Reappraisal of the Egyptian Predynastic." *In:* J. D. Clark and S. A. Brandt (eds.), q.v., pp. 65–73.

Healan, Dan M. (ed.)
1989 *Tula of the Toltecs.* Iowa City, IA: University of Iowa Press.

Henry, David O.
1989 *From Foraging to Agriculture: The Levant at the End of the Ice Age.* Philadelphia: University of Pennsylvania Press.

Herre, Wolf
1969 "The Science and History of Domestic Animals." *In: Science in Archaeology,* D. Brothwell and E. Higgs (eds.), New York: Frederick A. Praeger, pp. 257–272.

Higham, Charles and Tracey L.-D. Lu
1998 "The Origins and Dispersal of Rice Cultivation." *Antiquity,* **72**:867–877.

Hill, A., S. Ward, A. Deino, G. Curtis, and R. Drake
1992 "Earliest *Homo.*" *Nature,* **355**:719–722.

Hirsch, V. M., R. A. Olmsted, M. Murphey-Corb, R. H. Purcell, and

P. R. Johnson
1989 "An African Primate Lentivirus (SIVsm) Closely Related to HIV-2." *Nature* **339**:389–392.

Hodder, Ian (ed.)
1996 *On the Surface: Çatalhöyük, 1993–95*. London: David Brown.

Hoffecker, J. F., W. R. Powers, and T. Goebel
1993 "The Colonization of Beringia and the Peopling of the New World." *Science,* **159**: 46–53.

Hoffman, Michael A.
1991 *Egypt Before the Pharaohs* (Rev. Ed.). Austin: University of Texas Press.

Hole, Frank, Kent V. Flannery, and James A. Neely (eds.)
1969 *The Prehistory and Human Ecology of the Deh Luran Plain*. Ann Arbor: University of Michigan Museum of Anthropology.

Holloway, Ralph L.
1983 "Cerebral Brain Endocast Pattern of *Australopithecus afarensis* Hominid." *Nature,* **303**:420–422.

_____
1985 "The Poor Brain of *Homo sapiens neanderthalensis*." *In: Ancestors, The Hard Evidence,* E. Delson (ed.). New York: Alan R. Liss, pp. 319–324.

Holmes, C. E.
1996 "Broken Mammoth." *In:* West and West (eds.), q.v., pp. 312–318.

Hood, Sinclair
1973 *The Minoans*. London: Thames & Hudson.

Hooton, E. A.
1926 "Methods of Racial Analysis." *Science,* **63**:75–81.

Horr, D. A.
1975 "The Bornean Orangutan: Population Structure and Dynamics in Relationship to Ecology and Reproductive Strategy." *In: Primate Behavior: Developments in Field and Laboratory Research*, vol. 4, L. A. Rosenblum (ed.), New York: Academic Press.

Howell, F. Clark
1988 "Foreward." *In:* F. E. Grine (ed.), q.v., pp. xi–xv.

Howell, John H.
1987 "Early Farming in Northwestern Europe." *Scientific American,* **257**(5):118–126.

Hrdy, S. B.
1977 *The Langurs of Abu: Female and Male Strategies of Reproduction*. Cambridge: Harvard University Press.

Hrdy, Sarah Blaffer, Charles Janson, and Carel van Schaik
1995 "Infanticide: Let's not throw out the baby with the bath water." *Evolutionary Anthropology,* **3**(5):151–154.

Hublin, Jean-Jacques, F. Spoor, M. Braun, F. Zonneveld, and S. Condemi
1996 "A Late Neanderthal Associated with Upper Palaeolithic Artifacts." *Nature,* **38**:224–226.

Humphries, Rolfe
1955 *Ovid Metamorphoses*. Bloomington: Indiana University Press.

Hyslop, John
1984 *The Inka Road System*. Orlando: Academic Press.

Iseminger, William R.
1996 "Mighty Cahokia." *Archaeology,* **49**:(3):30–37.

Jarrige, Jean-Francois and Richard H. Meadow
1980 "The Antecedents of Civilization in the Indus Valley." *Scientific American,* **243**(2):122–133.

Jerison, H. J.
1973 *Evolution of the Brain and Behavior*. New York: Academic Press.

Jia, L. and R. Chakraborty
1993 "Extent of Within Versus Between Population Variations of VNTR Polymorphisms in Five Major Human Groups." *American Journal of Human Genetics,* 53 (Abstract #75).

Jia, L. and Huang Weiwen
1990 *The Story of Peking Man*. New York: Oxford University Press.

Jia, Lan-po
1975 *The Cave Home of Peking Man*. Peking: Foreign Language Press.

Jochim, Michael A.
1976 *Hunting-Gathering Subsistence and Settlement: A Predictive Model*. New York: Academic Press.

_____
1998 *A Hunter-Gatherer Landscape: Southwest Germany in the Late Paleolithic and Mesolithic*. New York: Plenum.

Johanson, Donald and Maitland Edey
1981 *Lucy: The Beginnings of Humankind*. New York: Simon & Schuster.

Johanson, Donald, F. T. Masao, et al.
1987 "New Partial Skeleton of *Homo habilis* from Olduvai Gorge, Tanzania." *Nature,* **327**:205–209.

Johanson, Donald C. and Tim D. White
1979 "A Systematic Assessment of Early African Hominids." *Science,* **202**:321–330.

Johanson, Donald C. and Maurice Taieb
1980 "New Discoveries of Pliocene Hominids and Artifacts in Hadar." International Afar Research Expedition to Ethiopia (Fourth and Fifth Field Seasons, 1975–77), *Journal of Human Evolution,* **9**:582.

Jolly, Alison
1985 *The Evolution of Primate Behavior* (2nd Ed.). New York: Macmillan.

Jonaitas, Aldona
1988 *From the Land of the Totem Poles*. Seattle: University of Washington Press.

Judge, W. James
1984 "New Light on Chaco Canyon." *In: New Light on Chaco Canyon*, David Noble (ed.), Santa Fe: School of American Research, pp. 1–12.

Kano, T.
1980 "The Social Behavior of Wild Pygmy Chimpanzees (*Pan paniscus*) of Wamba: A Preliminary Report." *Journal of Human Evolution,* **9**:243–260.

_____
1992 *The Last Ape. Pygmy Chimpanzee Behavior and Ecology*. Stanford: Stanford University Press.

Kantner, John
1999 "Anasazi Mutilation and Cannibalism in the American Southwest." *In: The Anthropology of Cannibalism*, Laurence R. Goldman, (ed.), Westport, CT: Bergin and Garvey, pp. 75–104.

Kappelman, John
1996 "The Evolution of Body Mass and Relative Brain Size in Fossil Hominids." *Journal of Human Evolution,* **30**:243–276.

Katz, D. and J. M. Suchey
1986 "Age Determination of the Male *Os Pubis*." *American Journal of Physical Anthropology* **69**:427–435.

Katz, S. H., M. L. Hediger, and L. A. Valleroy
1974 "Traditional Maize Processing Techniques in the New World." *Science,* **184**:765–773.

Kay, R., M. Cartmill, and M. Balow
1998 "The Hypoglossal Canal and the Origins of Human Vocal Behavior (abstract)." *American Journal of Physical Anthropology, Supplement,* **26**:137.

Keatinge, Richard W.
  1988   *Peruvian Prehistory*. Cambridge: Cambridge University Press.
Keeley, Lawrence H.
  1980   *Experimental Determination of Stone Tool Uses: A Microwear Analysis*. Chicago: University of Chicago Press.
Kelly, Robert L.
  1995   *The Foraging Spectrum: Diversity in Hunter-Gatherer Lifeways*. Washington, DC: Smithsonian Institution Press.
Kennedy, K. A. R.
  1991   "Is the Narmada Hominid an Indian *Homo erectus?*" *American Journal of Physical Anthropology*, 86:475–496.
Kennedy, Kenneth A. R. and S. U. Deraniyagala
  1989   "Fossil Remains of 28,000-Year-Old Hominids from Sri Lanka." *Current Anthropology*, 30:397–399.
Kenoyer, Jonathan Mark
  1998   *Ancient Cities of the Indus Valley Civilization*. Oxford: Oxford University Press.
Kent, Jonathan D.
  1987   "The Most Ancient South: A Review of the Domestication of the Andean Camelids." *In: Studies in the Neolithic and Urban Revolutions: The V. Gordon Childe Colloquium, Mexico, 1986*, Linda Mazanilla (ed.), Oxford: B.A.R., pp. 169–184.
Kenyon, Kathleen M.
  1981   *Excavations at Jericho*, Vol. 3. Jerusalem: British School of Archaeology.
Keyser, André W.
  2000   "New Finds in South Africa." *National Geographic*, (May), pp. 76–83.
Kimbel, William H.
  1988   "Identification of a Partial Cranium of *Australopithecus afarensis* from the Koobi Fora Formation, Kenya." *Journal of Human Evolution*, 17:647–656.
Kimbel, William H., Donald C. Johanson, and Yoel Rak
  1994   "The First Skull and Other New Discoveries of *Australopithecus afarensis* at Hadar, Ethiopia." *Nature*, 368:449–451.
Kimbel, William H., R. C. Walter, Donald C. Johanson, et al.
  1996   "Late Pliocene *Homo* and Oldowan Tools from the Hadar Formation (Kada Hadar Member), Ethiopia." *Journal of Human Evolution,* 31:549–561.
Kimbel, William H., Tim D. White, and Donald C. Johanson
  1988   "Implications of KNM-WT-17000 for the Evolution of 'Robust' *Australopithecus*." *In:* F. E. Grine (ed.), q.v., pp. 259–268.
King, Barbara J.
  1994   *The Information Continuum*. Santa Fe: School of American Research.
Kiple, Kenneth F.
  1993   *The Cambridge World History of Human Disease*. Cambridge: Cambridge University Press.
Klein, Richard G.
  1989   *The Human Career. Human Biological and Cultural Origins*. Chicago: University of Chicago Press.
Kolata, Alan L.
  1987   "Tiwanaku and Its Hinterland." *Archaeology*, 40(1):36–41.
Kooyman, Brian P.
  2000   *Understanding Stone Tools and Archaeological Sites*. Albuquerque, NM: University of New Mexico Press.
Kraeling, Carl H. and Robert McC. Adams (eds.)
  1960   *City Invincible*. Chicago: University of Chicago Press.
Kramer, Andrew
  1993   "Human Taxonomic Diversity in the Pleistocene: Does *Homo erectus* Represent Multiple Hominid Species?" *American Journal of Physical Anthropology*, 91:161–171.

Kramer, Samuel N.
  1963   *The Sumerians*. Chicago: University of Chicago Press.
Krause, D. W. and M. Maas
  1990   "The Biogeographic Origins of the Late Paleocene-Early Eocene Mammalian Immigrants to the Western Interior of North America." *In: Dawn of the Age of Mammals in the Northern Part of the Rocky Mountain Interior of North America*, T. M. Brown and K. D. Rose (eds.), Boulder, CO: Geological Society of America, pp. 71–105.
Krings, Matthias, Anne Stone, Ralf W. Schmitz, et al.
  1997   "Neandertal DNA Sequences and the Origin of Modern Humans." *Cell,* 90:19–30.
Kunzig, Robert
  1997   "Atapuerca, The Face of an Ancestral Child." *Discover,* 18:88–101.
Kus, James S.
  1984   "The Chicama-Moche Canal: Failure or Success? An Alternative Explanation for an Incomplete Canal." *American Antiquity*, 49(2):408–415.

Lack, David
  1966   *Population Studies of Birds*. Oxford: Clarendon.
Lalani, A. S., J. Masters, W. Zeng, et al.
  1999   "Use of Chemokine Receptors by Poxviruses." *Science,* 286:1968–71.
Lamberg-Karlovsky, C. C. and Jeremy A. Sabloff
  1995   *Ancient Civilizations: The Near East and Mesoamerica*. Prospect Heights, IL: Waveland.
Lambert, Joseph
  1997   *Traces of the Past: Unraveling the Secrets of Archaeology through Chemistry*. New York: Addison-Wesley Longman.
Lancaster, J. B. and C. S. Lancaster
  1983   "Prenatal Investment: The Hominid Adaptation." *In*: Ortner, D. J. (ed.), *How Humans Adapt. A Biocultural Odyssey*. Washington DC: Smithsonian Institution Press.
Lanning, Edward P.
  1967   *Peru Before the Incas*. Englewood Cliffs, NJ: Prentice-Hall.
Larick, Roy and Russell L. Ciochon
  1996   "The African Emergence and Early Asian Dispersals of the Genus *Homo*." *American Scientist*, 84:538-551.
Larsen, Clark Spencer
  1995   "Biological Changes in Human Populations with Agriculture." *Annual Reviews of Anthropology*, 24:185–213.
Leakey, M. D. and R. L. Hay
  1979   "Pliocene Footprints in Laetolil Beds at Laetoli, Northern Tanzania." *Nature*, 278:317–323.
Leakey, Meave G., Fred Spoor, Frank H. Brown, et al.
  2001   "New Hominin Genus from Eastern Africa Shows Diverse Middle Pliocene Lineages." *Nature*, 410:433–440.
Leakey, Meave G. et al.
  1995   "New Four-Million-Year-Old Hominid Species from Kanapoi: and Allia Bay, Kenya." *Nature*, 376:565–571.
Legge, Anthony J.
  1972   "Prehistoric Exploitation of Gazelle in Palestine." *In: Papers in Economic Prehistory*, E. S. Higgs (ed.), Cambridge: Cambridge University Press, pp. 119–124.
Legge, Anthony J. and Peter A. Rowley-Conwy
  1987   "Gazelle Killing in Stone Age Syria." *Scientific American*, 257(2):88–95.
Lehner, Mark
  1997   *The Complete Pyramids*. New York: Thames & Hudson.
Lerner, I. M. and W. J. Libby
  1976   *Heredity, Evolution, and Society*. San Francisco: W. H. Freeman.
Leroi-Gourhan, André
  1986   "The Hands of Gargas." *October* 37:18–34

Lewin, Roger
1986 "Damage to Tropical Forests, or Why Were There So Many Kinds of Animals?" *Science*, **234**:149–150.

Lewontin, R. C.
1972 "The Apportionment of Human Diversity." *In: Evolutionary Biology* (Vol. 6), T. Dobzhansky et al. (eds.), New York: Plenum, pp. 381–398.

Lieberman, Daniel, David R. Pilbeam, and Bernard A. Wood
1988 "A Probabilistic Approach to the Problem of Sexual Dimorphism in *Homo habilis*: A Comparison of KNM-ER-1470 and KNM-ER-1813." *Journal of Human Evolution*, **17**:503–511.

Linnaeus, C.
1758 *Systema Naturae.*

Lisowski, F. P.
1984 "Introduction." *In: The Evolution of the East African Environment.* Centre of Asian Studies Occasional Papers and Monographs, **59**, R. O. Whyte (ed.), Hong Kong: University of Hong Kong, pp. 777–786.

Livingstone, Frank B.
1980 "Natural Selection and the Origin and Maintenance of Standard Genetic Marker Systems." *Yearbook of Physical Anthropology*, **23**:25–42.

Lovejoy, C. O.
1993 "Modeling Human Origins: Are We Sexy Because We're Smart, or Smart Because We're Sexy?" *In:* D. T. Rasmussen (ed.), q.v., pp. 1–28.

Lowe, Gareth W.
1989 "The Heartland Olmec: Evolution of Material Culture." *In:* R. J. Sharer and D. C. Grove (eds.), q.v., pp. 33–67.

Loy, Thomas H. and E. James Dixon
1998 "Blood Residues on Fluted Points from Eastern Beringia." *American Antiquity,* **63**(1): 21–46.

Lucero, Lisa. J.
1999 "Classic Lowland Maya Political Organization: A Review." *Journal of World Prehistory,* **13**(2):211–263.

Lundelius, Ernest L., Jr. and Russell Graham
1999 "The Weather Changed." *Discovering Archaeology,* **1**(5):48–53.

Lynch, Thomas F.
1983 "The Paleo-Indians." *In: Ancient South Americans,* J. D. Jennings (ed.), San Francisco: W. H. Freeman, pp. 87–137.

_____
1990 "Glacial-Age Man in South America? A Critical Review." *American Antiquity,* **55**(1):12–36.

_____ (ed.)
1980 *Guitarrero Cave.* New York: Academic Press.

MacKinnon, J. and K. MacKinnon
1980 "The Behavior of Wild Spectral Tarsiers." *International Journal of Primatology,* **1**:361–379.

MacNeish, Richard S.
1964 "Ancient Mesoamerican Civilization." *Science,* **143**:531–537.

_____
1967 "A Summary of the Subsistence." *In:* D. S. Byers (ed.), q.v., pp. 290–310.

_____
1978 *The Science of Archaeology?* North Scituate, MA: Duxbury Press.

MacNeish, Richard S., et al.
1972 *The Prehistory of the Tehuacán Valley. Vol. 5: Excavations and Reconnaissance.* Austin: University of Texas Press.

Marcus, Joyce
1993 *Mesoamerican Writing Systems: Propaganda, Myth, and History in Four Ancient Civilizations.* Princeton, NJ: Princeton University Press.

Marcus, Joyce and Kent V. Flannery
1996 *The Zapotec Civilization.* New York: Thames & Hudson.

Marlar, Jennifer E. and Richard A. Marlar
2000 "Cannibals at Cowboy Wash; Biomolecular Archaeology Solves a Controversial Puzzle." *Discovering Archaeology,* **2**(5):30–36.

Marshack, A.
1972 *The Roots of Civilization.* New York: McGraw-Hill.

_____
1989 "Evolution of the Human Capacity: The Symbolic Evidence." *Yearbook of Physical Anthropology,* **32**:1–34.

Martin, Paul S.
1967 "Prehistoric Overkill." *In: Pleistocene Extinctions: The Search for a Cause,* P. S. Martin and H. E. Wright, Jr. (eds.), New Haven: Yale University Press, pp. 75–120.

_____
1982 "The Pattern of Meaning of Holarctic Mammoth Extinction." *In: Paleoecology of Beringia,* D. Hopkins, J. Matthews, C. Schweger, and S. Young (eds.), New York: Academic Press, pp. 399–408.

_____
1999 "The Time of the Hunters." *Discovering Archaeology,* **1**(5):40–47.

Mason, J. Alden
1968 *The Ancient Civilizations of Peru* (Rev. Ed.). London: Penguin Books.

Mayer, Peter
1982 "Evolutionary Advantages of Menopause." *Human Ecology,* **10**:477–494.

Mayr, Ernst
1970 *Population, Species, and Evolution.* Cambridge: Harvard University Press.

McConkey, Edwin H. and Ajit Varki
2000 "A primate genome project deserves high priority." Letters. *Science,* **289**:1295.

McGhee, Robert
1996 *Ancient People of the Arctic.* Vancouver: University of British Columbia Press.

McGrew, W. C.
1992 *Chimpanzee Material Culture. Implications for Human Evolution.* Cambridge: Cambridge University Press

_____
1998 "Culture in Nonhuman Primates?" *Annual Reviews of Anthropology,* **27**:301–328.

McHenry, Henry
1988 "New Estimates of Body Weight in Early Hominids and Their Significance to Encephalization and Megadontia in 'Robust' Australopithecines." *In:* F. E. Grine (ed.), q.v., pp. 133–148.

_____
1992a "Body Size and Proportions in Early Hominids." *American Journal of Physical Anthropology,* **87**:407–431.

_____
1992b "How Big Were Early Hominids?" *Evolutionary Anthropology,* **1**:15–20.

McKern, T. W. and T. D. Stewart
1957 "Age Changes in Young American Males, Technical Report EP-45." Natick, MA: U.S. Army Quartermaster Research and Development Center.

McNett, Charles W., Jr. (ed.)
1985 *Shawnee-Minisink: A Stratified Paleoindian-Archaic Site in the Upper Delaware Valley.* Orlando: Academic Press.

McRae, M.
1997 "Road Kill in Cameroon." *Natural History,* **106**:36–47.

Meadow, Richard H. and Jonathan M. Kenoyer
2000 "The Indus Valley Mystery." *Discovering Archaeology,* **2**(2):38–43.

Meehan, Betty
1982   *Shell Bed to Shell Midden*. Canberra: Australian Institute of Aboriginal Studies.

Mellaart, James
1975   *The Earlier Civilizations of the Near East*. London: Thames & Hudson.

Mellars, Paul and Petra Dark
1999   *Star Carr in Context: New Archaeological and Palaeoecological Investigations at the Early Mesolithic Site of Star Carr, North Yorkshire*. McDonald Institute Monographs. London: David Brown.

Mellars, P. and C. Stringer (eds.)
1989   *The Human Revolution*. Princeton, NJ: Princeton University Press.

Meltzer, David J.
1993a   "Is There a Clovis Adaptation?" *In:* Soffer and Praslov (eds.), q.v., pp. 293–310.

_____
1993b   *Search for the First Americans*. Washington, DC: Smithsonian Books.

Meltzer, David, James Adovasio, and Tom D. Dillehay
1994   "On a Pleistocene Human Occupation at Pedra Furada, Brazil." *Antiquity*, **68**:695–714.

Meltzer, David J. et al.
1997   "On the Pleistocene Antiquity of Monte Verde, Southern Chile." *American Antiquity*, **62**(4): 659–663.

Merriwether, D. Andrew, Francisco Rothhammer, and Robert E. Ferrell
1995   "Distribution of the Four Founding Lineage Haplotypes in Native Americans Suggests a Single Wave of Migration for the New World." *American Journal of Physical Anthropology*, **98**(4): 411–430.

Millon, René
1988   "The Last Years of Teotihuacán Dominance." *In: The Collapse of Ancient States and Civilizations*. N. Yoffee and G. Cowgill (eds.), Tucson: University of Arizona Press, pp. 102–164.

Moctezuma, Eduardo Matos
1988   *The Great Temple of the Aztecs*. New York: Thames & Hudson.

Molnar, Stephen
1983   *Human Variation. Races, Types, and Ethnic Groups* (2nd Ed.). Englewood Cliffs: Prentice-Hall.

Montet, Pierre
1981   *Everyday Life in Egypt in the Days of Ramesses the Great*. Philadelphia: University of Pennsylvania Press.

Moore, Andrew M. T.
1985   "The Development of Neolithic Societies in the Near East." *Advances in World Archaeology*, **4**:1–69.

_____
2000   *Village on the Euphrates: The Excavation of Abu Hureyra*. New York: Oxford University Press.

Moore, Lorna G. and Judith G. Regensteiner
1983   "Adaptation to High Altitude." *Annual Reviews of Anthropology*, **12**:285–304.

Moore, Lorna G. et al.
1994   "Genetic Adaptation to High Altitude." *In: Sports and Exercise Medicine*, S. C. Wood and R. C. Roach (eds.), New York: Marcel Dekker, pp. 225–262.

Moratto, Michael J.
1984   *California Archaeology*. New York: Academic Press.

Morin, Phillip A., James J. Moore, Ranajit Chakraborty, et al.
1994   "Kin Selection, Social Structure, Gene Flow, and the Evolution of Chimpanzees." *Science*, **265**:1193–1201.

Morris, Craig
1988   "A City Fit for an Inka." *Archaeology*, **41**(5):43–49.

Moseley, Michael E.
1975   *The Maritime Foundations of Andean Civilization*. Menlo Park: Cummings Publishing Company.

_____
1983   "Central Andean Civilization." *In: Ancient South Americans*, J. D. Jennings (ed.), San Francisco: W. H. Freeman, pp. 179–239.

_____
1992   *The Incas and Their Ancestors*. New York: Thames & Hudson.

Moseley, Michael E. and Kent Day (eds.)
1982   *Chan Chan: Andean Desert City*. Albuquerque: University of New Mexico Press.

Mountain, Joanna L., Alice A. Lin, Anne M. Bowcock, and L. L. Cavalli-Sforza
1994   "Evolution of Modern Humans: Evidence From Nuclear DNA Polymorphisms." *In:* M. J. Aitken et al. (eds.), q.v., pp. 69–83.

Murdock, George Peter
1959   *Africa: Its Peoples and Their Culture History*. New York: McGraw-Hill.

Murra, John V.
1972   "El 'control vertical' de una maximo de pisos ecologicos en la economia de los sociedades andines." *In: Vista de la Provincia de Leon de Huanaco (1562)*, J. V. Murra (ed.), Huanaco, Peru: Universidad Nacional Hermilio Valdizen, vol. 2, pp. 427–476.

Napier, J. R.
1967   "The Antiquity of Human Walking." *Scientific American*, **216**:56–66.

Napier, J. R. and P. H. Napier
1967   *A Handbook of Living Primates*. New York: Academic Press.

_____
1985   *The Natural History of the Primates*. London: British Museum (Natural History).

Nishida, T.
1968   "The Social Group of Wild Chimpanzees in the Mahale Mountains." *Primates*, **9**:167–224.

_____
1979   "The Social Structure of Chimpanzees of the Mahale Mountains." *In: The Great Apes*, D. A. Hamburg and E. R. McCown (eds.), Menlo Park: Benjamin Cummings, pp. 73–122.

Nishida, T., R. W. Wrangham, J. Goodall, and S. Uehara
1983   "Local Differences in Plant-feeding Habits of Chimpanzees between the Mahale Mountains and Gombe National Park, Tanzania. *Journal of Human Evolution*, **12**:467–480.

Nissen, Hans J.
1988   *The Early History of the Ancient Near East, 9000–2000 B.C.* Chicago: University of Chicago Press.

Noe, R., and R. Bshary
1997   "The Formation of Red Colobus-Diana Monkey Associations under Predation Pressure from Chimpanzees." *Proceedings of the Royal Society of London (B) Bioliogical Science*, **264**(1379):253–259.

Normille, D.
1997   "Yangtze Seen As Earliest Rice Site." *Science*, **275**:309.

Oakley, Kenneth
1963   "Analytical Methods of Dating Bones." *In: Science in Archaeology*, D. Brothwell and E. Higgs (eds.). New York: Basic Books, Inc.

O'Connor, Terry
2000   *The Archaeology of Animal Bones*. College Station, TX: Texas A&M University Press.

Odell, George H.
1998   "Investigating Correlates of Sedentism and
        Domestication in Prehistoric North America."
        American Antiquity, **63**(4):553–571.
Olliaro, Piero
1996   "Malaria, the Submerged Disease." *Journal of the
        American Medical Association*, **275**(3):230–233.
Olsen, Stanley J.
1985   *Origins of the Domestic Dog: The Fossil Record*. Tucson:
        University of Arizona Press.
Ovinnikov, Igor V., Anders Götherström, Galina P. Romanova, et al.
2000   "Molecular Analysis of Neanderthal DNA from the
        Northern Caucasus." *Nature*, **404**:490–493.
Owsley, Douglas W. and Richard L. Jantz
2000   "Biography in the Bones." *Discovering Archaeology*,
        2(1):56–58.

Parés, Josef M. and Alfredo Pérez-González
1995   "Paleomagnetic Age for Hominid Fossils at Atapuerca
        Archaeological Site, Spain." *Science*, **269**:830–832.
Parfit, Michael
2000   "Hunt for the First Americans." *National Geographic*,
        198(6):40–67.
Parpola, Asko
1994   *Deciphering the Indus Script*. Cambridge: Cambridge
        University Press.
Pauketat, Timothy R. and Thomas E. Emerson
1997   *Cahokia: Domination and Ideology in the Mississippian
        World*. Lincoln, NE: University of Nebraska Press.
Peres, C. A.
1990   "Effects of hunting on Western Amazonian primate
        communities." *Biological Conservation* **54**:47–59.
Phillips, K. A.
1998   "Tool use in Wild Capuchin Monkeys." *American Journal
        of Primatology*, **46**(3):259–261.
Phillipson, David W.
1984   "Early Food Production in Central and Southern Africa."
        In: J. D. Clark and S. A. Brandt (eds.), q.v., pp. 272–280.
Piggott, Stuart
1965   *Ancient Europe*. Chicago: Aldine.
Pinner, Robert W., Steven M. Teutsch, Lone Simonson, et al.
1996   "Trends in Infectious Diseases Mortality in the United
        States." *Journal of the American Medical Association*,
        275(3):189–193.
Piperno, Dolores R.
1988   *Phytolith Analysis: An Archaeological and Geological
        Perspective*. New York: Academic Press.
Piperno. Dolores and Deborah M. Pearsall
1998   *The Origins of Agriculture in the Lowland Neotropics*. San
        Diego: Academic Press.
Plog, Stephen
1997   *Ancient People of the American Southwest*. New York:
        Thames & Hudson.
Pope, G. G.
1984   "The Antiquity and Paleoenvironment of the Asian
        Hominidae." *In*: *The Evolution of the East Asian
        Environment*. Center of Asian Studies Occasional Papers
        and Monographs, No. 59, R. O. Whyte (ed.), Hong Kong:
        University of Hong Kong, pp. 822–847.
Possehl, Gregory L.
1990   "Revolution in the Urban Revolution: The Emergence of
        Indus Urbanization." *Annual Review of Anthropology*,
        19:261–282.

——— 1996   *Indus Age: The Writing System*. Philadelphia: University of
        Pennsylvania Press.

——— 1999   *Indus Age: The Beginnings*. Philadelphia: University of
        Pennsylvania Press.
Potts, Richard
1991   "Why the Oldowan? Plio-Pleistocene Toolmaking and
        the Transport of Resources." *Journal of Anthropological
        Research*, **47**:153–176.

——— 1993   "Archeological Interpretations of Early Hominid
        Behavior and Ecology." *In*: *The Origin and Evolution of
        Humans and Humanness*, D. T. Rasmussen (ed.), q.v.,
        pp. 49–74.
Potts, Richard and Pat Shipman
1981   "Cutmarks Made by Stone Tools from Olduvai Gorge,
        Tanzania. *Nature*, **291**:577–580.
Powledge, Tabitha M. and Mark Rose
1996   "The Great DNA Hunt." *Archaeology,* **29** (Sept./Oct.):
        36–44.
Pozorski, Shelia and Thomas Pozorski
1988   *Early Settlement and Subsistence in the Casma Valley, Peru*.
        Iowa City, IA: University of Iowa Press.
Pozorski, Thomas and Shelia Pozorski
1987   "Chavín, the Early Horizon, and the Initial Period."
        In: J. Haas et al. (eds.), q.v., pp. 36–46.
Prescott, William H.
1906   *History of the Conquest of Peru*. New York:
        Everyman's Library.
Price. T. Douglas
1995   "Social Inequality at the Origins of Agriculture."
        In: *Foundations of Social Inequality*, T. Douglas Price
        and Gary M. Feinman (eds.), New York: Plenum,
        pp. 129–151.

——— 2000   "Tracing the Migrants' Trail." *Discovering Archaeology*,
        2(4): 26–31.
Price, T. Douglas and Erik B. Petersen
1987   "A Mesolithic Camp in Denmark." *Scientific American*,
        265(3):113–121.
Proctor, Robert
1988   "From Anthropologie to Rassenkunde." *In*: *Bones, Bodies,
        Behavior. History of Anthropology* (Vol. 5), 6, W. Stocking,
        Jr. (ed.), Madison: University of Wisconsin Press,
        pp. 138–179.
Protzen, Jean-Pierre
1986   "Inca Stonemasonry." *Scientific American*, **254**(2):94–105.
Pulak, Cemal M.
1994   "1994 Excavation at Uluburnum: The Final Campaign."
        Institute for Nautical Archaeology Quarterly, **21**(4):21–34.

Rak, Y.
1983   *The Australopithecine Face*. New York: Academic Press.
Rasmussen, D. T. (ed.)
1993   *The Origin and Evolution of Humans and Humanness*.
        Boston: Jones and Bartlett.
Rathje, William
1971   "The Origin and Development of Lowland Classic Maya
        Civilization." *American Antiquity*, **36**(3):275–285.
Redman, Charles L.
1978   *The Rise of Civilization*. San Francisco: W. H. Freeman.
Reinhard, K. I. and Vaughan M. Bryant
1992   "Coprolite Analysis." *Archaeological Method and Theory*,
        14:245–288.
Relethford, John H. and Henry C. Harpending
1994   "Craniometric Variation, Genetic Theory, and Modern
        Human Origins." *American Journal of Physical
        Anthropology*, **95**:249–270.

Renfrew, Colin
1972   *The Emergence of Civilisation: The Cyclades and the Aegean in the Third Millenium B.C.* London: Methuen.

———
1983   "The Social Archaeology of Megalithic Monuments." *Scientific American,* 249(5):152–163.

Rice, Don, Arthur A. Demarest, and Prudence M. Rice
2001   *The Terminal Classic in the Maya Lowlands: Collapse, Transition, and Transformation.* Boulder, CO: Westview Press.

Richards, Martin, Melna Côrte-Real, Peter Forster, et al.
1996   "Paleolithic and Neolithic Lineages in the European Mitochondrial Gene Pool." *American Journal of Human Genetics,* 59(1):185–203.

Rightmire, G. P.
1981   "Patterns in the Evolution of *Homo erectus.*" *Paleobiology,* 7:241–246.

———
1990   *The Evolution of Homo erectus.* New York: Cambridge University Press.

———
1998   "Human Evolution in the Middle Pleistocene: The Role of *Homo heidelbergensis.*" *Evolutionary Anthropology,* 6:218–227.

Rindos, David
1984   *The Origins of Agriculture: An Evolutionary Perspective.* Orlando: Academic Press.

Roaf, Michael
1996   *Cultural Atlas of Mesopotamia and the Ancient Near East.* New York: Facts on File.

Roberts, Charlotte, with Keith Manchester
1997   *The Archaeology of Disease.* (2nd Ed.), Ithaca, NY: Cornell University Press.

Roberts, D. F.
1973   *Climate and Human Variability.* An Addison-Wesley Module in Anthropology, No. 34. Reading, MA: Addison-Wesley.

Roberts, Richard, Rhys Jones, and M. A. Smith
1990   "Thermoluminescence Dating of a 50,000-Year-Old Human Occupation Site in Northern Australia." *Nature,* 345:153–156.

Robinson, William J.
1990   "Tree-Ring Studies of the Pueblo de Acoma." *Historical Archaeology,* 24(3):99–106).

Rodman, P. S.
1973   "Population Composition and Adaptive Organisation among Orangutans of the Kutai Reserve." *In: Comparative Ecology and Behaviour of Primates,* R. P. Michael and J. H. Crook (eds.), London: Academic Press, pp.171–209.

Romer, Alfred S.
1959   *The Vertebrate Story.* Chicago: University of Chicago Press.

Roosevelt, Anna C. et al.
1996   "Paleoindian Cave Dwellers in the Amazon: The Peopling of the Americas." *Science,* 272 (19 April): 373–384.

Rose, M. D.
1991   "Species Recognition in Eocene Primates." *American Journal of Physical Anthropology,* Supplement 12, p. 153.

Rothschild, Nan A.
1979   "Mortuary Behavior and Social Organization at Indian Knoll and Dickson Mounds," *American Antiquity,* 44:658–675.

Ruben, John A., Christina Dal Sasso, Nicholas Geist, et al.
1999   "Pulmonary Function and Metabolic Physiology of Theropod Dinosaurs." *Science,* 283:514–516.

Ruff, C. B. and Alan Walker
1993   "Body Size and Body Shape." *In:* A. Walker and R. Leakey (eds.), q.v., pp. 234–265.

Ruhlen, M.
1994   "Linguistic Evidence for the Peopling of the Americas." *In: Method and Theory for Investigating the Peopling of the Americas,* Robson Bonnichsen and D. Gentry Steele (eds.), Corvallis, OR: Oregon State University, pp. 177–188.

Ruvolo, M., D. Pan, S. Zehr, T. Goldberg, et al.
1994   "Gene Trees and Hominoid Phylogeny." *Proceedings of the National Academy of Sciences,* 91:8900–8904.

Sabloff, Jeremy A. and William L. Rathje
1975   "The Rise of a Maya Merchant Class." *Scientific American,* 233(4):72–82.

Samuels, Stephen R. (ed.)
1991   *Ozette Archaeological Project Research Reports.* Pullman, WA: Washington State University.

Sandweiss, D. H., et al.
1996   "Geoarchaeological Evidence from Peru for a 5000 Years B.P. Onset of El Niño." *Science,* 273:1531–1533.

Sauer, Jonathan D.
1994   *Historical Geography of Crop Plants: A Select Roster.* Boca Raton: CRC Press.

Saunders, Joe W. et al.
1997   "A Mound Complex in Louisiana at 5400-5000 Years Before Present." *Science,* 277:1796–1799.

Savage-Rumbaugh, E. S.
1986   *Ape Language: From Conditioned Responses to Symbols.* New York: Columbia University Press.

Savage-Rumbaugh, S., K. McDonald, R. A. Sevic, W. D. Hopkins, and E. Rubert
1986a   "Spontaneous Symbol Acquisition and Communicative Use by Pygmy Chimpanzees (*Pan paniscus*)." *Journal of Experimental Psychology: General,* vol. 115, no. 3. pp. 211–235.

Savage-Rumbaugh, S. and R. Lewin
1994   *Kanzi. The Ape at the Brink of the Human Mind.* New York: John Wiley and Sons.

Schaller, George B.
1963   *The Mountain Gorilla.* Chicago: University of Chicago Press.

Schele, Linda and David Freidel
1990   *A Forest of Kings.* New York: William R. Morrow.

Schele, Linda and Mary Ellen Miller
1986   *The Blood of Kings: Dynasty and Ritual in Maya Art.* Fort Worth: Kimbell Art Museum.

Schoeninger, Margaret J.
1981   "The Agricultural 'Revolution': Its Effect on Human Diet in Prehistoric Iran and Israel." *Paléorient,* 7:73–92.

Schoeninger, M. J., M. J. Deniro, and H. Tauber
1983   "Stable Nitrogen Isotope Ratios of Bone Collagen Reflect Marine and Terrestrial Components of Prehistoric Human Diet." *Science,* 220:1381–1383.

Schurr, Theodore G.
2000   "The Story in the Genes." *Discovering Archaeology,* 2(1):59–60.

Schurr, T. G. et al.
1990   "Amerindian Mitochondrial DNAs Have Rare Asian Mutations at High Frequencies Suggesting a Limited Number of Founders." *American Journal of Human Genetics,* 46: 613–623.

Schwartzman, Stephen
1997   *Fires in the Amazon: An Analysis of NOAA-12 Satellite Data, 1996-1997.* Washington DC: Environmental Defense Fund.

Scott, K.
1980 "Two Hunting Episodes of Middle Paleolithic Age at La Cotte Saint-Brelade, Jersey (Channel Islands)." *World Archaeology*, **12**:137–152.

Sebastian, Lynne
1992 *The Chaco Anasazi: Sociopolitical Evolution in the Prehistoric Southwest*. Cambridge: Cambridge University Press.

Semaw, S., P. Renne, W. K. Harris, et al.
1997 "2.5-million-year-old Stone Tools from Gona, Ethiopia." *Nature*, **385**:333–336.

Senut, Brigette and Christine Tardieu
1985 "Functional Aspects of Plio-Pleistocene Hominid Limb Bones: Implications for Taxonomy and Phylogeny." *In: Ancestors: The Hard Evidence*, E. Delson (ed.), New York: Alan R. Liss, pp. 193–201.

Service, Alastair and Jean Bradbery
1997 *The Standing Stones of Europe: A Guide to the Great Megalithic Monuments*. (Rev. Ed.) London: Weidenfeld and Nicolson.

Seyfarth, Robert M.
1987 "Vocal Communication and its Relation to Language." *In:* Smuts et al., (eds), q.v., pp. 440–451.

Seyfarth, Robert M., Dorothy L. Cheney, and Peter Marler
1980a "Monkey Responses to Three Different Alarm Calls." *Science*, **210**:801–803.

_____
1980b "Vervet Monkey Alarm Calls." *Animal Behavior*, **28**:1070–1094.

Shackley, M. Steven (ed.)
1998 *Archaeological Obsidian Studies*. Berkeley and Los Angeles, CA: University of California Press.

Shaffer, Brian S. and Barry W. Baker
1997 "How Many Epidermal Ridges Per Linear Centimeter: Comments on Possible Pre-Clovis Human Friction Skin Prints from Pendejo Cave." *American Antiquity*, **62**(3):559–560.

Sharer, Robert J.
1996 *Daily Life in Maya Civilization*. Westport, CT: Greenwood Press.

Sharer, Robert J. and David C. Grove (eds.)
1989 *Regional Perspectives on the Olmec*. Cambridge: Cambridge University Press.

Sheets, Payson D.
1994 "Tropical Time Capsule." *Archaeology*, **47**(4):30–33.

Sherratt, A.
1981 "Plough and Pastoralism: Aspects of the Secondary Products Revolution." *In: Patterns of the Past: Studies in Honour of David Clarke*. Cambridge: Cambridge University Press, pp. 261–305.

Sibley, Charles and Jon E. Ahlquist
1984 "The Phylogeny of the Hominoid Primates as Indicated by DNA-DNA Hybridization." *Journal of Molecular Evolution*, **20**:2–15.

Sigurdsson, Haraldur
1999 *Melting the Earth: The History of Ideas on Volcanic Eruptions*. Oxford: Oxford University Press.

Simmons, Alan H.
1986 "New Evidence for the Use of Cultigens in the American Southwest." *American Antiquity*, **51**:73–89.

Simmons, J. G.
1989 *Changing the Face of the Earth*. Oxford: Basil Blackwell Ltd.

Simons, E.L.
1972 *Primate Evolution*. New York: Macmillan.

_____
1992 "Diversity in the Early Tertiary Anthropoidean Radiation in Africa." *Proceedings of the National Academy of Sciences, USA*, **89**:10743–10747.

Skelton, R. R., H. M. McHenry, and G. M. Drawhorn
1986 "Phylogenetic Analysis of Early Hominids." *Current Anthropology*, **27**:1–43; 361–365.

Slayman, A.
1997 "A Battle Over Bones." *Archaeology*, **50** (Jan./Feb.): 16–20.

Smith, Andrew
1992 "Pastoralism in Africa." *Annual Review of Anthropology*, **21**:125–141.

Smith, Andrew, Penny Berens, Candy Malherbe, and Matt Guenther
2000 *The Bushmen of Southern Africa: A Foraging Society in Transition*. Athens, OH: Ohio University Press.

Smith, Bruce D.
1985 "The Role of *Chenopodium* As a Domesticate in Pre-Maize Garden Systems of the Eastern United States." *Southwestern Archaeology*, **4**:51–72.

_____
1989 "Origins of Agriculture in Eastern North America." *Science*, **246**:1566–1571.

_____
1995 *Emergence of Agriculture*. New York: Scientific American Library.

_____
1997 "Reconsidering the Ocampo Caves and the Era of Incipient Cultivation in Mesoamerica." *Latin American Antiquity*, **8**: 342–383.

Smith, Christopher
1998 *Late Stone Age Hunters of the British Isles*. London: Routledge.

Smith, Fred H.
1984 "Fossil Hominids from the Upper Pleistocene of Central Europe and the Origin of Modern Europeans." *In: The Origins of Modern Humans*, F. H. Smith and F. Spencer (eds.), New York: Alan R. Liss, pp. 187–209.

Smith, Fred H., A. B. Falsetti, and S. M. Donnelly
1989 "Modern Human Origins." *Yearbook of Physical Anthropology*, **32**:35–68.

Smith, Fred H., Erik Trinkaus, Paul B. Pettitt, et al.
1999 "Direct Radiocarbon Dates for Vindija G_1 and Velika Pécina Late Pleistocene Hominid Remains." *Proceedings of the National Academy of Sciences*, **96**:12281–12286.

Smith, Patricia, Ofer Bar-Yosef, and Andrew Sillen
1984 "Archaeological and Skeletal Evidence for Dietary Change During the Late Pleistocene/Early Holocene in the Levant." *In:* Cohen and Armelagos (eds.), q.v., pp. 101–136.

Smuts, B. B.
1985 *Sex and Friendship in Baboons*. Hawthorne, NY: Aldine.

Smuts, B. et al. (eds.)
1987 *Primate Societies*. Chicago: University of Chicago Press.

Snow, Dean R.
1980 *The Archaeology of New England*. New York: Academic Press.

Soffer, Olga, and N. D. Praslov (eds.)
1993 *From Kostenki to Clovis: Upper Paleolithic—Paleo-Indian Adaptations*. New York: Plenum Press.

Stanford, C. B., J. Wallis, H. Matama, and J. Goodall
1994 "Patterns of Predation by Chimpanzees on Red Colobus Monkeys in Gombe National Park." *American Journal of Physical Anthropology*, **94**(2):213–228.

Steele, D. Gentry
2000 "The Skeleton's Tale." *Discovering Archaeology*, **2**(1): 61–62.

Steklis, Horst D.
1985 "Primate Communication, Comparative Neurology, and the Origin of Language Re-examined." *Journal of Human Evolution*, **14**:157–173.

Stocker, Terry, Sarah Meltzoff, and Steve Armsey
1980   "Crocodilians and Olmecs: Further Interpretations in Formative Period Iconography." *American Antiquity*, **45**:740–758.

Stoneking, Mark
1993   "DNA and Recent Human Evolution." *Evolutionary Anthropology*, **2**:60–73.

Straughan, Baird
1991   "The Secrets of Ancient Tiwanaku Are Benefiting Today's Bolivia." *Smithsonian*, **21**(11):38–49.

Straus, Lawrence Guy
1993   "Southwestern Europe at the Last Glacial Maximum." *Current Anthropology*, **32**:189–199.

_____
1995   "The Upper Paleolithic of Europe: An Overview." *Evolutionary Antrhopology*, **4**:4–16.

Strier, Karen B.
1999   *Primate Behavioral Ecology*. Boston: Allyn and Bacon.

Stringer, C. B. and P. Andrews
1988   "Genetic and Fossil Evidence for the Origin of Modern Humans." *Science*, **239**:1263–1268.

Struever, Stuart
1964   "The Hopewell Interaction Sphere in Riverine-Western Great Lakes Culture History." *In: Hopewellian Studies*, J. Caldwell and R. Hall (eds.), Springfield, Illinois, State Museum Scientific Papers, **12**:87–106.

Strum, S. C.
1987   *Almost Human. A Journey into the World of Baboons*. New York: W. W. Norton.

Suarez, B. K., J. D. Crouse, D. H. O'Rourke
1985   "Genetic Variation in North Amerindian Populations: The Geography of Gene Frequencies." *American Journal of Physical Anthropology*, **67**(3):217–232.

Sugiyama, Y. and J. Koman
1979   "Tool-using and -making Behavior in Wild Chimpanzees at Bossou, Guinea." *Primates*, **20**:513–524.

Susman, Randall L.
1988   "New Postcranial Remains from Swartkrans and Their Bearing on the Functional Morphology and Behavior of *Paranthropus robustus*." *In:* F. E. Grine (ed.), q.v., pp. 149–172.

Susman, Randall L.(ed.)
1984   *The Pygmy Chimpanzee: Evolutionary Biology and Behavior*. New York: Plenum Press.

Susman, Randall L., Jack T. Stern and William L. Jungers
1985   "Locomotor Adaptations in the Hadar Hominids." *In: Ancestors: The Hard Evidence*, E. Delson (ed.), New York: Alan R. Liss, pp. 184–192.

Sussman, Robert W.
1991   "Primate Origins and the Evolution of Angiosperms." *American Journal. of Primatology*, **23**:209–223.

Swisher, C. C. III, G. H. Curtis, T. Jacob, et al.
1994   "Age of the Earliest Known Hominids in Java, Indonesia." *Science*, **263**:1118–1121.

Swisher, C. C. III, W. J. Rink, S. C. Anton, et al.
1996   "Latest *Homo erectus* of Java: Potential Contemporaneity with *Homo sapiens* in Southwest Java." *Science*, **274**:1870–1874.

Szalay, Frederick S. and Eric Delson
1979   *Evolutionary History of the Primates*. New York: Academic Press.

Tagg, Martyn D.
1996   "Early Cultigens from Fresnal Shelter, Southeastern New Mexico." *American Antiquity*, **61**(2): 311–24.

Tattersal, Ian, Eric Delson, and John Van Couvering
1988   *Encyclopedia of Human Evolution and Prehistory*. New York: Garland Publishing.

Taylor, R. E. and M. J. Aitken
1997   *Chronometric Dating in Archaeology*. New York: Plenum.

Templeton, Alan R.
1996   "Gene Lineages and Human Evolution." *Science*, **272**:1363–1364.

Thieme, Hartmut
1997   "Lower Palaeolithic Hunting Spears from Germany." *Nature*, **385**:807–810.

Thomas, David H.
1985   *The Archaeology of Hidden Cave, Nevada*. Anthropological Papers of the American Museum of Natural History, 61, pt. 1. New York.

_____
2000   *Skull Wars: Archaeology and the Search for Native American Identity*. New York: Basic Books.

Thorne, A. G. and M. H. Wolpoff
1992   "The Multiregional Evolution of Humans." *Scientific American*, **266**:76–83.

Thorsby, Erik
1997   "Invited Anniversary Review: HLA Associated Diseases." *Human Immunology*, **53**:1–11.

Tiemel, Chen, Yang Quan, and Wu En
1994   "Antiquity of *Homo sapiens* in China." *Nature*, **368**:55–56.

Tishkoft, S. A., E. Dietzsch, W. Speed, et al.
1996   "Global Patterns of Linkage Disequilibrium at the CD4 Locus and Modern Human Origins." *Science*, **271**:1380–1387.

Tobias, Phillip
1971   *The Brain in Hominid Evolution*. New York: Columbia University Press.

_____
1983   "Recent Advances in the Evolution of the Hominids with Especial Reference to Brain and Speech." Pontifical Academy of Sciences, *Scrita Varia*, **50**:85–140.
1991   *Olduvai Gorge, Volume IV. The Skulls, Endocasts and Teeth of* Homo habilis. Cambridge: Cambridge University Press.

Todd, T. W.
1920–21 "Age Changes in the Pubic Bone." *American Journal of Physical Anthropology*, **3**:285–334; **4**:1–70.

Townsend, Richard F.
1992   *The Aztecs*. New York: Thames & Hudson.

Traverse, Alfred
1988   *Paleopalynology*. Boston: Unwyn Hyman.

Trigger, Bruce G., Barry J. Kemp, David O'Connor, and Alan B. Lloyd
1983   *Ancient Egypt: A Social History*. Cambridge: Cambridge University Press.

Tringham, Ruth
1971   *Hunters, Fishers, and Farmers of Eastern Europe, 6000–3000 B.C.* London: Hutchinson University Library.

Trinkaus, Erik and Pat Shipman
1992   *The Neandertals*. New York: Alfred A. Knopf.

Turner, Christy G.
1987   "Telltale Teeth." *Natural History*, **96**(1):6–10.

Turner, Christy G. and Jacqueline A. Turner
1999   *Man Corn: Cannibalism and Violence in the American Southwest and Mexico*. Salt Lake City: University of Utah Press.

Tuttle, Russell H.
1990   "Apes of the World." *American Scientist*, **78**:115–125.

United Nations Economic Commission for Europe/European Commission (EC-UN/ECE)
1996   Forest Conditions in Europe. Results of the 1995 Survey (EC-UN/ECE). Brussels.

Van Noten, Francis and Jan Raymaekers
1987   "Early Iron Smelting in Central Africa." *Scientific American*, **258**(6):104–111.

Varki, A.
2000   "A Chimpanzee Genome Project Is a Biomedical Imperative." *Genome Research*, **8**:1065–1070.

Verrengia, Joseph B.
1999   "First Americans from Europe? Study Clouds Asian Land Bridge Theory." The Associated Press (wire story), November 1, 1999.

Villa, Paola
1983   *Terra Amata and the Middle Pleistocene Archaeological Record of Southern France*. University of California Publications in Anthropology, Vol. 13, Berkeley: University of California Press.

Von Koenigswald, G. H. R.
1956   *Meeting Prehistoric Man*. New York: Harper & Brothers.

Vrba, E. S.
1988   "Late Pliocene Climatic Events and Hominid Evolution." *In:* F. Grine (ed.), q.v., pp. 405–426.

Walker, A.
1991   "The Origin of the Genus *Homo*." *In: Evolution of Life*, S. Osawa and T. Honjo (eds.), Tokyo: Springer-Verlag, pp. 379–389.

———
1993   "The Origin of the Genus *Homo*." *In:* D. T. Rasmussen (ed.), q.v., pp. 29–47.

Walker, Alan and R. E. Leakey (eds.)
1993   *The Nariokotome* Homo erectus *Skeleton*. Cambridge: Harvard University Press.

Wanpo, Huang, Russell Ciochon, et al.
1995   "Early *Homo* and Associated Artifacts from Asia." *Nature*, **378**:275–278.

Ward, Peter
1994   *The End of Evolution*. New York: Bantam.

Warren, Peter
1989   *The Aegean Civilizations*. New York: Peter Bedrick.

Washburn, S. L.
1963   "The Study of Race." *American Anthropologist*, **65**:521–531.

Watson, J. B. and F. H. C. Crick
1953a "Genetical Implications of the Structure of the Deoxyribonucleic Acid." *Nature*, **171**:964–967.

———
1953b "A Structure for Deoxyribonucleic Acid." *Nature*, **171**:737–738.

Weaver, Muriel Porter
1993   *The Aztecs, Maya, and Their Predecessors: Archaeology of Mesoamerica* (3rd Ed.). San Diego: Academic Press.

Weeks, Kent R.
1999   *The Lost Tomb*. New York: William Morrow.

Weiner, J. S.
1955   *The Piltdown Forgery*. London: Oxford University Press.

Weiner, Steve, Qinqi Xu, Paul Goldberg, Jinyi Liu, and Ofer Bar-Yosef
1998   "Evidence for the Use of Fire at Zhoukoudian, China." *Science*, **281**:251–253.

Weiss, Robin A. and Richard W. Wrangham
1999   "From *Pan* to Pandemic." *Nature*, **397**:385–386.

Wendorf, Fred and Romuald Schild
1989   *The Prehistory of Wadi Kubbaniya*. Dallas, TX: Southern Methodist University.

———
1994   "Are the Early Holocene Cattle in the Eastern Sahara Domestic or Wild?" *Evolutionary Anthropology*, **3**:118–128.

Wenke, Robert J.
1984   *Patterns in Prehistory* (2nd Ed.). New York: Oxford University Press.

West, Frederick Hadleigh and Constance West (eds.)
1996   *American Beginnings: The Prehistory and Palaeoecology of Beringia*. Chicago: University of Chicago Press.

Wheat, Joe Ben
1972   "The Olsen-Chubbuck Site: A Paleo-Indian Bison Kill." *American Antiquity*, **37**:1–180.

Wheeler, Mortimer
1968   *The Indus Civilization* (3rd Ed.). Cambridge: Cambridge University Press.

White, Tim D.
1980   "Evolutionary Implications of Pliocene Hominid Footprints." *Science*, **208**:175–176.

———
1983   Comment Made at Institute of Human Origins Conference on the Evolution of Human Locomotion (Berkeley, CA).

———
1992   *Prehistoric Cannibalism at Mancos SMTUMR-2346*. Princeton, NJ: Princeton University Press.

White, Tim D. and Donald C. Johanson
1989   "The Hominid Composition of Afar Locality 333: Some Preliminary Observations." *Hominidae*, Proceedings of the 2nd International Congress of Human Paleontology, Milan: Editoriale Jaca Book, pp. 97–101.

White, Tim D., Gen Suwa, and Berhane Asfaw
1994   "*Australopithecus ramidus*, a New Species of Early Hominid from Aramis, Ethiopia." *Nature*, **371**:306–312.

———
1995   "Corrigendum (White et al., 1994)." *Nature*, **375**:88.

Whiten, A., J. Goodall., W.C. McGrew, et al.
1999   "Cultures in Chimpanzees." *Nature*, **399**:682–685.

Whittaker, John C.
1994   *Flintknapping: Making and Understanding Stone Tools*. Austin: University of Texas Press.

Whittle, Alasdair
1985   *Neolithic Europe: A Survey*. Cambridge: Cambridge University Press.

Wicklein, John
1994   "Spirit Paths of the Anasazi." *Archaeology*, **47**(1):36–41.

Wilke, P. J., R. Bettinger, T. F. King, and J. F. O'Connell
1972   "Harvest Selection and Domestication in Seed Plants." *Antiquity*, **46**:203–208.

Williams, M. A. J.
1984   "Late Quaternary Prehistoric Environments of the Sahara." *In:* J. D. Clark and S. A. Brandt (eds.), q.v., pp. 74–83.

Williams, Robert C.
1985   "HLA II: The Emergence of the Molecular Model for the Major Histocompatibility Complex." *Yearbook of Physical Anthropology*, 1985, **28**:79–95.

Wills, W. H.
1989   *Early Prehistoric Agriculture in the American Southwest*. Santa Fe: School of American Research Press.

Wilson, David J.
1981   "Of Maize and Men: A Critique of the Maritime Hypothesis of State Origins on the Coast of Peru." *American Anthropologist*, **83**:931–940.

Wilson, Edward O.
1992   *The Diversity of Life*. Cambridge, MA: Harvard University Press.

Winslow, D. L. and J. R. Wedding
1997   "Spirit Cave Man." *American History*, **32** (March/April): 74.

Wittfogel, Karl A.
1957 *Oriental Despotism: A Comparative Study of Total Power.* New Haven: Yale University Press.

Wolpoff, Milford H.
1984 "Evolution in *Homo erectus:* The Question of Stasis." *Paleobiology,* **10**:389–406.

_____
1989 "Multiregional Evolution: The Fossil Alternative to Eden." *In:* P. Mellars and C. Stringer, q.v., pp. 62–108.

_____
1995 *Human Evolution* 1996 Edition. New York: McGraw-Hill College Custom Series.

_____
1999 *Paleoanthropology. (*2nd Ed.) New York: McGraw-Hill.

Wolpoff, Mildred H., Wu Xin Chi, and Alan G. Thorne
1984 "Modern *Homo sapiens* Origins." *In:* Smith and Spencer (eds.), q.v., pp. 411–483.

Wolpoff, M. et al.
1994 "Multiregional Evolutions: A World-Wide Source for Modern Human Population." *In:* Nitecki and Nitecki (eds.), q.v., pp. 175–199.

Wood, Bernard
1991 *Koobi Fora Research Project IV: Hominid Cranial Remains from Koobi Fora.* Oxford: Clarendon Press.

_____
1992a "Origin and Evolution of the Genus *Homo.*" *Nature,* **355**:783–790.

_____
1992b "A Remote Sense for Fossils." *Nature,* **355**:397–398.

Woolley, Leonard
1929 *Ur of the Chaldees.* London: Ernest Benn.

Wrangham, R. W.
1977 "Feeding Behaviour of Chimpanzees in Gombe National Park, Tanzania." *In: Primate Ecology,* T. H. Clutton-Brock (ed.). New York: Academic Press, pp. 503–538.

_____
1986 "Ecology and Social Relationships in Two Species of Chimpanzees." *In: Ecology and Social Evolution: Birds and Mammals,* D. I. Rubenstein and R. W. Wrangham (eds.), Princeton: Princeton University Press, pp. 352–378.

Wright, H. E.
1993 "Environmental Determinism in Near Eastern Prehistory." *Current Anthropology,* **34**:458–469.

Wu, Rukang and Xingren Dong
1985 "*Homo erectus* in China." *In: Palaeoanthropology and Palaeolithic Archaeology in the People's Republic of China,* R. Wu and J. W. Olsen (eds.), New York: Academic Press, pp. 79–89.

Wu, Rukang and S. Lin
1983 "Peking Man." *Scientific American,* **248**:(6)86–94.

Yamei, Hon, Richard Potts, Yaun Baoyin, et al.
2000 "Mid-Pleistocene Acheulean-like Stone Technology of the Bose Basin, South China." *Science,* **287**:1622–1626.

Yellen, John E.
1980 *Archaeological Approaches to the Present.* New York: Academic Press.

Yellen, John E. et al.
1995 "A Middle Stone Age Worked Bone Industry from Katanda, Upper Semliki Valley, Zaire." *Science,* **268**:553–556.

Yi, Seonbok and G. A. Clark
1983 "Observations on the Lower Palaeolithic of Northeast Asia." *Current Anthropology,* **24**:181–202.

Young, Biloine Whiting and Melvin L. Fowler
2000 *Cahokia: The Great Native American Metropolis.* Urbana, IL: University of Illinois Press.

Young, David
1992 *The Discovery of Evolution.* Cambridge: Natural History Museum Publications, Cambridge University Press.

Yudkin, J.
1969 "Archaeology and the Nutritionist." *In: The Domestication and Exploitation of Plants and Animals,* P. J. Ucko and G. W. Dimbleby (eds.), Chicago: Aldine, pp. 547–554.

Zubrow, Ezra
1989 "The Demographic Modeling of Neanderthal Extinction." *In:* Mellars and Stringer (eds.), q.v., pp. 212–231.

Photo Credits

Chapter opening photo: Cliff Palace, Colorado, PhotoDisc; **3**, Fig. 1–1a, Institute of Human Origins; **3**, Fig. 1–1b, Fig. 1–1c, Lynn Kilgore; **3**, Fig. 1–1d, Robert Jurmain; **7**, Fig. 1–2, Institute of Human Origins; **7**, Fig. 1–3, Courtesy, Eugenie Scott; **7**, Fig. 1–4, Courtesy, Judy Regensteiner; **9**, Fig. 1–5, William Turnbaugh, painting by Gilbert Stuart; **10**, Fig. 1–6, Courtesy, James D. Loy; **11**, Fig. 1–7, William Turnbaugh; **12**, Fig. 1–12, William Turnbaugh; **13**, Fig. 1–9, Whitney Powell-Cummer; **13**, Fig. 1–13, Gordon P. Watts, Jr.; **14**, Fig. 1–11, Harry Nelson; **19**, Fig. 1, Sarah Peabody Turnbaugh, Museum of Primitive Art and Culture; **19**, Fig. 2, Museum of Primitive Art and Culture; **20**, Fig. 3, Courtesy, Judy Regensteiner; **20**, Fig. 4, Courtesy, Russell Mittermeier; **21**, Fig. 5, Courtesy, Whitney Powell-Cummer; **21**, Fig. 6, Courtesy, Paul Sledzik; **22**, Fig. 7, Courtesy, Aaron Elkins; **22**, Fig. 8, Courtesy, David S. Robinson/Photo by Kevin J. Krisman; **26**, Fig. 2–1, Courtesy, Dept. of Library Services, American Museum of Natural History #318607; **27**, Fig. 2–2, Courtesy, Dept. of Library Services, American Museum of Natural History; **27**, Fig. 2–3, Corbis; **28**, Fig. 2–4, Corbis; **29**, Fig. 2–6, Courtesy, Dept. of Library Services, American Museum of Natural History #28000; **29**, Fig. 2–7, Courtesy, Dept. of Library Services, American Museum of Natural History #326671; **30**, Fig. 2–8, Courtesy, Dept. of Library Services, American Museum of Natural History #32670; **30**, Fig. 2–9, Courtesy, Dept. of Library Services, American Museum of Natural History #326672; **32**, Fig. 2–12, Lynn Kilgore; **33**, Fig. 2–13, Courtesy, Dept. of Library Services, American Museum of Natural History #326696; **34**, Fig. 2–14a, Michael Tweedie/Photo Researchers; **34**, Fig. 2–14b, Breck P. Kent/Animals Animals; **47**, Fig. 3–4, From Harrison, C. et al 1983. Cytogenics. Cell Genetics 35: 21–27, 1983. S. Karger, A. G., Basel; **53**, Fig. 3–9, Courtesy, Dept. of Library Services, American Museum of Natural History #238141; **60**, Fig. 3–13a, Fig. 3–13b, Corbis; **60**, Fig. 3–13c, Fig. 3–13d, Lynn Kilgore; **96**, Fig. 5–2, Norman Lightfoot/PhotoResearchers #7V3198; **99**, Fig. 5–3a, Renee Lynn/Photo Researchers #7U5895; **99**, Fig. 5–3b, George Holton/Photo Researchers #4E2925; **100**, Fig. 5–4a, Courtesy, William Pratt; **100**, Fig. 5–4b, Courtesy, L.G. Moore; **113**, Fig. 1, Lynn Kilgore; **114**, Fig. 2, Lynn Kilgore; **114**, Fig. 3, Fig. 4, Robert Jurmain; **115**, Fig. 5, Robert Jurmain; **115**, Fig. 6, Lynn Kilgore; **116**, Fig. 7, Lynn Kilgore; **116**, Fig. 9, Robert Jurmain; **117**, Fig. 10, Robert Jurmain; **117**, Fig. 11, Courtesy, Arthur Aufderheide; **118**, Fig. 12, Courtesy, Arthur Aufderheide; **118**, Fig. 13, Fig. 14, Robert Jurmain; **126**, see page for credits; **127**, see page for credits **133**, Fig. 6–11, Fig. 6–12, Courtesy, Fred Jacobs; **134**, Fig. 6–13, Courtesy, San Francisco Zoo; **134**, Fig. 6–14; Courtesy, Bonnie Pedersen/Arlene Kruse; **134**, Fig. 6–15, David Haring, Duke University Primate Zoo; **135**, Fig. 6–17, © Zoological Society of San Diego, photo by Ron Garrison; **135**, Fig. 6–18, Raymond Mendez/Animals Animals #MMO 080MER008 01; **136**, Fig. 6–20, Robert L. Lubeck/Animals Animals #MMO 210LUR003 01; **137**, Fig. 6–22, Robert Jurmain; **137**, Fig. 6–23a, Fig. 6–23b, Courtesy, Bonnie Pedersen/Arlene Kruse; **138**, Fig. 6–24, Robert Jurmain; **139**, Fig. 6–26, Lynn Kilgore; **139**, Fig. 6–27, Robert Jurmain, photo by Jill Matsumoto/Jim Anderson; **140**, Fig. 6–29a, Fig. 6–29b, Fig. 6–30a, Fig. 6–30b, Lynn Kilgore; **141**, Fig. 6–31a, Fig. 6–31b, Robert Jurmain, photo by Jill Matsumoto/Jim Anderson; **142**, Fig. 6–32, Courtesy, Ellen Ingmanson; **145**, Fig. 6–33, Courtesy, J. Oates; **150**, Fig. 7–1, Joe MacDonald/Animals Animals #MMO 090MCJ006 01; **152**, Fig. 7–2, Lynn Kilgore; **154**, Fig. 7–3, Fig. 7–4, Lynn Kilgore; **156**, Fig. 7–6, Lynn Kilgore; **157**, Fig. 7–7a, Robert Jurmain; **157**, Fig. 7–7b, Courtesy, Meredith Small; **157**, Fig. 7–7c, Lynn Kilgore; **157**, Fig. 7–7d, Courtesy, Arlene Kruse/Bonnie Pedersen; **158**, Fig. 7–8, Lynn Kilgore; **161**, Fig. 7–9a, Courtesy, David Haring, Duke University Primate Center; **161**, Fig. 7–9b, Courtesy, Arlene Kruse/Bonnie Pedersen; **161**, Fig. 7–9c, Robert Jurmain; **161**, Fig. 7–9d, © Tom McHugh/Photo Researchers, Inc. #7U5895; **161**, Fig. 7–9e, Robert Jurmain; **161**, Fig. 7–10, Harlow Primate Laboratory, University of Wisconsin; **165**, Fig. 7–11, Lynn Kilgore; **167**, Fig. 7–12, Courtesy, Rose A. Sevcik, Language Research Center, Georgia State University; photo by Elizabeth Pugh; **168**, Fig. 7–13, Lynn Kilgore; **187**, Fig. 8–11, Hansejudy Beste/Animals Animals; **187**, Fig. 8–12, J. C. Stevenson/Animals Animals; **188**, Fig. 8–13, Doug Wechsler/Animals Animals #MAM 130WED001 01; **188**, Fig. 8–14, **192**, Fig. 8–17, Robert Jurmain; **193**, Fig. 8–18, Courtesy, David Pilbeam; **208**, Fig. 9–3, Robert Jurmain; **208**, Fig. 9–4, Harry Nelson; **209**, Fig. 1, Courtesy of the L.S.B. Leakey Foundation; **211**, Fig. 9–5, Robert Jurmain; **213**, Fig. 9–6, Robert Jurmain; **228**, Fig. 10–5, Harry Nelson; **230**, Fig. 10–7, Tim D. White/Brill, Atlanta; **231**, Fig. 10–9, Lynn Kilgore; **232**, Fig. 10–10, Courtesy, Peter Jones; **232**, Fig. 10–11, Institute of Human Origins; **233**, Fig. 10–12a, Fig. 10–12b, Institute of Human Origins; **233**, Fig. 10–13, Institute of Human Origins, photo by Don Johanson; **235**, Fig. 10–14, David L. Brill/Atlanta; **236**, Fig. 10–15, National Museums of Kenya; **237**, Fig. 10–16, Reproduced with permission of the National Museums of Kenya, copyright reserved, courtesy of Alan Walker; **238**, Fig. 10–17a, Fig. 10–17b, Reproduced with permission of the National Museums of Kenya, copyright reserved; **239**, ER 1813, ER1470, Reproduced with permission of the National Museums of Kenya, copyright reserved; **239**, Stw 53, Courtesy, P. V Tobias (reconstruction by Ronald J. Clarke); **239**, OH 7, Harry Nelson; **240**, Fig. 10–19, Courtesy, Raymond Dart; photo by Alun Hughes; **240**, Fig. 10–20, Photo by Alun Hughes, reproduced by permission of Professor P. V. Tobias; **241**, Fig. 10–21, Wide World; **242**, Fig. 10–22, Transvaal Museum, South Africa; **244**, WT 17000, Reproduced with permission of the National Museums of Kenya, copyright reserved, courtesy Alan Walker; **244**, Lucy, Institute of Human Origins; **244**, L.H.-4, Institute of Human Origins; **244**, SK 48, Sts 5, Transvaal Museum, South Africa; **244**, Taung Child, Courtesy, P. V. Tobias; photo by Alun Hughes; **244**, "Zinj", Harry Nelson; **249**, ER 406, Reproduced with permission of the National Museums of Kenya, copyright reserved; **249**, OH 5, Harry Nelson; **249**, WT 17000, ER 729, ER 732, Reproduced with permission of the National Museums of Kenya, copyright reserved; **249**, SK 48, Transvaal Museum, South Africa; **259**, Fig. 11–01, Courtesy, Günter Bräuer; **260**, Dmanisi, Courtesy Günter Bräuer; **260**, ER 3733, Kenya Museums of Natural History; **260**, OH 9, Harry Nelson; **260**, WT 15000, Reproduced with permission of the National Museums of Kenya, copyright reserved; **260**, Salé, Courtesy, J. J. Hublin; **261**, Zhoukoudian, Lantian, Hexian, Harry Nelson; **261**, Trinil, Sangiran, Courtesy, S. Sartono; **263**, Fig. 11–4, Robert Jurmain; **264**, Fig. 11–3a, Fig. 11–3b, Harry Nelson; **264**, Fig. 11–3c, Fig. 11–3d, Robert Jurmain; **264**, Fig. 11–3e, From Franz Weidenreich, "Morphology of Solo Man," Anthropology Papers of the American Museum of Natural History, Vol. 43, part 3, 1951. Courtesy Public Affairs Department, The American Museum of Natural History; **264**, Fig. 11–3f, Harry Nelson; **265**, Fig. 11–5, The New York Academy of Medicine Library; **266**, Fig. 11–6, Courtesy, S. Sartono; **266**, Fig. 11–7, The New York Academy of Medicine Library; **267**, Fig. 11–8, Special Collections, American Museum of Natural History; **267**, Fig. 11–9, Special Collections, American Museum of Natural History #335794; **267**, Fig. 11–10, Robert Jurmain; **272**, Fig. 11–12a, Courtesy, Denis Etler; **272**, Fig. 11–12b, Courtesy, Denis Etler; **273**, Fig. 11–13, Fig. 11–14, Reproduced with permission of the Kenya Museums of Natural History; **278**, Fig. 11–16, Courtesy, The Museum of Primitive Art and Culture, Peace Dale, RI, photo by William Turnbaugh; **278**, Fig. 11–18a,

Fig. 11–18b, Robert Jurmain; **282**, Fig. 1, Goddard Space Flight Center; **282**, Fig. 2, Institute of Human Origins, photo by Nanci Kahn; **282**, Fig. 3, Reproduced with permission of the National Museums of Kenya, copyright reserved; **282**, Fig. 4, Institute of Human Origins, photo by Nanci Kahn; **283**, Fig. 5, Institute of Human Origins, photo by Nanci Kahn; **283**, Fig. 6, Fig. 7, Institute of Human Origins, photo by Don Johanson; **284**, Fig. 8, Fig. 9, Institute of Human Origins, photo by Don Johanson; **285**, Fig. 10, Robert Jurmain; **285**, Fig. 11, Fig. 12, Institute of Human Origins, photo by Don Johanson; **286**, Fig. 13, Institute of Human Origins, photo by Nanci Kahn; **286**, Fig. 14, Robert Jurmain; **289**, Fig. 12–1, Harry Nelson; **290**, Steinheim, Harry Nelson; **290**, Florisbad, Courtesy, Günter Bräuer; **290**, Kabwe, Harry Nelson; **290**, Arago, Courtesy, H. DeLumley; **291**, Fig. 12–2e, Courtesy, Xinzhi Wu; **295**, Fig. 12–4a, Fig. 12–4b, Harry Nelson; **300**, Fig. 12–7a, Fig. 12–7b, Courtesy, Milford Wolpoff; **300**, Fig. 12–7c, Fig. 12–7d, Courtesy, Fred Smith; **300**, Fig. 12–7e, Harry Nelson; **300**, Fig. 12–7f, Courtesy, Fred Smith; **301**, Fig. 12–8, Courtesy, Fred Smith; **301**, Fig. 12–9, Harry Nelson; **302**, Spy, Krapina, Courtesy, Milford Wolpoff; **302**, La Chapelle, La Ferrassie, Courtesy, Fred Smith; **302**, St. Césaire, Harry Nelson; **303**, Shanidar, Courtesy, Milford Wolpoff; **303**, Monte Circeo, Amud, Tabun, Courtesy, Fred Smith; **305**, Fig. 12–12a, Fig. 12–12b, Courtesy, Fred Smith; **305**, Fig. 12–13, Harry Nelson; **306**, Fig. 12–14, Courtesy, Milford Wolpoff; **319**, Cro-Magnon, Courtesy, David Frayer; **319**, Skhūl, Jebel Qafzeh, Omo, Border Cave, Klasies River Mouth, Courtesy, Fred Smith; **322**, Qafzeh 6, Border Cave, Skhūl, Courtesy, Fred Smith; **322**, Predmosti 3, Harry Nelson; **322**, Qafzeh 9, Courtesy, Fred Smith; **322**, Cro-Magnon I, Courtesy, David Frayer; **323**, Fig. 13–3a, Fig. 13–3b, Courtesy, David Frayer; **323**, Fig. 13–4a, Fig. 13–4b, Courtesy, David Frayer; **327**, Fig. 13–6a, Fig. 13–6b, Courtesy, David Frayer; **328**, Fig. 13–7, Courtesy, Milford Wolpoff; **329**, Fig. 13–8, Courtesy, Milford Wolpoff; **333**, Fig. 13–14a, Fig. 13–14b, Harry Nelson; **333**, Fig. 13–15, Jim Cartier/Photo Researchers; **335**, Fig. 13–17a, Fig. 13–17b, Jean-Marie Chauvet/Corbis Sygma; **346**, Fig. 14–1, Courtesy, Lena Sisco; **347**, Fig. 14–2, Courtesy, John Yellen; **348**, Fig. 1, Courtesy, William L. Rathje; **349**, Fig. 2, Courtesy, William L. Rathje; **350**, Fig. 14–3, Courtesy, Jennifer Hope Antes and the Museum of Natural History, Roger Williams Park, Providence, RI; **351**, Fig. 14–6, Courtesy, Museum of Primitive Art and Culture, Peace Dale, RI, photo by William Turnbaugh; **352**, Fig. 14–8, Courtesy, Larry Keeley; **353**, Fig. 14–9, William Turnbaugh; **357**, Fig. 14–12, Courtesy, Beta Analytic, Inc., Darden Hood, president; **358**, Fig. 14–13, William Turnbaugh; **362**, Fig. 14–15, Courtesy, Lena Sisco; **363**, Fig. 14–16, Stephanie M. Collins; **364**, Fig. 14–18, Fig. 14–19, Stephanie M. Collins; **365**, Fig. 14–20, Stephanie M. Collins; **365**, Fig. 14–21, Paul G. Richmond; **365**, Fig. 14–22, Stephanie M. Collins; **379**, Fig. 1, Courtesy, Museum of Primitive Art and Culture, Peace Dale, RI, photo by William Turnbaugh; **383**, Fig. 15–5, Courtesy, Tom Dillehay; **384**, Fig. 15–7, Courtesy, Peter Storck, Royal Ontario Museum; **385**, Fig. 15–8, Fig. 15–9, William Turnbaugh; **386**, Fig. 15–10, William Turnbaugh; **386**, Fig. 15–11, Reproduced with permission from George C. Frison, *Prehistoric Hunters of the High Plains*, New York; Academic Press, Copyright 1978; **387**, Fig. 15–13, William Turnbaugh; **389**, Fig. 15–15, Courtesy, Museum of Primitive Art and Culture, Peace Dale, RI, photo by William Turnbaugh; **394**, Fig. 15–20, Fig. 15–21, William Turnbaugh; **395**, Fig. 15–22, William Turnbaugh; **399**, Fig. 1, Fig. 2, Courtesy, The Public Archaeology Laboratory, Inc., Pawtucket, RI, and Donna Raymond; **400**, Fig. 3a, Fig. 3b, Fig. 4, William Turnbaugh; **401**, Fig. 5, Fig. 6, Fig. 7, William Turnbaugh; **402**, Fig. 8, Fig. 9, Courtesy, The Museum of Primitive Art and Culture, Peace Dale, RI; **402**, Fig. 10a, Fig. 10b, William Turnbaugh; **403**, Fig. 11, Fig. 12, William Turnbaugh; **403**, Fig. 13, Courtesy, The Museum of Primitive Art and Culture, Peace Dale, RI; **404**, Fig. 14, Fig. 15, Fig. 16, William Turnbaugh; **405**, Fig. 17a, Fig. 17b, Fig. 17c, Fig. 17d, Fig. 17e, William Turnbaugh; **406**, Fig. 18, Fig. 19, Courtesy, The Public Archaeology Laboratory, Inc., Pawtucket, RI, and Donna Raymond; **406**, Fig. 20a, Courtesy, The Public Archaeology Laboratory, Inc., Pawtucket, RI,

and Donna Raymond; **406**, Fig. 20b, William Turnbaugh; **407**, Fig. 21, Fig. 22, Fig. 23, Fig. 24, Courtesy, The Public Archaeology Laboratory, Inc., Pawtucket, RI, and Donna Raymond; **408**, Fig. 25, Courtesy, The Public Archaeology Laboratory, Inc., Pawtucket, RI, and Donna Raymond; **408**, Fig. 26, William Turnbaugh; **413**, Fig. 16–2, William Turnbaugh; **415**, Fig. 16–3, William Turnbaugh; **419**, Fig. 1, Reprinted by permission from "Use of Barley in the Egyptian Late Paleolithic," by F. Wendorf, et al., from *Science*, vol. 205, pp. 1,341–1,347, September 1979. Copyright September 1979 by the American Association for the Advancement of Science; **421**, Fig. 16–4, William Turnbaugh; **422**, Fig. 16–5, William Turnbaugh; **424**, Fig. 16–7, U.S. Department of Agriculture; **428**, Fig. 16–12, George Gerster/Photo Researchers, Inc.; **429**, Fig. 16–13, Harry Nelson; **429**, Fig. 16–14, U.S. Department of Agriculture; **435**, Fig. 16–17, William Turnbaugh, after model by C. A. Scott; **435**, Fig. 16–18, William Turnbaugh; **436**, Fig. 16–19, William Turnbaugh; **437**, Fig. 16–20, William Turnbaugh; **437**, Fig. 16–21, Courtesy, Museum of Primitive Art and Culture, Peace Dale, RI, photo by William Turnbaugh; **438**, Fig. 16–22, Fig. 16–23, William Turnbaugh; **439**, Fig. 16–24, Julian H. Steward, ed. *Handbook of South American Indians*, Vol. 1, plate 36. Washington, DC: U.S. Government Printing Office; **440**, Fig. 16–26, Courtesy, Museum of Primitive Art and Culture, Peace Dale, RI, photo by William Turnbaugh; **441**, Fig. 16–27, Courtesy, Katherine Pomonis; **450**, Fig. 17–2a, National Geographic Society; **450**, Fig. 17–2b, National Geographic Society; **450**, Fig. 17–2c, National Geographic Society; **450**, Fig. 17–2d, Dallas and John Heaton, Westlight; **450**, Fig. 17–2e, Walter H. Hodge, Peter Arnold, Inc.; **451**, Fig. 17–02f, National Geographic Society; **456**, Fig. 17–4, William Turnbaugh; **459**, Fig. 17–6, National Geographic Society; **460**, Fig. 17–7a, Fig. 17–7b, Courtesy, Museum of Primitive Art and Culture, Peace Dale, RI. Photos by William Turnbaugh; **461**, Fig. 17–8, After drawing by William Turnbaugh, based on specimen at Museum of Fine Arts, Boston; **462**, Fig. 17–9, Dallas and John Heaton/Westlight; **462**, Fig. 17–10, William Turnbaugh; **463**, Fig. 17–11, William Turnbaugh; **463**, Fig. 17–12, Courtesy, Bill Gamble, Ward's Scientific; **466**, Fig. 17–14, Courtesy, Susan Johnston; **467**, Fig. 17–15, National Geographic Society; **468**, Fig. 17–17, National Geographic Society; **469**, Fig. 17–18, Fig. 17–19, Paul G. Richmond; **471**, Fig. 17–21, Walter H. Hodge, Peter Arnold, Inc.; **471**, Fig. 17–22, After photograph of specimen in Herakleion Museum, Crete; **472**, Fig. 17–23, Leonard von Matt/Photo Researchers, Inc.; **472**, Fig. 17–24, National Geographic Society; **473**, Fig. 17–25, Courtesy, Museum of Primitive Art and Culture, Peace Dale, RI, photo by William Turnbaugh; **480**, Aztec, William Turnbaugh; **480**, Teotihuacán, Maya, Courtesy, Mark A. Gutchen; **480**, Inka, Courtesy, Carol Howell; **480**, Chimor, Wendell C. Bennett, "The Archaeology of the Central Andes," in Julian H. Steward, ed., *Handbook of South American Indians*, Vol. 2, plate 51. Washington, DC: Government Printing Office, 1947; **480**, Olmec, William Turnbaugh; **480**, Monte Albán, Courtesy, Mark A. Gutchen; **482**, Fig. 18–4, William Turnbaugh; **482**, Fig. 18–5, Bill Ross, Westlight; **483**, Fig. 18–6, Philip Drucker, Robert Squier, "Excavations at La Venta, Tabasco, 1955." *Smithsonian Institution, Bureau of American Ethnology Bulletin* 170, plate 20. Washington, DC: Government Printing Office, 1969; **483**, Fig. 18–7, Courtesy, Mark A. Gutchen; **484**, Fig. 18–8, Courtesy, Mark A. Gutchen; **485**, Fig. 18–9, Fig. 18–10, Courtesy, Mark A. Gutchen; **486**, Fig. 18–11, Fig. 18–12, Courtesy, Mark A. Gutchen; **486**, Fig. 18–13, William Turnbaugh; **489**, Fig. 18–14, Courtesy, Mark A. Gutchen; **491**, Fig. 18–15, Courtesy, Mark A. Gutchen; **495**, Fig. 18–18, William Turnbaugh; **496**, Fig. 18–19, After photograh by William Turnbaugh; **496**, Fig. 18–20, Drawings by William Turnbaugh, from photographs; **497**, Fig. 18–21, Paul G. Richmond; **497**, Fig. 18–22, Wendell C. Bennett, "The Archaeology of the Central Andes," in, Julian H. Steward, ed., *Handbook of South American Indians*, Vol. 2, plate 51. Washington, DC: Government Printing Office, 1947; **498**, Fig. 18–23, Courtesy, Katherine Pomonis; **499**, Fig. 18–24, Courtesy, Carol Howell; **500**, Fig. 18–25, William Turnbaugh, from a private collection

Index

Page numbers in **bold** refer to definitions. Page numbers in *italics* refer to illustrations or boxed material.

Major Archaeological Sites

BERING STRAIT [region]

OLD CROW

ALASKA
(U.S.) FAIRBANKS

CANADA

GREENLAND
(KALAALLIT NUNAAT)
(Den.)

ARCTIC CIRCLE

ICELAND

UNITED
KINGDOM
IRELAND
STAR CARR
STONEHENGE

CARNAC   (FR.)

LASCAUX
ALTAMIRA

PORTUGAL   SPAIN

AZORE IS.
(Port.)

MOROCCO

OZETTE   KENNEWICK

WILSON BUTTE   UNITED STATES
BUHL

DANGER CAVE   VAIL
LOVELOCK   MEADOWCROFT   SHAWNEE-MINISINK
MESA VERDE   COLBY   HOPEWELL
CHACO CANYON   CAHOKIA   CACTUS HILL
OLSEN-CHUBBUCK   INDIAN KNOLL
FOLSOM   EVA   TOPPER
NACO   CLOVIS   POVERTY
CASAS GRANDES   POINT
WATSON
BRAKE   WARM MINERAL SPRINGS

TROPIC OF CANCER

MEXICO   BAHAMAS

HAWAII
(U.S.)

TEOTIHUACÁN   LA VENTA   CHICHEN ITZÁ
TENOCHTITLÁN   CUBA   HAITI   DOMINICAN REP.
TEHUACÁN VALLEY   TIKAL   PUERTO   ANTIGUA & BARBUDA
MONTE ALBÁN   BELIZE   RICO (U.S.)   GUADELOUPE (Fr.)
SAN LORENZO   HONDURAS   DOMINICA
GUATEMALA   COPÁN   JAMAICA   MARTINIQUE (Fr.)
PALENQUE   NETHERLANDS   BARBADOS
EL SALVADOR   ANTILLES (Neth.)   GRENADA
NICARAGUA   TRINIDAD & TOBAGO
COSTA RICA   VENEZUELA

CAPE VERDE IS.   MAURITANIA   MALI

SENEGAL
GAMBIA   BURKINA
FASO
GUINEA BISSAU   GUINEA
SIERRA LEONE   IVORY
LIBERIA   COAST   GHANA

PANAMA   COLOMBIA   GUYANA
SURINAME
FRENCH GUIANA
(Fr.)

EQUATOR

GALAPAGOS IS.
(Ecuador)   ECUADOR   PEDRA PINTADA

EQUATORIAL G.

GUITARRERO CAVE

WESTERN
SAMOA   AMERICAN
SAMOA (U.S.)

SOCIETY IS.
(Fr.)   FRENCH
POLYNESIA
(Fr.)

TONGA
TAHITI (Fr.)

CHAN CHAN
MOCHE
CHAVÍN DE HUANTAR

BRAZIL

PERU
WARI   CUZCO
NAZCA   MACHU PICCHU
TIWANAKU   BOLIVIA

20°S

PARAGUAY

TROPIC OF CAPRICORN

PITCAIRN IS.
(U.K.)

EASTER ISLAND
(Chile)

CHILE

URUGUAY

ARGENTINA

MONTE VERDE

0   500   1000   1500 miles

0   1000   2000 km

Equatorial Scale

FALKLAND IS.
(U.K.)

FELL'S CAVE

ANTARCTIC CIRCLE